PARALEGAL
HANDBOOK

The West Legal Studies

Your options keep growing with West Legal Studies

Each year our list continues to offer you more options for every area of the law to meet your course or on-the-job reference requirements. We now have over 140 titles from which to choose in the following areas:

Administrative Law	Family Law
Alternative Dispute Resolution	Federal Taxation
Bankruptcy	Intellectual Property
Business Organizations/Corporations	Introduction to Law
Civil Litigation and Procedure	Introduction to Paralegalism
CLA Exam Preparation	Law Office Management
Client Accounting	Law Office Procedures
Computer in the Law Office	Legal Research, Writing, and Analysis
Constitutional Law	Legal Terminology
Contract Law	Paralegal Employment
Criminal Law and Procedure	Real Estate Law
Document Preparation	Reference Materials
Environmental Law	Torts and Personal Injury Law
Ethics	Will, Trusts, and Estate Administration

You will find unparalleled, practical support

Each book is augmented by instructor and student supplements to ensure the best learning experience possible. We also offer custom publishing and other benefits such as West's Student Achievement Award. In addition, our sales representatives are ready to provide you with dependable service.

We want to hear from you

Our best contributions for improving the quality of our books and instructional materials is feedback from the people who use them. If you have a question, concern, or observation about any of our materials, or you have a product proposal or manuscript, we want to hear from you. Please contact your local representative or write us at the following address:

West Legal Studies, 5 Maxwell Drive, P.O. Box 8007, Clifton Park, NY 12065

For additional information point your browser at
www.westlegalstudies.com

THOMSON

DELMAR LEARNING

PARALEGAL HANDBOOK

Vicki Brittain, J.D.
Terry Hull, J.D.

THOMSON
DELMAR LEARNING

Australia Canada Mexico Singapore Spain United Kingdom United States

THOMSON

DELMAR LEARNING

WEST LEGAL STUDIES

PARALEGAL HANDBOOK
Vicki Brittain, J.D. and Terry Hull, J.D.

Business Unit Executive Director:	**Executive Production Manager:**	**Executive Marketing Manager:**
Susan L. Simpfenderfer	Wendy A. Troeger	Donna J. Lewis
Senior Acquisitions Editor:	**Production Manager:**	**Channel Manager:**
Joan M. Gill	Carolyn Miller	Wendy Mapstone
Editorial Assistant:	**Production Editor:**	**Cover Design:**
Lisa Flatley	Betty L. Dickson	Dutton and Sherman Design

Printed in Canada
1 2 3 4 5 XXX 06 05 04 03 02

For more information contact Delmar Learning,
5 Maxwell Drive, PO Box 8007
Clifton Park, NY 12065.

Or find us on the World Wide Web at
http://www.westlegalstudies.com

For permission to use material from this text or
product, contact us by
Tel   (800)730-2214
Fax   (800)730-2215
www.thomsonrights.com

Library of Congress Cataloging-in-Publication Data

Hull, Terry, J.D.
    Paralegal handbook / Terry Hull, Vicki Brittain.
        p. cm. -- (The West Legal Studies series)
    Includes index.
    ISBN 0-7668-0772-X
    1. Legal assistants--United States--Handbooks,
manuals, etc. I. Brittain, Vicki. II. Title. III. Series.

KF320.L4 H85 2002
340'.023'73--dc21

                                        2002031292

NOTICE TO THE READER

Contents

Section Five: Legal Assistant Career Opportunities

13. *Exploring Career Opportunities*

14. *Securing Legal Assistant Career Opportunities*

Preface

For more than twenty years, we, as lawyers and paralegal educators, have had the pleasure of being a part of the dynamic growth of the paralegal/legal assistant profession. Although much of our involvement has been through research, writing, and teaching activities in the ivory tower of academia, we have also worked with paralegal/legal assistants both in the practice of law and as members of state and national academic and bar association committees and organizations striving to assist the profession to evolve from its infancy to its present stage. We remain committed to this profession and believe the profession offers society the best opportunity for making legal services more available to all segments of our society in a manner that will enable us to maintain the quality of legal services, yet reduce the cost, by judicious delegation to qualified, professional, competent legal assistants.

As the profession continues its evolution, we believe that the best contribution we can make at this time is to write a reference book that can be used as a resource on the history and evolution of the profession. We wrote this book with the following objectives:

- To draw parallels between the paralegal profession and other professions that have previously worked through these evolutionary stages

- To prompt questions concerning the future evolution of the profession

- To explore controversial issues and offer insight from divergent points of view

- To address important ethical issues and provide practical application of ethical principles

- To discuss survival skills that are necessary for practicing legal assistants and provides guidance to those who utilize legal assistants in both traditional and non-traditional legal working environments

- To provide employment information for entry-level and practicing paralegals as well as for those who employ legal assistants.

This multipurpose reference book is intended to appeal to many different audiences. It is a wonderful *career resource* for individuals interested in learning about the profession as a possible career choice. It is an effective *educational tool* to be used by educators to acquaint their entry-level paralegal students and their faculty with the development of the paralegal profession, with the substantive and ethical issues facing the profession at this time, with the options available for the profession in the future, and with practical survival skills and employment information. It is an important *reference work* for practicing paralegal/legal assistants working in traditional and in non-traditional legal working environments, allowing them access to the most up-to-date information concerning the issues facing the profession and offering them a guide for exploring and developing additional career opportunities. It is a helpful *employment resource* to be used by lawyer and non-lawyer employers seeking to understand the dynamics of the paralegal professional and the ethical utilization of legal assistants as valuable, income-producing members of the legal service delivery team. It is a *substantive reference work* that can be used by law faculty, law librarians, members of the judiciary, and legislators to obtain the necessary background information for academic lectures, evolving case law, and the consideration of future legislation relating to the profession.

In an effort to effectively communicate with the varied audiences and to achieve the multipurpose goal of this book, we have decided to use an objective, informative, plain-language writing style that can be easily understood by readers who currently are or plan to be involved in the evolution of the legal service delivery system.

Consistent with our desire to write a one-stop reference book for the profession, we decided that the best way to present the information was a hornbook approach that is utilized in many law texts. This approach includes explanatory narrative in all chapters but also includes excerpts from court cases and scholarly articles. In some chapters, the book includes the full text of statutes, landmark cases, and relevant scholarly articles. We have been careful to include endnotes at the conclusion of each chapter in order to provide additional information as well as citations to relevant primary and secondary authority. So that this reference book will remain a valuable resource even with the dynamic growth and expected rapid evolution of the profession, this book is being published in a manner that will enable us to update the necessary material by providing pocket-part updates.

In conclusion, we would like to thank those individuals who have inspired us, worked with us, and provided constructive feedback during the review and editing process. We commend this book to you with the hope that we have created a reference book that will be valuable as an evolutionary tool for the paralegal/legal assistant profession as well as an important resource for the individual members of the paralegal/legal assistant profession, the lawyers, employers, judges, legislators, educators, and members of the general public who benefit from the effective utilization of professional, competent, paralegals/legal assistants.

Vicki Brittain and Terry Hull
San Marcos, Texas

The Paralegal Profession

What Is a Paralegal?

INTRODUCTION

For decades, lawyers have employed staff persons to assist in the delivery of legal services. However, legal assistants or paralegals were not identified as a separate and distinct profession until the 1960s.

THE BIRTH OF A PROFESSION

This new profession was recognized by the American Bar Association[1] (ABA) in 1968 when a Special Committee was established to consider professional development and increased education and employment of legal assistants to enable lawyers to deliver legal services to the public more effectively.

The paralegal or legal assistant profession has experienced tremendous growth since that time, and the ABA's Special Committee has long since become a Standing Committee.[2] According to the U.S. Department of Labor statistics, paralegal employment is expected to grow faster than the average for all occupations through the year 2010,[3] and the government study predicts that job opportunities for paralegals will expand not only in private practices, but also in business organizations such as corporations, insurance companies, banks, title companies, and real estate firms.[4] This growth can be attributed to a number of factors, including endorsement by the ABA and state bar associations,[5] recognition and approval by the courts, acceptance and demand by the general public, and organization by paralegals themselves.

The Standing Committee on Legal Assistants of the ABA has devoted a webpage to "The Legal Assistant Career." The page includes information on compensation, utilization, and education for paralegals. It also includes links to additional helpful information, including the U.S. Department of Labor's outlook for the paralegal profession, the directory of ABA approved legal assistant education programs, and various articles located on other pages of the ABA website. These articles include information regarding the economic advantages of utilizing legal assistants in the law firm setting by emphasizing the profitable leveraging that legal assistants can provide, as well as improving the overall quality of legal services provided to the client (http://www.abanet.org/legalservices/legalassistants/career.html).

The ABA Commission on Nonlawyer Practice has recommended that the range of traditional paralegals be expanded, claiming that "[t]here are many ways that paralegals can enhance productivity, efficiency and quality in all law practice settings."[6] Their 1995 report went on to describe models currently in place in which paralegals ably perform quasi-legal services without lawyer assistance,[7] as well as innovative ways to expand the paralegal's role, including taking records depositions, appearing in court for uncontested matters and small probate hearings, signing form pleadings, and handling personal bankruptcies.[8]

Lawyers across the country hire paralegals because of the proclaimed economic benefits and the courts have validated the role of the paralegal as a viable member of the legal service delivery team in a law office by allowing paralegal fees to be recovered as an essential part of attorney fees.[9] In 1989, a United States Supreme Court Opinion stated the following:

> It has frequently been recognized in the lower courts that paralegals are capable of carrying out many tasks, under the supervision of an attorney, that might otherwise be performed by a lawyer and billed at a higher rate. Such work might include, for example, factual investigation, including locating and interviewing witnesses, assistance with depositions, interrogatories, and document production; compilation of statistical and financial data; checking legal citations; and drafting correspondence. Much such work lies in a gray area of tasks that might appropriately be performed by either an attorney or a paralegal.

The public has evidenced its support for the profession, as clients have begun to demand that the law firms they hire utilize the services of paralegals to ensure efficient and cost-effective legal services. Paralegals have also organized. There are paralegal organizations throughout the country, at the local, state, and national levels. These organizations have not only raised public consciousness, but have given paralegals a venue in which to express themselves and examine their goals and careers.

However, a great deal of uncertainty still exists regarding the use of paralegals. Although many employers have perfected their own "paralegal programs," this has usually been accomplished on a firm-by-firm, lawyer-by-lawyer basis. "Training a legal assistant to assist a lawyer is one thing; training a lawyer to utilize effectively the skills of a legal assistant may be quite another. Although these related concepts logically appear to be compatible, experience shows them frequently to be diverse and sometimes even antithetical."[10] Why? Because there are no strict standards or rules regarding the practical utilization of paralegals. In fact, there isn't even one widely shared or accepted definition of what a paralegal is.[11] The lack of a uniform set of standards or a definition places the paralegal profession in an interesting position. Obviously, it provides for a great deal of flexibility, but it delivers a great deal of uncertainty as well.

THE PARALEGAL IDENTITY ISSUE

Some in the field would call it a "paralegal identity issue" and many, including one of the authors, would call it an "identity crisis."[12] In fact, many cannot agree on whether the correct professional name is "paralegal" or "legal assistant." The following basic questions remain at issue:

- What is the correct occupational title for the person who is a member of a legal service delivery team and provides assistance to a supervising attorney which is non-clerical but does not involve the practice of law?
- What credentials does that person need to have?
- What competencies does that person need to possess?
- What educational background is required?
- What duties can that person perform?

What Is the Correct Occupational Title?

The answer to this question varies by market and by geographic region. Some members of the profession refer to themselves as "paralegals" while others refer to themselves as "legal assistants."[13] Historically there has been much debate regarding the preferred term and there are numerous arguments to support each.[14] For the most part, the titles are used interchangeably. Both the ABA and the National Association of Legal Assistants (NALA) use the term "legal assistant" in their definitions (see Appendix A); however, they also indicate that "legal assistants" are also known as "paralegals."[15] The American Association for Paralegal Education (AAfPE) prefers the occupational title of "paralegal" but also recognizes the term "legal assistant" in their literature and discussions.[16] This compromise is easy to make because it does not require absolute agreement by all involved in the profession; however, it does create confusion in the minds of the general public. Some individuals working in the field feel that the actual occupational title is crucial to the profession.[17] There is also growing evidence that private law firms may attempt to distinguish between the two terms by assigning the "legal assistant" title to entry-level positions and assigning the "paralegal" title to more experienced workers.[18] To add to the confusion, many organizations nationwide now refer to secretaries as "assistants."[19] For example, the NALS[20] has renamed its publication, formerly known as *Career Legal Secretary*, to *Basic Manual for the Lawyer's Assistant*; and the NALS Board has voted to use the term "lawyer's assistant" in lieu of "legal secretary" in its certifying examinations.[21] Motivated by these changes and the overall confusion, the NFPA adopted the following resolution:

Resolution adopted in 2002 regarding NFPA's Definition of a Paralegal.

WHEREAS, when this profession was first developed, the preferred term for those working in this field was "legal assistant". However, throughout the years, legal assistants came to also be called "paralegals"; and in 1995, a majority of NFPA's members voted to approve policy that NFPA prefers the term "paralegal" over the term "legal assistant"; and,

WHEREAS, despite the fact that statements were made early on that paralegal/legal assistant were equal and interchangeable terms for a single profession, there has traditionally been confusion and conflict within the public and the legal community as to these terms, and the roles and responsibilities associated therewith; and,

WHEREAS, our profession is facing additional confusion and conflict because in the last few years, an ever increasing number of: 1) law firms and other entities have begun calling their legal secretaries "legal assistants" and/or have begun tiering our profession such that individuals in entry-level positions are labeled "legal assistants" and those in more experienced positions are labeled "paralegals"; 2) legal secretaries have begun calling themselves, and signing correspondence which refers to themselves as, "legal assistants"; and,

WHEREAS, we, as paralegals and members of the legal community, have an ethical obligation to avoid misconceptions and to prevent confusion and even the appearance of an impropriety; and,

WHEREAS, the term "legal assistant" is now being used to refer to positions outside the paralegal definition, including, but not limited to, assistant county attorneys in some states and legal secretaries, it is no longer synonymous with the term "paralegal"; and, NFPA believes that it is in the best interest of our profession to promote the term "paralegal" as the proper nomenclature for members of this profession.

NOW THEREFORE, BE IT FURTHER RESOLVED, that NFPA hereby reaffirms Resolution 95M-4 that "Paralegal" is the preferred term for this profession; and,

BE IT FURTHER RESOLVED that Resolution 87-16 be revised as follows: RESOLVED that the NFPA adopt the following definition for Paralegal: A Paralegal is a person, qualified through education, training or work experience to perform substantive legal work that requires knowledge of legal concepts and is customarily, but not exclusively, performed by a lawyer. This person may be retained or employed by a lawyer, law office, governmental agency or other entity or may be authorized by administrative, statutory or court authority to perform this work. (emphasis added.)

BE IT FURTHER RESOLVED that all NFPA policy is hereby amended to coincide with this definition. However, in so doing, it is not the intent of this resolution or NFPA to exclude any member of this profession whose job duties fit the definition of paralegal but who is still called a legal assistant.[22]

Because of the unsettled nature of this controversy, the authors of this book use the two terms interchangeably.

What Are the Necessary Credentials, Competencies, and Educational Backgrounds?

When examining questions concerning necessary credentials, competencies, and educational backgrounds, many viewpoints should be carefully considered. In the late 1960s, someone prepared to work as a paralegal with "on-the-job training" primarily because no academic educational programs were available. A person became a paralegal simply by receiving training from the attorney that they worked for, who then, without any official sanction, bestowed the title of "paralegal." In the last several decades, a variety of educational programs have become available to prepare individuals for the paralegal profession. A myriad of such programs exist—six-week correspondence courses, continuing education programs, associate degree programs, baccalaureate programs, post-graduate programs, and graduate programs. Some proprietary programs are not connected to a traditional college or university and have differing standards of admission, ranging from a high school diploma to a four-year degree. This variety often causes confusion for both employers and potential employees. Although the market will define some parameters of education, markets vary across the country.

Under the auspices of its Standing Committee on Legal Assistants, the ABA House of Delegates conducts a program through which paralegal education programs may obtain ABA approval. "Promoting quality education for legal assistants has long been an important aspect of the work of the Standing Committee on Legal Assistants. This goal is met primarily through the approval of legal assistant education programs which is administered through the Standing Committee's Approval Commission."[23] This approval process is voluntary; all approved programs must meet guideline requirements[24] and undergo a full approval process every seven years. During the period of approval, programs are subject to ongoing reporting requirements, including submitting two regularly scheduled interim reports. Over 254 programs nationwide had received ABA approval as of August 2002.[25]

The AAfPE has also attempted to standardize educational programs for paralegals. In 1997, the AAfPE adopted a *Statement of Academic Quality* that describes the following "essential components of quality paralegal programs": curriculum development, facilities, faculty, marketing and promotion, instruction, administration, and student services. Also, in an attempt to better understand exactly what type of information paralegal programs should be delivering to students, an AAfPE task force appointed in 1994 developed a list of core competencies for paralegal programs. This document is located in Appendix B.

DISCUSSION QUESTIONS

As you review the Core Competency document, please consider the following:

1. If you have completed your paralegal studies, do you feel adequately prepared in each area described?

2. Do you feel the document is specific enough?

3. If you are currently a practicing paralegal, what areas would you add, if any? What could educators do to better prepare paralegals? Explain.

4. Do you feel that uniform education based on these core competencies will provide any sense of consistency for the paralegal profession?

What are Independent Paralegals and Legal Technicians?

Just as the general public became aware that paralegals were nonlawyers who provided non-clerical assistance to attorneys, other categories of nonlawyers began to draw media attention in the legal services arena. Nonlawyer legal service providers refer to themselves as "legal technicians," "document preparers," or "independent paralegals" and often offer their services directly to the public without supervision by a licensed attorney.[26] They should be distinguished from freelance paralegals who contract their services directly to employers but remain under the supervision of an attorney. Independent paralegals argue that they are not engaged in the unauthorized practice of law because they carefully limit their services to providing information concerning procedure, process, and forms. The state of California has recently enacted legislation that provides for the regulation of "legal document assistants."[27] The bill defines a legal document assistant as any person who provides any "self-help service"[28] to a member of the general public for compensation. The bill requires such persons to register in the county in which the services are provided and sets out standards of eligibility.[29] In continuing efforts to protect and inform consumers, it is likely that more states will pass similar legislation in an attempt to clarify by whom and under what circumstances these titles may be used.

DEFINITIONS ACROSS THE COUNTRY

One way to better understand the parameters of the paralegal profession is to closely review the existing definitions of a paralegal or legal assistant. Several definitions of paralegals and/or legal assistants are provided in Appendix A.[30] Generally speaking, the definitions make it clear that paralegals perform non-clerical, substantive legal work that is delegated by lawyers and are qualified to do so because of education, training, and/or experience. Also, most of the definitions indicate that a lawyer directs and supervises, or is at least responsible for, the work product of the paralegal. As an example, review the definition developed by the ABA's Standing Committee on Legal Assistants in 1997. The ABA definition is important because it is probably more often cited and adopted than any other source.

> A legal assistant or paralegal is a person, qualified by education, training, or work experience who is employed or retained by a lawyer, law office, corporation, governmental agency or other entity and who performs specifically delegated substantive legal work for which a lawyer is responsible.[31]

Now review the definition adopted by the NFPA. It recognizes that paralegals may perform, independently of attorneys, some activities that require substantive legal knowledge and are authorized by administrative, statutory, or court authority.

> A Paralegal is a person, qualified through education, training or work experience to perform substantive legal work that requires knowledge of legal concepts and is customarily, but not exclusively, performed by a lawyer. This person may be retained or employed by a lawyer, law office, governmental agency or other entity or may be authorized by administrative, statutory or court authority to perform this work.[32]

Finally, review the definition adopted by the NALA, which specifically speaks of the type of knowledge that paralegals have and the required supervision of an attorney.

> Legal assistants (also known as paralegals) are a distinguishable group of persons who assist attorneys in the delivery of legal services. Through formal education, training, and experience, legal assistants have knowledge and expertise regarding the legal system and substantive and procedural law which qualify them to do work of a legal nature under the supervision of an attorney.[33]

DISCUSSION QUESTIONS

1. Although the preceding three definitions are similar in many respects, they are not identical. Do you believe the differences are significant? In what ways?

2. Using these three definitions as a guide, draft one definition that you believe incorporates the best language of all three.

Sources of Definitions

Although paralegal definitions have been adopted by various national organizations, there are other sources as well, including state legislatures, state supreme courts, state case law, and state bar associations.

Maine has recently enacted legislation that specifically defines the terms "paralegals" and "legal assistants" as interchangeable and goes on to restrict use of those titles to those persons who fit the following definition:

> "Paralegal" and "legal assistant" mean a person, qualified by education, training or work experience, who is employed or retained by an attorney, law office, corporation, governmental agency or other entity and who performs specifically delegated substantive legal work for which an attorney is responsible.[34]

If a person violates this restriction, the statute provides for a fine of not more than $1,000.00. The California state legislature has enacted legislation that defines the term "paralegal", sets out required qualifications and typical tasks performed by paralegals, and requires continuing legal education for paralegals.[35] Other state legislatures that have either defined or addressed the paralegal profession in some way include Florida, Indiana, Oklahoma, Illinois, and Pennsylvania.[36]

State supreme courts, including those in Kentucky, Rhode Island, New Mexico, New Hampshire, South Dakota, and Virginia, have also addressed the definition of a paralegal.[37] These definitions range from listing specific duties[38] to vaguely defining a paralegal as someone who works under the control and supervision of a licensed attorney.[39] South Dakota includes minimum qualifications for a paralegal.

Sometimes, usually in connection with fee recovery disputes[40] or allegations of the unauthorized practice of law,[41] paralegals are defined in state case law. In over half of the states,[42] paralegals have been defined by state bar association sections and divisions, and through state bar association guidelines. In June 2000, the Florida Bar Board of Governors approved a rule amendment to prohibit anyone from using the title of "paralegal" or "legal assistant" unless that person works for a licensed attorney.[43] Also, the rule clarifies the practice parameters for paralegals in Florida by specifying that duties delegated to a paralegal by a lawyer do not require the presence or active involvement of the lawyer, but the lawyer must review, and will be held responsible for, the paralegal's work product.

DISCUSSION QUESTIONS

1. Describe some of the motivations by state legislatures and state courts for defining paralegals. Who is being protected or assisted by these definitions?
2. After reviewing the definitions in Appendix A, can you now define a paralegal? Can you develop a more precise definition?

A COMPARISON WITH THE PHYSICIAN ASSISTANT PROFESSION

Comparisons have often been made between the legal and medical professions for purposes of structure, education, and specialization.[44] In some respects, the medical profession has served as a model for the legal profession. With this type of history, it may be helpful to look to the medical profession, specifically the physician assistant (PA) profession,[45] in order to gather insight and perspective regarding the paralegal profession.

Physician assistants and paralegals share many areas of concern. For example, the pressure to increase prestige and credibility by identifying a minimum educational degree or background for entry into the profession; and the charge by some traditional practitioners[46] that the paraprofessionals will eventually erode distinct lines of practice and become competition for business. They also share a fundamental philosophy—a commitment to the team approach, because this type of interdependent relationship with traditional practitioners will best meet the needs of the public. The following discussion will further examine these and other comparisons and contrasts.

History and Prospects for the Future

In the mid-1960s, physicians and educators recognized a shortage and an uneven distribution of primary-care physicians. To expand the delivery of quality medical care, Dr. Eugene Stead of the Duke University Medical Center in North Carolina put together the first class of physician assistants in 1965.

As discussed previously, paralegals had been "identified" as early as 1968 by the ABA. Also, the ABA recognized by 1995 that increasing the public's access to the justice system and affordable assistance in law-related situations was an "urgent goal."[47]

Since their respective "foundings," the numbers of both physician assistants and paralegals have risen dramatically. As of January 2000, 40,000 individuals were eligible to practice as physician assistants, an increase of 75 percent since 1990.[48] Also, the U.S. Bureau of Labor Statistics (BLS) projected that the number of physician assistant jobs would increase by 53 percent between 2000 and 2010. As discussed earlier in this chapter, the BLS predicted that employment of paralegals would grow faster than the average for all occupations through the year 2010.[49]

The Preferred Title

As with the ongoing struggle among paralegals and other interested parties, physician assistants also have debated the best title for their profession. "Physician associates" was the first title chosen, but was later changed to "physician assistants."[50] This issue is still being debated because some believe that the title "physician associate" is a better description of the role they play; it suggests a higher level of competency and education than "assistant." However, opponents argue that the costs involved in changing the name of the profession at this stage of development are prohibitive. For example, federal and state laws and policies that currently provide for physician assistants would have to be amended,[51] not to mention the research costs involved in studying the issue.[52] For these reasons, the issue appears to be tabled.[53] However, a more recent concern for the physician assistant profession appears to be the need to distinguish itself from other similarly sounding professions. For example, the website for the American Academy of Physician Assistants includes essays that distinguish the PA profession from that of Anesthesiologist Assistants, Orthopedic Physician Assistants, and Radiology Practitioner Assistants.

DISCUSSION QUESTIONS

1. Do you see any similarities in the "title debate" facing both professions?
2. What lessons can be learned from the "title" controversies facing physician assistants?

Educational Criteria

Most physician assistant programs require applicants to have previous health care experience and/or two years of college education. The majority of students have a bachelor's degree and over four years of health-care experience. The average PA program curriculum is 24–25 months long and consists of classroom and laboratory instruction in the basic medical and behavioral sciences, followed by clinical rotations. In order for graduates to be eligible to take the Physician Assistant National Certifying Examination (PANCE), PA programs must be accredited by the Commission on Accreditation of Allied Health Education Programs. As of 1999, there were 110 accredited programs: 35 awarded master's degrees, four offered master's degree options, 60 awarded bachelor's degrees or a bachelor's degree option, eight awarded associate degrees, and 52 awarded certificates. Some programs offered more than one option.[54]

Admission requirements for paralegal programs vary widely and there is no required accreditation; however, some minimum requirements for those programs have been approved by the ABA. Specifically, the ABA Guidelines for the Approval of Legal Assistant Education Programs provide for the following:

> The program for legal assistants shall be:
> (a) At the postsecondary level of instruction;
> (b) At least sixty semester hours, or equivalent, which must include general education and legal specialty courses;
> (c) Offered by an institution accredited by an institutional accrediting agency acceptable to the committee.[55]

The guidelines go on to define and discuss legal specialty courses and general education requirements. As of 1997, there were 218 programs that had been approved by the ABA, including associate degree, baccalaureate degree, master's degree, certificate, and continuing education programs. As with the PA programs, some programs offered more than one option.

DISCUSSION QUESTION

A variety of educational options for career preparation is available in both professions. Does this lack of consistency provide necessary flexibility, or, does it promote confusion within these professions? Discuss.

A Question of Degree—the Debate.   A constant source of debate for both paralegals and physician assistants concerns the level of education that would be most appropriate for their profession. In 1998, this issue was raised at the American Academy of Physician Assistants (AAPA) National Conference when the Ohio State Chapter of physician assistants submitted a resolution that, after much discussion, was amended to read:

> After 1998, all Physician Assistant programs should either require a minimum of a baccalaureate degree upon entering the program or confer a minimum of a baccalaureate degree upon graduation.[56]

After much debate, the resolution was tabled and the House decided to refer the issue to the Education Council for review and research. The AAPA board of directors and APAP also formed a joint task force to discuss and research the implications of this issue to the profession and education of future PAs. As a basis for comparison, it is helpful to review the arguments being made both on behalf and against a minimum degree requirement; arguments made against such a requirement include:

- The original intent of the profession was to be competency-based and not degree-based.[57]
- Not enough information is available to determine what effect a minimum degree requirement would have on the profession.
- A baccalaureate degree would increase the cost of education for both the individual and the training institution, which may result in a loss of applicants and programs.[58]
- Potential PA students from rural or low-income areas may not have the funds to attend these degree programs.
- If too high a standard is required, for instance, a master's degree, then the profession risks losing diversity (existing programs may not be able to adapt to the master's degree model); requiring a master's degree might disenfranchise students who are unable to obtain a baccalaureate degree; those PAs who have less than a master's degree might feel at a competitive disadvantage with a resulting split in the profession; and lastly, if only some states require PAs to have a master's degree, then state-to-state mobility would be hindered.

Arguments made in favor of the baccalaureate degree as a minimum educational credential included the following:

- Many employers already require a baccalaureate degree for employment.
- The degree would allow PAs to remain competitive providers in the health-care field. Other health professionals, such as nurse practitioners, have established the master's degree as the minimum educational credential.
- The general public and those who are in a position to most influence the profession, such as physicians, hospital administrators, insurance companies and legislators, better understand and accept terms like baccalaureate degree than "competency-based learning."

Some even argue that a master's degree would be the most appropriate credential, for the following reasons:[59]

- A master's degree accurately reflects the level of academic training the physician assistants receive.
- Nurse practitioners have standardized their graduate degree to a master's, and, in a competitive market, physician assistants may be viewed as a lower-level service provider.
- A master's degree may hold more credibility with the public, employers, and lawmakers who do not fully understand the PA's training as a "competency-based" education.
- A master's degree allows for personal and professional growth in areas of research, administration, and academia, which will in turn spur growth, involvement, and credibility of the PA profession.

According to the 2000 AAPA Physician Assistant Census,[60] approximately 69 percent of physician assistants had a bachelor's degree before enrolling in a PA program. More than half (53 percent) received a bachelor's degree from a PA program and 13.8 percent received a master's-level PA degree. At the time, 61 percent of respondents held bachelor's degrees, 28 percent held master's degrees, and 2 percent held doctorates.

For the paralegal profession, the debate on this issue centers on the baccalaureate degree. The NFPA brought this issue to the forefront by developing a paralegal certification program that requires a bachelor's degree, completion of a paralegal program, and a minimum of two years of work experience as a paralegal in order to sit for the examination.[61] The NFPA supports these requirements by its research that indicates the current trend toward four-year degrees within the paralegal profession.[62] On the other hand, eligibility requirements for the NALA's certification examination range from a high school diploma and seven years of experience as a legal assistant, to graduation from an associate degree program and no experience requirements.

Even though the ABA has approved many programs that do not encompass or require a bachelor's degree, the ABA Guidelines provide the following criteria:

> The curriculum shall be constructed in such a way as to provide opportunity for students to achieve upward mobility. If credit is awarded, a maximum number of credits should be applicable toward further education for higher degrees or certificates with minimum loss of time and duplication of effort. *Graduates of associate degree programs should be encouraged to continue their education and to obtain a baccalaureate degree.* Each institution should make a good faith effort to enter into articulation agreements with other institutions to facilitate the transfer of students from two-year to four-year colleges.[63]

Currently, the profession is splintered on this issue and only the demands of the marketplace determine the acceptable education level for paralegals.

DISCUSSION QUESTIONS

1. Do you believe the minimum educational criteria for the paralegal profession will change? If so, how?

2. Review the arguments made in opposition to and in support of a baccalaureate degree as a minimum education credential for the physician assistant profession. Can any of these same arguments be made with respect to the paralegal profession? Which do you find most persuasive? Why?

Regulation

Only graduates of accredited PA programs are eligible to sit for the PANCE, and almost all states require certification. The PANCE is administered through the National Commission on Certification of Physician Assistants (NCCPA), an independent organization whose commissioners represent a number of different medical professions. Once a PA is certified, he/she must complete a continuous six-year cycle to keep his/her certificate current, including continuing medical education, passing the Physician Assistant National Recertifying Examination (PANRE) in the sixth year.[64]

One of the most obvious differences between these two professions is the certification requirement for physician assistants. Paralegals are currently not required to be certified or licensed in any state. Also, even though voluntary certification exists, it is offered at both the state and national levels by separate and distinct organizations instead of one unifying body. Similar to the PA certification, these voluntary certification schemes require continuing education to retain initial certification. However, unlike the PA plan, there in no recertification testing requirement.

DISCUSSION QUESTION

How do you think regulation affects a profession? How do you think it might affect the paralegal profession? See Chapter 7 of this book for an extensive treatment of this topic.

Importance of the Form of Regulation.   The AAPA recommends licensure for physician assistant regulation. Currently, states use three terms for the credential that they award: PAs are *licensed* in 37 jurisdictions, *certified* in nine, and *registered* in four.[65] The confusion is partly created by the nationwide certification program that exists for PAs and is further discussed below. The AAPA argues that licensing is generally considered to be the most rigorous form of credentialing and that physician assistants meet licensing requirements because they must pass an examination and possess certain educational and experience qualifications in virtually every state. Therefore, the procedure already exists and should consistently be referred to as licensure. It is the AAPA's position that physician assistants may be *certified* by the NCCPA, but they are *licensed* by states. This distinction is important to the physician assistant profession for several reasons. For example, many categories of health laws refer to "licensed providers." These laws usually intend to include health providers with a state-specified scope of practice. Therefore, the use of the terms registration or certification to identify physician assistants can create confusion and conflict with these health laws. Also, managed-care and third-party payers often make reference to "licensed providers" when determining reimbursement for services provided.[66] Finally, licensure creates credential parity with other medical professionals who perform a comparable role in providing health care. The term "unlicensed assistive personnel" is often used to describe medical assistants, nurse's aides, and others not specifically credentialed by the state; licensure will ensure that PAs are not confused with this class of worker. The AAPA makes it clear that licensure will not and does not imply nor create independent practice for physician assistants.

The subject of licensure for paralegals has often been debated. The NFPA supports licensure and offers its certification scheme as a model for state regulation. The NALA opposes licensure for the paralegal profession and argues that there is no demonstrated public need to regulate paralegals, regulation would increase the cost of paralegals to employers and to the public, and regulation does not allow for the growth of the paralegal profession nor encourage the utilization of paralegals in the delivery of legal services.[67]

DISCUSSION QUESTIONS

1. As discussed above, review the distinctions made in the physician assistant profession with respect to types of regulation. Could these types of distinctions also be important in the paralegal profession at some date in the future? Why or why not?

2. Physician assistants welcome licensure because it confers rights, obligations, and indicates "the most rigorous form of credentialing." The AAPA has even prepared model state legislation for adoption by state legislators,[68] some of which may be useful to the paralegal profession. For example, the physician assistant model legislation provides for physician supervision and details the physician assistant's scope of practice in terms of delegated authority and agency, as well as delineated services. It also offers options for regulatory bodies including the state board of medical examiners, a body composed solely of physician assistants, or regulation by a medical board with a physician assistant advisory committee. Qualifications for licensure include completion of a duly accredited PA program and certification through the NCCPA.

   Should paralegals be regulated? If so, should they adopt a method similar to that supported by the AAPA?

Scope of Responsibility

Physician assistants are regulated by state law and their scope of practice varies by state.[69] For example, most states specifically give physician assistants prescribing and dispensing authority, some for only non-controlled medications, some for controlled medications as well. In addition, states set out duties that can be performed by physician assistants, ranging from the broader—"duties and responsibilities assigned by the supervising physician"[70] and "acts that constitute the practice of medicine, as delegated by the supervising physician"[71]—to the more specific, such as

> taking histories, performing physical exams, ordering and/or performing diagnostic and therapeutic procedures, formulating a working diagnosis, developing and implementing a treatment plan, monitoring the effectiveness of therapeutic interventions, assisting at surgery, offering counseling and education, and making referrals.[72]

Generally, the type of medicine practiced by the PA corresponds to the supervising physician's practice; however, the extent of supervision required by the physician can vary widely from state to state. For example, in Alabama, oversight and direction are required, but not direct, on-site supervision. In Georgia, the supervising physician must be readily available and the Georgia State Board of Medical Examiners must approve utilization of a physician assistant in a satellite location. The ratio of physician assistants to physicians, once tightly restricted,[73] is becoming more flexible.[74] Regardless of the level and amount of supervision, the AAPA promotes the ideal that physician assistants are trained to "know their limits" and defer to physicians appropriately.

Paralegal duties vary widely depending on training, education, and experience, and are limited by the supervising attorney,[75] and by unauthorized practice of law (UPL) regulations. Broadly speaking, UPL regulations impact supervised paralegals by preventing them from giving legal advice directly to clients[76] and representing clients in a courtroom. Although most lawyers don't envision paralegals conducting trials, the ABA's Commission on Nonlawyer Practice found that at least some lawyers would like to see "court rules be changed to permit paralegals to appear in court for their law firm employers on routine matters such as calendar calls or previously agreed to matters such as child support calculations and small estate probate hearings."[77] Although specific ratios of paralegals to attorneys have not been mandated, case law, attorney guidelines, and UPL laws prohibit off-site supervision and require the lawyer to maintain a direct relationship with the client.

DISCUSSION QUESTIONS

1. Do you think it would be helpful to more specifically identify the "scope of practice" for paralegals? If so, who would it be helpful to—attorneys, consumers, paralegals?

2. Do you think state involvement and acknowledgement of the scope of practice of physician assistants has benefited that profession? If so, in what ways?

Contribution to the Field of Practice

The underlying philosophy for both the paralegal and physician assistant professions is to improve the efficiency and ultimate quality of the services provided by traditional practitioners.

> In their work with physicians, PAs routinely perform physical exams and take patient histories, order and interpret laboratory tests, diagnose and treat illness, suture lacerations and assist in surgery, write presciptions in nearly every state, and provide health education and patient counseling—all as delegated functions of the supervising physician. PAs work in complementary and synergistic ways with physicians. They foster an

integrated rather than a fragmented care system, assure continuity of care, and embrace the tenet that two heads are better than one.[78]

Also, physician assistants regard themselves as professionals who make a real contribution to the substance of the practice. For example, in an article describing the physician-physician assistant relationship, the AAPA states,

> The physician-PA team is effective because of the similarities in physician and PA training, the PA profession's commitment to practice with supervision, and the *efficiencies created by utilizing the strengths of each professional* in the clinical practice setting.[79]

It is at least arguable that the independent strengths of paralegals as professionals may not be as well promoted. One reason may be that the paralegal profession enjoys no such consistency and specificity among current state laws. While there are many state sources of definitions for paralegals, mostly these are couched in terms of "specifically delegated tasks" under the supervision of an attorney. To date, there are no existing regulations in any state that offer any real detail regarding the scope of a paralegal's practice; although recent attempts have been made,[80] there are also no statutes or court rules that set out regulatory requirements or disciplinary measures.

DISCUSSION QUESTIONS

1. There are many similarities between the PA and paralegal professions; however, there are also some important distinctions. Make three distinctions and explain why they are important.

2. Even though the two professions were established in the 1960s, physician assistants appear to have institutionalized themselves into mainstream medicine more quickly—they are better-defined as a profession and have in place a national required-certification scheme. Why do you think this is so?

CONCLUSION

Ideally, the members of the paralegal profession will be directly involved in deciding this issue. However, the profession does not speak with one voice. The two strongest national organizations, the NALA and the NFPA, cannot agree on a single standard. Although some feel that the ongoing debate between these two organizations is helpful, others feel it is a duplication of time, effort, and resources. The threat, real or perceived, is that outside influences will force decisions that the profession may not be ready to make.

Later chapters of this textbook consider whether the identity issue is best viewed as providing necessary flexibility to a new profession or as stymieing the progress and credibility of an established profession. By exploring various professional and ethical issues that face the paralegal profession, it will be easier to appreciate the evolution, accomplishments, and direction of this exciting field.

ENDNOTES

[1] The American Bar Association, founded in 1878, is the world's largest voluntary professional association, with more than 349,000 lawyer members and over 400,000 members overall. See *Profile of the American Bar Association, 1999*, ABA Division for Media Relations and Communication Services. As discussed in this book, the ABA has had a significant impact on the evolution of the paralegal profession.

[2] The ABA Standing Committee on Legal Assistants has jurisdiction over matters relating to the education, training, and use of legal assistants and other legal paraprofessionals. ABA, POLICY AND PROCEDURES HANDBOOK: 1994–95 46 (1994).

[3] U.S. DEP'T. OF LABOR, BUREAU OF LABOR STATISTICS, www.bls.gov <http://stats.bls.gov/emp/emptab3.htm> (last visited August 21, 2002).

[4] *Id.* See also Robert Sperber, *58% Paralegal Job Increase by Year 2005*, LEGAL ASSISTANT TODAY, May/June 1997.

[5] The ABA offers associate membership to paralegals and some state bar associations have created legal assistant/paralegal divisions within these organizations and have adopted rules for the utilization of legal assistants/paralegals.

[6] ABA COMM'N ON NONLAWYER PRACTICE, NONLAWYER ACTIVITIES IN LAW-RELATED SITUATIONS, *A REPORT WITH RECOMMENDATIONS*, 5 (August 1995).

[7] An example given was the federally funded Legal Counsel for the Elderly program and the use of paralegals to perform various services, such as assisting with medical care reimbursement. See Moore, *Improving the Delivery of Legal Services for the Elderly: A Comprehensive Approach*, 41 EMORY L.J. 805, 836, 845 (Summer 1992) for a discussion of this program.

[8] ABA COMM'N ON NONLAWYER PRACTICE, *supra* note 7, at 95–99.

[9] See *Missouri v. Jenkins*, 491 U.S. 274, 105 L. Ed. 2d 229, 109 S. Ct. 2463 (1989).

[10] Judy A. Toyer, *Teaching Lawyers How to Use the Skills of Legal Assistants Effectively*, Vol. 2, Number 1, SCOLA UPDATE xxx 1, 4, 5 (Fall 1999).

[11] See Lindsey Martin-Bowen, *Who Are You?*, NAT'L PARALEGAL REP., Year-end 1998.

[12] Merriam-Webster's Collegiate Dictionary defines "identity crisis" as "a state of confusion in an institution or organization regarding its nature or direction." Merriam-Webster Collegiate Dictionary/www.merriam-webster.com (last visited September 23, 2002).

[13] The terms "paralegal" and "legal assistant" will be used interchangeably for purposes of this book.

[14] One grammatical argument is that the term "legal assistant" should be used as the noun to describe the person and the term "paralegal" should be used as an adjective to describe the work performed. However, there is growing evidence that some firms distinguish between the two terms by assigning the title "legal assistant" to entry-level positions and the title "paralegal" to workers with many years of experience. See Cindy Collins, *Lower Paralegal Rates, Real Profits Fuel Law Firm Leverage In 1990s*, 14 No. 15 OF COUNSEL 1, 11 (August 7, 1995).

[15] See ABA By-Laws 21.12: "The terms legal assistant and paralegal are used interchangeably..."; Also see http//www.nala.org (Web site for the NALA).

[16] These organizations' Web sites use the terms interchangeably when reporting news or discussions that affect the profession. See http://www.aafpe.org and http://www.paralegals.org (Web site for the NFPA).

[17] For example, in Dallas, Texas, the members of the Dallas Area Legal Assistants voted to change their name to the Dallas Area Paralegal Association because the members perceived that there was a national trend to use the paralegal term over the legal assistant term. The president was quoted as saying, "Case law indicated that legal professionals with the title 'paralegal' versus 'legal assistant' have proven to be more effective in recovering legal fees." See Niccol Kording, *Don't Call Us DALA Anymore*, LEGAL ASSISTANT TODAY, Nov./Dec. 1995.

[18] Cindy Collins, *Lower Paralegal Rates, Real Profits Fuel Law Firm Leverage in 1990s*, 14 No. 15 OF COUNSEL 1, 11 (August 7, 1995).

[19] For example, at Southwest Texas State University, "office secretaries" have been renamed "administrative assistants."

[20] The NALS was formerly known as the National Association for Legal Secretaries, but now calls itself "the Association for Legal Professionals."

[21] See the NALS Web site at: http://www.nals.org/.

[22] NFPA, *Resolution adopted in 2002 regarding NFPA's Definition of a Paralegal,* at http://www.paralegals.org/Development/NFPA_def.htm (visited September 2002).

[23] ABA, *Guidelines for the Approval of Legal Assistant Education Programs,* FORWARD, 1997.

[24] The Guidelines impose minimum standards with respect to organization, administration, budget, advisory committee, educational programs, faculty, admissions, student services, placement, library, and physical facilities.

[25] ABA, *Standing Committee on Legal Assistants: History,* at http://www.abanet.org/legalassts/history.html (visited August 2000).

[26] "The plethora of titles commonly associated with non-lawyers who provide legal services causes confusion among professionals and laymen alike with regard to the definition and utilization of those individuals." Darcy L. Taylor, *What Is a Paralegal Anyway?* 37-JUL ADVOCATE (Idaho) 22, 22 (July 1994).

[27] California Business and Professions Code, Section 6400(c). "Under this legislation, 'legal document assistant' means any person who . . . provides, or assists in providing, or offers to provide, or offers to assist in providing, for compensation, any self-help service to a member of the public who is representing himself or herself in a legal matter, or who holds himself or herself out as someone who offers that service or has that authority."

[28] *Id.,* Section 6400(d). "'Self-help services' means all of the following: (1) Completing legal documents in a ministerial manner, selected by a person who is representing himself or herself in a legal matter, by typing or otherwise completing the documents at the person's specific direction. (2) Providing general published factual information that has been written or approved by an attorney, pertaining to legal procedures, rights, or obligations to a person who is representing himself or herself in a legal matter, to assist the person in representing himself or herself. This service in and of itself, shall not require registration as a legal document assistant. (3) Making published legal documents available to a person who is representing himself or herself in a legal matter."

[29] *Id.,* "To be eligible to apply for registration under this chapter as a legal document assistant, the applicant will possess at least one of the following: (a) a high school diploma or GED, and, either a minimum of two years of law-related experience under the supervision of a licensed attorney or a minimum of two years experience, prior to January 1, 1999, providing self-help service; (b) a baccalaureate degree in any field and either a minimum of one year of law-related experience under the supervision of a licensed attorney or a minimum of one year of experience, prior to January 1, 1999, providing self-help service; (c) a certificate of completion from a paralegal program that is institutionally accredited but not approved by the American Bar Association, that requires successful completion of a minimum of 24 semester units, or the equivalent, in legal specialization courses; (d) a certificate of completion from a paralegal program approved by the American Bar Association."

[30] Updated by the NALA as of 1/02.

[31] Adopted at the 1997 Annual Meeting of the ABA. www.abanet.org/legalassts/def98.html.

[32] www.paralegals.org/Development/NFPA_def.htm

[33] www.nala.org/terms.htm

[34] Sec. 1.4 MRSA c. 18, Sec. 921, 922.

[35] Calif. Business and Corporations Code, sec. 6450.

[36] See Appendix A.

[37] *Id.*

[38] See Appendix A, Kentucky, Rhode Island, and New Mexico.

[39] See Appendix A, New Hampshire.

[40] See Appendix A, Arizona, Oklahoma, and Washington.

[41] See Appendix A, New Jersey and South Carolina.

[42] See Appendix A.

[43] Rule 4-5.3. As of 6/8/2000, the Web site for the Florida Bar and the Florida Bar Rules (http://www.flabar.org) did not show that this change had been made.

[44] For example, see the ABA's "Nonlawyer Activity in Law-Related Situations," p. 95: "Several people . . . drew an analogy between legal paraprofessionals and medical paraprofessionals. They noted that the medical profession now uses paraprofessionals extensively . . . ."

[45] The sources for all information in this chapter regarding physician assistants were the APAP Web site at http://apap.org; and the AAPA Web site at http://www.aapa.org.

[46] The term "traditional practitioner" refers both to lawyers and physicians.

[47] ABA, COMM'N ON NONLAWYER PRACTICE, NONLAWYER ACTIVITY IN LAW-RELATED SITUATIONS 95 (August 1995).

[48] PHYSICIAN ASSISTANT CENSUS REPORT, AM. ACAD. OF PHYSICIAN ASSISTANTS (2001).

[49] OCCUPATIONAL OUTLOOK HANDBOOK (2002–03 ed., Government Printing Office, 2002) at 232.

[50] The Yale program is still known as the physician associate program.

[51] At the federal level these laws include the Social Securities Act, the Labor-HHS Appropriations, and policies such as the OSHA Standards, DEA, and Department of Health and Human Services. At the state level, a name change would affect legislative acts regulating physician assistants' scope of practice and reimbursement in nursing homes and hospitals, under individual insurance policies, Medicaid, and state laws regarding prescription privileges.

[52] An estimate by the AAPA is $125,000.00.

[53] The 1999 AAPA House of Delegates voted against a resolution that would have required an informal membership survey on this issue. See http://saapa.aapa.org//hottopics/ht9902.htm.

[54] AAPA, Facts at a Glance (1999) http://www.aapa.org/glance.html.

[55] ABA, STANDING COMM. ON LEGAL ASSISTANTS, GUIDELINES FOR THE APPROVAL OF LEGAL ASSISTANT EDUCATION PROGRAMS, 1997.

[56] Student Association of the American Academy of Physician Assistants, *Hot Topics #2—The Degree Issue,* at http:saaapa.aapa.org//hottopics/ht9902.htm (last visited Jan. 11, 2001).

[57] Physician assistant education is generally touted as being competency-based as opposed to degree-based, meaning that "students must demonstrate proficiency in various areas of medical knowledge and must meet behavioral and clinical learning objectives."

[58] However, applicants to physician assistant programs must complete roughly two years of college courses in basic science and behavioral science as prerequisites to PA training. This is analogous to pre-med studies that are required of medical students. The average PA program curriculum is 24–25 months long and consists of classroom and laboratory instruction in the basic medical and behavioral sciences, followed by clinical rotations.

[59] See *A Standardized Degree: Time to Move the Debate Forward,* J. FOR THE AM. ACAD. OF PHYSICIAN ASSISTANTS (November 1998).

[60] Survey forms were mailed to all individuals, both AAPA members and non-members, who were believed to be eligible to practice as PAs in the United States as of March 1, 1999, and for whom address information was available. In total, forms were mailed to 42,762 people—accounting for 92 percent of the 45,311 individuals eligible to practice as PAs as of the census expiration date. Completed surveys were received from 19,278 people or 43% of all individuals eligible to practice as physician assistants. http://www.aapa.org/research/intro2000.html (last visited January 11, 2001).

[61] The NFPA does provide a "grandfathering period" for those who do not have a bachelor's degree but do have a minimum of four years work experience as a paralegal.

[62] See National Federation of Paralegal Associations at www.paralegals.or/PACE/pacedev.html.

[63] ABA STANDING COMM. ON LEGAL ASSISTANTS, EDUCATIONAL PROGRAMS, G-301(D), GUIDELINES FOR THE APPROVAL OF LEGAL ASSISTANT EDUCATION PROGRAMS, 12, 13 (September 1997) (emphasis added).

[64] http://www.nccpa.net/CER_process.asp

[65] STANDARDIZATION OF REGULATORY TERMS: LICENSURE FOR PHYSICIAN ASSISTANTS, AAPA, 1999, http://www.aapa.org/gandp/license.html. Note: Mississippi has no physician assistant practice act; the District of Columbia licenses physician assistants.

[66] The AAPA is quick to point out, however, that physician assistants do not seek independent reimbursement, but reimbursement to their employer.

[67] *Issues related to licensure and governmental regulation of paralegals,* at http://www.nala.org.

[68] The AAPA has noted that

> Great progress has been made in standardizing the regulation of physician assistants. All jurisdictions, except Mississippi, have enacted fairly detailed statutes and regulations that define physician assistants, describe their scope of practice, discuss supervision, designate the agency that will administer the law, set application and renewal criteria, and establish disciplinary measures for specified violations of the law.

State Regulation of Physician Assistant Practice, November 1999, at http://www.aapa.org/gandp/statelaw.html.

[69] *Summary of State Regulation of Physician Assistant Practice* (Arkansas) at http://www.aapa.org/gandp/statelaw.html; see also Alaska.

[70] *Id.,* Colorado.

[71] *Id,* Alabama; also see Arizona.

[72] Early state laws governing PA practice frequently put a limit on the number of PAs that could be

supervised by a single physician, generally 2:1 and sometimes 1:1. See AAPA, *Ratio of Physician Assistants to Supervising Physicians,* December 1999, at www.aapa.org/gandp/ratio.html.

[73] The American Medical Association Council on Medical Service has stated, "Supervising physicians are the most knowledgeable of their own supervisory abilities and practice style, as well as the training and experience of physician extenders in their practice . . . . Specified ratios of supervisory physicians to physician extenders might restrict appropriate provision of care and could reduce access to care." See AMERICAN MEDICAL ASSOCIATION, *Ratio of Physicians to Physician Extenders,* COUNCIL ON MEDICAL SERVICE REPORT 10, December 1998.

[74] Most state bars have promulgated ethical guidelines for the utilization of paralegals/legal assistants by supervising attorneys.

[75] Without prior approval by the supervising attorney.

[76] ABA COMM'N ON NONLAWYER PRACTICE, NON-LAWYER ACTIVITY IN LAW-RELATED SITUATIONS, A REPORT WITH RECOMMENDATIONS, at 6 (August 1995).

[77] ASS'N OF PHYSICIAN ASSISTANT PROGRAMS, INTO THE FUTURE: PHYSICIAN ASSISTANTS LOOK TO THE 21ST CENTURY, 1999.

[78] AM. ACAD. OF PHYSICIAN ASSISTANTS, *The Physician-PA Team* (December 1998), at http://www.aapa.org/gandp/team/html (emphasis added).

[79] In 1998, the New Jersey Supreme Court Committee on Paralegal Education and Regulation issued a report that recommended a licensing plan for paralegals; however, the Supreme Court of New Jersey declined the recommendation and instead requested a less comprehensive plan.

[80] *Model State Legislation for Physician Assistants,* at http://www.aapa.org/gandp/modelaw.html.

Appendix A

NALA Summary of Definitions of Terms: Legal Assistant and Paralegal

From http://www.nala.org/terms.htm (accessed September 24, 2002). Released: January 23, 1997 (updated 1/02). Reprinted with permission of the National Association of Legal Assistants, Inc. 1516 S. Boston #200, Tulsa, OK 74119; www.nala.org.

[From http://www.nala.org/terms.htm]

Summary of Definitions of Terms:
Legal Assistant and Paralegal
Released: January 23, 1997 (updated 1/02)
National Association
of Legal Assistants, Inc.
1516 S. Boston, #200
Tulsa, Oklahoma 74119
(918) 587-6828; FAX (918) 582-6772

INTRODUCTION

The National Association of Legal Assistants, Inc., is a professional association composed of individual members and 92 state and local affiliated associations, representing over 18,000 legal assistants. Established in 1975, NALA goals and programs were developed by 800 charter members to:

increase the professional standing of legal assistants throughout the nation

provide uniformity in the identification of legal assistants

establish national standards of professional competence for legal assistants

provide uniformity among the states in the utilization of legal assistants

One of the services of this association is tracking legislative, court and bar association activities related to the paralegal profession. The following is a summary of the various definitions of the terms "paralegal" and "legal assistant" as of June, 1998, from 27 states, the United States Supreme Court, the American Bar Association, and the National Association of Legal Assistants.

DEFINITION OF LEGAL ASSISTANT/PARALEGAL

National associations, bar associations, legislatures and supreme courts have addressed the definition of legal assistants and paralegals. Through discussions within each group, similarities in the identification and duties of legal assistants are emerging with routine consistency. The common threads in these definitions and discussions are:

Legal Assistants:
1) have received specialized training through formal education or many years of experience;
2) work under the supervision and direction of an attorney; and

3) perform non-clerical, substantive legal work in assisting an attorney.

This paper summarizes these definitions.

National Organizations

The definition of "legal assistant" adopted in 1984 by the National Association of Legal Assistants is as follows:

> Legal assistants (also known as paralegals) are a distinguishable group of persons who assist attorneys in the delivery of legal services. Through formal education, training, and experience, legal assistants have knowledge and expertise regarding the legal system and substantive and procedural law which qualify them to do work of a legal nature under the supervision of an attorney.

In 1986, the American Bar Association adopted the following definition:

> A legal assistant is a person, qualified through education, training or work experience, who is employed or retained by a lawyer, law office, governmental agency, or other entity, in a capacity or function which involves the performance, under the ultimate direction and supervision of an attorney, of specifically-delegated substantive legal work, which work, for the most part, requires a sufficient knowledge of legal concepts that, absent such assistant, the attorney would perform the task.

In 1997, the American Bar Association amended this definition. The 1997 version is:

> A legal assistant or paralegal is a person qualified by education, training or work experience who is employed or retained by a lawyer, law office, corporation, governmental agency or other entity who performs specifically delegated substantive legal work for which a lawyer is responsible.

Both definitions recognize the terms "legal assistant" and "paralegal" as identical terms.

In fact, in recognition of the similarity of the definitions and the need for one clear definition, in July 2001, the NALA membership approved a resolution to adopt the ABA definition.

State Legislatures

Legislatures among the United States have also addressed this question. The State of Florida statute 57.104, effective 10/1/87, specifically states that legal assistants work under the direction of the supervision of an attorney.

Similar legislation was introduced in 1993 in the states of Indiana and Oklahoma. These bills call for the recoverability of legal assistant time in attorney fee awards. The Indiana bills (House Bill 1583; Senate Bill 424), passed April 27, 1993; now public law 93-6. They define paralegals as persons (1) qualified through education, training or work experience, and (2) employed by a lawyer, law office, governmental agency or other entity to work under the direction of an attorney in a capacity that involves the performance of substantive legal work that usually requires a sufficient knowledge of legal concepts and would be performed by the attorney in the absence of the paralegal. This definition is, essentially, the same as the definition adopted by the American Bar Association.

Oklahoma House Bill 1628 defined legal assistants in the same manner, using the ABA definition as a basis. This bill passed the Oklahoma House of Representatives on February 15, 1993. It did not reach the Senate floor during the session.

The California legislature recently enacted a statute governing the use of the terms paralegal and legal assistant. See Chapter 5.6 Paralegals 6450 of the Business and Professions Code. This law. effective January 1, 2001, defines "paralegal" as follows:

> 6450. (a) "Paralegal" means a person who either contracts with or is employed by an attorney, law firm, corporation, governmental agency, or other entity and who performs substantial legal work under the direction and supervision of an active member of the State Bar of California, as defined in Section 6060, or an attorney practicing law in the federal courts of this state, that has been specifically delegated by the attorney to him or her. Tasks performed by a paralegal include, but are not limited to, case planning, development, and management; legal research; interviewing clients; fact gathering and retrieving information; drafting and analyzing legal documents; collecting, compiling, and utilizing technical information to make an independent decision and recommendation to the supervising attorney; and representing clients before a state or federal administrative agency if that representation is permitted by statute, court rule, or administrative rule or regulation.

> 6454. The terms "paralegal," "legal assistant," "attorney assistant," "freelance paralegal," "independent paralegal," and "contract paralegal" are synonymous for purposes of this chapter.

Illinois Senate Bill 995, passed and signed by the governor on July 7, 1995, sets forth a definition of a paralegal. Effective January 1, 1996, the bill amended the Statute on Statutes by adding Section 1.35 as follows:

> Sec. 1.35. Paralegal. "Paralegal" means a person who is qualified through education, training, or work experience and is employed by a lawyer, law office, governmental agency, or other entity to work under the direction of an attorney in a capacity that involves the performance of substantive legal work that usually requires a sufficient knowledge of legal concepts and would be performed by the attorney in the absence of the paralegal. A reference in an Act to attorney fees includes paralegal fees, recoverable at market rates.

The Pennsylvania legislature has addressed paralegals in its unauthorized practice of law statutes. Effective July 11, 1996, Section 2524(a) of Title 42 of the Pennsylvania Consolidated Statutes now reads:

> (a) General rule.—Except as provided in subsection (b), any person, including, but not limited to, a paralegal or legal assistant, who within this Commonwealth shall practice law, or who shall hold himself out to the public as being entitled to practice law, or use or advertise the title of lawyer, attorney at law, attorney and counselor at law, counselor, or the equivalent in any language, in such as a manner to convey the impression that he is a practitioner of the law of any jurisdiction, without being an attorney at law or a corporation complying with 15 Pa.C.S. Ch. 29 (relating to professional corporations), commits a misdemeanor of the third degree[.] upon a first violation. A second or subsequent violation of this subsection constitutes a misdemeanor of the first degree.

This statute is in response to widespread concern that some individuals using the terms "paralegal" or "legal assistant" as their occupational title and in advertisements were doing so in a way that lead potential customers to believe they are authorized to deliver legal services. This legislation prohibits use of the terms "paralegal" and "legal assistant" in this fashion.

Rather than serving as a definition of what paralegals may do, the statute informs the public that paralegals and legal assistants do not deliver legal services without attorney supervision and cannot hold themselves out as individuals entitled to practice law.

The State of Maine statutorily defined the terms "legal assistant" and "paralegal" in 1999. By passage of LD 0724 the legislature has not only defined the terms, it provides that a person who claims to be a paralegal or legal assistant and does not meet the statutory definition commits a civil violation for which a forfeiture of up to $1000 may be adjudged. The adopted definition is:

> "Paralegal" and "legal assistant" mean a person, qualified by education, training or work experience, who is employed or retained by an attorney, law office, corporation, governmental agency or other entity and who performs specifically delegated substantive legal work for which an attorney is responsible."

Supreme Court Recognition

The United States Supreme Court encourages and recognizes the use of legal assistants working under the supervision of an attorney.

It has frequently been recognized in the lower courts that paralegals are capable of carrying out many tasks, under the supervision of an attorney, that might otherwise be performed by a lawyer and billed at a higher rate. *Missouri v. Jenkins*, 491 U.S. 274, S.Ct. At 2471-72 (1989).

State supreme courts have also addressed the definition of "legal assistant" or "paralegal" in their rules and in their opinions. Many of the state supreme court findings are included in this section. Further, the definitions of legal assistants or paralegals adopted by bar associations that are regulated by supreme courts are included in this section.

Kentucky   Among the earliest to address the utilization of paralegals in its rules is the Kentucky Supreme Court in adoption of rule 3.700 on September 4, 1979. The rule, revised through 1989, lists the following definition:

> For the purposes of this Rule, a paralegal is a person under the supervision and direction of a licensed lawyer, who may apply knowledge of law and legal procedures in rendering direct assistance to lawyers engaged in legal research; design, develop or plan modifications or new procedures, techniques, services, processes or applications; prepare or interpret legal documents and write detailed procedures for practicing in certain fields of law; select, compile and use technical information from such references as digests, encyclopedias or practice manuals; and analyze and follow procedural problems that involve independent decisions.

Michigan   Effective January 1, 2001, the Michigan Supreme Court amended its rules to provide the following:

> Rule 2.626 Attorney Fees. An award of attorney fees may include an award for the time and labor of any legal assistant who contributed nonclerical, legal support under the supervision of an attorney, provided the legal assistant meets the criteria set forth in Article 1, Section 6 of the Bylaws of the State Bar of Michigan.

Article 1, Section 6 of the Bylaws of the State Bar of Michigan states:

> Any person currently employed or retained by a lawyer, law office, governmental agency or other entity engaged in the practice of law, in a capacity or function which

involves the performance under the direction and supervision of an attorney of specifically delegated substantive legal work, which work, for the most part, requires a sufficient knowledge of legal concepts such that, absent that legal assistant, the attorney would perform the tasks and which is not primarily clerical or secretarial in nature, and;

(a) who has graduated from an ABA approved program of study for legal assistants and has a baccalaureate degree; or

(b) has received a baccalaureate degree in any field, plus not less than two years of in-house training as a legal assistant; or

(c) who has received an associate degree in the legal assistant field, plus not less than two years of in-house training as a legal assistant; or

(d) who has a minimum of four years of in-house training as a legal assistant; may upon submitting proof thereof at the time of application and annually thereafter become a Legal Assistant Affiliate Member of the State Bar of Michigan.

Rhode Island   In Rhode Island Supreme Court Provisional Order No. 18, effective February 1,1983 and revised through October 31, 1990, "legal assistant" is defined as follows:

A legal assistant is one who under the supervision of a lawyer, shall apply knowledge of law and legal procedures in rendering direct assistance to lawyers, clients and courts; design, develop and modify procedures, techniques, services and processes; prepare and interpret legal documents; detail procedures for practicing in certain fields of law; research, select, access, and compile information from the law library and other references; and analyze and handle procedural problems that involve independent decisions.

The guidelines accompanying this definition emphasize that legal assistants shall work under the direction and supervision of a lawyer who shall be ultimately responsible for their work product.

New Mexico   The New Mexico Supreme Court Judicial Pamphlet 16, 1986, states that:

A 'legal assistant' means a person, not admitted to the practice of law, who provides assistance to a licensed lawyer and for whose work that licensed lawyer is ultimately responsible. The assistance may include, but is not limited to, record and statistical research; investigation; analysis of records, documents and facts; problem analysis; preparation of legal memoranda; assistance in drafting legal documents, interrogatories and correspondence; completion of forms which have been prepared by or under the supervision of the supervising attorney; location of reported decisions, cite checking and shepardizing; and interviews of clients and witnesses. These and other types of assistance must be provided under the supervision and direction of a licensed attorney. . . .

The commentary to this definition includes references to the fact that the definition of "legal assistant" is intended to cover those persons usually designated as "legal assistants," "paralegals" and "lawyers assistants."

In 1995 the Supreme Court amended SCRA 1986, 24-101 of the Rules Governing the New Mexico Bar to establish a division of the bar for legal assistants, affirming the definition and listing qualifications for division membership.

New Hampshire   Supreme Court Administrative Rule 35, Guidelines for the Utilization by Lawyers of the Services of Legal Assistants Under the New Hampshire Rules of Professional Conduct, amended through 1987, define a legal assistant as:

a person not admitted to the practice of law in New Hampshire who is an employee of or an assistant to an active member of the New Hampshire Bar, a partnership comprised of active members of the New Hampshire Bar or a Professional Association within the meaning of RSA Chapter 294-A, and who, under the control and supervision of an active member of the New Hampshire Bar, renders services related to but not constituting the practice of law.

South Dakota   In Rule 92-5, March 6, 1992, the Supreme Court of South Dakota adopted the following definition of legal assistants.

Legal assistants (also known as paralegals) are a distinguishable group of persons who assist attorneys in the delivery of legal services. Through formal education, training, and experience, legal assistants have knowledge and expertise regarding the legal system and substantive and procedural law which qualify them to do work of a legal nature under the direct supervision of a licensed lawyer.

The rule further states that "any person having been convicted of a felony shall not serve as a legal assistant in the State of South Dakota, unless upon application to the Supreme Court of South Dakota, establishing good moral character and restoration of full civil rights, and its approval thereof."

The South Dakota rule goes on to list seven minimum qualifications as follows:

(1) Successful completion of the Certified Legal Assistant (CLA) examination of the National Association of Legal Assistants, Inc.; or

(2) Graduation from an ABA approved program of study for legal assistants; or

(3) Graduation from a course of study for legal assistants which is institutionally accredited but not ABA approved, and which requires not less than the equivalent of sixty semester hours of classroom study; or

(4) Graduation from a course of study for legal assistants, other than those set forth in (2) and (3) above, plus not less than six months of in-house training as a legal assistant; or

(5) A baccalaureate degree in any field, plus not less than six months in-house training as a legal assistant; or

(6) A minimum of three years of law-related experience under the supervision of a lawyer, including at least six months of in-house training as a legal assistant; or

(7) Two years of in-house training as a legal assistant.

Indiana   The Indiana Supreme Court adopted Guidelines on the Use of Legal Assistants January 1, 1994, which are part of the Indiana Rules of Professional Conduct. The rules provide:

"A legal assistant shall perform services only under the direct supervision of lawyer authorized to practice in the State of Indiana and in the employ of the lawyer or the lawyer's employer. Independent legal assistants, to-wit, those not employed by a specific firm or by specific lawyers are prohibited. A lawyer is responsible for all of the professional actions of a legal assistant performing legal assistant services at the lawyer's direction, and should take reasonable measures to insure that the legal assistant's conduct is consistent with the lawyer's obligations under the Rules of Professional Conduct."

The guidelines provide that a lawyer may delegate to a legal assistant any task normally performed by the lawyer; however, any task prohibited by statute, court rule, administrative rule or regulation, controlling authority, (or the) *Indiana Rules of Professional Conduct* may not be assigned to a non-lawyer. They also provide that a lawyer may charge for the work performed by a legal assistant. Finally, the guidelines set forth a statement of legal assistant ethics and provide that all lawyers who employ legal assistants in the State of Indiana shall assure that such legal assistants conform their conduct to be consistent with stated ethical standards.

North Dakota   Amendments to the North Dakota Rules of Professional Conduct adopted December 11, 1996 by the North Dakota Supreme Court, with an effective date of March 1, 1997, include rules which govern legal assistants/paralegals in North Dakota. Rules 1.5 (Fees), 5.3 Responsibilities Regarding Nonlawyer Assistants, 7.2 Firm Names and Letterheads and the Terms section of the NDRPC include a definition of "legal assistant", suggested minimum standards, and comments related to supervision of legal assistants, the unauthorized practice of law and billing for work performed by a legal assistant.

The rules state the following definition:

> "Legal Assistant" (or paralegal) means a person who assists lawyers in the delivery of legal services, and who through formal education, training, or experience, has knowledge and expertise regarding the legal system and substantive and procedural law which qualifies the person to do work of a legal nature under the direct supervision of a licensed lawyer.

Virginia   On March 8, 1996, the Virginia State Bar Standing Committee on the Unauthorized Practice of Law adopted a resolution stating that a legal assistant working under direction of a member of the Virginia State Bar in conformance with the Standards and Guidelines would not be engaged in the unauthorized practice of law and that the employment or supervision by a Virginia State Bar member of legal assistants who conform to the Standards and Guidelines would be in the best interest of the public.

The resolution recommends that members of the Virginia State Bar make all reasonable efforts to encourage all legal assistants to subscribe and conform to the Standards and Guidelines. This resolution adopts the following definition of a legal assistant (paralegal):

> "as one who is a specially trained individual who performs substantive legal work that requires a knowledge of legal concepts and who either works under the supervision of an attorney, who assumes professional responsibility for the final work product, or works in areas where lay individuals are explicitly authorized by statute or regulation to assume certain law-related responsibilities."

Cases

Arizona   In *Continental Townhouses E. Unit One Ass'n v. Brockbank*, 152 Ariz. 537, 733P.2d 1120, 73 A.L.R.4th 921 (1986), the Arizona Court of Appeals considered whether the time of a non-lawyer employee may be included in attorney fee awards. In its opinion, the Court relied upon the definition of "legal assistant" formulated by the American Bar Association. The court also used the terms "legal assistant" and "paralegal" interchangeably.

New Jersey   In 1990, the New Jersey Committee on Unauthorized Practice of Law issued Opinion No. 24 which held that legal assistants or paralegals who contract their services to attorneys are engaged in the unauthorized practice of law. The New Jersey Committee on the Unauthorized Practice of Law is appointed by the Supreme Court, thus its findings and opinions become Supreme Court Rule. This opinion was appealed to the New Jersey Supreme Court. The Supreme Court issued its Opinion on May 14,1992, and held:

The evidence does not support a categorical ban on all independent paralegals practicing in New Jersey. Given the appropriate instructions and supervision, paralegals, whether as employees or independent contractors, are valuable and necessary members of an attorney's work force in the effective and efficient practice of law.

The court further stated that charges for non-lawyers' time that properly fall within the definition of "attorney fees" are those that are clearly shown to have been made (1) for the delegated performance of substantive legal work, that (2) would otherwise have to be performed by a lawyer, (3) at a rate higher than that charged for non-lawyers' time.

Oklahoma   In *Taylor v. Chubb*, 874 P.2d 806 (Okla. 1994), the Oklahoma Supreme Court held that charges for legal assistants could and should be included by courts in attorney fee award decisions. In its decision, the court refers to the definition of a legal assistant as promulgated by the American Bar Association, and specifically enumerated a list of duties that may be properly performed by legal assistants as follows:

1. Interview clients
2. Draft pleadings and other documents
3. Carry on legal research, both conventional and computer aided
4. Research public records
5. Prepare discovery requests and responses
6. Schedule depositions
7. Summarize depositions and other discovery responses
8. Coordinate and manage document production
9. Locate and interview witnesses
10. Organize pleadings, trial exhibits and other documents
11. Prepare witness and exhibit lists
12. Prepare trial notebooks
13. Prepare for the attendance of witnesses at trial
14. Assist lawyers at trials

South Carolina   In *The State of South Carolina v. Robinson*, Opinion No 24391, filed March 18,1996, the court stated the function of a paralegal was addressed In re: Easler, 275, S.C.400, 272 S.E.2d 32 (1980):

Paralegals are routinely employed by licensed attorneys to assist in the preparation of legal documents such as deeds and mortgages. The activities of a paralegal do not constitute the practice of law as long as they are limited to work of a preparatory nature, such as legal research, investigation, or the composition of legal documents, which enable the licensed attorney-employer to carry a given matter to a conclusion through his own examination, approval or additional effort. Id. at 400, 272 S.E.2d at 32-33.

The opinions stated that while there are no regulations dealing specifically with paralegals, requiring a paralegal to work under the supervision of a licensed attorney ensures control over his or her activities by making the supervising attorney responsible. See Rule 5.3 of the Rules of Professional Conduct, Rule 407SCACR (supervising attorney is responsible for work of non-lawyer employees). Accordingly, to legitimately provide services as a paralegal, one must work in conjunction with a licensed attorney."

Washington   Adopted 12/3/94, the Washington State Bar Association Board of Governors has established guidelines for the utilization of legal assistant services. The guidelines are based on the ABA Model Guidelines for Utilization of Legal Assistants and adopt the definition of legal assistant/paralegal promulgated by the American Bar Association.

In *Absher Construction Company v. Kent School District*, 29 Wn. App. 841, (1995),the Washington Court of Appeals considered the question of the award of non-lawyer time in attorney fee awards if the non-lawyer is a legal assistant. The Court defined a legal assistant as one who is "qualified through education, training, or work experience, is employed or retained by a lawyer, law office, governmental agency or other entity in a capacity or function which involves a performance, under the ultimate direction and supervision of an attorney, of specifically delegated legal work, which work, for the most part requires a sufficient knowledge of legal concepts that, absent such assistant, the attorney would perform the task." The Court set forth the following criteria relevant in determining whether such services should be compensated:

1. The services performed by the nonlawyer personnel must be legal in nature.

2. The performance of these services must be supervised by an attorney.

3. The qualifications of the person performing the services must be specified in the request for fees in sufficient detail to demonstrate that the person is qualified by virtue of education, training, or work experience to perform substantive legal work.

4. The nature of the services performed must be specified in the request for fees in order to allow the reviewing court to determine that the services performed were legal rather than clerical.

5. As with attorney time, the amount of time expended must be set forth and must be reasonable; and

6. The amount charged must reflect reasonable community standards for charges by that category of personnel.

BAR ASSOCIATION ACTIVITY

Bar associations in the following states have defined legal assistants as qualified and educated individuals working under the supervision of attorneys:

Alaska

Arizona

California (Santa Barbara Bar)

Colorado Connecticut

Florida

Illinois

Iowa

Kansas

Kentucky

Massachusetts

Michigan

Minnesota

Missouri

New Mexico

New Hampshire

North Carolina

North Dakota

Ohio

Oregon

Rhode Island

South Carolina

South Dakota

Tennessee

Texas

Virginia

West Virginia

Wisconsin

The following are examples of bar resolutions or guidelines adopted by the associations to assist attorneys in the utilization of paralegal services.

Bar Association Sections and Divisions

Michigan   The Bylaws of the State Bar of Michigan, Article 1, Sec. 6, defines "legal assistant" for the purposes of membership in the State Bar Legal Assistant Section, as follows:

> Any person currently employed or retained by a lawyer, law office, governmental agency or other entity engaged in the practice of law, in a capacity or function which involves the performance under the direction and supervision of an attorney of specifically delegated substantive legal work, which work, for the most part, requires a sufficient knowledge of legal concepts such that, absent that legal assistant, the attorney would perform the tasks and which is not primarily clerical or secretarial in nature, and;
>
> (a) who has graduated from an ABA approved program of study for legal assistants and has a baccalaureate degree; or
>
> (b) has received a baccalaureate degree in any field, plus not less than two years of in-house training as a legal assistant; or

(c) who has received an associate degree in the legal assistant field, plus not less than two years of in-house training as a legal assistant; or

(d) who has a minimum of four years of in-house training as a legal assistant . . .

On April 23, 1993, the Michigan State Board of Commissioners announced approval of Michigan Guidelines for the Utilization of Legal Assistants. In recognition of the professional status of legal assistants, the guidelines cite *Missouri v. Jenkins* in allowing that a fee arrangement with a client may include a reasonable charge for work performed by legal assistants at market rates.

Nevada   As part of the creation of a Division of Legal Assistants, the State Bar of Nevada has adopted the following definition of a legal assistant: (12/94)

> A legal assistant (also known as a paralegal) is a person, qualified through education, training or work experience, who is employed or retained by a lawyer, law office, governmental agency, or other entity in a capacity or function which involves the performance, under the ultimate direction and supervision of an attorney, of specifically delegated substantive legal work, which work, for the most part, requires sufficient knowledge of legal concepts that, absent such an assistant, the attorney would perform the task.

This definition is identical to that adopted by the American Bar Association in 1986.

Texas   As early as 1981, the Board of Directors, State Bar of Texas, adopted General Guidelines for the Utilization of the Services of Legal Assistants by Attorneys. These guidelines require that a legal assistant work under the supervision of an attorney and shall not give legal advice or otherwise engage in the unauthorized practice of law. An attorney may allow a legal assistant under his or her supervision and direction to perform delegated services in the representation of that attorney's clients provided: 1) the client understands the legal assistant is not an attorney; 2) the attorney maintains a direct relationship with the client; 3) the attorney directs and supervises the legal assistant; and 4) the attorney remains professionally responsible for the client and the client's legal matters. The State Bar of Texas was the first state to establish a membership division for legal assistants within its bar association.

Bar Association Guidelines

Colorado   One of the first states to establish guidelines for paralegals in July 1986, the Colorado Bar has adopted the following definition of a paralegal:

> Legal assistants (also known as paralegals) are a distinguishable group of persons who assist attorneys in the delivery of legal services. Through formal education, training and experience, legal assistants have knowledge and expertise regarding the legal system and substantive and procedural law which will qualify them to do work of a legal nature under the direct supervision of a licensed attorney.

Connecticut   From a December 11, 1985 Report of Connecticut Bar Association Special Inter-Committee Group to Study the Role of Paralegals, the committee sets forth recommendations as to what the professional obligations of lawyers should be in relation to paralegals. The report uses "paralegal" and "legal assistant" as having identical meanings and define the terms as follows:

> persons employed by law offices who are not admitted to practice law but a major part of whose work is performing tasks commonly performed by lawyers and who are under the general supervision and control of lawyers. Paralegals may be salaried employees or independent contractors such as freelance paralegals utilized on occasion by lawyers for special assignments.

The Connecticut Bar Association offers associate membership to paralegals.

Georgia   Georgia Advisory Opinion No. 21, revised May 20, 1983, sets forth the following definition of legal assistant as follows:

> For the purposes of this opinion, the terms 'legal assistant,' 'paraprofessional,' and 'paralegal' are defined as any lay person not admitted to the practice of law in this state who is an employee of or an assistant to, an active member of the State Bar of Georgia or of a partnership or professional corporation comprised of active members of the State Bar of Georgia and who renders services relating to the law to such member, partnership or professional corporation under the direct control, supervision and compensation of a member of the State Bar of Georgia.

Idaho   In State Bar Resolution 94-7, adopted November, 1994, the Idaho State Bar urged the Supreme Court to adopt the ABA Model Standards and Guidelines for Utilization of Legal Assistant Services, which includes the definition of a legal assistant/paralegal promulgated by the American Bar Association.

Maryland   In 2001, the Maryland State Bar Association began offering associate membership to legal assistants. The definition and requirement states:

> Paralegal/Legal Assistant. A paralegal/legal assistant is a person qualified through education, training or work experience to perform work that requires knowledge of legal concepts and is customarily, but not exclusively, performed by a lawyer. This person shall be retained or employed by a lawyer, law office, governmental agency or other entity or be authorized by administrative, statutory, or court authority to perform this work. A paralegal/legal assistant may apply for associate membership if sponsored by an active lawyer member of the Association.

New York   The New York State Bar Association Committee on Law Office Economics and Management Subcommittee on Legal Assistants published a pamphlet entitled "The Expanding Role of the Legal Assistant in New York State." This references guidelines for the utilization of legal assistants, published in 1976, and adopts the definition of a legal assistant as promulgated by the American Bar Association.

Oklahoma   During its meeting on August 20, 1999, the Oklahoma Bar Association Board of Governors adopted a resolution defining the terms "legal assistant" and "paralegal" to provide guidance to members of the bar. The board approved the following definition as a guide to

Oklahoma attorneys, corporations or other entities to utilize the services of legal assistants/paralegals and bill their clients separately for such services:

> A legal assistant or paralegal is a person qualified by education, training or work experience who is employed or retained by a lawyer, law office, corporation, governmental agency or other entity who performs specifically delegated substantive legal work for which a lawyer is responsible, and absent such assistant, the lawyer would perform the task.

Effective September 15, 2000, the Oklahoma Bar Association adopted minimum qualification standards to serve as a guide for Oklahoma attorneys. The guidelines include the above quoted definition, prescribes standards for qualified legal assistants, and includes a recommendation for continuing legal education. Click here to review the guidelines in their entirety.

Oregon   The Oregon State Bar Association has published a pamphlet entitled "The Lawyer and the Legal Assistant" (undated). This states the terms "legal assistant" and "paralegal" are synonymous terms, and that legal assistants must work under the direct supervision of a licensed attorney.

Utah   As published in January 1994, the Office of Attorney Discipline of the Utah State Bar has set forth standards related to the ethical use of paralegals in the practice of law. The office has reviewed the National Association of Legal Assistants Guidelines for Utilizing Paralegals as well as the ABA Model guidelines for Utilization of Legal Assistant Services and "in an attempt to provide a safe harbor for those lawyers utilizing paralegals until the Supreme Court Advisory Committee on Discipline formally considers amending Rule 5.3 and 5.5(b) of the Rules of Professional Conduct, promulgates standards and guidelines." The guidelines require attorney supervision of legal assistants, and list general duties and responsibilities of a legal assistant.

West Virginia   During its annual meeting held July 16-17, 1999, The West Virginia State Bar Board of Governors approved the following definition:

> A legal assistant is a person, qualified through education, training or work experience, who is employed or retained by a lawyer, law office, governmental agency, or other entity, in a capacity or function which involves the performance, under the ultimate direction and supervision of an attorney, of delegated substantive legal work, which work, for the most part, requires a sufficient knowledge of legal concepts that, absent such assistance, the attorney would perform the task.

The members of the The State Bar Legal Assistant Committee felt the adoption of the definition of a legal assistant/paralegal by The State Bar is important to the legal profession in providing uniformity in the identification of legal assistants.

Wisconsin   The following definition of a paralegal has been approved by the Wisconsin State Bar Paralegal Task Force, November 1996:

> A 'paralegal' is an individual qualified through education and training, who is supervised by a lawyer licensed to practice law in this State, to perform substantive legal work requiring a sufficient knowledge of legal concepts that, absent the paralegal, the attorney would perform the work.

SUMMARY

All definitions describe a professional group working under the direct supervision of an attorney, and acknowledge that the terms "paralegal" and "legal assistant" are used synonymously. They intentionally exclude persons who do not work under attorney supervision even though they may perform law related work. This direct supervision is required whether the legal assistant is utilized in the course of full time employment or is being utilized on a contractual basis by an attorney or firm. In both instances, the work product of the legal assistant becomes merged into the final product of the supervising attorney.

Bar association definitions may be found in guidelines and informational materials developed by the bar associations to assist their members in understanding more about the utilization of legal assistants and how this may assist their practice. In addition, bar associations that offer associate membership to legal assistants include a definition of "legal assistants" or "paralegals" within the membership requirements.

Appendix B

AAfPE Core Competencies for Paralegal Programs

Report of the Task Force on Core Competencies

From http://www.aafpe.org/core.html (accessed September 24, 2002). Web page dated 06/23/2002. © American Association for Paralegal Education.

Core Competencies Task Force:

Thomas Eimermann, Illinois State University, Chair

David Dye, Missouri Western State College

Lynn Kickingbird, Oklahoma City University

Kathryn Myers, Saint Mary-of-the Woods College

Clark Moscrip, St. Mary's College

Diane Petropulos, Sonoma State University

Jules Tryk, Cuyahoga Community College

PREAMBLE

In order to be a successful paralegal/legal assistant, a person must not only possess a common core of legal knowledge, but also must have acquired vital critical thinking, organizational, communication, and interpersonal skills. All paralegal education programs, regardless of the specialty areas they choose to emphasize, should provide an integrated set of core courses that develop the following competencies.

This is an inspirational document developed by an AAfPE Task Force for the benefit of paralegal educators. It was approved and adopted by the Board of Directors at their meeting in San Francisco, California, on October 11, 1994.

SKILL DEVELOPMENT

A. Critical Thinking Skills

Paralegal education programs should be able to demonstrate that their courses incorporate learning strategies which develop their students' abilities to:

1. analyze a problem by identifying and evaluating alternative solutions;
2. logically formulate and evaluate solutions to problems and arguments in support of specific positions;
3. identify interrelationships among cases, stat-utes, regulations, and other legal authorities;
4. apply recognized legal authority to a specific factual situation;
5. recognize when and why varied fact situations make it appropriate to apply exceptions to general legal rules;
6. determine which areas of law are relevant to a particular situation;

7. apply principles of professional ethics to specific fact situations;

8. distinguish evidentiary facts from other material and/or controlling facts; and

9. identify factual omissions and inconsistencies.

B. Organizational Skills

Paralegal education programs should be able to demonstrate that their courses incorporate learning strategies which develop their students' abilities to:

1. categorize information;

2. prioritize information;

3. organize information; and

4. utilize time efficiently.

C. General Communication Skills

Paralegal education programs should be able to demonstrate that their courses incorporate learning strategies which develop their students' abilities to:

1. read with comprehension;

2. listen effectively and accurately interpret nonverbal communication;

3. write in clear, concise, and grammatically correct English;

4. speak in clear, concise, and grammatically correct English;

5. use language to persuade; and

6. tailor the nature of the communication to maximize understanding in the intended audience, including those with different levels of education and different cultural backgrounds.

D. Interpersonal Skills

Paralegal education programs should be able to demonstrate that their courses incorporate learning strategies which develop their students' abilities to:

1. establish rapport and interact with lawyers, clients, witnesses, court personnel, co-workers, and other business professionals;

2. be diplomatic and tactful;

3. be flexible and adaptable;

4. be assertive without being aggressive;

5. work effectively as part of a team when appropriate.; and

6. work independently and with a minimal amount of supervision when appropriate.

E. Legal Research Skills

Legal research involves the application of the critical thinking, organizational, and communications skills listed above. Courses should teach students how to apply these skills to be able to:

1. use the resources available in a standard law library to locate applicable statutes, administrative regulations, constitutional provisions, court cases, and other primary source materials;

2. use LEXIS, WESTLAW, and/or other computer assisted legal research programs to locate applicable statutes, administrative regulations, constitutional provisions, court cases, and other primary source materials;

3. use the resources of a standard law library to locate treatises, law review articles, legal encyclopedia, and other secondary source materials that help to explain the law; and

4. "cite check" legal sources.

F. Legal Writing Skills

Legal writing involves the application of the critical thinking, organizational, and communications skills listed above. Courses should teach students how to apply these skills to be able to:

1. report legal research findings in a standard interoffice memo or other appropriate format;

2. use appropriate citations for sources;

3. use the proper format and appropriate content in drafting client correspondence and legal documents; and

4. modify standardized forms found in form books, pleadings files, or a computer data bank.

G. Computer Skills

Although it is certainly possible for an individual to perform many paralegal tasks without the use of computers, increasing levels of computer literacy will be demanded in the future. Courses should teach students how to:

1. use the basic features of at least one commonly used word processing program, database program, and spreadsheet program; and

2. use the basic features of a computer assisted legal research program and other electronic resources.

H. Interviewing and Investigation Skills

Interviewing and investigation involve the application of the critical thinking, organizational, and communications skills listed above. Courses should teach students how to:

1. identify witnesses or potential parties to a suit;

2. conduct an effective interview and record appropriate, accurate statements;

3. gain access to information that is commonly kept by government agencies; and

4. prepare releses and requests to gain access to medical and corporate records.

ACQUISITION OF KNOWLEDGE

Although paralegals work in a variety of specialty areas, there is a common core of legal knowledge that all paralegals should possess.

A. Organization and Operation of the Legal System

Paralegal education programs should be able to demonstrate that their curricula include courses or segments of courses which provide their students with an understanding of:

1. the major functions the law serves in modern society;
2. how common law traditions are reflected in today's legal system; how law is classified on the basis of its source and its function; the difference between substantive and procedural law; and the difference between civil and criminal law;
3. the general structure of the U.S. legal system at the federal, state, and local levels;
4. the detailed structure of the state and local courts in the state within which the paralegal program is located;
5. the differences in function and procedure among trial courts, appellate courts, and administrative hearings; and
6. the functions performed by the various officials involved in the court system (e.g., police, lawyers, judges, court clerks, court reporters).

B. Organization and Operation of Law Offices

Paralegal education programs should be able to demonstrate that their curricula include courses or segments of courses which provide their students with an understanding of:

1. the various types of practice arrangements lawyers use for the delivery of legal services to the general public and the indigent, as well as in corporations and government agencies;
2. the functions performed by the various people typically working in a law office, including attorneys (partners and associates), paralegal/legal assistants, clerical personnel, investigators, and others; and
3. the organizational structure and the administrative procedures (including time-keeping and billing systems) that are commonly used in law offices.

C. The Paralegal Profession and Ethical Obligations

Paralegal education programs should be able to demonstrate that their curricula include courses or segments of courses which provide their students with an understanding of:

1. the factors which lead attorneys to employ paralegals/legal assistants;
2. the types of duties paralegal/legal assistants perform when working in various areas of the law;
3. definitions that are most commonly used for the following terms: paralegal, legal assistant, independent paralegal, legal technician, freelance paralegal, certification, registration, and licensure;
4. an understanding of the ethical responsibilities that have been established by statutes, court decisions, and court rules affecting paralegals/legal assistants and lawyers (including conflict of interest, confidentiality, competence, solicitation, fees and billing, obligations of attorneys to clients, and protection of client funds); and
5. the nature of the supervision that must be present in order to avoid situations that constitute the unauthorized practice of law.

D. Contracts

Although it is certainly possible for paralegals/legal assistants to work in some specialty areas without an extensive knowledge of contracts, an understanding of some of the most basic principles of contracts is very useful in a wide variety of specialty areas. Paralegal education programs should be able to demonstrate that their curricula include courses or segments of courses which provide their students with an understanding of:

1. the manner in which contracts are formed and what elements must be present for a contract to be valid;

2. the rights and obligations of the various parties to contract, as well as the rights of third parties; and

3. remedies that are available when contracts are breached and the steps that must be taken to invoke those remedies.

E. Torts

Although it is certainly possible for paralegals/legal assistants to work in some specialty areas without an extensive knowledge of torts, the basic principles of this area of law are applicable to such a large number of matters as to justify its inclusion among the core competencies needed for quality paralegal programs. Paralegal education programs should be able to demonstrate that their curricula include courses or segments of courses which provide their students with an understanding of:

1. the concepts of negligence, duty, breach, proximate cause, intentional torts, and strict liability; and

2. the various types of damages that can be awarded and what needs to be established to collect such damages.

F. Business Organizations

Although it is certainly possible for paralegals/legal assistants to work in some specialty areas without an extensive knowledge of business organizations, the basic principles of this area of law are applicable to a large enough number of matters as to justify its inclusion among the core competencies needed for quality paralegal programs. Paralegal education programs should be able to demonstrate that their curricula include courses or segments of courses which provide their students with an understanding of:

1. the basic forms and functions of business organizations, including sole proprietorships, partnerships, limited partnerships, for profit corporations, and not-for-profit corporations.

G. Litigation Procedures

Although it is certainly possible for paralegals/legal assistants to work in jobs where they are not directly involved in litigation, the number of matters that are litigated are great enough to justify its inclusion among the core competencies needed for quality paralegal programs. Paralegal education programs should be able to demonstrate that their curricula include courses or segments of courses which provide their students with an understanding of:

1. the basic differences between civil and criminal procedure;
2. the nature of the remedies that are available through civil litigation;
3. the form, content, and function of the legal documents that are typically prepared as part of the litigation process; and
4. the types of calendaring and tickler systems that are frequently used as part of a "case management" system.

Paralegal Associations and Organizations

INTRODUCTION

Membership in a paralegal organization carries distinct advantages for practicing paralegals, including support, professional networks, job banks, continuing legal education, access to seminars, and social opportunities. Professional organizations can serve as a resource for information and news about the paralegal profession and often publish newsletters or journals. They also conduct surveys of the membership to determine salaries and other conditions of employment. Survey results are extremely useful when conducting a job search, or from an employer's perspective, a search for an employee.

Another important role often played by these organizations is that of a representative of the profession. This role becomes more critical as the paralegal profession evolves and becomes more closely scrutinized by both the legal community and the general public.

Finally, it is important for paralegal students to be aware that some paralegal organizations offer scholarships and discounted memberships for students.

LOCAL AND STATE PARALEGAL ORGANIZATIONS

Almost every state in the country boasts a statewide professional organization for legal assistants, as well as one or more local organizations. Usually the statewide organization will be located in the state's capital city and the local organizations are located in the larger metropolitan areas. These organizations may or may not be affiliated with the state or local bar associations. States where bar associations permit paralegals to participate as associate members or in selected sections include Alaska, California, Colorado, Florida, Illinois, Kansas, Maryland, Michigan, Minnesota, Nevada, New Jersey, New Mexico, North Dakota, Ohio, Rhode Island, Texas, Utah, Virginia, and Wisconsin.[1] In the following excerpt, both disadvantages and advantages to paralegal involvement in bar associations are considered.

Advantages, Disadvantages and Methods to Accomplish
Reasons for Pursuing Bar Association Involvement

- Paralegals benefit from assisting attorneys to realize the nature of paralegal education that qualifies them to perform legally substantive tasks. If attorneys understand paralegal qualifications, paralegals may receive more challenging tasks and increased responsibility.

- Paralegals benefit from assisting attorneys to understand the complex legal tasks they are capable of performing. If attorneys understand the level of work paralegals can perform, paralegals may be better utilized and become respected members of the legal team.

- Paralegals benefit from assisting attorneys to recognize their continuing legal education needs. If attorneys understand that paralegal knowledge is directly related to the quality and quantity of work paralegals are capable of producing, attorneys may be more likely to sponsor attendance at CLE seminars, which in turn improves paralegals' knowledge and capabilities.

Consequence: The entire legal community wins when attorneys recognize that paralegals have the education and experience to perform legally substantive tasks. When attorneys believe that paralegals are qualified, paralegals receive increased responsibility and more substantive work, and their work is more satisfying and challenging. They develop a sense of pride and ownership in the work and in its result. They become loyal and dedicated employees and more valued members of the profession.

Types of Involvement

- Be a conduit of information about the paralegal profession, the local paralegal association and NFPA.

- Plan and present seminars for attorneys that promote the cost-efficient utilization of paralegal skills in the delivery of legal services.

- Interact with members of the bar to increase attorney awareness of paralegal education, roles, responsibilities and utilization.

- Create a bar association paralegal committee to address issues specific to paralegals in the delivery of legal services.

- Join the bar association as associate members.

Potential Disadvantages of Becoming Involved with Bar Associations

NFPA members have determined that the paralegal profession should be independent and self-directed, a premise which may not be supported by members of the bar.

For every paralegal who joins a local or state bar association, the local or state paralegal association stands to lose the participation, dues revenues or support of that paralegal.[2]

Bar associations are created to address issues related to attorneys, not paralegals; therefore, the majority of issues with which the bar association deals will not affect paralegals.

The goals and purposes of bar associations may differ significantly from those of paralegal associations.

If the bar association does not support paralegals or afford paralegals a vote on issues which affect them and their participation in the delivery of legal services, the paralegal members or committee may not have an impact on attorneys' views towards paralegals.

Most tangible membership benefits available through bar associations are available through NFPA and/or local paralegal associations, *e.g.*, car rental discounts, group disability, life and medical insurance, credit cards, express delivery discounts and credit unions.

Potential Advantages of Becoming Involved with Bar Associations

For paralegals to consider becoming involved in bar associations, one or more of the following factors should be present:

- Most importantly, paralegals have a vote in decisions that affect them;
- Paralegals are permitted to join bar association committees, sections and divisions;
- Paralegals receive the same or equivalent benefits of membership that are provided to other members of the bar association;
- Paralegals are encouraged to write for publications that promote the cost-efficient utilization of paralegal services, and those publications are supported and/or published by the bar association;
- Paralegals are consulted on matters before the bar which directly affect utilization of paralegals in the delivery of legal services;
- Paralegals' opinions pertaining to the role of paralegals are valued by members of the bar; and
- Opportunities for the advantages listed above are not available through paralegal association membership.

Potential Benefits of Becoming Involved with Bar Associations

- To obtain the advantages listed above under "Potential Advantages."
- To have the right to offer opinions concerning issues that affect paralegal participation in the delivery of legal services.
- To obtain the membership discounts available to bar association members on items such as copying services, travel-related services and bar-sponsored publications.
- To obtain reduced registration fees to attend bar association-sponsored continuing legal education seminars, functions and meetings.
- To participate in committees, sections or divisions related to a paralegal's specialty area of law, *e.g.*, real estate, matrimonial, litigation, probate.
- To participate in committees focusing on law office management, *pro bono* legal services, the unauthorized practice of law, legal ethics and other issues not directly related to a specialty, but of interest to paralegals.

- To participate in activities relating to paralegal regulation, such as on task forces and committees.

- To assist attorneys to understand that the paralegal profession is self-directed.

Steps Which May Be Taken to Facilitate Paralegal Involvement with Bar Associations

Ask what you can do for the bar association, not what the bar association can do for you.

Contact bar association leaders to make them aware of paralegal interest in bar association activities that affect paralegals.

Provide bar association members information and publications aimed at increasing their awareness of paralegal participation in the delivery of legal services and issues currently affecting the paralegal profession, e.g., the local association's newsletter and NFPA's *Model Code of Ethics and Professional Responsibilities and Guidelines for Enforcement*.

Offer to plan or conduct attorney seminars that promote paralegal utilization.

Contribute to publications for members of the bar to increase their awareness about paralegals on issues such as educational opportunities, paralegal tasks and responsibilities, profitability of paralegals, increased productivity through paralegal utilization, and ethical responsibilities of attorneys concerning paralegals.

Advertise the paralegal association's job bank and opportunities for attorneys to locate or recruit qualified paralegals by using the job bank.

Present a proposal which demonstrates the value of paralegal associate membership to the bar association for the purpose of increasing attorney awareness about paralegals.[2]

DISCUSSION QUESTIONS

1. Carefully review the "potential disadvantages" for paralegal involvement in bar associations as cited in the preceding article. Which, in your opinion, are the most significant? How might these disadvantages be addressed?

2. Now review the "potential advantages" for paralegal involvement in bar associations. Again, identify those which you feel are the most significant. Can these advantages be obtained by other methods than membership in a bar association?

3. Consider your local bar association. Do they offer memberships for paralegals? If so, do you believe that this membership has helped to create a constructive dialogue between the legal and paralegal professions?

NATIONAL ORGANIZATIONS

The two major paralegal national membership organizations are the National Association of Legal Assistants (NALA) and the National Federation of Paralegal Associations (NFPA). Both are composed of local and state-level paralegal associations, educational programs, and individual members.

The NALA was an outgrowth of the National Association of Legal Secretaries (NALS), now known as "The Association for Legal Professionals." The NALS offered a

Professional Legal Secretary exam and had worked with the ABA Special Committee on Legal Assistants since 1968. In 1974, the NALS established a task force to determine whether a national certifying test or process was appropriate for the newly developing legal assistant field. The task force determined that a separate association was appropriate and, by 1975, the NALA had been incorporated. As of this writing, the NALA has a membership of over 18,000 paralegals, comprising both individual members and members of 91 state and local affiliated associations. The NFPA was formed in 1974 and is a professional organization of state and local paralegal associations from across the United States and Canada, representing over 17,000 paralegals.[3]

Both offer their members a variety of benefits, including seminars, newsletters, ethical guidelines, an Internet connection, and credentialing examinations (discussed later in this chapter). Each organization presents an exhaustive description of the services that they provide, at their respective Web sites.[4] They also act as representatives of the profession and will offer testimony when appropriate, or even file amicus briefs in cases where a legal principle affecting paralegals is at issue.

Often, it is not necessary to join as an individual because the local organization that you join may already be affiliated with a national organization.[5]

One notable aspect regarding these organizations is their unwillingness to join forces. Although they both profess to exist in order to protect and promote the best interests of the paralegal profession, there is arguably inherent conflict in the fact that they both exist. Some practicing paralegals have bemoaned the confusion and divisiveness caused by having two national organizations instead of one.[6] Each organization attempts to position itself as the one, true representative of the paralegal profession, but some of their core beliefs and ideologies vary, including the nature and extent of any competency exams that are developed for paralegals, and even the role that paralegals should play in the delivery of legal services.

DISCUSSION QUESTIONS

1. Review again the NFPA and NALA definitions of a paralegal as set out in Chapter 1. How are these definitions similar? How do they vary? Are the variations significant? In what way? Which definition do you agree with? Why?

2. Do you think it would be better for the profession to be represented by just one national organization or do you think the profession's diversity is better served by having more than one?

PROFESSIONAL ASSOCIATIONS AND THEIR ROLE IN THE SOCIALIZATION OF PARALEGALS

An examination of the various organizations and associations available to paralegals leads to an inquiry regarding the role that these organizations do or should play in the development of the paralegal profession. Much has been written regarding the role that the organized bar plays in the continuing development of the legal profession, and a review of some of this analysis may be instructive. Consider the following claim:

> Professional associations, which had been "formal vehicles for professional improvement and 'social centers' that would foster collegiality and solidarity,[7] have become the place where law school education and on-the-job training may be integrated in a practical way with the profession's views on professional standards, goals, and values.[8]

This author suggests that professional associations can play a key role in the socialization of lawyers. "The term 'socialization,' used . . . in the context of the legal profession, refers to the process of educating new entrants to a profession by teaching them appropriate role behaviors, developing their work skills and abilities, and helping them adjust to the work group's norms and values."[9] The author discusses two specific organizations in the context of membership requirements, activities, and the extent of their efforts to influence others by the use of (1) information exchange and networking; (2) continuing education programs and publications; (3) other educational efforts such as computer research groups and foundations to support research; and (4) law reform efforts, including amicus curiae briefs, lobbying, and public relations activities.

DISCUSSION QUESTIONS

1. Examine the paralegal associations that you belong to or are aware of. How would you assess these associations in the four categories set out previously?

2. Do you believe that professional associations should play a role in the socialization of paralegals? If not by associations, are there other ways in which the socialization process could be accomplished? Could it be accomplished by law firms?

CRITIQUE OF PROFESSIONAL ASSOCIATIONS _____

Professional associations have been criticized too, primarily from the belief that they focus on exclusivity to the ultimate disadvantage of the consumer. In the following excerpt, the author discusses the bar as a club and its effects on the professionalism of lawyers:

> One lesson that history reveals, not surprisingly, is that some of the cynicism about professionalism is justified. The heritage of Bar Associations like that of all trade organizations rests initially in self-interest and protectionism rather than any noble spirit of public service. Our medieval predecessors established guilds to control competition, not to encourage it, and until relatively recently we happily continued that tradition. But before we leap to the conclusion that we should therefore condemn our past, we should realize two things: self-interest can in fact produce public benefits, and our his-

tory predicts much of the ambivalence with which we today approach professional ethics and professionalism.

A useful perspective from which to view the growth and popularity of professional organizations is that of the economic theory of "clubs."[10] This theory holds that social organizations even this informal do not arise by accident, but because they serve some purpose for their members.[11] It would be a mistake to assume, however, as many do, that those purposes are essentially "negative"—that is, to control behavior in ways that benefit that group but not the larger community (for example, to stifle competition). To the contrary, social groupings of this kind can in fact originate out of an interest to enhance economic efficiency, not avoid it.[12]

The basic efficiency-enhancing feature that clubs can provide is predictability.[13] In situations of great uncertainty—where social circumstances are in flux or the nature and quality of a product are not readily apparent—individuals with similar interests may organize to provide each other with consistent, comprehensible feedback, and to provide outsiders with a standard against which the members of the club might be assessed. The essential function of the group, consequently, is informational. Membership tells members something about each other—it helps them predict the kind of interaction they will have with members they do not otherwise know well—and it likewise tells non-members something about those in the club . . . . Thus, in order to serve this information function, club membership must mean something; but to mean something, clubs must in turn be able to exercise serious control over entry into the group and the behavior of their members.[14] The danger here, of course, is that rigor and consistency can devolve into rigidity and stagnation, and the organization can destroy its social usefulness.[15]

DISCUSSION QUESTIONS

1. Does membership in either the NALA or the NFPA provide any sort of specific information about a person? Does your local paralegal association have membership requirements?

2. Is the paralegal profession one that can be fairly described as a situation where "the nature and quality of a product are not readily apparent"? If so, is it important that membership in a professional association for paralegals be subject to control or restriction?

CERTIFICATION AND SPECIALIZATION EXAMS OFFERED THROUGH PROFESSIONAL ORGANIZATIONS

Although some states have imposed restrictions,[16] generally speaking, the paralegal profession is composed of persons with a wide variety of educational and experiential backgrounds. Partly in response to the profession's need to distinguish and credential itself, various organizations provide voluntary credentialing examinations for paralegals, including certification and specialization.

NALA—Certified Legal Assistant Program (CLA)

The NALA offers a voluntary national certification program to be designated a Certified Legal Assistant (CLA). The NALA's CLA program was established in 1976 and boasts that, through January 2002, over 11,000 paralegals had achieved this credential. To be eligible to sit for the CLA, a paralegal must meet one of the following conditions: (1) Prove graduation from a paralegal program that meets specified requirements; *or* (2) have a bachelor's degree plus one year experience as a paralegal,[17] *or* (3) have a high school diploma or equivalent plus seven years experience as a paralegal plus a minimum of 20 hours of continuing legal education completed within two years prior to application. The examination covers verbal and written communication skills, judgment and analytical abilities, ethics, human relations, legal terminology, and legal research. A substantive law section requires completion of one test covering the American legal system and four subtests chosen from a list of nine practice areas. After successful completion of this two-day examination, a paralegal may designate himself/herself as a Certified Legal Assistant or CLA. Because of this designation, it is inaccurate for someone with a "certificate of completion" from a paralegal program to identify him or herself as "certified."[18] Instead, that person would be "certificated."[19] A minimum number of hours of relevant continuing education is required in order to maintain the CLA designation, which must be renewed every five years.[20]

The NALA claims that the CLA credential is recognized nationwide. The organization cites a 1993 ABA Section of Law Practice Management publication that states

> The legal assistant who can use the CLA designation has a number of advantages, not the least of which is that a hiring lawyer can assume from the CLA appellation that he or she is dealing with an experienced legal assistant who has performed to a high standard. It would be safe to assume that a CLA can immediately bring experience and capability to the practice.[21]

Also, the NALA claims that numerous bar associations include the CLA credential among the eligibility requirements for associate membership, that courts have awarded higher fees to paralegals with the CLA designation, and that paralegals with the CLA credential receive higher salaries nationwide.[22]

The NALA also offers a CLA Specialty credential for those who have "demonstrated advanced knowledge and skills in a specialty area of practice." Specialty examinations are available in civil litigation, probate and estate planning, corporate and business law, real estate, bankruptcy, intellectual property, and criminal law and procedure. For the specialty examination, an applicant must be a Certified Legal Assistant in good standing. As of December 2001, over 900 persons have achieved specialist status. In addition, the NALA has teamed up with legal assistant associations in California, Florida, and Louisiana to offer state certification programs to "recognize expertise in state laws and procedures . . . ."

California Advanced Specialist Certification.   The California Advanced Specialist (CAS) Certification was created in 1995 for paralegals who already hold the CLA designation and wish to demonstrate advanced knowledge in California law and procedure. Specialty certification is available in the areas of civil litigation, business organizations, business law, real estate, estates and trusts, and family law. As of December 1999, 30 paralegals had received the CAS credential.

Florida Certification Program.   The certified Florida Legal Assistant CFLA program was established in 1980 and is available to persons who have already received their CLA designation. The exam is administered by the Paralegal Association of Florida, Inc., an affiliate of the NALA. The examination is limited to Florida law and takes approximately three hours. Upon successful completion of the CFLA examination, a paralegal becomes authorized to use the designation CFLA along with the CLA or CLAS designation, as appropriate. Continuing legal education regarding Florida law is required to maintain the CFLA certification. There are over 120 CFLAs in the state of Florida.[23]

Louisiana Certified Paralegal Program.   The Louisiana Certified Paralegal Program requires the applicant to take both the CLA and the LCP (Louisiana Certified Paralegal) examinations. The LCP examination is designed to test knowledge and understanding of the Louisiana legal and judicial system, Louisiana general law, ethics, civil procedure, and four areas of substantive law.

NFPA—Paralegal Advanced Competency Exam (PACE)

The NFPA offers the Paralegal Advanced Competency Exam (PACE) to "test the competency level of experienced paralegals." The NFPA offers this exam for paralegals who have at least two years experience and who meet specific educational requirements. Tier One of the exam is designed to test critical-thinking skills and problem-solving abilities, and includes general legal questions and incorporates ethics throughout the exam. Tier Two tests knowledge of specific legal practice areas.

The original resolution by the NFPA membership to develop the PACE was approved in 1994. The expressed goals of the NFPA were not only to offer practicing paralegals a means by which to validate their experience and job skills and establish credentials, but also to offer state entities and regulating bodies a standard to measure advanced competency for experienced paralegals.

One of the most controversial aspects of the PACE is the requirement that paralegals must possess a four-year degree in order to sit for the exam. This decision was criticized by the majority of the membership of the AAfPE and by the NALA. However, the NFPA defends this requirement as follows:

> In an effort to set the stage for future growth and expansion, it was critically important that paralegals have adequate educational training. Accordingly, the membership made a conscious decision to require a four-year degree to take the exam after the initial grandparenting period has expired. The decision to require a four-year degree was part of the original resolution approved in 1994 and was reaffirmed in 1995 after delegates readdressed the decision to require a four-year degree.[24]

Recognizing that many paralegals already have extensive experience, the NFPA agreed to waive the educational requirements if a minimum of four (4) years experience as a paralegal was obtained by December 31, 2002.[25] Paralegals who successfully complete the PACE receive the designation of PACE—Registered Paralegal or RP.

Texas Legal Assistant Specialty Certification

In 1993, the Supreme Court of Texas endorsed the concept of specialty certification for paralegals. This was the first paralegal credentialing program in the nation to be affiliated with a state bar. In fact, it is patterned after the Board Certification Program for Texas attorneys and is administered through the same entity—the Texas Board of Legal Specialization.

This examination is offered to the paralegal with *advanced* skills and expertise, not to the beginner. In order to sit for the examination, you must have at least five years experience as a paralegal, three of which must have been in Texas law. You also must satisfy specific educational requirements (or, have an additional four years of experience), and you must have completed a minimum of 30 hours of continuing legal education in the three years prior to your application. Paralegals who successfully complete the four-hour written examination are designated as Board Certified Legal Assistant—[area]—Texas Board of Legal Specialization. Specialty certification is offered in the following areas: civil trial law, family law, personal injury trial law, real estate law, and estate planning/probate law.

Specialization or Homogeneity?

The acceptance of specialization within the practice of law is relatively recent. There was a time when lawyers believed that the concept of a unified bar would be threatened by specialization and the resulting stratification. In order to appreciate the possible effects of specialization on the paralegal profession, it is important to understand the debate regarding the same issue in the legal profession.

In 1921, Alfred Z. Reed began an eight-year, nationwide study of attorneys' education, work, and role in society for the Carnegie Foundation for the Advancement of Teaching. He noted that attorneys were focusing their efforts on certain types of clients and client needs and suggested that the profession formally recognize the reality of specialization. He also concluded that there was no such thing as a "standard lawyer." The bar was widely differentiated, *based in large part on the educational background of the lawyer.* Instead of striving for the unattainable—the unitary bar—Reed proposed formal recognition of a stratified bar based both upon the type of legal education the lawyer received and the lawyer's functions in the community. Despite Reed's recommendation, those devoted to raising educational standards believed that keeping a place for "superficial" law schools—and, of course, for "superficially" trained lawyers—would result in a lessening of professionalism. Ultimately, the bar rejected Reed's report and instead opted to increase educational standards.

In 1961, the ABA created a Special Committee on Recognition and Regulation of Specialization in Law Practice, which proposed a plan to formally certify lawyers. Opponents conceded the existence and inevitability of legal specialization, but voiced three areas of concern: (1) what effect formally acknowledging differences among bar members would have on the "cohesiveness of the bar" and on competition generally; (2) whether specialization would narrow lawyers' vision, preventing them from seeing the big picture; and (3) the practicalities of administering a nationwide specialization program.[26] The proposal was abandoned a year later. The issue was debated through 1969, when the ABA determined that specialization should not be conducted at the national level and left the experiment to the individual state bars. Although specialization is determined on a state-by-state basis, the ABA supports such state efforts and has created a model certification plan and model standards for specialty areas.

DISCUSSION QUESTIONS

1. The paralegal profession can also be described as widely differentiated, based in large part on the educational background of the paralegal. What do you think of applying Reed's argument to the paralegal profession—instead of striving for the unattainable, a unitary paralegal profession, formally recognize a stratified paralegal profession based both upon the type of legal education the paralegal received and the paralegal's functions in the legal environment?

2. Arguably, the paralegal profession is increasing educational requirements and accepting specialization, although not by any national consensus. Instead, the market in individual states seems to drive educational requirements and specialty standards, if any. Would an effort more national in scope promote and support the paralegal profession more effectively?

CONCLUSION

Professional organizations for paralegals exist at the local, state, and national levels. As discussed in this chapter, these organizations perform a critical service to the paralegal profession and offer a variety of benefits to their members. However, do these organizations affect the perceptions of those outside the paralegal profession? Does membership result in any type of recognition or acceptance by the general public? Certification schemes are offered in a variety of formats and at differing competency levels. But again, what do these examinations communicate to those outside of the profession? These types of questions require careful study by the paralegal profession in the search for its identity.

1 National Ass'n of Legal Assistants, Summary of Bar Associate Membership Requirements, State and Local Bars 1–12 (Aug. 1998); http://www.nala.org/terms.htm.

2 http://www.paralegals.org/Development/bar.html

3 *Statement on Issues Affecting the Paralegal Profession* http://www.paralegals.org/Development/statement/parapro2.html.

4 The NALA's Web site is located at http://www.nala.org, and the NFPA's Web site is at http://www.paralegals.org. See www.paralegals.org/Members/benefits.htm and www.nda.org/benefits.htm for detailed listing of specific benefits.

5 See Appendices C and D for a listing of membership organizations for both the NALA and the NFPA, respectively.

6 Membership survey, 23 no. 4 Dallas Area Paralegal Newsletter, at 1, April 1999.

7 Terence C. Halliday, Beyond Monopoly: Lawyers, State Crisis, and Professional Empowerment 60–61 (1987) (analyzing the Chicago Bar Association). The earliest lawyer associations in the United States were local bar associations established on the east coast from 1760 to 1820. (See p. 61.)

8 Judith Kilpatrick, *Specialty Lawyer Associations: Their Role in the Socialization Process,* 33 Gonz. L. Rev. 501, 504 (1997–1998).

9 *Id.* at 504; with footnote 11: "In social science parlance, 'organizational socialization is the process by which employees are transformed from organization outsiders to participating and effective members.'" Daniel C. Feldman, *The Multiple Socialization of Organization Members,* 6 Acad. Of Mgmt. Rev. 309 (1981).

10 See James M. Buchanan, *An Economic Theory of Clubs,* Economica 1 (1965). See also Mark V. Pauly, *Clubs, Commonality, and the Core: An Integration of Game Theory and the Theory of Public Goods,* 34 Economica 314 (1967); Mark. V. Pauly, *Cores and Clubs,* 9 Pub. Choice 53 (1970); (definition of club as a "voluntary group deriving mutual benefit from sharing one or more of the following: production costs, the members' characteristics, or a good characterized by excludable benefits").

11 Buchanan, *supra* note 12, at 1–2 and n.1.

12 *Id.*

13 *Id.* at 2–6, 7–11.

14 *Id.* at 13.

15 Terrell and Wildman, *Rethinking Professionalism,* 41 Emory L.J. 403, 409–410 (Spring, 1992).

16 South Dakota Supreme Court Rule 92-5 defines, restricts, and sets out qualifications for legal assistants or paralegals; the states of Maine and Florida restrict use of the title "legal assistant" or "paralegal" to those persons working under the supervision of a lawyer or authorized business entity; also see *State v. Robinson,* Op. # 24391, South Carolina: "Accordingly, to legitimately provide services as a paralegal, one must work in conjunction with a licensed attorney."

17 Successful completion of at least 15 semester credit hours (or 22 1/2 quarter hours or 225 clock hours) of substantive legal assistant courses is equivalent to the one-year experience requirement.

18 The NALA has copyrighted the use of the CLA and CLA Specialist designations.

19 This designation also causes some confusion in the employment arena, where an employer may intend to hire an employee with a "certificate of completion" from a paralegal program, but will advertise for a "certified legal assistant."

20 This requirement may also be partially met by successful completion of a NALA specialty examination, relevant coursework, teaching experience, and/or publications.

21 http://www.nala.org/98CLA_impact.htm.

22 http://www.nala.org/98CLA_impact.htm.

23 See http://www.pafinc.org.

24 http://www.paralegals.org/PACE/pacedev.html.

25 To be eligible for the Tier Two waiver, applicants must have at least six years of experience as a paralegal.

26 Judith Kilpatrick, *Specialist Certification for Lawyers: What is Going On?* 51 U. Miami L. Rev. 273, 280–282 (Jan. 1997).

Appendix C
NALA Affiliated Associations

From http://www.nala.org/Affiliated_Associations_Info.htm (accessed September 24, 2002). Last Update: 04/23/2002.

Alabama

Alabama Association of Legal Assistants
Legal Assistant Society of Virginia College
Samford University Paralegal Association

Arizona

Arizona Paralegal Association
Legal Assistants of Metropolitan Phoenix
Tucson Association of Legal Assistants

Arkansas

Arkansas Association of Legal Assistants

California

Santa Barbara Paralegal Association
Los Angeles Paralegal Association (Pending)
Orange County Paralegal Association
Palomar College Paralegal Studies Club (San Marcos)
Paralegal Association of Santa Clara County
San Joaquin Association of Legal Assistants
Ventura County Association of Legal Assistants

Colorado

Association of Legal Assistants of Colorado
Legal Assistants of the Western Slope

Florida

Central Florida Paralegal Association
Gainesville Association of Legal Assistants
Jacksonville Legal Assistants

Northwest Florida Paralegal Association

Paralegal Association of Florida, Inc.

South Florida Paralegal Association

Southwest Florida Paralegal Association, Inc.

Volusia Association of Paralegals

Georgia

Georgia Legal Assistants

South Georgia Association of Legal Assistants

Southeastern Association of Legal Assistants of Georgia

Idaho

Gem State Association of Legal Assistants

Illinois

Central Illinois Paralegal Association

Indiana

Indiana Legal Assistants

Iowa

Iowa Association of Legal Assistants

Kansas

Heartland Association of Legal Assistants (Kansas City)

Kansas Association of Legal Assistants

Kentucky

Western Kentucky Paralegals

Louisiana

Louisiana State Paralegal Association

Northwest Louisiana Paralegal Association

Michigan

Legal Assistants Association of Michigan

Mississippi

Mississippi Association of Legal Assistants

University of Southern Mississippi Society for Paralegal Studies

Missouri

PSI SIGMA CHI Paralegal Society of Springfield College

St. Louis Association of Legal Assistants

Montana

Montana Association of Legal Assistants

Nebraska

Nebraska Association of Legal Assistants

Nevada

Clark County Organization of Legal Assistants

Sierra Nevada Association of Paralegals

New Jersey

Legal Assistants Association of New Jersey

North Carolina

Coastal Carolina Paralegal Club

Metrolina Paralegal Association

North Carolina Paralegal Association

North Dakota

Red River Valley Legal Assistants

Western Dakota Association of Legal Assistants

Ohio

Toledo Association of Legal Assistants

Oklahoma

City College Legal Association

Northeastern State University Legal Assistant Association

Oklahoma Paralegal Association
TCC Student Association of Legal Assistants
Tulsa Association of Legal Assistants

Oregon

Pacific Northwest Legal Assistants

Pennsylvania

Keystone Legal Assistant Association

Puerto Rico

Puerto Rico Association of Legal Assistants

South Carolina

Central Carolina Technical College Paralegal Association
Charleston Association of Legal Assistants
Greenville Association of Legal Assistants
Tri-County Paralegal Association

South Dakota

South Dakota Paralegal Association
American University Student Association of Legal Assistants

Tennessee

Greater Memphis Paralegal Alliance, Inc.
Tennessee Paralegal Association

Texas

Capital Area Paralegal Association
El Paso Association of Legal Assistants
Legal Assistants Association/Permian Basin
Legal Assistants of North Texas Association
Northeast Texas Association of Legal Assistants
Southeast Texas Association of Legal Assistants
Texas Panhandle Association of Legal Assistants

Tyler Area Association of Legal Assistants
West Texas Association of Legal Assistants

Utah

Legal Assistants Association of Utah

Virgin Islands

Virgin Islands Association of Legal Assistants

Virginia

Peninsula Legal Assistants, Inc.
Richmond Association of Legal Assistants
Roanoke Valley Paralegal Association
Tidewater Association of Legal Assistants

West Virginia

Legal Assistants of West Virginia

Wisconsin

Madison Area Paralegal Association

Wyoming

Legal Assistants of Wyoming

Appendix D

NFPA Member Associations

http://www.paralegals.org/Members/regions.html (accessed September 24, 2002). Updated 8/9/02.
Copyright 1994–2001 National Federation of Paralegal Associations, Inc., Kansas City MO.

NFPA REGIONS

Region I

Alaska Association of Paralegals
E-Mail: Alaska@paralegals.org

Arizona Association of Professional Paralegals, Inc.
E-Mail: Arizona@paralegals.org

Hawaii Paralegal Association
E-Mail: Hawaii@paralegals.org

Oregon Paralegal Association
E-Mail: Oregon@paralegals.org

Paralegal Association of Southern Nevada
E-Mail: SouthernNevada@paralegals.org

Sacramento Association of Legal Assistants
E-Mail: Sacramento@paralegals.org

San Diego Association of Legal Assistants
E-Mail: SanDiego@paralegals.org

San Francisco Paralegal Association
E-Mail: SanFrancisco@paralegals.org

Washington State Paralegal Association
E-Mail: Washington@paralegals.org

Region II

Dallas Area Paralegal Association
E-Mail: Dallas@paralegals.org

Illinois Paralegal Association
E-Mail: Illinois@paralegals.org

Kansas City Paralegal Association
E-Mail: KansasCity@paralegals.org

Kansas Paralegal Association
E-Mail: Kansas@paralegals.org

Minnesota Paralegal Association
E-mail: Minnesota@paralegals.org

New Orleans Paralegal Association
E-mail: NewOrleans@paralegals.org

Paralegal Association of Wisconsin, Inc.
E-mail: Wisconsin@paralegals.org

Rocky Mountain Paralegal Association
E-mail: RockyMountain@paralegals.org

Region III

Cincinnati Paralegal Association
E-mail: Cincinnati@paralegals.org

Cleveland Association of Paralegals
E-mail: Cleveland@paralegals.org

Georgia Association of Paralegals, Inc.
E-mail: Georgia@paralegals.org

Greater Dayton Paralegal Association
E-mail: Dayton@paralegals.org

Greater Lexington Paralegal Association, Inc.
E-mail: Lexington@paralegals.org

Gulf Coast Paralegal Assocaition
E-mail: GulfCoast@paralegals.org

Indiana Paralegal Association
E-mail: Indiana@paralegals.org

Memphis Paralegal Association
E-mail: Memphis@paralegals.org

Michiana Paralegal Association
E-mail: Michiana@paralegals.org

Middle Teneessee Paralegal Association
E-mail: MiddleTennessee@paralegals.org

Northeast Indiana Paralegal Association, Inc.
E-mail: NortheastIndiana@paralegals.org

Northeastern Ohio Paralegal Association
E-mail: NorthEasternOhio@paralegals.org

Palmetto Paralegal Association
E-mail: Palmetto@paralegals.org

Paralegal Association of Central Ohio
E-mail: CentralOhio@paralegals.org

Tampa Bay Paralegal Association
E-mail: TampaBay@paralegals.org

Region IV

Central Pennsylvania Paralegal Association
E-mail: CentralPennsylvania@paralegals.org

Chester County Paralegal Association
E-mail: ChesterCounty@paralegals.org

Delaware Paralegal Association
E-mail: Delaware@paralegals.org

Fredericksburg Paralegal Association
E-mail: Fredericksburg@paralegals.org

Lycoming County Paralegal Association
E-mail: Lycoming@paralegals.org

Maryland Association of Paralegals
E-mail: Maryland@paralegals.org

Montgomery County Paralegal Association
E-mail: Montgomery@paralegals.org

National Capital Area Paralegal Association
E-mail: NationalCapital@paralegals.org

Philadelphia Association of Paralegals
E-mail: Philadelphia@paralegals.org

Pittsburgh Paralegal Association
E-mail: Pittsburgh@paralegals.org

South Jersey Paralegal Association
E-mail: SouthJersey@paralegals.org

Region V

Central Connecticut Paralegal Association, Inc.
E-mail: CentralConnecticut@paralegals.org

Central Massachusetts Paralegal Association
E-mail: CentralMassachusetts@paralegals.org

Connecticut Association of Paralegals, Inc.
E-mail: Connecticut@paralegals.org

Long Island Paralegal Association
E-mail: LongIsland@paralegals.org

Manhattan Paralegal Association, Inc.
E-mail: Manhattan@paralegals.org

Massachusetts Paralegal Association
E-mail: Massachusetts@paralegals.org

New Haven County Association of Paralegals, Inc.
E-mail: NewHaven@paralegals.org

Paralegal Association of New Hampshire
E-Mial: NewHampshire@paralegals.org

Paralegal Association of Rochester
E-mail: Rochester@paralegals.org

Rhode Island Paralegal Association
E-mail: RhodeIsland@paralegals.org

Southern Tier Paralegal Association
E-mail: SouthernTier@paralegals.org

Vermont Paralegal Organization
E-mail: Vermont@paralegals.org

West/Rock Paralegal Association
E-mail: WestRock@paralegals.org

Western Massachusetts Paralegal Association
E-mail: WesternMassachusetts@paralegals.org

Western New York Paralegal Association, Inc.
E-mail: WesternNewYork@paralegals.org

Ethics and Professional Responsibility

3

Rules, Guidelines, and Codes

INTRODUCTION

The current trend in regulating behavior is to codify rules of ethics. Sometimes these rules are purely aspirational in nature, and sometimes they provide for mechanisms of enforcement. Ethical rules generally provide parameters or boundaries for acceptable behavior in given situations. Ethical rules for lawyers have gone through various transformations, beginning with moral admonitions and resulting in an unequivocal enforceable disciplinary code. Ethical rules for paralegals also vary, although they generally reflect many of the rules in place for lawyers. This chapter will discuss the current ethical rules promulgated for both lawyers and paralegals, as well as ask important questions about the effectiveness of these rules.

RULES, GUIDELINES, AND CODES—LAWYERS

In order to deter lawyer misconduct and provide guidance, the American Bar Association has promulgated three successive sets of regulation for the legal profession that articulate standards and set out rules of application. In 1908, the ABA set forth the Canons of Professional Ethics (Canons), the legal profession's first official statement of its code of conduct. In 1969, the ABA adopted the Code of Professional Responsibility (Code). Unlike the Canons, the Code provided specific and binding rules. In 1983, the ABA expanded and restructured the Code and adopted the Model Rules of Professional Conduct (Model Rules). Currently, a majority of the states have adopted some version of the Model Rules, while others have retained some version of the Code.[1] About thirty amendments to the original Model Rules have been adopted by the ABA since 1983.[2] More recently, in an attempt to update the Model Rules and encourage more uniformity among the states, the ABA established the Commission on the Evaluation of the Rules of Professional Conduct, or "Ethics 2000," in order to reevaluate the Model Rules. After much discussion and debate of the Commission's final proposal, this reevaluation resulted in additional amendments to the Model Rules.[3]

Why Are These Rules Significant for Paralegals?

The Model Rules are significant for paralegals because supervising attorneys can be held responsible for violations of the rules committed by nonlawyer staff. Also, the Model Rules address specific restrictions placed on nonlawyers.[4] Model Rule 5.3 provides the following in part:

> [A] lawyer having direct supervisory authority over the nonlawyer shall make reasonable efforts to ensure that the person's conduct is compatible with the professional obligations of the lawyer . . . .*A lawyer shall be responsible for conduct of such a person that would be a violation of the rules of professional conduct . . .* [5]

Therefore, it is incumbent upon any practicing paralegal to familiarize himself or herself with all applicable disciplinary codes, rules, or guidelines that have been promulgated by or for lawyers. Sanctions for lawyers who violate the Disciplinary Rules can range from disbarment to reprimand by their local state bar, as well as prosecution for any criminal or civil violations incurred in connection therewith.

Guidelines for the Utilization of Paralegal Services

Other ethical guidelines that exist for lawyers include guidelines for the utilization of paralegal services. The ABA has published Model Guidelines, and many individual states have followed suit. The guidelines can be categorized to reflect concerns in the following two main areas:

- The paralegal's conduct should be consistent with the disciplinary rules that bind lawyers (including prohibitions against the unauthorized practice of law, relating client confidences, entering into conflicts of interest, and sharing legal fees).
- The paralegal should disclose his/her status as a paralegal and a non-lawyer.

Before we move on to rules specifically targeted at the paralegal profession, it may be instructive to consider the structure of the current disciplinary system in place for most lawyers, the purported purposes for discipline, and some of the criticisms of the system. The traditional form of supervision for most lawyers in the United States empowers state supreme courts to regulate their officers, including the attorneys who practice before them.[6] This supervision ranges from volunteer lawyer ethics committees to more professional state disciplinary agencies.[7] Purposes for supervision and discipline encompass the goals of (1) cleansing; (2) deterrence; and (3) improving the public image of lawyers.[8] The goal of cleansing involves identifying and removing all deviant members from the profession. "Deterrence" implies maximizing compliance with professional rules through imposition of penalties. Finally, the public image of lawyers might be improved if the public perceives a level of response from the bar sufficient to adequately deal with violations of the Professional Rules and wayward lawyers in general.[9]

Criticisms of the current system vary. For example, there has been some debate regarding the autonomy of the bar in attorney regulation.[10] Some commentators believe that volunteer lawyer ethics committees are preferable over more formal, professional groups because lawyers are less likely to feel disenfranchised if they have input in the disciplinary process.[11] On the other hand, history warns that state disciplinary systems can become decentralized, resulting in inconsistent discipline and sometimes reluctance to discipline at all.[12] For example, particularly in smaller communities, the ethics committee may be composed of "friends" of the accused who may be reluctant to impose discipline.

Other criticisms and concerns involve the purposes for supervision and discipline as described above. For example, "cleansing" the profession assumes that the disciplinary system will identify and remove "unfit" lawyers. The "deterrence" goal assumes that fear of sanctions will motivate lawyers to behave. Both of these goals rely, in main part, on the ability and willingness of clients to report lawyer misconduct. Reports by clients likely occur under primarily the most egregious circumstances. It is arguable that most clients would prefer preventive measures and access to mediation for disputes with their lawyers.[13]

DISCUSSION QUESTIONS

1. What can paralegals learn from lawyer disciplinary systems?

2. What is the current disciplinary system for lawyers in your state? What is your perception of it? Is it effective? Does it accomplish the goals identified above?

3. Review the publication for your state bar association. Does it have a section that reports violations of your state's professional rules and the resulting penalties imposed? What kinds of violations are attorneys most disciplined for? How might paralegals help prevent some of these violations?

4. In addition to the Professional Rules, are there more general ways that lawyers can and should increase overall professional service to their clients?

5. What types of preventative measures could be instituted to further protect clients? Is there a role for paralegals?

RULES, GUIDELINES, AND CODES—PARALEGALS _____

Local, state, and national organizations across the country promulgate ethical codes and guidelines for paralegals. For example, the two prominent paralegal national organizations, the National Association of Legal Assistants (NALA) and the National

Federation of Paralegal Associations (NFPA) have published ethical standards, codes, guidelines, and opinions for the paralegal profession. The NFPA has even adopted guidelines for the enforcement of its code of ethics. Sanctions include (1) a letter of reprimand; (2) required attendance at a selected ethics course; and (3) imposition of a fine. The NFPA guidelines also threaten suspension or revocation of license or authority to practice, which is a premature threat at best. Local paralegal associations, whether independent or associated with the state or local bar, also publish ethical rules and codes. Commentators believe that the "ethics code trend" will continue as states "continue to grapple with the questions concerning the licensing or regulating of the paralegal profession."[14] The abundance of ethics codes can be somewhat disconcerting to the new paralegal professional; however, they all have some themes in common. For example, consider the NALA and NFPA standards, codes, and guidelines in Appendices F and G. Both sets of standards and codes emphasize abiding by disciplinary rules of conduct that bind lawyers, guarding client confidences, avoiding conflicts of interest, avoiding the unauthorized practice of law, and disclosing one's status as a paralegal and a non-lawyer.

DISCUSSION QUESTIONS

1. Under the NALA model standards and guidelines, what specific standards may be used to determine an individual's qualifications as a paralegal/legal assistant? Do you agree?

2. Why is it important that any work done by a paralegal lose its separate identity and become merged with that of the attorney?

3. These rules contain a directive that the paralegal inform a client or other person immediately of his/her status if the paralegal becomes aware that the client or other person believes that the paralegal is an attorney. Will the level of sophistication of the client or other person make a difference in the type and/or frequency of this disclosure?

4. What kinds of tasks may an attorney delegate to a paralegal? If you were a state legislator, would you allow any additional tasks and/or responsibilities? Does our changing society and legal system affect your response? Explain.

5. Is it important for paralegals to receive continuing education?

6. Is there any difference between revealing confidential client information and engaging in indiscreet communications regarding clients?

THE UNIQUE POSITION OF THE PARALEGAL

This section of the book addresses ethical considerations and obligations of paralegals in the legal environment by the use of applicable rules, guidelines, ethical opinions and case law. Unfortunately, however, the realities of the workplace often present situations that the rules and guidelines are unable to adequately address. As you study the following chapters, it is important to think of the issues that are presented in the context of the uniquely difficult role that paralegals play in the legal environment. Although paralegals are held to high standards of conduct, they are usually in subordinate positions with little or no control over ultimate decisions. What if one of the decisions made by a supervising attorney violates a Model Rule of Professional Conduct? Much has been written regarding the associate attorney's dilemmas in similar settings,[15] but few answers have been found. Rule 5.2 of the Model Code declares that subordinate attorneys are bound by the Model Rules, regardless of whether they are acting at the direction of another person. However, this rule also allows the subordinate attorney to defer to a supervising attorney on arguable questions of professional duty. As mentioned earlier in this chapter, paralegals are subject to ethical rules and guidelines that have been promulgated by various organizations, including bar associations and professional groups, as well as state legislatures and case law. Still, these rules and guidelines provide little legal or moral comfort to paralegals who feel uncomfortably close to ethical violations through the acts of their supervising attorneys. In the following excerpt, a young lawyer discusses ethical dilemmas that he encountered at an insurance defense firm in connection with billable hours:

> There was a rule for this particular client that no more than 15 hours of paralegal time could be billed for a single case. If you had to use more than that, you had to get permission in advance from an adjuster . . . . The lawyers often got too busy and they asked paralegals to do work that lawyers were supposed to do . . . . In some cases the paralegals would come in and say, "I've hit my 15 hour limit" and stop . . . . Other times they would work and work and work, and bill and bill and bill. Then you'd get a pre-bill that said "Paralegal time: 65 hours." If the bill went to the insurance company that way, the adjuster would just . . . subtract 50 hours . . . So when the pre-bill came out, if there were more than 15 hours of paralegal time, we were told to turn them into attorney time. In other words, you didn't do the work, but just say you did. I am not sure whether the client was billed at attorney rates for the same number of hours worked or whether the firm computed the difference in the billing rate and reduced the number of hours accordingly . . . but I think they didn't bother to change the rate. One of the outgoing associates who had resigned as I was coming in mentioned to me: "You know this place is so ridiculous, it's so unethical. They routinely . . . bill any paralegal time over 15 hours to the attorneys, and they don't even change the rate." On one occasion I went to my partner and said, "There's all this paralegal work on the pre-bill that is over the 15 hour limit . . . . What should I do about it?" He said, "Well whatever is over, just make sure that the narrative describing the work reads properly and then change the initials to yours." I said, "But I wasn't even at the firm when this work was done!" He said, "Well then, bill it as the attorney who was here during that time period so there won't be any question . . . ." I said, "Who's going to do the math?" He gave me this really scared blank look. I said, "There's a difference in rate between attorneys and paralegals." He said, "Oh, oh yeah, bring it to accounting. They will do it." I did bring it to accounting. I have no idea whether they ever did anything about it or not.[16]

DISCUSSION QUESTIONS

1. Although the type of conduct described in the preceding excerpt is not typical, the pressure to bill does exist. As a result, associate attorneys and paralegals (subordinate employees who are required to bill) are often placed in a vulnerable position. Using your instincts, what do you think the associate attorney should have done in this situation? If the paralegals had been aware, what should they have done? Generally, Model Rule 5.2 provides for some insulation for subordinate lawyers who are acting in accordance with a supervisory lawyer's "reasonable resolution of an arguable question of a professional duty." On the other hand, Model Rule 8.3, requires lawyers to inform the "appropriate professional authority" when he or she has knowledge that another lawyer has committed a violation of the Model Rules. What are the ethical obligations for attorneys faced with this type of situation? Should it be any different for paralegals?

2. Review the Guidelines and Standards promugated by NALA and NFPA (Exhibits F and G). Were any of these rules violated by the facts given in the above excerpt?

CONCLUSION

One of the obvious drawbacks of ethical rules in general is the inability to predict every conceivable ethical dilemma. Although ethical rules can affect specific conduct if it is addressed, these rules alone do not instill ethical ideals and professional values. The Model Code of Responsibility for lawyers focuses on instances of possible malpractice or attorney misconduct; not on the social values and moral implications of practicing law.

Paralegals can learn a great deal from the current debates surrounding lawyer disciplinary systems and professional rules. A paralegal is likely to be subjected to the same types of ethical dilemmas that face lawyers. As a result, they should be subjected to the same amount of ethical reflection. In addition, paralegals can face unemployment and lose credibility if they fail to abide by the Model Rules for lawyers that have been adopted in their state. Finally, ethical practice may lead to an intrinsically happier life. In *Ethics in the New Millennium*, the Dalai Lama suggests that a life focused on ethically positive conduct is more likely to result in happiness and satisfaction than one that does not.[17]

ENDNOTES

[1] Jeffrey A. Maine, *Importance of Ethics and Morality in Today's Legal World*, STETSON L. REV. 1073, 1076 (Spring 2000); Carol M. Langford and David M. Bell, *"What Needs Fixing?" Finding a Voice: The Legal Ethics Committee*, 30 HOFSTRA L. REV. 855, 862 (Spring 2002) .

[2] E. Norman Veasey, *Ethics 2000: Thoughts and Comments on Key Issues of Professional Responsibility in the Twenty-First Century*, 2002 DEL. L. REV. 1. E. Norman Veasey served as the Chair of the Commission on Evaluation of the Rules of Professional Conduct (nicknamed "Ethics 2000").

[3] *Id.* at 3.

[4] Rule 5.5 prohibits a lawyer from assisting a non-lawyer in the unauthorized practice of law, as further discussed in Chapter 4. Rule 5.4 prohibits a lawyer from sharing fees with a non-lawyer, although nonlawyer employees may be included in a compensation or retirement plan that is based on a profit-sharing arrangement.

[5] AM. BAR ASS'N, MODEL RULES OF PROFESSIONAL CONDUCT, Rule. 5.3 (2002 ed.) (emphasis added).

[6] *Lawyer's Responsibilities to the Profession: Decoding the Ethics Codes*, 107 HARV. L. REV. 1581 (May, 1994) (no author available).

[7] Carol M. Langford and David M. Bell, *"What Needs Fixing?" Finding a Voice: The Legal Ethics Committee*, 30 HOFSTRA L. REV. 855 (Spring 2002).

[8] George L. Hampton, *Toward An Expanded Use of the Model Rules of Professional Conduct*, 4 GEO. J. LEGAL ETHICS 655 (Winter 1991).

[9] *Id.* at 657.

[10] Langford and Bell, *supra.*

[11] Langford and Bell, *supra* at 857.

[12] *See generally* SPECIAL COMM. ON EVALUATION OF DISCIPLINARY ENFORCEMENT, ABA, PROBLEMS AND RECOMMENDATIONS IN DISCIPLINARY ENFORCEMENT (1970).

[13] Thomas D. Morgan & Ronald D. Rotunda, *Professional Responsibility* 51–56 (5th ed., Foundation Press 1991).

[14] Hope Viner Samborn, *Conflicts and Confidences— Codes Address Ethics for Paralegals and Impact on Lawyers*, 82 A.B.A. J. 24 (June 1996).

[15] DEBORAH L. RHODE AND DAVID LUBAN, LEGAL ETHICS, 375–388 (Foundation Press 1992).

[16] Lisa G. Lerman, *Scenes From a Law Firm*, 50 RUTGERS L. REV. 2153, 2162 (1998).

[17] See generally DALAI LAMA, ETHICS FOR THE NEW MILLENNIUM (1999).

Appendix E

ABA Model Guidelines for the Utilization of Legal Assistant Services

From http://www.abanet.org/legalassts/modguide.html (accessed September 24, 2002). © The American Bar Association. All rights reserved. Reprinted by permission.

The following Guidelines were adopted by the ABA's policy making body, the House of Delegates, in 1991. Lawyers are the intended audience of these Guidelines. The Guidelines, therefore, are addressed to lawyer conduct and not directly to the conduct of legal assistants and paralegals. Both the National Association of Legal Assistants (NALA) and the National Federation of Paralegal Associations (NFPA) have adopted guidelines of conduct that are directed to legal assistants and paralegals.

The Guidelines were developed to conform with the ABA's Model Rules of Professional Conduct, decided authority, and contemporary practice. Lawyers are to be directed to Model Rule 5.3 of the Model Rules of Professional Conduct and nothing in these Guidelines is intended to be inconsistent with Rule 5.3. For more information see, the ABA Center for Professional Responsibility.

Note: The terms "legal assistant" and "paralegal" are used interchangeably. Annotations and commentary to the Guidelines (which were not adopted as official policy in 1991 by the House of Delegates) are not included below. They are currently being reviewed by the Standing Committee on Legal Assistants to see if they should be revised in light of current case law. A copy of the Guidelines with annotations and commentary is available through the ABA Legal Assistants Department staff office. (Phone: 312/988-5616; Fax: 312/988-5677; E-Mail: legalassts@abanet.org).

GUIDELINE 1:

A lawyer is responsible for all of the professional actions of a legal assistant performing legal assistant services at the lawyer's direction and should take reasonable measures to ensure that the legal assistant's conduct is consistent with the lawyer's obligations under the ABA Model Rules of Professional Conduct.

GUIDELINE 2:

Provided the lawyer maintains responsibility for the work product, a lawyer may delegate to a legal assistant any task normally performed by the lawyer except those tasks proscribed to one not licensed as a lawyer by statute, court rule, administrative rule or regulation, controlling authority, the ABA Model Rules of Professional Conduct, or these Guidelines.

GUIDELINE 3:

A lawyer may not delegate to a legal assistant:

(a) Responsibility for establishing an attorney-client relationship.

(b) Responsibility for establishing the amount of a fee to be charged for a legal service.

(c) Responsibility for a legal opinion rendered to a client.

GUIDELINE 4:

It is the lawyer's responsibility to take reasonable measures to ensure that clients, courts, and other lawyers are aware that a legal assistant, whose services are utilized by the lawyer in performing legal services, is not licensed to practice law.

GUIDELINE 5:

A lawyer may identify legal assistants by name and title on the lawyer's letterhead and on business cards identifying the lawyer's firm.

GUIDELINE 6:

It is the responsibility of a lawyer to take reasonable measures to ensure that all client confidences are preserved by a legal assistant.

GUIDELINE 7:

A lawyer should take reasonable measures to prevent conflicts of interest resulting from a legal assistant's other employment or interests insofar as such other employment or interests would present a conflict of interest if it were that of the lawyer.

GUIDELINE 8:

A lawyer may include a charge for the work performed by a legal assistant in setting a charge for legal services.

GUIDELINE 9:

A lawyer may not split legal fees with a legal assistant nor pay a legal assistant for the referral of legal business. A lawyer may compensate a legal assistant based on the quantity and quality of the legal assistant's work and the value of that work to a law practice, but the legal assistant's compensation may not be contingent, by advance agreement, upon the profitability of the lawyer's practice.

GUIDELINE 10:

A lawyer who employs a legal assistant should facilitate the legal assistant's participation in appropriate continuing education and pro bono publico activities.

Appendix F

NALA Professional Standards

From http://www.nala.org/stand.htm (accessed September 24, 2002). Last Update: 04/23/2002. Copyright 2001, National Association of Legal Assistants, Inc., 1516 S. Boston, #200, Tulsa, OK 74119. Reprinted with permission.

Legal assistants and paralegals are individuals who assist lawyers in the delivery of legal services. Legal assistants and paralegals cannot give legal advice to consumers of legal services. Legal advice may only be relied upon if given by an attorney. All states require attorneys to be licensed and most have statutes imposing penalties for the unauthorized practice of law.

TABLE OF CONTENTS:

Note: On the NALA Links of Interest page, there are links to bar association codes of ethics. Members of the National Association of Legal Assistants are bound by a Code of Ethics and Professional Responsibility. Any violation of this code is cause for removal of membership. Also, NALA affiliated associations must adopt the NALA Code of Ethics and Professional Responsibility as their standard of conduct.

NALA CODE OF ETHICS AND PROFESSIONAL RESPONSIBILITY

A legal assistant must adhere strictly to the accepted standards of legal ethics and to the general principles of proper conduct. The performance of the duties of the legal assistant shall be governed by specific canons as defined herein so that justice will be served and goals of the profession attained. (See Model Standards and Guidelines for Utilization of Legal Assistants, Section II.)

The canons of ethics set forth hereafter are adopted by the National Association of Legal Assistants, Inc., as a general guide intended to aid legal assistants and attorneys. The enumeration of these rules does not mean there are not others of equal importance although not specifically mentioned. Court rules, agency rules and statutes must be taken into consideration when interpreting the canons.

Definition: Legal assistants, also known as paralegals, are a distinguishable group of persons who assist attorneys in the delivery of legal services. Through formal education, training and experience, legal assistants have knowledge and expertise regarding the legal system and substantive and procedural law which qualify them to do work of a legal nature under the supervision of an attorney.

Canon 1.

A legal assistant must not perform any of the duties that attorneys only may perform nor take any actions that attorneys may not take.

Canon 2.

A legal assistant may perform any task which is properly delegated and supervised by an attorney, as long as the attorney is ultimately responsible to the client, maintains a direct relationship with the client, and assumes professional responsibility for the work product.

Canon 3.

A legal assistant must not: (a) engage in, encourage, or contribute to any act which could constitute the unauthorized practice of law; and (b) establish attorney-client relationships, set fees, give legal opinions or advice or represent a client before a court or agency unless so authorized by that court or agency; and (c) engage in conduct or take any action which would assist or involve the attorney in a violation of professional ethics or give the appearance of professional impropriety.

Canon 4.

A legal assistant must use discretion and professional judgment commensurate with knowledge and experience but must not render independent legal judgment in place of an attorney. The services of an attorney are essential in the public interest whenever such legal judgment is required.

Canon 5.

A legal assistant must disclose his or her status as a legal assistant at the outset of any professional relationship with a client, attorney, a court or administrative agency or personnel thereof, or a member of the general public. A legal assistant must act prudently in determining the extent to which a client may be assisted without the presence of an attorney.

Canon 6.

A legal assistant must strive to maintain integrity and a high degree of competency through education and training with respect to professional responsibility, local rules and practice, and through continuing education in substantive areas of law to better assist the legal profession in fulfilling its duty to provide legal service.

Canon 7.

A legal assistant must protect the confidences of a client and must not violate any rule or statute now in effect or hereafter enacted controlling the doctrine of privileged communications between a client and an attorney.

Canon 8.

A legal assistant must do all other things incidental, necessary, or expedient for the attainment of the ethics and responsibilities as defined by statute or rule of court.

Canon 9.

A legal assistant's conduct is guided by bar associations' codes of professional responsibility and rules of professional conduct.

NALA MODEL STANDARDS AND GUIDELINES FOR UTILIZATION OF LEGAL ASSISTANTS

NALA's study of the professional responsibility and ethical considerations of legal assistants is ongoing. This research led to the development of the NALA Model Standards and Guidelines for Utilization of Legal Assistants. This guide summarizes case law, guidelines and ethical opinions of the various states affecting legal assistants. It provides an outline of minimum qualifications and standards necessary for legal assistant professionals to assure the public and the legal profession that they are, indeed, qualified. The following is a listing of the standards and guidelines.

The annotated version of the Model was revised extensively in 1997. It is on-line—NALA Model Standards and Guidelines—and may be ordered through **NALA Headquarters.**

Introduction

Proper utilization of the services of legal assistants affects the efficient delivery of legal services. Legal assistants and the legal profession should be assured that some measures exist for identifying legal assistants and their role in assisting attorneys in the delivery of legal services. Therefore, the National Association of Legal Assistants, Inc., hereby adopts these Model Standards and Guidelines as an educational document for the benefit of legal assistants and the legal profession.

Standards

A legal assistant should meet certain minimum qualifications. The following standards may be used to determine an individual's qualifications as a legal assistant:

1. Successful completion of the Certified Legal Assistant certifying (CLA) examination of the National Association of Legal Assistants;
2. Graduation from an ABA approved program of study for legal assistants;
3. Graduation from a course of study for legal assistants which is institutionally accredited but not ABA approved, and which requires not less than the equivalent of 60 semester hours of classroom study;
4. Graduation from a course of study for legal assistants, other than those set forth in (2) and (3) above, plus not less than six months of in-house training as a legal assistant.
5. A baccalaureate degree in any field, plus not less than six months in-house training as a legal assistant;
6. A minimum of three years of law-related experience under the supervision of an attorney, including at least six months of in-house training as a legal assistant; or
7. Two years of in-house training as a legal assistant.

For purposes of these Standards, "in-house training as a legal assistant" means attorney education of the employee concerning legal assistant duties and these Guidelines. In addition to review and analysis of assignments the legal assistant should receive a reasonable amount of instruction directly related to the duties and obligations of the legal assistant.

Guidelines

These guidelines relating to standards of performance and professional responsibility are intended to aid legal assistants and attorneys. the responsibility rests with an attorney who employs legal assistants to educate them with respect to the duties they are assigned to supervise the manner in which such duties are accomplished.

Guideline 1
Legal assistants should:

1. Disclose their status as legal assistants at the outset of any professional relationship with a client, other attorneys, a court or administrative agency or personnel thereof, or members of the general public;

2. Preserve the confidences and secrets of all clients; and

3. Understand the attorney's Code of Professional Responsibility and these guidelines in order to avoid any action which would involve the attorney in a violation of that Code, or give the appearance of professional impropriety.

Guideline 2
Legal assistants should not:

1. Establish attorney-client relationships; set legal fees, give legal opinions or advice; or represent a client before a court; nor

2. Engage in, encourage, or contribute to any act which could constitute the unauthorized practice of law.

Guideline 3
Legal assistants may perform services for an attorney in the representation of a client, provided:

1. The services performed by the legal assistant do not require the exercise of independent professional legal judgment;

2. The attorney maintains a direct relationship with the client and maintains control of all client matters;

3. The attorney supervises the legal assistant;

4. The attorney remains professionally responsible for all work on behalf of the client, including any actions taken or not taken by the legal assistant in connection therewith; and

5. The services performed supplement, merge with and become the attorney's work product.

Guideline 4
In the supervision of a legal assistant, consideration should be given to:

1. Designating work assignments that correspond to the legal assistant's abilities, knowledge, training and experience.

2. Education and training the legal assistant with respect to professional responsibility, local rules and practices, and firm policies;

3. Monitoring the work and professional conduct of the legal assistant to ensure that the work is substantively correct and timely performed;

4. Providing continuing education for the legal assistant in substantive matters through courses, institutes, workshops, seminars and in-house training, and

5. Encouraging and supporting membership and active participation in professional organizations.

Guideline 5

Except as otherwise provided by statute, court rule or decision, administrative rule or regulation, or the attorney's Code of Professional Responsibility; and within the preceding parameters and proscriptions, a legal assistant may perform any function delegated by an attorney, including but not limited to the following:

1. Conduct client interviews and maintain general contact with the client after the establishment of the attorney-client relationship, so long as the client is aware of the status and function of the legal assistant, and the client contact is under the supervision of the attorney.

2. Locate and interview witnesses, so long as the witnesses are aware of the status and function of the legal assistant.

3. Conduct investigations and statistical and documentary research for review by the attorney.

4. Conduct legal research for review by the attorney.

5. Draft legal documents for review by the attorney.

6. Draft correspondence and pleadings for review by and signature of the attorney.

7. Summarize depositions, interrogatories, and testimony for review by the attorney.

8. Attend executions of wills, real estate closings, depositions, court or administrative hearings and trials with the attorney.

9. Author and sign letters provided the legal assistant's status is clearly indicated and the correspondence does not contain independent legal opinions or legal advice.

The notes to accompany the NALA Model Standards and Guidelines for Utilization of Legal Assistants are updated regularly by the NALA Professional Development Committee. The standards and guidelines are adopted by the NALA membership, and changes to these provisions must be brought before NALA members during their annual meeting in July.

Appendix G

Model Code of Ethics and Professional Responsibility and Guidelines for Enforcement

From http://www.paralegals.org/Development/modelcode.html (accessed September 24, 2002). Created 10-97; updated 5/16/02. Reprinted courtesy of National Federation of Paralegal Associations, Inc.

PREAMBLE

The National Federation of Paralegal Associations, Inc. ("NFPA") is a professional organization comprised of paralegal associations and individual paralegals throughout the United States and Canada. Members of NFPA have varying backgrounds, experiences, education and job responsibilities that reflect the diversity of the paralegal profession. NFPA promotes the growth, development and recognition of the paralegal profession as an integral partner in the delivery of legal services.

In May 1993 NFPA adopted its Model Code of Ethics and Professional Responsibility ("Model Code") to delineate the principles for ethics and conduct to which every paralegal should aspire.

Many paralegal associations throughout the United States have endorsed the concept and content of NFPA's Model Code through the adoption of their own ethical codes. In doing so, paralegals have confirmed the profession's commitment to increase the quality and efficiency of legal services, as well as recognized its responsibilities to the public, the legal community, and colleagues.

Paralegals have recognized, and will continue to recognize, that the profession must continue to evolve to enhance their roles in the delivery of legal services. With increased levels of responsibility comes the need to define and enforce mandatory rules of professional conduct. Enforcement of codes of paralegal conduct is a logical and necessary step to enhance and ensure the confidence of the legal community and the public in the integrity and professional responsibility of paralegals.

In April 1997 NFPA adopted the Model Disciplinary Rules ("Model Rules") to make possible the enforcement of the Canons and Ethical Considerations contained in the NFPA Model Code. A concurrent determination was made that the Model Code of Ethics and Professional Responsibility, formerly aspirational in nature, should be recognized as setting forth the enforceable obligations of all paralegals.

The Model Code and Model Rules offer a framework for professional discipline, either voluntarily or through formal regulatory programs.

§1. NFPA MODEL DISCIPLINARY RULES AND ETHICAL CONSIDERATIONS

1.1 A PARALEGAL SHALL ACHIEVE AND MAINTAIN A HIGH LEVEL OF COMPETENCE.

Ethical Considerations

EC-1.1(a)   A paralegal shall achieve competency through education, training, and work experience.

EC-1.1(b)   A paralegal shall aspire to participate in a minimum of twelve (12) hours of continuing legal education, to include at least one (1) hour of ethics education, every two (2) years in order to remain current on developments in the law.

EC-1.1(c)   A paralegal shall perform all assignments promptly and efficiently.

1.2 A PARALEGAL SHALL MAINTAIN A HIGH LEVEL OF PERSONAL AND PROFESSIONAL INTEGRITY.

Ethical Considerations

EC-1.2(a)   A paralegal shall not engage in any ex parte communications involving the courts or any other adjudicatory body in an attempt to exert undue influence or to obtain advantage or the benefit of only one party.

EC-1.2(b)   A paralegal shall not communicate, or cause another to communicate, with a party the paralegal knows to be represented by a lawyer in a pending matter without the prior consent of the lawyer representing such other party.

EC-1.2(c)   A paralegal shall ensure that all timekeeping and billing records prepared by the paralegal are thorough, accurate, honest, and complete.

EC-1.2(d)   A paralegal shall not knowingly engage in fraudulent billing practices. Such practices may include, but are not limited to: inflation of hours billed to a client or employer; misrepresentation of the nature of tasks performed; and/or submission of fraudulent expense and disbursement documentation.

EC-1.2(e)   A paralegal shall be scrupulous, thorough and honest in the identification and maintenance of all funds, securities, and other assets of a client and shall provide accurate accounting as appropriate.

EC-1.2(f)   A paralegal shall advise the proper authority of non-confidential knowledge of any dishonest or fraudulent acts by any person pertaining to the handling of the funds, securities or other assets of a client. The authority to whom the report is made shall depend on the nature and circumstances of the possible misconduct, (e.g., ethics committees of law firms, corporations and/or paralegal associations, local or state bar associations, local prosecutors, administrative agencies, etc.). Failure to report such knowledge is in itself misconduct and shall be treated as such under these rules.

1.3 A PARALEGAL SHALL MAINTAIN A HIGH STANDARD OF PROFESSIONAL CONDUCT.

Ethical Considerations

EC-1.3(a)   A paralegal shall refrain from engaging in any conduct that offends the dignity and decorum of proceedings before a court or other adjudicatory body and shall be respectful of all rules and procedures.

EC-1.3(b)   A paralegal shall avoid impropriety and the appearance of impropriety and shall not engage in any conduct that would adversely affect his/her fitness to practice. Such conduct may include, but is not limited to: violence, dishonesty, interference with the administration of justice, and/or abuse of a professional position or public office.

EC-1.3(c)   Should a paralegal's fitness to practice be compromised by physical or mental illness, causing that paralegal to commit an act that is in direct violation of the Model Code/Model Rules and/or the rules and/or laws governing the jurisdiction in which the paralegal practices, that paralegal may be protected from sanction upon review of the nature and circumstances of that illness.

EC-1.3(d)   A paralegal shall advise the proper authority of non-confidential knowledge of any action of another legal professional that clearly demonstrates fraud, deceit, dishonesty, or misrepresentation. The authority to whom the report is made shall depend on the nature and circumstances of the possible misconduct, (e.g., ethics committees of law firms, corporations and/or paralegal associations, local or state bar associations, local prosecutors, administrative agencies, etc.). Failure to report such knowledge is in itself misconduct and shall be treated as such under these rules.

EC-1.3(e)   A paralegal shall not knowingly assist any individual with the commission of an act that is in direct violation of the Model Code/Model Rules and/or the rules and/or laws governing the jurisdiction in which the paralegal practices.

EC-1.3(f)   If a paralegal possesses knowledge of future criminal activity, that knowledge must be reported to the appropriate authority immediately.

1.4 A PARALEGAL SHALL SERVE THE PUBLIC INTEREST BY CONTRIBUTING TO THE IMPROVEMENT OF THE LEGAL SYSTEM AND DELIVERY OF QUALITY LEGAL SERVICES, INCLUDING PRO BONO PUBLICO SERVICES.

Ethical Considerations

EC-1.4(a)   A paralegal shall be sensitive to the legal needs of the public and shall promote the development and implementation of programs that address those needs.

EC-1.4(b)   A paralegal shall support efforts to improve the legal system and access thereto and shall assist in making changes.

EC-1.4(c)   A paralegal shall support and participate in the delivery of Pro Bono Publico services directed toward implementing and improving access to justice, the law, the legal system or the paralegal and legal professions.

EC-1.4(d)   A paralegal should aspire annually to contribute twenty-four (24) hours of Pro Bono Publico services under the supervision of an attorney or as authorized by administrative, statutory or court authority to:

1. persons of limited means; or
2. charitable, religious, civic, community, governmental and educational organizations in matters that are designed primarily to address the legal needs of persons with limited means; or
3. individuals, groups or organizations seeking to secure or protect civil rights, civil liberties or public rights.

1.5 A PARALEGAL SHALL PRESERVE ALL CONFIDENTIAL INFORMATION PROVIDED BY THE CLIENT OR ACQUIRED FROM OTHER SOURCES BEFORE, DURING, AND AFTER THE COURSE OF THE PROFESSIONAL RELATIONSHIP.

Ethical Considerations

EC-1.5(a)   A paralegal shall be aware of and abide by all legal authority governing confidential information in the jurisdiction in which the paralegal practices.

EC-1.5(b)   A paralegal shall not use confidential information to the disadvantage of the client.

EC-1.5(c)   A paralegal shall not use confidential information to the advantage of the paralegal or of a third person.

EC-1.5(d)   A paralegal may reveal confidential information only after full disclosure and with the client's written consent; or, when required by law or court order; or, when necessary to prevent the client from committing an act that could result in death or serious bodily harm.

EC-1.5(e)   A paralegal shall keep those individuals responsible for the legal representation of a client fully informed of any confidential information the paralegal may have pertaining to that client.

EC-1.5(f)   A paralegal shall not engage in any indiscreet communications concerning clients.

1.6 A PARALEGAL SHALL AVOID CONFLICTS OF INTEREST AND SHALL DISCLOSE ANY POSSIBLE CONFLICT TO THE EMPLOYER OR CLIENT, AS WELL AS TO THE PROSPECTIVE EMPLOYERS OR CLIENTS.

Ethical Considerations

EC-1.6(a)   A paralegal shall act within the bounds of the law, solely for the benefit of the client, and shall be free of compromising influences and loyalties. Neither the paralegal's personal or business interest, nor those of other clients or third persons, should compromise the paralegal's professional judgment and loyalty to the client.

EC-1.6(b)   A paralegal shall avoid conflicts of interest that may arise from previous assignments, whether for a present or past employer or client.

EC-1.6(c)   A paralegal shall avoid conflicts of interest that may arise from family relationships and from personal and business interests.

EC-1.6(d)   In order to be able to determine whether an actual or potential conflict of interest exists a paralegal shall create and maintain an effective recordkeeping system that identifies clients, matters, and parties with which the paralegal has worked.

EC-1.6(e)   A paralegal shall reveal sufficient non-confidential information about a client or former client to reasonably ascertain if an actual or potential conflict of interest exists.

EC-1.6(f)   A paralegal shall not participate in or conduct work on any matter where a conflict of interest has been identified.

EC-1.6(g)   In matters where a conflict of interest has been identified and the client consents to continued representation, a paralegal shall comply fully with the implementation and maintenance of an Ethical Wall.

1.7 A PARALEGAL'S TITLE SHALL BE FULLY DISCLOSED.

Ethical Considerations

EC-1.7(a)   A paralegal's title shall clearly indicate the individual's status and shall be disclosed in all business and professional communications to avoid misunderstandings and misconceptions about the paralegal's role and responsibilities.

EC-1.7(b)   A paralegal's title shall be included if the paralegal's name appears on business cards, letterhead, brochures, directories, and advertisements.

EC-1.7(c)   A paralegal shall not use letterhead, business cards or other promotional materials to create a fraudulent impression of his/her status or ability to practice in the jurisdiction in which the paralegal practices.

EC-1.7(d)   A paralegal shall not practice under color of any record, diploma, or certificate that has been illegally or fraudulently obtained or issued or which is misrepresentative in any way.

EC-1.7(e)   A paralegal shall not participate in the creation, issuance, or dissemination of fraudulent records, diplomas, or certificates.

1.8 A PARALEGAL SHALL NOT ENGAGE IN THE UNAUTHORIZED PRACTICE OF LAW.

Ethical Considerations

EC-1.8(a)   A paralegal shall comply with the applicable legal authority governing the unauthorized practice of law in the jurisdiction in which the paralegal practices.

§2. NFPA GUIDELINES FOR THE ENFORCEMENT OF THE MODEL CODE OF ETHICS AND PROFESSIONAL RESPONSIBILITY

2.1 BASIS FOR DISCIPLINE

2.1(a)   Disciplinary investigations and proceedings brought under authority of the Rules shall be conducted in accord with obligations imposed on the paralegal professional by the Model Code of Ethics and Professional Responsibility.

2.2 STRUCTURE OF DISCIPLINARY COMMITTEE

2.2(a)   The Disciplinary Committee ("Committee") shall be made up of nine (9) members including the Chair.

2.2(b)   Each member of the Committee, including any temporary replacement members, shall have demonstrated working knowledge of ethics/professional responsibility-related issues and activities.

2.2(c)   The Committee shall represent a cross-section of practice areas and work experience. The following recommendations are made regarding the members of the Committee.

1) At least one paralegal with one to three years of law-related work experience.

2) At least one paralegal with five to seven years of law related work experience.

3) At least one paralegal with over ten years of law related work experience.

4) One paralegal educator with five to seven years of work experience; preferably in the area of ethics/professional responsibility.

5) One paralegal manager.

6) One lawyer with five to seven years of law-related work experience.

7) One lay member.

2.2(d)   The Chair of the Committee shall be appointed within thirty (30) days of its members' induction. The Chair shall have no fewer than ten (10) years of law-related work experience.

2.2(e)   The terms of all members of the Committee shall be staggered. Of those members initially appointed, a simple majority plus one shall be appointed to a term of one year, and the remaining members shall be appointed to a term of two years. Thereafter, all members of the Committee shall be appointed to terms of two years.

2.2(f)   If for any reason the terms of a majority of the Committee will expire at the same time, members may be appointed to terms of one year to maintain continuity of the Committee.

2.2(g)   The Committee shall organize from its members a three-tiered structure to investigate, prosecute and/or adjudicate charges of misconduct. The members shall be rotated among the tiers.

2.3 OPERATION OF COMMITTEE

2.3(a)   The Committee shall meet on an as-needed basis to discuss, investigate, and/or adjudicate alleged violations of the Model Code/Model Rules.

2.3(b)   A majority of the members of the Committee present at a meeting shall constitute a quorum.

2.3(c)   A Recording Secretary shall be designated to maintain complete and accurate minutes of all Committee meetings. All such minutes shall be kept confidential until a decision has been made that the matter will be set for hearing as set forth in Section 6.1 below.

2.3(d)   If any member of the Committee has a conflict of interest with the Charging Party, the Responding Party, or the allegations of misconduct, that member shall not take part in any hearing or deliberations concerning those allegations. If the absence of that member creates a lack of a quorum for the Committee, then a temporary replacement for the member shall be appointed.

2.3(e)   Either the Charging Party or the Responding Party may request that, for good cause shown, any member of the Committee not participate in a hearing or deliberation. All such requests shall be honored. If the absence of a Committee member under those circumstances creates a lack of a quorum for the Committee, then a temporary replacement for that member shall be appointed.

2.3(f)   All discussions and correspondence of the Committee shall be kept confidential until a decision has been made that the matter will be set for hearing as set forth in Section 6.1 below.

2.3(g)   All correspondence from the Committee to the Responding Party regarding any charge of misconduct and any decisions made regarding the charge shall be mailed certified mail, return receipt requested, to the Responding Party's last known address and shall be clearly marked with a "Confidential" designation.

2.4 PROCEDURE FOR THE REPORTING OF ALLEGED VIOLATIONS OF THE MODEL CODE/DISCIPLINARY RULES

2.4(a)   An individual or entity in possession of non-confidential knowledge or information concerning possible instances of misconduct shall make a confidential written report to the Committee within thirty (30) days of obtaining same. This report shall include all details of the alleged misconduct.

2.4(b)   The Committee so notified shall inform the Responding Party of the allegation(s) of misconduct no later than ten (10) business days after receiving the confidential written report from the Charging Party.

2.4(c)   Notification to the Responding Party shall include the identity of the Charging Party, unless, for good cause shown, the Charging Party requests anonymity.

2.4(d)   The Responding Party shall reply to the allegations within ten (10) business days of notification.

2.5 PROCEDURE FOR THE INVESTIGATION OF A CHARGE OF MISCONDUCT

2.5(a)   Upon receipt of a Charge of Misconduct ("Charge"), or on its own initiative, the Committee shall initiate an investigation.

2.5(b)   If, upon initial or preliminary review, the Committee makes a determination that the charges are either without basis in fact or, if proven, would not constitute professional misconduct, the Committee shall dismiss the allegations of misconduct. If such determination of dismissal cannot be made, a formal investigation shall be initiated.

2.5(c)   Upon the decision to conduct a formal investigation, the Committee shall:

1) mail to the Charging and Responding Parties within three (3) business days of that decision notice of the commencement of a formal investigation. That notification shall be in writing and shall contain a complete explanation of all Charge(s), as well as the reasons for a formal investigation and shall cite the applicable codes and rules;

2) allow the Responding Party thirty (30) days to prepare and submit a confidential response to the Committee, which response shall address each charge specifically and shall be in writing; and

3) upon receipt of the response to the notification, have thirty (30) days to investigate the Charge(s). If an extension of time is deemed necessary, that extension shall not exceed ninety (90) days.

2.5(d)   Upon conclusion of the investigation, the Committee may:

1) dismiss the Charge upon the finding that it has no basis in fact;

2) dismiss the Charge upon the finding that, if proven, the Charge would not constitute Misconduct;

3) refer the matter for hearing by the Tribunal; or

4) in the case of criminal activity, refer the Charge(s) and all investigation results to the appropriate authority.

2.6 PROCEDURE FOR A MISCONDUCT HEARING BEFORE A TRIBUNAL

2.6(a)   Upon the decision by the Committee that a matter should be heard, all parties shall be notified and a hearing date shall be set. The hearing shall take place no more than thirty (30) days from the conclusion of the formal investigation.

2.6(b)   The Responding Party shall have the right to counsel. The parties and the Tribunal shall have the right to call any witnesses and introduce any documentation that they believe will lead to the fair and reasonable resolution of the matter.

2.6(c)   Upon completion of the hearing, the Tribunal shall deliberate and present a written decision to the parties in accordance with procedures as set forth by the Tribunal.

2.6(d)   Notice of the decision of the Tribunal shall be appropriately published.

2.7 SANCTIONS

2.7(a)   Upon a finding of the Tribunal that misconduct has occurred, any of the following sanctions, or others as may be deemed appropriate, may be imposed upon the Responding Party, either singularly or in combination:

1) letter of reprimand to the Responding Party; counseling;

2) attendance at an ethics course approved by the Tribunal; probation;

3) suspension of license/authority to practice; revocation of license/authority to practice;

4) imposition of a fine; assessment of costs; or

5) in the instance of criminal activity, referral to the appropriate authority.

2.7(b)   Upon the expiration of any period of probation, suspension, or revocation, the Responding Party may make application for reinstatement. With the application for reinstatement, the Responding Party must show proof of having complied with all aspects of the sanctions imposed by the Tribunal.

2.8 APPELLATE PROCEDURES

2.8(a)   The parties shall have the right to appeal the decision of the Tribunal in accordance with the procedure as set forth by the Tribunal.

DEFINITIONS

"Appellate Body" means a body established to adjudicate an appeal to any decision made by a Tribunal or other decision-making body with respect to formally-heard Charges of Misconduct.

"Charge of Misconduct" means a written submission by any individual or entity to an ethics committee, paralegal association, bar association, law enforcement agency, judicial body, government agency, or other appropriate body or entity, that sets forth non-confidential information regarding any instance of alleged misconduct by an individual paralegal or paralegal entity.

"Charging Party" means any individual or entity who submits a Charge of Misconduct against an individual paralegal or paralegal entity.

"Competency" means the demonstration of: diligence, education, skill, and mental, emotional, and physical fitness reasonably necessary for the performance of paralegal services.

"Confidential Information" means information relating to a client, whatever its source, that is not public knowledge nor available to the public. ("Non-Confidential Information" would generally include the name of the client and the identity of the matter for which the paralegal provided services.)

"Disciplinary Hearing" means the confidential proceeding conducted by a committee or other designated body or entity concerning any instance of alleged misconduct by an individual paralegal or paralegal entity.

"Disciplinary Committee" means any committee that has been established by an entity such as a paralegal association, bar association, judicial body, or government agency to: (a) identify, define and investigate general ethical considerations and concerns with respect to paralegal practice; (b) administer and enforce the Model Code and Model Rules and; (c) discipline any individual paralegal or paralegal entity found to be in violation of same.

"Disclose" means communication of information reasonably sufficient to permit identification of the significance of the matter in question.

"Ethical Wall" means the screening method implemented in order to protect a client from a conflict of interest. An Ethical Wall generally includes, but is not limited to, the following elements: (1) prohibit the paralegal from having any connection with the matter; (2) ban discussions with or the transfer of documents to or from the paralegal; (3) restrict access to files; and (4) educate all members of the firm, corporation, or entity as to the separation of the paralegal (both organizationally and physically) from the pending matter. For more information regarding the Ethical Wall, see the NFPA publication entitled "The Ethical Wall - Its Application to Paralegals."

"Ex parte" means actions or communications conducted at the instance and for the benefit of one party only, and without notice to, or contestation by, any person adversely interested.

"Investigation" means the investigation of any charge(s) of misconduct filed against an individual paralegal or paralegal entity by a Committee.

"Letter of Reprimand" means a written notice of formal censure or severe reproof administered to an individual paralegal or paralegal entity for unethical or improper conduct.

"Misconduct" means the knowing or unknowing commission of an act that is in direct violation of those Canons and Ethical Considerations of any and all applicable codes and/or rules of conduct.

"Paralegal" is synonymous with "Legal Assistant" and is defined as a person qualified through education, training, or work experience to perform substantive legal work that requires knowledge of legal concepts and is customarily, but not exclusively performed by a lawyer. This person may be retained or employed by a lawyer, law office, governmental agency, or other entity or may be authorized by administrative, statutory, or court authority to perform this work.

"Pro Bono Publico" means providing or assisting to provide quality legal services in order to enhance access to justice for persons of limited means; charitable, religious, civic, community, governmental and educational organizations in matters that are designed primarily to address the legal needs of persons with limited means; or individuals, groups or organizations seeking to secure or protect civil rights, civil liberties or public rights.

"Proper Authority" means the local paralegal association, the local or state bar association, Committee(s) of the local paralegal or bar association(s), local prosecutor, administrative agency, or other tribunal empowered to investigate or act upon an instance of alleged misconduct.

"Responding Party" means an individual paralegal or paralegal entity against whom a Charge of Misconduct has been submitted.

"Revocation" means the recision of the license, certificate or other authority to practice of an individual paralegal or paralegal entity found in violation of those Canons and Ethical Considerations of any and all applicable codes and/or rules of conduct.

"Suspension" means the suspension of the license, certificate or other authority to practice of an individual paralegal or paralegal entity found in violation of those Canons and Ethical Considerations of any and all applicable codes and/or rules of conduct.

"Tribunal" means the body designated to adjudicate allegations of misconduct.

The Unauthorized
Practice of Law

INTRODUCTION

The prohibitions against the unauthorized practice of law have been hotly debated in a variety of contexts and heavily criticized for a variety of reasons including allegedly restricting "access to justice" and interfering with proposals for multidisciplinary practice.[1] This chapter will discuss the purported rationales for the prohibition, acquaint you with various methods used to identify the unauthorized practice of law, and introduce you to some of the arguments and issues in this particularly controversial area.

RATIONALE FOR THE PROHIBITION

Arguably, we as a society believe that we will be better protected from the ignorant and the unscrupulous if various professionals and tradesmen are required to be licensed to perform certain functions on behalf of others. This licensing process gives the public some assurance that minimum standards of education or training have been received and that required information or procedures have been mastered. Through the years the legal profession has maintained that only licensed attorneys are qualified to engage in the practice of law. The rationale could be explained as follows:

> Functionally, the practice of law relates to the rendition of services for others that call for the professional judgment of a lawyer. The essence of the professional judgment of the lawyer is his educated ability to relate the general body and philosophy of law to a specific legal problem of a client; and thus, the public interest will be better served if only lawyers are permitted to act in matters involving professional judgment.[2]

In the following excerpt, the commentator supports this sentiment with some traditional arguments commonly made by the organized bar:

> The problem, of course, is that most unlawful practitioners lack any, or sufficient, knowledge of the law, and their illicit activities are totally unregulated . . . . Among the many problems with nonlawyer practice is that involving the holding out of oneself as competent to perform legal services when only the opposite is true. Such representations run counter to everything the organized bar has ever championed. It was the ABA, after all, that took legal interns from the drafty 19th century reading rooms of law offices and made them students in a regulated legal system of education that is so universally recognized as the best way to prepare for a life of legal service to the public. One wonders what lawyering skills might best be sharpened by retreating from that level of preparedness . . . . And after all is said and done, who but lawyers will have to right the wrongs inflicted upon the unsuspecting victims of untrained or improperly trained, unknowledgeable, effectively unregulated, and, probably in most cases, uncaring nonlawyer practitioners?[3]

However, this reasoning has not been unanimously embraced. At least one commentator has questioned not only the motives behind unauthorized practice of law (UPL) prohibitions, but also the constitutionality of such doctrine.[4] Deborah Rhode, a distinguished scholar who has published extensively on this and related topics,[5] has questioned the broad constraints on the ability of nonlawyers to give and receive legal assistance, particularly in a culture where law plays so dominant a role. In his article, *Nonlawyers and the Unauthorized Practice of Law: An Overview of the Legal and Ethical Parameters,*[6] Derek Denckla argues that many of the assumptions made to support arguments in favor of restrictive UPL rules are erroneous. For example, the argument that UPL restrictions protect the public presupposes that lawyers are more knowledgeable in any specific area than nonlawyers, and, that lawyers have more integrity because they operate within the confines of disciplinary rules. Denckla cites studies that support his claim that lawyers aren't necessarily more competent than laypersons and are rarely disciplined for incompetence, and he makes the point that other professions are also guided by ethical guidelines.

Perhaps the public is unsupportive because they are simply unaware of the potential dangers. Recently, a group of lawyers in Illinois discussed the problems caused by the unauthorized practice of law and suggested that a database be developed to document these problems.

> The conferees placed their greatest emphasis, however, on the immediate need for the bar association to initiate a program to educate the public. The public needs to understand why it is to their advantage to consult attorneys and how the prohibitions on the unauthorized practice of law are designed for their protection. The conferees envisioned an effort on behalf of the legal profession as a whole, not one that features selected interest groups within the bar. They concluded that this type of educational program is imperative, or lawyers will be unable to avoid the perception that they are merely trying to protect their turf.[7]

DISCUSSION QUESTIONS

1. Do you believe that if the dangers of the unauthorized practice of law were better documented that the public would be more supportive of the bar's enforcement of these laws?

2. Is it easier to document and understand the dangers of unauthorized practice in other occupations, such as medicine?

3. Paralegal professionals are in a unique position to both appreciate the subtleties and complexities of the practice of law, as well as obtain a high level of competency in some aspects of the practice of law. Based on your experiences thus far, which arguments do you find most compelling?

4. Do you believe that unauthorized practice of law prohibitions are anticompetitive? If so, can the resulting additional costs to society be justified?

5. Related concerns include the often unilateral determination by members of the bar as to whether a violation has occurred and the potential bias of the "enforcers" who have an economic stake in the outcome.[8] What do you think of this line of argument? Would a more objective determination garner more support or credibility?

WHAT IS THE UNAUTHORIZED PRACTICE OF LAW?

The prohibition against the unauthorized practice of law (UPL) is at once an ambiguous yet exacting rule. It appears to be a straightforward admonition, but upon closer examination questions quickly arise regarding the precise parameters. The Model Rules of Professional Conduct promulgated by the ABA do not define the "practice of law." Rule 5.5 of the Model Rules, entitled "Unauthorized Practice of Law," simply states the following:

> A lawyer shall not:
> (a) practice law in a jurisdiction where doing so violates the regulation of the legal profession in that jurisdiction; or
> (b) assist a person who is not member of the bar in the performance of activity that constitutes the unauthorized practice of law.[9]

The Comment to this rule goes on to state that "[t]he definition of the practice of law is established by law and varies from one jurisdiction to another."

How Have the Individual States Defined UPL?

Individual states admit that UPL is often vaguely defined. Consider the following definition of the practice of law found in the Texas Government Code, Section 81.101:

(a) In this chapter the "practice of law" means the preparation of a pleading or other document incident to an action or special proceeding or the management of the action or proceeding on behalf of a client before a judge in court as well as a service rendered out of court, including the giving of advice or the rendering of any service requiring the use of legal skill or knowledge, such as preparing a will, contract, or other instrument, the legal effect of which under the facts and conclusions involved must be carefully determined.

(b) The definition in this section is not exclusive and does not deprive the judicial branch of the power and authority under both this chapter and the adjudicated cases to determine whether other services and acts not enumerated may constitute the practice of law.

(c) In this chapter, the "practice of law" does not include the design, creation, publication, distribution, display, or sale, including publication, distribution, display, or sale by means of an Internet web site, of written materials, books, forms, computer software, or similar products if the products clearly and conspicuously state that the products are not a substitute for the advice of an attorney. This subsection does not authorize the use of the products or similar media in violation of Chapter 83 and does not affect the applicability or enforceability of that chapter.

Note the language in subsection (b), which states that this definition is not exclusive and leaves room for interpretation and elaboration by the Texas courts. In fact, Texas courts have stated that, "[c]ourts inherently have the power to determine what is the practice of law on a case by case basis."[10] In *Cortez*, the Texas Supreme Court held that the judge, *not* the jury, should determine whether particular undisputed actions constitute the unauthorized practice of law. The Court rationalized this by stating that even though it was in the jury's province to determine what conduct is restricted in other professions, such as medicine, that the relationship between the court and the legal profession is different because of the court's responsibility to police the legal profession.[11] Recently, the Supreme Court of South Carolina reaffirmed that "it is neither practicable or wise to attempt a comprehensive definition by way of a set of rules. Instead, we are convinced that the better course is to decide what is and what is not the unauthorized practice of law in the context of the actual case or controversy.[12] Similarly, the Indiana Bar's Unauthorized Practice of Law Committee decided that the filing of specific cases would be the proper avenue to help better define what constitutes UPL.[13] The State Bar of Michigan recently acknowledged that Michigan's prohibitions against UPL were not precise; however, the Bar's representative felt that sufficient cases had been litigated to narrow the definition of the practice of law.[14] These attitudes are representative of most state bars and supreme courts across the country; as a result, courts are often left to decide what is and what is not the practice of law on a case-by-case, and state-by-state basis.

Generally, most descriptions of the kinds of activities that constitute the practice of law may be divided into three broad categories: (1) in-court representation, (2) document drafting, and (3) the giving of legal advice. Since many of the definitions are broad and overinclusive, determining which fact scenarios fall within these categories has been the subject of much case law across the country.

Case Law: Tests

As discussed previously, state courts have assumed the burden of determining what is and what is not the unauthorized practice of law. Unfortunately, no clear guidelines have emerged, and even the tests that have been developed by courts are applied in an often inconsistent and sometimes contradictory manner. In the following excerpt, the author identifies and examines the various tests applied by courts when determining what constitutes the unauthorized practice of law.

1. The "Commonly Understood" Test and its Variations.

    Courts that apply the "commonly understood" test define the practice of law as those activities that are "commonly understood to be the practice of law."[15] This broad definition includes those activities that lawyers perform outside of any court and that have no immediate relation to proceedings in court. It embraces the giving of legal advice on a large variety of subjects and the preparation of legal instruments covering an extensive field . . . . Once it is determined that a service customarily has been provided by lawyers, nonlawyers are precluded from also providing that service[16]—unless the court is one that recognizes exceptions to this rule.

    a. "Incidental" exception to the "Commonly Understood" Test.

        . . . This exception is usually justified on the grounds that the exclusion of non-lawyers from so broad a spectrum of activities would too greatly circumscribe the activities of other professionals—including accountants, insurance agents, and trust and title company agents[17] and would not serve the public interest. A few of those courts that recognize the "incidental" exception limit it to activities that are not merely incidental but also "necessary" to the primary business . . . .[18]

    b. "Difficult Question" Standard.

        . . . Still other courts circumscribe the "incidental" test by requiring that no "difficult question of law" be involved.[19] Under the "no difficult question" standard, a nonlawyer may provide services commonly understood to be the practice of law only if those services are incidental and no complex or difficult questions of law are involved . . . .[20]

2. The "Client Reliance" Test

    A second test focuses on whether a client believes that he is receiving legal services. Under this standard, an individual is engaged in the practice of law if he is "perceived by the parties as performing the traditional role of advice giving."[21] The reason given for labeling such services the practice of law is the likelihood that consumers will rely on them as qualified legal services . . . .[22]

3. The "Relating Law to Specific Facts" Test

    Another test identifies the practice of law as "relating the general body and philosophy of law to a specific legal problem of a client."[23] [The author generally discusses three cases that apply this test to sales of divorce kits] . . . . These three courts applied the "relating law to specific facts" test to similar situations in three different ways. The *Dacey*[24] court focused on whether the information provided the consumer was general or tailored to a particular individual in his or her particular situation. In *Gilchrist,*[25] the court enjoined personal contact between employees of the divorce kit company and consumers because, with personal contact, the general advice became specific. In *Stupica,*[26] the court enjoined the sale of the divorce kits altogether because the selecting of the proper forms was itself deemed "comprehensive and specific" legal advice.[27]

4. The "Affecting Legal Rights" Test

A fourth test identifies services as the practice of law when they affect legal rights. The court in *Baron v. City of Los Angeles*[28] held that one is engaged in the practice of law if he furnishes "legal advice and counsel and prepares . . . legal instruments and contracts by which legal rights are secured although such matter may or may not be pending in a court."[29] The court in *State Bar v. Guardian Abstract & Title Co.*[30] stated that "rendering a service that requires the use of legal knowledge" or "preparing instruments and contracts by which legal rights are secured" indicates the practice of law[31] Applying this standard, the court in *Palmer v. Unauthorized Practice Committee*[32] held that "the exercise of judgment in the . . . selecting of the proper form of instrument, necessarily affects important legal rights. The reasonable protection of those rights . . . requires that the persons providing such services be licensed members of the legal profession."[33]

5. The "Attorney-Client Relationship" Test

A fifth test focuses on the . . . relationship with the client.[34] In holding that the mere sale of a legal self-help kit does not constitute the practice of law, the *Dacey* court mentioned the lack of "that relation of confidence and trust so necessary to the status of attorney and client [that] is the essential of legal practice."[35] *Cramer* picked up this theme, stating that the defendant in *Dacey* was not engaged in the unauthorized practice of law because "there [was] no personal contact or relationship with a particular individual."[36]

DISCUSSION QUESTIONS

1. Is there one perfect test, or is a combination better? Which of the preceding tests makes the most sense to you? Why?

2. Review the following excerpt from *Stovall v. Martinez*, 996 P.2d 371, 374–375, (Kan. App. 2000) and apply the tests discussed by Morrison. Which tests could be appropriately applied to this scenario?

The essential facts are as follows: After working for a number of years as an insurance adjuster and claims examiner for State Farm Insurance Company, defendant established his own business as an insurance claims consultant. In the course of his business, defendant heavily advertised his services as an alternative to representation by an attorney. Defendant represented claimants under a contingency fee contract. The contract stated defendant had a right to a lien on the claimant's recovery. In representing a claimant, defendant compiled a settlement packet of relevant information, made written demand upon the insurance company, advised the claimant regarding the reasonableness of a settlement, and negotiated with the insurance company. Defendant was not licensed to practice law . . . . Defendant contends the trial court erred in finding he engaged in the unauthorized practice of law. Defendant does not dispute the underlying facts, but primarily argues that because he performed the same services as an employee of State Farm Insurance Company, either he was not practicing law in his insurance consulting business or all insurance adjusters and claims examiners are unlawfully practicing law. From that assumption, defendant launches an equal protection argument . . . . The primary flaw in defendant's reasoning is that it disregards the role defendant assumed in relation to individual clients. Our Supreme Court has the inherent power to define and regulate the practice of law. What constitutes the unauthorized practice of law must be determined on a case-by-case basis. *State ex rel. Stephan v. Williams*, 246 Kan. 681, 689, 793 P.2d 234 (1990). Our Supreme Court has repeatedly recognized the actions of counseling and advising clients on their legal rights and rendering services requiring knowledge of legal principles to be included within the definition of practicing law. See, e.g., *Williams*, 246 Kan. at 689, 793 P.2d 234.

Purporting to be an expert, defendant offered a service, the performance of which clearly required knowledge of legal principles. Defendant induced his clients to place their trust in his judgment and skill in framing their claims. Defendant's financial interest in settlement without litigation conflicted with the client's interest in getting a fair settlement. That relationship to the client distinguishes the service defendant offered from the work he did while employed by an insurance company. Defendant's business is distinguished from the service offered by, for instance, ombudsmen and union representatives by his profit motive and potential conflict of interest. The court does not concern itself with the results of the service. See *State ex rel. Schneider v. Hill*, 223 Kan. 425, 426, 573 P.2d 1078 (1978). Unquestionably, the trial court did not err in finding defendant's consulting services involved the practice of law.

Case Law: Common Areas of Concern

Common areas of concern to UPL committees and state courts include the following: (1) administrative agency practice (discussed later in this chapter); (2) "forms" practices such as estate planning (including wills preparation), bankruptcy, real estate, and immigration; and (3) areas in which the nonlawyer attempts to act as a representative or agent for a consumer, such as an insurance adjuster for personal injury claims.

Providing Forms.   Courts generally hold that a nonlawyer may sell legal forms[37] and may even fill in blanks on standardized forms with the exact words supplied by others. However, any instructions or personalized assistance in filling out the forms may constitute the unauthorized practice of law.[38] This is true even if the forms were initially prepared by lawyers.[39] The prototype scenario often involves the sale of "kits," which include legal forms and detailed instructions on how to use them. Courts are divided as to whether the sale of these "kits" is unlawful.[40] Obviously the burgeoning area of computer software also requires this analysis. For example, recently a United States District Court judge held that the *Quicken Family Lawyer* software program constituted the illegal practice of law in the State of Texas. The court argued that the program's use of interactive questions to craft a customized document for consumers involved the use of "professional judgment" and created a false "air of reliability" about the documents created.[41] However, in view of the legislation since adopted in the state of Texas,[42] as long as the required disclosure is made that the product is not a substitute for the advice of an attorney, it is doubtful that the Court would reach the same conclusion today.[43]

Sometimes, providing forms constitutes only a small part of services provided to others by nonlawyers. In their article, "The Thin Red Line: An Analysis of the Role of Legal Assistants in the Chapter 13 Bankruptcy Process,"[44] the authors provide a detailed summary of bankruptcy court decisions that have specified actions that, if performed by nonlawyers, constitute the unauthorized practice of law in a bankruptcy case. These actions include the following:

- advising a debtor as to legal rights regarding secured collateral, describing the difference between a Chapter 13 filing and a Chapter 7 filing, and selecting the debtor's exemptions[45]
- advising a debtor whether or not to file a Statement of Intention and directing a client to refer to a list of exemptions from which to select assets[46]
- soliciting information from clients that is reformulated and typed into the bankruptcy petition[47]
- advising debtors to file a Chapter 13 petition and composing an insufficient Chapter 13 plan[48]
- drafting and preparing legal documents, including bankruptcy petitions, statements, and schedules[49]
- defining terms in bankruptcy schedules such as "creditors holding secured claims," "real property," and "executory contracts"[50]
- determining whether property should be claimed as exempt, whether the client had any co-debtors, or whether the client was a party to executory contracts and/or expired leases[51]
- advising clients to list all debt and the option of voluntary repayment[52]

The authors, quoting *In re Bachman*,[53] also set out the types of services that may be performed by nonlawyers: (1) typing bankruptcy forms, provided they copy only written information furnished to them; (2) selling bankruptcy forms; (3) selling to the public printed material purporting to explain bankruptcy practice and procedure; and (4) advertising secretarial, notary, and typing services.

Other services that constitute the unauthorized practice of law include preparing and filing lien affidavits and claims and releases of liens affecting title to property[54] where a nonattorney ran a debt collection business for construction, medical, and business clients.

DISCUSSION QUESTIONS

1. In *The Florida Bar v. Catarcio*, 709 So. 2d 96, (Fla. 1998), the defendant operated a business under the name of "American Paralegal Center, Inc." and used

a business card that identified him as "Richard T. Catarcio, J.D." although he was not licensed to practice law in any state. Review the following excerpt where the court takes note of the actions of Catarcio that constituted the unauthorized practice of law, and, discusses supporting precedent:[55]

[T]he referee concluded that Catarcio had engaged in the unlicensed practice of law by (1) advising Cooper and Caron as to various legal remedies available to them and possible courses of action; (2) taking information from Cooper orally to complete the bankruptcy petition and amendment when the forms being completed were not forms approved by this Court; (3) having direct contact with Cooper and Caron in the nature of consultation, explanation, recommendations, advice and assistance in the provision, selection, and completion of legal forms; (4) inducing Cooper to place reliance upon him in the preparation of his bankruptcy forms; (5) advising Cooper and Caron to file a joint bankruptcy petition when they were not married in contravention of 11 U.S.C. § 302(a), which states that joint bankruptcy petitions are filed by a debtor and the debtor's spouse, and by advising Caron to fraudulently sign her name as "Cooper" even though she told him that she was divorced from Cooper and that her legal name at the time was Caron; (6) offering "Free Consultation" in advertising his legal forms preparation service in that it holds him out as able to provide legal services in the nature of consultation and because it goes beyond the limitations placed on nonlawyer advertising by offering more than secretarial and notary services and selling legal forms and general printed materials; and (7) by using the designation "J.D." on his business card in conjunction with his offer of the preparation of legal forms and the depiction of the Scales of Justice.

After arriving at the above conclusions, the referee recommended that this Court find that Catarcio engaged in the unlicensed practice of law based on his conduct in the preparation of Cooper and Caron's joint bankruptcy petition, as well as the manner in which Catarcio advertised his legal forms preparation service. The referee then recommended that Catarcio be enjoined from the unlicensed practice of law and taxed for the costs of these proceedings. We approve the report of the referee . . . .

This Court has issued numerous decisions proscribing the type of conduct engaged in by Catarcio. See *Florida Bar v. Davide*, 702 So. 2d 184 (Fla. 1997) (adopting uncontested referee's report finding nonlawyers engaged in unlicensed practice of law by, among other things, advising persons regarding bankruptcy exemptions); *Florida Bar v. Warren*, 655 So. 2d 1131, 1132–33 (Fla. 1995) (enjoining nonlawyer from, among other things, counseling persons as to "the advisability of their filing for protection under the United States bankruptcy laws"); *Florida Bar v. Schramek*, 616 So. 2d 979, 984 (Fla. 1993) (finding nonlawyer engaged in unlicensed practice of law in many areas, including bankruptcy, by providing services "which require[d] a knowledge of the law greater than that possessed by the average citizen"); *Florida Bar v. King*, 468 So. 2d 982, 983 (Fla. 1985) (adopting uncontested referee's report finding nonlawyer engaged in unlicensed practice of law by, among other things, having "direct contact in the nature of consultation, explanation, recommendations, advice and assistance in the provision, selection and completion of forms"); *Florida Bar v. Martin*, 432 So. 2d 54 (Fla. 1983) (approving referee's report finding nonlawyer's use of designation "J.D." in conjunction with his name constituted unlicensed practice of law); *Brumbaugh*, 355 So. 2d at 1194 (enjoining nonlawyer from advising clients as to various available remedies, making inquiries or answering questions as to particular forms which might be necessary, how best to fill out such forms, and where to properly file such forms).

This Court has also adopted rules regulating the unlicensed practice of law which proscribe the type of conduct engaged in by Catarcio. See *R. Regulating Fla. Bar* 10-2.1(a) (1997) (restricting nonlawyer oral communications solely to those eliciting factual information for the completion of forms approved by this Court); see also *Florida Bar Re Approval of Forms Pursuant to Rule 10-1.1(b) of the Rules Regulating The Florida Bar,* 591 So. 2d 594, 595 (Fla. 1991) (approving "fill-in-the-blank" forms developed by the Bar for use in "areas amenable to a forms practice").

Federal bankruptcy courts sitting in Florida have found similar conduct constituted the unlicensed practice of law. See *In re Samuels,* 176 B.R. 616, 621–22 (Bankr. M.D. Fla. 1994) (providing exhaustive list of activities constituting the unlicensed practice of law in bankruptcy context in Florida and other jurisdictions, and stating that "[t]he Florida Supreme Court and Florida bankruptcy courts have made it clear that persons wanting to provide services in the bankruptcy area are limited to typing or transcribing written information provided to them by a consumer onto pre-prepared forms"); *In re Calzadilla*, 151 B.R. 622, 625–26 (Bankr. S.D. Fla. 1993) (providing what bankruptcy services a nonlawyer may and may not provide); *In re Bachmann*, 113 B.R. at 773–75 (applying this Court's Brumbaugh decision in bankruptcy context).

a. Generally, Florida allows nonlawyers to provide limited services in connection with form preparation. List the restrictions as identified by this opinion.

b. In view of the restrictions placed on "typing services," why do you think anyone would be interested in operating this type of business?

2. Review the following excerpt from *Fadia v. UPL Comm.*, 830 S.W.2d 162, 164 (Tex. App.—Dallas, 1992).

Vijay Fadia owns and operates County Homestead Service Agency in Torrance, California. He publishes a will manual entitled "You and Your Will: A Do-It-Yourself Manual" that he distributes in several states, including Texas. Fadia is not a licensed attorney in any state and has not attended law school. Fadia admits that no Texas attorney has reviewed or updated the book. He sold approximately 200 manuals in Texas for $24.95 each. Fadia's will manual contains information on how to prepare a will. The manual covers topics such as executors, legal guardians, holographic wills, joint wills, simultaneous death provisions, incontestability clauses, specific bequests, community property, and pourover wills. The will manual also includes "fill-in-the-blank forms" for specific situations and several documents he calls "statutory" will forms from other states . . . .

UNAUTHORIZED PRACTICE OF LAW

In his first point of error, Fadia argues that the publishing, marketing, and distribution of the will manual cannot constitute the practice of law. He contends that his will manual contains general information about wills and that his book encourages the public to seek the advice of a lawyer for complicated estate matters. Because a will secures legal rights and involves the giving of advice requiring the use of legal skill or knowledge, the preparation of a will involves the practice of law. *Palmer v. Unauthorized Practice of Law Comm. of the State Bar of Texas,* 438 S.W.2d 374, 376 (Tex. Civ. App.—Houston [14th Dist.] 1969, no writ); Tex. Gov't Code Ann. 81.101 (Vernon 1988). No phase of law requires a more profound learning on the subject of trusts, powers, taxation law, legal and equitable estates, and perpetuities than preparing a will. An unlicensed person, untrained in such complex legal subjects, cannot perform these duties for someone else. *Palmer*, 438 S.W.2d at 376. Fadia urges this Court to reject *Palmer* and accept the new age of legal self-help clinics. See, e.g., *People v. Landlords Professional Serv.*, 215 Cal. App. 3d 1599, 264 Cal. Rptr. 548, 553 (Cal. Ct. App.1989) (clerical services do not constitute the practice of law, but personal advice to a specific individual does constitute the practice of law); *Florida Bar v. Brumbaugh*, 355 So. 2d 1186, 1194 (Fla. 1978) (the sale of legal forms and their instructions to the general public rather than to a specific individual for a particular legal problem does not constitute thepractice of law); *Oregon State Bar v. Gilchrist*, 272 Or. 552, 538 P.2d 913, 919 (1975) (advertisement and sale of divorce kits without personal advice to the customer does not constitute the practice of law). To grant Fadia's request to overrule *Palmer* would require us to legislate from the bench. See *Ex Parte Salter*, 452 S.W.2d 711, 713 (Tex. Civ. App.—Houston [1st Dist.]

1970, writ refused). Changes to section 81.101, however, must come from the legislature. *Salter*, 452 S.W.2d at 713. A review of the summary judgment evidence shows that:

(1) the will manual covers topics in which only an attorney may advise a client, like specific bequests, residuary estates, executor powers, self-proving affidavits, intestacy, and attestation clauses,

(2) the manual contains fill-in-the-blank forms that can easily confuse nonlawyers,

(3) one section of the manual contains a "create-your-own-will" section and tells persons how to use the clauses contained in the manual to create their own wills,

(4) the manual contains certain statutory wills that are not valid in Texas,

(5) no attorney licensed in Texas reviewed the manual for legal accuracy, and

(6) Fadia is not a licensed attorney in any state.

Fadia's will manual goes well beyond simple layman's advice. The will manual contains "fill-in-the-blank forms" and a "create-your-own-will" section. The selection of the proper legal form affects important legal rights. *Palmer*, 438 S.W.2d at 377. Fadia purports to advise a layperson on how to draft a will. This advice constitutes the practice of law. *Id.* Fadia's advertisements and will manual lead the public to falsely believe that testamentary dispositions can be standardized. Reliance on his forms leads to a false sense of security and often unfortunate circumstances for the general public. *Palmer*, 438 S.W.2d at 376.

The selling of legal advice is the practice of law. Fadia sold his advice for $24.95. *Cf. Cortez*, 692 S.W.2d at 50. The State Bar has not only the right but also the obligation to prevent legal advice clothed in the robes of simplicity from adversely affecting the estates of the unsuspecting public. Because a nonlawyer cannot and should not give advice to any other person on the drafting and executing of wills, we conclude that Fadia's publication and distribution of his will manual constitutes the practice of law. We overrule his first point of error.

a. The court stated that "Fadia's advertisements and will manual lead the public to falsely believe that testamentary dispositions can be standardized."

Why is this significant?

b. How much did Fadia charge for his will manual? Do you think the price mattered?

c. Where did the court draw the line? In other words, at what point did Fadia's forms become the "unauthorized practice of law"?

3. Read the following excerpt from *The Florida Bar v. American Senior Citizens Alliance (ASCA)*, 689 So. 2d 255 (Fla. 1997):

ASCA, a for-profit corporation owned and managed exclusively by nonlawyers, was in the business of creating and selling complex estate planning documents including living trusts, wills, durable powers of attorney and other related legal documents. ASCA was headquartered in Orlando but operated throughout Florida. ASCA employed licensed attorneys as in-house counsel but relied upon paralegals, customer service representatives and salespeople to contact customers and sell them estate planning devices. ASCA solicited prospective customers through direct mass mailings which offered the preparation of a living will at no charge if a customer contacted the company and set up an appointment to meet with a salesperson in the customer's home. At the appointment, the salesperson made a standardized sales pitch designed to convince the customer that estate planning devices such as wills, joint tenancies, and the like were inferior to the ASCA living trusts. The sales pitch was a "high-pressure" presentation designed to exploit the elderly customer's common fears and misunderstandings surrounding probate processes. The pitch included a detailed description of how living trusts work, the duties of a trustee and how one should be chosen, and the legal process concerning a person's death, disability or incompetency. The salespersons regularly answered specific legal questions for the customer and gave tailored legal advice regarding how a particular estate planning device would affect the customer's particular life circumstances. Finally, the customer was told that an attorney would be drafting her living trust. When a customer bought a living trust from ASCA, the salesperson gathered information about the assets the customer owned and collected at least half of the drafting fee, ranging from $695 to $1,495, at the appointment. None of this money was placed in a protective escrow but instead was deposited into respondent's general account. The fee, along with the package drawn up by the salesperson, was then sent to ASCA's Orlando office. A paralegal in the Orlando office received the information and prepared the trust and related documents using standardized forms on ASCA's computer data base. These forms contained approximately fifty pages of boilerplate language, and in most cases only two pages were modified. When a paralegal received several packages at one time, one of ASCA's managers—none of whom were lawyers—prioritized the packages based primarily on monetary considerations (i.e., trusts for which money was still owed were completed first so that ASCA would promptly receive additional payment). Paralegals also prepared the deeds and other papers necessary for funding a customer's trust. Finally, an in-house attorney reviewed the completed trust package. The customer did not choose the attorney who reviewed her paperwork. Many trusts contained incorrect information, which was not corrected even if known, or were inadequately funded and resulted in negated trusts. The ASCA nonlawyer owner and managers had access to all customer files and attorney work product. Confidential personal information that ASCA customers gave to salespersons was secretly provided to an insurance/annuity affiliate of ASCA to be used later for "prospecting." Most ASCA customers never had any communication with

ASCA in-house attorneys either by telephone or in writing. Nor did the ASCA lawyers normally ascertain whether the individual customer knew what a living trust was or whether the trust was appropriate for her. Customers who called with legal questions were deliberately routed to a nonlawyer employee, and the few appointments made with attorneys at the ASCA offices were kept to a maximum of forty-five minutes by employees interrupting and falsely stating that the lawyer had another appointment. Because decisions on whether a particular customer needed a living trust and the type of trust best suited for that customer were made by the lay salesperson at the time of the sales presentation, the in-house lawyer's role at the last stage of ASCA's trust processing was limited to making a cursory review of the forms before the documents were mailed back to the customer for execution of the trust. The referee found that ASCA improperly solicited customers for the purchase of legal instruments; made repeated misrepresentations; shared fees with nonlawyers; commingled advance fee payments with operating funds; restricted the exercise of independent professional judgment of corporate lawyers; made repeated advertising violations; failed or refused to communicate with clients; and disclosed confidences for profit. The referee further found that customers paid for legal advice that was never received and the ASCA practices resulted in great harm to elderly members of the public.

Additionally, the referee found that respondent improperly relied upon the language in *Florida Bar re Advisory Opinion—Nonlawyer Preparation of Living Trusts*, 613 So. 2d 426, 428 (Fla. 1992), as permitting ASCA's practice of entering the homes of its elderly victims and giving legal advice rather than merely gathering information. Because respondent's unlicensed conduct was based, at least in part, on a purported misconstruction of this Court's case law, the referee recommended that this Court issue an opinion in this case clarifying the language in its prior decisions and more specifically defining what is meant by "gathering the necessary information" in connection with living trusts . . . . Under the untenable guise of "gathering information," nonlawyer ASCA employees answered specific legal questions; determined the appropriateness of a living trust based on a customer's particular needs and circumstances; assembled, drafted and executed the documents; and funded the living trusts in direct violation of our clear admonitions to the contrary in *Brumbaugh*[56] and *Living Trusts*.[57] The particularized legal advice and services rendered by ASCA's nonlawyer employees clearly constituted the unlicensed practice of law. Pursuant to the referee's request, we find that ASCA's conduct here constituted the unlicensed practice of law and was far more than the mere "gathering of the necessary information for a living trust."

    a. Do you think it would have made a difference in the outcome of the case if the in-house lawyers had played a larger role in the provision of services?

    b. Based on this opinion, develop the type of "living trust" business that would have been allowed by the court.

    c. At what point did merely "gathering information" become the unauthorized practice of law?

4. In view of the holdings in *Fadia* and *ASCA*, consider the following hypothetical:[58]

Rose was sued by the Unauthorized Practice of Law Committee of State Y because she had prepared a will for her Uncle Sam using computer software. Uncle Sam was legally blind and bedridden. Rose had purchased the computer software, which she used to generate the will, prior to meeting with Uncle Sam.

This particular software program did not allow editing or provide options as to the type of form or provision to be included; it merely asked questions of the user, the answers to which generated the final document. According to Rose, she simply read the questions to Uncle Sam, and he provided the answers. Moreover, Rose never held herself out to Uncle Sam as competent to do anything more than simply complete forms; nor did she ever attempt to advise Uncle Sam on the legal effects of his decisions.

Based on this information, the court held that "Rose acted as nothing more than a scribe in assisting Uncle Sam with his will and thus, she did not engage in the practice of law. We are aided in reaching our conclusion by the unfortunate result that would obtain if we held otherwise. A person in Uncle Sam's position, mentally competent yet legally blind and requiring assistance for certain basic tasks such as reading and writing, would not be able to dispose of his property as he pleases without incurring the expense of hiring an attorney to write his will. In such situations, public policy should support one person's assisting another by simply filling in blanks on a pre-printed, uneditable form, at the specific direction of the other, without advising as to the legal effects of such requests."

a. The court placed special emphasis on the fact that Uncle Sam was blind. Should the disability of a recipient be a factor in determining whether someone providing services has engaged in the unauthorized practice of law? What about the ecomomic standing of the recipient?

b. What are the distinguishing facts between *Fadia, ASCA* and the preceding hypothetical?

Agent or Representative.   Clearly, representing another person in a public tribunal constitutes the practice of law. Less clear is whether representation of another person in other scenarios is also practicing law. For example, third-party insurance claim adjusters seek compensation from insurance companies on behalf of claimants for losses due to personal injury or property damage. Recently, in Utah, the state supreme court held that this type of "third-party" adjusting constituted the unauthorized practice of law.[59] As support for its holding, the court cited several cases from other jurisdictions finding that third-party adjusters engaged in the practice of law even though the adjusters did not perform courtroom services.[60] The arguments made by these courts included the following rationales: "[t]he conduct of litigation is by no means all of legal practice;"[61] "[a] person may confer legal advice not only by word of mouth but also by a course of conduct that encourages litigation and the prosecution of claims;"[62] and "[f]actual determinations that affect liability and damage issues and negotiation [of] legal positions and issues . . . clearly involve the practice of law."[63]

A potentially confusing area in which representatives often argue their right to represent others is when they hold a power of attorney for that other person. The courts are clear that a power of attorney does not grant the holder the authority to act as an attorney at law.[64] However, consider the following dissenting opinion in a case where a nephew, holding a power of attorney and attempting to protest a real property valuation on behalf of his "physically and mentally infirm" elderly aunt, was held to be engaged in the unauthorized practice of law:

> PFEIFER, J. dissenting.
>
> This case presents an example of an opinion of this court being taken to an illogical extreme. My vote in *Sharon Village*[65] was based on the facts of that case—a third-party agent, unrelated to the entities seeking revisions, filed applications with the Licking County Board of Revision. I saw that decision as one affecting freelancers soliciting and filing applications for revision without having a real relationship with the taxpayer. I considered that practice to be potentially harmful to taxpayers. With this case, we have finally reached the level of *reductio ad absurdum* regarding *Sharon Village*. Here, Frieda Fravel (the aunt) has given Dorn (the nephew) the legal power to step into her shoes. He is operating as Frieda Fravel, not merely on her behalf. By all accounts, this is a loving relative, trusted to take control of Fravel's estate, doing what is clearly in the best interest of the estate. This does not come close to involving the perceived perils involved with *Sharon Village*. I accordingly dissent, ...

DISCUSSION QUESTIONS

1. In the preceding dissenting opinion, the judge wants to distinguish between unrelated third-party agents and "loving relatives." Do you think this is a justifiable distinction?

2. Read the excerpt of *Brown v. Unauthorized Practice of Law Comm.*, 742 S.W.2d 34, 37–43 (Tex. App.—Dallas, 1987). Note the court's discussion of how a course of conduct can implicitly result in the practice of law. Do you agree with the court's reasoning?

> At trial, Brown admitted that he was not an attorney; however, he stated that he did have legal training. He explained that he went to the Brownwood Institute for paralegal study for one year. He also stated that he worked for various attorneys on a freelance basis. The record reflects the following undisputed facts. Ron Brown conducted a business in which he entered contracts with individuals to represent them in resolving their personal injury and/or property damage claims on a contingent fee basis. Brown correctly argues that the record nowhere reveals any evidence of one of his clients directly testifying, "Ron Brown advised me of my rights and of the advisability of making a claim," or "Ron Brown advised me as to whether to accept an offered sum of money in settlement of my claim," or "Ron Brown advised me of my rights, duties, and privileges under the laws." Because there is no direct testimony on those three fact findings, Brown maintains that there is no evidence to support them. For the reasons given below, we disagree with Brown's contention.
>
> A person may confer legal advice not only by word of mouth but also by a course of conduct that encourages litigation and the prosecution of claims. *Quarles v. State Bar of Texas*, 316 S.W.2d 797, 800, 802, & 804 (Tex. Civ. App.—Houston 1958), pet. denied for writ of cert. to Supreme Court of Texas, 368 U.S. 986, 82 S. Ct. 601, 7 L. Ed. 2d 524 (1962). We agree with Brown that there is no evidence that he ever verbally told his

clients their rights. This may be due to the fact that Brown, not being an attorney, did not know himself what his client's legal rights were. Brown's course of conduct nevertheless encouraged litigation and the prosecution of claims and, at least implicitly, advised his clients of what he perceived to be their legal rights. Determining the legal liability, the extent of legally compensable damages, and the legal rights and privileges of personal injury and property damage claimants, by their very nature, require legal skill and knowledge. We now illustrate how Brown's course of conduct provides both legally and factually sufficient evidence to support the trial court's findings of fact.

We first address whether Brown advised persons as to their rights and the advisability of making claims for personal injuries and/or property damages. Brown contends that he merely handled undisputed and uncontested claims and that he never advised clients of their rights or the advisability of making claims because, "When they come to me, they already feel they have a case. When they come to me, they're usually already involved in an accident, and they know whose [sic] at fault." [However], [t]hese persons apparently "felt" they had a claim, and the fact that Brown undertook to represent them regarding their claims illustrates that he impliedly advised them that they did indeed have legal rights and that they certainly should make a claim. Brown emphasizes that he handles only undisputed and uncontested claims. On the issue of liability, this may be so. However, the evidence abundantly shows that Brown negotiated settlements on damages. Ruth Hunter, a claims representative for Members Insurance, testified that she negotiated with Brown on perhaps six different claims. Van Simms, a claims supervisor with Fireman's Insurance, testified that Brown wanted to settle Eunice King's damages on an estimated basis, which meant calculating future medical expenses. It is self-evident that if damages are undisputed and uncontested, then negotiation would not be necessary; because the evidence shows that Brown negotiated, at least on damage issues, we cannot agree that Brown handled only undisputed and uncontested cases.

Brown denied negotiating; he contends that he merely processed claims and that his clients determined their own damages and that he merely inserted their figure and thereafter acted as a go-between . . . . If Brown did in fact merely act as a go-between, and if he merely asked for the damages his clients asked for, then Brown again was impliedly advising his clients that the damages for which they asked were in fact the only damages to which they were entitled. From the above evidence, we hold that the evidence is both legally and factually sufficient to support the finding that Brown advised persons as to their rights and the advisability of making claims for personal injuries and/or property claims.

We now address whether Brown advised persons as to whether to accept an offered sum of money in settlement of claims for personal injuries and/or property damages. Brown's contract with White provides that neither he nor she may settle her claim without the other's approval in writing. When Brown approves a settlement he again impliedly advises his client to accept the sum of money offered in settlement. We hold that this evidence is both legally and factually sufficient to support this finding.

The last fact finding we must address is whether Brown advised his clients of their rights, duties, and privileges under the law. The practice of law embraces in general all advice to clients and all action taken for them in matters connected with the law. *Quarles*, 316 S.W.2d at 803. When a person acts for himself or others and undertakes to advise prospective employers or clients by word or course of conduct concerning their legal rights and the prospects of settling personal injury, accident, or other legal claims, thereby encouraging the assertion or prosecution of claims or lawsuits, this person steps beyond the bounds of a legitimate investigation facts and engages in the unauthorized practice of law. *Id.* at 800, 802–03 . . . . Contracting with persons to represent them with regard to their personal causes of action for property damages and/or personal injury constitutes the practice of law. *Quarles*, 316 S.W.2d at 801 & 804; cf. *Davies v. Unauthorized Practice Committee of State Bar of Texas*, 431 S.W.2d 590, 594 (Tex. Civ. App.—Tyler 1968, writ ref'd n.r.e.) (acting in representative capacity in the presentation of claims). Advising persons as to their rights and the advisability of making claims for personal injuries and/or property damages constitutes the practice of law. See *Quarles*, 316 S.W.2d at 800 & 804. Advising persons as to whether to accept an offered sum of money in settlement of claims for personal injuries and/or property damages entails the practice of law. *Cf. Stewart Abstract Co. v. Judicial Commission*, 131 S.W.2d 686, 689 (Tex. Civ. App.—Beaumont 1939, no writ) (all advice to clients connected with the law). Entering into contracts with persons to represent them in their personal injury and/or property damage matters on a contingent fee together with an attempted assignment of a portion of the person's cause of action involves the practice of law. *Quarles*, 316 S.W.2d at 800–01 & 803. Entering into contracts with third persons which purport to grant the exclusive right to select and retain legal counsel to represent the individual in any legal proceeding constitutes the practice of law. *Cf. id.* at 804 (peddling and offering to attorneys legal business of claimants).

Brown argues that the Texas Insurance Code authorizes persons such as himself to handle undisputed and uncontested claims and claims arising under life, accident, and health insurance policies, provided the person merely performs clerical duties and does not negotiate with the other parties on the disputed and contested claims. Tex. Ins. Code Ann. art. 21.07-4, § 1(b)(5) & (6) (Vernon Supp. 1987). We conclude that Brown's reliance on this statute is misplaced for the following reasons. First, Brown has not been enjoined from performing clerical duties and there is no contention that purely clerical duties, such as recording a client's responses to questions on a form, is the unauthorized practice of law. Second, we disagree with Brown that the evidence shows that he only handled undisputed and uncontested claims. Brown apparently believes that if the issue of liability is uncontested, that the claim is undisputed and uncontested. A claim or cause of action for personal injury and/or property damage also involves the issue of damages, and as long as the damage issue is unresolved, the claim is a disputed and contested claim. There is ample proof in this record that Brown negotiated the amount of damages to be paid on behalf of parties other than himself. This activity required the use of legal skill and knowledge and, thus, constituted the practice of law. *Cortez*, 692 S.W.2d at 50. Consequently, we hold that Brown's course of conduct does not fall within the activities authorized under article 21.07-4, section 1(b)(5) and (6) of the Texas Insurance Code. Brown's first six points of error are overruled.

ACCESS TO JUSTICE

In 1992 the American Bar Association established the Commission on Nonlawyer Practice (Commission) and directed it to conduct research, hearings, and deliberations to determine the implications of nonlawyer practice for society, the client, and the legal profession. In 1995, the Commission released a report that identified three major conclusions from the data it had collected: (1) Increasing access to affordable assistance in law-related situations is an urgent goal; (2) Protecting the public from harm from persons providing assistance in law-related situations is also an urgent goal; and (3) When adequate protections for the public are in place, nonlawyers have important roles to perform in providing affordable access to justice.[66]

When reviewing current UPL positions by the various states, it is important to recognize this "access to justice" argument. It has been argued that UPL restrictions are the main barrier blocking the development of affordable legal service options for the public.[67]

DISCUSSION QUESTIONS:

1. Is increasing the use of nonlawyers the best way to expand access to justice?
2. When we speak of access to justice, which should be prioritized—quantity of access or quality of access?
3. Is the cost of a lawyer's services the primary factor undermining access to justice?

LIABILITY CONCERNS

Thus far this chapter has focused on defining, understanding and identifying the unauthorized practice of law. In addition to these concerns, you should also understand and appreciate the liability that individuals are exposed to, both supervising lawyers and paralegals, if they violate the ethical rules in connection with UPL. Although currently only lawyers are subject to professional discipline in the form of disbarment, suspension, and/or reprimand, both lawyers and paralegals are subject to the general legal system that may provide a variety of remedies for those who are injured by another's negligence.

Supervising Attorney Liability

Rule 5.5 of the ABA Model Rules, entitled "Unauthorized Practice of Law," states in part that "a lawyer shall not . . . assist a person who is not member of the bar in the performance of activity that constitutes the unauthorized practice of law." In addition, Rule 5.3, entitled "Responsibilities Regarding Nonlawyer Assistants," states that a lawyer is responsible for making reasonable efforts to ensure that the nonlawyer assistant's conduct is compatible with the professional obligations of the lawyer. Therefore, lawyers can be disciplined for allowing their nonlawyer staff to engage in the unauthorized practice of law. Many of the cases in this area involve situations where the lawyer has allowed the nonlawyer too much discretion and responsibility in handling a case.[68] Sometimes the lawyer will attempt to practice law from more than one location and will allow a nonlawyer staff member to "manage" one office while the lawyer is at the second office. In managing the office, the nonlawyer might enter into fee agreements, allow the client to be confused as to the status of the non-lawyer, and attempt to negotiate on behalf of the lawyer.[69]

Other scenarios that will result in liability for the nonsupervising attorney are those in which the lawyer enters into a business arrangement with the nonlawyer that involves the unauthorized practice of law by the nonlawyer.[70]

Lawyers are also held responsible for any malpractice committed by their non-lawyer staff. In *Musselman v. Willoughby Corp.*, 230 Va. 337, 337 S.E.2d 724 (1985), the paralegal, who the court notes was "untrained," played an instrumental role in a real estate closing and committed legal malpractice while performing his duties. The jury found against the attorney in the amount $243,722.99, which was the amount of the loss suffered by the client.

Paralegal Liability

Paralegals or other nonlawyers engaged in the unauthorized practice of law can find themselves not only enjoined from such practice, as discussed previously in this chapter, but also sued by the local district attorney for violations of any applicable statutes,[71] and by any client who was harmed by their actions. Like any other citizen, paralegals are personally liable for any harm that they do to others. This includes any negligent acts, as well as any intentional torts such as embezzlement. A more difficult question is whether paralegals can be guilty of legal malpractice. In the following excerpt, the author discusses the evolving standards of nonlawyer liability:

> A more difficult question is whether a paralegal may be sued individually and held personally liable for fraudulent or negligent conduct. In short, can a nonlawyer be guilty of malpractice? This is an interesting question, particularly since the traditional legal malpractice action requires as a first element, the existence of an attorney-client relationship, which goes to establish the standard of care. [72]
>
> Recently, an Illinois Appellate Court reviewed a complaint seeking a citation to recover assets that had been transferred to a lawyer's paralegal, because, the plaintiffs claimed, the paralegal breached her fiduciary duties to the lawyer's client, an elderly man who had lived alone for the last part of his life.[73] Apparently, the gist of the claim was that the paralegal had exerted undue influence on the client, who had come to depend on the paralegal for grocery shopping and other services.
>
> Paralegals are not fiduciaries, as a matter of law, to their employer-lawyer's clients, the appeals court held, explaining that "paralegals do not independently practice law, but simply serve as assistants to lawyers. They are not equal or autonomous partners."[74] The paralegal could not be sued for breach of fiduciary duty as if she were a lawyer.
>
> As the Illinois Appellate Court pointed out, there "is very little case law from Illinois or any jurisdiction generally discussing paralegals."[75] That which exists seems to conflict, as exemplified by the split of authority in decisions from Ohio and Nevada.
>
> In 1988, an Ohio appeals court concluded in a terse opinion without extensive analysis that a paralegal could not be liable in legal malpractice because she was not a lawyer. Furthermore, a malicious prosecution claim in another count of the complaint was dismissed because the paralegal did not prosecute the original action.[76]

By contrast, several years later, the Nevada Supreme Court determined in *Busch v. Flangas*[77] that a lawyer's law clerk could be sued in legal malpractice individually for failing to perfect a client's security interest in the sale of business assets. The client contacted the law clerk directly in the lawyer's office seeking completion of documents necessary to sell a bakery.

Although the law clerk "is not an attorney, he can be subject to a legal malpractice claim if he attempts to provide legal services,"[78] the majority concluded, relying on *Bowers v. Transamerica Title Insurance Company*,[79] decided by the Supreme Court of Washington in 1983 . . . . [In that case], the Supreme Court ruled that a lay escrow agent may be held to the same duties and standard of care as an attorney escrow agent. When a "layman attempts to practice law" he or she "is liable for negligence [citation omitted]. The duties of an attorney practicing law are also the duties of one who without a license attempts to practice law."[80]

It appears the Nevada Supreme Court decision in Busch, declaring the duties of law clerks, who like paralegals are supervised by lawyers, rests on the duties established for nonlawyers who are not under a lawyer's supervision, imposing the same standard of care as that imposed on lawyers. The Busch Court did not explain why it adopted this standard of care.

However, some insight might be gleaned from one well-regarded treatise on legal malpractice: [w]hen the paralegal undertakes tasks requiring legal skills and experience, the same standard which would apply to the attorney should determine liability. The earlier case law involving law clerks and nonlawyers performing legal services appear to justify this conclusion.[81]

At this point the most that can be said safely is that the law establishing the duties and legal accountability of paralegals is in the process of development.[82]

DISCUSSION QUESTIONS

1. In *Webb v. Pomeroy*, 8 Kan. App. 2d 246, 655 P.2d 193 (1983), the court held that an independent document preparer (nonlawyer) was amenable to suit for malpractice reasoning that the nonlawyer had the same fiduciary duties as that of a lawyer and should have known the proper procedures to secure the contractual rights of the persons he served. Can you make a distinction between a paralegal working under the supervision of an attorney and an independent legal technician or document preparer?

2. The author also discussed theories of liability resulting from fraud, misrepresentation, and unlawful trade practices, particularly where the nonlawyer made representations that his or her work was the same quality as an attorneys.[83] Again, can you distinguish between these situations and a properly supervised paralegal?

3. What do you think the standard of care should be for paralegals? Should paralegals be held to a higher standard of care than other nonlawyer staff?

CONCLUSION

This chapter not only presents the reader with various examples of activities that constitute the unauthorized practice of law, but also provides an in-depth appreciation for the subtleties and complexities of this issue. The question of what constitutes the unauthorized practice of law is continually being studied and reevaluated by legislatures and courts across the country, and only a careful study of relevant case law and statutory law will provide the necessary parameters.

ENDNOTES

1 See John S. Dzienkowski & Robert J. Peroni, *Multidisciplinary Practice and the American Legal Profession: A Market Appraoch to Regulating the Delivery of Legal Services in the Twenty-First Century,* 69 FORDHAM L. REV. 83 (2000); Michael W. Price, *A New Millennium's Resolution: The ABA Continues Its Regrettable Ban on Multidisciplinary Practice,* 37 HOUS. L. REV. 1495 (2000); Jacqueline M. Nolan-Haley, *Lawyers, Nonlawyers, and Mediation: Rethinking the Professional Monopoly from a Problem-Solving Perspective,* 7 HARV. NEGOT. L. REV. 235 (2002); Jonathan Rose, *Unauthorized Practice of Law in Arizona: A Legal and Political Problem That Won't Go Away,* 34 ARIZ. ST. L. J. 585 (2002).

2 AMER. BAR ASS'N, MODEL CODE OF PROFESSIONAL RESPONSIBILITY E.C. para. 3-5 (1969).

3 Robert Ostertag, *Nonlawyers Should Not Practice,* A.B.A. J., May 1996, at 116.

4 Deborah L. Rhode, *Policing the Professional Monopoly: A Constitutional and Empirical Analysis of Unauthorized Practice Prohibitions,* 34 STAN. L. REV. 1 (1981).

5 See Deborah L. Rhode, *Delivery of Legal Services by Non-Lawyers,* 4 GEO. J. LEGAL ETHICS 209 (1990); Deborah L. Rhode, *Policing the Professional Monopoly, supra*; Deborah L. Rhode, *Professionalism in Perspective: Alternative Approaches to Nonlawyer Practice,* 22 N.Y.U. REV. L. & SOC. CHANGE 701 (1996).

6 Derek A. Denckla, *Nonlawyers and the Unauthorized Practice of Law: An Overview of the Legal and Ethical Parameters,* 67 FORDHAM L. REV. 2581 (1999).

7 Ellen E. Deason, *Allerton House Conference '98: Confronting and Embracing Changes in the Practice of Law,* 86 ILL. B.J. 628, 630 (1998).

8 *Id.* at 52.

9 ABA, MODEL RULES OF PROFESSIONAL CONDUCT (2002 ed.)

10 *UPL Comm., State Bar of Texas v. Cortez,* 692 S.W.2d 47 (Tex. 1985); *cert. den'd* 474 U.S. 980 (U.S. Tex. 1985).

11 Sometimes the state court's possessiveness of this particular issue is resisted by the federal courts. For example, in *Texas UPL Comm., State Bar of Texas v. Paul Mason & Associates,* 46 F.3d 469 (5th Cir. Tex. 1995) the United States District Court held that federal bankruptcy laws that allowed nonlawyers to provide assistance to creditors preempted any state law disallowing such representation.

12 *In the Matter of Lexington County Transfer Court,* 512 S.E.2d 791, 793 (S.C. 1999) (quoting from *In re Unauthorized Practice of Law Rules Proposed by the South Carolina Bar,* 422 S.E.2 123, 124 (S.C. 1992).

13 Michael R. Heppenheimer, *Report of the Unauthorized Practice of Law Comm.,* RES GESTAE, September 1998, at 28.

14 Elizabeth S. Holmes, *What is the Unauthorized Practice of Law and How is it Regulated?* 76 MICH. B.J. 580 (1997).

15 *Connecticut Bank & Trust,* 145 Conn. at 234, 140 A.2d at 870 (quoting *Grievance Comm v. Payne,* 128 Conn. 325, 330, 22 A.2d 623, 626 (1941); see also *State Bar of Arizona v. Arizona Land Title & Trust.* 90 Ariz. 96 at 87, 366 P.2d 1 at 9 (Ariz.

1961) ([T]hose activities, whether performed in court or in the law office, which lawyers customarily have carried on from day to day through the centuries, must constitute "the practice of law").

16 *State Bar of Arizona v. Arizona Land Title & Trust, id.* at 91, 366 P.2d at 12 (nonlawyer prohibited from performing services commonly understood to be the practice of law even though incidental and no difficult question involved).

17 *State Bar v. Cramer,* 399 Mich. 116, 149, 249 N.W.2d 1, 14 (1976) (Levin, J., dissenting)("In the borderline areas between the professions, it is laymen—accountants, real estate brokers, insurance agents, trust officers—who make a judgment . . . of where the practice of one discipline ends and the practice of law begins and of whether to call in a lawyer."); *Auerbacher,* 139 N.J.Eq. at 603, 53 A.2d at 802 ("Bankers, liquor dealers and laymen generally possess rather precise knowledge of the laws touching their particular business or profession. A good example is the architect, who must be familiar with zoning, building and fire prevention codes . . . This is not practicing law."); see also MODEL RULES OF PROFESSIONAL CONDUCT Rule 5.5 comment (1980) ("claims adjusters, employees of financial or commercial institutions, social workers, accountants and persons employed by government agencies [are] nonlawyers whose employment requires knowledge of law").

18 See *Arizona Land Title & Trust,* Ariz. At 91, 366 P.2d at 11 ("The testimony of several witnesses indicates that these practices are not necessary concomitants to the title insurance business."); *Auerbacher,* 139 N.J.Eq. at 601, 53 A.2d at 801 ("[N]o one handling industrial relations, or acting as a consultant, can render effective service unless he is familiar with such statutes and regulations . . . [K]nowledge of the law, and . . . use of that knowledge as a factor in determining what measures [to] recommend, do not constitute the practice of law.").

19 *Agran,* 127 Cal. App. 2d Supp. at 817, 273 P.2d at 626; *Gardner,* 234 Minn. at 468, 48 N.W.2d at 788; *Guardian Abstract & Title,* 91 N.M. at 439, 575 P.2d at 948.

20 234 Minn. 468, 48 N.W.2d 788 (1951).

21 WISCONSIN STATE BAR STANDING COMM. ON PROFESSIONAL ETHICS, Formal Op. E-79-2 (1979), WIS. B. BULL., Jan. 1980, at 61; see also *Arizona*

Land Title & Trust, 90 Ariz. at 87, 366 P.2d at 9 (client reliance is key to attorney-client relationship).

22 Comment, *The Attorney as Mediator-Inherent Conflict of Interest?,* 32 UCLA L. REV. 986, 995, 1002 (1985).

23 MODEL CODE OF PROFESSIONAL RESPONSIBILITY EC 3-5 (1980); see also MARYLAND ETHICS OP. ("[I]t is possible for a mediator . . . to engage in the practice of law by applying general legal principles to the specific problems of his clients.").

24 *New York County Lawyer's Association v. Dacey,* 21 N.Y.2d 694, 287 N.Y.S.2d 422, 234 N.E.2d 459 (mem.) rev'g 28 A.D.2d 161, 283 N.Y.S.2d 984 (1967).

25 *Oregon State Bar v. Gilchrist,* 272 Or. 552, 538 P.2d 913 (1975).

26 *Florida Bar v. Stupica,* 300 So. 2d 683 (Fla. 1974)

27 Although the defendants were enjoined from selling divorce kits, the court distinguished the kits from a "mere collection" of forms. *Id.*

28 2 Cal. 3d 535, 469 P.2d 353, 86 Cal. Rptr. 673 (1970).

29 *Id.* at 542, 469 P.2d at 357, 86 Cal. Rptr. At 677 (quoting *People v. Merchants' Protective Corp.,* 189 Cal. 531, 535, 209 P. 363, 365 (1922) (quoting *Eley v. Miller,* 7 Ind. App. 529, 535, 34 N.E. 836, 837–38 (1893); see also *Agran v. Shapiro,* 127 Cal. App. 2d Supp. 807, 811, 273 P.2d 619, 622 (1954).

30 91 N.M. 434, 575 P.2d 943 (1978).

31 *Id.* at 439, 575 P.2d at 948 (quoting *State ex rel. Norvell v. Credit Bureau,* 85 N.M. 521, 526, 514 P.2d 40, 45 (1973)); see also *People v. Sipper,* 61 Cal. App. 2d Supp., 844, 846, 12 P.2d 960, 962 (1943); *People v. Ring,* 26 Cal. App. 2d Supp. 768, 771, 70 P.2d 281, 283 (1937). The Guardian court here applies the "incidental" and "difficult question of law" exceptions to the "acting legal rights" test. The court reasons that, although legal rights were affected by the filling in of blanks in real estate instruments, such action was not the practice of law since no difficult question of law was involved.

32 438 S.W.2d 374 (Tex. Civ. App. 1969).

33 *Id.* at 377 (quoting *Cape May County Bar Ass'n v. Ludlam,* 45 N.J. 121, 126, 211 A.2d 780, 782 (1965)); see also *Clark v. Rearden,* 231 Mo. App. 666, 104 S.W.2d 407 (1937). Similar language is found in *State Bar v. Arizona Land Title & Trust Co.,* 90 Ariz. 76, 88, 366 P.2d 1, 10 (1961)

("The title company employee, in 'filling in a form', obviously exercises his own discretion as to what forms should be used . . . this kind of quasi-legal counseling [has been] condemned."), modified on other grounds, 97 Ariz. 293, 371 P.2d 1020 (1962).

34 See VA. RULES OF COURT 6:1, 216 Va. 941, 1062 (1976) (defining the practice of law in terms of the relationship between attorney and client).

35 *New York County Lawyer's Ass'n v. Dacey,* 28 A.D.2d 161, 174, 283 N.Y.S.2d 984, 998, rev'd, 21 N.Y.2d 694, 287 N.Y.S.2d 422, 234 N.E.2d 459 (1967) (mem.)

36 *State Bar v. Cramer,* 399 Mich. 116, 137, 249 N.W.2d 1,9 (1976) (quoting Dacey, 28 A.D.2d at 171, 283 N.Y.S.2d at 998). Article by Andrew S. Morrison, *Is Divorce Mediation the Practice of Law? A Matter of Perspective,* 75 CALIF. L. REV. 1093 (1987).

37 See People ex rel. *Atty. Gen. v. Bennet,* 74 P.2d 671 (1937); *The Florida Bar v. American Legal and Business Forms, Inc.,* 274 So. 2d 225 (1973); *New York County Lawyer's Assoc. v. Dacey,* 234 N.E.2d 459 (1967); *Oregon State Bar v. Gilchrist,* 538 P.2d 913 (1975).

38 *Fadia v. UPL Comm.,* 830 S.W.2d 162 (Tex. Civ. App.—Dallas, 1992, *writ den'd); State Bar of Michigan v. Cramer,* 399 Mich. 116 (1976); also see *The Florida Bar v. Miravalle,* 2000 WL 633010 (Fla. 2000) a potentially relevant case in which the court found a "typing service" to be involved in the unauthorized practice of law where the "typing service" used forms not approved by the Florida State Bar, crafted custom documents based on information provided by individuals, engaged in legal research in order to prepare these documents, and drafted and typed these documents.

39 *Coffee County Abstract and Title Company v. State, Ex Rel Norwood,* 445 So. 2d 852 (Ala. 1983).

40 See generally, Patricia Jean Lamlin, *Sale of Books or Forms Designed to Enable Laymen to Achieve Legal Results Without the Assistance of Attorney as Unauthorized Practice of Law,* 71 A.L.R. 3d 1000 (1976), current through the June 1999 Supplement Annotation.

41 *Unauthorized Practice of Law Committee v. Parsons Technology,* 1999 WL 47235 (N.D. Tex. 1999).

42 See Texas Government Code 81.101(c), enacted by the Texas legislature in 1999.

43 The Texas UPL Committee had been investigating NOLO Press for a similar type of violation when this legislation was passed; as a result, the investigation was subsequently dropped.

44 Gary E. Sullivan, Jeffrey W. Wagnon, David G. Epstein *The Thin Red Line: An Analysis of the Role of Legal Assistants in the Chapter 13 Bankruptcy Process,* 23 J. LEGAL PROF. 15 (1998–1999).

45 *In re Anderson,* 79 B.R. 482, 484–86 (Bankr. S.D. Cal. 1987).

46 *In re McCarthy,* 149 B.R. 162, 165–67 (Bankr. S.D. Cal. 1992).

47 *In re Bachman,* 113 B.R. 769, 774 (Bankr. S.D. Fla. 1990).

48 *Id.*

49 *Id.* at 773.

50 *In re Herren,* 138 B.R. 989, 994–95 (Bankr. D. Wyo. 1992).

51 *In re Harris,* 152 B.R.440, 441, 445 (Ankr. W.D. Pa. 1993).

52 *Herren,* 138 B.R. at 995.

53 *In re Bachman,* 113 B.R. 769, 774 (Bankr. S.D. Fla. 1990).

54 *Crain v. UPL Comm.,* 11 S.W.3d 328 (Tex. App.—Houston [1st. Dist.], 2000).

55 *The Florida Bar v. Catarcio,* 709 So. 2d 96, 99–100 (Fla. 1998).

56 *Florida Bar v. Brumbaugh,* 355 So. 2d 1186 (Fla. 1978); the court noted that had Brumbaugh limited her activities to selling printed material purporting to explain legal practices in general, or selling sample legal forms, such activities would not have fallen under the aegis of practicing law. *Id.* at 1194. Additionally, had Brumbaugh typed forms for her clients, provided she copied only the information given to her in writing by her clients, this too would have been acceptable.

57 *Florida Bar re Advisory Opinion—Nonlawyer Preparation of Living Trusts,* 613 So. 2d 426, 428 (Fla. 1992); "Gathering the necessary information for the living trust does not constitute the practice of law, and nonlawyers may properly perform this activity."

58 Based on the facts of *In re Estate of Shumway,* 1999 WL 688265 (Ariz. App. Div. 1 1999) in which the court found that preparation of the will did not constitute the unauthorized practice of law; however, this case has been granted review by the Arizona Supreme court.

59 *Utah State Bar v. Summerhayes & Hayden,* 905 P.2d 867 (Utah 1995).

60 See *Fitchette v. Taylor,* 254 N.W. 910 (Minn. 1934); *Brown v. Unauthorized Practice of Law*

Committee, 742 S.W.2d 34 (Tex. App. 1987, no writ); and *Idaho State Bar v. Villegas,* 879 P.2d 1124 (Idaho 1994).

[61] *Fitchette, supra* note at 911.

[62] *Brown, supra* note at 140.

[63] *Villegas, supra* note at 1126. Also see *Cincinnati Bar Association v. Cromwell,* 695 N.E.2d 243, 244 (Ohio 1998) where a nonlawyer was providing representative services under the business name of "Paralegal Service Group."

[64] *Fravel v. Stark County Board of Revision,* 728 N.E.2d 393, 394 (Ohio 2000) ("Obtaining a power of attorney from a principal does not insulate a non-attorney from violating the unauthorized practice of law statutes when the non-attorney performs a legal act in representing the principal").

[65] *Sharon Village Ltd. v. Licking Cty. Bd. Of Revision,* 678 N.E.2d 932 (Ohio 1997).

[66] See generally Commission on Nonlawyer Practice, American Bar Ass'n, Nonlawyer Activity in Law-Related Situations (1995).

[67] Derek A. Denckla, supra at 2599; see also Charles W. Wolfram, Modern Legal Ethics 825 (practioner's ed. 1986).

[68] See *Attorney Grievance Commission of Maryland v. Hallmon,* 681 A.2d 510 (Md. 1996) (attorney was suspended from practice for ninety days because of failure to supervise nonlawyer and assisting nonlawyer in unauthorized practice of law). Also see *Mays v. Comm. on Prof. Conduct,* 938 S.W.2d 830 (Ark. 1997), where attorney was reprimanded for failure to establish and sustain attorney-client relationship and was held responsible for misdeeds of nonlawyer staff.

[69] *Louisiana State Bar Association v. Edwins,* 540 So. 2d 294 (La. 1989); *Florida Bar v. Lawless,* 640 So. 2d 1098 (S. Ct. Fla. 1994) (lawyer suspended for 90 days for failing to supervise paralegal's activities in immigration matters); *Glover Bottled Gas Corp. v. Beverage Barn, Inc.,* 129 A.D. 678, 514 N.Y.S.2d 440 (1987) (employing lawyer liable for improper supervision); *Moore v. State Bar,* 62 Cal. 2d 74, 41 Cal. Rptr. 151, 396 P.2d 577 (1964); *Lane v.*

Williams, 521 A.2d 706 (Me. 1987); *Chavez v. Nevell Mgmt. Co.,* 69 Misc. 2d 718, 330 N.Y.S.2d 890 (1972).

[70] See *In re Morin,* 319 Or. 547, 878 P.2d 393 (1994) (sale of living trust packages).

[71] See *People v. Landlords Professional Services,* 264 Cal. Rptr. 548 (1989), where a nonlawyer was not only enjoined from acts that constituted unauthorized practice of law, but was also fined $17,000 for violations of the state Business and Professions Code.

[72] RESTATEMENT, THIRD, THE LAW GOVERNING LAWYERS, Sec. 71, Elements and Defenses Generally (Tent. Draft No. 7, April 7, 1994).

[73] *Divine v. Giancola,* 263 Ill. App. 3d. 799, 635 N.E.2d 581 (Ill. App. 1st Dist. 1994).

[74] *Id.,* 635 N.E.2d at 588.

[75] *Id.,* 635 N.E.2d at 587.

[76] *Palmer v. Westmeyer,* 48 Ohio App. 3d 296, 549 N.E.2d 1201 (1988).

[77] 108 Nev. 821, 837 P.2d 438 (1992).

[78] *Id.,* 108 Nev. At 824, 837 P.2d at 440. The dissent countered that a law clerk, paralegal or other employee, as an employee of a lawyer, owed no duty to the client, and thus could not be liable, although the employee owed a duty to the lawyer.

[79] 100 Wash. 2d 581, 675 P.2d 193 (1983).

[80] *Id.,* 100 Wash. 2d at 587, 675 P.2d at 198. The law in Washington appears to be well established that "nonlawyers are held to the standard of care equivalent to that of a lawyer." *Hangman Ridge Training Stables, Inc. v. Safeco Title Ins. Co.,* 33 Wash. App. 129, 131, 652 P.2d 962, 964 (Div. 3 1982).

[81] MALLEN & SMITH, n.1, Sec 5.5, at 277.

[82] Cornelia Wallis Honchar, *Evolving Standards of Nonlawyer Liability,* PROF. LAW, May 1995, at 14, 15.

[83] See *Ford v. Guarantee Abstract & Title Co.,* 553 P.2d 254 (S. Ct. Kan. 1976); *Webb v. Pomeroy,* 8 Kan. App. 2d 246, 655 P.2d 193 (1983); and *Banks v. Dist of Columbia Dept. of Consumer & Regulatory Affairs,* 634 A.2d 433 (D.C. App. 1993).

THE UNAUTHORIZED PRACTICE OF LAW—REFORMS AND EXCEPTIONS

INTRODUCTION

Increasingly, various states are revising traditional notions of what constitutes the unauthorized practice of law. Evidence of revision consists of amended and less restrictive definitions, delegations of authority to nonlawyers in limited law-related services, and a willingness to allow nonlawyer representation in front of some state agencies. This chapter will explore recent revisions and the forces that are responsible for these changes.

EXAMPLES OF UNAUTHORIZED PRACTICE OF LAW REFORM

In the following excerpt, the author discusses attempts by various states to reform their unauthorized practice of law rules.

A. Washington's Limited Practice Rule

In 1983, the Supreme Court of Washington adopted a "limited practice rule" allowing certain lay persons to engage in the practice of law in some real estate transactions.[1] The rule created a supreme court-appointed Limited Practice Board[2] and vested it with the power to certify "limited practice officers."[3] The officers are required to pass an examination[4] and certification is subject to continuing educational requirements.[5] Additionally, the officers must demonstrate the financial ability to cover damages that may result from their negligent acts.[6]

Washington's Limited Practice Rule also requires that officers make appropriate disclosures to their clients[7] and use only pre-approved legal forms. Moreover, when practicing under this rule, the officers are held to the same standard of care as an attorney.[8] The Washington approach apparently is succeeding. The Board has issued over 1200 licenses since 1984, and only twelve complaints had been filed against the limited practice officers through 1989.[9]

B. Florida's "Unlicensed" Practice of Law Rules

Another method used to regulate the unauthorized practice of law is the adoption of rules by bar associations. Bar association rules are not enacted by the legislature, and therefore, like court rules, they do not encounter separation of powers problems. The Florida Bar Association recently amended its rules to reform Florida's regulation of the unauthorized practice of law.

. . . On January 1, 1987, the new "unlicensed" practice of law rules went into effect and extensively altered the regulation of the unauthorized practice of law in Florida.[10] The new rules provide that the Florida Bar refer all unlicensed practice of law complaints to the state attorney for prosecution.[11] Consequently, the legal profession distances itself from such prosecutions[12] and weakens the perception that the enforcement of the unlicensed practice prohibition is a protectionist measure.[13] Further, the rules allow for more nonlawyer participation in the investigation and enforcement of the laws that regulate the unlicensed practice of law.[14] They establish a system whereby the public can obtain advisory opinions from a state bar committee concerning issues related to the unlicensed practice of law.[15] The rules also were amended to allow nonlawyers to engage in "limited oral communications" to help individuals complete certain pre-approved legal documents.[16]

C. California's "Legal Technician" Proposal.

For almost five years the California State Bar worked to devise, draft, and implement reform of its regulation of the unauthorized practice of law.[17] California's approach is unique because it provides reform through a joint effort of all three branches of government: the executive, the legislative, and the judicial.[18] In 1986, the California State Bar created the Public Protection Committee to research and design a system that would effectively regulate the unauthorized practice of law.[19] The Committee concluded that there was an unmet need for legal services that could be met by nonlawyers ("legal technicians").[20] The Committee recommended that the state bar support reform allowing legal technicians to practice law,[21] but specifically advised that the bar itself refrain from any role in enforcing such regulation.[22] The bar adopted the findings of the Committee and created the Commission of Legal Technicians to draft rules and provide guidelines for legal technicians to insure the protection of the public.[23] The Commission recommended that the state bar propose a supreme court rule that would allow nonlawyers to perform legal services in specified areas.[24] The Commission also suggested that the bar sponsor legislation to create an independent paralegal regulatory system under the supervision of the Department of Consumer Affairs.[25]

The recommendations were designed to create a comprehensive and coordinated reform, involving all three branches of government.[26] First the judicial branch, through the California Supreme Court, authorizes nonlawyer participation in the legal profession and delegates regulation of such participation to the Department of Consumer Affairs.[27] Second, the legislature passes the enabling statutes.[28] Finally, the executive branch, through the Department of Consumer Affairs, implements the program.[29] The Commission assigned responsibility to all three branches of government in an effort to avoid any separation of powers problems.[30]

. . . Although ultimately rejected,[31] California's proposal involving all three branches of government provides a detailed model that is potentially useful to other states considering unauthorized practice of law reform.

The experiences in Washington, Florida, and California provide insight into the complexities involved in regulating the unauthorized practice of law.[32] Any attempt at reform must recognize the need to protect the public, while at the same time consider public needs for affordable legal services, public opinion, and constitutional constraints.[33]

DISCUSSION QUESTIONS

1. The proposals vary in their approaches and scope. Identify the proposals, or parts of proposals, which you think are best. Why do you think so?

2. Can you think of a better way to deal with this issue?

3. In 1999, the State Bar of Texas formed a task force to evaluate the regulation of the unauthorized practice of law in the state of Texas. In the June 2000 issue of the *Texas Bar Journal*, the task force issued a preliminary report recommending that current statutory law be amended to more "carefully and realistically" regulate this subject, as follows:

   > In some instances, however, licensure requirements may need to be more relaxed— where the legal service being provided can be readily determined to be of a simple nature and/or where others have skills, training, and ethical standards which provide some assurance of protection to the public. The task force's goal has been to identify those areas where the public can be adequately served by persons other than lawyers licensed by the State of Texas and to allow for such in the proposed statutory revision.[34]

   a. Do you think that this type of "reevaluation" of UPL statutes will become more widespread?

   b. What might state bars gain by relaxing licensing requirements?

   c. What might they lose?

FUNCTIONS AUTHORIZED BY STATUTE, COURT RULINGS, AND/OR ADMINISTRATIVE RULINGS

In some instances federal and state agencies, court rules, and various statutory laws specifically authorize nonlawyers to perform or provide legally related services. The following discussion examines these authorities by citing specific examples and presents arguments both supporting and opposing this type of expansion in the provision of legal services.

Statutes

Sometimes federal or state legislatures give express permission to nonlawyers to perform certain functions that may otherwise constitute the practice of law. Areas of law in which this is commonly done include family law,[35] real estate,[36] immigration,[37] and matters that can be resolved in small claims court.[38] As previously discussed, this permission may be given in the context of performing "incidental legal services" in connection with another profession, or permission may be given because the legislature has determined that doing so would be in the best interest of the public.

Court Rulings

Under some local court rules, paralegals are allowed to make in-court appearances in uncontested matters. This is consistent with the findings recently made by the ABA's Commission on Nonlawyer Practice, which recommended that the range of activities of traditional paralegals should be expanded, with lawyers remaining responsible for their activities. In its report the Commission stated the following:

> The Commission found that lawyers use the services of paralegals in innovative ways to save time and reduce costs to clients. Several lawyers recommended to the Commission, for example, that court rules be changed to permit paralegals to appear in court for their law firm employers on routine matters such as calendar calls or previously agreed-to matters such as child support calculations and small estate probate hearings.[39]

Self-Help Centers.   Some states have begun to consider self-help centers as ways to assist self-represented persons access the legal system and legal services. For example, the following excerpt describes a program recently initiated in Florida, designed to assist *pro se* litigants and to be implemented through local court rules:

> In *In re Family Court Steering Committee* (Fla. Aug. 22, 1996) (Administrative Order), then Chief Justice Kogan directed the Family Court Steering Committee to recommend, among other things, "ways courts can assist self-represented litigants access the family courts through the use of standardized simplified forms, self-help centers, technological innovations, and other mechanisms, as appropriate." Pursuant to that directive, the steering committee has petitioned this Court to adopt proposed Florida Family Law Rule 12.750, entitled "Family Self-Help Programs."
>
> According to the steering committee's petition, approximately sixty-five percent of initial filings in family law cases are filed by self-represented litigants and approximately eighty percent of modification and enforcement cases involve at least one unrepresented litigant. The steering committee asserts that the rule is needed to encourage self-represented litigants to obtain legal advice; to provide information concerning pro bono legal services, low cost legal services, and lawyer referral services; to provide forms, general information about the judicial process, and other information necessary to assist those who represent themselves; to clearly define the services provided to ensure that self-help programs do not provide legal advice through nonlawyers; to facilitate but not encourage self-representation; to assist in obtaining legislative funding for the programs; and to establish uniformity throughout the state to provide certain basic services in all circuits. Specifically, the proposed rule (1) directs that self-help programs be established by local rule; (2) sets forth definitions; (3) sets forth the services that can be performed and the limitations on those services; (4) sets forth activities that are not to be considered the practice of law; (5) provides that the information provided is not confidential or privileged; (6) provides that there is no conflict of interest in providing services to both parties; (7) provides for a disclaimer to be

provided to persons receiving services; (8) provides that self-help personnel need not identify themselves on the form unless the personnel actually record information on the form; (9) provides that self-help programs are to be made available to all unrepresented litigants unless otherwise provided by statute; (10) provides that self-represented litigants may be required to pay for the costs of services if so directed by statute; (11) provides that all records of a self-help program are public records; and (12) creates an exclusion for domestic violence cases to allow for assistance in domestic violence matters as directed by Florida Family Law Rule 12.610.

The proposed rule was published in The Florida Bar News and a number of comments were received . . . . According to the comments, the pilot programs may resolve some concerns regarding the unlicensed practice of law . . . . As noted by the steering committee, the proposed rule was submitted pursuant to the Chief Justice's request to address a major access-to-the-courts problem. Additionally, nineteen of the twenty circuits are currently operating some type of self-help program without any guidelines for operation. Accordingly, we adopt the proposed rule . . . . However, we will consider modifications to the rule as necessary should the information obtained from the pilot programs so mandate.

In drafting the proposed rule, the steering committee has attempted to reach a balance between the need to provide services to self-represented litigants and the need to limit nonlawyer self-help program personnel from providing legal advice or otherwise engaging in the unauthorized practice of law. The steering committee acknowledges that defining the practice of law is difficult. In drafting the proposed rule, the steering committee relied upon court precedent in determining what activities constitute the practice of law and attempted to draft the rule accordingly. However, the steering committee acknowledges that the provisions in the rule may exceed restrictions placed on the forms and on information nonlawyers may provide to self-represented litigants. For instance, currently, under Rule Regulating the Florida Bar 10-2.1, which governs in part the unauthorized practice of law, only Florida Supreme Court Approved forms may be provided by nonlawyers to self-represented litigants. Under the proposed rule, self-help program personnel not only may provide approved forms, they also may provide forms approved by the chief judge of a circuit that are not included in and are not inconsistent with the approved forms . . . . [O]ur experience with the mandatory forms in domestic violence cases indicates that local provisions regarding family law cases vary greatly from circuit to circuit. Accordingly, we find that local circuits should be able to use forms that are approved by the chief judge of the circuit and that are in substantial compliance with and not inconsistent with the Supreme Court approved forms. We need not amend rule 10-2.1 to be consistent with our holding here because the proposed rule specifically directs that the services listed in the rule, when performed by nonlawyer personnel in a self-help program, will not constitute the unauthorized practice of law.

The comments also ask that self-help personnel be allowed to provide litigants with forms appropriate to a litigant's needs and to provide information about those forms. They note that, unlike situations involving the unlicensed practice of law, self-help program personnel will be trained and supervised by attorneys; they also will be working with court-approved forms and operating in the context of nonprofit, court-approved programs. We find that self-help personnel should be able to provide information about the forms and to recommend specific forms so long as they do not provide advice or recommendations as to any specific course of action to be taken. In *Florida Bar v. Brumbaugh*, 355 So. 2d 1186 (Fla. 1978), we did hold that nonlawyers were prohibited from assisting litigants in preparing forms, from asking questions as to the particular forms, and from advising them how to fill out such forms and where to file them. However, as noted by the comments, unlike the situation at issue in *Brumbaugh* where the unauthorized practice of law was at issue, the self-help programs are nonprofit, court-sanctioned programs that will be operated under the supervision of attorneys. Notably, under the rule as proposed, no lawyer-client relationship will form between the litigant and the self-help center, and any information provided by the litigant is not confidential or privileged; a disclosure ("notice requirement") of these conditions is required under the rule. We have modified the rule accordingly.

Next, we are asked to allow self-help program personnel to direct litigants to appropriate statutes and rules and to provide them with definitions of terms. Under the rule as proposed, personnel may "provide, either orally or in writing, citations of statutes and rules, without advising whether or not a particular statute or rule is applicable to the self represented litigant's situation" . . . . the steering committee stresses that personnel should not be able to advise a litigant as to which rule or statute applies because that would constitute the practice of law. Additionally, the steering committee notes that confidential information should never be imparted to program personnel. We adopt the steering committee's proposal and have amended the rule accordingly.

In *re Amendments to the Florida Family Law Rules of Procedure (self help)* 725 So. 2d 365 (Fla. 1998).

DISCUSSION QUESTIONS

1. Do you know if any self-help legal programs are available in your state? If so, how are they administered?

2. The court notes that in drafting the rule, the steering committee tried to strike a balance between providing services and the "need to limit nonlawyer self-help program personnel from providing legal advice or otherwise engaging in the unauthorized practice of law." What safeguards are included in the rule that help alleviate fears in this area?

3. How does the court distinguish the facts in *Florida Bar v. Brumbaugh*, 355 So. 2d 1186 (Fla. 1978) from this self-help program?

4. Why is it important that no "lawyer-client" relationship will form between the litigant and the self-help center and that no confidential information will be imparted to the self-help center's personnel?

Administrative Rulings

Many federal and state administrative agencies allow nonlawyers to represent parties in agency proceedings and provide advice and assistance with agency forms. At the federal level the scope of this type of representation is determined by each individual agency; however, at the state level, state courts often ultimately decide the scope of the nonlawyer's role. This discussion will explore this difference and provide specific examples of nonlawyer assistance and representation in both federal and state administrative agencies.

Federal Agencies   The Administrative Procedure Act allows federal agencies to determine whether or not nonlawyers will be allowed to represent others in front of them, and the Agency Practice Act of 1965 allows federal agencies to establish their own qualifications for such representation. Examples of federal agencies that allow nonlawyer representation include: Board of Immigration, Internal Revenue Service, U.S. Patent Office, Social Security, and the Worker's Compensation Appeals Board.[40] Although, representation by nonlawyers is allowed, there is still some debate among the individual federal agencies. Consider the following excerpt.[41]

> Those who oppose the appearance of nonlawyers before federal agencies generally focus on the need for a lawyer's professional judgment. This view emphasizes the fundamental need for legal knowledge in order to preserve a client's interests.[42] Although nonlawyers may possess superior expertise in a specific area, the various legal remedies that are available to a claimant and the ability to obtain those remedies are not known until the case has been investigated thoroughly.[43] This argument concludes that although the specialized abilities of a nonlawyer remain essential, legal training is required to coordinate and utilize the nonlawyer's talents effectively . . . .[44]
>
> Proponents of nonlawyer representation focus on the need to balance the interests of protecting the public from inadequate representation with the need for efficient resolution of extra-judicial disputes. At least four rationales are suggested for permitting nonlawyer representation: (1) nonlawyers possess specialized competence in particular fields; (2) the issues presented before federal agency proceedings involve simple and less dominant legal issues; (3) a sufficient number of lawyers are not available to perform the services; and (4) in choosing its representation, the public has a freedom of choice . . . .[45]

DISCUSSION QUESTIONS

1. Some commentators believe that lawyers take a paternalistic approach by dismissing the public's ability to adequately assess the competence of its representatives and by dismissing the public's right of free choice in choosing representation. What do you think of this argument? Is the public in the best position to make this determination? Does this depend on the sophistication level of the "public" in question?

2. Proponents of nonlawyer representation also contend that the predominant questions during administrative proceedings usually involve economic, scientific, financial, or technical expertise, and the legal issues that arise rarely involve a client's substantive rights. Do you agree? Can you think of any circumstances in which a client's substantive rights could be jeopardized?

3. What about client confidentiality? Disputed issues may ultimately be decided by a court of law; opponents are concerned that prior communications between a nonlawyer and a client could be subject to discovery. Is this a valid concern?

4. Review the following excerpt from *Florida Bar re Advisory Opinion on Nonlawyer Representation in Securities Arbitration*, 696 So. 2d 1178, 1181 (Fla. 1997) in which the Supreme Court of Florida considers the issue of whether nonlawyers, for compensation, may represent investors in securities arbitration against a broker:

> The proposed opinion asserts that this Court may—and should—enjoin the activities of nonlawyer securities arbitration representatives because no federal or state rules or regulations specifically authorize these nonlawyer representatives to engage in such activities. The proposed opinion explains that securities arbitration is conducted before self-regulatory organizations (SROs), which are private bodies and not federal offices or agencies. The rules governing the SROs at issue here, namely the National Association of Securities Dealers (NASD), the New York Stock Exchange (N.Y.S.E.), and the American Stock Exchange (AMEX), are approved by the Securities and Exchange Commission (SEC). The Committee acknowledges, however, that the rules governing the SROs do not expressly prohibit nonlawyer representation, and that the Arbitrator's Manual published jointly by the SROs and the Securities Industry Association indicates that parties in securities arbitration "may choose to appear pro se (on their own) or be represented by a person who is not an attorney, such as a business associate, friend, or relative." Nevertheless, the Committee maintains first that neither the rules provision, nor the Manual, constitutes federal legislation preempting this Court's regulatory authority, and, second, that these very general, permissive guidelines do not condone the nonlawyer representation for compensation at issue here. Rather, the Committee maintains in its proposed opinion that these provisions merely recognize, in an informal manner, the right of an investor to appear pro se, either by representing himself or with the uncompensated help of a business associate, relative or friend. That practice would not be affected by the opinion. However, the proposed opinion concludes that the representation of an investor in securities arbitration by a nonlawyer for compensation is both unlicensed and unauthorized, and subject to regulation by this Court. Lastly, the proposed opinion points to several ways in which the public is harmed by the activities of nonlawyer representatives in securities arbitration. Most importantly, the Committee notes that because the stock brokerage industry arbitration forums have no qualification procedures, and nonlawyer representatives—unlike attorneys—are not supervised or subject to discipline by a state bar or any other regulatory body, instances of misleading advertising, ineffective representation and the unethical conduct of nonlawyer representatives are prevalent but unsanctionable. Specifically, nonlawyers who have been disciplined or suspended by the securities industry or from the practice of law can represent investors in arbitration forums and are not required to meet any ethical standards in their practice. Settlement negotiations and the handling of client's money on deposit goes unregulated. Testimony before the Committee indicated that nonlawyer representatives are sometimes improperly motivated to settle claims rather than arbitrate because they are unable to go to court to confirm or collect an arbitration award on behalf of their client or defend against a broker's attempt to have the award vacated. Moreover, where claims are not

settled and litigation does occur, the investor represented by a nonlawyer is sorely disadvantaged because, at least in the securities setting, the defendant broker or firm is always represented by well-resourced attorneys. And, to make matters worse, investors have no recourse against their compensated representatives for the ineffective representation. After hearing oral argument, reviewing the proposed advisory opinion, and considering the comments of the interested parties, we are persuaded of the need for some regulation of these compensated representatives and approve the UPL Standing Committee's proposed opinion. We conclude that compensated nonlawyer representatives in securities arbitration are engaged in the unauthorized practice of law and pose a sufficient threat of harm to the public to justify our protection. In *State ex rel. Florida Bar v. Sperry*, 140 So. 2d 587 (Fla. 1962), this Court set out the framework for determining whether specific activities constitute the practice of law, which bears repeating here. We explained: [I]t is not the nature of the agency or body before which the acts are done, or even whether they are done before a tribunal of any sort or in the private office of an individual, that determines whether that which is done constitutes the practice of law. The best test, it seems to us, is what is done, not where, for the safest measure is the character of the acts themselves. If they constitute the practice of law the fact that they are done in the private office of the one who performs them or before a nonjudicial body in no way changes their character . . . .

It is generally understood that the performance of services in representing another before the courts is the practice of law. But the practice of law also includes the giving of legal advice and counsel to others as to their rights and obligations under the law and the preparation of legal instruments, including contracts, by which legal rights are either obtained, secured or given away, although such matters may not then or ever be the subject of proceedings in a court. We think that in determining whether the giving of advice and counsel and the performance of services in legal matters for compensation constitute the practice of law it is safe to follow the rule that if the giving of such advice and performance of such services affect important rights of a person under the law, and if the reasonable protection of the rights and property of those advised and served requires that the persons giving such advice possess legal skill and a knowledge of the law greater than that possessed by the average citizen, then the giving of such advice and the performance of such services by one for another as a course of conduct constitute the practice of law.

Although we recognize that arbitration was set up to be a nonjudicial alternative for dispute resolution, it is clear that, in light of our caselaw thoroughly discussing the activities that constitute the practice of law, the services provided by nonlawyer representatives in the alternative but still adversarial context of securities arbitration constitutes the practice of law. As the Committee pointedly and accurately notes in its proposed opinion, nonlawyer representatives give specific legal advice and perform the traditional tasks of the lawyer at every stage of the arbitration proceeding in an effort to protect the investor's important legal and financial interests. We cannot ignore such a situation. Because such activities—when performed by nonlawyers—are wholly unregulated and unsanctionable, we further agree with the proposed opinion that these activities must be enjoined. In these circumstances, the public faces a potential for harm from incompetent and unethical representation by compensated nonlawyers which cannot otherwise be remedied. See *Florida Bar v. Moses*, 380 So. 2d 412, 417 (Fla. 1980) (stating that the "single most important concern in th[is] Court's defining and regulating the practice of law is the protection of the public from incompetent, unethical, or irresponsible representation").

Finally, we also must reject the position of the interested parties that this Court has been preempted from regulating the unlicensed practice of law in this instance. Specifically, the interested parties maintain that we are precluded from regulating the activities at issue here because the general rules governing the SROs do not prohibit nonlawyer representation, and the Arbitrator's Manual, which serves as a handbook for the arbitration process, expressly authorizes lay representation. In *Moses*, we found that a lay representative appearing before the Public Employees Relations Commission (PERC) was engaged in the unlicensed practice of law, and that, in the absence of authorizing legislation, it was within our purview to regulate it. We explained: This Court has no control over the agencies of this state, and any attempt to exercise it would violate article II, section 3 of the constitution which states:

> No person belonging to one branch shall exercise any powers appertaining to either of the other branches unless expressly provided herein.

In the absence of legislative authorization for lay representation, there would be no question that conduct which constitutes the practice of law, wherever performed, is subject to our constitutional responsibility to protect the public from the unauthorized practice of law. We have so held in finding that, absent legislative governing authority, the preparation and filing of a corporate charter constitutes the unauthorized practice of law. *The Florida Bar v. Town*, 174 So. 2d 395 (Fla. 1965), followed in *The Florida Bar v. Keehley*, 190 So. 2d 173 (Fla. 1966); *The Florida Bar v. Fuentes*, 190 So. 2d 748 (Fla. 1966); and *The Florida Bar v. Scussel*, 240 So. 2d 153 (Fla. 1970). See also *In re The Florida Bar*, 355 So. 2d 766 (Fla. 1978). But the legislature has constitutional authorization to oust the Court's responsibility to protect the public in administrative proceedings under article V, section 1 of the Florida Constitution, and when it does so any "practice of law" conduct becomes, in effect, authorized representation. 380 So. 2d at 417. In that case, however, we found that "PERC is unquestionably subject to the APA [the Administrative Procedure Act], and the APA has unquestionably authorized representation before PERC by nonlawyers. Sections 120.52(1)(b), 120.62(2), Florida Statutes (1975)." *Id.* at 417–18. That is not the case here. We agree with the proposed opinion that neither the SRO rules nor the language in the Arbitrator's Manual constitutes federal or state legislative displacement of our authority to protect the public from harm by regulating the unauthorized practice of law. We do acknowledge that the Securities and Exchange Commission, the federal agency responsible for oversight of securities arbitration, easily could—and may very well choose—to preempt us in enjoining nonlawyer representation by authorizing or regulating the activities of these professionals. Nevertheless, we think that compensated nonlawyer representatives in securities arbitration are engaged in the unauthorized practice of law and the protection of the public requires us to step in where there is no such legislation or regulation. Accordingly, we enjoin nonlawyers from representing investors in securities arbitration proceedings for compensation from the date this opinion becomes final and we approve the Committee's proposed opinion. It is so ordered.

a. This opinion makes a distinction between representation by a business associate, friend, or relative at no charge to the investor, and nonlawyer representation for compensation. Why does it matter whether or not the nonlawyer was paid for his or her services?

   b. This opinion also distinguishes this situation from one in which federal legislation has preempted the Court's regulatory authority. Do you agree with the
court's reasoning?

   c. In the court's own words, arbitration was set up to be a nonjudicial alternative
for dispute resolution; however, the court believes that the services of lawyers
are still necessary. List the justifications argued by the court. Do you agree?

State Agencies   Although courts will usually recognize preemption of their authority
by federal agencies, this acquiescence has not been uniformly adopted with regard to
state agencies. A determination must first be made as to whether or not nonlawyer
representation constitutes the unauthorized practice of law.

> The divergent theories among the states regarding legislative regulation of the practice
> of law can be characterized as a continuum. A restrictive view allows legislative enact-
> ments only if the reviewing court finds the legislative intent "congenial" with existing
> judicial regulatory policies. A more compatible view allows the legislature to provide "a
> guiding influence" to move the courts in directions they would not otherwise take. The
> most expansive view explicitly recognizes a legislative role to regulate concurrently the
> practice of law . . . .[46]

Even though the prevailing state view allows the judiciary to regulate the unauthorized practice of law, the following three trends have emerged:

1. If there is express legislative authority or the agency allows it, courts will generally allow nonlawyer representation, citing public policy reasons.[47]

2. Usually it is an agency-by-agency determination.

3. An Attorney General's Opinion often formulates the acceptable standards.[48]

State courts also make determinations by considering the formality of the proceedings, whether the issue involved will demand legal skills to resolve, whether the
proceedings are governed by the rules of evidence, and whether the nonlawyer will
receive a fee for his or her services. In *Hunt v. Maricopa County Employees Merit System
Commission*,[49] the Arizona Supreme Court developed a test to allow nonlawyer representation if (1) the nonlawyer representative provides his services without a fee and
(2) the amount in controversy does not exceed one thousand dollars.

As with federal agencies, opponents cite similar arguments against nonlawyer representation.

> Judicial appeal universally is allowed for a party who has exhausted all administrative
> remedies. These appeals, however, often are limited to questions of law and additional
> evidence may not be introduced on appeal. Thus, preparation of an adequate record
> is vital to the protection of a client's interests. Under the "professional judgment"
> model, the nonlawyer does not possess the training, skill, or even the motivation to
> develop an adequate record for appeal.

In the following excerpt, the author comments on Tennessee House Bill 1482,
which allows the State Board of Equalization ("Board") the power to certify persons to

appear as official representatives and serve as counsel for clients in a quasi-judicial setting. The author also identifies and discusses the need for standards to address the proper scope of nonlawyer representation before state agencies:

> The conflicting views among the states exemplify the difficulty of developing a standard that adequately addresses both the procedural and substantive protections the public deserves . . . . The amorphous language used by the judiciary allows the courts to selectively apply existing laws. The resulting confusion prevents the development of consistent standards concerning the proper role for nonlawyers appearing as representatives before state administrative agencies.
>
> The lack of guidance within a particular state may be the result of a power struggle between the legislative and judicial branches. In contrast to the decentralized federal regulatory structure, state supreme courts maintain ultimate regulatory control over the practice of law. The overlap of legislative and judicial functions that inevitably occurs in a quasi-judicial legislative proceeding presents an additional question not present at the federal level: Which is the proper body to control practice before state administrative proceedings? Whether a result of comity considerations or a failure to recognize the potential hazards to the public, neither the judiciary nor the legislature authoritatively has defined these standards.
>
> The failure to address adequately the proper scope of nonlawyer representation before state agency proceedings could undermine the public's right to adequate representation. A subtle recognition of this potentially serious problem seems to be emerging. The long history of permitting lay representation without express statutory authorization demonstrates that both branches, at least implicitly, recognize a legitimate role for the nonlawyer during state administrative proceedings. A definite trend toward a balancing approach among the states that have considered the issue exists. The balancing analysis recognizes that individual agencies are sufficiently unique to warrant separate consideration and allows competing policy objectives to be considered on a case by case basis . . . .
>
> House Bill 1482[50] contains safeguards designed to address the potential conflicts that may arise. First, requiring disclaimers by nonlawyers prevents misrepresentation and allows the public to make an informed choice.[51] Second, allowing de novo review for judicial appeals from the Board protects a client's substantive legal rights.[52] Finally, although the magnitude of interests are often significant in controversies before the Board,[53] the sophistication and overall competence of the majority of clients required to appear before the Board should prevent the selection of incompetent counsel . . . .[54]

DISCUSSION QUESTIONS

1. Which branch should determine whether nonlawyer representation should be allowed before state agencies: the judiciary, the legislature, or the agency itself?

2. House Bill 1482 contains "safeguards." Do you think these are sufficient to address the concerns of opponents to nonlawyer representation before state agencies?

3. Consider the following excerpt from *Turner v. Kentucky Bar Association:*

We have been called upon to decide whether non-lawyer "workers' compensation specialists" in the Kentucky Department of Workers' Claims may assist ill or injured workers in processing their claims and, if so, what type and degree of assistance the specialists may offer. To resolve this issue, we must first determine whether KRS 342.320(9) is a legislative trespass upon judicial authority, in violation of the separation of powers provisions of the Constitution of Kentucky . . . . We must then determine whether specific tasks performed by workers' compensation specialists, as outlined in KRS 342.329(1)(a)–(e), are permissible paralegal duties or whether the performance of these tasks by non-attorneys constitutes the unauthorized practice of law. See KRS 524.130 (which prohibits the unauthorized practice of law).

I. BACKGROUND

This case arose from the extensive reform of Kentucky's workers' compensation system, which included undertakings to make the claims resolution process less dependent on litigation and rely more on informal administrative proceedings. In 1994, the General Assembly enacted KRS 342.329, which established an ombudsman program within the Kentucky Department of Workers' Claims (hereinafter Department). In December 1996, in an extraordinary session, the General Assembly amended KRS 342.329. The amendment expanded the services offered by the Department of Workers' Claims information personnel and established a new job classification, workers' compensation specialist. As amended, the statute provides:

(1) The commissioner shall establish a Division of Ombudsman and Workers' Compensation Specialist Services. The functions of the division shall include:

(a) Serving as an information source for employees, employers, medical, vocational, and rehabilitation personnel, carriers, and self-insurers;

(b) Responding to inquiries and complaints relative to the workers' compensation program;

(c) Advising all parties of their rights and obligations under this chapter;

(d) Assisting workers in obtaining medical reports, job descriptions, and other materials pertinent to a claim for benefits and preparing all documents necessary for a claim application; and,

(e) Performing other duties as required by the commissioner through administrative regulations promulgated by the commissioner.

KRS 342.329(1)(a)–(e).

The only new job duties added by the 1996 amendment are those appearing in subsection (d). In addition to the foregoing, in 1996, the General Assembly passed another statute which stated that "Notwithstanding any provisions of law to the contrary, the provisions of this chapter shall not be construed or interpreted to prohibit nonattorney representation of injured workers covered by this chapter." KRS. 342.320(9).

As a result of the 1996 legislation, the Kentucky Bar Association (hereinafter KBA) received inquiries whether the 1996 amendments authorize unqualified persons to engage in the practice of law. The KBA Board of Governors referred the matter to its Unauthorized Practice of Law Committee of the KBA. Following the Committee's report, the KBA Board of Governors adopted KBA U-52 as a formal advisory opinion. See SCR 3.530(2). This opinion addressed KRS 342.320(9) and KRS 342.329(1)(c)–(d), and held that 1) non-lawyers may not represent parties before the Department, and 2) non-lawyers may not serve as workers' compensation specialists for the Department.

KBA U-52 concluded that the duties assigned the non-attorney workers' compensation specialists would be duties normally performed by an attorney and would therefore constitute the unauthorized practice of law. Following the release of this advisory opinion in the Summer 1997 issue of Bench and Bar, the official publication of the KBA, the Commissioner of the Department and ten individuals employed as workers' compensation specialists requested that this Court review KBA U-52 pursuant to SCR 3.530(5). Prior to review of KBA U-52, we must examine KRS 342.320(9) for constitutional defects and also determine whether the specialists' job duties are consistent with those duties authorized to be performed by paralegals.

II. CONSTITUTIONALITY OF KRS 342.320(9)

[1] The first issue to be addressed is whether KRS 342.320(9) violates the constitutional principle of separation of powers. This statutory provision states:

Notwithstanding any provisions of the law to the contrary, the provisions of this chapter shall not be construed to prohibit nonattorney representation of injured workers covered by this chapter. KRS 342.320(9).

Although phrased in the negative, KRS 342.320(9) clearly authorizes non-lawyers to represent injured workers, employers, and insurance carriers in proceedings before the Department and prohibits any construction to the contrary. As a result of the statute, the workers' compensation specialists, in the performance of their statutory duties, are exempt from criminal sanctions for the unauthorized practice of law. See KRS 524.130. And as the Supreme Court has no regulatory control over non-attorneys, specialists would provide legal representation without being subject to the professional standards applied to lawyers. The determinative constitutional issue, therefore, is whether the legislature exceeded its authority by enacting KRS 342.320(9), a statute that infringes upon the power of the judicial branch. The separation of the legislative and judicial branches of government is mandated by sections 27, 28, and 116 of the Constitution of Kentucky. Section 27 provides that the powers of government shall be divided between three distinct bodies: legislative, executive, and judicial. Section 28 forcefully articulates the bedrock separation of powers principle that "No person or collection of persons, being of one of those departments, shall exercise any power properly belonging to either of the others, except in the instances hereinafter expressly directed or permitted." Section 116, enacted as part of the Judicial Article effective January 1, 1976, states in relevant part that the "Supreme Court shall have the power to prescribe . . . rules of practice and procedure for the Court of Justice." Longstanding decisional law supports the exclusive authority of the Supreme Court to promulgate the rules of legal practice and procedures. This authority was clearly articulated in *Hobson v. Kentucky Trust Co.*, 303 Ky. 493, 197 S.W.2d 454, 457 (1946):

> The making of rules of practice in courts, as well as out of courts, in matters pertaining to the rights of individuals under the law, is inherently possessed by courts and judges, in carrying out the functions of persons as between each other and as between them and the government. Such authority is universally accepted by the courts as properly embraced within the Judicial Department of the government.

Similarly, in *Ratterman v. Stapleton*, Ky., 371 S.W.2d 939, 941 (1963), the court stated:

> The right to prescribe such rules as are necessary to qualify, regulate, and control attorneys as officers of the court is a right of self-preservation inherent in

the court and is not derived from or dependent upon any act of the Legislature or any express provision of the Constitution. [footnote omitted]

The correct principle, as we view it, is that the legislative function cannot be so exercised as to interfere unreasonably with the functioning of the courts, and that any unconstitutional intrusion is per se unreasonable, unless it be determined by the court that it can and should be tolerated in a spirit of comity. Undoubtedly, the separation of powers principles strictly prohibit the legislature from infringing upon the judiciary's exclusive power to make rules governing the practice of law, court procedures, and any exceptions thereto. In the case at bar, the legislature has authorized non-attorneys in the Department to act as legal representatives in workers' compensation cases. This is not within its purview. The legislature has no power to make rules relating to the practice of law or create exceptions to the settled rules of this Court. Thus KRS 342.320(9) is unconstitutional. We have not overlooked the principle of comity. However, KRS 342.320(9) is not the type of statutory provision this Court should accept, despite its unconstitutionality, based upon considerations of comity. For this Court to extend comity, the statute must be a " 'statutorily acceptable' substitute for current judicially mandated procedures." *Foster v. Overstreet*, Ky., 905 S.W.2d 504, 507 (1995) (citing *Drumm v. Commonwealth*, Ky., 783 S.W.2d 380 (1990); *Gaines v. Commonwealth*, Ky., 728 S.W.2d 525 (1987). KRS 342.320(9) is not a "statutorily acceptable" substitute for current procedures. Instead, it represents an attempt to change the fundamental nature of legal practice to include persons who are not qualified to practice law, who are not required to meet professional licensing standards, and who are not subject to the disciplinary authority of this Court. Despite our respect for the legislative branch of government, we cannot grant comity to a statute that grants non-lawyers the right to practice law.

III. THE WORKERS' COMPENSATION SPECIALISTS

The next issue is whether the duties performed by the workers' compensation specialists are consistent with guidelines set by this Court for permissible duties of paralegals or whether those duties constitute the unauthorized practice of law. Workers compensation specialists may perform duties that do not involve the practice of law as defined by SCR 3.020 and that are consistent with SCR 3.700. This Court has defined the practice of law as any service rendered involving legal knowledge or legal advice, whether of representation, counsel or advocacy in or out of court, rendered in respect to the rights, duties, obligations, liabilities, or business relations of one requiring the services. SCR 3.020. The Court has also promulgated guidelines relating to the employment and duties of paralegals:

> A paralegal is a person under the supervision and direction of a licensed lawyer, who may apply knowledge of the law and legal procedures in rendering direct assistance to lawyers engaged in legal research; design, develop or plan modifications or new procedures, techniques, services, processes or applications; prepare or interpret legal documents and write detailed procedures for practicing in certain fields of law; select, compile and use technical information from such references as digests, encyclopedias or practice manuals; and analyze and follow procedural problems that involve independent decisions.

SCR 3.700, Preliminary statement.

The fundamental qualification of the performance of these duties is that the paralegal must work under the supervision and direction of a licensed lawyer. The KBA contends that two specific subsections of KRS 342.329 authorize workers' compensation specialists to perform duties that should only be undertaken by licensed attorneys. The statutory duties the KBA takes issue with are:

> (c) Advising all parties of their rights and obligations under this chapter; and
> (d) Assisting workers in obtaining medical reports, job descriptions, and other materials pertinent to a claim for benefits and preparing all documents necessary for a claim application. KRS 342.329(1)(c)–(d).

To properly consider the KBA's contention, it is necessary to review not only these statutorily authorized duties, but also the actual practices of workers' compensation specialists. The duties of a specialist begin with the fielding of a telephone call. The Department provides an 800 telephone line for insurance carriers, employees, employers, medical providers, and attorneys to call for information on workers' compensation laws and procedures. Prospective claimants are told in the beginning of the conversation that the specialist is neither an advocate nor an attorney. Every case is documented on a "request for assistance" form. In current practice, an attorney, presently Cathy Costelle, supervises the specialists. While Ms. Costelle is not usually present during these telephone conversations, she reviews each request form for accuracy and legal sufficiency. Her knowledge would be necessarily limited to the content of the assistance form. A primary responsibility of a specialist is to mediate the dispute so that a filed claim will not be necessary. If mediation does not resolve the problem, the claimant is advised of his or her right to file a claim either *pro se* with the assistance of the specialist, or through private counsel. If the claimant elects to utilize the specialist's aid in preparation of Form 101, the application is reviewed by Ms. Costelle prior to signature by the claimant and filing. Specialists are allowed to assist the *pro se* claimants at arbitration, a procedure that normally does not require the cross-examination of witnesses or presentation of legal arguments as is typical in adversarial proceedings. After the informal arbitration proceeding, there is a right of appeal to an administrative law judge for a *de novo* hearing under courtroom conditions at which representation by an attorney is required. Most of the tasks performed by the specialist are procedural and administrative in nature. SCR 342.329(1)(a)–(e), supra p. 2. These tasks do not require any interpretation or analysis of the law, and they are precisely the type of duties authorized by SCR 3.700. Additionally, each call to a specialist is documented, and the documentation is reviewed by a supervising attorney, the chief specialist. Although the chief specialist is not required by statute to be an attorney, in practice it is imperative for this person to be a qualified attorney who can properly supervise the non-attorney specialists just as any other attorney takes supervisory responsibility for any paralegal employees pursuant to SCR 3.700. Although the statutory scheme does not require an attorney as chief specialist and supervisor, in practice such hierarchy has been implemented, and but for what appears to be settled policy to keep an attorney as chief specialist, our opinion might well be different. Therefore, in dispensing information via the telephone, by completing the "request for assistance" forms, by mediating disputes, and by assisting claimants in filling out their claim forms, while under the direct supervision of an attorney who shall be responsible for their conduct, specialists do not engage in the unauthorized practice of law. Thus, subject to the qualifications set forth herein, we hold that non-lawyers may serve as workers' compensation specialists and overrule the part of KBA U-52 that holds to the contrary.

On the other hand, we agree with the conclusion in KBA U-52 that non-lawyers may not represent parties before the Department. Legal representation by a lay person before an adjudicatory tribunal, however informal, is not permitted by SCR 3.700, as such representation involves advocacy that would constitute the practice of law. The swift and expeditious resolution of claims is of importance to the efficient functioning of Kentucky's workers' compensation system. The use of non-attorney personnel, such as workers' compensation specialists, is acceptable as a means to facilitate communication and to resolve simple disputes, provided an attorney supervisor oversees the work of non-attorney personnel in the resolution of these simple cases. Yet when representation before a tribunal is required, this Court has a duty to ensure that such representation is from a individual with a court-mandated duty of loyalty to the client and one who must comply with the Rules of Professional Conduct. SCR 3.130, *et seq.* The authority of an attorney supervisor can not meet the required standard.

IV. CONCLUSION

For the foregoing reasons, the advisory opinion issued by the KBA Board of Governors, designated as KBA U-52, is hereby affirmed in part and reversed in part. Workers' compensation specialists who are not attorneys may process claims, as long as their work is supervised by a licensed attorney. However, such specialists may not represent parties before any adjudicative tribunal.

Turner v. Kentucky Bar Association, 980 S.W.2d 560 (Ky. 1998).

a. In this decision, the first issue decided by the Court was whether a state statute allowing nonlawyer representation was a legislative trespass upon judicial authority, in violation of the separation of powers provisions of the Constitution of Kentucky. This court sent a clear message that the Kentucky legislature had overstepped its bounds. How do you think this opinion will affect future legislation? Was the legislation too sweeping in nature (e.g., by allowing nonattorney representation without further restriction)? Review KRS 342.320(9).

b. The second issue decided by the court was whether the duties performed by the "worker's compensation specialists" constituted the unauthorized practice of law. In its analysis, the court discussed the definition of paralegals in the state of Kentucky, although the statute didn't mention "paralegals." Why do you think the court decided to include paralegals in its analysis?

c. Ultimately the court determined that some of the duties performed by the "worker's compensation specialists" were allowable because, in practice, an attorney reviewed and was responsible for legal opinions and documents. The court stated, "[a]lthough the statutory scheme does not require an attorney as chief specialist and supervisor, in practice such hierarchy has been implemented." What do you think will happen if the chief specialist is not an attorney?

Mediation—Drawing a Fine Line Mediation is becoming more and more widely adopted and accepted by our society, with applications in both personal and business settings. State court systems have embraced the concept of mediation as a method by which to expedite justice and streamline the docket. However, one effect of this movement has been increasing legal ethics inquiries regarding mediation and its possible categorization as the unauthorized practice of law.[55] State bars differ in their approach and analysis of this issue, as discussed in the following excerpt:

> The State Bar of Michigan consistently has held that attorneys who mediate represent neither party in a mediation and do not practice law as they mediate.[56] In Tennessee, lawyer-mediators have been deemed not to be practicing law, but nevertheless have been held to the ethical standards of an attorney.[57] Additionally, Oregon and Florida have permitted their attorneys to mediate conflicts with other non-legal professionals.[58] Oregon's State Bar Association Board of Governors has held that a lawyer-mediator who mediated disputes with psychologists neither violated Model Rule 5.3 nor aided in the unlawful practice of law because mediation need not implicate the practice of law.[59] The Florida State Bar Association Committee on Professional Ethics has considered whether a law firm ethically may operate a separate mediation department employing non-lawyer mediators.[60] While approving the project, the Florida Committee required the firm to hold its non-lawyer mediators to the Model Rules,[61] suggesting that mediation may prove similar but still distinct from the practice of law . . . .

The author also addresses the ethical obligations for lawyers and nonlawyers who mediate, as follows:

> Even at the margins of practicing law, the Model Rules[62] suggest clear boundaries. Non-lawyers approaching the practice of law are considered equal to attorneys for the purpose of deciding inquiries into unethical conduct.[63] Even when a non-lawyer professional escapes censure, the Model Rules clearly hold supervising attorneys accountable for the acts of their non-legal staff.[64]

Finally, the author discusses the need for further reform and evolution of existing ethical standards to meet the challenge of new services provided by lawyers and non-lawyer professionals, as follows:

> A relatively clear preference by courts and ethics associations for applying traditional rules of professional conduct to the expanding practice of law by non-legal professionals and lawyer-mediators, however, invites rather than discourages further ethical inquiries. Simply asserting the applicability of current ethics rules to avant guard ethical dilemmas ignores the force of popular movements in the legal market place.[65]Client and attorney enthusiasm for new practices such as assigning greater responsibility to legal assistants or offering mediation as a choice among the menu of established legal services may push ethics decision-makers to adjust their initial conservatism and further reform ethical standards to accommodate these marginal practices of law . . . . Clarifying a precise definition for what the practice of law encompasses may help resolve current queries such as, is the law practiced by non-lawyer practitioners and are the services performed by non-lawyer mediators the practice of law? Like any good formalist definition, realist developments eventually will erode the utility of precise language.[66] Lawyers, as agents of principals with increasingly developing demands, should posit a dynamic definition of legal services that accommodates an appropriate, rather than an antiquated, code of ethics.[67]

DISCUSSION QUESTIONS

1. Do you believe mediation constitutes the practice of law? Which attributes of mediation are similar to practicing law? Which are distinguishable?
2. Do you think that the existing Model Rules of Professional Conduct sufficiently address the ethical concerns involved in mediation?

CONCLUSION

As the push for affordable legal services and ways to avoid the overburdened court system continue, the paralegal profession will continue to be closely scrutinized and lines will continue to be redrawn. It is imperative that paralegals be fully informed of these changes and the societal pressures that are responsible for them. Although increased responsibility may be attractive in some contexts, the potential for increased liability should be considered and weighed as well.

ENDNOTES

1 Wash. Ct. R. Ann., ADMISSION TO PRACTICE RULE 12. The rule authorizes "certain lay persons to select, prepare and complete legal documents incident to the closing of real estate and personal property transactions and to prescribe the conditions and limitations upon such activities." *Id.* ADMISSION TO PRACTICE RULE 12 (a).

2 *Id.* ADMISSION TO PRACTICE RULE 12(b)(1).

3 *Id.* ADMISSION TO PRACTICE RULE 12(b)(2)(i).

4 *Id.* ADMISSION TO PRACTICE RULE 12(b)(2)(ii)

5 *Id.* ADMISSION TO PRACTICE RULE 12(f)(1).

6 *Id.* ADMISSION TO PRACTICE RULE 12(f)(2). The Board accepts as proof of financial solvency a $100,000.00 individual errors and omissions insurance policy, an agency policy, or a financial responsibility form from a corporate surety . . . .

7 *Id.* ADMISSION TO PRACTICE RULE 12 (d).

8 *Id.* ADMISSION TO PRACTICE RULE 12(g)(5). . .

9 STATE BAR OF CALIFORNIA, REPORT OF THE STATE BAR OF CALIFORNIA COMMISSION ON LEGAL TECHNICIANS 17, 47 (1990) (This report discusses the efforts in Washington.)

10 One of the alterations made by the new rules changed the name of "unauthorized practice of law" to "unlicensed practice of law." See RULES REG. FLA. BAR 10-1.1(b). The name was changed to reinforce the notion that anyone who practices law must pass the bar exam, that is, the person must be licensed. See H. Glenn Boggs, *The New Face of the Unlicensed Practice of Law,* Fla. B. J., July/August 1987, at 55.

11 RULES REG. FLA. BAR 10-1(d).

12 *Id.* at 10-7.

13 H. Glenn Boggs, The New Face of the Unlicensed Practice of Law, 1987 FLA B. J. at 56.

14 RULES REG. FLA. Bar 10.1-1(d) mandates that at least five members of the standing committee shall be nonlawyers.

15 See *The Florida Bar re Amendment to Rules Regulating the Florida Bar,* 510 So. 2d 596 (1987) (promulgated as part of RULES REG. FLA. BAR 10-1(b). Specifically, "limited oral communication" includes such assistance as informing the individual of the number of copies of the document that must be filed "and other matters of a routine administrative nature necessary to assure that the matter goes forward.")

16 *Id.* at 597.

17 See Deborah L. Rhode, *Policing the Professional Monopoly: A Constitutional and Empirical Analysis of Unauthorized Practice Prohibitions,* 34 Stan. L. Rev. 1, 55 (1981).

18 *Id.* at 1.

19 See State Bar of California, Report of the Public Protection Committee 7, 2 (1988)

20 See *Id.* at 1 n.1 (defining "legal technician" as a nonlawyer who is permitted to practice law).

21 *Id.* at 1.

22 *Id.* at 8. The Committee explained that "the public will not view the Bar's efforts as 'public protection'; rather it will be viewed as an effort by the organized bar to protect the self-interests of its constituents." *Id.*

23 State Bar of California, Report of the State Bar of California Commission on Legal Technicians 17 (1990) [hereinafter 1990 Report], at 8.

24 *Id.* at 1. The areas specified by the report were bankruptcy, family law, and landlord-tenant law.

25 *Id.*

26 *Id.* at 28.

27 *Id.*

28 *Id.*

29 *Id.*

30 See Kathleen E. Justice, *Comment, There Goes the Monopoly: The California Proposal to Allow Nonlawyers to Practice Law,* 44 Vand. L. Rev. 179, 204 (1991).

31 In August 1991, the Board of Governors rejected the proposed rule. Some members of the board believed the plan allowed too many nonlawyers to practice law and provided too few safeguards to protect the public, and some believed it did not allow enough nonlawyers to practice law. See Don J. DeBenedictis, *California Bar Drops Technician Plan,* A.B.A. J., Nov. 1991 at 36.

32 Judicial decrees provide yet another example of reform in the regulation of this area. In a recent Nevada case, the state district court set forth guidelines allowing nonlawyers to perform some legal services in the areas of family law and bankruptcy. *State Bar of Nevada v. Johnson,* No. CV89-5814 (Nev. Dist. Ct. Apr. 12, 1990). Evidence that legal needs of low-income people were largely unmet prompted the court's "deregulation" of these "scrivener services." *Id.*

Another reform alternative is a constitutional amendment. The voters of Arizona

amended their constitution to change Arizona's unauthorized practice of law rules . . . . This approach avoids conflicts with the separation of powers doctrine associated with a legislative enactment. A properly enacted constitutional amendment is immune from legislative or judicial attack, and can be repealed only by a subsequent amendment. See, e.g., Ariz. Const. Art. XXI.

33 Ryan J. Talamante, *We Can't All Be Lawyers . . . Or Can We? Regulating the Unauthorized Practice of Law in Arizona,* note, 34 Ariz. L. Rev. 873, 878–883 (Winter 1992).

34 State Bar of Texas Unauthorized Practice of Law Task Force, *Preliminary Recommendation of a New Statutory Definition for the "Practice of Law,* 63 Tex. B.J. 543 (June 2000).

35 For example, in Connecticut, petitions for the termination of parental rights may be filed by social workers of the department of children and families; See Conn. General Statutes Sec. 17a-112; and Conn. Supreme Court Rules of Practice; Practice Book (1998 Rev.) Sec. 26-1 (l), formerly Sec. 1023.1 (l); also see *In re Darlene,* 717 A.2d 1242 (Conn. 1998) in which the Supreme Court of Connecticut upheld this practice.

36 Virginia's Consumer Real Estate Settlement Protection Act (CRESPA) (Va. Code §§ 6.1-2.19–2.29) authorizes certain qualified nonlawyers (licensed real estate brokers, financial institutions, title insurance companies and title agents) to provide escrow, closing and settlement services in transactions involving the purchase and financing of real estate containing not more than four residential dwelling units.

37 In Washington, "immigration assistants" may accept compensation for assistance with immigration issues, and those assistants are specifically prohibited from giving legal advice. Wash. Rev. Code sec. 19.154.020(1); .060; .080(6). Assistance is limited to mostly clerical duties such as translating, supplying birth and marriage certificates, making referrals to attorneys and transcribing responses to a government form selected by the customer, without advising the customer how to answer the form. Wash. Rev. Code sec. 19.154.020. Federal law allows "reputable individuals" of good moral character to represent persons on immigration matters as long as the represen-

tation is without remuneration, is on an individual case basis, and is based on a pre-existing relationship (such as family or friend) with the person entitled to representation. 8 C.F.R. sec. 92.1(a)(3). Most important, the representative must be approved by an immigration official and must not be a person "who regularly engages in immigration and naturalization practice or preparation, or holds himself out to the public as qualified to do so." 8 C.F.R. sec. 292.1(a)(3)(iv).

[38] Tex. Prop. Code sec. 24.011 allows nonlawyer representation in forcible entry and detainer suits (eviction actions) heard in justice courts (small claims); Also see *Holz v. Busy Bees Contracting, Inc.,* 589 N.W.2d 633 (Wis. App. 1998.); "We hold that an appeal in a small claims action is an "action or proceeding" pursuant to sec. 799.06(2), Wis. Stat., which permits a nonlawyer to commence, prosecute or defend a small claims action if the nonlawyer is a "full-time authorized employee" of the entity on whose behalf the nonlawyer acts." *Id.* at 634.

[39] NONLAWYER ACTIVITY IN LAW-RELATED SITUATIONS: A REPORT WITH RECOMMENDATIONS, August 1995, at 6.

[40] For an exhaustive list, an excellent source is WILLIAM. P. STATSKY, PARALEGAL ETHICS AND REGULATION, (West Publishing Co. 2d ed., 1993).

[41] Gregory T. Stevens, Note, *The Proper Scope of Nonlawyer Representation in State Administrative Proceedings: A State Specific Balancing Approach,* 43 VAND. L. REV. 245, 264–265 (January 1990).

[42] Robert G. Heiserman, *Nonlawyer Practice Before Federal Administrative Agencies Should be Discouraged,* 37 ADMIN. L. REV. 375, 378 (1985) (proceedings of the colloquium sponsored by the ABA Standing Comm. on Lawyer's Responsibility for Client Protection).

[43] *Id.* at 376. Heiserman noted that "[n]onlawyers might fail to recognize legal issues outside their particular areas of competency." *Id.* at 380.

[44] *Id.* at 376–79.

[45] Jonathan Rose, *Nonlawyer Practice Before Federal Administrative Agencies Should Be Encouraged,* 37 ADMIN. L. REV. 363, 365 (1985) (proceedings of the colloquium sponsored by the ABA Standing Comm. on Lawyer's Responsibility for Client Protection).

[46] Stevens, *supra* note 41, at p. 259.

[47] In Michigan, if there is explicit legislative authority for a nonlawyer to represent the interests of others before a proceeding held pursuant to administrative regulations, there is an exception to the unauthorized practice prohibition. *State Bar of Michigan v. Galloway,* 124 Mich. App. 271 (1983).
In *Unauthorized Practice of Law Committee v. Employers Unity, Inc.,* while acknowledging that the representation by nonlawyers in front of a state agency constituted the unauthorized practice of law, the Colorado Supreme Court justified nonlawyer representation on public policy grounds.

[48] See Opinion No. H-974, issued April 7, 1977, by the Texas Attorney General's office. This opinion stated that representation by nonlawyers before the Industrial Accident Board and the State Board of Insurance was not the unauthorized practice of law as long as permitted by these agencies. The Opinion was also quick to point out that this determination involved these two agencies only. "Any prohibition of such representation by nonlawyers must result from an assessment of the public welfare. In our view, the Legislature and the agency involved are in the best position to make such an assessment."

[49] 127 Ariz. 259, 619 P.2d 1036, (1980) (en banc).

[50] Act of Mar. 17, 1988, ch. 619, 1988 Tenn. Pub. Acts 265 (codified at TENN. CODE ANN. Secs. 67-5-1511(b), -1514 (Supp. 1988).

[51] See TENN. CODE ANN. Sec. 67-5-1514(g) (Supp. 1988)

[52] See TENN. CODE ANN. Sec. 67-5-1511(b) (Supp. 1988)

[53] See Op. Att'y Gen. Colo. File No. OLS8804271/AQT (Sept. 1, 1988).

[54] This argument states: "[M]any persons appearing before the agencies are sophisticated and intelligent. They have specialized knowledge about their cases and thus can assess the competency of potential representatives, either lawyers or nonlawyers. In addition, they often are corporate entities that employ a large number and wide variety of intelligent and specially trained employees. Corporate entities have available vast expertise on their relationships with government, and they usually are experienced in choosing competent representatives. These features make them

infrequent victims of misrepresentation or manipulation." Gregory T. Stevens, Note, *The Proper Scope of Nonlawyer Representation in State Administrative Proceedings: A State Specific Balancing Approach,* 43 Vand. L. Rev. 245, 273–274 (January 1990).

[55] One concern is that the mediator often applies a legal standard to the facts of a dispute, therefore practicing law.

[56] Michigan Bar Standing Comm. on Professional and Judicial Ethics, Op. RI-118 (1994).

[57] Tennessee S. Ct. Bd. of Professional Responsibility, Formal Op. 90 F-124 (1990).

[58] Florida Bar Ass'n Comm. on Professional Ethics, Op. 94-6 (1995); Oregon Bar Ass'n Bd. of Governors, Formal Op. 1991-101 (1991).

[59] Oregon Bar Ass'n Bd. of Governors, Formal Op. 1991-101 at 1 (1991).

[60] Florida Bar Ass'n Comm. on Professional Ethics, Op. 94-6 at 1 (1995).

[61] *Id.* The committee did not address whether non-lawyers employed in the mediation practice would be considered non-legal practitioners subject to supervision by the attorneys under Model Rule 5.3.

[62] Model Rules of Professional Conduct Rules 5.3, 5.5, and 5.7 (1983).

[63] *Id.* Rule 5.3(a).

[64] *Id.* Rule 5.3(c).

[65] See Carrie Menkel-Meadow, *Ethics in Alternative Dispute Resolution: New Issues, No Answers from the Adversary Conception of Lawyers' Responsibilities,* 38 S. Tex. L. Rev. 407, 452 (1997) (predicting that lawyers will develop practical rules of ethics related specifically to alternative dispute resolution problem-solving).

[66] For example, the definition of "ancillary services" in the original Model Rule 5.7, Model Rules Rule 5.7(b) (1995), proved insufficient to account for "law-related services" not addressed in the current Model Rule 5.7.

[67] Jonathan A. Beyer, *Non-Lawyer Practitioner: Practicing Law at the Margins: Surveying Ethics Rules for Legal Assistants and Lawyers Who Mediate,* 11 Geo. J. Legal Ethics 411, 417–420 (Winter 1998).

Conflicts of Interest, Confidentiality, and Risk Management

INTRODUCTION

Although it is critical that paralegals be familiar with all of the ethical, professional, and/or disciplinary rules discussed in Chapter 3 of this book, the following discussion will focus on the rules associated with conflicts of interest and confidentiality, and, how these rules impact and promote risk management in the legal environment.

CONFLICTS OF INTEREST

The duty of loyalty that an attorney owes to his or her client is both historically rooted[1] and widely recognized in legal circles. Generally, this duty prohibits lawyers from undertaking representation or entering into business transactions that are directly adverse to a client's interests. The ABA Model Rules contain six separate rules[2] and several pages of commentary that focus specifically on identifying and prohibiting conflicts of interest. Probably one of the more litigated types of conflict-of-interest scenarios are those involving former clients. Unlike many of the other disciplinary rules, a violation of a conflict of interest of a former client, or "side-switching" as it is commonly called, can mean disqualification of the offending attorney and his or her entire law firm.

Conflicts of Interest—Former Clients

ABA Model Rule 1.9 provides that without prior consent, a lawyer who has formerly represented a client in a matter shall not thereafter represent another person in the same or a substantially related matter adverse to the former client. According to the comments following this rule, the purpose is to protect client confidences that were presumed to be disclosed during the prior representation. If a conflict is found to exist, the lawyer can be disqualified from representing the new client. When determining conflicts questions, courts are often inconsistent and unpredictable. Various schools of thought exist throughout the country as to when a conflict with a former client should result in disqualification.

Vicarious Disqualification   Lawyers in the same law firm are presumed to share information with each other regarding clients. Therefore, if one lawyer in a firm has a conflict because of representation of a former client, then an irrebuttable presumption arises that confidences have been shared and the entire firm is disqualified. This is known as *vicarious disqualification*,[3] and has been the subject of debate and discourse within the legal profession for many years. Some states apply the rule strictly, while others apply a more functional analysis of the circumstances to determine if disqualification is appropriate.[4] Some states allow lawyers to rebut or refute the presumption by creating "ethical screens" or "chinese walls" to insulate the tainted lawyer and allow the firms to present evidence that client confidences were not revealed.

Application of this rule to legal assistants and other nonlawyers in the law office depends on the court hearing the case. Many courts attempt to distinguish nonlawyer personnel from lawyers and thus give them less restrictive treatment. Some courts have refused to extend vicarious disqualification to nonlawyers at all, and those that have usually allow nonlawyers to rebut the presumption that confidences have been shared.[5] However, a few states have determined that nonlawyers and lawyers should be held to the same standard,[6] arguing, "[t]o hold otherwise would grant less protection to the confidential and privileged information obtained by a nonlawyer than that obtained by a lawyer."[7] Because many of the states have varying standards regarding this issue, including the factors that trigger it,[8] the reader should carefully review the relevant ethical and case law opinions in his or her home state.

The ABA's Committee on Ethics and Professional Responsibility has addressed this issue and determined that a law firm that employs a nonlawyer with a prior conflict of interest may continue representation if (1) the new firm effectively screens the nonlawyer from participating in matters involving that client, and (2) the nonlawyer does not disclose any information about those clients to the new firm.[9] This opinion has been criticized for its underlying rationale for treating lawyers differently than nonlawyers.[10] In the following excerpt, the author questions the ABA's position, as well as the case law opinions that make distinctions between lawyers and paralegals for conflict-of-interest purposes:[11]

> Arguably these opinions make artificial distinctions. While focusing on the lawyer/ nonlawyer nomenclature, the courts fail to distinguish within the nonlawyer class and lump together secretaries, office managers, and other staff members, as well as paralegals.[12] The inherent problem with this analysis is that there are clearer and more important distinctions between the work performed by other support staff and paralegals than that performed by paralegals and attorneys. Like attorneys, paralegals are often involved with client matters from the time of interview through final resolution.

Paralegals are involved in strategy sessions. They draft discovery requests and become familiar with the types of evidence needed. They perform research and understand the issues involved. Paralegals assist at trial and hearings. Most important, paralegals often act as a direct contact for clients, taking phone calls, alleviating apprehensions, and generally being available . . . .

Job mobility is another argument used to distinguish nonlawyers from lawyers.[13] The subject of vicarious disqualification of nonlawyers was addressed by the American Bar Association in Informal Opinion 88-1526 (issued June 22, 1988). That opinion addressed a situation wherein a paralegal with substantial knowledge relating to the representation of a client "switched sides." The Committee concluded that the law firm should not be disqualified as long as the paralegal was screened from all contact with the case, and did not disclose any client confidences. The Committee felt that the employment opportunities of nonlawyer employees should be protected, explaining:

> It is important that nonlawyer employees have as much mobility in employment opportunity as possible consistent with the protection of clients' interests. To so limit employment opportunities that some nonlawyers trained to work with law firms might be required to leave the careers for which they are trained would disserve clients as well as the legal profession. Accordingly, any restrictions on the nonlawyer's employment should be held to the minimum necessary to protect confidentiality of client information.

This argument is patently artificial when used to distinguish between lawyers and paralegals. Lawyers face the same mobility concerns which have been discussed in case law involving imputed disqualification of lawyers.[14] As stated in a different context: "More importantly, we cannot perceive a real distinction, in terms of the 'substantial relationship' test, between legal work and non-legal work, or between a requisite minimum of legal advice and mere peripheral legal participation."[15] Case law distinctions which appear to provide a safe harbor for paralegals are easily refuted. For this reason, the focus should not be so much on treating paralegals differently from attorneys, but instead on finding a rule which allows appropriate screening mechanisms for all legal professionals.[16]

DISCUSSION QUESTIONS

1. Are the distinctions made by the ABA and the courts between lawyers and paralegals valid with respect to this issue?

2. Should "ethical walls" alone be sufficient to avoid vicarious disqualification? In *Phoenix Founders Inc. v. Marshall*, 887 S.W.2d 831 (Tex. 1994), the Court identified certain factors to help determine whether or not the screening had been effective: substantiality of the relationship between the former and current matters; time elapsing between the matters; size of the firm; number of individuals presumed to have confidential information; nature of involvement in the former matter; and timing and features of any measures taken to reduce the danger of disclosure. How important are these other factors in determining the effectiveness of the wall? Can a two-person law firm ever create an effective wall?

CONFIDENTIALITY

More encompassing than the duties owed under general agency law and the attorney-client privilege is Rule 1.6 of the ABA Model Rules of Professional Conduct. This rule requires lawyers to keep virtually all information concerning a client completely confidential. In fact, this rule imposes confidentiality on information relating to the representation even if it is acquired before or after the relationship existed. According to the comments following this rule, the justification for such a broad reach is to ensure free and open discussion between lawyer and client so the lawyer can be fully informed and better able to counsel the client.

It is also important that paralegals protect client confidences. Nearly all states that have guidelines for the utilization of legal assistants require the lawyer "to instruct legal assistants concerning client confidences" and "to exercise care to ensure that legal assistants comply" with the Code in this regard. Also, NFPA Model Disciplinary Rule 1.5 and NALA Model Guideline I require legal assistants to preserve confidential information.

Privileged Client Communications. As stated above, the rule protecting client confidences encompasses all information protected by the attorney-client privilege as well. The attorney-client privilege is an evidentiary rule that applies to judicial and other proceedings in which an attorney may be called as a witness or otherwise be required to produce information concerning a client. Under the attorney-client privilege, the lawyer can refuse to disclose communications in any form that are confidential in nature and that relate to the subject matter of the representation. The attorney-client privilege is designed to encourage full and frank communication between a client and his or her attorney, and it protects the substance of confidential communications from discovery or involuntary disclosure in a trial or other proceeding. The privilege belongs to the client, not the attorney, and although attorneys may invoke the privilege on behalf of their client, they may not invoke it if the client has waived the privilege. Attorneys also may not waive the privilege without the client's consent.

It has been held that the attorney-client privilege, as a matter of evidentiary law, is broad enough to encompass the nonlawyers working under a lawyer's direct supervision and control.[17] Courts rationalize that since paralegals are extensions of the attorneys that they work for, allowing discovery of confidential communications between a client and a paralegal would erode the attorney-client relationship.[18]

DISCUSSION QUESTION

Commentators generally agree that the attorney-client privilege is important to the administration of justice for the following reasons: (1) Legal matters can be effectively handled only if all available facts are disclosed to the attorney; (2) clients will be more likely to seek legal advice if they know that their disclosures will be kept confidential; (3) clients will more likely comply with regulatory laws because their attorney will advise them to do so after disclosure; and (4) disclosure may discourage frivolous lawsuits because the attorney will be able to determine the weakness of a client's case.[19]

Do you think these reasons are applicable to nonlawyer representatives as well?

Paralegal Work Product. Sometimes, in preparation for a case, a lawyer will prepare a document that does not contain client communications, but was prepared in anticipation of the litigation. Under the work-product rule, this document would be protected from discovery by the opposing side. Work product consists of any notes, working papers, memoranda, or similar documents and tangible things prepared by a lawyer in anticipation of litigation. In the following excerpt, the author discusses the work product doctrine and its applicability to nonlawyers.

> Three particularly troublesome issues are: who can create work product; who can assert work product immunity; and what constitutes waiver of the immunity. Although these questions have been discussed and litigated extensively, no clear resolution has emerged. Thus, the practicing attorney, his client, and their agents cannot determine with certainty whose work will be protected . . . .
>
> A. Who Can Create Work Product
>
> The 1970 amendment to rule 26(b)(3) ostensibly settled the question of who can create work product by adding protection for the work product of non-lawyers. The question, however, remains unsettled even though the policies underlying the work product doctrine favor granting equal treatment to lawyers and nonlawyers and provide the basis for resolving any uncertainties.
>
> 1. Development of Work Product Immunity for Nonlawyers.
>
> Before the 1970 amendment to rule 26(b)(3), the courts split among three main positions on whether to extend protection to nonlawyer work product. First, under *Alltmont v. United States*[20] position, courts extended the Hickman rationale for immunity to all documents prepared for use at trial.[21] Second, courts following the *Southern Railway v. Lanham*[22] position held that only mental impressions of nonlawyers receive work product protection.[23] Finally, courts following *Burke v. United States*[24] protected only work supervised by an attorney and involving legal skill.[25] The 1970 amendment to rule 26(b)(3) expanded the scope of protection to the work of a party's "consultant, surety, indemnitor, insurer, or agent."[26] The Advisory Committee notes regarding this concluded that "the weight of authority affords protection of the preparatory work of both lawyers and nonlawyers (though not necessarily to the same extent)."[27] Although the parenthetical contradicts the absolute nature of the rule and would buttress a case of discovery of nonlawyer work product, no reported cases refer to it for support . . . .
>
> Perhaps a fuller explanation by the Committee of its protection of nonlawyer work product would have lead [sic] to fewer anomalous holdings since rule 26(b)(3)'s enactment. For example, some courts abide by the rule and grant protection to nonlawyer work product, formulating their analyses solely in terms of anticipation of litigation.[28] Other courts, however, flatly ignore the rule and apply the gamut of pre-amendment analyses. . . . .[29]

2. Justifications for Protecting Nonlawyer Work Product
The policies underlying the work product doctrine support protection of nonlawyer work product. Broad coverage of both lawyer and nonlawyer work product preserves the functional integrity of the various professionals involved in preparing a case. If the work product doctrine did not protect nonlawyer work product, lawyers might take over the roles now performed by nonlawyers in order to ensure that the work product doctrine protected the material now usually prepared by nonlawyers. Professionals should not distort their roles in order to abuse work product protection;[30] a lawyer, for example, should not play the role of investigator in order to qualify the resulting investigative material for immunity. Broad coverage thus encourages two fundamental goals of the adversary system—greater efficiency and accuracy. With such coverage, attorneys have more time to prepare for trial[31] because they need not perform investigative work . . . .
Further . . . if nonlawyer work is denied protection, attorneys will not delegate even marginally legal functions to their agents. As the Supreme Court recognized in *United States v. Nobles*,[32] such delegation is necessary in modern litigation. . . . .[33]

3. Analysis and Recommended Formulation
Protection of ordinary work product should depend on whether material was prepared in anticipation of litigation, and not on the preparer's status as an attorney or nonattorney.[34] Admittedly, equal treatment of lawyers and nonlawyers creates evidentiary problems in applying the anticipation-of-litigation test, but courts can use various rules of thumb when making that determination. By viewing the "who can create work product" question as almost entirely a question of anticipation of litigation, courts achieve a more efficient allocation of legal resources. Lawyers will have more time for preparation and parties who attempt their own investigations will not be penalized. Also, the anticipation-of-litigation framework provides a more forthright approach to denying work product protection to nonlawyers than does a routine application of the "ordinary course of business" exception.[35]

Protected work product has been held to include materials prepared by paralegals in anticipation of litigation.[36] But where a party was trying to gain access to indexes of documents and the adverse party argued that the indexes were work product, the New York Supreme Court held that "work product" has been narrowly construed to include only material prepared in an attorney's professional capacity and which necessarily involved professional skills. Documents which could have been prepared by a layman are not covered.[37]

RISK MANAGEMENT

Ethical responsibilities for paralegals do not end with an understanding and appreciation of the ethical rules and codes. Paralegals can be of great assistance in taking positive steps to ensure these rules and codes are being followed and, at the same time, lessen the likelihood of malpractice claims.[38] One way to incorporate this understanding of ethical responsibilities is through the concept of "risk management." Although many law firms practice this concept within the general framework of professional responsibility codes, a more formal, systematic program might be more effective in preventing malpractice, and in helping the law firm better meet client expectations.[39] The most effective risk management programs usually include policies in the areas of (1) prevention, (2) maintenance, and (3) review.[40] Paralegals, in the unique intermediary role that they often play in the law office, can contribute in all three areas.

Preventative policies might focus on being aware of client confidentiality concerns and including safeguards at all relevant aspects of a client matter. As an intermediary between office staff and lawyers, paralegals are often in an ideal position to impose and apply these safeguards.[41] Prevention might also include ensuring quality in the delivery of legal services.[42] Two ways to do this is to ensure adequate supervision and consultation throughout the handling of a matter. Paralegals and their supervising attorneys should identify points during the handling of a matter when they should either meet or confirm the progress that has been made. Finally, maintaining calendars, tickler systems, and organized files are classic paralegal responsibilities that are critical to any risk management program.

Maintenance includes "keeping the case moving forward."[43] Clients often complain about lack of communication or inaction on their matters. Paralegals can play a key role in ensuring that client matters are being attended to and that client phone calls are being returned. Although paralegals must be cautioned against giving legal advice, the paralegal is in the ideal position to interact with clients and provide them with assurance and assistance.

Finally the risk management program itself should be reviewed and "fine-tuned" as lessons are learned from individual incidents. Are the identified procedures being complied with? Have errors decreased? Has overall client satisfaction increased? What steps or safeguards should be added? Paralegals should help gather this information and reduce it to a formal, systematic process.

CONCLUSION

This chapter has focused on client confidences and the responsibilities and rights of lawyers and paralegals in protecting those confidences, including avoiding conflicts of interests. The rules that we have discussed ensure that clients may enter into a confidential relationship with an attorney and know that the attorney will vigorously represent them and protect their interests. The increasingly responsible role that paralegals play in the law office means that they have an obligation to thoroughly appreciate these rules and their interpretation and application, as well as assist in risk management.

ENDNOTES

1 Deborah L. Rhode & David Luban, LEGAL ETHICS 446 (Foundation Press 1992): "By the 1880s, however, conflicts of interest were generally thought to be improper, and the 1887 Alabama Bar Code of Ethics—the distant ancestor of today's Codes and Model Rules—prohibited representation of conflicting interests unless the parties had consented."

2 See Rules 1.7 (general rule), 1.8 (prohibited transactions), 1.9 (former clients), 1.10 (imputed disqualification), 1.11 (successive government and private employment), and 1.12 (former judge or arbitrar).

3 See ABA Model Rule 1.10, "Imputed Disqualification: General Rule."

4 For an example, see Wash. D.C. Rules of Prof. Conduct, Rule 1.10, Comment 10: "A rule based on a functional analysis is more appropriate for determining the question of vicarious disqualification. Two functions are involved: preserving confidentiality and avoiding positions adverse to a client."

5 *Phoenix Founders Inc. v. Marshall*, 887 S.W.2d 831 (Tex. 1994). After holding that a conclusive, or irrebuttable, presumption arose that the paralegal received client confidences and secrets, the Court allowed the law firm to refute or rebut the presumption that those confidences had been shared. However, the Court set out two situations in which disqualification would be required: 1) when confidential information had in fact been disclosed and 2) when the screening would be ineffective; the court then discussed the factors that would be considered to determine the effectiveness of the screening. See also *Kapco Manufacturing Company, Inc. v. C & O Enterprises, Inc.*, 637 F. Supp. 1231 (N.D. Ill. 1985); the court applied a similar analysis, deciding that even though the presumption of receipt of confidences at the first firm was not rebutted; the sharing of those confidences at the second firm was rebutted.

6 *Ciaffone v. District Court*, 945 P.2d 950 (Nev. 1997); Also see *Creighton University v. Hickman*, 512 N.W.2d 374 (Neb. 1994) (however, the nonlawyer in *Creighton* who was found to have a conflict had formerly worked as an attorney in the first firm. The court specifically stated that "Canon 9 requires an attorney to avoid even the appearance of impropriety. Employing, in any capacity, one who was an attorney on the other side of a case carries with it the appearance of impropriety." *Id.* at 378.

7 *Ciaffone* at 953.

8 Opinion RI-284, State Bar of Michigan (1997): screening is required if employee typed, filed, copied, proofread or processed confidential information; North Carolina State Bar Association Opinion 176 (1994): screening is required if the paralegal's involvement was negligible; *In re American Home Products Corp.*, 985 S.W.2d 68 (Tex. 1998): freelance consultants must meet the same screening requirements as regular employees.

9 ABA Comm. on Ethics and Professional Responsibility, Formal Op. 88-1526 ("Imputed Disqualification Arising from Change of Employment by Nonlawyer Employee").

10 M. Peter Moser, *Chinese Walls: a Means of Avoiding Law Firm Disqualification When a Personally Disqualified Lawyer Joins the Firm*, 3 GEO. J. LEGAL ETHICS 399, 403, 407 (1990); *Ciaffone v. District Court*, 945 P.2d 950, 953 (Nev. 1997); John M. Burman, *Conflicts of Interest in Wyoming*, 35 LAND & WATER L. REV. 79, 177-179 (2000).

11 See also John Burman, *Support Staff Conflicts of Interest*, WYO. LAW., October 1997, at 12, wherein the author also questions the distinctions made by the ABA. *Id.* at 14.

12 However, even this "lumping" is sometimes ineffective to argue that a distinction should be made. In *Esquire Care, Inc. v. Maguire*, 532 So. 2d 740 (Fla. Dist. Ct. App. 1988) the court applied an "access to information standard" analysis and stated the following:

In determining whether an individual is privy to attorney-client confidences, a court should not look to what tasks the employee performs so much as to his or her access to the same types of privileged materials that lawyers would receive. That a secretary may make no lawyerlike decisions, or counsel clients, does not mean he or she is not privy to confidential communications. *Id.* at 741.

13 See *Herron v. Jones*, 637 S.W.2d 569, 571 (Ark. 1982); *In re Complex Asbestos Litigation*, 283 Cal. Rptr. 732, 746–47 (Cal. App. 1991).

14 Courts have expressed a concern for the restricted mobility of attorneys unless they are allowed to rebut vicarious disqualification. *Schloetter v. Railoc of Indiana, Inc.*, 546 F.2d 706, 712 n. 11 (7th Cir. 1976), cited the decision in *Silver Chrysler Plymouth* with approval, as follows:

[A] different result in . . . *Silver Chrysler* might have severely restricted mobility within the legal profession. For law firms would be understandably reluctant to hire a young lawyer who had previously worked at a large law firm if it were to mean full automatic disqualification from any case involving a party represented by the young lawyer's former employer.

15 *NCK Organization Ltd. v. Bregman*, 542 F.2d 128, 132 (2d.Cir. 1976). Although in this case the Second Circuit was considering whether duties performed by an attorney as officer of a corporation were somehow exempt from the restrictions of the Disciplinary Rules, this type of analysis could easily be transferred to paralegals and the type of services that they traditionally perform.

16 Terry L. Hull, *Conflicts of Interest—What Guidance for Paralegals?* J. OF PARALEGAL EDUC. AND PRAC., Spring 1995, at 1, 19–23.

17 Section of Litigation, ABA, The Attorney-Client Privilege and the Work-Product Doctrine, I.C.3 (1989). Also see *Samaritan Foundation v. Superior Court in and for the County of Maricopa*, 844 P.2d 593 (Ariz. App. Div. 1, 1992), review granted, *aff'd* in part, vacated in part, *Samaritan Foundation v. Goodfarb*, 862 P.2d 870 (Ariz. 1993) (lawyers do not forfeit the attorney-client privilege by receiving otherwise privileged client communications through the conduit of a properly supervised paralegal employee; *Pennsylvania v. Mrozek*, 657 A.2d 997 (Pa. 1995).

18 *In re French*, 145 B.R. 991 (Bankr. S.D. 1992) and 162 B.R. 541 (Bankr. S.D. 1994).

19 Emily Jones, *Keeping Client Confidences: Attorney-Client Privilege and Work Product Doctrine in Light of United States v. Adlman*, 18 PACE L. REV. 419, 424 (Spring 1998).

20 177 F.2d 971 (3d Cir. 1949), cert. denied, 339 U.S. 967 (1950).

21 "[W]e think that [Hickman's] rationale has a much broader sweep and applies to all statements of prospective witnesses which a party has obtained for his trial counsel's use . . . [W]e can see no logical basis for making any distinction between statements of witnesses secured by a party's trial counsel personally in preparation for trial and those obtained by others for use of the party's trial counsel." *Alltmont v. United States*, 177 F.2d at 976; see also *Bredice v. Doctors Hosp., Inc.*, 50 F.R.D. 249, 251 (D.D.C. 1970); 8 C. Wright and A. Miller, Federal Practice and Procedure, Sec. 2024, at 205–06 (1970). ("But if statements of witnesses are to be protected from discovery at all, the protection should not depend on who obtained the statement").

22 403 F.2d 119 (5th Cir. 1968).

23 The Fifth Circuit in Lanham held that the ordinary work product of a claims agent is not protected because "[s]uch statements are usually essential to the proper defense of the action," and because allowing discovery would not be likely to alter defendant's activities." 403 F.2d at 129. As the court noted: "It is not likely that defendants in accident cases will cease taking statements simply to avoid discovery." *Id*. The Court added, however, that discovery of "documents reflecting the mental processes and impressions of claim agents or investigators should be conditioned upon a strong showing of 'necessity or justification." *Id*. at 131; see also *Richards-Wilcox Mfg. Co. v. Young Spring & Wire Corp.*, 34 F.R.D. 212, 213 (N.D. Ill. 1964) (purely factual statements gathered by observer are not work product).

24 32 F.R.D. 213 (E.D.N.Y. 1963).

25 The court in *Burke* denied protection for a non-lawyer's work product because "[t]here is no showing that the materials represent the product of the training, skill or knowledge of an attorney which the work product privilege is aimed at protecting." *Id*. at 214; see also *Groover, Christie & Merritt v. Lo Bianco*, 336 F.2d 969, 973–4 (D.C. Cir. 1964)(Wright, C.J., dissenting) (documents prepared by unsupervised defendant are not work product).

26 Fed. R. Civ. P. 26(b)(3).

27 Fed. R. Civ. P. 26 advisory committee note, 48 F.R.D. 487, 502 (1970) (emphasis added).

28 Footnote omitted.

29 See, e.g., *Virginia Elec. & Power Co. v. Sun Shipbuilding & Dry Dock Co.*, 68 F.R.D. 397 (E.D. Va. 1975) (in discussing work product, no references to 1970 rule or any cases post-1970, but extensive citation of pre-1970 cases).

30 Footnote omitted.

31 See *Hickman v. Taylor*, 329 U.S. 495, 510 (1947) (attorneys should be free to prepare for trial without constant interruptions from other parties).

32 422 U.S. 225 (1975).

33 *Id.* at 238 ("[A]ttorneys often must rely on the assistance of investigators and other agents in the compilation of materials in preparation for trial. It is therefore necessary that the [work product] doctrine protect material prepared by agents for the attorney . . . ").

34 See, e.g., *United States v. Chatham City Corp.*, 72 F.R.D. 640, 642–43 (S.D. Ga. 1976).

35 Anderson, Cadieux, *et al.*, *The Work Product Doctrine*, 68 Cornell L. Rev. 760, 865–869 (August 1983).

36 See *Toyota Motor Sales, U.S.A., Inc. v. Heard*, 774 S.W.2d 316 (Tex. Civ. App.—Houston [14th Dist], 1989); *Gould, Inc. v. Alter Metals Co.*, No. 91C20371, 1993 WL 394765 (N.D. Ill. 1993) (not reported in F.Supp.).

37 See *Bloss v. Ford Motor Co.*, 126 A.D.2d 804 (1987).

38 See Robert W. Martin, Jr., *The Golden Age of Paralegals and Risk Managers: Acceptance, Appreciation and Shared Goals*, W. Va. Law, Nov. 1995, at 18, 19–21.

39 Norman K. Clark, *Risk Management Protects Profitability, Creates Competitive Advantage*, 43-AUG Res Gestae 33 (1999).

40 *Id* at 34.

41 See Robert W. Martin, Jr., *The Golden Age of Paralegals and Risk Managers: Acceptance, Appreciation and Shared Goals*, W. Va. Law, Nov. 1995 at 18, 19–21.

42 Clark, *supra* n. __, at 34.

43 *Id.*

Issues Facing the Profession

SUBSTANTIVE ISSUES FOR THE LEGAL ASSISTANT PROFESSION

The legal assistant profession began in the late 1960s. In 1968, the ABA Special Committee on the Availability of Legal Services recognized the use of nonlawyer services to "free a lawyer from tedious and routine detail."[1] Great strides were made in the 1970s, 1980s, and 1990s as the American Bar Association (ABA) and state bar associations began to embrace the paralegal concept and endorse it through the creation of legal assistant divisions and the adoption of rules for the utilization of legal assistants.[2] The courts have validated the role of the legal assistant as a viable member of the legal service delivery team in a law office by allowing legal assistant fees to be recovered as an essential part of attorney fees.[3] Consistent with the 1997 update to the 1994 study published by the U.S. Department of Labor's Bureau of Labor Statistics[4] that projected a 58 percent nationwide increase in legal assistant jobs between 1994 and 2005, the legal assistant profession has continued to grow in numbers and in status. (See Figure S-1.)

The government study predicted that job opportunities for legal assistants would expand not only in private law firms but also in business organizations such as corporations, insurance companies, banks, title insurance, and real estate firms.[5] The public has evidenced its support for the profession as clients have begun to demand that the law firms that they hire utilize the services of legal assistants to ensure efficient and cost-effective legal services.

Throughout this exciting, evolutionary process the profession has made substantial gains and has overcome diverse obstacles. It is ironic that now, in its fourth decade, the profession continues to wrestle with many of the same substantive issues that existed at its inception. These continuing issues have stirred strong emotions and

1. Personal and home care aides	119%	16. Special education teachers	53%
2. Home health aides	102%	17. Amusement and recreation attendants	52%
3. Systems analysts	92%	18. Correctional officers	51%
4. Computer engineers	90%	19. Operations research analysts	50%
5. Physical and corrective therapy assistants and aides	83%	20. Guards	48%
6. Electronic pagination systems workers	83%	21. Speech language pathologists and audiologists	46%
7. Occupational therapy assistants and aides	82%	22. Private detectives and investigators	44%
8. Physical therapists	80%	23. Surgical technologists	43%
9. Residential counselors	76%	24. Dental hygienists	42%
10. Human services workers	75%	25. Dental assistants	42%
11. Occupational therapists	72%	26. Adjustment clerks	40%
12. Manicurists	69%	27. Teacher aides and educational assistants	39%
13. Medical assistants	59%	28. Data processing equipment repairers	38%
14. Paralegals	**58%**	29. Nursery and greenhouse managers	37%
15. Medical record technicians	56%	30. Securities and financial service sales representatives	37%

Figure S-1 Fastest growing occupations by percentage, 1994–2005 (as compiled by the Bureau of Labor Statistics).

BUREAU OF LABOR STATISTICS, U.S. DEP'T OF LABOR, BLS BULLETIN 2472, THE EMPLOYMENT OUTLOOK: 1994–2005 (Dec. 1997). Copyright 2002 James Publishing, Inc. Reprinted courtesy of LEGAL ASSISTANT TODAY magazine. For subscription information call (800) 394-2626, or visit http://www.legalassistanttoday.com.

debate among the various stakeholders and will continue to be emotionally charged in the future. This section examines professionalization and regulation issues from the viewpoints of various stakeholders, including legal assistants, lawyers, law office managers, educators, and the general public.[6]

[1]See *Paralegal Institute, Inc. v. American Bar Association*, 475 F. Supp. 1123, 1126 (E.D.N.Y. 1979), *aff'd*, 622 F.2d 575 (2nd Cir. 1980).

[2]See *supra* Chapters 1–3.

[3]See *Missouri v. Jenkins*, 491 U.S. 274 (1989), in which the Supreme Court held that a legal fee may include a charge for legal assistant services at market rates rather than actual cost.

[4]BUREAU OF LABOR STATISTICS, U.S. DEP'T OF LABOR, BLS BULLETIN 2472, THE EMPLOYMENT OUTLOOK: 1994–2005 (Dec. 1997). This study shows the "paralegal" profession as one of the 15 fastest-growing professions in the United States. *See supra* Figure S-1. See DOL Bureau of Labor Standards Web site at http://www.bls.gov, which contains updated occupational outlook information, projections, and employment and wage estimates for paralegals and legal assistants SOC Code number 23-2011.

[5]*Id. See also* Robert Sperber, *58% Paralegal Job Increase by Year 2005*, LEGAL ASSISTANT TODAY, May/June 1997, at 24, 25.

[6]See discussion *infra* Chapter 1 (the professional identity "issue" or "crisis").

The Regulation Issue

INTRODUCTION

Closely connected to the professional identity issue, which was discussed in detail in Chapter 1, is the issue of regulation of the legal assistant profession. The proponents of regulation posit that a regulatory scheme is necessary in order to protect the public, resolve the professional identity crisis, and provide structure and order to the profession, which in turn will benefit all stakeholders. The opponents of regulation believe that a regulatory scheme is not necessary because the status quo is effective in protecting the public. They raise the concerns that a regulatory scheme will confine the profession and exclude individuals from pursuing their chosen careers. The concept of regulation of the profession is not a new idea; it has been the subject of many meetings, surveys, opinion polls, task forces, and public hearings throughout the history of the profession. Increasingly, legal assistants, legal assistant organizations, state bar committees, lawyers, educators, legislators, consumer advocate groups, and members of the public are discussing the pros and cons of various regulatory schemes. Many commentators have drawn parallels between the legal assistant profession and the legal profession, and they believe that the real question is not whether legal assistants will be regulated, but when and by whom.

WHAT TYPES OF REGULATORY SCHEMES ARE BEING CONSIDERED?

The potential regulatory schemes proposed for the paralegal profession fall into three categories, as shown in Figure 7-1: certification, registration, and licensure.

DEFINITIONS OF REGULATORY MECHANISMS

CERTIFICATION VOLUNTARY	LICENSURE MANDATORY	REGISTRATION MANDATORY
Function of private agency or association	Function of government	Function of government
Administered by leaders of the profession or career field	Administered by governmental agency with some involvement from the profession	Administered by governmental agency with some involvement from the profession
Can easily respond to changes in the field	Not as quick to respond; subject to governmental red tape	Not applicable; this process is least affected by change
Privately funded by the profession	Funding subject to governmental appropriations	Funding subject to governmental appropriations
Purpose to recognize exceptional achievement	Purpose to control entry to a career field; to protect public/consumers	Purpose to identify members of a career field
Profession established standard for all those in the career field	Governmentally established standard subject to extreme variability among the states	Governmentally established standard

Figure 7-1 NALA graph of regulation options

Copyright 2001. Reprinted with permission of the National Association of Legal Assistants, 1516 S. Boston, #200, Tulsa, OK 74119, http://www.nala.org.

- *Certification* is generally discussed as a voluntary procedure but could be designed as a mandatory procedure enforced by the certification-awarding entity. In a certification process, a (self-ordained) non-governmental entity awards "certification" to individuals who have met certain qualifications. Qualifications could include education, work experience, passing a qualifying examination, or other criteria specified by the certification awarding entity.

- *Registration* can be structured as either a voluntary or a mandatory procedure and would be a governmental function. The purpose of a registration process would be to identify the members of the profession.

- *Licensure* would be a mandatory procedure. It would be a legal condition for employment, as prescribed by legislation enacted through the exercise of police power for the protection of the public interest and administered by state agencies.

WHAT CERTIFICATION OPTIONS CURRENTLY EXIST? _____

Currently, both of the nationwide legal assistant membership organizations offer voluntary certification examinations. The National Association of Legal Assistants (NALA) offers certification to its members through the Certified Legal Assistant (CLA) examination. This examination and certification option was first available in 1976 and is recognized by many as a standard for paralegal competency testing. The NALA-CLA program was created to achieve four goals: to establish a professional standard for legal assistants, to create a mechanism for identification of individuals who meet the standard, to create a credentialing program that will strengthen and support expansion of the career field, and to offer a voluntary program of self-regulation that encourages substantive growth in the career field. According to the NALA Web site (http://www.nala.org), "As of January 2002, there are 11,164 Certified Legal Assistants and 966 Certified Legal Assistant Specialist in the United States. Over 21,000 legal assistants have participated in this program." Under the certification program provided by NALA, if a legal assistant passes the examination, the designation of "CLA" can be used after his or her name in legal-related matters. In addition, the NALA offers an examination that tests competency in certain specialty areas. If the second examination is passed, the individual can add the designation "CLAS" behind the CLA.

In 1994, the membership of the National Federation of Paralegal Associations (NFPA) voted to develop an examination that would test the competency level of experienced legal assistants and that would offer experienced legal assistants an opportunity to establish credentials and a means of validating their experience and knowledge. The reasons underlying the decision to develop and offer the examination are explained on the NFPA Web site (http://www.paralegals.org), as follows: "The overwhelmingly positive vote to develop this exam is a conscientious effort by these paralegals to direct the future of the paralegal profession and acknowledges the vital role of paralegals within the legal service industry. It is also a direct response to states that are considering regulation of the paralegal profession and are seeking a method to measure job competency."

In 1996, the NFPA developed and began to administer an examination that was originally intended as an advanced examination for senior-level legal assistants. This examination is called the Paralegal Advanced Placement Examination (PACE). The PACE has a two-tier design: The first tier is composed of general legal and ethical questions and is also available in state-specific modules; the second tier is for specialty sections. A legal assistant must pass the first tier of the exam in order to be eligible to take the second tier and must also have additional paralegal work experience. A legal assistant who passes the first tier of PACE and otherwise meets the NFPA requirements may use the designation "PACE-Registered Paralegal" or "RP."

Both the NALA and the NFPA offer the use of their examinations to state regulatory bodies as potential testing tools in a state regulatory scheme. Although these certification options are currently available, there is not agreement in the field concerning their value and there is concern that the multiple tests, multiple designations, and lack of uniformity have created more problems for the profession by adding to the confusion.

Some state bar associations and other groups have provided other certification options for legal assistants. For example, the Texas Board of Legal Specialization offers legal assistant examination in several specialty areas;[1] the Houston Paralegal Association offers credentialing for members only; the Institute of Law Clerks of Ontario, Canada (ILCO) allows its Fellow members to use a specific designation if they pass an advanced specialty course.

In addition to the existing certification examinations, the American Association for Paralegal Education (AAfPE) has appointed a task force to study the development of an entry-level legal assistant examination that would be administered to a student upon completion of a paralegal educational program and prior to entry into the profession. Such an examination, which would be administered by all educational programs nationwide, would have two benefits: First, it would provide an assessment tool for educators to determine whether their programs were accomplishing their goals; second, it would provide a uniform entry-level examination to test competencies of those entering the profession. Although some within the AAfPE support the development of such an entry-level examination, opponents argue that the profession is still too new to be able to assess competency properly; that developing an examination at this point would be too limiting to the profession; and that to add yet another examination to those already in place (the CLA exam and the PACE exam) would create even more credentialing confusion for the profession, the public, and potential employers.

HOW DO LEGAL ASSISTANTS VIEW REGULATION?

As with many of the continuing issues involving the legal assistant profession, different stakeholders have opposing opinions, and even within each group of stakeholders there are opposing opinions. For example, a nationwide opinion poll conducted by *Legal Assistant Today* asked practicing legal assistants the question, "Should paralegals be regulated?" Article 7-1 provides an analysis of the results of that poll.

Legal assistants as a group cannot agree on the regulation issue. It is a critical issue for the profession because ultimately it will control entry into the profession. Many legal assistants who have on-the-job training and experience but lack formal, academic training and education are concerned that a regulatory scheme may adversely affect their continued paralegal employment. Other legal assistants have other, more global concerns, including the cost of the regulatory process to legal assistants, employers, and to the public and the lack of need for any change to the existing system.

The NFPA has issued a position paper on the issue of regulation in which it endorses the concept of regulation that would expand the roles and responsibilities of legal assistants and allow them to perform duties beyond what they are currently permitted to perform. The NFPA has proposed a two-tier licensing program as a preferred form of regulation. Article 7-2 is a conference paper that sets forth the NFPA position on regulation, including the NFPA's Model Act For Paralegal Licensure.[2]

Should Paralegals be Regulated?

Yes, but . . . while the majority of you felt that both supervised and unsupervised parale-gals should be regulated, your opinions differed on the best way to regulate the profession without limiting responsibilities and opportunities.

Professionalism again and again echoed in your comments as the driving force behind the majority's push for regulation of paralegals who work under the direct supervision of an attorney (65%). "Certification would help to upgrade professionalism and distinguish paralegals from secretaries," said one respondent. "I believe that regulation may be a step toward gaining professional recognition by showing attorneys that a paralegal has attained at least a minimum standard of competency," said another.

Should paralegals who work under the supervision of an attorney be regulated?

Yes   65%
No   35%

Out of the 35% opposed to regulation of supervised paralegals, many view it as a threat to paralegals who acquired their professional status through on-the-job training rather than formal education. "If licensure or certification were to be imposed on the paralegal profession, there could be many paralegals who lose their jobs due to noncompliance because they have attained their professional status and competence through work expe-rience, rather than attending school," commented one opponent. Others feel that regula-tion of supervised paralegals is simply not necessary. "Since attorneys are directly responsible for the work of the paralegals they supervise, I see no need for licensure, certi-fication, or registration," said another opponent.

With agreement bordering on unanimous, 99% of you felt that paralegals who deliver services directly to the public should be regulated. "I believe they should be licensed, certi-fied, and required to carry professional liability insurance or post a bond in an amount which would reflect the type of exposure for the kind of cases they are engaged in," said one.

What form of regulation is appropriate? For the paralegal under the supervision of an attorney, it was a toss up, with 37% of you in favor of licensure and another 37% of you in favor of certification. You were more decisive about which form of regulation should apply to paralegals directly serving the public: 59% of you said licensure and another 23% favored limited licensure, with only 12% for certification. Registration was the least favored form of regulation for both supervised and unsupervised legal assistants.

Quite a few of you had your own ideas for solving the issue of regulating the profession. "If we as paralegals hope to obtain recognition as professionals in the legal community, we must submit to the same type of regulation as attorneys. That regulation will only enhance the professional status of paralegals everywhere," suggested one respondent.

Your number one choice for administrator of the regulatory program was a mixed panel (72%). Second to the mixed panel was the court system with a low 9%. A few of you sug-gested regulation via the schools. "The easiest way to handle all of this controversy is to do it through the paralegal schools—making all the courses the same, offering a curricu-lum much like law school," proposed one.

Article 7-1 Results from the July/August Legal Assistant Today opinion poll.

Should Paralegals Be Regulated? LEGAL ASSISTANT TODAY, Sept./Oct. 1992, at 90. Copyright 2002 James Publishing, Inc. Reprinted courtesy of LEGAL ASSISTANT TODAY magazine. For subscription information call (800) 394-2626, or visit http://www.legalassistanttoday.com.

Should paralegals who deliver services directly to the public (e.g., legal technicians) be regulated?

Yes   99%
No   1%

Surprisingly, men, at 71%, were more likely to favor regulation of supervised paralegals than women, at 63%. "Some form of organized regulation would legitimize and lend greater respect to the profession," said one male paralegal manager.

There are, as you alluded to in your comments, many issues to consider in the debate over regulation of paralegals. The underlying theme is, without a doubt, professionalism and improvement of the occupation. Putting it all into perspective, one respondent said, "I think some form of regulation is important, not only to protect the public, but also to protect the integrity of our profession. I think coordination with the Bar Association is important because we are partners in the legal process, not adversaries."

Article 7-1 Continued

National Federation of Paralegal Associations, Inc.

The National Federation of Paralegal Associations, Inc. (NFPA) is a non-profit, professional organization comprising 55 state and local paralegal associations throughout the United States. NFPA affirms the paralegal profession as an independent, self-directed profession which supports increased quality, efficiency, and accessibility in the delivery of legal services. NFPA promotes the growth, development, and recognition of the profession as an integral part in the legal services team.

Position on Regulation

NFPA members have adopted a position that endorses any form of regulation of paralegals as long as that form would enable paralegals to do more under the regulatory plan than they were previously permitted to do. Included with NFPA's position on regulation for paralegals working in an expanded role are provisions for:

- a preference for a two-tiered licensing plan, which constitutes mandatory regulation;
- recognition that another form of regulation, *e.g.,* certification or registration, may be appropriate in a given state;
- standards for ethics;
- standards for discipline;

Article 7-2 1999 AAfPE Conference Workshop on Regulation, October 15, 1999, Boston Park Plaza.

Nat'l Fed'n of Paralegal Ass'ns, Conference Paper, Position on Regulation, presented at the 1999 American Association for Paralegal Education Workshop on Regulation, October 15, 1999, at 1–8. Nat'l Fed'n of Paralegal Ass'ns, Model Act for Paralegal Licensure, at 286–300. Available at http://www. paralegals.org/regulation.html. Courtesy of National Federation of Paralegal Associations, Inc.

- standards for education;
- a method to assess advanced competency of paralegals;
- establishing a disciplinary process; and
- defining those tasks that may be performed by paralegals in numerous specialty areas of law.

NFPA's preferred form of regulation is licensure. NFPA has developed a Model Act for Paralegal Licensure (see attachment) that can be used by any state or other regulatory agency considering licensing. The Act encompasses a 2-tier regulatory scheme consisting of licensing and specialty-licensing. The licensing programs contain minimal educational standards and provide for an expanded role for qualifying paralegals. As part of that 2-tier regulatory scheme, the Paralegal Advanced Competency Exam (PACE) was developed (see attachment). The prerequisites to sit for the exam are a bachelor's degree, completion of a paralegal program within an institutionally accredited school, and a minimum of two years work experience. Successful completion of PACE awards the "Registered Paralegal (RP)" credential. Strict adherence to attendance of continuing education programs is mandatory to maintain the standard of excellence embodied in the credential.

NFPA's Model Code of Professional Responsibility and Guidelines For Enforcement represents another component of its regulatory system (see attachment).

Pros & Cons of Regulation as It Affects NFPA's Members:

Proper utilization of paralegal services increases the consumer's access to legal services by making legal services more available, more efficient, and less costly. However, it is extremely important that adequate protections for the public be implemented and that there be a method by which to gauge nonlawyer competence and accountability.

Regulation of the paralegal profession will provide consumers standards by which they can measure the quality of the professional help they seek. There is potential for harm to both the public and the profession when untrained and unqualified individuals identify themselves as paralegals to members of the public. This potential has become a reality in far too many instances throughout the United States and has been the subject of actions taken by State Committees on the Unlicenced Practice of Law.

Since the early 1980's, the judicial system has recognized the important role that paralegals perform in the delivery of legal services. Courts began awarding fees for paralegal services and consistently noted that if the work had not been done by paralegals, it would have been necessary for attorneys to perform the work, resulting in increased legal fees to the client. Likewise, paralegal fees are being charged to the consumer as part of fee arrangements entered into between lawyers and clients. The consumer/client is being made aware that the cost of the delivery of legal services on his or her behalf is being reduced by the utilization of paralegals performing substantive legal work as part of the legal services team. Thus, it is imperative that standards be established to ensure that while the cost of the delivery of legal services is being reduced, the quality of those services is not.

NFPA believes that paralegals can play a vital role in increasing access to justice. The public is demanding greater access to the legal system and changes to the methods by which legal services are delivered. All members of the legal profession must work together in the reformation of the legal system to meet the needs of the public. Regulation of the paralegal profession by a method that would identify and provide for an expansion of the roles and responsibilities of paralegals will provide the means by which to fulfill the unmet needs for affordable legal assistance to the public. Regulation would ensure that the highest quality of legal services are being delivered, would ensure only individuals who meet strict educational criteria be permitted to deliver legal services, would require professional accountability, and would mandate that the public be protected.

Opponents of mandatory regulation for paralegals argue that it will restrict entry into the profession by imposing educational, financial, and bureaucratic requirements that will result in a decrease in the number of paralegals and thus decrease the ability to utilize paralegal services. NFPA would submit that parallel professions, such as dental technicians and physicians assistants, have experienced no such phenomena by the implementation of regulation. Conversely, there has been an increase in the ability to attend to the public's medical needs by the utilization of the services of these professionals. NFPA believes that by raising standards and implementing means in which to ensure that every member of the legal services team has met certain requirements, the quality of legal services being delivered will be greatly enhanced.

Need to Regulate the Paralegal Profession:

The continued existence of unmet legal needs is of paramount concern to lawyers, paralegals, and nonlawyers alike. The legal community must strive to provide a greater variety of legal services in order to allow more freedom of choice, easier access to professional services for the public, and reduced costs.

The ability of unqualified and untrained individuals to use the title "paralegal" dilutes the integrity of the entire legal profession and places members of the public at risk for harm.

Increasing access to affordable assistance and protecting the public from harm have been the foundation upon which NFPA's positions on paralegal education, ethics, and regulation are based. NFPA believes that when adequate protections for the public are in place, nonlawyers can play an important role in providing affordable access to justice.

Appropriate Forum to Encourage the Developmental Process of Regulation:

NFPA agrees that nonlawyer activity is best addressed at the state level. NFPA does not currently have a policy on a preferred body to implement regulation of the paralegal profession. However, NFPA is currently researching this issue, and as more information becomes available, NFPA will be in a position to consider adopting a policy in this regard.

Through its research, NFPA has determined that most of the states have taken the position that the court system is the appropriate authority in which to regulate the practice of law. The New Jersey Report reinforces this finding. It must be noted, however, that legislative bodies also regulate the practice of law by the passage of various bills that impact that practice. State bars also have regulatory authority by virtue of their codes of professional responsibility.

NFPA's preferred position on the issue of regulation would have paralegals retaining primary control of the paralegal profession. It also supports participation by members of the legal community, paralegal educators, and the public in making policies regarding regulation of the profession.

Conclusion:

NFPA endorses regulation of the paralegal profession, and its preferred form of regulation is licensure. During the past 25 years, NFPA has taken steps to lay the necessary foundation for a regulatory scheme by developing a Model Act for Licensure, the Paralegal Advanced Competency Exam, and the Model Code of Professional Responsibility and Guidelines For Enforcement.

The Determinations on the Report of the Committee on Paralegal Education and Regulation issued by the New Jersey Supreme Court last spring urged the paralegal community and the attorney bar to work together to lay the groundwork to enhance the pro-

Article 7-2 Continued

fession. In doing so, the New Jersey Supreme Court indirectly suggested that the Conclave's participating organizations work together to form a foundation for defining, improving, and promoting the paralegal profession. Currently, the Conclave is embarking on a project to develop a uniform definition of the title "paralegal." It is hoped that this effort will lead to the development of a uniform Model Code of Ethics. Uniformity in these two areas can provide further groundwork for regulatory efforts. Other professions, such as physicians assistants, have achieved regulation and professional status with the assistance and support of their related national professional associations. NFPA hopes that the efforts of the Conclave projects will prove to be as successful.

NFPA's Model Act for Paralegal Licensure

MODEL ACT FOR PARALEGAL LICENSURE

Licensure of Paralegals is defined by NFPA as the process by which an agency or governmental entity authorizes general practice in the Paralegal profession and the use of the title "Paralegal", to individuals meeting predetermined qualifications that include: a) an educational requirement; b) the passage of a proficiency based examination; c) continuing legal education; d) adherence to a code of ethics; and e) other criteria as required by the agency or governmental entity.

This Model Act is provided for assistance in developing and drafting Paralegal Licensure legislation and reflects NFPA's policy on paralegal regulation. Each jurisdiction should modify this Model to its particular needs and requirements.

CHAPTER 1.
LICENSED PARALEGALS

CHAPTER 2.

SPECIALTY LICENSED PARALEGALS

CHAPTER 1

I. PURPOSE

The purpose of this Act, to be known as the State Licensed Paralegal Act, is to:

1. acknowledge the need for cost effective legal services;
2. recognize that some services can be provided by qualified paralegals;
3. promote professional standards of performance for those engaged in Paralegal Practice by regulating use of the title and work performed by paralegals, and by setting standards of qualification, training, education and experience for those who seek to engage in and remain in Paralegal Practice;
4. expand those duties paralegals may perform as authorized practice; and
5. provide public protection from unauthorized, unprofessional and/or unethical conduct by implementing regulatory authority over persons who purport to be paralegals.

II. DEFINITIONS

As used in this Act, unless the context otherwise requires:

1. "Act" shall mean the State Licensed Paralegal Act;
2. "Board" shall mean the State Board of Licensed Paralegal Practice;
3. "Code of Ethics" shall mean the rules of professional conduct for paralegals as adopted by the Board;
4. "Continuing Legal Education" ("CLE") shall mean any legal or other educational activity or program which is designed to maintain and improve the professional competency of practicing Paralegals and is defined and approved by the Board, and/ or is accredited CLE for attorneys;

Article 7-2 Continued

5. "Lawyer" or "Attorney" shall mean any person licensed or authorized to practice law under the laws of this state;

6. "License" shall mean authority granted by the Board under Chapter 1 of this Act to practice as a paralegal in this state, as evidenced by issuing of a license document;

7. "Licensed Paralegal" shall mean a Paralegal who holds a valid License under the provisions of this Act;

8. "Specialty License" shall mean authority granted by the Board under Chapter 2 of this Act to practice as a Paralegal with a recognized legal specialty;

9. "Paralegal"[1] shall mean a person qualified through education, training or work experience to perform substantive legal work that requires knowledge of legal concepts and is customarily, but not exclusively, performed by a lawyer. This person may be retained or employed by a lawyer, law office, governmental agency or other entity or may be authorized by administrative, statutory or court authority to perform this work;

10. "Paralegal Practice" shall mean offering to provide or providing any substantive legal service or work not prohibited by any other state or federal statute or Supreme Court Rule, the adequate performance of which requires Paralegal education, training, and experience in the application of special knowledge of legal concepts and skills to that legal service;

11. "Paralegal School" shall mean an institution of post-secondary education or program either approved by the American Bar Association or in substantial compliance with the ABA Guidelines for Paralegal Programs, that offers the minimum educational requirements necessary for qualification for licensure as determined by the Board;

12. "Person" shall mean any individual, public or private corporation, political subdivision, governmental agency, municipality, partnership, association, firm, trust, estate, or other entity whatsoever;

13. "State" shall include any state, district, commonwealth, territory, insular possession, and any other area subject to the legislative authority of the United States of America.

1. *Historically, the terms paralegal and legal assistant have been used synonymously, but recently two separate professions have emerged. For the purposes of this act, a legal assistant meeting the definition set forth herein for paralegal, shall be included within the definition.*

III. LICENSE REQUIRED—RESTRICTION ON USE OF NAME OR TITLE

1. No person shall purport to be a Paralegal, or assume the duties incident to those of a Paralegal in this State, or use the title "Paralegal", "Licensed Paralegal," or the designation "LP," or any words or letters which indicate or tend to indicate to the public that the person is a Paralegal unless the requirements of this Act are met and a valid, current License from the Board is held by such person. A Paralegal License shall be conspicuously displayed in the Paralegal's place of business or employment.

2. NON LAWYER DISCLOSURE.
   No Paralegal shall engage in the practice of law, nor shall a Paralegal represent himself/herself or allow himself/herself to be represented as a licensed attorney nor shall he/she use the title of attorney nor shall he/she associate or allow to be associated with his/her name any term which would suggest that he/she is qualified to engage in the practice of law. The Paralegal shall clearly identify himself/herself by appropriate identification as a Paralegal.

IV. STATE BOARD OF PARALEGAL PRACTICE

A. BOARD MEMBERSHIP—APPOINTMENT—TERM—OATH—QUORUM

1. There is hereby created an independent Board of state government to be known as the "State Board of Licensed Paralegal Practice," which shall promulgate and administer administrative regulations necessary to effectuate the provisions of this Act and shall have complete supervision over the administration of the provisions of this Act. The Board shall consist of seven (7) members, appointed by the Governor.

2. All seven (7) members of the Board shall be current residents of this State who have resided in this State continuously for at least six (6) months prior to appointment. Three (3) members shall be Licensed Paralegals as defined by this Act, two (2) members shall be Attorneys licensed to practice in this State and can demonstrate that they have been actively involved with the Paralegal profession as an employer of Paralegals; one (1) member of the Board shall be a paralegal educator, who is not an attorney from an institution that is either ABA approved or in substantial compliance with the ABA Guidelines for Paralegal Programs; and one (1) member shall be a citizen at large who is not associated with or financially interested in Paralegal or legal practice.

3. The Board members shall be appointed by the Governor with initial appointments for three (3) members including the citizen at large, for terms of three (3) years; two (2) members for terms of two (2) years; and two (2) members for a term of one (1) year. Thereafter, the members shall be appointed by the Governor for staggered terms of three (3) years. No member shall serve more than two (2) full consecutive terms. Initial terms shall begin on the effective date of this Act. Every unexpired term shall be filled only for the remainder of that term.

4. The initial Paralegal appointees to the Board shall not be required to be licensed, but rather shall, by their sworn statement in writing, signed, and verified, have engaged in continuous Paralegal Practice for at least ten (10) years immediately preceding their appointment, the last five (5) of which were within this State, and be eligible to be licensed under Chapter 1, Section V B of this Act. All subsequent Paralegal members shall be Licensed Paralegals as defined under this Act.

5. Whenever an appointment of a Licensed Paralegal is to be made to the Board, the Paralegal Association(s) in this State shall be requested to submit to the Governor the names of three (3) persons for each vacancy to be filled by a Licensed Paralegal. Whenever an appointment of an attorney is to be made to the Board, the Bar Association(s) in this State shall be requested to submit to the Governor the names of three (3) persons for each vacancy to be filled by an attorney. Whenever an appointment of a paralegal educator is to be made to the Board, the institutions offering ABA approved paralegal education programs in this State shall be requested to submit to the Governor the names of three (3) persons for each vacancy to be filled by a paralegal educator. Whenever an appointment of a citizen at large is to be made to the Board, the appointment shall be made at the pleasure of the Governor. All persons recommended shall be qualified for membership on the Board, and the Governor shall appoint one (1) of the three (3) recommended. Names

Article 7-2 Continued

shall be submitted to the Governor at least sixty (60) days prior to the appointment date.

6. A majority of the Board shall constitute a quorum. The concurring vote of a majority of the Board shall be considered as the action of the Board, except in matters involving suspension, revocation or reinstatement of a License, in which case, an affirmative vote of at least five (5) members of the Board shall be required.

7. The Governor may suspend or remove any member of the Board for misfeasance, malfeasance, gross inefficiency or misconduct, or upon any of the constitutional grounds upon which officers may be suspended by the Governor of this State.

8. In the event a Board member is removed, the removal shall be effective and a vacancy shall be deemed to exist as of the date of the Governor's finding. Any Board member so removed shall be entitled to appeal the removal in a court of competent jurisdiction.

9. Any vacancy which occurs on the Board for any reason shall be filled for the unexpired term according to Section (5), above.

B. MEETINGS OF THE BOARD

The Board shall meet annually for the purpose of electing from its members a President, a Vice President, and a Secretary/Treasurer. The Board shall hold at least two (2) regular meetings each year. Additional meetings may be held upon call of an officer of the Board or at the written request of any two (2) members of the Board. All meetings of the Board shall be open to the public except that the Board may hold executive sessions to prepare, approve, grade or administer examinations, or upon the request of an applicant who fails an examination, prepare a response indicating the cause of such failure; or other reasons for privacy as allowed by law.

C. POWERS AND DUTIES OF THE BOARD

1. The Board shall administer, coordinate, and enforce the provisions of this Act; evaluate the qualifications of applicants; supervise the administration of the examination of applicants, including setting, assessing and collecting reasonable fees for examination, licensing and renewals, penalties and other monies; create and maintain a log or database of persons who are issued a License; and may issue subpoenas, examine witnesses, and administer oaths, and shall conduct confidential investigations of persons engaging in practices which may violate the provisions of this Act.

2. The Board shall prescribe the time, place, method, manner, scope and subjects of examinations; provided, however, at least two (2) examination sessions shall be held each calendar year.

3. The Board shall conduct such hearings and keep such records and minutes as shall be necessary to effect an orderly dispatch of business.

4. The Board shall adopt and interpret rules and regulations, which include but are not limited to, qualifications for a license, renewal of a license, discipline and enforcement proceedings, establishment of ethical standards of practice, and may amend or repeal the same.

5. Every person who holds a License to practice as a Paralegal in this State shall be governed and controlled by the Code of Ethics adopted by the Board.

6. The conferral or enumeration of specific powers elsewhere in this Act shall not be construed as a limitation of the general powers conferred by this Act.

D. LICENSE—BOARD TO ISSUE—WHEN

The Board shall issue a License to all applicants who meet the requirements of this Act and who pay to the Board the initial licensing fee and subsequent fees and any penalties assessed as prescribed by Board regulations. The License shall be issued within sixty (60) days of completion of all requirements.

E. REVOLVING FUND FOR BOARD

All monies received by the Board under this Act shall be paid to the Secretary/Treasurer of the Board. All monies shall be deposited in the State Treasury into a separate fund for the exclusive use of the Board. No part of this fund shall revert to the general funds of this State. The Board shall be financed solely and individually from income accruing to it from fees, licenses, and other charges collected by the Board and all such monies are hereby appropriated to the Board. All salaries and expenses as approved by the Board shall be paid from the monies deposited in this fund, the amounts of which shall be set by the Board.

F. BOARD MEMBERS—COMPENSATION

Each member of the Board shall receive as compensation a reasonable amount as determined by the Board and approved by the legislature for each day or part thereof spent in the performance of official duties, including time spent in reasonable and necessary travel, and, in addition, shall be reimbursed for all reasonable and necessary travel and incidental expenses incurred in connection with said duties.

The compensation provided by this Act and all reasonable expenses incurred under this Act shall be paid from the revolving fund as set forth in Section IV (E) above. No such compensate or expense shall be a charge against the general funds of the State.

G. BOARD TO EMPLOY NECESSARY PERSONNEL

The Board shall employ, and at its discretion discharge, any employees as shall be deemed necessary, and shall outline their duties and fix their compensation. The amount of per diem mileage and expense money paid to employees shall be established by Board regulation.

H. IMMUNITY OF BOARD

Members of the Board, its agents, and employees shall be immune from suit in any action civil or criminal, which is based upon any official act or acts performed by them in good faith.

I. REQUEST TO BOARD FOR OPINION ON ACTIONS WHICH MAY CONSTITUTE UNACCEPTABLE CONDUCT

1. In order to assist a Licensed Paralegal in determining if an action would constitute unacceptable conduct under the provisions of this Act, the Licensed Paralegal may request opinion of the Board by written request submitted to the Secretary/Treasurer. The Board may, at its discretion, cause a formal written opinion to be written and distributed publicly if the request addresses an issue of such public interest that the Board's opinion on the subject is deemed desirable. Otherwise, an informal letter opinion to the requester shall become a part of the procedural record of the Board.
2. In formulating a response to a request, the Board may request an opinion from any related professional association or consumer related interest group; however, the Board shall not be bound by the supplemental opinion.

Article 7-2 Continued

3. The Board shall keep a permanent record of all the requests made and the response thereto. The Board may publish its opinions.

V. QUALIFICATIONS FOR LICENSURE

A. MANDATORY REQUIREMENTS

Any person, to be eligible for a License under this Act, shall:

1. Be eighteen (18) years of age or older; AND
2. Be of good moral character; AND
   a. Not have been convicted of a felony; AND
   b. Not have been suspended or disbarred from the practice of law in any state; AND
   c. Not have been convicted of the unauthorized practice of law in any state; AND
3. Pass a proficiency-based general legal knowledge examination for paralegals, which will include but will not be limited to ethics, general legal and State specific sections; AND
4. Not be currently under suspension, termination or revocation of a certification, registration or license to practice by a professional organization, court, disciplinary board or agency in any jurisdiction; AND
5. Meet one of the following minimum educational requirements:
   (a) Bachelor's degree in Paralegal studies, including 24 semester credit hours or equivalent of legal specialty courses; OR
   (b) Bachelor's degree in any subject PLUS 24 semester credit hours or equivalent of legal specialty courses; AND
6. PROOF OF FINANCIAL RESPONSIBILITY
   Each person licensed to practice as a Paralegal under the provisions of this act, who provides services directly to the public shall maintain professional liability insurance or other indemnity against liability for professional malpractice. The amount of insurance which each such person shall carry as insurance or indemnity against claims for professional malpractice shall be determined by the State Board of Paralegal Practice.

B. WAIVER OF REQUIREMENTS

As of the date of the enactment of this Act, paralegals with a minimum of three (3) consecutive years of experience as a Paralegal immediately prior to application for a License may waive the minimum educational requirements. Paralegals with a minimum of five (5) consecutive years of experience as a Paralegal immediately prior to application for a License may waive the minimum educational requirements, and further, will be required to take and pass only the ethics portion of the proficiency-based general legal knowledge examination. A signed and notarized Affidavit, setting forth the applicant's qualifications for a waiver under this Section, must be submitted to the Board with each request for a waiver under this Section.

The ethics section of the examination, and the character and fitness requirements, will not be waived under any circumstances.

This section shall expire three (3) years from the effective date of this Act.

VI. FEES

A. EXAMINATION FEE

Any person who qualifies under the provisions of this Act and who desires to take the proficiency-based examination shall pay to the Board a reasonable fee for the initial examination. This fee shall be determined by regulation of the Board and shall be payable at the time of application for examination.

Re-examination, as provided in this Act, shall be given to the same applicant for an additional fee, as determined by the Board, for each subject or part thereof in which the applicant is re-examined.

B. LICENSE FEE

Any person who qualifies to be Licensed Paralegal under the provisions of this Act and who desires to apply for a License in this State shall pay to the Board a reasonable fee as determined by regulation of the Board. The License shall be renewed every two years by the Board. Any renewal of the License as provided for in this Act shall be subject to payment of a reasonable renewal fee as determined by regulation of the Board. The Board may, in its discretion, reduce or waive the above fee requirements in extraordinary circumstances.

VII. APPLICATION FOR AND METHOD OF EXAMINATION

1. An applicant for a License under this Act, shall file with the Board an application setting forth the name and age of the applicant, the place or places of education, the hours accrued in a Paralegal program, or courses of study, and the applicant's legal experience. Each applicant must submit proof by certified transcript that he or she meets the minimum educational requirements as set forth in Section V. Each application shall contain a statement that it is made under oath or affirmation that its representations are true and correct to the best knowledge and belief of the person signing same, subject to the penalties of making a false affidavit or declaration. The application fee, as determined by regulation of the Board, shall accompany the application, and shall not be refundable.

2. Examinations shall be administered at least two (2) times annually as determined by the Board. Notice of each examination session shall be given at least sixty (60) days prior to the scheduled date of examination.

3. Examinations shall be written and shall consist of an ethics examination and a proficiency based general legal knowledge examination.

4. Within sixty (60) days of the examination date, the Board shall notify the applicant of the results and issue the License.

VIII. EXPIRATION DATE OF LICENSE; RENEWAL; AND CONTINUING LEGAL EDUCATION REQUIREMENTS

1. Every License initially issued to a Paralegal in this State shall expire two years after the issue date unless sooner revoked, suspended, or canceled. Subsequent Licenses issued to a Paralegal in this State shall expire two years after the issue date unless sooner revoked, suspended, or canceled. In both cases, the date of expiration shall be printed on such License.

2. All Licensed Paralegals shall, on or before the License expiration, renew his/her License by payment to the Board of a renewal fee as set by regulation of the Board, and upon submission of proof and a statement of compliance with the Continuing Legal Education requirements as made mandatory in Section VIII (3) of this chapter[2]. A notice shall be sent by certified mail to the Licensed Paralegal thirty (30) days after the renewal date if such renewal

Article 7-2 Continued

has not been made. If the Licensed Paralegal fails to meet the requirements of renewal within sixty (60) days after the renewal date, the Board shall automatically suspend the License. Notice of the automatic suspension shall be issued to the Licensed Paralegal by the Board within seven (7) days after the aforesaid sixty (60) day period expires. Notice of any suspension shall be published in a statewide legal publication. Any License thus suspended may be restored within one (1) year after the automatic suspension upon application to the Board and compliance with the requirements of renewal and the payment of a reinstatement fee as determined by regulation of the Board. Restoration shall be subject to approval by the Board.

3. Upon application for renewal, the Licensed Paralegal shall submit to the Board evidence satisfactory to the Board that such Licensed Paralegal has accumulated the required number of hours of Continuing Legal Education[2] in accordance with regulations adopted by the Board.

4. Inactive status may be granted to a Licensed Paralegal upon application to the Board and for good cause shown. Such a request will be considered only if the Licensed Paralegal is in good standing at the time of application. A paralegal may request inactive status for a period of up to two (2) years. Removal from inactive status may be granted only if application for reactivation is filed with the Board six (6) months prior to the expiration of the period of inactive status. After the license has been reactivated, the Licensed Paralegal shall have six (6) months in which to submit evidence to the Board that the Licensed Paralegal has met one quarter of the Continuing Legal Education requirement as set forth above.

2. NFPA recommends 12 hours of CLE within 2 years.

IX. COMPLAINTS—NOTICE

Upon a written complaint, verified by affidavit, of any person setting forth facts which, if proven, would constitute grounds for discipline, suspension or revocation of the License under this Act, the Board shall investigate the actions of the Licensed Paralegal. A hearing by the Board must be held within ninety (90) days of receipt by the Board of the written complaint. At least thirty (30) days prior to the date set for a hearing concerning the written complaint, the Board must serve written notice of the scheduled hearing and a copy of the written complaint on the Licensed Paralegal. Service may be accomplished by personal delivery or registered or by certified mail to the Licensed Paralegal's last known address. The Board shall direct the Licensed Paralegal to file a written answer to the complaint within twenty (20) days of receipt of the service. Failure to file such answer may result in the automatic suspension or revocation of the License prior to the scheduled hearing.

Except for automatic suspension, no License shall be revoked, suspended or reinstated without a hearing. The Board may at any time proceed against a Licensed Paralegal on its own initiative either on the basis of information contained in its own records or on the basis of information obtained through its investigation, utilizing the process described in the preceding paragraph. Such information shall be held strictly confidential until such time as a License is revoked or suspended. The Board shall keep a certified record of the proceedings of any hearing held.

X. REVOCATION OR SUSPENSION OF, OR REFUSAL TO GRANT, ISSUE, OR RENEW LICENSE

After notice and hearing as provided in this Act, the Board may revoke or suspend any License issued under this Act; may refuse to grant, issue or renew any License; may censure the Licensed Paralegal; or may place any Licensed Paralegal on probation for any one or any combination of the following causes:

(a) Fraud or deceit in procuring or attempting to procure the License;
(b) Dishonesty, fraud or willful, wanton misconduct resulting in negligence in Paralegal Practice;
(c) Deception, misrepresentation or unethical conduct in Paralegal Practice;
(d) Violation of any of the provisions of this Act or rules or regulations promulgated by the Board under this Act;
(e) Violation of any section of the Code of Ethics promulgated by the Board;
(f) Conviction of any felony or a crime involving moral turpitude under the laws of any State or of the United States;
(g) Revocation or suspension of, or refusal to grant, issue or renew the authority to practice as a Licensed Paralegal in any State, territory or foreign nation, if at least one of the grounds for that action is the same as or equivalent to of [sic] one of the grounds for the same action as set forth in this Act;
(h) Suspension or revocation of the right to practice before any State or Federal agency;
(I) Failure of a Licensed Paralegal to renew an expired License to practice within five (5) years from the expiration date of the License to practice last obtained or renewed by said Licensed Paralegal.
(j) Advertising paralegal services in a manner that is false or misleading to the public.

XI.   VIOLATIONS—PENALTIES

1. Any person who practices or offers to practice as a Licensed Paralegal without being duly certified according to this Act, or whose License had been suspended or revoked, is guilty of a crime as defined by this State.
2. Notwithstanding the existence or pursuit of any other remedy, civil or criminal, the Board may institute rules and administrative regulations, and/or orders of the Board, and maintain actions to restrain or enjoin any violation of this Act.
3. Any person who willfully makes any false representation to the Board in applying for a License under this Act is guilty of a violation of this Act and, upon notice by the Board, shall post a bond in an amount sufficient to cover any judgment, criminal penalties and interest which may be assessed by the Board in its sole discretion.
4. The Board may impose penalties for violations of this Act, in an amount determined at the Board's discretion, and may require a bond to be posted in an amount sufficient to cover any judgment, interest and penalties which may be assessed.

XII. APPEAL FROM AN ORDER OF THE BOARD

1. Any person aggrieved by an order of the Board may, within thirty (30) days after notice thereof, appeal to a court of competent jurisdiction. The court shall decide the appeal upon the certified record received from the Board and no new evidence or additional evidence shall be heard or considered by the court.
2. A party aggrieved by a final order of a court of competent jurisdiction may appeal further in accordance with the Rules of Civil Procedure.

Article 7-2 Continued

XIII. VOLUNTARY SURRENDER OF LICENSE

Any Licensed Paralegal notified of impending revocation of his/her License for violation of any of the rules or regulations of the Board or provisions of this Act, may apply to surrender his/her License in lieu of revocation.

XIV. PETITION FOR NEW LICENSE AFTER REVOCATION—PROBATION PERIOD

1. Except for those Licensed Paralegals who have been disciplined pursuant to this Act, causes for denial, probation, suspension or revocation of a License, a Licensed Paralegal whose License has been revoked or voluntarily surrendered in lieu of revocation may, after two (2) years from the effective date of the revocation order, petition the Board for a reinstatement of such License.
2. Reinstatement shall be at the sole discretion of the Board. Reinstatement shall not be issued unless the applicant submits evidence satisfactory to the Board that the applicant meets the requirements of this Act and is able to resume Paralegal Practice.
3. If the Board reinstates such License under the circumstances described in this section, the Licensed Paralegal shall be under probation for a period of not less than two (2) years nor more than five (5) years as determined by the Board. Any subsequent violation during the probation period shall result in automatic revocation of the License.

XV. RECIPROCITY

1. The Board may, upon application and payment of a fee to be established by regulation of the Board, issue a License to persons who hold a certificate of qualification or valid License issued to them by proper authority of any state which has licensing and educational standards equal to or greater than this State, as set forth herein. Such persons may be Licensed without examination upon payment of the regular application fee, the successful completion of the written ethics examination, and meeting the character and fitness requirements as described by this Act.
2. The Board may promulgate regulations governing the matter of reciprocity with other States.

CHAPTER 2

I. INCORPORATION BY REFERENCE

All Sections of Chapter 1 shall apply to Specialty Licensed Paralegals and are incorporated herein by reference, and 1 shall be supplemented with additional requirements as provided in this Chapter 2.

II. SUPPLEMENTAL DEFINITION

As used in the Act unless the context otherwise requires:
1. "Specialty Licensed Paralegal" shall mean a Paralegal who holds a valid Specialty License under the provisions of this Chapter.

III. SPECIALTY LICENSE REQUIRED—RESTRICTION ON USE OF NAME OR TITLE

No person shall purport to be a Specialty Licensed Paralegal or assume the duties incident to those of a Specialty Licensed Paralegal in this State, or use the title "Specialty Licensed

Paralegal" or any words or letters which designate or tend to designate to the public that the person is a Specialty Licensed Paralegal unless the requirements of this Act are met and a valid, current Specialty License from the Board is held. A Specialty Paralegal License shall be conspicuously displayed in the Paralegal's place of business or employment.

IV. SUPPLEMENTAL QUALIFICATIONS FOR LICENSURE

Any person applying for a Specialty Paralegal License, under this Act, shall:

1. Meet the requirements of Chapter 1, Section V; AND
2. Have been a Licensed Paralegal for a minimum of four (4) years; AND
3. Pass a Specialty examination.

As of the date of the enactment of this Act, a Paralegal qualifying for licensure under Chapter 1, Section V(8) may waive the requirement to have been a Licensed Paralegal for four (4) years and may sit for Specialty examination. This section shall be applicable for a period of four (4) years following the effective date of this Act.

V. APPLICATION FOR AND METHOD OF EXAMINATION—ADDITIONAL REQUIREMENTS

1. An applicant for a Specialty License under this Act, shall include in the application filed with the Board, proof that the Paralegal has met the requirements of Chapter 2, Section IV, above.
2. Specialty License examinations shall consist of a written examination of such specialty area of law as to test in a satisfactory manner the qualifications of the applicant to specialize in the legal area for which the license is sought.
3. Under no circumstances shall the Specialty License examinations described in Chapter 2, Section V(2) be waived.

Article 7-2 Continued

The NALA advocates professional self-regulation through voluntary certification instead of licensure. Article 7-3 is a conference paper that sets forth the NALA position on licensure and governmental regulation of paralegals.[3]

Some stakeholders, including consumer advocacy groups, believe that any of the proposed regulation schemes would erect barriers that would restrict the public access to legal services. Article 7-4, which was published in the American Bar Association Journal, contains contrasting viewpoints on licensing.

Increasingly, state legislatures are becoming interested in the regulatory issue.[4] For example, in 1991 the Minnesota legislature considered the creation of a licensure or regulatory scheme for legal assistants and asked the Minnesota Supreme Court to appoint a committee to study the desirability of establishing a regulatory system. The committee concluded that since the practice of law was already a regulated profession, licensing legal assistants was not necessary. In July 1998, the New Jersey Supreme Court Committee on Paralegal Education and Regulation issued a report that, among other things, included recommendations for utilization of legal assistants in the delivery of

Issues Related to Licensure and Governmental Regulation of Paralegals
A Presentation to:
The American Association for Paralegal Education
Annual Conference
October 15, 1999
Boston, Massachusetts
Vicki Voisin, CLAS, President
National Association of Legal Assistants
Tulsa, Oklahoma
www.nala.org

Issues Related to Licensure and Governmental Regulation of Paralegals

Introduction

In July, 1998, the New Jersey Supreme Court Committee on Paralegal Education and Regulation issued a report which sets forth several recommendations concerning the attorneys' use of paralegals in the delivery of legal services. The report sets forth a system of licensure for paralegals. It is apparent from the report that the purpose of the licensing procedure is to identify individuals who meet a set of educational requirements and who pass a written examination on the subject of ethics and to qualify them to work as paralegals under the supervision of licensed attorneys. The duties and responsibilities of licensed paralegals would be no different than they are today; and, absent a licensed paralegal, any employee may perform these duties although they may not use the title "paralegal." Further, the licensure requirements establish rules and regulations concerning the employer/employee relationship of attorneys with assistants.

NALA submitted a statement to the court which stated that the association cannot support the proposed system of licensure for several reasons[1]. Among these reasons:

1. There is no demonstrated public need to regulate paralegals.
2. This procedure would increase the cost of paralegals to employers.
3. This procedure would increase the cost of legal services to the public.
4. This procedure does not allow for the growth of the paralegal profession nor does it encourage the utilization of paralegals in the delivery of legal services.

In a report dated May 24, 1999, the New Jersey Supreme Court issued its determination regarding the committee's recommendations. Essentially, the Court found that regulation of paralegals by Court-directed licensing is not necessary. It stated:

> regulation of paralegals should be conducted in a form that best serves the needs of the public, the bar, and the Judiciary . . . the Court has concluded that direct oversight of paralegals is best accomplished thorough attorney supervision.

Article 7-3 Voisin, Issues Relating to Licensure

Vicki Voisin, Conference Paper, Issues Related to Licensure and Governmental Regulation of Paralegals, *presented at the 1999 American Association for Paralegal Education Workshop on Regulation, October 15, 1999, at 1–18. Copyright 2001, National Association of Legal Assistants, 1516 S. Boston, #200, Tulsa, OK 74119; http://www.nala.org. Reprinted with permission.*

The Court, however, found that a system of professional certification of legal assistants and paralegals may be helpful to the legal community in identifying and recognizing competent professionals.

The issues of licensure of a profession are very complicated and rest on two factors: 1) a person's fundamental right to engage in his or her chosen profession; and 2) protection of the health, welfare and safety of the public. Often, in today's discussions concerning paralegal licensure, the needs of members of the profession are confused with the needs of the public. Some view licensure as the same as establishment of professional standards—this is a misstatement. This article will present the issue of licensure from a legislature's point of view and will address the questions of what licensure is, why it is created, and the criteria for licensure used by legislatures to evaluate licensing proposals.

There are at least 12 states which include information in the statutes about what is required in order to establish a licensing procedure.[2] The states and statutes reviewed for this article are as follows:

California	Title 2, Div. 2, Part 1, Chapter 1.5, Article 8. Legislative oversight of state board formation and licensed professional practice. Secs. 9148.4, 9148.10.
New Mexico	Ch. 12, Article 9A. Sunrise Act. Secs.12-9A-1-12-9A-6.
Colorado	24-34-104.1 General assembly sunrise review of new regulation of occupations and professions
South Dakota	Ch. 36-1A
Florida	Title III. 11.62 Legislative review of proposed regulation of unregulated functions.
Vermont	Title 26. Ch. 57 Review of licensing statutes, boards and commissions. Sec. 3105.
Georgia	Title 43. Ch. 1A. Occupational regulation legislation review
Virginia	Title 54.1, Subtitle 1, Chapter 1. Sec. 54.1-100-54.1-311.
Hawaii	Division 1, Title 4, Ch. 26H Hawaii Regulatory licensing reform act
Washington	Title 18. Ch. 18.118 Regulation of business professions
Maine	Title 32, Ch. 1-A, Subchapter II. Sunrise review procedures. Sec. 60-J-60L
Wisconsin	Criteria for evaluating need to draft a regulatory legislative proposal of the State of Wisconsin Dept.of Regulation & Licensing

See also Revised Statutes of Nebraska Annotated, Chapter 71. Public Health and Welfare; Article 62. Nebraska Regulation of Health Professions Act. Although this statute deals specifically with the regulation of health professions, its review is instructive.

The Pennsylvania legislature has also looked at the broad question of regulating occupations. Consider the following from a report of the Committee on Professional Licensure, House of Representatives of the State of Pennsylvania, issued in 1991 (House Bill 1401, Introduced May 15, 1991)

. . . Requiring certain information to be solicited in connection with the consideration of legislation by the general assembly; and providing for the licensing, registration, or certification of members of an occupation or profession.

Provides that

(1) Regulation should be imposed on occupation or profession only when necessary to the protection of the public interest.

Article 7-3 Continued

(2) Establishing the system for reviewing the necessity of regulating an occupation or profession prior to enacting laws for such regulation will better enable it to evaluate the need for the regulation and to determine the least restrictive regulatory alternative consistent with public interest.

(3) Expanding the scope of practice of an occupation or profession necessitates the systematic review of the impact of the proposed expansion on health, safety and welfare of the public. Neither house of the general assembly shall vote on any legislation which proposes the regulation of any unregulated professional or occupational group or which proposes to expand the scope of practice of any regulated professional or occupational group until the legislative budget and finance committee has submitted to the committee of the house in which the legislation originated a sunrise evaluation report covering 24 items.

Licensure Defined

Several of the above listed statues included definitions of licensure, as follows:

Georgia: 43-1A-3. (6) "License," "licensing," or "licensure" means authorization to engage in a business or profession which would otherwise be unlawful in the state in the absence of authorization. A license is granted to those individuals who meet prerequisite qualifications to perform prescribed business or professional tasks, who use a particular title, or who perform those tasks and use a particular title.

South Dakota: Chapter 36-1A-4 For the purposes of this chapter, licensure is a process by which a board grants to an individual, who has met certain prerequisite qualifications, the right to perform prescribed professional and occupational tasks and to use the title of the profession or occupation.

Washington: RCW 18.118.020 (7) "License," "licensing," and "licensure" mean permission to engage in a business profession which would otherwise be unlawful in the state in the absence of the permission. A license is granted to those individuals who meet prerequisite qualifications to perform prescribed professional tasks and for the use of a particular title.

In summary, licensure grants a practitioner the legal right to work in his or her chosen occupation, by law, and restricts this right to only those persons who hold a license. Licensure is a mandatory legal condition for employment, generally enacted by legislation and administered by state agencies.

Why License an Occupation—Legislative Intent

The driving force behind a legislature to take action to license a profession is the health, welfare, and safety of the public. Consider the following statements of intent from the statutes:

Colorado 24-34-104.1(1) the general assembly finds that regulation should be imposed only on an occupation or profession only when necessary for the protection of the public interest.

Florida. 11.62. (2) It is the intent of the legislature:

(a) That no profession or occupation be subject to regulation by the state unless the regulation is necessary to protect the public health, safety, or welfare from significant and discernible harm or damage and that the police power of the state be exercised only to the extent necessary for that purpose; and

(b) That no profession or occupation be regulated by the state in a manner that unnecessarily restricts entry into the practice of the profession or occupation or inversely affects the availability of the professional or occupational services to the public.

Hawaii Code Annotated 26H-2, 26H-5 and 26H-6

26H-2 Policy: The legislature hereby adopts the following policies regarding the regulation of certain professions and vocations:

(1) The regulation and licensing of profession and vocations shall be undertaken only when reasonably necessary to protect the health, safety, or welfare of consumers of the services; the purpose of regulation shall be the protection of the public welfare and not that of the regulated profession or vocation;

Vermont Sec.3105 Criteria and standards. (a) A profession or occupation shall be regulated by the state only when:

1. It can be determined that the unregulated practice of the profession or occupation can clearly harm or endanger the health, safety, or welfare of the public, and the potential for the harm is recognizable and not remote or speculative;
2. The public can reasonably be expected to benefit from an assurance of initial and continuing professional abilities; and
3. The public cannot be effectively protected by other means.

Virginia. 54.1.100 Regulations of professions and occupations.

The right of every person to engage in any lawful profession, trade or occupation of his choice is clearly protected by both the Commonwealth of the Va. Code Ann.@54.1-100 (1998) United States and the Constitution of the Commonwealth of Virginia. The Commonwealth cannot abridge such rights except as a reasonable exercise of its police powers when it clearly found that such abridgment is necessary for the preservation of the health, safety and welfare of the public. No regulation shall be imposed upon any profession or occupation except for the exclusive purpose of protecting the public interest when:

1. The unregulated practice of the profession or occupation can harm or endanger the health, safety or welfare of the public, and the potential for harm is recognizable and not remote or dependent upon tenuous argument;
2. The practice of the profession or occupation has inherent qualities peculiar to it that distinguish it from ordinary work and labor;
3. The practice of the profession or occupation requires specialized skill or training and the public needs, and will benefit by, assurances of initial and continuing professional and occupational ability; and
4. The public is not effectively protected by other means.

These statements demonstrate the legislatures' views toward protection of the public as well as the use of licensing as a last resort. For example, the Florida and Virginia statues both refer to the police powers of the state—strong language demonstrating how reluctant a state may be to license an occupation.

Criteria to Determine Whether an Occupation Should be Licensed

Each of the statutes defined some criteria against which applications for licensure are measured. The criteria are quite similar from statute to statute. The following from the State of Wisconsin is typical of this criteria and the information needed to substantiate each:

Article 7-3 Continued

Criterion 1. Regulation should address the single purpose of promoting the general welfare of the consumer of services.
1. Has the public been harmed because this profession/service entity has not been regulated?
2. What constitutes harm? Please list examples.
3. To what extent has the public's economic well-being been harmed? Is the harm wide-spread or isolated? Please explain.
4. Is potential harm recognizable or remote?
5. To what can the harm be attributed?
    a. Lack of knowledge
    b. Lack of skills
    c. Lack of ethics
    d. Other
6. Can potential users of the service be expected to possess the knowledge needed to properly evaluate the quality of the service? If no, why not?

Criterion 2. The functions and responsibilities of individuals working in the occupation shall require independent judgment and action based on a substantive body of skill and knowledge.
The questions to be raised in regard to this criterion have to do with autonomy and accountability.
1. What is the extent of autonomy of work?
2. Is there a high degree of independent judgment required?
3. How much skill and experience is required in making these judgments?
4. Do practitioners customarily work on their own or under supervision?
5. If supervised, by whom, how frequently, where, and for what purpose?
6. If the person is infrequently, or unsupervised, to whom is he/she accountable? To whom is the supervisor accountable?

Criterion 3. The public cannot be effectively protected by means other than regulation.
1. Can existing problems be handled through strategies on the part of the applicant group?
    a. Has the occupational group established a code of ethics? To what extent has it been accepted and enforced?
    b. Has the group established complaint handling procedures for resolving disputes between practitioners and the consumer? How effective has this been?
    c. Has a non-governmental certification program been established to assist the public in identifying qualified practitioners?
2. Could the use of existing laws or existing standards solve problems?
    a. Use of unfair and deceptive trade practice laws.
    b. Use of civil laws such as injunctions, cease and desist orders, etc.
    c. Use of criminal laws such as prohibition against cheating, false pretense, deceptive advertising, etc.

Criterion 4. Benefits of regulation should outweigh potentially adverse effects.
1. What are the potential benefits?
    a. How will regulation help the public identify qualified services?
    b. How will regulation assure that practitioners are competent?

    c. What assurance will the public have that the individuals credentialed by the state have maintained their competence?

    d. How will complaints of the public against the practitioners be handled?

    e. Will licensure increase the availability of services and decrease costs?

    f. What is the impact of this action on consumer choice? Are choices increased, or maintained, or limited?

2. What are the potential adverse effects?

    a. Will the occupational group control the supply of practitioners?

    b. Will regulation act as an entry barrier?

    c. Will regulation prevent the optimal utilization of personnel?

    d. Will regulation increase the cost of services to the consumer? Consider: license fees, bonding costs, record keeping.

    e. Will stringent and/or additional educational requirements increase the cost of entry into the occupation and subsequently increase the cost of the services?

    f. Will regulation decrease availability of practitioners?

3. Do the benefits more than compensate for potentially adverse effects?

How do legislatures look at this information.

Attached to this article is a chart furnished by the California Department of Consumer Affairs which is used to rank the need for regulation, from low to high, based on the information provided to substantiate each criterion. The chart lists each criterion and gives examples of findings that would lead to a conclusion of a low need, or a high need. This chart is quite informative of the views and concern of the legislature concerning governmental regulation of a profession. Note that in the first criterion the legislature is not persuaded at all by a request which only demonstrates that licensure procedure is sought only by the profession, not the public. This leads us to a more general discussion of licensure and the needs of the paralegal profession.

Licensure and the Regulated Profession—What does this mean?

Licensure allows one to demonstrate proficiency for entry into a profession, with such minimal competency defined legislatively. Because the license is the same thing as a permission to gain employment in a certain occupation, there is tremendous pressure to develop the licensing program to address or define the lowest level of professional competence. In addition, among the statutes reviewed for this article, many differentiate the forms of regulation, from registration to certification to licensure. The statutes further state that the form of regulation chosen must be the least restrictive, consistent with the public interest. Not only, then, are legislatures pressured to define the lowest level of competence, they are encouraged to use the least restrictive form of regulation, if regulation is determined to be needed.

    A license merely controls entry into a profession, it does not establish professional standards, nor is that its purpose. This is an important distinction to keep in mind. It requires careful consideration of the purpose of a licensure program before deciding if it is in the best interest of the profession. In fact, because licensure programs are created to serve the public, the rules and regulations which drive the licensure process are developed with the needs of the public in mind, not the needs of the profession. In instances where these needs may compete, the public will be served. Closely related to this point is the fact that licensure programs are the responsibility of government or the agency overseeing the

Article 7-3 Continued

process, **not** the profession. A licensure program may or may not include the involvement or even the interests of members of the profession.

The requirements and procedures for obtaining a license vary from state to state. Therefore, unless some sort of reciprocity agreement has been created between states, it may not be easy for a professional licensed in one state to obtain a license in another. This fact is among the reasons this issue has nationwide implications for the paralegal profession.

A licensing procedure—a statute—does not ensure competence or ethical performance. For example, NALA's files are full of newspaper articles describing cases in which individuals are charged with the unauthorized practice of law and where states are considering legislation to toughen UPL penalties. There is no reason to believe the licensure of legal assistants would have any effect on the practices of these individuals.

Protecting the Title: Legal Assistant or Paralegal

Some view licensing as the only means available to a profession to protect the title. However, a licensing procedure is not always necessary to accomplish this. Many states have taken some sort of action to define the terms "paralegal" and "legal assistant" through case law, supreme court rule, model guidelines for utilization of legal assistants adopted by the states, or ethical opinions. These documents form the basis for challenging one's use of the term incorrectly.

In 1996, the Supreme Court in the State of South Carolina heard a case in which one of the issues was whether the defendant had a first amendment right to advertise himself as a paralegal (*State v. Robinson*, Opinion Number 24391; filed March 18, 1996). The defendant was operating a business which consisted of the delivery of legal services without attorney supervision. The defendant contended that advertising himself as a paralegal is not false since there are no regulations requiring any qualifications to be a paralegal in the state. The Supreme Court found the following:

> This court has addressed the function of a paralegal <u>In re: Easler</u>, 275 S.C. 400, 272 S.E.2d 32 (1980):

> Paralegals are routinely employed by licensed attorneys to assist in the preparation of legal documents such as deeds and mortgages. The activities of a paralegal do not constitute the practice law as long as they are limited to work of a preparatory nature, such as legal research, investigation, or the composition of legal documents, which enable the licensed attorney-employer to carry a given matter to a conclusion through his own examination, approval or additional effort.

> <u>Id</u>. at 400, 272 S.E.2d at 32–33. While there are not regulations dealing specifically with paralegals, requiring a paralegal to work under the supervision of a licensed attorney ensures control over his or her activities by making the supervising attorney responsible. *See* Rule 5.3 of the Rules of Professional Conduct, Rule 407 SACR (supervising attorney is responsible for work of nonlawyer employees). Accordingly, to legitimately provide services as a paralegal, one must work in conjunction with a licensed attorney. Robinson's advertisement as a paralegal is false since his work product is admittedly not subject to the supervision of a licensed attorney.

> Further, the ad's statement, "If your civil rights have been violated—call me," is an unlawful solicitation. It is unlawful for one who is not a licensed attorney to solicit the cause of another person. S.C. Code Ann. Sec. 40-5-310 (Supp. 1994). We find Robinson should be enjoined from advertising himself as a paralegal or soliciting the representation of others.

Is the New Jersey Situation Unique?

New Jersey is not the only state to have considered this matter. In 1995, a representative of the Hawaii Department of Consumers and Consumer Affairs spoke with members of the Hawaii Paralegal Association about procedures for regulating a profession. It was reported the representative stated that professional regulation hinges upon whether consumers need to be protected from abuses by unscrupulous persons practicing in a particular profession. In Hawaii there was no demonstrated public need for regulation of paralegals.

The Minnesota legislature, in 1991, asked the Supreme Court to appoint a committee to study the feasibility of the delivery of legal services by those who would be called specialized legal assistants. The study was to include consideration of a licensure procedure. In March, 1994, the committee issued its report and discussed the following concerning the licensure of the specialized legal assistants as summarized below:

> The Minnesota statutes provided that no regulation shall be imposed upon any occupation unless retained for the safety and well-being of the citizens of the state. This statute indicates that the purpose of a professional license requirement is to protect the citizens of the state by limiting entry into a profession to those people who demonstrated that they possess at least a minimum level of skill and knowledge related to the practice of the profession. License requirements are intended to protect the service consuming public from harm that can be caused by unqualified practitioners.
>
> The report concluded that licensing legal assistants does not fit into the analytical framework created by this statute because the practice of law is already a regulated profession. Further, the license requirement would increase the cost of licensed people's services by limiting the number of people who can perform a task. The committee also identified the fact that a licensure mechanism for legal assistants would require the creation of a regulatory system similar to that for lawyers, with the same expense and complexity. Creating this would only be justified if it would result in significantly cheaper costs to the consumers of legal services without unacceptable risk. It is not apparent to the committee how independent licensure would achieve these goals. The cost of doing business alone would be no different than those costs of lawyers and the fees charged by nonlawyers to remain in business would be unaffordable for many people.

Even in a situation in which nonlawyers would deliver legal services directly to the public, the report did not find any benefit in creating a licensure or regulatory scheme for these individuals.

Options

As demonstrated in this short summary, licensing procedures are complicated, designed with the public in mind, and with regard to professions, allow a licensed person to do something—perform some function that cannot be performed by an unlicensed person. There are many ways in which an occupation can establish standards for itself.

In is [sic] May 24 report, the New Jersey Supreme Court encouraged the consideration of proposals that would involve the voluntary certification of individuals to provide a means of recognizing qualified paralegals.

Those professions that do not offer services or products directly to the public often embrace a certification procedure. Certification programs are generally conducted by pro-

Article 7-3 Continued

fessional associations and are widely recognized by courts and state and federal agencies as valid programs which identify competent professionals. The fact that certification programs are voluntary, not mandatory, does not lessen the impact of these programs. Certification programs must operate under specific rules and requirements designed to insure the fairness and objectivity of the programs as well as the reliability and validity of the examination itself. It is generally agreed throughout the literature that certification programs are more flexible, more responsive to the career field, and establish standards for a profession that licensing programs are unable to do. Like licensing programs, certification programs generally include an element of discipline of certified individuals who do not adhere to professional standards. In short, certification programs have all the perceived benefits in terms of professional standards—and none of the governmental red tape.

Some state associations have recognized the benefit of voluntary certification processes for legal assistants. This includes the efforts of the California Alliance of Paralegal Associations in establishing the California Advanced Specialist program, the Louisiana State Paralegal Association in establishing the Louisiana Certified Paralegal program, and Florida Legal Assistants, Inc., in establishing the Certified Florida Legal Assistant which use the CLA as the basis of their programs. The State Bar of Texas, Legal Assistants Division has also developed a certification process.

Other states have approached this by establishing guidelines and rules that attorneys may use in the utilization of legal assistants. In addition to providing this guidance, the Court rule may also be helpful in governing the use of the phrases "paralegal" and "legal assistant" as found in the South Carolina case. Bar associations in several states have taken the lead in developing these guidelines and many have worked with state legal assistant organizations. Guidelines for the utilization of legal assistants have been established in the following states. Those states whose guidelines are adopted as a Supreme Court Rule or by a Supreme Court case are indicated with an (*). Those states whose guidelines are those of state legal assistant organizations are indicated with an (**):

California**	Maine	Oklahoma*
Colorado	Michigan	Oregon
Connecticut	Minnesota	Pennsylvania
Florida	Mississippi	Rhode Island*
Georgia	Missouri	South Carolina
Hawaii	Montana	South Dakota*
Idaho	Nevada	Texas
Illinois	New Hampshire*	Utah
Indiana*	New Jersey**	Virginia
Iowa*	New Mexico*	Washington
Kansas	New York	West Virginia
Kentucky*	North Carolina	
Louisiana**	North Dakota*	

Model guidelines have also been developed by the American Bar Association and the National Association Legal Assistants. As with the discussion concerning professional certification and licensure, guidelines and Supreme Court rules are an attractive way to deal with the issues of professional regulation because they may be drafted and amended by those involved in the legal profession—not by the government or a legislature. Further, guidelines and Supreme Court rules are more directly related to a Supreme Court's jurisdiction over those licensed to practice law than attempting to govern those who are not licensed and are, essentially, members of another profession.

Summary

The issues of professional regulation through creation of a statute, through self-regulatory mechanisms or through Supreme Court rule are complex matters. The decision to embrace one scheme over another rests on what is best for the profession from a global perspective based on research and knowledge, and not on individual experience. Critical in the decision process is the perception of the future growth and development of the career field. Throughout the United States, the utilization of legal assistants has become accepted, acceptable, important and, indeed, necessary to the efficient practice of law. Any system of regulation should be based on this recognition and acceptance of the legal assistant profession and provide for its continued growth.

One final observation—why does this matter? The profession continues to debate the issue of licensure, often to the detriment of the growth of our career field. Within these debates, the issues of the perceived need for professional recognition are confused with the purposes of governmental regulation. The issue of an individual's responsibility to advance himself within his chosen career field is confused with the perception of licensing as a mechanism which will ensure job opportunities. The issue of protecting the profession is confused with the issue of protecting the public. This confusion of issues has led us into non-productive, time wasting debates. Let us be smart about our direction and the growth of our profession—let us choose a path for the career field that is definable and achievable, controlled by our profession with its growth as the driving force.

Vicki Voisin, CLAS
President, National Association
of Legal Assistants

December 14, 1998
Updated: August 25, 1999

Table 1. Criteria Rating Form

This is an example of legislative analysis of each criterion for establishing a licensing process from the California Dept. of Consumer Affairs. The chart lists each criterion to be met to establish a licensing procedure, and gives examples of findings that would lead to a conclusion of a low need, or high need.

Criteria	Little need for regulation	High need for regulation
Unregulated practice of this occupation will harm or endanger the public health, safety, and welfare	Regulation sought only by practitioners. Evidence of harm lacking or remote. Most effects secondary or tertiary. Little evidence that regulation would correct inequities.	Significant public demand. Patterns of repeated and severe harm, caused directly by incompetent practice. Suggested regulatory pattern deals effectively with inequity. Elements of protection from fraudulent activity and effective practice are included.

Article 7-3 Continued

Criteria	Little need for regulation	High need for regulation
Existing protections available to the consumer are insufficient	Other regulated groups control access to practitioners. Existing remedies are in place and effective. Clients are generally groups or organizations with adequate resources to seek protection.	Individual clients access practitioners directly. Current remedies are ineffective or nonexistent.
No alternatives to regulation will adequately protect the public	No alternatives considered. Practice unregulated in most other states. Current system for handling abuses adequate.	Exhaustive search of alternatives find them lacking. Practice regulated elsewhere. Current system ineffective or nonexistent.
Regulation will mitigate existing problems	Little or no evidence of public benefit from regulation. Case not demonstrated that regulation precludes harm. Net benefit does not indicate need for regulation.	Little or no doubt that regulation will ensure consumer protection. Greatest protection provided to those who are least able to protect themselves. Regulation likely to eliminate current existing problems.
Practitioners operate independently, making decisions of consequence	Practitioners operate under the supervision of another, regulated profession or under the auspices of an organization which may be held responsible for services provided. Decisions made by practitioners are of little consequence.	Practitioners have little or no supervision. Decisions made by practitioners are of consequence, directly affecting important consumer concerns.
Functions and tasks of the occupation are clearly defined	Definition of competent practice unclear or very subjective. Consensus does not exist regarding appropriate functions and measures of competence.	Important occupational functions are clearly defined, with quantifiable measures of successful practice. High degree of agreement regarding appropriate functions and measures of competence.
The occupation is clearly distinguishable from other occupations that are already regulated	High degree of overlap with currently regulated occupations. Little information given regarding the relationships among similar occupations.	Important occupational functions clearly different from those of currently regulated occupations. Similar non-regulated groups do not perform critical functions included in his occupation's practice.

Criteria	Little need for regulation	High need for regulation
The occupation requires possession of knowledges, skills and abilities that are both teachable and testable	Required knowledge undefined. Preparatory programs limited in scope and availability. Low degree of required knowledge or training. Current standard sufficient to measure competence without regulation. Required skills objectively determined; not teachable and/or not testable.	Required knowledge clearly defined. Measures of competence both objective and testable. Incompetent practice defined by lack of knowledge, skill or ability. No current standard effectively used to protect public interest.
Economic impact of regulation is justified	Economic impact not fully considered. Dollar and staffing cost estimates inaccurate or poorly done.	Full analysis of all costs indicate net benefit of regulation is in the public interest

NATIONAL ASSOCIATION OF LEGAL ASSISTANTS

LICENSURE OF PARALEGALS

The National Association of Legal Assistants has been monitoring the issue of governmental regulation of paralegals by licensure programs since the association's inception in 1975. Most recently, NALA submitted an extensive report to the New Jersey Supreme Court in response to a report and recommendations of the Supreme Court Committee on Paralegal Education and Regulation outlining the association's view of this complex issue.

This report and supplemental information appear on the NALA web site at www.nala.org.

NALA Position on Governmental Regulation of Paralegals

Quite simply, licensure grants a practitioner a legal right to work in his or her chosen occupation, by law, and restricts this right to only those persons who hold a license. Licensure is a mandatory legal condition for employment, generally enacted by legislation and administered by state agencies.

There is a general lack of understanding regarding the subject of occupational licensure and, as a result, many are misled regarding the capabilities of a licensing mechanism and how it may affect the profession from a positive, growth standpoint. Statutes in at least 12 states define information that is required before a state will establish a licensing mechanism. Within these statues [sic] are statements of legislative intent—statements that illuminate the reasons a legislature will enact a licensing procedure. Examples of these statements are:

Article 7-3 Continued

> The general assembly finds that regulation should be imposed only on an occupation or profession only when necessary for the protection of the public interest.
>
> The regulation and licensing of professions and vocations shall be undertaken only when reasonably necessary to protect the health, safety, or welfare of consumers of the services; the purpose of regulation shall be the protection of the public welfare and not that of the regulated profession or vocation.

Foremost in the discussion of this subject is the identification of this as a very complex and complicated issue which rests on two factors: 1) a person's fundamental right to engage in his or her chosen profession, and 2) protection of health, welfare and safety of the public. Licensing mechanisms exist to control entry into a profession—no more, no less. They do not exist as professional recognition programs nor do they exist to protect the licensed profession, as stated in the above quote.

Unless an occupation involves the delivery of services directly to the public, without supervision by a licensed profession, or there is some compelling public interest in establishing a licensing procedure, a legislature will most likely dismiss a licensing procedure.

Pros and Cons

There are very few pros involved in the governmental regulation of an occupation that cannot be accomplished in some other fashion. The cons to a licensing procedure for the legal assistant profession, as it is presently defined, are overwhelming: 1) there is no demonstrated public need; 2) the procedure would increase the cost of paralegals to employers; 3) the procedure would increase the cost of legal services to the public, and, 4) the procedure does not allow for the growth of the paralegal profession nor does it encourage the utilization of paralegals in the delivery of legal services.

As stated in the Administrative Determination of the New Jersey Supreme Court, the professional credentialing programs of professional associations are the appropriate means to identify and recognize competent practitioners. In its determination, the Court further stated that paralegal oversight is best conducted by the supervising attorneys who are responsible for all legal work done by paralegals.

Summary

Throughout the United States, the utilization of legal assistants has become accepted, acceptable to the courts, important to the public, and indeed, necessary to the efficient practice of law. Any system of regulation should be based on this recognition and acceptance and provide for the continued growth of the paralegal profession.

---

[1] NALA supported Recommendation 6 of the committee which suggests the Supreme Court modify the Rules of Professional Conduct to incorporate ethics and performance standards governing New Jersey lawyers in using the services of paralegals. This recommendation essentially asks the Court to provide more guidance to attorneys in the utilization of paralegals.

[2] The Utah legislature is considering similar legislation. Special thanks to Mary Catherine Perry, Office of Legislative Research and General Counsel, for providing this information to NALA.

Legal Assistants
Has the time arrived for state-by-state licensing?

The paralegal profession, which continues to grow in numbers and status, may soon be approaching a watershed. At its annual meeting in September, the National Federation of Paralegal Associations voted to promote licensing as the preferred form of regulation for legal assistants who work under the supervision of attorneys.

The endorsement came with a caveat—that licensing ought to expand, and not limit, a paralegal's duties.

Hope Viner Samborn, a lawyer and an instructor at the Loyola University Institute for Paralegal Studies in Wilmette, Ill., believes that licensing is the best way to ensure professionalism and competence.

Attorney supervision, registration or voluntary certification programs are inadequate to guarantee that minimal qualifications are met, says Samborn.

Not so, says Theresa Meehan Rudy, director of education and research for Help Abolish Legal Tyranny (HALT), in Washington, D.C. She believes that licensing is just another market barrier that will restrict access to legal services.

Why regulate, says Rudy, when there is no clear proof that the public is being harmed under the present system?

Yes: Enhance Professionalism
By Hope Viner Samborn

The number of paralegals or legal assistants working in the United States is expected to increase from 90,000 in 1990 to 167,000 in 2005, according to projections of the U.S. Department of Labor.

Accompanying this projected increase is a need for state-by-state licensing of paralegals who work under attorneys' direct supervision. Licensing would benefit consumers by enhancing low-cost, high-quality legal services.

Now anyone can call himself or herself a paralegal or legal assistant. No state licenses these professionals. Each state should act now.

For licensing, states should require paralegals to take a practical proficiency test, to pass character evaluations, and to meet such minimum educational requirements as a bachelor's degree from an accredited institution.

In addition, states should enact criminal penalties for individuals who hold themselves out as paralegals but fail to meet stringent licensing requirements. A state licensing body should include paralegals, attorneys and paralegal educators who would ensure that license tests keep pace with the changing profession.

Despite some additional governmental expense, licensing is the only way to ensure that the work of paralegals meets the professional standards of the legal profession.

Some organizations will argue that certification, registration or attorney supervision alone, rather than licensing, will protect these high standards.

Certification doesn't work. First, it is voluntary. The National Association of Legal Assistants (NALA) offers a two-day certification test. Only about 5,000 paralegals have

Article 7-4 Legal Assistants: Has the Time Arrived for State-By-State Licensing?

Hope Viner Samborn and Theresa Meehan Rudy, Legal Assistants: Has the time arrived for state-by-state licensing? A.B.A. J., Dec. 1992, at 42. Reprinted by permission of the ABA JOURNAL.

been certified this way, according to NALA statistics. This is less than six percent of the paralegals working in 1990.

Second, the NALA test does not focus on state law issues paralegals routinely face. Paralegal practice varies by state. Without rigorous state-by-state tests, certification fails.

Registration also is inadequate. It would identify individuals as paralegals, but it would not increase professional standards.

Attorney supervision also fails to ensure professional standards. Many attorneys are uncertain how to assess the experience and qualifications of paralegals.

In some cases, attorneys are timid about using paralegals because even routine matters often involve nuances only trained professionals can spot.

Assures Proficiency

If paralegals were licensed and properly trained, attorneys could be assured of a minimum proficiency for even entry-level paralegals. Now it is a roulette game.
Current educational programs vary. As the field has grown, so too have the number of programs offering "paralegal" training.

As of August 1992, only 162 of the more than 600 paralegal programs met the ABA's stringent educational standards for program approval, according to the ABA Standing Committee on Legal Assistants.

Without licensing, schools have little incentive to seek this approval. Licensing would weed out some inferior programs.

Consumers also would be better served by dual mechanisms for oversight of paralegals. Attorneys would continue to supervise and be responsible for paralegal work. However, licensing authorities also could sanction paralegals for failing to maintain high professional standards.

The demand for quality, low-cost legal services continues to escalate. Highly skilled and well-trained paralegals who work under attorney supervision are one means of meeting this demand. They can and do augment the legal profession by handling routine matters.

The paralegal's role can and should continue to expand if paralegals are qualified as professionals. The benefits of state licensing to consumers are obvious: legal services at a cheaper cost. It's efficient. It's workable.

No: Another Roadblock
By Theresa Meehan Rudy

Licensing of lawyers has given them a stranglehold on legal services, with consumers losing out. As the absence of competition drove prices up, the public grew annoyed with the extravagant fees lawyers charged.

As a result, lawyers began to employ paralegals who, under lawyer tutoring and supervision, could reduce the costs to the client. Now, in the face of the "threat" of an open market for paralegals, the bar and even some paralegals are insisting on licensing traditional paralegals.

Studies of licensing in professions—from electricians to plumbers to lawyers—prove that schemes such as these do little to protect the consumer from unscrupulous or incompetent practitioners. On the contrary, they tend to drive up consumers' costs by limiting who can and cannot get into the occupation.

For once, let's ask what consumers want before licensing yet another occupation. They want the widest range of choices available in the marketplace, they want access to affordable service providers, and they want to be protected from unethical, incompetent providers.

Will paralegal licensing answer their needs? No.

Licensing schemes create all sorts of barriers to entering (and staying in) an occupation. The candidate must attain a certain level of education, take—that is, pay to take—a licensing examination, and renew, through additional test-taking or dues, their license. These barriers are put in place, proponents argue, to ensure competence in the service provider.

Increases Costs

Yet meeting the general qualifications for a license (put another way, being a good test-taker) is not sufficiently related to being a good paralegal, electrician or plumber. Just take a look at the number of medical and legal malpractice suits filed each year. What's more, as the upfront costs of entering the profession are increased, those costs are passed to the consumer.

Mandatory licensing of traditional paralegals is particularly unnecessary and undesirable from the consuming public's point of view. Licensing will limit the number and diversity of people working as paralegals, increase the cost of legal services, and provide little or no consumer protection.

Not that the public needs to be directly protected from paralegals. Not a single study, survey or opinion poll exists to show that consumers feel harmed by the work traditional paralegals do.

Some argue that licensing, because it imposes uniform education and/or testing requirements, will create a pool of qualified and competent candidates and make hiring prospective paralegals easier for lawyers. Not so.

It is transparent that traditional paralegals, and some lawyers, are pursuing licensing for their own benefit, using the guise of public protection. They know that licensing tends to freeze an occupation. Yet, since no one knows the full potential of the paralegal movement, it's much too early to think of locking it up with licensing.

Licensing has never, in any occupation, established more than minimal standards. Besides, all paralegal schools are not the same and paralegals, like other workers, will possess different amounts of knowledge and experience when they complete their education.

In fact, most will learn their skills on the job. Lawyers still need to discern which candidates are qualified—licensing will not make hiring any easier or quicker.

Licensing schemes, because of their anti-competitive effects, should only be used if substantial and irreparable harm to consumers exists. Whatever the decision, if paralegals are to be regulated, let's not make the same mistakes twice: no self-regulation.

The public, consumer regulators and legislators must be the ones in charge of regulating paralegals—not paralegals or bar officials.

Article 7-4 Continued

legal services and a proposed system for legal assistant licensure. Notwithstanding the report, the New Jersey legislature did not adopt a licensing scheme for legal assistants. Article 7-5 is a statement submitted by the NALA to the New Jersey Supreme Court setting forth its opposition to the proposed licensing scheme.

In February 2000, the Rhode Island Bar Association's Committee on Paralegals submitted a report proposing a voluntary registration scheme for Rhode Island paralegals. In August 2000, the Hawaii Supreme Court proposed new rules to regulate the use of legal assistants based on the recommendation for mandatory regulation made by the Hawaii State Bar Association Task Force on Paralegal Certification. Although the proposal did not actually provide a licensing mechanism, it would have the effect of controlling entry into the profession. Both the NALA and the NFPA have filed responses to the proposal, which can be found on their respective Web sites. In August 2000, the Wisconsin State Bar Board of Governors approved the Paralegal Practice Task Force Report recommending paralegal licensure, subject to the court's willingness to take on paralegal regulations. In September 2000, the Oklahoma Bar Association adopted minimum standards and qualifications for legal assistants. In 2001, the Maryland State Bar Association began offering associate membership to legal assistants and established a definition of legal assistant/paralegal. In April 2002 the Florida Supreme Court amended its rules regulating the Florida bar, restating a definition of legal assistants. Although stakeholders are increasingly seeking to define legal assistants, establish minimum standards for legal assistance, and even propose various regulation options, to date, no state has established a licensing system. During the next decade, the regulation issue will continue to be in the forefront in many states.

HOW DO LAW OFFICE MANAGERS AND EMPLOYERS VIEW REGULATION?

The members of the Legal Assistant Managers Association (LAMA) are supervisors and managers of legal assistant employees. The members of LAMA do not endorse certification as a mandatory hiring or promotional criterion.[5] They believe that employers must retain discretion to hire individuals with credentials to match their hiring needs. Article 7-6 discusses the position paper that LAMA developed concerning the issue of regulation.

HOW DO LEGAL ASSISTANT EDUCATORS VIEW REGULATION?

As with all groups of stakeholders, there is no agreement among educators on the issue of regulation. As discussed previously, the AAfPE in 1996 began discussing the creation of a credentialing examination for entry-level legal assistants. Although no consensus has been reached, many believe that another examination by yet another self-ordained authority would not be helpful and may, in fact, simply add more confusion to the field. Article 7-7, although not representative of the opinions of all educators, contains a scholarly analysis of the historical background underlying the certification and regulation debate.

The following statement was submitted to the New Jersey Supreme Court on January 5, 1999. For related information, see a companion article entitled "Issues Related to Licensure and Governmental Regulation of Paralegals."

Response to the Report of the New Jersey Supreme Court Committee on Paralegal Education and Regulation

Introduction

The report of the Committee on Paralegal Education and Regulation, published on July 27, 1998, sets forth several recommendations concerning the attorneys' use of paralegals in the delivery of legal services, sets forth a system of licensure and prerequisites, promulgates a code of professional conduct for paralegals, suggests modifications to the Rules of Professional Conduct concerning attorneys' use of paralegals, and discusses the administrative body and organization required to effect the recommendations.

This statement will focus on several key aspects of the report in light of the corporate mission and responsibility of the National Association of Legal Assistants to support the development of the paralegal profession. This includes supporting and enhancing the professional growth of those within the field; as well as promoting the paralegal occupation as an excellent career option for those just entering the workforce.

By way of introduction, the National Association of Legal Assistants (NALA) was formed and incorporated in 1975 as a nonprofit organization in recognition of, and in response to, the burgeoning use of legal assistants and paralegals in the delivery of legal services throughout the United States. Today, the National Association of Legal Assistants represents over 18,000 paralegals through its individual members and 87 affiliated state and local associations. The Association is governed by a national Board of Directors elected by voting members of NALA, and managed by a professional staff of eight employees. Headquartered in Tulsa, Oklahoma, NALA is a nonprofit organization under IRS Code 501(c)(6) and has an annual budget of approximately $900,000. NALA members are located throughout the United States. The Legal Assistants Association of New Jersey is an affiliated association of NALA, with approximately 300 members. There are approximately 100 individual NALA members in New Jersey.

At its inception, members charged NALA with a variety of responsibilities to meet their needs and the needs of the community the association serves. Uppermost on the list was to provide standards and professional development programs for its members. To reach the goal of advancing paralegal excellence, the Association established the following:

1. a code of ethics for legal assistants;
2. a national professional credentialing program;
3. model standards and guidelines for use of legal assistants by attorneys;
4. a national periodical for the dissemination of vital educational information to members of the paralegal profession.

Article 7-5 Response to the Report of the New Jersey Supreme Court

Detailed information regarding these programs was provided to the Court previously.[1] NALA established the Code of Ethics and Professional Responsibility for Legal Assistants on May 1, 1975, making this the first document to promulgate professional standards for paralegals as a self-regulatory mechanism. Individual members of NALA and members of NALA affiliated associations are bound by the provisions of this Code; any member found in violation of the Code may be subject to discipline which could result in membership expulsion. A copy of the Code may be found in the appendix.

The NALA Model Standards and Guidelines for Utilization of Legal Assistants serves as an educational tool for bar association committees and supreme courts interested in establishing similar guidelines. The Model provides a summary of guidelines and ethical opinions adopted by the various states regarding legal assistants. Adopted by the NALA membership in 1984, and updated most recently in 1997, the Model is a helpful service provided by this Association. A copy of the Model may be found in the appendix.

Recognizing the special responsibility of professional associations to encourage professional growth of those within the field, to establish a national standard of achievement and excellence, to identify those who have reached the standard, and to bring the recognition of legal assistants to a professional standing, NALA established the Certified Legal Assistant (CLA) professional credentialing program in 1976. Today, over 9000 legal assistants have achieved the CLA credential; the certification process has received recognition as a positive program encouraging the professional growth of legal assistants; and those who achieve the CLA credential have been recognized by employers through increased compensation and increased support of participation in continuing education programs which is required to maintain the credential. In addition to this national recognition, the CLA program is the foundation of certification programs for legal assistants administered by professional associations in the states of California, Florida, and Louisiana. Information describing the CLA program in greater detail may be found in the appendix.

NALA publishes a comprehensive publication entitled FACTS & FINDINGS which provides members of the paralegal profession with topical and educational information on the paralegal profession, including, most significantly, summaries of case law and ethical opinions concerning the legal assistant. This information is also available to NALA members through NALA's online information service, NALA NET.

Through adoption of the NALA Model Standards and Guidelines for Utilization of Legal Assistants in 1984, the NALA membership established the following definition of a legal assistant:

> Legal assistants (also known as paralegals) are a distinguishable group of persons who assist attorneys in the delivery of legal services. Through formal education, training, and experience, legal assistants have knowledge and expertise regarding the legal system and substantive and procedural law which qualify them to do work of a legal nature under the supervision of an attorney.[2]

NALA recognizes the ethical ramifications of performance of legal assistants' work and emphasizes, through self-regulatory ethical codes and guidelines, that legal assistants shall not undertake tasks which are required to be performed by attorneys, such as setting fees, giving legal advice, or giving the appearance of practicing law. NALA codes and guidelines stress that all work of a legal nature which is performed by the legal assistant must be delegated and supervised by an attorney who assumes full professional responsibility for the work product.

Legal assistants are regulated through several means. In addition to the self-regulatory mechanisms of their professional associations, legal assistants are regulated through the license of employers. The attorney licensing mechanism sets forth those responsibilities which an attorney may delegate to nonlawyer personnel, the duties and responsibilities which are reserved solely for attorneys, and consequences of violating these duties and responsibilities. The attorney's license demands that the attorney take measures to discipline or terminate the employment of a nonlawyer whose work is incompetent or who acts in a manner contrary to the attorney's ethical code and legal obligations. Finally, legal assistants are regulated by the marketplace - competent legal assistants will find employment; those who do not meet the demands of the job or conduct themselves in a manner that would jeopardize the attorney's license will have a difficult time with employment.

The National Association of Legal Assistants believes the report and recommendations of the New Jersey Committee on Paralegal Education and Regulation involves matters of vital interest to paralegals in New Jersey as well as those throughout the United States. It is the position of NALA that the Committee's recommendation No. 6 provides guidance to attorneys regarding utilization of legal assistants and, while many of the rules may be repetitive of other rules of professional conduct, the recommendation would serve to further clarify the supervisory role of attorney-employers of legal assistants and other lay personnel.

It is also the position of NALA that the proposal for licensure of paralegals in the State of New Jersey is harmful to the growth of the profession and is anti-competitive. This proposal is not based on any occupational or professional research, is subjective and would be costly, and would result in the loss of jobs. Further, the licensing proposal effectively minimizes the accountability of supervising attorneys by rending the issue of paralegal conduct and accountability away from the law office and thrusting it into an administrative maze of plenary and restricted licenses for paralegals that operates independently of attorney licensing. This specific licensing proposal is tantamount to using a full-body cast to treat a sprained ankle; and it creates a myriad of other unnecessary and debilitating problems in the process. With the exception of recommendation No. 6, the Committee recommendations do not encourage the use of paralegals.

Points

1. The paralegal's role is accepted and necessary in the efficient practice of law.

Today, there is little question that the utilization of legal assistants in the delivery of legal services is an acceptable practice in the modern office. Utilization of legal assistants results in a more efficient law practice and serves to reduce the cost of legal fees to clients. In the November 29, 1990 *Law Journal*, the New Jersey Committee on Professional Ethics published Opinion No. 647 which stated the following with reference to New Jersey paralegals:

> **It cannot be gainsaid that the utilization of paralegals has become, over the last ten years, accepted, acceptable, important and indeed, necessary to the efficient practice of law. Lawyers, law firms and, more importantly, clients benefit greatly by their work. Those people who perform paraprofessionally are educated to do so. They are trained and truly professional. They are diligent and carry on their functions in a dignified, proper, professional manner. They understand ethical inhibitions and prohibitions. Lawyers assign them work expecting**

Article 7-5 Continued

them to respect confidences which they obtain and to themselves in the best traditions of those who serve in legal area . . . It is too late in the day to view these paraprofessionals with suspicion of their morals or ethics. [126 NJLJ, index page 1526].

In the Court's decision in its review of Opinion 24, the court stated:

Given the appropriate instructions and supervision, paralegals, whether as employees or independent contractors, are valuable and necessary members of an attorney's work force in the effective and efficient practice of law.

The positive impact of the utilization of paralegals in the practice of law has also been recognized by appellate federal courts. In the 1989 case of *Missouri v. Jenkins*, 491 U.S. 274, 109 S.Ct. 2463, 105 L.Ed. 2d 229 (1989), the Supreme Court of the United States held that an award of attorneys' fees may include the market value of services rendered by paralegals, stating the following:

It has frequently been recognized in the lower courts that paralegals are capable of carrying out many tasks, under the supervision of an attorney, that might otherwise be performed by a lawyer and billed at a higher rate. Such work might include, for example, factual investigation, including locating and interviewing witnesses; assistance with depositions, interrogatories, and document production; compilation of statistical and financial data; checking legal citations; and drafting correspondence. Much such work lies in a gray area of tasks that might appropriately be performed either by an attorney or a paralegal. [Id., 109 S.Ct., at 2471-2472].

The United States Supreme Court added that paralegal services may encourage cost-effective legal services by reducing the spiraling cost of litigation. [Id., 109 S. Ct. at 2471].

2. The Supreme Court permits the use of nonlawyers by New Jersey attorneys.

In addition to the Court's recognition of the value of paralegals in the delivery of legal services, Rules of Professional Conduct 5.3 recognizes that a New Jersey attorney may use the services of a nonlawyer by stating the following:

With respect to a nonlawyer employed or retained by or associated with a lawyer:

(a) every lawyer or organization authorized by the Court Rules to practice law in this jurisdiction shall adopt and maintain reasonable efforts to ensure that the conduct of nonlawyers retained or employed by the lawyer, law firm, or organization is compatible with the professional obligations of the lawyer.

(b) a lawyer having direct supervisory authority over the nonlawyer shall make reasonable efforts to ensure that the person's conduct is compatible with the professional obligations of the lawyer; and

(c) a lawyer shall be responsible for conduct of such a person that would be a violation of the Rules of Professional Conduct if engaged in by a lawyer if:

(1) the lawyer orders or ratifies the conduct involved; or

(2) the lawyer has direct supervisory authority over the person and knows of the conduct at a time when its consequences can be avoided or mitigated but fails to take reasonable remedial action.

(3) the lawyer has failed to make reasonable investigation of circumstances that would disclose past instances of conduct by the nonlawyer incompatible with the professional obligations of a lawyer, which evidence a propensity for such conduct.

3. "No rational basis exists for the disparate way in which Advisory Opinion No. 24 treats employed and independent paralegals. The testimony overwhelmingly indicates that independent paralegals were subject to direct supervision by attorneys and were sensitive to potential conflicts of interests."—New Jersey Supreme Court Opinion In Re Opinion No. 24 of the Committee on the Unauthorized Practice of Law.3. "No rational basis exists for the disparate way in which Advisory Opinion No. 24 treats employed and independent paralegals. The testimony overwhelmingly indicates that independent paralegals were subject to direct supervision by attorneys and were sensitive to potential conflicts of interests."—New Jersey Supreme Court Opinion In Re Opinion No. 24 of the Committee on the Unauthorized Practice of Law.

When the New Jersey Committee on the Unauthorized Practice of Law issued Opinion No. 24 the Supreme Court and those interested in the issue carefully studied whether there is such a vast difference in the professional responsibilities and duties of legal assistants who are employed by law firms or corporations and legal assistants who contract their work to attorneys ("independent paralegals") that they should be considered as two separate classes of paraprofessionals. In the Supreme Court's opinion, there is no rational basis for the disparate way in which Opinion No. 24 treated employed and independent paralegals. Although independent paralegals may have a greater potential for conflicts, the risk is not essentially different from that experienced by paralegals who change jobs. Further, as paraprofessionals who work solely under the supervision of attorneys, independent paralegals were not found to be engaged in the practice of law.

The Supreme Court also recognized that:

1. Paralegals who are supervised by attorneys do not engage in the unauthorized practice of law. The availability of legal services to the public at an affordable cost is an important goal. The use of paralegals provides a means of achieving that goal while maintaining the quality of legal services. Requiring paralegals to be full-time employees of law firms would deny attorneys not associated with large law firms valuable paralegal services.

2. No judicial, legislative, or other rule-making body excludes independent paralegals from its definition of paralegal. New Jersey ethics rules recognize independent paralegals; language in RPC 5.3 indicates that it applies to independently retained paralegals and not just to employed paralegals. Moreover, Rule 4:42-9(b) permits the award of counsel fees to include paralegal service; this rule does not distinguish between employed or retained paralegals.

Article 7-5 Continued

3. Under both federal law and New Jersey law, and under both the American Bar Association (ABA) and New Jersey Ethics Rules, attorneys may delegate legal tasks to paralegals if the attorneys maintain direct relationships with their clients, supervise the paralegal's work and remain responsible for the work product. Neither case law nor statutes distinguish paralegals employed by an attorney or law firm from independent paralegals retained by an attorney or a law firm. Rather, the key is attorney supervision, whether the paralegal is employed or retained.

4. Any system of regulation or guidelines should encourage the use of paralegals while providing both attorneys and paralegals with standards that together with RPC's can guide their practices.

The Court's findings of its review of Opinion No. 24 recognized that additional regulations and guidelines need to be established to further clarify the role of legal assistants in the practice of law and suggested consideration to be given to regulations to address the problems that the work practices of all paralegals may create.

The Court's suggestion included regulations concerning conflicts of interest and any concerns resulting from paralegals sending correspondence directly to clients without attorney review and approval. The apparent question which the Court sought to address is what constitutes proper supervision by attorneys of the nonlawyer employees and contractors with whom they work.

It is respectfully submitted that because the Supreme Court has jurisdiction over the admission to the practice of law and the discipline of persons admitted to practice, any regulations suggested by the Committee would necessarily relate to those who are subject to Supreme Court regulation—New Jersey attorneys. The Committee's report and proposal assumes that the New Jersey Supreme Court has jurisdiction to license nonlawyers, although the report does not state any specific basis for this assumption. Even if the New Jersey Supreme Court has jurisdiction to mandate an independent licensing mechanism for nonlawyers, a separate but related issue is whether the Supreme Court should exercise its authority in the manner proposed by the Committee.

Another issue related to this discussion involves members of other professions who may be performing paralegal work. Many professional duties of those within other occupations may relate to either the practice of law or to duties and responsibilities of paralegals.[3] For example, In Re Opinion No. 26 of the Committee on the Unauthorized Practice of Law, the Supreme Court was presented with the question as to whether the real estate closing practice in South Jersey, which consists largely of closings in which neither the buyer nor the seller is represented by counsel, constitutes the unauthorized practice of law. In this instance the Court determined that:

> It is the public interest that determines the outcome of any prohibition and in serving that public interest, it may be necessary to impose conditions to ensure that the public is served. Today's holding is consistent with previous treatment of this issue. Given the history and experience of the South Jersey practice, however, the court concludes that the public interest will not be compromised by allowing the practice to continue so long as the parties are adequately informed of the conflicting interest of brokers and title officers and other risks involved in proceeding without a lawyer.

The above quote, along with the question presented by opinion No. 26, is interesting to this entire discussion. First, in recognizing that some professions skirt and may overlap the practice of law, a question arises as to whether the licensure of legal assistants would also include regulation of those in other occupations who may be performing paralegal duties. Secondly, the Court's statement that the public interest is the determinent factor in questions such as this is central to the issue of licensure of paralegals.

4. A licensure mechanism must be developed in response to a demonstrated need; based upon objective, quantifiable research; and must serve the public interest.

By their very nature, licensure mechanisms are designed to protect the health, safety, and well-being of citizens.[4] Licensure mechanisms are, for the most part, established by governments through their legislative bodies to serve the public interest. In New Jersey, for example, the legislature has established 33 boards which regulate the activities of 60 professions and occupations; 600,000 New Jersey citizens are regulated by these boards which range from medicine, dentistry and nursing to plumbing, psychological counseling and engineering.

A licensure mechanism is appropriate in instances where the public may be harmed by incompetent products or services.[5] In connection with this report, the Committee has not demonstrated a public need for the licensure of paralegals. Rather, the Committee's report focuses solely on the relationship between the legal assistant and the attorney/employer and the regulation of those who are admitted to the practice of law. It may be assumed that the Committee's ultimate interest is the safety and well-being of citizens of New Jersey. However, this does not appear to be the driving force of the Committee's recommendations.

The Committee's licensure recommendation sets forth a complicated system of plenary licenses and restricted licenses, divides the paralegal profession into two groups based on conditions of employment, although there is no rational basis for this segmentation, and classifies paralegals according to their education and experience. Among the elements basic to a licensing mechanism is the definition of the profession which it regulates. The Committee's approach to defining the career field into separate segments has no basis, particularly when these segmented groups have identical duties and responsibilities.

It is critical that any licensing or professional certification program must relate to and reflect real-world situations. Professional licensing mechanisms are designed to protect the public and to control entry into an occupation. Licensing mechanisms are not aspirational goals that may be adopted by those within the profession nor can they serve to strong-arm the growth and development of a career field. The Committee's report and recommendations with regard to a licensing mechanism seem to dismiss the present day realities of the practice of law and the paralegal occupation.

No occupational research is offered to substantiate the Committee's fragmentation of the career field or creation of the admission requirements. In fact, while the Committee estimates there are approximately 1,000 paralegals in New Jersey, a recent article in the *New Jersey Lawyer* states that in 1996 there were approximately 3,600 paralegals according to the latest data from the State Department of Labor's occupational survey.[6] Occupational research is fundamental to the development of a licensing mechanism.[7]

Attached to this statement is a copy of the 1997 National Utilization and Compensation Survey Report of the National Association of Legal Assistants for the Court's review.[8] The report shows that approximately 41% percent of those employed as paralegals have received a bachelor's degree; 29% report a high school diploma as their highest level of general education. The data describing participation in legal assistant edu-

Article 7-5 Continued

cational programs show that 30% have received an associate degree; 19% have received an undergraduate certificate; 16% have received a post baccalaureate certificate; 22% report they have not completed a legal assistant educational program. Interestingly, those who report completion of high school as their highest level of general education have been employed longer with the current employer and have more years of experience than all other legal assistants. Further, years of experience and years on the current job are statistically significant factors related to compensation and billing rates. This finding clearly demonstrates that, as a practical matter, law firms recognize the value of the experience of their nonlawyer employees. As a matter of fact, the level of general education was not found to be statistically significant at all to salary and compensation levels, and barely significant to billing rates.

In contrast, the licensure mechanism proposed by the Committee prohibits qualification for employment as a paralegal on the basis of years of experience alone, and further segments those who are employed as paralegals and have a bachelor's degree in any field and only in-house paralegal training. This latter group of paralegals may only seek employment with law offices; they are not eligible for employment as paralegals in corporations, government, or on a contract basis. Also, with regard to this class of employees, the licensing scheme prescribes the number of paralegals a law firm may employ with this qualification and by whom they are supervised. Finally, the licensing mechanism prohibits qualification and employment of paralegals by virtue of years of experience after three years of the rule's inception.[9] It is respectfully submitted that a majority of those currently employed as paralegals in New Jersey have achieved their positions by virtue of experience and in-house training.

The restricted license proposed by the committee is contemptuous of all in-house training for legal assistants; yet in-house training of competent individuals is a time-honored method of training for legal assistants. To reject this method of instruction by relegating it to the restricted license category is an affront to every legal assistant who is trained in this manner as well as to the lawyers who have educated and supervised them through the years. The requirements for a plenary license do not consider in-house training as a viable means of qualification as legal assistant; yet the committee proposes that a person can meet the threshold educational requirements by earning 60 college credits from an accredited four-year institution in *any* field plus a certificate from an ABA-approved training program. Thus, someone with 60 hours of college credits in animal husbandry and a certificate may qualify for the license; one with over ten years of experience and in-house training as a paralegal does not qualify. The licensing scheme advanced by the Committee is filled with similar contradictions, restrictions on attorneys' practices, and arbitrary lines in the sand.

An interesting aspect of the Committee's recommendation and qualifications for the license is its reliance on and endorsement of the American Bar Association's school approval process for legal assistant programs. The National Association of Legal Assistants supports this process and funds a seat on the ABA School Approval Commission. Also, graduates of ABA approved schools may qualify for NALA membership and may qualify to sit for the CLA examination. It is the position of NALA, however, that the Committee's reliance on ABA approved schools as the sole provider of paralegal education is not based on fact nor substantiated by research, and places and [sic] undue burden on schools and students. This proposal is certainly anti-competitive in that it prevents the creation of any new programs for paralegal education after the adoption of the rules. To be licensed as a paralegal in New Jersey, a person must have graduated from an ABA approved program or from a program that has applied for ABA approval and receives it within two years of the individual's application. However, a program cannot apply for ABA approval until it has graduated its first class. This takes approximately two years; thus, the program's first graduates can never apply for licenses as paralegals in New Jersey. In practical terms, this means that no one considering a career as a legal assistant would want to be among the first graduating class of any program, no matter how qualified its curriculum, because the graduate could not get a job and there is *no guarantee* the program would be ABA approved.

Further, by the adoption of the ABA school approval process as the sole means of paralegal education, there is an implied assumption that all the graduates of an ABA approved program are qualified to begin work as a legal assistant. Marginal students graduate from ABA approved degree programs, just as marginal students graduate from all degree programs.

Finally, this proposal would effectively cause paralegal programs in New Jersey that are not ABA approved to go out of business when, in fact, some programs cannot qualify for ABA approval for reasons extraneous to paralegal curriculum. These reasons include cost and the competing requirements of the ABA and marketplace realities. Many educators believe the ABA's curricula requirements are nearly ten years behind the times and, for this reason, have chosen not to seek the ABA credential.

It is respectfully submitted that the Committee's report and recommendations could cause public harm by arbitrarily defining those citizens who may or may not qualify for employment as a paralegal and by unnecessarily restricting the delivery of paralegal education.

5. It is respectfully submitted that this report and recommendations could cause public harm by unnecessarily increasing the cost of legal services to consumers and eliminating the benefits of the utilization of nonlawyers in the delivery of legal services.

The curious aspect of this licensing mechanism is really quite simple: Why would an elaborate system of licensing be created, and why would individuals subject themselves to it, if the license does not grant the person any rights or permission to do something? Generally, licensing mechanisms are helpful to the public because they provide information to consumers that assists them in judging the value of a product or service. In this instance, however, the license provides no information to the consumer. With reference to someone interested in becoming a legal assistant, it appears that the sole purpose for seeking licensure is to be able to use the title "paralegal" or "legal assistant" in their work environment. In this proposal, the license does not control one's work product. In fact, any lawyer or nonlawyer could perform paralegal duties in the law office. We suggest this is exactly how firms will respond to this burdensome regulatory scheme.

The licensing of paralegals through this system does not increase the efficiency of delivery of legal services nor reduce the cost. It does not streamline the practice of law by allowing paralegals to perform functions generally reserved for attorneys. On the contrary, it adds substantially to the cost of legal services through direct costs, such as licensing fees, and indirect costs related to the methods by which firms supervise the services of paralegals. For example, under the restricted license category a law firm may not employ more than one in-house trained paralegal for each one to 10 lawyers, the supervising lawyer of in-house trained paralegals must have been admitted to practice for at least five years, and a supervising lawyer may supervise no more than one restricted licensed paralegal at any given time.

Article 7-5 Continued

With regard to definition and licensing of contract paralegals, the procedure severely limits the number of contract paralegals who are qualified for the license and certainly prohibits any growth in numbers of those who offer their services in this fashion. This has the potential of unfairly prejudicing the sole practitioner. The sole practitioner or small firm practitioner who cannot afford to hire a full-time legal assistant has two options in terms of handling routine work: (1) utilizing independent legal assistants on a per case basis as needed while properly supervising the work product, or (2) performing these tasks him/herself. Since the licensing mechanism does not encourage the growth of contract paralegals and severely reduces the numbers of those who may offer these services, the sole practitioner would have no choice but to perform the paralegal tasks. It is inevitable, then, that either the attorney or the client will unjustly bear a heavy financial loss for time spent by the attorney on routine matters.[10]

Other indirect costs associated with the licensing mechanism would include the cost of separate malpractice insurance for paralegals as licensed individuals. The Committee states that attorneys should be absolved of primary responsibility for ethical violations committed by a paralegal if the breach of conduct is outside the attorney's control. It goes on to state that legal assistants must be independently responsible for breaches of conduct and subject to discipline. Thus the need for malpractice insurance, which would be exceptionally costly considering the numbers of individuals involved.

The final cost category associated with this mechanism is the cost to the public not only in terms of increased cost of legal services but also in terms of the public funds required for initial and on-going capitalization of the program. While the report includes an estimated budget for the first year of operation, from NALA's 20+ years of experience with the Certified Legal Assistant credentialing program, the estimated cost appears low, particularly considering the complicated nature of the process. Compounding the administrative expenses, it is most likely a procedure such as this would be challenged in the courts. Clearly, the revenues generated by licensing and renewal fees cannot be depended upon to provide financial support for this process. First, the market is quite limited regardless of whether there are 1000 or 3600 paralegals in the state. Second, as pointed out earlier, there is no reason for one to seek a license as a paralegal.

In summary, the cost of this program hits on all fronts: increased costs of legal services to the public, increased cost to those working as paralegals, and increased demand for public funds. Any cost-saving benefits related to the utilization of paralegals in the delivery of legal services will be lost and replaced with rising costs.

6. Professional associations offer viable alternatives to governmental regulation.

The Committee's report focuses primarily on the development of a system of governmental or judicial regulation of members of an occupation that is already regulated by the license of the employers. The proposed licensing mechanism for paralegals includes completion of a written examination covering a code of professional conduct for paralegals that is, for the most part, simply a restatement of the attorneys' code. The recommendation to establish a licensing procedure is offered at a time when governments are overburdened and the term "deregulation" is loudly spoken. At the end of 1980, it was estimated that federal regulations cost Americans over 1 billion dollars a year. A typical family of four paid an extra $1,800 annually for goods and services simply because excessive federal regulations added to the cost of these goods and services.[11]

Against this backdrop, one begins to question the purpose of the paralegal license. Because the license does not allow a paralegal to perform any functions that he or she does not perform already, one must surmise the purpose of the license is to identify paralegals within the state, and to discipline paralegals for violation of a code of professional conduct to which they are already committed and must follow to retain their employment. We submit the mechanism described is not a licensing procedure but a registration procedure. Other mechanisms already exist in New Jersey that would serve this purpose. For example, since 1989 the New Jersey State Bar Association has permitted paralegals who meet their membership requirements to join the association. This process could easily be transformed into a system of registration.

In addition, no consideration is given to the important role played by professional associations in this arena. In addition to the New Jersey State Bar Association, the Legal Assistants Association of New Jersey, established in 1982, also provides professional development programs for paralegals, has established a code of ethics and professional responsibility for paralegals, and, through its membership requirements, has established standards for entry into the field.[12] The valuable role professional associations play in the area of credentialing and self-regulation has long been recognized in our society. Self-regulation, defined as a process whereby an interorganizational network (such as a trade association, professional society, or other third party) sets and enforces standards relating to the conduct of firms and/or individuals in an industry or profession,[13] is one of the highest and best traditions in American society, and is a fundamental goal of virtually every individual professional. Self-regulatory programs are usually voluntary programs and are subject to the control by the marketplace, by the value of the standards which they promulgate, and by governmental regulation. In summary:

> Courts and government agencies generally have recognized that a private, non-profit association, board, or other similar organization serves the public interest by establishing and measuring against quality standards. The self-regulation of a profession or field of endeavor by an organization typically is assumed to benefit the public by promulgating information that particular individuals or institutions have achieved and maintained accepted criteria of quality, such as in professional practice or in programs of education.[14]

Summary

Like the Supreme Court Committee on Paralegal Education and Regulation, the National Association of Legal Assistants is vitally concerned that those within the paralegal profession adhere to stringent standards of conduct and ethics. The legal profession is built solely on a foundation of trust and adherence to a code of professional conduct by paralegals is the most crucial element in the growth and acceptance of this career field. However, governments and associations can only deal with an individual's actions. Licensing procedures control entry into an occupation or profession; they do not ensure ethical behavior. A licensing procedure will not change the actions and attitudes of those who are unscrupulous in our society. For example, those individuals who call themselves paralegals and deliver services directly to the public seem to pay little attention to unauthorized practice of law statutes.

The Committee's report is important to the development of the career field by initiating these discussions and examining the purposes and impact of licensing mechanisms. We respectfully submit, however, that it is the attorney who maintains the supervision of nonlawyer personnel and who is solely responsible for their conduct. The guidelines and rules presented under recommendation No. 6 provide helpful information to attorneys

Article 7-5 Continued

regarding their utilization of paralegals and other non-lawyers in the delivery of legal services.

> Respectfully submitted,
> Vicki Voisin, CLAS
> President, National
> Association of Legal
> Assistants

1 See *amicus* brief and appendix filed by the National Association of Legal Assistants In Re Opinion No. 24 of The Committee on the Unauthorized Practice of Law. March 21, 1991.

2 For a more detailed discussion of the way different states have defined the terms "paralegal" and "legal assistant," see **Summary of Definitions of Terms: Legal Assistant and Paralegal**, National Association of Legal Assistants, June 1998, which may be found in the appendix.

3 There is a renewed interest in this issue throughout the legal community, particularly with the passage of the Internal Revenue Service reform bill which extends the traditional lawyer-client privilege to cover some communications between taxpayers and their accountants. On August 4, 1998, the ABA President appointed a Commission on Multidisciplinary Practice to study and report on the manner and extent to which nonlawyer professional service firms are seeking to provide legal services. See "ABA President Creates Commission To Review Multidisciplinary Practice Issues," *ABA-BNA Lawyers' Manual on Professional Conduct*, Vol. 14, No. 15, P 390. August 19, 1998.

4 "Essentially, there are three forms of individual credentialing - licensing, certification, and registration. . . . Licensure is the most restrictive of the three forms of credentialing and generally refers to the mandatory governmental requirement necessary to practice in a particular profession or occupation. . . . Licensure implies both practice protection and title protection, in that only individuals who hold the license are permitted to practice and to use a particular title. Certification, on the other hand, is usually a voluntary process instituted by a nongovernmental agency in which individuals are recognized for advanced knowledge and skill. . . . In some instances individuals who seek certification are ready hold a license. . . . Certification implies title protection as only those who are certified may use a particular title. The ultimate intent of licensure is to directly protect the public from incompetent practitioners. The intent of certification, on the other hand, normally is to inform the public that individuals who have achieved certification have demonstrated a particular degree of knowledge and skill. Its only potential direct method of public protection is through ethics enforcement. . . . Registration, also used for title protection, is normally a mandatory process that only requires individuals to apply for the title through the appropriate governmental or private agency. As such, registration is generally the least restrictive form of credentialing, most often used when public protection is less critical." See, **Certification, A NOCA Handbook,** National Organization for Competency Assurance, 1200 19th St. NW, #300, Washington, DC 20036-2422, 1996, P 3.

5 See Appendix E, "Issues Related to Licensure and Governmental Regulation of Paralegals," and "Summary of Review Criteria for Use In Determining Whether an Occupation or Profession Should be Licensed or Regulated by a State." These articles summarize sunrise legislation in other states.

6 7 NLJ 1818 (Monday, August 3, 1998)

7 The United States Supreme Court has addressed professional credentialing programs of associations on many occasions. Recently, in *Peel v. Attorney Registration and Disciplinary Committee of Illinois*, 110 S.Ct. 2281 (1990), in allowing an attorney's use of a specialty credential available from a professional association, the Court suggested that a claim of certification is truthful and not misleading if:

1. the claim itself is true.
2. the bases on which certification was awarded are factual and verifiable
3. the certification in question is available to **all professionals in the field who meet relevant, objective, and consistently applied standards** [emphasis added] and
4. the certification claim does not suggest any greater degree of professional qualification than reasonably may be inferred from an evaluation of the certification program's requirements.

The opinion of the Court is relevant to discussions of licensure mechanisms by further emphasizing the fact that the programs must be relevant and objective.

8 Since 1986, the National Association of Legal Assistants has conducted a national survey of the utilization and compensation of legal assistants on a bi-annual basis. The survey provides detailed information tracking the growth, duties, responsibilities, and compensation of legal assistants. This research is conducted by professionals in the field and offers reliable and valid national data. NALA's 1988 National Utilization and Compensation Survey Report is referenced in the opinion of the United States Supreme Court in *Missouri v. Jenkins*, 491 U.S. 274, 289 n. 11, 109 S.Ct. 2463, 105 L.Ed. 2d 229 (1989).

9 A person who is employed full-time as a paralegal for two years at any time during the five years immediately preceding application for licensure and who successfully completes an ethics examination may qualify for a plenary license provided the person applies for license within three years after the effective date of the rule. Otherwise, the person does not qualify for any license.

10 According to information supplied by the New Jersey Office of Attorney Ethics, it may be estimated that "almost three-quarters of all law firms (74.25%) were single practice firms. Two person firms represented 11.97% of all private practice firms, while firms of between 3 to 5 comprised 8.70%. Only 5.08% of all of the law firms in New Jersey had 6 or more attorneys."

11 **Certification and Accreditation Law Handbook,** Jacobs, Jerald A., American Society of Association Executives, Washington, DC., 1992, P 9, quoting Carol E. Dinkins, U.S. Deputy Attorney General, "The Role of Self-Regulation in Regulatory Reform," in *The White House Conference on Association Self-Regulation*, 1984, 68.

12 The requirements for voting membership in the Legal Assistants of New Jersey are as follows: (1) Certification as a Certified Legal Assistant; or (2) Graduation from a legal assistant program that is approved by the American Bar Association; or (3) Graduation from a program that is institutionally accredited and includes not less than 60 semester hours of study of which 15 semester hours are substantive legal courses; or (4) Graduation from a legal assistant program which does not meet the above requirements plus 6 months of in-house training as a legal assistant; or (5) A bachelor's degree in any field plus 6 months of in-house training as a legal assistant; or (6) Three-years law related experience under the supervision of a licensed attorney plus 6 months of in-house training as a legal assistant.

13 **Current Principles and Practices in Association Self-Regulation,** Lad, Lawrence J., DBA, American Society of Association Executives, 1992, P 45.

14 **Certification and Accreditation Law Handbook**, Jacobs, Jerald A., American Society of Association Executives, 1992, P. 9.

Article 7-5 Continued

LAMA Opposes Mandatory Regulation of Traditional Paralegals

However, association position paper states it would consider licensing requirements for independents only.

By Robert Sperber

Traditional legal assistants should not be licensed, announced the Legal Assistant Management Association (LAMA) in a just-released position paper.

The approximately 400-person association, which represents legal assistant managers in the United States and Canada, joins a rancorous debate that has paralegal associations, legislators, state bars and other professionals divided.

"LAMA is currently opposed to mandatory regulation of legal assistants," the organization states in its position paper. "In particular, LAMA is not in favor of broad-based state or provincial licensing of legal assistants."

In issuing the position paper, LAMA throws its weight behind the American Bar Association's Standing Committee on Legal Assistants, which states that "the public is protected by the license of the lawyer through whom the legal assistant must act." Some individual LAMA officials have expressed opposition to licensing in the past, but the association has not taken an official position until this opinion. This paper was originally written in October but, due to changes on LAMA's board, not released to the public until April.

Independent Paralegals

While opposed to broad-based licensing of all paralegals, LAMA leaves the door open for regulation of independent legal assistants who work directly for the public.

"Strong arguments can be made in favor of licensing non-lawyer direct service providers to ensure their competency and their accountability," the position paper states. While the paper does not actually advocate such licensing, the association is not against it because such licensing would be a way of protecting the public, said LAMA President Patricia Hicks.

Hicks, manager of corporate services for the Toronto firm of Blake, Cassels & Graydon, said that licensing traditional paralegals could limit managers in the paralegals they hire. For instance, LAMA members sometimes hire nurse consultants as paralegals. It would be unfair to demand these nurses to obtain legal certification, she said.

"Licensing of traditional legal assistants would create an unwieldy bureaucracy that would have the potential to limit the flexibility and discretion employers need in hiring," the position paper states. "Regulation may unnecessarily restrict who is classified as a legal assistant. As a result, employers may find themselves unable to hire individuals who are otherwise qualified but do not meet the regulatory standards."

LAMA also argues that licensing may preclude firms from collecting court-approved fees for legal assistants who do not meet regulation criteria.

Article 7-6 LAMA position paper

Robert Sperber, LAMA Opposes Mandatory Regulation of Traditional Paralegals, Legal Assistant Today, July/Aug. 1997, at 20. Copyright 2001 James Publishing, Inc. Reprinted courtesy of Legal Assistant Today magazine. For subscription information call (800) 394-2626, or visit http://www.legalassistanttoday.com.

Proponents of licensing often argue that such licensing would lead to further expansion of the role legal assistants play in delivering legal services. LAMA takes the opposite tact, arguing that "broad-based state licensing may hinder legal assistant professional growth by placing limits on legal assistant responsibilities."

Voluntary Regulation

While opposing state regulation of the profession, LAMA is in favor of continuing voluntary regulation through such vehicles as NALA's Certified Legal Assistant exam or NFPA's Paralegal Advanced Competency Exam, as well as registration with an association or agency, and government-allowed nonlawyer direct service providers before governing administrative agencies.

"Each employer should use its discretion to determine the value of voluntary regulation when making hiring or other employment decisions," LAMA states.

Article 7-6 Continued

Paralegal Licensing Standards: The Educational Perspective

Allan M. Tow*

Legal Assistant regulation is on the horizon in one form or another [and possibly in many forms]. It is imperative that we approach the regulation "can of worms" from an informed and knowledgeable vantage point, and that we participate in the formative process.

—Gail White Nicholson, Vice President,
Greenville Association of Legal Assistants 1991[1]

I. Introduction

The debate concerning the regulation of paralegals raises issues of great concern for paralegal educators. As teachers in a primarily vocational environment, paralegal educators can have a profound impact upon both the form and the content of future paralegal regulation and licensing. Regulation and licensing necessarily implicate the determination of educational standards as preconditions to professional status. Similar to the law school experience with the licensing of attorneys, paralegal schools are faced with determining the pedagogical requirements for professional qualification. For the past several years, the pendency of paralegal regulation has prompted a variety of pronouncements from educators, paralegals themselves, and a surprising number of sources from outside of the paralegal profession. Viewed together, these pronouncements suggest that the standards for both educational qualification and the parameters of permissible professional activity for paralegals are already in place, and in practice. In some instances, regulatory provisions that authorize the "practice of law" by non-attorneys already establish standards for profes-

Article 7-7 Journal of Paralegal Education and Practice

Alan Tow, Paralegal Licensing Standards: The Educational Perspective, 14 J. PARALEGAL EDUC. AND PRAC. 59–90 (1998). Courtesy of the American Association for Paralegal Educators.

sional legal services. Moreover, some of these provisions establish fairly exacting requirements and are thus harbingers of the licensing provisions to come.

This article examines the problem of determining the standards for paralegal licensing and its implications for paralegal educators. Beginning with a brief history of the debate, the article traces the issues from the initial discussions by the host and paralegal profession. Observers and commentators have provided insight into the problem of determining standards for the emerging paralegal profession. Of particular note is the role of the paralegal educator in the politics of the licensing debate. Together, those views and the views of those actively engaged in the profession call for greater recognition and autonomy for the paralegal profession.

More telling are the specific requirements of those outside the profession. Practical standards established by state and, particularly, by federal regulations for non-attorney representation before administrative agencies are strong evidence of emerging practice standards.

This article posits that the debate over licensing standards will center largely upon educational requirements. Thus, it suggests that the pedagogical standards established by paralegal educators should be made with a view towards preparing students for the authorized practice of law. Moreover, by expanding the areas of practice taught in paralegal schools, educators may gain further recognition of the tasks that their graduates undertake in the legal profession.

II. Historical Background

Only recently have paralegals begun to enjoy appreciation as legal professionals "whose labor contributes to the work product."[2] Courts have expressly embraced the notion that employing paralegals "'encourages [the] cost-effective delivery of legal services.'"[3] As a legal professional, a paralegal's litigation expertise is compensable as attorneys fees under the federal Civil Rights Act,[4] the Equal Access to Justice Act,[5] the Bankruptcy Code,[6] and several other statutes.[7] Access to a paralegal's expertise may even satisfy a litigant's constitutional right of access to the courts.[8] Some of the professional tasks performed by a paralegal now carry the accolade of "discretion and independent judgment . . . [with] the power to make *independent* choice, free from immediate direction or supervision and with respect to matters of *significance*."[9] Buoyed by optimistic projections for employment opportunities, the paralegal profession has been touted as the fastest growing in the country.[10] Yet, all of this praise and glowing optimism for the paralegal profession is relatively new.

The prospect that anyone other than a licensed attorney could perform legal tasks has traditionally been met with strident hostility from the legal profession. Under the general rubric of public protection "from incompetent lay persons,"[11] and public need "for integrity and competence of those who undertake to render legal services,"[12] the practice of law is limited only to those licensed by the state to do so. It is a highly controlled activity, and engaging in that activity without permission may result in sanctions.[13] However, like obscenity, "there is no clear, accepted definition of what constitutes the unauthorized practice of law."[14] Nevertheless, the bar's enforcement of these laws may be vigorous and at times "vindictive,"[15] despite the lack of public demand for such protection.[16] It is no surprise then that the "real" motivation for the enforcement of unauthorized practice laws has been perceived as protection of the attorneys' professional monopoly.[17]

Born of legal secretaries performing more than clerical tasks,[18] paralegals still struggle against the hierarchy of their host profession, "organized lawyerdom, a powerful adversary"[19]—a profession which still disparages[20] and demands that paralegals "[u]nderstand the chain of command."[21] Moreover, the dynamics of gender and hierarchy replete in the legal profession contribute to the continued subjugation of paralegals.[22] Manifestly, the struggle for recognition as professionals through regulation has been accurately viewed as "ultimately political; it is a question of power and control."[23] As discussed, *infra,*[24] licensing will ultimately become the prime indication of autonomous professional status for paralegals. The distinction conferred by a governmentally granted license will grant paralegals entry, albeit limited, into the legal profession. More importantly, the license will permit paralegals to distinguish themselves from the lay public at large. Once licensed, paralegals will no longer be merely "non-attorneys." It is against this background that the debate over regulation is occurring.

III. The Certification and Licensing Debate

The future of the paralegals' professional status and recognition will center largely on the nature and privilege of a conferred credential rather than merely the occupational title itself. Anyone may call him or herself a "paralegal." As a practical matter, there are no formal educational qualifications or direct legal regulation of paralegals. "Like 'midwife,' 'computer consultant' and 'financial planner,' 'paralegal' can mean almost anything. Because most states have no official certification programs for paralegals, people with all sorts of training and experience quite properly and legally use this term."[25] And then, some not so properly. Without a required or recognized credential, "the responsibility for competence through education and skills rests firmly with paralegals themselves as well as the lawyers who employ them."[26] And perhaps therein lies the problem. Even today, as members of a profession that has experienced steady growth, development, and hard-earned recognition over the past thirty years,

> [m]any paralegals express . . . frustration over what they felt was a lack of respect for their professional status. They rankle at the fact that some lawyers allow secretaries and other clerical and other personnel to call themselves paralegals, even though they haven't had any formal paralegal training and don't really do paralegal work.[27]

Thus, the lack of an identifiable credential, which would otherwise distinguish paralegals to the exclusion of untrained encroachers, continues to relegate the profession to an ill-defined status. Furthermore, the boundaries of that status will remain elusive regardless of a commonly accepted level of education or training, unless there is a vehicle that can quantify the ability to perform legal tasks and become a recognized reference both in and outside of the legal profession. While more than 500 paralegal training programs have emerged, many conferring associate or baccalaureate degrees recognized by state laws on higher education,[28] the attainment of a specific level of academic achievement is apparently insufficient for the maintenance of a cognizable professional status.

Nevertheless, the role of education and training for a paralegal is an essential, if not indispensable, part of becoming a respected professional. As a practical matter, "[e]mployers are increasingly demanding evidence that they are hiring well-trained employees."[29] In the larger arena, evidence of a paralegal's education provides "the public, legislators, and paralegal graduates with a means of measuring acquired abilities."[30] Within paralegal education, implementing measurements such as core competencies and credentialing exams "prepare . . . students to handle an expanded role" [and to] "take a more active role in the delivery of legal services."[31] By teaching the theories of substantive law, their practical applications, and the skills necessary to perform legal tasks, educators prepare paralegal students for direct entry into the legal profession. Thus, if "[t]he question now is not

Article 7-7 Continued

whether the field will be regulated, but what form the regulation will take,"[32] educators occupy a unique position "to recommend the [necessary] educational standards [to] develop fair proficiency examinations, and [to] help write the ethical and disciplinary rules."[33] Hence, "[t]he issue of regulation is closely tied in with that of educational standards."[34] And it is the development of educational standards that will provide the formative basis for the progression of the paralegal profession into an autonomous profession with an ethic of "service to the legal profession, to clients and the community."[35]

In an ideal professional community, educators would "work with paralegals and lawyers to identify the specific skills and the specific bodies of knowledge that paralegal graduates need to possess in order to be effective in the workplace."[36] There has been regular and meaningful cooperation and exchange between educators and paralegals for many years, both engaging themselves in "joint efforts" [designed to] "strengthen the relationship between [them]."[37] Working with lawyers, however, has been a more complex matter.

IV. Paralegal Education and the American Bar Association

The American Bar Association (ABA) has long been the predominant voice regarding the standards for practice and the education of the nation's lawyers. After its inception in 1878, the ABA immediately began promulgating standards for the training and licensing of attorneys.[38] Through its accreditation process, the ABA virtually dictates the educational standards for law schools to the extent that "all 50 states and the District of Columbia consider graduation from an ABA accredited law school sufficient for the legal education requirement of bar admission."[39] With control of the legal profession and leadership from the profession's elite,[40] the ABA has faithfully and zealously guarded the lawyers' monopoly, often taking surprisingly unpopular positions.[41] Nonetheless, the ABA recognized early on that delegating legal tasks to lay persons "will enable [the lawyer] to render his professional services to more people, thereby making legal services more fully available to the public."[42] Indeed, in 1971, the ABA's House of Delegates recommended its Special Committee on Legal Assistants consider "[t]he nature of the *training* . . . to develop competence and proficiency," and "[t]he desirability of recognizing competence . . . by *academic recognition* or other suitable means."[43] Soon after, the ABA resolved to develop "standards for ascertaining the proficiency of legal professionals."[44] To some observers, "the use of some type of certification or licensing arrangement seemed to be the logical next step."[45] Yet, at public hearings held during the mid-1970's, the notion of establishing standards for certification or licensure was met with substantial opposition and was eventually rejected.[46]

Ultimately, the proposal for paralegal regulation by either certification or licensure was still premature in the mid-1970's.[47] Because the profession had begun only a decade before,[48] there was insufficient experience in working with legal para-professionals to create qualifying criteria. Indeed, by 1975, "the competencies required to perform the roles and functions of legal assistants had not yet been adequately defined."[49] As a nascent profession, paralegals had only begun to become known within the legal profession at large. "For example, when paralegal [training] programs were first offered in the late sixties, many were developed without the general knowledge, much less the sanction of lawyers."[50] Nevertheless, the ABA's tenor remained positive and supportive. Its 1975 conclusions recognized the continued growth of the occupation, its dynamic development, and the possibility that paralegal certification could make legal services more widely available and more affordable.[51] More significantly, as a strong indication of its approval, the report also recommended that the ABA "continue to exercise the initiative" [along with] "the joint cooperation of appropriate and representative national associations of legal assistants . . . *educators,* and the general public."[52]

A decade later, the ABA's position had become noticeably restrained. In 1986, the ABA's Standing Committee's position paper (1986 Report) on voluntary certification starkly concluded that,

(1) Certification of minimal or entry-level paralegal competence is not appropriate.

(2) Voluntary certification of advanced paralegal competence or proficiency in specialty areas of the law might be appropriate if it is administered by the appropriate body.

(3) The ABA is not the appropriate body to undertake a program of certifying paralegals in advanced competence or proficiency in specialty areas of the law.

(4) A voluntary program of certifying advanced paralegal competence or proficiency in specialty areas of the law, if undertaken at all, should be undertaken on a national basis by a board that includes lawyers, paralegals, educators, and members of the general public.

(5) Since such a board does not presently exist, there should not be any certification at this time.[53]

The 1986 Report signaled a significant retreat from the ABA's earlier support for the growth of the paralegal profession, particularly in light of existing studies.[54] The circular reasoning used to justify abandonment of past initiatives, the absence of any further recognition of the paralegal's value to the delivery of legal services, and the ABA's abject refusal to invest any more "time and expense"[55] were altogether telling: "as a practical consequence, it can be said that the ABA is opposed to *any* certification."[56] Moreover, the ABA's simultaneously adopted definition of "legal assistant"[57] has been seen as "a clear political message to paralegals—they are to have no professional autonomy, . . . [there is] top down control of paralegals by lawyers and the American Bar Asociation."[58] The 1986 Report's conclusions, that neither the ABA nor any other organization was "appropriate" for certifying paralegals, effectively excluded any consideration of certification in the near future. Through the 1986 report, the ABA asserted its supremacy over the entire legal profession.

The ABA's opposition to certification preemptively foreclosed consideration of licensing for paralegals. "A major detriment the ABA [saw] is that such certification could evolve into Licensure . . . ."[59] Licensure, even in limited form, legitimates the professional status of not only the paralegal, but also (and more importantly) the paralegal's tasks. Licensure, the governmental imprimatur for engaging in professional activities from which non-licensed individuals are prohibited, would require lawyers to share a part of their jealously-guarded realm of professional tasks. While symbolic accolades such as voluntary certification[60] or associate bar membership[61] may help substantially to dignify the paralegal profession, the paralegal is still relegated to performing tasks consisting of "tedious or routine detail"[62]—tasks that still could be performed by any non-attorney or non-paralegal.

The ABA asserted its primacy and control over paralegal education as well. The 1986 Report "recommend[ed] ABA approval of paralegal education programs as the *best method* of assuring legal assistant quality."[63] In 1972, the Standing Committee on Legal Assistants had begun a voluntary "approval" process for paralegal schools. However, "in 1981, the House of Delegates of the ABA instructed its Committee on Legal Assistants to terminate the ABA's involvement in the approval process."[64] To mollify the objections of paralegal schools that had already received approval, the ABA created what is now known as the Legal Assistant Program Approval Commission whose recommendations are passed to the Standing Committee on Legal Assistants "which in turn makes its recommendations to the [ABA's] House of Delegates . . . . The major difference between the Committee and the Commission is that the latter must contain nonlawyer members."[65] Of the eleven Commission seats, only four must be filled by lawyers.[66] Significantly, the remaining seats belong to educators, paralegals, and the general public,[67] creating a balanced commission.

Article 7-7 Continued

There were also moderating voices within other parts of the ABA. The 1986 Report itself mentioned the notion of "limited licensing of paralegals."[68] Moreover, the ABA members noted that, "it can no longer be claimed that lawyers have the exclusive possession of the esoteric knowledge required and are therefore the only ones available to advise clients on any matter concerning the law."[69] Still, those views "drew the ire"[70] of other members of the ABA, and for the time being remained voices in the dark.

Since its inception, ABA approval for paralegal schools has been controversial. To many, the decisions and criteria for establishing educational standards for the training of paralegals should not be left to lawyers alone. For those who favor a measurable degree of autonomy for paralegals, input must be more balanced. Allowing the ABA to control educational training cedes a large part of control over the paralegal profession to those who may be more interested in exploiting paralegals. As one noted commentator has confirmed,

> [s]ince a major objective of lawyers is to increase their profits by the use of paralegals, critics argue that it is a conflict of interests for lawyers to control the field totally. When regulatory decisions must be made on matters such as the approval of schools, whose interests would the lawyers be protecting in making these decisions? The interests of paralegals? The interests of the public? Or the profit interest of the lawyer regulators?[71]

Indeed, the traditional analysis used to justify the delegation of legal tasks to paralegals focuses primarily upon economic benefits—to attorneys. An early ABA commissioned study that sanctioned the notion of para-professionals in law found that using paralegals can be a key element to profitability in law firms. "The secret . . . is to have each [legal]procedure completed by the least expensive person competent to handle that procedure."[72] Yet this mentality of exploitation should come as no surprise. An observer of the paralegal movement has long noted that "[p]owerful autonomous professional groups [such as the ABA], though deeply valued by their members, are condemned by others as economically self-serving and socially oppressive."[73] Thus, control over paralegal education and hence the paralegal profession by lawyers can only result in a top down hierarchical form of regulation bereft of input by those subject to the regulation—the paralegals themselves. To be sure, the primary focus of the ABA's attention on paralegals has been upon the benefits that the lawyers receive. As the preeminent professional organization for the nation's attorneys, the ABA exists for attorneys and not for paralegals.

Still, there is cause for hope that the ABA, and lawyers in general, will view the status of paralegals with greater generosity. This hope is based on modern sociological theory that, in a larger realm, "the transition to post-industrial society entails the abandonment of traditional top-down bureaucratic models of organization and control in favor of 'flatter' organizations stressing flexibility, participation, and full use of human potential . . . [and] a 'socially conscious entrepreneurship.'"[74] Specifically, "in a society which values knowledge, information and technical specialties, power will gravitate to the possessors of those things, i.e., the professionals . . . [those who] understand their importance to society and have a rich sense of their professional responsibility to society."[75]

This optimistic view of modern organizational politics may already [sic] becoming a reality. Within the past few years, the ABA's activities have indicated a more flexible view towards the use of paralegals. In 1993, the ABA Commission on Nonlawyer Practice recommended that the bar "'[e]ncourage innovative methods which simplify and make less expensive the rendering of legal services.'"[76] More significantly, in 1995, a report from the same ABA commission specifically recommended the expanded use of paralegals.[77] With its stated purpose of "[i]ncreasing the [p]ublic's [a]ccess to the [j]ustice [s]ystem and to [a]ffordable [a]ssistance [w]ith [i]ts [l]egal and [l]aw-[r]elated [n]eeds,"[78] the ABA Nonlawyer

Report went further to advocate the employment of freelance paralegals. In so doing, the ABA Nonlawyer Report noted that

> [s]olo practitioners or small law firms who cannot afford a full-time paralegal may employ on a contract basis part-time or case-by-case services of paralegals. The paralegals may work either through temporary employment agencies or out of their own offices. Under these arrangements, the lawyers still provide either supervision or accountability to the client for the paralegal's work.[79]

Thus with its emphasis upon accountability, public access, and cost effective delivery of legal services, the 1995 ABA Nonlawyer Report echoed a higher purpose and provided a substantial accommodation to the realities of modern law practice and social responsibility, common goals for both paralegals and attorneys. Certainly the encouragement and, in particular, the recognition of freelance paralegals in the ABA Nonlawyer Report reflects a positive evolution in the thinking of the paralegal profession.[80] The newly found sense of social responsibility has even infiltrated into the ABA's stated goals in establishing guidelines for its approval program: "'to promote meaningful access to legal representation and the American System of justice for all persons regardless of their economic or social condition' and 'to make the judicial system more understandable, accessible and affordable.'"[81]

The progression of the paralegal's status must be viewed as an evolutionary process. Sociologists have observed that "[t]he likely path an emerging profession will take toward the development of its identity and maturation can be predicted by observing the histories of older, established professions and noting the stages evidenced in their evolution."[82] Sociologists have noted that "[p]rofessionalism is possible for the assisting profession when it is in the best interests of the hosting profession."[83] That lawyers and the ABA view paralegals "with pecuniary favor"[84] is a positive sign of the profession's impending maturation.

Once the assisting profession has emerged in response to a needed and specialized lower echelon division of labor, "specific training and skill acquisition are required."[85] At this point in the "assisting profession's" development, the educational requirements become paramount indicia of the paralegal's progress toward professionalization. Moreover, as "agitated voices"[86] call for self-regulation and autonomy, the paralegal profession may perhaps now be seen as entering the final stages of maturation. Through the standardization of educational requirements, formation of a professional code[87] and membership criteria, "[t]he occupation becomes a profession."[88]

V. The Search for Standards in Paralegal Education

The formulation of commonly recognized educational requirements necessarily precedes more formal determinations of competency such as voluntary certification or governmental license.[89] "[With] the lack of standardization in training and the ability to enter the profession with unknown abilities, paralegals are learning that the time has come to more clearly define their place in the legal community."[90]

The paralegal's place in the legal community has only recently been capable of clearer definition. Early in the licensing debate, disagreements over what standards would be used for determining competency played heavily in the abandonment of initiatives for licensing paralegals. One report found that standards for determining competency at such a premature stage of professional development "are difficult or impossible to formulate."[91] However, as the role and the specific knowledge and technical skills required for profes-

Article 7-7 Continued

sional performance by paralegals became more well defined, the need for discernable standards for paralegal training became more apparent. Initial determinations of the educational requirements prescribed a wide-range of options for meeting minimum qualifications.[92] Recently, however, these options have become narrowed. Recent surveys of potential employers across the country indicate that most law firms require "four-year degrees—in any field—*and* paralegal certificates from ABA-accredited schools."[93] While some debate still rages over the formalization of educational requirements,[94] "[t]here is a growing call for proclaiming the bachelor's degree [in paralegal studies] as the only acceptable level of paralegal education . . . "[95] Paralegal associations themselves have also redefined their position in favor of the general trend favoring a four-year degree as an entry level requirement.[96] The emergence of a standardized educational requirement is a clear sign of professionalization. "As criteria for membership evolve, the credentials necessary to enter the profession become increasingly uniform."[97] With the establishment of uniform educational standards comes professional identity. "Such a change can only come about through a consensus between the assisting profession (paralegals) and the established hosting profession (lawyers) concerning formal entry requirements. And as entry requirements are established, informal access to the assisting profession will become increasingly less likely."[98]

In addition to moving toward a four-year degree, there needs to be a standardization of the paralegal curriculum through the definition of the necessary knowledge base and skills for entry into the profession. This becomes an integral part of the professionalization process. With educational standards established, the paralegal profession may then garner greater acceptance. "And as they define the profession by means of qualifying standards for membership, they will seek endorsements of those standards by government officials and agencies as well as the ABA."[99]

Thus, viewed in a more constructive light, the ABA's role in paralegal education through its approval process has been credited with stimulating growth in the number of paralegal schools across the country,[100] and "fostering the growth of the paralegal market."[101] While some paralegal schools, have decided to forego ABA approval for "philosophical and economic reasons,"[102] schools that have received ABA approval have done so with the explicit acknowledgment that "some employers do use graduation from an approved program as one of the criteria considered in their selection process."[103] In fact, the distinction of ABA approval has now become "the only kind of specialized recognition of paralegal educational programs available,"[104] and ABA approval can be used as a marketing tool implicitly "stressing the benefits of one program over other similar programs."[105] The ABA approval process and the corresponding ABA Guidelines have become, in fact, a commonly accepted educational standard as degrees conferred in accordance with ABA Guidelines have become an accepted credential and an assurance as to the quality of a paralegal's training.

At the very least, the ABA Guidelines help provide a sound contextual foundation for paralegal education and lend a high degree of credibility to paralegal educators and the paralegal profession. With its stated purpose of "[p]romoting quality education for legal assistants,"[106] the ABA Guidelines prescribe a program's requirements in the areas of "curriculum, admissions, faculty, administration, staff, facilities, finances, library, and support programs (for instance, placement)."[107] Although the bulk of its provisions outline administrative and structural parameters for a paralegal program,[108] the ABA Guidelines also establish paralegal education firmly within the mainstream of higher education.[109] The ABA Guidelines affirm the standard of paralegal education at an accredited post-secondary level.[110] Furthermore, a paralegal program situated within a college or university must be "organized and administered"[111] with resources "comparable" with other departments within the institution.[112] Because "the intrusion of paralegal programs into undergraduate offerings on some campuses has been viewed with dismay and sometimes even hostility,"[113] this guideline has been particularly welcome.

The same resource allocation provisions of the ABA Guidelines also greatly benefit paralegal educators.[114] The Guidelines' requirement that paralegal faculty be treated equally with other academic departments in a college or university provides an important foothold in the academic setting.[115] As "new players in higher education,"[116] paralegal faculty find themselves in an environment that "traditionally has not included a niche for faculty teaching in professional practice-oriented programs."[117] By requiring that paralegal programs be treated comparably with other academic units within a college or university, the ABA Guidelines provide that paralegal faculty are entitled to the same respect, credibility, and tenure as other full-time faculty.[118]

Other ABA Guidelines also assist in assuring that students in paralegal education are well-rounded and acclimated to the academic rigors of a college or university. Guideline G-303(b) establishes the minimum quantitative standard for paralegal education "[a]t sixty semester hours, or equivalent, which must include general education and legal specialty courses."[119] Comments following this guideline prescribe that at least eighteen hours consist of "legal specialty" courses and at least another eighteen hours consist of "general education" courses, which are defined as "those courses designed to give a student a broadly based liberal arts education."[120] Further comments to the same guideline require distribution of general education courses among "at least three different disciplines, such as social sciences, natural sciences, mathematics, humanities, foreign language and English."[121] There is also a college level writing proficiency requirement and accommodations for high school advance placement courses, nationally recognized equivalency tests, and even relevant work experience.[122]

While the provisions of the ABA Guidelines establish an appropriate model for a paralegal program,[123] there are some points of concern for paralegal educators and administrators of paralegal programs. For example, at a time of concern over declining enrollment,[124] the provisions of the ABA Guidelines governing admissions may inadvertently give rise to additional tensions for paralegal programs seeking approval or reapproval from the ABA. Where there is competition for students among schools, admissions offices at colleges or universities may feel compelled to apply inappropriate admissions criteria. In particular, financial pressures to accept as many students as possible clash with high or particularized academic admissions criteria that have been established by the ABA. Four-year schools that accept and indeed depend upon large numbers of transfer students from non-ABA approved schools find themselves on the horns of a peculiar dilemma.

ABA Guidelines on admissions[125] do not themselves legislate the usual admissions criteria such as grade point averages or SAT scores. A high school diploma or its equivalent is the only objective standard set out by the admissions guideline. Other provisions of the same guideline only require rationality and consistency of admissions process or projected success of the applicant. However, in establishing minimum quantitative standards for paralegal education,[126] the guidelines define "general education" in the negative. "Examples of courses that are *not* considered general education include, but are not limited to, physical education, performing arts, accounting, computers, technical writing, business mathematics, keyboarding and business law."[127]

By categorically rejecting many courses from the "general education" requirement, the ABA Guidelines may arguably be encroaching upon accepted notions of academic freedom—the holy grail in liberal arts education. Under the ABA Guidelines, courses in the

Article 7-7 Continued

areas of "physical education, performing arts, accounting, computers, technical writing, business mathematics, keyboarding, and business law,"[128] may not qualify as "general education" courses.[129] To be sure, the implicit purpose for the exclusion of courses from those areas is to ensure that the "general education" of paralegals include only subjects of commonly acknowledged academic rigor. Understandably, courses in physical education and keyboarding may not "provide the students with critical reasoning and writing skills."[130] Yet, one can easily justify including many of those courses that do teach those skills, and comprise an integral part of a "broadly based liberal arts education."[131] The sweep of the guideline is too broad and may cause paralegal programs to incur additional and unwarranted tensions from their institutional peers.

As educational standards that are "the only kind of specialized recognition of paralegal educational programs available,"[132] the ABA Guidelines provide a meaningful foundation for recognition of paralegal education. Still, the ABA Guidelines offer no guidance for more definitive standards regarding the specific skills required of paralegals in the working legal world. At best, the Guidelines' provisions for "legal specialty" courses offer only a few suggested courses which, by definition, might emphasize the practical skills a paralegal uses.[133] As a whole, the ABA Guidelines outline professional educational standards of quality in education for paralegals, but only in the most general fashion. Perhaps this is a good thing. With the evolution of the paralegal culture and "a generation of experience"[134] and expertise, paralegal educators are perfectly positioned to provide the necessary details to the general framework for paralegal education established by the ABA Guidelines. Certainly the time has come to ask "what exactly does constitute quality paralegal education and whether the ABA Guidelines should be the only measure of that quality."[135] The autonomy and professionalization that paralegals (and their educators) seek requires them to "[s]trengthen the curriculum by clearly defining the necessary skills and knowledge base . . . required to be effective in the profession."[136] And they have.

VI. The American Association for Paralegal Education

AAfPE, the nation's only service organization for paralegal educators, has been an active voice promoting paralegal education and the profession. As the overseers of paralegal education, the association occupies a central position in establishing standards of instruction. Having "wrestled with the issue of education standards" for years,[137] AAfPE began "looking at curricular standards which exceed the ABA's Approval Guidelines."[138] Quite plainly, the ABA Guidelines were substantively sparse and overly fixated upon structure and administration. Moreover, the guidelines' austere generality were thought to bestow "'standards without standardization.'"[139] Hence, educational credentials molded by the ABA Guidelines alone represented "'formal degrees rather than performance capacity.'"[140] To avoid this "undesirable dichotomy,"[141] AAfPE published the Core Competencies for Paralegal Programs[142]—a "procla[mation] . . . of distinct and identifiable skills and knowledge."[143]

Identifying no less than fifteen substantive areas, each with as many as nine specific points, the Core Competencies delineate the skills and knowledge "that paralegal educators must strive to instill in [their] students."[144] In the areas classified as skills, paralegal educators are exhorted to teach students a comprehensive spectrum, ranging from the intrinsic ability of critical thinking to behavioral adeptness at interpersonal skills.[145] Examples of professionally oriented skills include the ability to "use . . . primary [and] secondary source materials,"[146] and the ability to "conduct an effective interview," or "gain access to [public] information."[147]

The knowledge base desired by the Core Competencies expresses a "common core of legal knowledge that all paralegals should possess."[148] The substantive areas of law prescribed by the Core Competencies represent a sequenced progression of "functionally organized courses,"[149] much resembling a first year law school curriculum. This part of the paralegal's curriculum prescribes foundation informational on the legal system and the profession, as well as basic principles of law also "useful in a wide variety of specialty areas."[150]

The design of both the skill and the knowledge components of the Core Competencies mirrors initial pedagogical standards set by the American Association of Law Schools.[151] After a period of considerable disagreement over the definition of "legal skills," law schools questioned whether they were "producing *reliable professional competence.*"[152] The result, a "1944 report of the AALS Curriculum Committee, . . . was apparently the first organized attempt to isolate legal skills and so to articulate the rationales underlying legal education."[153] The Core Competencies perform the same functions for paralegals and define educational policy for paralegal educators. With the express purpose of providing "[a]ll paralegal education programs . . . [with] an integrated set of core courses,"[154] the Core Competencies have finally standardized paralegal education with sufficient specificity. In so doing, the Core Competencies establish paralegal education as a credible and uniformly acceptable professional credential.[155]

AAfPE has also established educational criteria for matters beyond the paralegal curriculum. Its Statement of Academic Quality[156] adds additional detail to the generalized administrative provisions of the ABA Guidelines in areas such as faculty, facilities, and student services.[157] The Statement of Academic Quality also links its structural qualifications to the substantive provisions of the Core Competencies under the rubrics of "paralegal instruction" and "related competencies," lending a cohesiveness and consistency to both. Laudably, the Statement of Academic Quality requires that [q]uality programs strive to achieve diversity in the composition of the faculty" [and] "their student body."[158] Most significantly, the Statement of Academic Quality defines paralegal solely by education; "[A] person is qualified as a paralegal with (1) an associate or baccalaureate degree or equivalent course work; and (2) a credential in paralegal education completed in any of the following types of educational programs: associate degree, baccalaureate degree (major or minor), certificate, or master's degree."[159]

AAfPE declarations such as the Core Competencies and the Statement of Academic Quality comprise call for autonomy and self-regulation. However, AAfPE membership still remains largely dependent upon ABA standards. Institutional membership is "[a]vailable to institutions offering paralegal and legal assistant education programs, either approved by the American Bar Association or in substantial compliance with its guidelines."[160] It is likely that the ABA Guidelines continue to be used as a convenience. Yet, the functional specificity attained by both the Core Competencies and the Statement of Academic Quality, could themselves embody membership criteria for AAfPE.[161] While the Core Competencies and the Statement of Academic Quality speak to the desired "skills and knowledge" of paralegal students, they speak more to the attributes and quality of paralegal education. AAfPE, less than twenty years old, is younger than the paralegal profession,[162] and is itself undergoing a maturation process. As recent additions to their academic institutions teaching a newly recognized profession, paralegal educators are emerging as a new breed of vocational college professors, defining their own identities and professional status.

As a form of membership criteria *and* educational credential, both documents will profoundly impact upon a wide population of institutions, faculty, administrators and students. Years in the making, the AAfPE Core Competencies was the result of a long process among high-ranking and well-recognized members of the association and its officers. Given the ongoing evolution of paralegals and likewise of paralegal education, "we must

Article 7-7 Continued

continuously re-examine ourselves and the profession,"[163] including documents such as the Core Competencies. There is a foreseeable need to amend the Core Competencies.

For example, a source of inspiration for the Core Competencies was the notion that "'an educated person will be somebody who has learned how to learn, and who continues learning, especially by formal education, throughout his or her lifetime.'"[164] However, that ideal appears nowhere in the document. Given the need for continuing legal education,[165] and the "aspirational"[166] nature of the Core Competencies, paralegal educators ought, as a matter of educational policy, encourage more heuristic forms of instruction. Shouldn't paralegal educators teach a love of learning?

Another policy concern involves issues more politic. The Core Competencies' somewhat didactic tenor implies a hierarchical modality of instruction. Among its several provisions, there is a lack of opportunity for students to develop an ability for open-ended appraisal. At best, the Core Competencies suggest teaching the ability to "recognize when and why varied fact situations make it appropriate to apply exceptions to general legal rules."[167] For many clients' situations, this is an overly polite way of saying that the law is determinative, and often times wrong. As seasoned practitioners, most paralegal educators know this to be the case more often than they care to admit. They have observed and experienced the frequent conflicts between law, ethics, morality and truth. From those experiences alone they have learned how to think critically. Under the general rubric of "critical thinking," the Core Competencies command that paralegal educators teach only the ability "to analyze, . . . to evaluate, . . . to apply, . . . to identify, . . . to recognize, . . . to determine, . . . [and] to distinguish . . ."[168] Yet, critical thinking skills at the very least require a dauntless and unwavering ability to question.

If paralegal educators have "demonstrated a confidence in our positions and policies,"[169] dare we teach students to question authority? After all, the paralegal movement began by questioning whether lawyers exclusively could possess the esoteric knowledge needed to practice law. Paralegal educators have questioned rules proscribing the unauthorized practice of law.[170] And they continue to question the professional monopoly, academe, and the ABA. Therefore, if the Core Competencies require students be taught that "the modern functions of law serves in modern society,"[171] it must also be taught that the law "is incorherent [sic] where it presents itself as logical, and that it is loaded in favor of one class where it appears to be accessible to all, and that it operates not to produce clear doctrines but to mask essential contradictions."[172] Likewise, when paralegal educators abide by the Core Competencies and teach "the functions performed by the various people typically working in a law office,"[173] they should clarify that those functions reflect an entrenched hierarchy of questionable legitimacy.[174] Thus, paralegal educators may well teach their students that entry into a law office, and indeed the legal profession, is at their own risk and for their own reward.

VII. The Continuing Search for Standards

If paralegal educators are willing "to lead in providing answers to the questions of what is a paralegal, what are they able to do, and what do they need to know,"[175] we must maintain "an informed evaluation of the capabilities of our graduates."[176] For it is in the real world that paralegal education will be observed, measured, and judged. Moreover, the expectations by their employers and by segments of the legal community may furnish additional standards and mandates for the continuing evolution of curricular issues in paralegal education. These expectations also suggest future paralegal tasks and serve as a source for the expansion of the permissible scope of "task boundaries." Further research into some of these areas should be part of the educator's continuing vigilance for not just the "capabilities of our graduates," but also for "what . . . they need to know."

In the continuing search for standards, the paralegal educator must also consider the accidental by-product of the collision between federal and state law which permits paralegals to appear before federal administrative agencies.[177] As creations of state law, the prohibitions against the unauthorized practice of law have been preempted by federal regulations that permit paralegals to "practic[e] law in a manner that is remarkably similar to an attorney's representation of a client in court."[178] Even in many states, paralegals may perform the same legal tasks before state administrative bodies.[179] While the state regulations permitting nonlawyer administrative appearances would still subject paralegals to its unauthorized practice rules requiring supervision and accountability, paralegals practicing under the federal authority are not.[180] In fact, even the ABA has recognized that rules authorizing nonlawyer representation before administrative bodies "obviate the attorney's responsibility for the [paralegal's] work[;] it does change the nature of the attorney supervision."[181] Under both state or federal rules, "[t]he opportunity to use such legal assistant services has particular benefits."[182] An examination of some of the regulations that permit paralegal administrative representation may reveal the need to teach more specialized skills and additions to the knowledge base comprising a quality education of a "well-educated paralegal graduate."[183]

In the area of Social Security, representation by nonlawyers has been long permitted and recognized as surprisingly successful.[184] Recent additions to the federal regulations that authorize paralegals to appear as legal representatives indicate a growing acknowledgment of the necessity for standards of educational proficiency. Title 42 U.S.C. § 406(a)(1), authorizes persons "other than attorneys" to represent claimants in the Social Security Administration, who are "possessed of the necessary qualifications to enable them to render such claimants valuable service . . . ; and . . . competent to advise and assist such claimants in presentation of their cases."[185] The tasks and skills required of a nonlawyer representative in these cases is no different from attorneys. "The regulatory scheme provides that a representative, once appointed may obtain information on behalf of the claimant; submit evidence, submit statements 'about facts and law;' and may 'make any request or give any notice about the proceedings . . . '"[186] Seizing these opportunities, paralegal educators may provide the skills of case presentation, administrative advocacy, and client counseling, as well as the substantive law of the administrative agency. Indeed, paralegal representation before administrative agencies "is not an undertaking to be viewed lightly; nor is it one to be taken absent careful preparation and understanding."[187]

The same education and practice opportunities abound in other federal administrative areas as well. Initial feasibility inquiries into immigration law as an area for paralegal practice found a great need for immigration law training for paralegals.[188] This study presents a model in the methodology for the identification of the skills and training needed in specialty areas of law. With the use of surveys as well as analyses of substantive tasks, the study delineated no less than seven specific tasks that could be performed by paralegals.

Regulatory provisions promulgated by federal agencies differ greatly in the scope of allowable nonlawyer practice. In immigration matters, 8 C.F.R. § 292.1(a)(4), provides that accredited representatives"[189] may represent a person in Immigration Court and its appellate body, the Board of Immigration Appeals. To qualify as an "accredited representative," an individual must demonstrate "experience and knowledge of immigration and naturalization law and procedure."[190] The professional representation of "accredited representative" is limited to "non-profit religious, charitable, [and] social service agencies."[191] However most other regulatory provisions permitting direct representation by nonlawyers permit no such limits and present greater opportunities for paralegal practice. Further

Article 7-7 Continued

examination of those provisions reveal, in some cases, qualifying educational standards for practice. More significantly, these regulations are limited forms of *de facto* licensing for paralegals who do qualify under such regulations.[192]

Significantly, in many administrative regulations, the qualifications for nonlawyer representation require education and experience. In proceedings before the Secretary of Housing and Urban Development, a nonlawyer representative may appear before the administrative agency "upon an adequate showing . . . that the individual possesses the legal technical or other qualifications necessary to advise and assist in the presentation of the case."[193] Other administrative agencies are more exacting in their requirements for nonlawyer representation. For instance, in proceedings before the Interstate Commerce Commission, a "non-attorney applicant . . . must have completed 2 years . . . of post secondary education and must possess technical knowledge or experience in the field of transportation . . . or a bachelor's degree and . . . one year [experience in the field of transportation]."[194] Certainly the most exacting requirements come from the U.S. Patent Office. Title 35 U.S.C. § 31 permits the appearance of "agents, attorneys or other persons. [sic]"[195] before the Patent Office. Federal Regulations promulgated pursuant to the statute require intending practitioners, both attorneys and non-attorneys, to submit "satisfactory proof of good moral character and repute and of sufficient basic training in scientific and technical matters."[196] The same provision requires both attorneys and non-attorneys "to pass a rigorous examination, strictly regulates their advertising, and demands that '(a)ttorneys and agents appearing before the Patent Office conform to the standards of ethical and professional conduct generally applicable to attorneys before the courts of the United States.'"[197]

Whatever its provisions, regulatory authority for practice opportunities for paralegals makes it incumbent upon paralegal educators to identify other skills and knowledge bases that may also become part of a quality paralegal education. This should be true even in areas of administrative practice that have no qualifying criteria for representation before the agency.[198] These and many other areas of practice offer additional educational mandates for paralegal educators. By including these areas of administrative practice in the paralegal curriculum, educators would affirm their commitment to high standards in paralegal education, and assure that our students would "become capable and successful paralegals."[199]

VIII. Future Implications for Paralegal Licensing

Professor Eimermann has stated the essential problem in formulating reasonable standards for assessing competency:

> Critics have long argued that arbitrary measures of training and experience are overemphasized and that real competence to do the job is not measured. Although standardized examinations can be used to test knowledge of basic legal principles and procedures, there is disagreement over what types of knowledge are essential. At the present time lawyers are expected to be qualified as generalists, and bar examinations are designed to test all major fields of legal knowledge. Should paralegals be required to be generalists also?[200]

Attempts by professional paralegal associations to formalize competency criteria through standardized certification exams have followed a generalist approach. The Certified Legal Assistant Examination is, like most bar exams, a two-day ordeal, and "encompass[es] a *general* knowledge and understanding of the entire profession and capabilities far exceeding minimal requirements."[201] A review of its summary outline reveals a litany of areas from legal terminology, including "Latin phrases," to ethics and human relations. A substantive law section includes a list of subject matters ranging from "a" (Administrative Law) to "z" (Real Estate—zoning).[202] In fact, the outline of the exam's coverage looks very much like the Core Competencies, in many respects. NFPA has begun its own certification know [sic] as the Paralegal Advanced Competency Exam,[203] which also tests a generalized spread of "five areas of job competency."[204] Both exams are entirely objective, consisting of multiple choice, true/false and matching, in the case of the CLA exam; and all multiple choice questions without "negatively worded stems, such as 'none of the above,'" for PACE.[205] As such, both resemble the multi-state portion of a bar exam. Yet, the future trend for paralegal licensing may be more limited, in form and scope.

Given "our federal constitutional system, [authoritative regulation of paralegals] will almost certainly be at the state level of government."[206] Whether as "associate members" of the state bar or members of a separate "state-level commission . . . set up to oversee matters of paralegal regulation,"[207] a licensed paralegal will have met educational criteria that is proscribed by standards similar to those in the Core Competencies and the Statement of Academic Quality. The education of the licensed paralegal will be obtained at institutions that are accredited by the state as well as by the ABA, by AAfPE, or by both. The model of paralegal regulation and licensing will probably consist of two forms.

In the first form, a paralegal, whether an employee or a freelance independent contractor, would be permitted to practice various forms of law, including giving of advice if under the supervision, or ultimate supervision, of an attorney. Thus similar to the status of paralegals in New Jersey and Kentucky,[208] the concerns of competency and accountability would be adequately mollified by the implementation of accepted educational requirements and the supervision of an attorney.

The second form or layer of licensing would enable an already licensed paralegal of advanced or highly specialized standing to perform an additional limited range of legal services, such as drafting simple wills or conducting real estate closings. In a surprising conclusion, the ABA Commission on Nonlawyer Practice noted that, "lawyers . . . should have to compete with properly licensed paraprofessionals. The continuing high cost of legal services requires that such approaches be considered if clients of ordinary means are to be served at all."[209] In its final form, the ABA Nonlawyer Report went further. As a specific recommendation, the ABA encouraged states to "assess what level of regulation, if any, is appropriate for particular activities."[210] More significantly, the ABA Nonlawyer Report encouraged the notion of limited licensing by the states. By listing a number of activities eligible for limited licensing, the ABA Nonlawyer Report has suggested a realistic and workable model for paralegals to obtain a clearly defined professional status.

Whether paralegal licensing comes by way of statute, regulation, court rules,[211] or bar rules,[212] the role of education is unquestionably central. Paralegal educators have persistently declined to take a position on "whether nonlawyers should be allowed to provide legal representation directly to clients."[213] They have been forewarned that "[p]aralegal educators should not choose sides."[214] And the leadership of paralegal education cautions that "we, as educators, should not take a position on whether regulation of paralegals is needed or appropriate."[215] Quite plainly, it is not "necessary for paralegal educators to favor or oppose regulation of the paralegal profession."[216] The role of the paralegal educator is a narrow one: To ensure that our students receive the highest possible quality of paralegal education. In doing this, paralegal educators promote the paralegal profession in no small measure. By promulgating standards of excellence, they may educate not only their students but also the lawyers, legislators, employers, and the public as to "what constitutes quality paralegal education and why it should be a component of any regulatory scheme."[217]

Article 7-7 Continued

IX. Conclusion

Early calls for paralegal regulation were premature. Central to the problem were the lack of definition for the role that paralegals would assume and the tasks that they could accomplish. Furthermore, educational standards, a key ingredient to any regulation, were nonexistent and difficult to formulate. There were, moreover, political and social dynamics that increased the debate. However, after more than three decades of evolution and experience, the paralegal profession is now on the verge of regulation. Paralegal education and the establishment of educational standards contribute not only to the status of paralegals but also to the possibility of their regulation. Paralegal educators have, in large part, succeeded in institutionalizing paralegal education. More significantly, educators have also provided workable and practical educational standards for paralegals. These competency based standards have the function of conferring a credible educational credential as a precondition for any future regulation. Licensing paralegals may ultimately occur in both general and limited form, thus recognizing both the general and special competence that may be provided by a quality paralegal education.

*   Allan Tow is Assistant Professor, Paralegal Studies, Suffolk University, Boston, Massachusetts. He has a B.A., Anthropology, from Brandeis University, and a J.D. from Boston College Law School.

1.   WILLIAM P. STATSKY, INTRODUCTION TO PARALEGALISM: PERSPECTIVES, PROBLEMS AND SKILLS 186 (5th ed. 1997).

2.   *Missouri v. Jenkins*, 491 U.S. 274, 285 (1989).

3.   *Id.* at 288, *quoting Cameo Convalescent Center v. Senn*, 738 F.2d 836, 846 (7th Cir. 1984), *cert. denied*, 469 U.S. 1106 (1985).

4.   42 U.S.C. § 1988 (1997); *Jenkins*, 491 U.S. 274.

5.   28 U.S.C. § 2412 (1997); *Andrews v. United States*, 122 F.3d 1367 (11th Cir. 1997); *Stockton v. Shalala*, 36 F.3d 49 (8th Cir. 1994) (Social Security); *Harris v. Railroad Retirement Bd*, 990 F.2d 519 (10th Cir. 1993) (Railroad Retirement Act).

6.   11 U.S.C. § 330 (a) (1998); In Re: Busy Beaver Building Centers, Inc., 19 F.3d 833 (3d Cir. 1994).

7.   Fair Labor Standards Act, 29 U.S.C. § 216(b)(1998); *Bankston v. Illinois*, 60 F.3d 1249 (7th Cir. 1995); consumer matters, 15 U.S.C. § 1989(a) (1998), *Strebel v. Milton Wagstaff Motor Co., Inc.*, 46 F.3d 1152 (10th Cir. 1995); certain Internal Revenue Service matters, 28 U.S.C. § 7430(c)(4)(A) (1998), *Miller v. Alamo*, 983 F.2d 856 (8th Cir. 1993); antitrust, 15 U.S.C. § 15 (1998), *American Computech v. National Medical Care, Inc.*, 959 F.2d 239 (9th Cir. 1992); securities fraud, 15 U.S.C. § 78j(b) (1998), *Harmon v. Lyphomed, Inc.*, 945 F.2d 969 (7th Cir. 1991).

     For an early discussion, see Anthony M. Piazza, *Fee-Shifting Statutes and Paralegal Services*, 2 J. PARALEGAL EDUC. & PRAC. 141 (1985). See also Marni Pilafian Lee, *Court-Awarded Paralegal Fees: An Update*, 5 J. PARALEGAL EDUC. & PRAC. 11 (1988).

8.   *Lewis v. Casey*, 578 U.S. 343 (1996).

9.   *U.S. Department of Labor v. Page & Addison*, No 3:91–CV –2655-P (N.D. Texas 1991) (emphasis provided), *reported generally*, Betsy Covington, *Paralegal Professionalism and the Department of Labor*, THE PARALEGAL EDUCATOR, Dec. 1994, at 21.

10. 1988 JOBS RATED ALMANAC; BARBARA BERNARDO, PARALEGAL: AN INSIDER'S GUIDE TO THE FASTEST-GROWING OCCUPATION OF THE 1990s (1990); The Economy, FORTUNE, Aug. 22, 1994 at 62.

11. Katherine A. Currier, *The Unauthorized Practice of Law: Does Anyone Know What It Is?* 8 J. PARALEGAL EDUC. & PRAC. 21, 23 n. 7 (1991).

12. *Id., quoting* MODEL CODE OF PROFESSIONAL RESPONSIBILITY, EC3-1.

13. Deborah L. Rhode, *Policing the Professional Monopoly: A Constitutional and Empirical Analysis of Unauthorized Practice Prohibitions*, 34 STAN. L. REV. 1, 11 n.39 (1981); Currier *supra* note 11, at 22 n.1.

14. *Id.* at 23, n.35 (citing *Jacobellis v. Ohio*, 378 U.S. 184, 197 (1964) (Stewart, J., concurring).

15. WILLIAM P. STATSKY, THE REGULATION OF PARALEGALS: ETHICS, PROFESSIONAL RESPONSIBILITY, AND OTHER FORMS OF CONTROL 13 (1988) (citing a *60 Minutes* television program episode regarding folk hero Rosemary Furman, *60 Minutes* (CBS television broadcast, Nov. 4, 1984).

16. RALPH WARNER, THE INDEPENDENT PARALEGAL'S HANDBOOK 2/25 (3d 1994).

17. Rhode, *supra* note 13, at n.1; Currier, *supra* note 11, n.7.

18. [M]any legal secretaries found themselves performing paralegal-type functions in addition to their secretarial tasks. For instance, it was common for a legal secretary to draft as well as type legal documents. As legal secretaries handled more para-professional tasks and fewer clerical ones, the new profession was born.
    BERNARDO, *supra* note 10, at 10.

19. WARNER, *supra* note 16 at 2 (1994).

20. Quintin Johnstone, *The Future of the Paralegal Profession,* 6 J. PARALEGAL EDUC. & PRAC. 27, 33 (1989).

21. THE NATIONAL ASSOCIATION OF LEGAL ASSISTANTS, INC., MANUAL FOR LEGAL ASSISTANTS 59 (1992).

22. The paralegals' struggle to establish themselves as an autonomous profession pits a largely female population against an established institution which has had a "long history of male domination." Patricia A. Cain, *The Future of Feminist Legal Theory,* 11 WIS. WOMEN'S L.J. 367, 368 (1997). While there is no extant empirical data, at least one paralegal educator and gender scholar has noted the fact that the majority of paralegal students are female, Lynne D. Dahlborg, *Gender Issues in the Paralegal Profession and Education,* 13. J. PARALEGAL EDUC. & PRAC. 21, 24 (1997). The fact that most working paralegals are women had been recognized early on. Edward M. Wheat, *Paralegal Regulation And The New Professionalism,* 3 J. PARALEGAL EDUC. & PRAC. 1, 8 (1986).

    The paralegals' plight is further compounded by the rigid structure of the professional milieu. "Nowhere is hierarchy more entrenched than in the legal profession." Deborah W. Post, *Critical Thoughts About Race, Exclusion, Oppression and Tenure,* 15 PACE L.REV. 69,85 (1994). The classic dialectic on the top-down structure of the legal profession, DUNCAN KENNEDY, LEGAL EDUCATION AND THE REPRODUCTION OF HIERARCHY: A POLEMIC AGAINST THE SYSTEM (1983), heralded the famous Critical Legal Studies movement. See Calvin Trillon, *Reporter at Large: Harvard Law,* NEW YORKER (Mar. 26, 1984) at 53.

23. Wheat, *supra* note 22, at 2.

24. See discussion *infra* at 87.

25. WARNER, *supra* note 16, at 5/6.
    "[A] 'paralegal' may be a legal secretary with years of experience, a retired school teacher with an interest in law, or a law clerk who failed the bar exam and wanted to remain in the field." Donald Green, et al., *The Professionalization of the Legal Assistant: Identity, Maturation States, and Goal Attainment,* 7 J. PARALEGAL EDUC. & PRAC. 35, 36 (1990).

26. THERESE A. CANNON, ETHICS AND PROFESSIONAL RESPONSIBILITY FOR LEGAL ASSISTANTS 271 (2d ed. 1996).

27. Thomas E. Eimermann, *Establishing Qualitative Standards for Paralegal Education,* THE PARALEGAL EDUCATOR, June 1992, at 3.

28. CANNON, *supra* note 26, at 271.

29. Sarah Donohue, *Entry-Level Credentialing Exam: Can We Afford Not to Develop It?,* THE PARALEGAL EDUCATOR, Sept. 1996, at 9.

30. *The Most Frequently Asked Questions About the Credentialing Exam,* THE PARALEGAL EDUCATOR, Sept. 1996, at 7.

31. Diane Petropulos, *Letter to the ABA,* THE PARALEGAL EDUCATOR, March/April 1996, at 9.

32. Clark G. Moscrip, *Regulation Report,* THE PARALEGAL EDUCATOR, June 1992, at 12.

33. *Id.* At 13.

34. Eimermann, *supra* note 27, at 3.

Article 7-7 Continued

35. Wheat, *supra* note 22, at 12.
36. *Id.*
37. Patricia Hicks, *A Response to AAfPE's Policy Statement on Legal Assistant Education,* The Paralegal Educator, Dec. 1997, at 7.
38. "'The best system would be . . . to require that all applicants should learn the principles of law in a school, then apply them for at least a year in an office, and finally pass a public examination by impartial examiners appointed by the courts.'" Robert Stevens, Law School-Legal Education in American from The 1850s to The 1990s 27–28 (1983) (quoting Lewis Delafield, President of the American Social Science Association, 1876).
39. *Massachusetts School of Law v. American Bar Association,* 107 F.3d 1026, 1031 (3d Cir. 1997).
40. Tommy Prud'homme, *The Need For Responsibility Within the Legal Profession,* 26 Gonz. L. Rev. 443, 452 (1991).
41. See *e.g., Bates v. State Bar of Ohio,* 443 U.S. 350 (1977) (ABA opposed First Amendment claims for lawyer advertising); *Goldfarb v. Virginia State Bar,* 421 U.S. 773 (1975) (ABA claimed exemption from antitrust laws and vigorously supported notion of minimum legal fees).
42. Thomas E. Eimermann, Fundamentals of Paralegals 8–9 (3rd ed. 1992) (quoting ABA Special Comm. On Legal Assistants, Liberating the Lawyer: The Utilization of Legal Assistants by Law Firms in the United States (1971) [hereinafter ABA Liberating the Lawyer].
43. *Id.* (italics supplied).
44. Eimmerman, *supra* note 27, at 51 (quoting ABA Certification at 7).
45. *Id.* In retrospect, the ABA's recognition of the paralegal profession rose meteorically. After endorsing the concept of the paralegal in 1967, the ABA established its Special Committee on Legal Assistants which in 1975 became a Standing Committee that is still in operation today. Cannon, *supra* note 26, at 12.
46. The majority of fifty-odd organizations participating in the public hearings expressed opposition to the notion of certification or licensure. *Id.*
47. Conclusion 4 of the ABA's Special Committee Report on Certification specifically noted that further development of the roles and functions of legal assistants was needed before certification could be attempted. ABA Special Committee on Legal Assistants, Certification of Legal Assistants 28 (1975), [hereinafter "ABA Certification"], quoted in Eimermann, *supra* note 27, at 76.

    A major paralegal organization also agreed that the certification efforts at the time were premature. "The paralegal profession is still a new one and the tremendous diversity in the functions and classifications of its members makes it extremely difficult to create generalized standards that can be fairly applied." Statsky, *supra* note 15, at 119, quoting Judith Current, past president, National Federation of Paralegal Associations [hereinafter NFPA].
48. "The use of specifically educated nonlawyers to assist lawyers in the delivery of legal services is a relatively new phenomenon in the history of American law: The concept is a little less than 30 years old." Cannon, *supra* note 26, at 12.
49. Eimmerman, *supra* note 27, at 51.
50. Green, et al., *supra* note 25, at 36.
51. ABA Certification, *supra* note 47.
52. *Id.* (italics supplied).
53. ABA Position Paper—Question of Legal Assistant Licensure or Certification (1986) [hereinafter ABA Position Paper], from Statsky, *supra* note 15, at 124.
54. The Legal Services Section of the State Bar of California had found that, "certification . . . would have a significant impact not only on individual paralegals, attorneys and educators but also on the way legal services are delivered to the public." *Economics of Law Practice Committee Proposal for State Bar Certification of Legal Assistants* 4, quoted in Statsky, *supra* note 15, at 125 (emphasis omitted).
55. *Id.*

56. *Id.* at 125.
57. A legal assistant is a person, qualified through education, training or work experience, who is employed or retained by a lawyer, law office, governmental agency, or other entity in a capacity or function which involves the performance, under the ultimate direction and supervision of an attorney, of specifically delegated substantive legal work, which work, for the most part, requires a sufficient knowledge of legal concepts that, absent such assistant, the attorney would perform the task.
    ABA Position Paper, *supra* note 53, at 4.
        The ABA's choice of words has been noted with some significance: "It is also interesting that the phrase 'legal assistant' is used rather than 'paralegal,' a practice that is also followed by NALA. Paralegal is a much harder-edged term than legal assistant and carries with it connotations of competence and self direction." Wheat, *supra* note 22, at 2.
58. *Id.* at 2–3.
59. *Id.*
60. The National Association of Legal Assistants' [hereinafter NALA] "highly successful" certification exam rewards a successful applicant with the designation of Certified Legal Assistant (CLA). According to data gathered from NALA, "figures show that CLAs earn approximately $2,000 more than those who are not CLAs." EIMMERMANN, *supra* note 42, at 50.
61. In the early 1980's, the ABA and some state bar associations supported the idea of creating a new category of associate membership for paralegals. The ABA established such a category in 1987. BERNARDO, *supra* note 10, at 163. Bar associations in Texas and Ohio have enrolled large numbers of paralegals into their ranks as associate members. North Carolina's Academy of Trial Lawyers admits paralegals as "Legal Assistant Affiliate Members." Supporters claim that associate bar membership encourages greater communication between lawyers and paralegals, fosters greater recognition and expanded responsibilities of paralegals and provides greater public awareness of paralegals. STATSKY, *supra* note 15, at 108–09. More recently, the North Carolina Bar Association's Board of Governors unanimously approved the creation of a Legal Assistant Division. See Camille Stuckey Stell, CLAS, *The Status of North Carolina Paralegals,* THE PARALEGAL EDUCATOR April/May 1998, at 22–23.
62. EIMERMANN, *supra* note 42, at 8–9 (quoting ABA Liberating the Lawyer, *supra* note 43, at 43.)
63. ABA Position Paper, *supra* note 54.
64. STATSKY, *supra* note 15, at 102.
65. *Id.*
66. *Id.* at 102.
67. *Id.*
68. *Id.* at 25.
69. *Id.*
70. *Id.*
71. STATSKY, *supra* note 15, at 101.
72. EIMERMANN, *supra* note 42, at 6 (quoting ABA Liberating the Lawyer, *supra* note 42, at 43).
73. Wheat, *supra* note 22, at 5.
74. *Id.* at 7.
75. *Id.* at 7–8
76. CANNON, *supra* note 26, at 16 (quoting ABA Commission on Nonlawyer Practice, (1993)).
77. Report of ABA Commission on Nonlawyer Practice (hereinafter ABA Nonlawyer Report), Nonlawyer Activities in Law-Related Situations 94 (August 1995).
78. *Id.* at 73.
79. *Id.* at 96–97.

Article 7-7 Continued

80. The notion that paralegals could work independently as freelance professionals has only recently gained acceptance. See *e.g.*, WARNER, *supra* note 16; In re Opinion 24 of Committee on Unauthorized Practice of Law, 128 N.J. 114, 607 A.2d 962 (1992), holding that independent paralegals working on a case-by-case basis under the supervision of an attorney are not engaged in the unauthorized practice of law; and Kentucky Supreme Court Rule 3.700, sub-rule two which states,

    [f]or purposes of this rule, the unauthorized practice of law shall not include any service rendered involving legal knowledge or legal advice, whether representation, counsel or advocacy, in or out of court, rendered in respect to the acts, duties, obligations, liabilities or business relations of the one requiring services where:

    A.   The client understands that the paralegal is not a lawyer;

    B.   The lawyer supervises the paralegal in the performance of his duties; and

    C.   The lawyer remains fully responsible for such representation, including all actions taken or not taken in connection therewith by the paralegal to the same extent as if such representation had been furnished entirely by the lawyer and all such actions had been taken or not taken directly by the lawyer.

    D.   The services rendered under this Rule shall not include appearing formally in any court or administrative tribunal except under Sub-rule 3 below, nor shall it include questioning of witnesses, parties or other persons appearing in any legal or administrative action including but not limited to depositions, trials, and hearings.

81. AMERICAN BAR ASSOCIATION STANDING COMMITTEE ON LEGAL ASSISTANTS, GUIDELINES FOR THE APPROVAL OF LEGAL ASSISTANT EDUCATION PROGRAMS 1 (1997) [hereinafter ABA Guidelines](quoting ABA's formal mission statement).

82. Green, et al., *supra* note 25, at 35.

83. *Id.* at 36.

84. *Id.*

85. *Id.*

86. *Id.* at 40. "'Agitation' is a means by which new groups assert independence and establish autonomy." *Id.* at 39.

    A shining example of a paralegal educator's call for greater recognition through "agitation" can be found in Bernard G. Helldorfer, *AAfPE's Response to ABA Proposed Definition*, AAfPE SIDEBAR, July / August 1997, at 3, in which the American Association for Paralegal Education's [hereinafter AAfPE] President informed the ABA,

    [B]y not providing any opportunity for input from those most affected by the definition, namely the paralegals, the new definition cannot be said to represent a consensus within the profession. . . . [W]e believe that the [ABA] has severely diminished the value and contribution of formal education to the profession . . . . In light of our concerns, please be advised that the AAfPE Board of Directors has voted to develop an AAfPE definition of paralegal/legal assistant which will advance and promote the paralegal profession and the value of formal paralegal education.

    See also *supra*, notes 29 through 38 and accompanying text.

87. See *e.g.*, NATIONAL ASSOCIATION OF LEGAL ASSISTANTS, INC., MODEL STANDARDS AND GUIDELINES FOR UTILIZATION OF LEGAL ASSISTANTS (Sept. 1997) [hereinafter "NALA Standards"].

88. Green, et al., *supra* note 25, at 40.

89. See *e.g.*, Qualifications for Eligibility for NALA's Certification Examination.

    In order to take the NALA certification examination, the applicant must meet the requirements of one of the three categories listed below:

    1.   Graduation from a legal assistant program that is:

        a) Approved by the American Bar Association, or

        b) An associate degree program, or

        c) A post-baccalaureate certificate program in legal assistant studies, or

        d) A bachelor's degree program in legal assistant studies, or

e) A legal assistant program which consists of a minimum of 60 semester (or equivalent quarter) hours of which at least 15 semester hours (or equivalent quarter) are substantive legal courses.

   2. A bachelor's degree in any field plus one (1) year's experience as a legal assistant.

   3. A high school diploma or equivalent plus seven (7) years' experience as a legal assistant under the supervision of a member of the Bar plus evidence of a minimum of twenty (20) hours of continuing legal education credit to have been completed within a two-year period prior to the examination date.

EIMERMANN, supra note 42, at 77.

90. Katherine Jordan, *It's Time to Set Standards in Growing Paralegal Field,* BOSTON BUS. J., Sept. 3–9, 1993, at 11.

91. Illinois State Bar Association, *Report on the Joint Study Committee on Attorney Assistants,* June 21, 1977 at 6, quoted in STATSKY, *supra* note 15, at 50.

92. For instance, NALA Standards provide for no less than seven options:

   A legal assistant should meet certain minimum qualifications. The following standards may be used to determine an individual's qualifications as a legal assistant:

     1. Successful completion of the Certified Legal Assistant ("CLA") certifying examination . . . ;

     2. Graduation from an ABA approved program of study for legal assistants;

     3. Graduation form [sic] a course of study for legal assistants which is institutionally accredited but not ABA approved, and which requires not less than the equivalent of 60 semester hours of classroom study;

     4. Graduation from a course of study for legal assistants, . . . plus not less than six months of in-house training as a legal assistant;

     5. A baccalaureate degree in any field, plus not less than six months in-house training . . . ;

     6. A minimum of three years of law-related experience under the supervision of an attorney, including at least six months of in-house training . . . ; or

     7. Two years of in-house training as a legal assistant.

NALA Standards, *supra* note 87, at 7.

   Consistent with this wide-ranging offering, see note 91, *supra.*

93. Elaine Bieberly, *Hiring Trends,* NATIONAL PARALEGAL REPORTER, Summer 1997, at 11.

   This, apparently, is not news. A survey conducted in 1988 under the combined auspices of the ABA, AAfPE, LAMA, NALA, NFPA, and the Association of Legal Administrators, had determined that "[t]he majority of this country's paralegal employers, from medium- to large-size private law firms and corporations now believe that the successful applicant for a job should carry a bachelor's degree." Kathleen G. Anderson, Research Note, *The Changing Face of Paralegal Education In the Marketplace,* 6 J. PARALEGAL EDUC. & PRAC. 55, 55 (1989).

94. See *e.g.,* Sharon E.D. Gerst and Stephanie M. Landstrom, *Should There Be Educational Requirements For Paralegals?,* LEGAL ASSISTANT TODAY, May/June 1994, at 24–25.

95. Bernie Helldorfer, *AafPE's Mission: A Time to Check the Compass,* THE PARALEGAL EDUCATOR, March/April 1997 at 5. But see, *AAfPE, Proposed Statement on Educational Component of Legislation Regulating or Defining Paralegals,* THE PARALEGAL EDUCATOR, April/May 1998, at 7. "The American Association for Paralegal Education recommends that a person is qualified as a paralegal with . . . an <u>associate or baccalaureate</u> degree or equivalent course work, and a credential in paralegal education." *Id.* (underscore in original).

96. While NFPA members recognized that a two-year degree with an emphasis in paralegal studies is acceptable to employers in some markets as the <u>*minimum criteria*</u> for individuals to enter the paralegal profession, NFPA recommends that, based upon current hiring trends, future practitioners should have a four-year degree to enter the profession.

Article 7-7 Continued

Susan A. Kaiser, *NFPA Refines Its Position on Paralegal Education,* NATIONAL PARALEGAL REPORTER, Spring 1996, at 8 (emphasis added).

LAMA's [Legal Assistant Management Association] position is that a baccalaureate degree should be the minimum requirement for employment as a legal assistant . . . . Working with complex legal issues requires that a legal assistant possess clear writing, research and critical thinking abilities. Because a strong academic background is essential, a baccalaureate degree should be the minimum requirement for employment as a legal assistant. LAMA believes this *accepted professional standard* of academic achievement lends greater credibility and respect to the legal profession.

LAMA, *Position Paper On Legal Assistant Education,* THE PARALEGAL EDUCATOR, Sept. 1997 at 13 (footnote omitted) (italics added).

97. Green, et al., *supra* note 25, at 38.
98. *Id.* at 37.
99. *Id.*
100. *Paralegal Institute, Inc. v. American Bar Association,* 475 F. Supp. 1123, 1131 (E.D.N.Y. 1979), aff'd, 622 F.2d 575 (2d Cir. 1980). Concluding that the ABA guidelines for paralegal schools do not violate antitrust laws, the Court noted that

when the ABA's accreditation program was instituted in 1973, there were approximately 37 paralegal training programs throughout the United States; by February of 1978, there were approximately 224 such programs nationwide. In the New York market area (New York City plus a 100 mile radius), where three paralegal institutions operated in 1972, 17 such institutions are currently operating. Contrary to plaintiff's contentions, the ABA accreditation program appears to have had a positive effect on competition in the paralegal training market.

475 F. Supp. at 1131.
101. *Id.* at 1132.
102. EIMERMANN, *supra* note 42, at 46. As of 1988, "the majority of programs have decided *not* to apply for approval." STATSKY, *supra* note 15, at 101 (italics in original). This apparently has remained true to today. The 1995 ABA Nonlawyer Report noted that "[t]here are approximately 700 paralegal education programs in the United States." ABA Nonlawyer Report, *supra* note 77, at 56. Of these 700-odd programs, only about 210 have obtained ABA approval. Marilyn Barmash, *Update on ABA Activities,* THE PARALEGAL EDUCATOR, Mar./ Apr. 1997, at 27.
103. EIMERMANN, *supra* note 42, at 46.
104. CANNON, *supra* note 26, at 271.
105. Mary M. Flaherty, *Marketing Through the Employer Survey,* THE PARALEGAL EDUCATOR, Apr./May,1998, at 3.
106. ABA Guidelines, *supra* note 81, at 1.
107. CANNON, *supra* note 26, at 271.
108. The paralegal program must be staffed with an experienced and knowledgeable director who is committed to the education of paralegals and whose full-time efforts will be devoted to the program's leadership in all aspects. Guideline G-401, 402. The students, faculty must have access to a law library, and to sufficient and suitable physical plant facilities for the program's operation and administration. Guidelines G-601, G-701, 702, 703. A carefully and specifically constituted advisory committee must meet regularly and play an active role in assisting the director to accomplish her enumerated duties. Guideline G- 203. ABA Guidelines, *supra* note 81.
109. Similar to the experience of computer training schools, advertisements for paralegal training are now only rarely seen on matchbook covers or as offered in correspondence schools.
110. "The Program of Education for Legal Assistants shall be:
(a)   At the postsecondary level of instruction;
(b)   . . . Offered by an institution accredited by an institutional accrediting agency acceptable to the committee."
ABA Guidelines, Guideline G-303.

111. ABA Guidelines, Guideline G-201.
112. ABA Guidelines, Guideline G-202.
113. Elizabeth Horowitz, *Paralegal Education And Academia: Institutional Issues*, 2 J. PARALEGAL EDUC. & PRAC. 1,8 (1985).

   The "hostility" experienced by many university housed paralegal programs is a result of the "tension" created by the academics' disparagement of vocational goals—a traditional conflict between "scholars versus practitioners, learning knowledge for its own sake versus learning knowledge with immediate practical application, teaching versus research . . . " *Id.* See also Jill E. Martin, *Paralegal Programs in the Liberal Arts*, 4 J. PARALEGAL EDUC. & PRAC. 1 (1987).

114. The comments following ABA Guideline G-202, list as factors to be considered in determining "comparability . . . [s]tatus of the program director; . . . [t]reatment of faculty . . . ; [s]upport for professional development; [and] [p]articipation in academic affairs and decision making." ABA Guidelines, Guideline G-202, comments.
115. *Id.*
116. Margaret T. Stopp and Susan W. Harrell, *Tenure and Promotion Standards for Paralegal Faculty*, 13 J. PParalegal [SIC] EDUC. & PRAC. 1,1 (1997).
117. *Id.*
118. "It may be that the reasons for this dismay [over paralegal programs by academe] are political and budgetary, rather than based on a view of paralegal studies as intellectually inferior." *Id.* A contrary view as to the effect of ABA Guidelines is acknowledged.

   Approval by the . . . [ABA] . . . may actually decrease the credibility of the program among those unfamiliar with the paralegal profession. Most ABA-approved programs offer certain courses because the ABA recommends they do so. Such curriculum decisions are normally made by faculty. Liberal arts faculty members are concerned about the governance of their institution and do not like an outside non-academic organization telling them what should be offered.

   Martin, *supra* note 113, at 8.
   Regarding the availability of tenure to paralegal educators, see STOPP, *supra* note 116.
119. ABA Guidelines, Guideline G-303(b).
   Earlier ABA Guidelines required thirty (30) semester units of college level work before entering a paralegal program. Horowitz, *supra* note 113, at 6 n. 6.
120. *Id.*
121. *Id.*
122. ABA Guidelines, Guideline G-303, comments H and J.
123. Sprinkled among its provisions are several mandates which further a paralegal program's social responsibility. The guidelines prohibit discrimination in an acceptably broad range of grounds, including sexual orientation. Guideline G-204. There are consumer protection-like provisions which prohibit false and misleading advertising, Guideline G-501, comment D. Guideline G-502, mandates student support services in the forms of advising, counseling and placement; and requires student input into curriculum and program evaluation.
124. See Ruth-Ellen Post, *Paralegal Enrollments: Has the Bubble Burst?*, THE PARALEGAL EDUCATOR, Dec. 1997, at 10.
125. ABA Guidelines, Guideline G-501.
126. ABA Guidelines, Guideline G-303.
127. *Id.,* comment F (italics added).
128. ABA Guidelines, Guideline G-303, comment F.
129. *Id.*
130. *Id.*

Article 7-7 Continued

131. The exclusion of courses from the "performing arts" is particularly bothersome. Courses that teach and improve upon the skills of public speaking, for instance, certainly may be a valid part of a "broad based liberal arts education." Or certainly "emphasize[ ] [paralegal] skills . . . and are pertinent to the [paralegal's] performance on the job." ABA Guidelines, Guideline G-303, command D(2) and (3). Much more can be said to support the acceptance of courses in acting and theater arts. "In acting the heart teaches the intellect." James Maxwell, Note, *Acting and Legal Education*, 17 Vt. L. Rev. 533, 533 (1993).

132. Cannon, *supra* note 26, at 271.

133. ABA Guidelines, Guideline G-303, comment D(2).

134. Diane Petropulos, *President's Column, Educational Standards: AAfPE's Obligation to the Profession,* The Paralegal Educator, Mar./ Apr. 1996, at 6.

135. Bernie Helldorfer, *President's Column—The Year in Perspective*, The Paralegal Educator, Sept. 1997, at 4. Surely, a parting shot agitating for autonomy. See note 86, *supra*.

136. Green, et al., *supra* note 25, at 41.

137. David Dye, *AAfPE's History,* The Paralegal Educator, June 1992, at 5.

138. *Id.*

139. Ann Yarbro McCoin, *President's Column, Communication is Key,* The Paralegal Educator, Dec. 1994, at 4 (quoting Peter Druker, *The Age of Social Transformation,* The Atlantic Monthly, Nov. 1994.).

140. *Id.*

141. *Id.* at note 139.

142. AAfPE, Core Competencies for Paralegal Programs (1994)[hereinafter Core Competencies].

143. Bernard Helldorfer, *Taking the Next Step: Uniting the Profession and Finishing the Job,* The Paralegal Educator, Sept. 1996, at 6.

144. *Id.* If the Core Competencies can be viewed as providing "what to teach," a contemporaneous effort offers instructors "how to teach." Anita Tebbe, Strategies and Tips for Paralegal Educators (1995).

145. Core Competencies, I(A) and (D).

146. *Id.,* I(E)(1) and (3).

147. *Id.,* I(H)(2) and (3).

148. *Id.,* II.

149. Stevens, *supra* note 38, at 214–215.

150. Core Competencies, II, D. The Core Competencies section on the Acquisition of Knowledge enumerates in fairly specific detail legal principles in the substantive areas of contracts, torts, business organizations, and litigation procedures. *Id.*

151. Stevens, *supra* note 38, at 178. Founded in 1900, the American Association of Law Schools (hereinafter "AALS") is the national service association for the nation's law schools. Its membership, purposes, and activities are similar to those of AAfPE.

152. *Id.* at 214 (italics in original).

153. *Id.*

154. Core Competencies, Preamble.

155. Other unifying activities which also have the affirmative effect of standardizing curricula include drafting Model Syllabi. See *e.g.,* Deborah A. Howard, *Education Committee Undertakes New Syllabi,* The Paralegal Educator, Apr./May 1998, at 16.

156. AAfPE, Statement of Academic Quality (1997).

157. For instance, ABA Guideline G-401, states that "[t]he program director and instructors must possess education, knowledge and experience in the legal assistant field." *Id.* Proportedly [sic], the guideline establishes qualifications for paralegal faculty. However, neither the guideline nor the comments which follow it specify what constitutes "education, knowledge and experience." Anyone can call themselves a paralegal, or a paralegal educator for that matter. The Quality

Statement substantially narrows the field. "The faculty of a quality paralegal education programs [sic] consists of legal professionals . . . who . . . hold a graduate degree or possess exceptional expertise in the legal subject to be taught . . . ."

158. *Id.*

159. *Id.* Compare with ABA Position Paper's definition, *supra* note 57. For new professions, such as paralegals, semantic changes underscore the evolution of role clarification and self-awareness. Toward those ends, AAfPE even has its own Paralegal Definition Task Force. Paul Guymon, *Task Force Drafts Proposed Definition,* THE PARALEGAL EDUCATOR, Dec. 1997, at 17.

160. AAfPE, AAfPE DIRECTORY 2 (1997).

161. That AAfPE-generated educational standards could also function as membership criteria had been considered well before completion of the Core Competencies. "We have looked at [educational standards as] . . . criteria . . . for institutional membership." Dye, *supra* note 137.

   However, AAfPE's official policy is that the Core Competencies "*should* be required of all graduates of member schools." AAfPE Board, *Policy Statement, Statement to ABA Commission on Nonlawyer Practice,* THE PARALEGAL EDUCATOR, Sept., 1993, at 7 (italics supplied).

162. See note 48, *supra;* CANNON, *supra* note 26, at 12; Dye, *supra* note 137.

163. Helldorfer, *supra* note 143.

164. McCoin, *supra* note 139.

165. See ABA MODEL GUIDELINES FOR THE UTILIZATION OF LEGAL ASSISTANT SERVICES, Guideline 10 (1991), CANNON, *supra* note 26, at 272.

166. Core Competencies, Preamble.

167. Core Competencies, I, A, 5.

168. *Id.,* I, A.

169. Helldorfer, *supra* note 143.

170. Currier, *supra* note 11.

171. Core Competencies, II, A, 1.

172. Trillon, *supra* note 22, at 70.

173. Core Competencies, II, B, 2.

174. See note 22, *supra.*

175. Clark Moscrip, *AAfPE Must Stand for Excellence,* THE PARALEGAL EDUCATOR, Apr./May 1998, at 6.

176. *Id.*

177. 5 U.S.C. § 555(b)(1967), *Sperry v. Florida* ex rel. Florida Bar, 373 U.S. 379 (1963). This, of course, is not a new fact. See A.L. Humphreys, et al., *Paralegal Representation Before The Social Security Administration,* 9 J. PARALEGAL EDUC. & PRAC. 23 (1993). As a matter of fact, these provisions have existed for decades. F. Trobridge vom Baur, Standards of Admission to Practice Before Federal Administrative Agencies, Survey of the Legal Profession (1953), chart summary reproduced in Federal Bar Association (Rodolphe J. de Seife, ed.), Practice of Laymen Elsewhere in Government, 15 F. BAR J. THE PRACTICE OF NON-LAWYERS BEFORE ADMINISTRATIVE AGENCIES, 227, 228–235 (1955).

178. WILLIAM P. STATSKY, ESSENTIALS OF PARALEGALISM 188.

179. Gregory T. Stevens, *The Proper Scope of Nonlawyer Representation in State Administrative Proceedings: A State Specific Balancing Approach,* 43 V AND. L. REV. 245 (1990); [*Unauthorized Practice of Law Committee v. State of Rhode Island*], 543 A.2d 662 (R.I. 1988); Formal Opinion 1988-103 California State Bar Committee on Professional Responsibility and Conduct.

180. *Sperry,* 373 U.S. 389.

181. ABA MODEL GUIDELINES FOR THE UTILIZATION OF LEGAL ASSISTANT SERVICE, Comment to Guideline 2 (1991).

182. *Id.*

183. Moscrip, *supra* note 175.

Article 7-7 Continued

184. DSS/OHA, Participant Involvement in Request for Hearing Cases for Fiscal 1983, Table 6, (May, 1984), also cited in WILLIAM P. STATSKY, *supra* note 15, at 34 (1988); see also A.L. Humphreys, et al., *supra*, note 177.

185. 42 U.S.C. § 406(a)(1)(1998); 20 C.F.R. § 404.1705(1998).

186. Jeffrey S. Wolfe, *In Quest of the Challenge—The Role of Non-Lawyer Representatives Before the Office of Hearings and Appeals,* FACTS & FINDINGS, February 1998, at 9, quoting 20 C.F.R. §§ 404.1707, 404,1710, 404.1710(1998)(footnotes omitted).

187. *Id.* at 11.

188. Allan H. Wernick, *The Education and Utilization of Paralegals in the Practice of Immigration Law,* 7 J. PARALEGAL PRAC. & EDUC. 35 (1990).

189. The regulation provides pertinently as follows:"

§ 292.1 Representation of others.

(a)   A person entitled to representation may be represented by any of the following:

. . .

(4)   Accredited representatives. A person representing an organization described in § 292.2 of this chapter who has been accredited by the Board."

190. 8 C.F.R. § 292.2(d)(1998).

191. 8 C.F.R. § 292.2(a)(1998).

192. The earliest forms of limited licensing by administrative agencies for nonlawyers have been in existence since 1860's. Presently codified in 38 U.S.C. § 5904, nonlawyers have been able to assist veterans seeking disability benefits since the Civil War. ABA Nonlawyer Report at 25. The practice of allowing nonlawyers known as "patent agents" to represent individuals before the U.S. Patent Office has been in existence since 1869. *Sperry,* 373 U.S. 379.

193. 24 C.F.R. § 26.7(d)(1998).

194. 49 C.F.R. § 1103.3(b)(1998).

195. 35 U.S.C. § 31(1998).

196. 37 C.F.R. § 10.7(b)(1998).

197. *Sperry,* 373 U.S. at 395–96 (citations omitted).

198. A number of administrative agencies permit nonlawyer representation without qualifications for education or training. See *e.g.,* 12 C.F.R. § 308.6(1998)(Federal Deposit Insurance Corporation); 16 C.F.R. § 4.1(a)(2)(1998) (Federal Trade Commission); 20 C.F.R. § 802.202(d)(2)(1998) (Benefits Review Board); 29 C.F.R. § 18.34(a)(1998) (Department of Labor); 21 C.F.R. § 1316.50(1998) (Drug Enforcement Administration); 29 C.F.R. § 1601.7(a)(1998)(Equal Employment Opportunity Commission).

199. Clark G. Moscrip, *AAfPE Is Living In Interesting Times,* THE PARALEGAL EDUCATOR, Dec. 1997, at 6.

200. EIMERMANN, *supra* note 42, at 50.

201. VIRGINIA KOERSELMAN, CLA REVIEW MANUAL 2 (1993) (italics added).

202. *Id.* at 3–6.

203. Also known by its acronym, the PACE exam was administered for the first time in June 1996. Therese A. Cannon, *Setting the PACE for the Paralegal Profession,* NATIONAL PARALEGAL REPORTER, Spring 1996, at 26.

204. *Id.*

205. KOERSELMAN, *supra* note 201, at 3.

206. *Id.;* see also Wheat, *supra* note 22, at 11.

207. *Id.,* at 9.

208. See *supra* note 80.

209. Report of ABA Commission on Nonlawyer Practice (11993), quoted in CANNON, *supra* note 26, at 16.

210. ABA Nonlawyer Report at 136.

211. See Robert LeClair, *Paralegal Certification Through Local Court Rule: A Different Perspective on an Old Problem,* THE PARALEGAL EDUCATOR, Apr./May 1998, at 23.

212. A proposed Alaska Bar Rule has approached the issue of regulation of nonlawyers by redefining the types of activities that may be considered the practice of law. Susan Howery, *Alert! One State Considers Licensing Paralegals,* The Paralegal Educator, Apr./May 1998, at 22.
213. AAfPE Board, *supra* note 161, at 8.
214. Clark G. Moscrip, *Legislative Report,* The Paralegal Educator, June 1993, at 9.
215. Diane Petropulos, *Where We Go from Here,* The Paralegal Educator, Sept. 1997, at 7.
216. *Id.*
217. *Id.*

Article 7-7 Continued

CONCLUSION

The regulation issue is central to the professional identity issue and it is interwoven with the unauthorized practice of law issue. It remains a concern to legal assistants, educators, students, legislators, state bar associations, judges, and lawyers, although there is no agreement on the crux of the issue: whether regulation is needed to protect the public. Absent a public need, the state lacks authority to use its police power to require mandatory licensing. However, that fact would not prevent other forms of regulation, including certification and registration. Even the stakeholders who support regulation do not agree on the appropriate regulatory scheme. The regulation debate will continue to be a focus during the coming years.

DISCUSSION QUESTIONS

1. Do you feel regulation is necessary for the profession? Why or why not?
2. Of the proposed regulation options discussed, which option do you prefer and why?

ENDNOTES

[1]*See* discussion *infra* Chapter 2 (certification and specialization examinations).
[2]To obtain updated information concerning the view of the NFPA on the regulation issue, see its Web site at http://www.paralegals.org/ Development/Updates/home.html.
[3]To obtain updated information concerning the view of the NALA on the regulation issue, see its Web site at http://www.nala.org.

[4]*See* 1998–2000 NFPA Legislative Committee Bill Activity/Status Report as of July, 1999 (report contains a chart summarizing legislative activity relating to regulation in all 50 states). Visit the following Web sites for updated information concerning the status of regulation activities: http://www.nala.org and http://www.paralegals. org.
[5]*See* Robert Sperber, *LAMA Opposes Mandatory Regulation of Traditional Paralegals,* Legal Assistant Today, July/Aug. 1997, at 20.

The Exempt Employee Issue

INTRODUCTION

The regulation issue is interwoven with the paralegal identity issue because regulation is seen as a method of defining who a legal assistant is and what a legal assistant has qualifications to do. Also interwoven with these issues is the question of whether a legal assistant is an exempt employee under the Fair Labor Standards Act (FLSA). If a legal assistant is an exempt employee, he or she is not entitled to overtime pay; on the other hand, if a legal assistant is a nonexempt employee, the employer is required to pay him or her overtime pay. Some stakeholders in the field strongly believe that if the profession is going to progress, a legal assistant must be classified as an exempt employee, consistent with the exempt status accorded to the other professional income-producing employees in the law firm. Other stakeholders, though agreeing that legal assistants should be accorded the benefits of professional status, argue that they are nonexempt under the FLSA and thus should be paid overtime.

WHAT IS THE FAIR LABOR STANDARDS ACT (FLSA)?

The Fair Labor Standards Act of 1938[1] is the federal law, administered and enforced by the U.S. Department of Labor, that establishes minimum wage and hours for employees working in the private and public sector. The Act requires employers to pay overtime compensation to certain classes of employees. However, under the Act, certain categories of employees are exempt from the wage and hour restrictions contained in the act. If an individual is exempt under the FLSA, they can be required to work in excess of 40 hours per week without being paid overtime. There are three exempt categories, as follows:

- Executive
- Professional
- Administrative

The *executive exemption* applies to any employee who is guaranteed a salary of at least $250.00 per week, whose primary duty is managing an enterprise or a recognized department or subdivision thereof, and who customarily and regularly directs the work of at least two other employees. This exemption could apply to a supervising legal assistant.

The *professional exemption* applies to any employee whose work assignments require a knowledge of an advanced type in a field of science or learning customarily acquired by a prolonged course of specialized intellectual instruction and study, as distinguished from a general academic education. This exemption has been applied to physician's assistants[2] and to legal assistants. In *Oxman v. Hamilton & Samuels*, the California Division of Labor Standards Enforcement held that the legal assistants in question were professionally exempt because they performed duties that required discretion, the use of independent judgment, and were cost-effective replacements for associates.[3] Factors that the Division felt were significant included that the firm required its legal assistants to have certificates from ABA-approved legal assistant programs, that the legal assistants were a distinct group within the firm with authority to delegate work to the firm's secretaries, and that the firm's clients paid substantial hourly rates ($100.00 or more) for the legal assistant's work. However, it should be noted that this case is a departure from the DOL's position that legal assistants would normally not be granted a professional exemption.

The *administrative exemption* applies to any employee who is guaranteed a salary of at least $250.00 per week, whose primary duty consists of performing office or non-manual work directly related to the management policies or general business operations of the employer or the employer's clients, and who customarily and regularly exercises discretion and independent judgment. The DOL has taken the position that legal assistants, as a general rule, do not qualify for the administrative exemption. However, this position has been criticized by commentators who believe that the DOL has not responded to the evolution and current realities of the legal assistant profession.

Who Decides Whether a Legal Assistant Is an Exempt Employee Under the FLSA?

In the FLSA, Congress authorized the Secretary of Labor to define the terms executive, professional, and administrative. In line with this delegated authority, the Wage and Hour Division of the DOL develops guidelines and regulations which attempt to clarify what types of employees fall within each exemption category. The DOL has consistently taken the position that, as a general rule, legal assistants do not fall within any exempt category and therefore must be paid overtime compensation. However, notwithstanding the rigid position of the DOL, whether a particular legal assistant employee falls within an exempt category will be determined by the trier of fact on a case-by-case basis. As a practical matter, because of the varied job descriptions, credential requirements, and qualifications for legal assistants, it is very possible that a jury could find one legal assistant within a law firm to be exempt and another to be nonexempt. The decision will turn on the type of tasks performed, the amount of independent judgment and discretion required, and the educational background, criteria, and credentials required for the position.

In the case of *Reich v. Page Addison*[4] the jury was asked to determine whether 23 current and former legal assistant employees in a Dallas-based law firm were exempt under the FLSA. The DOL had audited the compensation practices of the law firm and had determined that the law firm had violated the FLSA by failing to pay overtime compensation to the legal assistants. After hearing evidence at the trial concerning the type of duties performed by the legal assistants, the federal court jury found that the legal assistants were exempt employees under the administrative exemption. They found that the legal assistants in question exercised independent judgment and discretion in the performance of their duties or responsibilities even though their work was subject to approval and possible rejection by a supervising attorney. The DOL appealed the decision, but in September of 1994 abandoned the appeal with prejudice (i.e., with the understanding that the action may not be brought again).

Do Legal Assistants Want to Be Exempt Under the FLSA?

Some legal assistants want to be considered as exempt employees under the FLSA, other legal assistants don't. According to surveys conducted nationwide, approximately 50 percent of legal assistants believe that they have the educational background and qualifications to exercise independent judgment and discretion as they perform paralegal tasks and that they fall within the exemptions under the FLSA. The remaining 50 percent do not want to be considered exempt under the FLSA because they want to receive overtime compensation.[5]

Article 8-1 contains an analysis of exempt/nonexempt issues and includes comments by practicing legal assistants that will provide insight into this issue from a practicing legal assistant perspective.

In Article 8-2, the author reacts to *Page & Addison* and predicts the effect that case will have on legal assistants and their employers.

In Article 8-3, the author provides insight into the opinions of practicing legal assistants in private law firms and corporate legal departments on the exempt/nonexempt issue.

Exempt vs. Nonexempt

A decision based on another large issue was reached in 1994. In 1991, the U.S. Department of Labor (DOL) was auditing the compensation practices of a Dallas-based firm, Page & Addison. Determining that the law firm had violated federal laws by refusing to pay overtime compensation to 23 former and current legal assistants, it sued. In March 1994, a federal jury found in favor of the law firm.

Despite this landmark decision, the DOL continues to have definite ideas about the status of legal assistants and overtime pay: legal assistants are not nonexempt employees entitled to overtime compensation.

Its rationale is based on the wording of the Fair Labor Standards Act (FLSA) of 1938. Under the FLSA, only doctors, lawyers and teachers are blankly exempt from overtime compensation requirements by their very job titles; only agriculture is exempt as an industry. From there, three classifications exist under part 541 of the Fair Labor Standards Act (FLSA) that allow for additional exemptions: the executive, administrative, and professional.

"The idea," wrote Diane Patrick, in "To Be Or Not To Be (Exempt)," *LEGAL ASSISTANT TODAY*, September/October 1992, "was to encourage employers to hire more employees, thus creating more jobs." Overtime pay was not to be treated as some sort of employee "benefit," but rather as a penalty on an employer for not hiring another person to do the work requiring the additional hours.

"These exemptions . . . were created to cover situations where it would clearly not be feasible for an employer to hire extra people for the particular job; that is, situations where there was a clear uniqueness to the particular employee's job tasks," says Patrick. "(It is) for this reason there are only three categories of job tasks—and this is job tasks, not job titles—that are considered to be exempt."

In the case of Page & Addison, it was the description of the job tasks handled by the legal assistants that led a federal jury to find in the law firm's favor. The DOL—ever consistent—originally appealed the decision, but on September 22, 1994, chose to abandon its appeal with prejudice.

Since that time, in a letter that was published in April of 1996, the DOL's Wage and Hour Division Deputy Assistant Administrator Daniel Sweeney once again turned down exemption status for a law firm paralegal, stating that his review of the paralegal's tasks indicated the paralegal was a "production worker." Stacey Hunt, who reported on the article for LAT, wrote: "The paralegal earned a $30,000 annual salary and received a certificate from an ABA-approved school. The paralegal's duties included drafting federal complaints, drafting and responding to discovery requests, interviewing witnesses and preparing affidavits, creating and maintaining files, interacting with clients on a regular basis, trial preparation, preparing subpoenas for witnesses records, medical releases, correspondence and summarizing deposition trials, hearings and medical records."

Professional Classifications

What is important to note is that the DOL—and, actually, many members of the legal community—do not feel that overtime compensation should be seen as a bad thing. Hunt

Article 8-1 The Issues Affecting Paralegals Then and Now ("Exempt vs. Nonexempt")

Gina M. Gladwell, The Issues Affecting Paralegals Then and Now, LEGAL ASSISTANT TODAY, Sept./Oct. 1997, at 65–68. Copyright 2002 James Publishing, Inc. Reprinted courtesy of LEGAL ASSISTANT TODAY magazine. For subscription information call (800) 394-2626, or visit www.legalassistanttoday.com.

states that "Sweeney points out that nothing derogatory is meant by the Department of Labor in not classifying paralegals as professionals. 'It is merely a defined term in the regulations,' he says, 'not a reflection of anyone's work quality or dedication.'"

Linda Katz, manager of legal assistants at Baker & Botts, L.L.P. in Houston, agrees. "Legal assistants should be treated as professionals . . . . It shouldn't be assumed that legal assistants who are paid overtime aren't professionals and, conversely, legal assistants who are classified as exempt may be treated as clerical. The issue is not whether legal assistants are classified as exempt or nonexempt, but how they are treated (that is important)."

Some paralegals are not convinced. "It helps provide another layer of professionalism to our profession. As long as your [sic] treated fairly and are considered for bonuses, I'm willing to put in the time," says Oaks.

"If you are exempt and the secretarial staff is nonexempt, that's a way of showing you as a professional employee," says Barbara S. Wallace, a third party administrator at Cigna in Wilmington, Delaware. "A lot of employers make that distinction."

M. Ann Heyer, CLA, a legal assistant at Johnstone Adams Bailey Gordon & Harris, L.L.C. in Mobile, Alabama, says she would give up her overtime pay "if it meant more recognition—more professionalism."

At the organization level, NALA and NFPA have stated that because their members have not reached a consensus, they have not taken any formal position. AAfPE, LAMA and the ABA also have no formal position. Legal assistants, as evidenced, are split.

"I see both sides of it, but I just think the exempt people generally are not being compensated fairly," says Holmes. "In my experience, you work many more hours then [sic] if you were just being compensated for that. The level of salaries hasn't made up for (no overtime pay)."

Tiers and the Senior Paralegal

One solution that has been around for about five years is having firms implement "tiers" of legal assistant positions. Lower level legal assistants, who are generally handling more production-level tasks, are paid hourly and receive overtime compensation. Upper level legal assistants, who work on substantive projects requiring "regular exercise of discretion and independent judgment" (as required by the FLSA), are salaried at higher rates of pay. "That's a sign of how sophisticated and how substantive the position has become," says Katz. "It allows law firms to retain their best legal assistants by having a career path, and it's a benefit to clients because their services can be performed more cost efficiently."

It also raises the respect level, and substantive work level, afforded senior legal assistants. "More and more, the paralegals are being used for jobs that ordinarily would have been completed by first- and second-year lawyers, including preparation for trial and actually attending trials," says Nelson.

"The breadth of responsibility that the paralegals are able to take on, and the fact that they are included more in the actual decision making on how to manage a case, is exciting," agrees Laurie P. Roselle, litigation paralegal coordinator at Rogers & Wells in New York City. "We've turned up the heat, and you see paralegals doing things now that five and 10 years ago you never saw them doing."

In some specialties, legal assistants with experience are so high in demand that law firms actively seek recruits from around the country. Eighteen months ago, San Francisco-based Cooley, Godward, Castro, Huddleston & Tatum advertised a $500 signing bonus for corporate paralegals with at least one year of experience in "venture financings, public offerings and public and/or private company corporate maintenance." The firm had also created a "specialist" spot above the senior legal assistant position to provide upward mobility for paralegals with 12-plus years of experience. To receive the designation, paralegals had to have consistently high reviews and a developed expertise in an area of specialty; provide mentoring and in-house educational training classes; and bill 1,950 hours annually. In return, their salaries were equivalent to those of second- and third-year associates, they were eligible for substantial bonuses, and they received a special perk of a coveted health club membership.

Indeed, among the paralegals interviewed for this article, those that have a minimum of 10 years' experience have seen their incomes rise, on average, by $31,000 since they began their careers. A handful have seen their pay increase in excess of $55,000 a year. And on top of these lucrative salaries, many enjoy an often unparalleled level of confidence from top firm management. Barbara McClorey, a senior legal assistant at White & Case in New York City says: "I find more partners coming to me asking for guidance on a certain tax matter—the way to prepare a return, or fiduciary matter. When I first started, it was junior attorneys, or interns that asked me. Now, I'm being relied on more than before at a top level within the firm."

Article 8-1   Continued

"Exempt from overtime pay"

The effect of the *DOL vs. Page & Addison* decision on paralegals and their employers

By Dorene Ridgway

Finally, a court has set a precedent for an issue that's been plaguing paralegals for years—should paralegals be exempt or nonexempt from overtime pay? Or is it a precedent? Here's what happened.

Litigation

On September 22, 1994, the United States Department of Labor (DOL) abandoned its appeal with prejudice in *DOL vs. Page & Addison, P.C.,* U.S. Dist. Court, Northern District of Texas, Dallas Division No. 3:91-CV-3655-P (*Page & Addison*). There will be no written Fifth Circuit Court decision filed in New Orleans Appellate Court No. 94-10435 affirming or overturning the District Court's jury finding that 23 paralegals at the 10-lawyer firm are exempt from the overtime requirements of the Fair Labor Standards Act enacted in 1938 (FLSA). The jury's decision, entered on March 10, 1994, is binding. Its decision is based upon the administrative exemption as set forth in 29 CFR § 541.1 and 541.101 through

Article 8-2   Exempt from Overtime Pay

Dorene Ridgway, "Exempt from Overtime Pay": The Effect of the DOL vs. Page & Addison Decision on Paralegals and Their Employers, NATIONAL PARALEGAL REPORTER, Spring 1995, at 31–32. Courtesy of the National Federation of Paralegal Associations, Inc.

541.119. Exempt status applies to *Page & Addison's* Paralegals because each one was found to exercise independent judgment and discretion when she performed her duties and fulfilled her responsibilities, even though a supervisory attorney must approve or reject the paralegal's work.

The *Page & Addison* decision is fact-specific; it relates only to paralegals employed by that firm. This decision may trigger additional litigation to exempt paralegals from overtime on a case-by-case basis because a decision from the United States District Court, Northern District of Texas, may have no effect upon paralegals in other parts of the country. At this time, no opinion letter of the Wage-Hour Administrator exempting paralegals as a class from the Act is forthcoming. The DOL considers paralegals as a class nonexempt from the FLSA. If other court cases are decided in the future, the DOL may schedule comment periods or hearings to propose a change to the Regulations. The DOL might re-examine the issue to establish clear guidelines for a firm to make a reasonable determination about the status of its paralegals. Each law firm would have to determine its paralegals' status based upon job descriptions and the duties it delegates to paralegals.

Compensation

Surveys show that about 50% of employers pay paralegals for overtime and the other half do not pay them overtime for the same tasks. The surveys also indicate that exempt paralegals are not necessarily delegated more responsible tasks than are nonexempt ones. Attorneys do not distinguish between exempt and nonexempt tasks. Thus, it has not been determined if exemption for paralegals as a class will expand duties in the paralegal profession.

Paralegals favoring overtime pay contend that exempt paralegals are not paid at a higher rate to compensate them for the added hours worked. According to the July 1994 *Law Office Management & Administrator Report,* exempt paralegals average $32,798 per year and nonexempt paralegals average $30,312. Although it appears that the FLSA intended exempt employees to be paid more than an average salary, the regulations requiring a minimum of $250 per week ($13,000 per year) be paid to exempt employees have not been changed since 1974 due to political reasons.

Some paralegals are not convinced that they gain the financial rewards, status, and the perceived professional image that go along with exemption from the Act. The price of giving up overtime pay, mastering the knowledge necessary to perform profitable tasks for their employers, and taking the risks necessary to excel to top-notch levels in this profession may not reward paralegals their expected benefits.

Because no clear consensus on this issue exists among paralegals and their employers, NFPA delegates have decided to continue monitoring the issue and not to take a formal position on it yet. Paralegals and legal administrators could work with their employers on defining the issue. Unless government regulations are changed, other law firms may find themselves in the same position as *Page & Addison.* At this point, paralegals and attorneys nationwide must accept the DOL's policy of nonexempt status for paralegals as a class. If a law office or department is not paying its paralegals overtime, it should review its policies to ensure it complies with federal and state laws. The prudent employer must use not only the *Page & Addison* court decision, but also the regulations or an amendment to statutes as guides to avoid exposing its firm to noncompliance.

With the absence of regulations that apply specifically to the paralegal profession, it is up to the employer to delegate appropriate tasks to its paralegals to allow exemption from the FLSA on a case-by-case basis and to comply with 29 U.S.C. § 213(a)(1). The employer always carries the burden of proving the exemption. An employer who repeatedly and willfully violates the Act could be subject to a fine of $10,000 and imprisonment of up to six months. The employer violating the Act is potentially liable to the employee in the amount of overtime, together with an additional amount as liquidated damages and a reasonable attorney fee.

Dorene Ridgway chairs NFPA's Ad Hoc Committee on Exempt/Nonexempt Status and has served on various committees with the Washington State Paralegal Association since 1980. A collection and commercial litigation paralegal at the Seattle law firm Lane Powell Spears Lubersky, she holds a B.S. in Business and Legal Administration.

Article 8-2   Continued

Exempt to non-exempt—a blessing or curse?

By Frances Beall Whiteside

Apparently, it's a hot topic.

"Thanks for continuing to study this issue," wrote one respondent to *The Reporter's* "Are you exempt or non-exempt?" This paralegal was one of 51 who responded to the survey that ran in the Summer 1994 *NPR*.

Not surprisingly, the results were divided.

More than half (53%) of the respondents were non-exempt. Of those 27, almost half (48% or 13 paralegals) believe their positions should be classified as exempt. (Employers of 13 respondents had changed paralegals to non-exempt status within the past two years.) None of the 24 exempt paralegals believes the exempt position he or she holds should be re-classified as non-exempt.

Certainly, the survey's responses reflect how controversial this issue is to paralegals. Those against changing an exempt classification to non-exempt believe the latter obstructs upward mobility; whereas an exempt rating helps maintain professional status.

A corporate paralegal argued, "To be demoted to a non-exempt employee is a step down and does not accurately portray my job responsibility and duties." She added that only paralegals within her corporation had been singled out for a change from exempt to non-exempt.

Another paralegal detailed how a change to non-exempt status cost her dearly. "Although I volunteer to stay and help on emergency projects (and not because I need the money)," she wrote, "my offers have been refused because attorneys must think about budget, and so my overtime hours will not be authorized. I lose the opportunity to

Article 8-3   Exempt to Non-Exempt—A Blessing or Curse?

Frances Beall Whiteside, Exempt to Non-Exempt—a Blessing or a Curse? NATIONAL PARALEGAL REPORTER, *Winter 1994, at 28. Courtesy of the National Federation of Paralegal Associations, Inc.*

advance to [a higher rating] level because non-exempt employees cannot be raised above [a certain grade] level." This status change also caused the employee's eligibility for a third week of vacation to be moved four years into the future.

"I cannot advance unless I give up being a paralegal, and my professionalism is diminished," she concluded. "My employer loses, too."

Some exempt employees pointed out abstract compensation that comes with exempt status: "I can arrive late, leave early, and take a long lunch hour, as long as the work gets done," one exempt employee wrote. "I have the freedom to come and go as I please," another echoed.

In contrast, those who promote non-exempt status for paralegals reason that exempt status could be just another tool to help employers exploit legal assistants.

"It's a profit deal," one respondent quoted from Steve Martin's *The Jerk*. "Paralegals will never be promoted to partner or given any opportunity to earn large salaries [like] attorneys."

Another grimly observed, "There's no hope that exempt status will bring more prestige, responsibility and compensation."

A Southern paralegal argued, "Lawyers would have us working 24 hours a day, especially during trial, with no additional compensation. We earn the overtime."

And one working mother explained, "I have a family and cannot work more than 35 hours a week. If considered exempt, I would be expected to work as many hours as necessary with no additional compensation."

One respondent cautioned that NFPA should not work to change the DOL ruling "until paralegals are licensed in some respect and earn higher salaries. Overtime pay is the only way paralegals are close to being compensated adequately for the tasks performed."

Finally, some paralegals suggested what might be the best compromise: the tier solution, which classifies some paralegals exempt, some non-exempt.

"We work in diverse settings and have very different jobs," one such respondent commented. "Some are properly non-exempt, but some paralegals have overriding responsibilities, especially in corporate/financial settings."

Frances Beall Whiteside writes the column, "After Hours" for Legal Assistant Today.

WHAT ARE THE POSITIONS OF THE NATIONWIDE ASSOCIATIONS ON THE EXEMPT/NONEXEMPT ISSUE?

Both the NALA and the NFPA have surveyed their membership to ascertain their members' opinions on whether legal assistants should be considered as exempt employees under the FLSA. Both organizations have studied the issue in committee and discussed the issue at meetings. The membership in both organizations are split on this issue. Each organization has stated that it will not take a formal position on the issue because there is not consensus in its membership.

No formal position has been taken by the American Association for Paralegal Education (AAfPE), the Legal Assistant Manager Association (LAMA), or the American Bar Association (ABA).

Article 8-4, published in the Washington University Law Quarterly, provides an in-depth analysis of the exempt/nonexempt issue and concludes that the ABA should take

Text continues on page 258

FLSA: Exempting Paralegals from Overtime Pay

I. Introduction

The practice of law in the United States has undergone significant transformation in response to the changing economic, social and political climate of American society. Americans are often recognized for their litigious nature, and recent statistics support this position.[1] In order to provide clients with quality legal representation without imposing severe financial and administrative costs, law firms have increasingly turned to paralegals[2] or legal assistants to aid them in performing legal services.[3] This trend has resulted in confusion as to appropriate limits on paralegal responsibilities[4] and the proper classification of paralegals under state and federal employment stautes.[5]

The Fair Labor Standards Act of 1938 ("FLSA")[6] exempts certain classes of employees from the right to receive overtime pay[7] based on the salary received, the type of work performed and the amount of discretion and individual judgment exercised.[8] Paralegals once performed mostly clerical tasks including filing, pulling cases off shelves and photocopying. Today, paralegals often engage in tasks involving more sophisticated legal skills. Nonetheless, the Department of Labor ("DOL") maintains that paralegals are not exempt under the FLSA and are, thus, entitled to overtime pay.[9] In March 1994, for example, the DOL filed suit against a Texas law firm[10] alleging violations of the FLSA overtime pay requirements. Although the DOL emphasizes the need to evaluate each exemption claim on a case-by-case basis,[11] to date, it has not exempted paralegals under the Act.

The problem with labelling all paralegals "non-exempt" is that law firms and paralegals disagree as to whether exemption is appropriate in this context. For example, one survey revealed that only fifty-eight percent of paralegals questioned believed that they should receive overtime pay.[12] Furthermore, the approaches adopted by law firms lack uniformity.[13] Under the FLSA, the penalties for failure to pay required overtime wages can be severe, leaving law firms open to liability if they erroneously classify their paralegals.[14]

The question then remains whether paralegals should be exempt from the overtime pay requirements of the FLSA. This Note argues that the American Bar Association ("ABA") should develop consistent standards of certification in order to exempt all paralegals. The benefits of such a scheme would be uniformity, increased morale among paralegal employees, and more productive and efficient use of paralegal skills. The occupational status of paralegal practice is currently unsettled because paralegals do not clearly fall within or without the definition of exemption found in the regulations accompanying the FLSA.[15] Careful analysis, however, reveals that exemption is both consistent with the modern definition, and a mutual benefit to all parties involved.

Part II of this Note addresses the criteria for executive, administrative, and professional exemption under the FLSA. Part III explores penalties for overtime pay violations. Part IV discusses the history of paralegals in American law firms, their roles in the legal process, and the dangers inherent in delegating paralegal responsibilities. Part V enumerates and analyzes the various arguments for and against paralegal exemption, and suggests possible methods of fitting paralegals within the exemption definitions. Part VI concludes that paralegals should be exempt from overtime pay under the FLSA, and offers proposals for implementation of this new status.

Article 8-4   FLSA: Exempting Paralegals from Overtime Pay

Allison Engel, FLSA: Exempting Paralegals from Overtime Pay, 74 Wash. U. L.Q. 253–82 (1996). Courtesy of Washington University in St. Louis School of Law.

II. Exemption Under the Fair Labor Standards Act of 1938

Although the FLSA exempts executives, administrators and professionals from minimum pay and maximum hour requirements,[16] the Act's legislative history provides no guidance for this exclusion.[17] One author[18] suggests alternative reasons for the exemptions: the Act's primary purpose of protecting workers who are most susceptible to exploitation;[19] the drafters' fears about the constitutionality of covering these employees;[20] absence of a need for government regulation;[21] unattractive financial burdens on employers;[22] or potential infeasibility of regulating these employees.[23] The author enumerates problems with each of these rationales, however,[24] and concludes that the "professional-managerial" exemptions should be eliminated altogether.[25]

Given the unlikelihood of eliminating the FLSA exemptions, it is necessary to understand their operations to assess whether employees meet the criteria.[26]

A. Operation of the Exemptions

Whether an employee falls within one of the exemptions enumerated in the FLSA is determined by the trier of fact.[27] In the Act, Congress authorized the Secretary of Labor ("the Secretary") to define the terms "executive," "administrative" and "professional."[28] The guidelines developed by the Wage and Hour Division of the DOL do not carry the force of law, but courts generally accept the guidelines as valid.[29] The Act states that executive, administrative and professional employees—exempt employees—need not receive compensation for hours worked in excess of the standard work week.[30] However, the FLSA does not further classify the types of employees covered.[31] The regulations advanced by the Wage and Hour Division of the DOL ("Wage and Hour Regulations") purport to clarify what types of employees fit within each of these categories,[32] but there is disagreement as to the application of the delineations.[33] Further complicating the analysis, neither title[34] nor salary[35] alone determines exemption status.

1. Executive Exemption

The Wage and Hour Regulations set forth six requirements for executive exemption. First, the employee's primary duty must be management of the employing establishment.[36] Second, the employee must "customarily and regularly direct the work of two or more employees."[37] Third, the employer must have authority to hire, fire, and promote employees directly or through influential suggestions.[38] Fourth, the employer must "customarily and regularly" exercise discretionary powers.[39] Fifth, the employer must devote only a limited amount of time to non-exempt activities.[40] Finally, the employer must compensate the employee on a salary basis.[41]

This "long test" applies to employees earning less than $250 per week.[42] Employees earning over $250 per week need only satisfy the requirements of the "short test." These include regularly overseeing two or more supervisors, and exercising discretionary powers.[43] Courts give only three of the "short" and "long test" requirements significant attention and explanation.

First, executives must "customarily and regularly" exercise discretionary powers.[44] This requirement does not entail routine decisionmaking, but rather "discretion as to policy."[45] Employee discretion must involve decisions beyond those made by experienced, skilled workers in their daily activities.[46] However, the existence of "well-defined employer policies" is not enough to automatically remove an employee from this category.[47] In *Anderson v. Federal Cartridge Corp.*,[48] the Federal Court for the District of Minnesota held that because no business can operate effectively without such policies, exemption cannot logically depend on the ability to change them.[49]

Second, executives must devote a limited amount of time to nonexempt work.[50] In *George Lawley & Son Corp. v. South*,[51] an employer wanted the court to exempt an employee from the FLSA requirements.[52] The employer contended that "not devot[ing] more than 20 percent"[53] of work hours to nonexempt activities referred to twenty percent of the hours worked by all nonexempt employees, not just the employee whose status was in question.[54] The First Circuit concluded that such an interpretation would create an anomalous result by exempting every employee with five or more individuals working under him.[55]

The third issue receiving judicial scrutiny is the requirement that executives be compensated "on a salary basis at a rate of not less than $155 per week."[56] If an employee's salary falls within this range, exemption is possible but not conclusive.[57] The reviewing court must still apply the "salary basis" test.[58]

The salary basis test requires that an employee receive fixed compensation regardless of work quality or hours worked.[59] This requirement exposes employers to unanticipated liability by placing otherwise exempt employees outside the exemption, thereby entitling them to back-pay.[60] For example, an employer who denies an employee overtime pay for two years by claiming exemption, may become liable for that money by making salary deductions for jury duty.[61] A 1992 study indicated that private-sector employers may be liable for over thirty-nine billion dollars in unpaid overtime wages, yet fail to modify their practices to avoid liability.[62]

In practice, application of the executive exemption to employees has not resulted in a uniform standard.[63] Courts emphasize different aspects of the definition and focus on different facts in reaching their conclusions.[64] For example, a Michigan Federal District Court exempted a bookkeeper under the FLSA because he monitored his employer's banking activities and heavily influenced his superiors' decisions.[65] In contrast, an Oklahoma Federal District Court did not exempt a bookkeeper who supervised his employer's business transactions and monitored company payments.[66] Ultimately, executive status does not guarantee exemption. Exemption determinations focus on the particular employee's duties, not on job titles or wages.

2. Administrative Exemption

Qualification as an administrative[67] employee may also be accomplished under either a "short test"[68] or "long test."[69] The "short test" applies to employees earning at least $250 per week,[70] and requires that (1) the employee primarily perform work directly related to "management policies or general business operations of his employer or his employer's customers,"[71] and (2) the employee "customarily and regularly exercise discretion and independent judgment."[72] In contrast, the "long test" requires satisfaction of both elements of the "short test," as well as the remaining provisions of the Wage and Hour Regulations.[73] Because most employees satisfy the $250 threshold, courts rarely apply the "long test."[74]

One part of the "short test" analyzes the level of employee discretion and independent judgment.[75] Under this test, an employee must "choose a course of action from among a number of possible alternatives" to qualify for exemption.[76] A primary concern is whether the employee actually has authority to make decisions.[77] One court defined this as requiring "more discretion than an experienced, skilled worker might exercise . . . in his day-to-day activities."[78]

Article 8-4   Continued

Although courts consider how frequently superiors reverse or review discretionary decisions, this factor alone will not automatically preclude a finding of exemption.[79] Courts evaluate the tests performed to assess the validity of exemption. In *Schockley v. City of Newport News,*[80] the Fourth Circuit held that "media relations sergeants"—police sergeants who collect information off the "crime line," develop broadcasts, and handle press relations[81]—were not administrators under the Act because they lacked the requisite authority and discretion.[82] Similarly, in *Berg v. Newman,*[83] the Federal Circuit Court of Appeals refused to categorize air traffic control repairmen as exempt administrators because, despite their expertise, they did not exercise discretion on a daily bassis.[84] Both *Schockley* and *Berg* indicate that administrators must maintain some level of autonomy to qualify for exemption.

Additionally, courts require that decision-making employees possess a significant degree of choice regarding matters of substantial importance to the employer's operations.[85] For example, even though New York State police investigators have a primary duty to prevent and investigate crimes, the Northern District of New York refused to exempt them because they did not administer the business affairs of the agency.[86] Thus, absent an ability to affect the employer's business, even employee autonomy is insufficient for exemption.

A second element of the "short test" requires employees to engage in work "directly related to management policies."[87] According to one article,[88] work must be broken down into "production" tasks and "administrative" tasks.[89] Employees are not administratively exempt unless they perform duties beyond the basic services of the employer's business.[90] For example, in *Schockley,* the Fourth Circuit refused to find that media relations sergeants were exempt employees because none of their duties rose to the level of discretionary authority or managerial decisionmaking.[91]

3. Professional Exemption

The DOL scrutinizes employee education when applying the professional exemption test.[92] The "short test" requires that the employee engage in work requiring "knowledge of an advanced type in a field of science or learning customarily acquired by a prolonged course of specialized intellectual instruction and study as distinguished from a general academic education and from an apprenticeship and from training in the performance of routine mental, manual, or physical processes."[93] It also requires consistent exercise of judgment or discretion, and applies to employees earning over $250 per week.[94] Employees who do not meet the $250 salary threshold must satisfy all requirements of the wage and hour regulations.[95] The educational requirement for this exemption distinguishes it from both the executive and administrative exemptions.[96] Thus, analysis of this criterion is essential in determining whether the professional exemption applies.

The Wage and Hour Regulations make "knowledge of an advanced type"[97] necessary for professional exemption.[98] The regulations require an employee to acquire a degree beyond a high school diploma.[99] Although this will often lead to an advanced degree, it is the knowledge and not the degree that is most important.[100] For example, in *Otis v. Mattila,*[101] the Minnesota Supreme Court refused to exempt an accountant notwithstanding his advanced accounting degree, because he failed to exercise the requisite discretion.[102]

Furthermore, courts analyze exempt status by scrutinizing the duties performed, not by deferring to the employee's title.[103] For example, in *Walling v. Morris,*[104] the Sixth Circuit refused to exempt an individual working as "superintendent of maintenance" because he devoted twenty-five percent of his working hours to routine tasks identical to those performed by those he supervised.[105]

B. Penalties for Overtime Pay Violations

Employers who do not comply with the FLSA requirements[106] leave themselves vulnerable to rather severe penalties. Section 216(b) of the Act provides that a violation of the minimum wage and maximum hour requirements will result in liability to the affected employee "in the amount of their unpaid minimum wages, or their unpaid overtime compensation," as well as an equal amount in liquidated damages.[107] Furthermore, repeat violations may result in a civil penalty of up to $1,000 per violation.[108]

A recent case, *Reich v. Newspapers of New England, Inc.,*[109] provides an example of the heavy monetary penalties employers may face for misclassifying their employees. The defendant, a small New England newspaper, failed to pay its reporters, editors, and photographers overtime wages, believing they were professionally exempt under the FLSA.[110] The Federal District Court of New Hampshire found the paper liable for $10,445.80 in unpaid overtime.[111] *Reich* illustrates the importance of properly classifying employees' positions under the FLSA.

III. The Historical Role of the Paralegal

A. Definition of Paralegal

Because the FLSA focuses on duties performed and authority exercised, the definition of "paralegal" is crucial in determining how such employees will be treated.[112] A general definition of "paralegal" is a person qualified through education, training, or work experience, to perform substantive legal work under the supervision of a practicing attorney.[113] However, because the breadth of authority and duties given paralegals varies by firm, individual firms may manipulate the work description of their paralegals to fall within or without the FLSA's coverage. Thus, because paralegals' positions are defined by the specific tasks they perform, paralegals may fall under different FLSA classifications.

B. Origins of the Paralegal Profession

The recent growth of the paralegal profession began in the early 1970s.[114] In 1968, the ABA Special Committee on the Availability of Legal Services formally recognized the use of nonlawyer services to "free[ ]a lawyer from tedious and routine detail."[115] The Committee also created another special committee to determine the necessary training, the appropriate tasks and the foreseeable benefits of paralegals.[116]

The use of paralegals started gaining prominence in the 1970s as the increasing complexity of legal casework necessitated the use of legal assistants to continue effective representation and maintain reasonable financial costs.[117] This prompted the increased need for paralegal schools and led to the creation of representative paralegal institutions.[118] After several years of investigative studies and reports, the ABA Committee issued guidelines for accreditation of paralegal training institutions in 1974.[119] That same year, the National Federation of Paralegal Associations ("NFPA") formed to "maintain[ ] a communications network to assist in the development of the paralegal profession."[120] The paralegal market's rapid expansion led to the creation of a second nation-wide association. In 1975, the National Association of Legal Secretaries ("NALS"), recognizing the new trend towards alternative legal services, created a section for legal assistants.[121] Within a year, the section severed ties with the NALS and organized as the National Association of Legal

Article 8-4   Continued

Assistants ("NALA").[122] Thirteen years later, the Supreme Court validated the importance of paralegal services in *Missouri v. Jenkins*,[123] holding that paralegal time must be included in the reimbursement of attorneys' fees.[124]

Today, paralegals remain an important part of law firm communities. Paralegals' recent success in the recession[125] evidences their importance. In a fall 1993 report, the DOL predicted that the number of paralegals will increase eighty-three percent between 1992 and 2005.[126] The existence of approximately 77,000 paralegals in the United States legal industry demonstrates the importance of their services to law firms.[127] Between 1989 and 1992, paralegals' billable hours increased by 5.7%, with the average paralegal billing 1,429 hours in 1992.[128] These figures indicate not only the dramatic increase in demand for paralegal services, but also their established role in law firms.

C. Scope of Paralegal Duties

Paralegal duties vary significantly.[129] First, different law firms have different expectations of paralegals' roles and require varying skill levels.[130] Second, because there are currently no uniform paralegal licensing requirements, there is a wide range of skills and ability, especially at the entry-level.[131] Although the ABA has developed accreditation criteria for paralegal training institutes,[132] not all paralegals attend facilities with ABA approval. Many law firms preferring to hire individuals without any formal paralegal education nonetheless opt to specially train them in-house.[133] Consequently, while some paralegals could actually be classified as "legal secretaries" or "clerks," others engage in more substantive legal tasks.

For example, Firm A may limit paralegal responsibilities to filing legal documents, locating cases and writing letters, while Firm B may allow its paralegals to write briefs, attend depositions and prepare motions.[134] Given their lack of authority and discretion, paralegals in Firm A appear nonexempt under the FLSA.[135] Classifying paralegals in firms that fall in between is substantially more difficult.[136]

For paralegals who are not clearly nonexempt under the FLSA, an important issue arises regarding the duties they perform. At what point do paralegal responsibilities cross the line into the realm of "unauthorized practice of law" ("UPL")? [137]

D. The Unauthorized Practice of Law

States vary in their definitions of what constitutes UPL.[138] However, most UPL statutes prohibit any individual who is not a licensed attorney from providing legal services or representation.[139] The ABA Model Code of Professional Responsibility[140] contains the following broad definition:

> It is neither necessary nor desirable to attempt the formulation of a single, specific definition of what constitutes the practice of law. Functionally, the practice of law relates to the rendition of services for others that call for the professional judgment of a lawyer. The essence of the professional judgment of the lawyer is his educated ability to relate the general body and philosophy of law to a specific legal problem of a client; and thus, the public interest will be better served if only lawyers are permitted to act in matters involving professional judgment . . . .[141]

To assist attorneys' effective use of paralegal services, the ABA adopted Model Guidelines for the Utilization of Legal Assistant Services.[142] These guidelines allow attorneys to delegate tasks to legal assistants so long as the law does not specifically prohibit them.[143] Under the Guidelines, prohibited tasks include: providing legal advice, discussing legal fees with clients, retaining clients, writing briefs for court submission, and falsely identifying oneself as an attorney.[144]

The growth of the paralegal profession has created a debate among attorneys, legal scholars and paralegals regarding the rules governing the unauthorized practice of law. While many attorneys insist on insulating the legal practice from outside infiltration,[145] paralegals and paralegal supporters contend that the practical benefits of allowing non-lawyer practitioners to perform more important tasks justify relaxing the rules.[146]

Opponents of nonlawyer services argue that increasing paralegal duties will result in increased UPL and undermine attorney services.[147] Another concern is that paralegals do not receive formal legal training, and therefore are not competent to perform complicated legal tasks.[148] Therefore, opponents argue that clients are better served by having attorneys working on their cases.[149]

Proponents of nonlawyer practitioners focus on the necessity of legal services in segments of our society that cannot otherwise afford quality representation. They argue that clients should have a choice between expensive attorney fees and cheaper paralegal services.[150] Other proponents view increased job responsibility as integral to the sustained demand for paralegals,[151] whose services are invaluable in today's expensive legal market.

Because it is the duties performed that determine exemption, resolving the UPL issue is a critical factor in deciding whether paralegals merit exemption from overtime pay.[152] Although exempting paralegals means granting them more responsibility, UPL may be thwarted by ensuring that an attorney supervises the work performed. Thus, in the private sector, UPL may become a secondary concern.

IV. The Debate over the Exemption of Paralegals

In *Reich v. Page & Addison,*[153] a jury found paralegals administratively exempt from overtime pay under the FLSA.[154] The case has raised the question whether and to what extent paralegals should be exempt.[155] Answering this inquiry is rather difficult because the DOL, law firms, paralegal associations and even paralegals themselves do not agree on the proper response.[156] The DOL claims to evaluate each situation on a case-by-case basis,[157] but to date, the Department has never exempted a paralegal.[158] The NFPA has refrained from adopting a position, reasoning that its members are split on the issue.[159] The division among paralegals confirms the NFPA's posture. Some paralegals support exemption while others covet the overtime pay they receive as nonexempt employees.[160] These conflicting positions will be examined below.

A. The Argument for Nonexemption

The DOL has consistently held that paralegals do not qualify for exemption under the FLSA. A Letter Ruling issued by the DOL on August 17, 1979,[161] determined that paralegals "generally are not involved in the performance of duties . . . required by the regulations for exemption."[162] Specifically, the Department found that paralegals use "skills rather than discretion and independent judgment."[163] Another Letter Ruling, issued approximately one month later,[164] defined specific duties paralegals perform.[165] These included, "interviewing clients, identifying and refining problems[,] . . . drafting pleadings and petitions[,] . . . acting as general litigation assistant[,] . . . conducting formal and informal hearings . . . and performing outreach services." The DOL found all of these duties nonexempt because they necessitated attorney supervision and did not require independent judgment.[166]

Article 8-4 Continued

A significant segment of the paralegal community does not view itself as executively, administratively or professionally exempt and supports the DOL's position.[167] These paralegals enjoy their entitlement to overtime pay and refuse to sacrifice this compensation for a "title."[168] Some of these paralegals believe that law firms are merely attempting to evade paying paralegals their just compensation.[169]

One consistently advanced argument is that if paralegals actually perform tasks with discretion and judgment, they necessarily are engaging in UPL.[170] This argument receives little recognition among private sector paralegals working in law firms because most have attorney supervision.[171]

Attorneys who support the DOL's position—that paralegals should remain nonexempt employees under the FLSA—may fear that exempting paralegals could undermine their practice. Many attorneys want to maintain their status as the only professionals licensed to practice law.[172] Exempting paralegals would grant greater standing and legitimacy to non-lawyers by recognizing them as executives, administrators or professionals who possess the discretion and authority to work on legal matters. The recent movement to deregulate independently practicing paralegals[173] probably concerns attorneys who believe that their importance in society will diminish.

Paralegals who oppose exemption generally believe that they receive great benefits from overtime pay, emphasizing their perceived monetary gain.[174] Working in excess of forty hours per week entitles nonexempt employees to time and a half, double time or some other overtime pay schedule.[175] To these paralegals, overtime compensation is worth more to them than the prestige or increased duties that flow from exemption.

A final concern with FLSA exemption is the potential unfairness of exempting paralegals with vastly disparate job descriptions. Because some paralegals are trained by law firms while others obtain certification, their duties vary widely.[176] It is arguably unfair to lump all such paralegals together and exempt individuals who are closer to "legal secretaries" than "administrators," "executives" or "professionals."[177] Thus, exemption potentially raises both equity and feasibility issues. Who is entitled to exemption, and how should that determination be made?

B. The Argument for Exemption

Proponents of paralegal exemption focus on the quality of their legal responsibilities.[178] Paralegals on this side of the debate are typically certified and have formal training. Exemption proponents believe that the primary issue is respect, not money, and they perceive benefits accruing to both paralegals and firms.[179]

The first argument supporting exemption recognizes that labelling paralegals as exempt affords them greater status and thus increases their job satisfaction and performance.[180] Lawyers often view paralegals as members of the "support staff" and exclude them from important meetings concerning case dispositions.[181] This alienates paralegals who feel that they contribute substantially to legal representation and who also feel they possess the qualifications to participate in discussions relating to their work.[182] Although paralegals recognize that ultimate decisions rest with the attorneys and clients, they believe that their unique perspectives on the cases can provide invaluable assistance.[183] Granting paralegals exempt status would confer greater respect and integrate them into the firm community, thereby enhancing their ultimate performance.[184]

Another factor supporting exemption is the ambiguous qualifications for "overtime." Under the FLSA, nonexempt employees working in excess of forty hours per week must be paid at least one and a half times their regular wage for each additional hour.[185] Unfortunately, the wage calculations become very complicated when employees work short weeks or have fluctuating hours.[186] Exemption proponents argue that employers do not uniformly follow the time and a half policy, and that overtime schedules often provide no added wages at all, thus eliminating the ostensible benefit.[187]

In addition to time and a half, employers also utilize double time and straight time systems. Under the double time system, employers pay employees twice their regular wage rate for each hour worked in excess of forty.[188] Under the straight time system, employers compensate employees at their standard wage rate for each overtime hour worked.[189] Some paralegals perceive overtime as an illusory concept that appears to increase income but in practice keeps employees at a set pay level.[190] Firms either refuse to pay overtime at all, or they pay overtime but correspondingly reduce base pay to compensate.[191] Thus, proponents argue that paralegals receive greater benefits from exemption because overtime pay does not necessarily supplement regular earnings at all.

Firms may also benefit from exempting paralegals by increasing the quality of work, thereby facilitating competition and ensuring longevity of the paralegal staff.[192] Almost all workers want their employers to recognize and appreciate their contributions. Furthermore, satisfied employees produce better results, keep their jobs longer, and become a valuable asset to their employers.[193] Ultimately exemption imbues paralegals with self-worth and respect, qualities that are likely to increase the value of both employees and the businesses that employ them.[194]

Exemption proponents also cite employee exemption in similar professions.[195] Although the DOL determines exemption on a case-by-case basis,[196] it is useful to compare the duties performed by other similar employees who receive exemption under the FLSA. A profession closely analogous to paralegals is physicians' assistants. In 1974,[197] the DOL determined that physicians' assistants are professionals within the FLSA exemptions.[198] Even though these physicians' assistants were technically outside the FLSA exemptions because they lacked bachelor's degrees, the DOL granted an exception. The DOL reasoned that they were "directly engaged in the practice of medicine, subject to the physician's approval, while performing duties requiring considerable analysis, interpretation and discretion."[199]

In distinguishing paralegals from physicians' assistants, the DOL explained that paralegals lack discretion and independent judgement.[200] However, just as physicians' assistants may make decisions about patients subject to doctor approval, paralegals may make decisions regarding cases subject to attorney approval. The arguably similar discretion possessed by physicians' assistants and legal assistants lead exemption proponents to question the DOL's measuring criteria.[201] Furthermore, as evidenced by the District Court's ruling in *Reich v. Page & Addison, P.C.,* at least one court has refused to automatically exclude paralegals from FLSA exemptions.[202]

Notwithstanding the positive results exemption would create, paralegals must still meet the requirements of the executive, administrative or professional exemptions of the FLSA.[203]

1. Executive Exemption

The executive exemption most readily applies to paralegals occupying managerial positions within a firm. Many firms employ supervisory paralegals to oversee the entire legal assistant staff because they are "uniquely qualified to recruit, manage and evaluate legal assistants."[204] These paralegals exercise the requisite authority for FLSA exemption because they typically earn a sufficient salary, exercise discretion, and supervise numerous other employees.[205]

Article 8-4   Continued

2. Administrative Exemption

Paralegals may be considered administratively exempt if they meet the work performance qualifications under the FLSA.[206] First, paralegals must perform duties directly related to "management policies or general business operations" of the firm's clients.[207] Paralegals perform essential services for law firms because they analyze data and draw conclusions which are "important to the determination of, or which, in fact, determine financial, merchandising, or other policy . . . ."[208] Additionally, paralegals frequently analyze case data and offer opinions and evaluations based on their research.[209]

Paralegals also exercise "discretion and independent judgment" in their job capacities.[210] Legal problems vary in their nature and complexity, and paralegals often apply their knowledge and skill to each unique issue. Thus, a paralegal's duties may include "a careful analysis of the problem, deciding what information is required for resolution, determining the form the resolution should take, or ascertaining the documentation required to prove a case."[211] These duties involve discretion and judgment as required by the FLSA.

3. Professional Exemption

Proponents of paralegal exemption have not focused on the professional exemption.[212] However, a recent case, *Oxman v. Hamilton & Samuels,*[213] provided a significant step towards recognition of paralegals as professionals.[214] In *Oxman,* the California Division of Labor Standards Enforcement found that "an ABA-approved course of study for legal assistants does meet the educational criteria of the professional exemption."[215] Although no court has adopted a similar finding, *Oxman* suggests that proper accreditation may satisfy the requirements for professional exemption under the FLSA.

V. Proposed Exemption of Paralegals

Given paralegals' disparate skills and duties, they have had difficulty finding a uniform standard of education, training, and classification that would entitle them to FLSA exemption. The lack of uniformity has created confusion among employers and paralegals, and apprehension among paralegals' organizations. This Note now addresses how the legal community should alleviate these problems and create a practical standard.

Legislators, paralegal organizations, and employers should require paralegals to obtain a license from a competent training institution. In September 1992, the NFPA approved licensing to regulate paralegals working under attorney supervision.[216] However, the NFPA found expansion of paralegal duties to be the crucial aspect of such licensing.[217] One author proposed implementing state-by-state licensing to assure a minimum level of proficiency among even entry-level paralegals.[218] Under a licensing proposal, a paralegal would receive a license by attaining a minimum score on an examination designed to assess character and test legal proficiency. Further, no applicant could take the examination unless he or she fulfilled a minimum education standard. Although certification programs currently exist, they are wholly voluntary, and fail to account for the divergent practices among various states.[219] Licensing would ensure that every paralegal would enter the profession with the same basic skills, making regulation more feasible and equitable.

Presumably, employers would recognize licensing as conferring heightened authority and would grant paralegals greater responsibilities, including increased discretion over the disposition of cases. The promotion would not only ensure higher morale, but also improve the final work product. Firms would be confident and secure in the competence of their paralegals, and ultimate attorney supervision would remain as a check on the UPL.[220] Although some firms would still prefer to train their paralegals in-house to maintain uniform methods, licensing would start paralegals at a higher plateau in the legal community.

Some firms have implemented "tiers of paralegals," with entry-level employees performing more clerical tasks and advanced employees tackling more substantive issues.[221] Such a system, on its face, alleviates the problem of disparate skills among paralegals. However, the problem of where to draw the line between exempt and non-exempt employees still remains. At what point do "clerical paralegals" become "administrative paralegals" or "professional paralegals?"[222] In addition, paralegal dissension may develop if some paralegals are exempted while others are not. Tiering alone will not rectify the problem, but if used in conjunction with licensing, it may create a valuable incentive program to keep paralegals motivated and satisfied with their job prospects.

Assigning paralegals responsibilities that automatically entitle them to exemption will serve the interests of uniformity and equality. Automatic exemption eases implementation and protects law firms from liability for misclassification. Of course, the DOL still requires analysis on a case-by-case basis[223] when disputes arise, but disputes would decrease under a simple, uniform classification system. In addition, automatic exemption is equitable because it treats all paralegals uniformly. If all paralegals receive the same training, they all would be entitled to exemption and the attendant increase in responsibilities that exemption bestows.

VI. Conclusion

The complexity of legal issues in today's society has resulted in a growing need for paralegal services. Attorneys must often delegate various tasks to legal assistants so they may concentrate their efforts on a client's key legal questions. An efficient, well-trained paralegal staff is crucial to the law firm community. Uniform licensing requirements would ensure that all paralegals are proficient in the fundamentals of paralegal research and job responsibilities, thereby improving the overall quality of legal representation.

Paralegals are often an under-utilized resource, in part because attorneys are unsure about their level of aptitude. Uniform licensing would provide attorneys with some measure of a paralegal's skill, and enhance any individualized training mandated by each firm. As client expectations increase, law firms must find effective ways to meet the new demands. Improving the paralegal staff is an easy way to satisfy client needs, and ensure employee longevity and job satisfaction.

Allison Engel

1. The Federal system is inundated with lawsuits. In 1991, plaintiffs filed 207,610 new cases in United States District Courts. ADMIN. OFFICE OF THE U.S. COURTS, FEDERAL JUDICIAL WORKLOAD STATISTICS 2 (1993). By 1993, plaintiffs had filed 228,162 cases. *Id.*

   Not all commentators agree that the United States is overly litigious. *See e.g.,* Randall R. Bovbjerg et al., *Juries and Justice: Are Malpractice and Other Personal Injuries Created Equal?,* 54 LAW & CONTEMP. PROBS. 5, 8 (1991) (noting that although many consider Americans highly litigious, most malpractice victims do not file claims); Marc Galanter, *Reading the Landscape of Disputes: What We Know and Don't Know (and Think We Know) About Our Allegedly Contentious and Litigious Society,* 31 UCLA L. REV. 4, 5–6 (1983) (rebutting claims of an American litigation explosion); Marc S. Klein, *Megatrends in International Product Liability Law,* 949 A.L.I.-A.B.A 113, 120 (Aug. 19, 1994) (questioning whether America's unique products liability system results from the litigious nature of Americans).

Article 8-4   Continued

2. In this Note, the term "paralegal" includes "legal assistants," "nonlawyer practitioners," James Podgers, *Legal Profession Faces Rising Tide of Non-Lawyer Practice*, ARIZ. ATT'Y, Mar. 1994, at 24, and "nonlawyer assistants," David B. Isbell & Lucantonio N. Salvi, *Ethical Responsibility of Lawyers for Deception by Undercover Investigators & Discrimination Testers: An Analysis of the Provisions Prohibiting Misrepresentation Under the Model Rules of Professional Conduct*, 8 GEO. J. LEGAL ETHICS 791 (1995), employed by law firms. Paralegals working in prisons are not addressed in this Note. For a discussion of prison paralegals, see James K. Haslam, *Prison Labor Under State Direction: Do Inmates Have the Right to FLSA Coverage and Minimum Wage?*, 1994 B.Y.U. L. REV. 369, 372 (1994) (concluding that the FLSA should not cover prisoner paralegals because Congress did not intend the statute to extend this far and because it would undermine public policy supporting prisoner incarceration). *See also* Prisoners' Legal *Ass'n v. Roberson*, 822 F. Supp. 185, 190–91 (D.N.J. 1993) (stating that interference with paralegal inmates' rights to assist other prisoners with complaints, appeals, and petitions would violate the Fourteenth Amendment right to Due Process).

   This Note similarly omits self-employed paralegals that the legal community commonly refers to as "legal technicians." *See* Rosalind Resnick, *Looking at Alternative Services: The Lawyer/Non-Lawyer Wall Continues to Erode*, NAT'L L.J., June 10, 1991, at 1, 32. Legal technicians are non-lawyers who fill out legal forms, assist in real estate transactions, and finalize divorces. *Id.* Supporters of legal technicians argue that they provide assistance to an otherwise forgotten area of society, namely poor and middle-class Americans, by charging lower fees, offering convenient locations, and taking on smaller cases. Roselind Resnick, *Legal Technicians Face Regulation*, NAT'L LAW J., June 22, 1992, at 42. Opponents argue that legal technicians often engage in the "unauthorized practice of law" ("UPL") by performing duties reserved for licensed attorneys. *Id.* A discussion of the concerns raised by legal technicians is beyond the scope of this Note given the extensive number of articles written on the subject. *See, e.g., id.*; Jeff Simmons, *Nonlawyer Practice Rules: No Turning Back*, ARIZ. ATT'Y, Mar. 1994, at 19. For a discussion of UPL as it relates to law firm paralegals, see *infra* notes 139–52 and accompanying text.

   For an explanation of the overtime pay exemption as it relates to public sector employees, see Exemptions From Minimum Wage and Overtime Compensation Requirements of the Fair Labor Standards Act; Public Sector Employers, 57 Fed. Reg. 37,666 (1992).

3. In the 1970s, law firms generally consisted of attorneys, financial support staff, and secretaries. *See* Richard S. Granat and Dana K. Saewitz, *Paralegals Move Up to Management*, NAT'L L.J., Jan 30, 1989, at 19. Today, increased competition among firms has restrained partners' availability to perform basic legal tasks and thus necessitated increased delegation of routine duties and administrative practices. *Id.*

4. For a discussion of the ethical and legal limits of paralegal practice, *see infra* notes 138–52 and accompanying text.

5. This Note addresses paralegal classification under the Fair Labor Standards Act of 1938. 29 U.S.C. § 206 (1988 & Supp. IV 1992). For examples of similar state classifications, see ALASKA STAT. § 23.10.055 (Supp. 1994); CONN. GEN. STAT. ANN. § 31–76 (1995); MINN. STAT. ANN. § 177.23 (West 1993); IDAHO CODE § 67-5302 (1989).

6. 29 U.S.C. §§ 201–219 (1988).

7. Section 213 of the FLSA provides that "the provisions of sections 206 . . . and section 207 of this title shall not apply with respect to—(1) any employee employed in a bona fide executive, administrative, or professional capacity . . . " 29 U.S.C. § 213(a)(1) (1988 & Supp. IV 1992). Section 206 provides:
   (a) Employees engaged in commerce . . .
   Every employer shall pay to each of his employees who work in any workweek is engaged in commerce or in the production of goods for commerce, or is employed in an enterprise engaged in commerce or in the production of goods for commerce, wages at the following rates:
   (1) except as otherwise provided in this section, not less than $3.35 an hour during the period

ending March 31, 1990, not less than $3.80 an hour during the year beginning April 1, 1990, and not less than $4.25 an hour after March 31, 1991; . . .

29 U.S.C. § 206 (1988 & Supp. IV 1992). Section 207 provides that "it is important to note that exemption does not become an issue under the FLSA until it is determined that the employee is 'covered' by the Act. That is, unless the employee is engaged in commerce or in the production of goods for commerce, determination of exemption is unnecessary." 29 U.S.C. § 207 (1988 & Supp. IV 1992). *See also Krill v. Arma Corp.,* 76 F. Supp. 14, 17 (E.D.N.Y. 1948) (refusing to find an employee covered by the Act when he did "not engage in commerce or in the production of goods for commerce").

8.   29 C.F.R. §§ 541.01–541.602 (1993).

9.   The DOL expressed its opinion in its brief filed in *Reich v. Page & Addison*, No. 3:91-CV-2655-P, slip op. (N.D. Tex. March 10, 1994) Despite DOL opposition, the court in *Page & Addison* held that the paralegals employed at the Page & Addison law firm were administratively exempt from the FLSA and thus not entitled to overtime compensation. *Id. See infra* notes 153–59 and accompanying text (discussing *Page & Addison*). The DOL did not challenge this ruling. *Reich v. Page & Addison*, No. 94-10435, slip op. (5th cir. Sept. 21, 1994) (dismissing appeal)

10. Brief for the Department of Labor, *Reich v. Page & Addison*, P.C., (N.D. Tex. 1994) (No. 3:91-CV-2655-P).

11. Telephone Interview with Vonda Marshall, Staff Attorney, Department of Labor (Sept. 26, 1994) [hereinafter Marshall Interview].

12. Richard T. Cassidy & Jan L. Browning, *Paralegal Overtime: Yes, No, or Maybe*, Tex. Bar J., Jan. 1994, at 32 (citing Legal Assistant Today, May/June 1992).

13. *Id.* Sixty-three percent of the survey respondents reported that their firms did not pay them overtime wages. *Id.*

14. 29 U.S.C. § 216 (1988 & Supp. IV 1992) (imposing fine of up to $1000 for each violation of sections 206 or 207).

15. *See, e.g.,* Executive Office of the President, Office of management and Budget, Standard Industrial Classification Manual 369 (1987) (listing paralegals as providing "miscellaneous business services").

16. 29 U.S.C. § 213(a)(1) (1988).

17. *See, e.g., Joint Hearings Before the Committee on Education and Labor on S. 2475 and H.R. 7200,* 75th Cong., 1st Sess. 45 (1937).

18. Peter D. DeChiara, *Rethinking the Managerial-Professional Exemption of the Fair Labor Standards Act,* 43 Am. U.L. Rev. 139 (1993).

19. *Id.* at 161.

20. *Id.* at 162.

21. *Id.* at 165.

22. *Id.* at 176.

23. *Id.* at 182.

24. *Id.* at 160–86.

25. *Id.* at 189. The author explains that Congress adopted the exemptions when only a small portion of the workforce was "managerial-professional." *Id.* at 153–60. "Managerial-professionals" were predominantly male, enjoyed a high level of respect and stature, worked fewer hours and almost never experienced unemployment. *Id.* The author suggests that such justifications no longer exist because of recent changes in size, composition, stature, hours, and stability of "managerial-professional" occupations. *Id.* He proposes that the hours of managers and professionals should be regulated, with such workers receiving mandatory "comp time" instead of overtime pay, *Id.* at 186–88. *See also* Rosabeth M. Kanter, When Giants Learn to Dance:

Article 8-4   Continued

Mastering the Changes of Strategy, Management and Careers in the 1990s 267–80 (1989); Juliet B. Schor, The Overworked American: The Unexpected Decline of Leisure 66–67 (1991), *cited in DeChiara, supra* note 18, at 140 n.4.

26. The executive, administrative and professional exemptions have been an integral part of the FLSA since its passage in 1938. Congress has never indicated an intent to change this exemption policy.

27. *See, e.g., Walling v. General Indus. Co.,* 330 U.S. 545, 546–47 (1947) (indicating that the district court made "special findings of fact" in exempting employees under the FLSA); *see also Hoyt v. General Ins. Co. of America,* 249 F.2d 589, 590 (9th Cir. 1957) (stating that authorities are "uniform" in analyzing the question of employee exemption as "an ultimate question of fact").

28. 29 U.S.C. § 213(a)(1) (1988).

29. *But see Hoyt,* 249 F.2d at 590 (finding that although courts may use the regulations of the Wage and Hour Division as guidelines, they do not constitute binding authority).

30. 29 U.S.C. § 213 (1988). Conversely, non-exempt employees are entitled to overtime pay for each hour worked beyond the standard 40 hours per week. 29 U.S.C. § 206 (1988 & Supp. IV 1992).

31. 29 U.S.C. § 213 (1988).

32. 29 C.F.R. §§ 541.1–541.3 (1995).

33. The large number of exemption disputes between employers and employees underscores the ambiguity of the exemption classification. *See, e.g., Dalheim v. KDFW-TV,* 918 F.2d 1220 (5th Cir. 1990) (granting overtime pay to general-assignment reporters, producers, directors and assignment editors); *Jackson v. Kentucky,* 892 F. Supp. 923 (E.D. Ky. 1995) (granting employees overtime pay after misclassification as exempt administrators); *Mueller v. Thompson,* 858 F. Supp. 885 (W.D. Wis. 1994) (finding state employees properly exempt under FLSA and not entitled to overtime pay); *Freeman v. National Broadcasting Co., Inc.,* 846 F. Supp. 1109 (S.D.N.Y. 1993) (finding employees of news division of television network not exempt as professionals or administrators); *Hilbert v. Washington, D.C.,* 784 F. Supp. 922 (D.D.C. 1992) (granting overtime pay to police captains and lieutenants given their failure to qualify for executive, administrative or professional exemption); *Harris v. District of Columbia,* 741 F. Supp. 254 (D.D.C. 1990) (granting overtime pay to supervisory housing inspectors); *Palardy v. Horner,* 711 F. Supp. 667 (D. Mass. 1989) (finding technical employees of Department of Navy not exempt as administrators or professionals); *Pezzillo v. General Tel. & Electronics Info. Sys., Inc.,* 414 F. Supp. 1257 (M.D. Tenn. 1976) (denying administrative exemption for computer programmers). Unfortunately, courts have failed to resolve the cases consistently. *See, e.g., Quark v. Baltimore County, MD,* 895 F. Supp. 773 (D. Ma. 1995) (finding emergency medical service captains exempt executives); *Amshey v. United States,* 26 Cl. Ct. 582 (Cl. Ct. 1992) (granting overtime pay to sergeants and lieutenants in Secret Service). For examples of occupations deemed both exempt and non-exempt, see 29 U.S.C.A. § 213 (West 1988).

34. *See, e.g., Justice v. Metropolitan Gov't of Nashville, Davidson City, Tenn.,* 4 F.3d 1387 (6th Cir. 1993) (noting that classification of employees as exempt depends upon responsibilities and tasks, not titles). The label attached to a given job cannot be the only factor in deciding exemption because of potential injustice. *See Freeman v. Nat'l Broadcasting Co., Inc.,* 846 F. Supp. 1109 (S.D.N.Y. 1993) (titles can be had cheaply and are of no determinative value) (citing § 541.201(b)). A secretary entitled to overtime pay could be deprived of these wages by changing her title to "administrative assistant." Similarly, a non-executive, administrative, or professional job title does not automatically remove an employee from exemption. Because job titles do not necessarily reflect the actual duties performed, they often are insufficient indicators of exempt status.

35. *See George Lawley & Son Corp. v. South,* 140 F.2d 439, 444 (1st Cir.), *cert. denied,* 322 U.S. 746 (1944). The *Lawley* court indicated that salary alone does not exempt an employee from overtime wages: because "the component parts of [the Wage and Hour Division's] regulations are stated in the conjunctive, an employee must come within all of them in order to be exempt."

Id. at 444. Thus, compliance with the salary requirement is insufficient to exempt an employee absent compliance with the other requirements.

36. 29 C.F.R. § 541.1(a) (1995).
37. *Id.* § 541.1(b).
38. *Id.* § 541.1(c).
39. *Id.* § 541.1(d).
40. *Id.* § 541.1(e).
41. *Id.* § 541.1(f). The complete definition of "executive" as advanced in the Wage and Hour Division Regulations is as follows:

   The Term *employee employed in a bona fide executive . . . capacity* in section 13(a)(1) of the Act shall mean any employee:
   (a) Whose primary duty consists of the management of the enterprise in which he is employed or of a customarily recognized department of subdivision thereof; and
   (b) Who customarily and regularly directs the work of two or more other employees therein; and
   (c) Who has the authority to hire or fire other employees or whose suggestions and recommendations as to the hiring or firing and as to the advancement and promotion or any other change of status of other employees will be given particular weight; and
   (d) Who customarily and regularly exercises discretionary powers; and
   (e) Who does not devote more than 20 percent . . . of his hours of work in the workweek to activities which are not directly and closely related to the performance of the work described in paragraphs (a) through (d) of this section: . . . ; and
   (f) Who is compensated for his services on a salary basis at a rate of not less than $155 per week . . . exclusive of board, lodging, or other facilities; *Provided,* That an employee who is compensated on a salary basis at a rate of not less than $250 per week . . . exclusive of board, lodging, or other facilities, and whose primary duty consists of the management of the enterprise in which the employee is employed or of a customarily recognized department or subdivision thereof, and includes the customary and regular direction of the work of two or more other employees therein, shall be deemed to meet all the requirements of this section.
   29 C.F.R. § 541.1 (1995).

42. Bruce McLanahan, Fair Labor Standards Act Checklist (PLI Litig. & Admin. Practice Course Handbook Series no. H4-5219, 1995). The $250 threshold is subject to change. *See* Karen L. Corman, Employment Regulations, Overview and Update (PLI Litig. & Admin. Practice Course Handbook Series no. H4-5189, 1994).
43. 29 C.F.R. § 541.1(f) (1995). *See also* McLanahan, *supra* note 42, at 612–13.
44. 29 C.F.R. § 541.1(d) (1995).
45. *See Carstarphen v. Windleg,* 112 F. Supp. 692, 694 (E.D.N.C. 1953).
46. *Schanck v. Lehigh Valley R.R.,* 52 N.Y.S.2d 491, 492 (N.Y. City Ct. 1944).
47. *Anderson v. Federal Cartridge Corp.,* 62 F. Supp. 775, 781 (D. Minn. 1945), *aff'd,* 156 F.2d 681 (8th Cir. 1946).
48. 62 F. Supp. 775.
49. *Id.* at 781.
50. 29 C.F.R. § 541.1(e) (1995). Exempt employees may not spend more than 20% of their time on non-exempt activities. *Id.*
51. 140 F.2d 439 (1st Cir.), *cert. denied,* 322 U.S. 746 (1944).
52. *Id.* at 443.
53. 29 C.F.R. § 541.1(e) (1994).
54. 140 F.2d at 444.
55. *Id.*

Article 8-4   Continued

56. 29 C.F.R. § 541.1(f) (1995).
57. *See George Lawley & Son Corp. v. South*, 140 F.2d at 444.
58. The "salary basis" test is identical for executives and administrators. *See* 29 C.F.R. §§ 541.1(f), 541(e)(1) (1995). For professionals, the test only differs by fifteen dollars. *See* 29 C.F.R. § 541.1 (f), 541.2(e)(1) (1994)). Thus, the "salary basis" test covers all three exemptions.
59. The Wage and Hour Regulations define "salary basis" as follows:
    (a) An employee will be considered to be paid "on a salary basis" within the meaning of the regulations if under his employment agreement he regularly receives each pay period on a weekly, or less frequent basis, a predetermined amount constituting all or part of his compensation, which amount is not subject to reduction because of variations in the quality or quantity of the work performed.
        29 C.F.R. § 541.118(a) (1995). However, as commentators indicate, paying an employee a "salary" as opposed to an hourly wage does not satisfy this definition. *See* Matthew M. Smith & Steven H. Winterbauer, *Overtime Compensation Under the FLSA: Pay Them Now or Pay Them Later,* 19 EMP. REL. J. 23, 25 (1993). The authors also note that the DOL has interpreted "salary basis" as not allowing exempt employees to receive salary deductions for missing a few hours of work. *Id.*
60. *See* Smith & Winterbauer, *supra* note 59, at 25. See *infra* notes 106–10 and accompanying text for a description of the penalties for provision violations.
61. *Id.*
62. *See* Smith & Winterbauer, *supra* note 59, at 25, 47 n.5 (citing *The Private Sector Costs of the Department of Labor's Pay Docking Policy,* Policy Paper, Employment Policy Foundation, 1992). Authors Smith and Winterbauer identified six policies likely to subject employers to liability:
    (1) salary deductions for part-day absences;
    (2) benefits deductions for part-day absences from sick, personal, or vacation leave;
    (3) payment of additional compensation, including overtime pay or compensatory time off, tied directly to the number of extra hours worked;
    (4) suspensions without pay for disciplinary infractions;
    (5) salary deductions for absences caused by jury duty, attendance as a witness, or temporary military leave; and
    (6) suspensions without pay for temporary budget-related business requirements.
    Id. at 25.
63. *Compare Wells v. Radio Corp. of America*, 77 F. Supp. 964 (D.N.Y. 1948) (finding foreman was an exempt executive); *Hoff v. North American Aviation*, 67 F. Supp. 375 (D. Tex. 1946) (holding foreman of airplane factory was an exempt executive); *with Anderson v. Federal Cartridge Corp.*, 72 F. Supp. 639 (D. Minn. 1947) (finding shift foreman was not an exempt executive); *Gibson v. Atlantic Co.*, 63 F. Supp. 492 (D. Ga. 1945) (holding night foreman was not an exempt executive).
64. *See* cases cited *supra* note 63.
65. *Burke v. Lecrone-Benedict Ways*, 63 F. Supp. 883, 885–86 (E.D. Mich. 1945).
66. *Patton v. Williams*, 61 F. Supp. at 884, 885–86 (E.D. Okla. 1943).
67. The Wage and Hour Division's regulations define an "administrative" employee as one:
    (a) Whose primary duty consists of either:
        (1) The performance of office or nonmanual work directly related to management policies or general business operations of his employer or his employer's customers, or
        (2) The performance of functions in the administration of a school system . . . ; and
    (b) Who customarily and regularly exercises discretion and independent judgment; and
    (c) (1) Who regularly and directly assists a proprietor, or an employee employed in a bona fide executive or administrative capacity (as such terms are defined in the regulations of this subpart), or
        (2) Who performs under only general supervision work along specialized or technical lines requiring special training, experience, or knowledge, or
        (3) Who executes under only general supervision special assignments and tasks; and

(d) Who does not devote more than 20 percent . . . of his hours worked in the workweek to activities which are not directly and closely related to the performance of the work described in paragraphs (a) through (c) of this section; and

(e) (1) Who is compensated for his services on a salary or fee basis at a rate of not less than $155 per week . . . exclusive of board, lodging, or other facilities, or

(2) Who, in the case of academic administrative personnel, is compensated for services as required by paragraph (e)(1) of this section, or on a salary basis . . . .

29 C.F.R. §§ 541.2(a)–541.2(e)(2) (1995).

68. *See Ahern v. New York*, 807 F. Supp. 919, 925 (N.D.N.Y. 1992) (explaining the "short test").

69. *See Schockley v. City of Newport News*, 997 F.2d 18, 25 (4th Cir. 1993) (distinguishing the "short" and "long test").

70. McLanahan, *supra* note 42, at 612–13.

71. 29 C.F.R. § 541.2(a)(1).

72. *Id.* § 541.2(b).

73. *See Ahern*, 807 F. Supp. at 924–26.

74. *See* McLanahan, *supra* note 42, at 61. The author notes that because the $250 threshold is so low, "almost all employees having any responsibility will qualify." *Id.*

75. *Id.* at 925. *See also* 29 C.F.R. § 541.2(b) (1995).

76. Smith & Winterbauer, *supra* note 59, at 34.

77. *Id.*

78. *See Schanck v. Lehigh Valley R.R.*, 52 N.Y.S.2d 491, 492 (N.Y. City Ct. 1944).

79. *See Dymond v. U.S. Postal Serv.*, 670 F.2d 93 (8th Cir. 1982) (finding administrative exemption viable for employee notwithstanding supervisor reversal).

80. 997 F.2d 18 (4th Cir. 1993).

81. *Id.* at 28.

82. *Id.* at 28–29.

83. 982 F.2d 500 (Fed. Cir. 1992).

84. *Id.* at 503.

85. *See Christenberry v. Rental Tools, Inc.*, 655 F. Supp. 374, 376 (E.D. La. 1987). *See also* 29 C.F.R. § 541.207.

86. *See Ahern v. New York*, 807 F. Supp. 919, 926 (N.D.N.Y. 1992).

87. *Id.* at 925. *See also* 29 C.F.R. § 541.2(a)(1)(1995).

88. Smith & Winterbauer, *supra* note 59, at 23.

89. *Id.* at 36.

90. *Id.*

91. 997 F.2d 18, 28–29 (4th Cir. 1993).

92. Marshall Interview, *supra* note 11.

93. 29 C.F.R. § 541.301(a) (1995). *See* McLanahan, *supra* note 42, at 612.

94. *Id.* § 541.301(e). *See* McLanahan, *supra* note 42, at 612.

95. *See* McLanahan, *supra* note 42, at 612.

96. *Id.* § 541.301(a).

97. *Id.* § 541.301(b).

98. The Wage and Hour Regulations define a "professional employee" as one:

(a) Whose primary duty consists of the performance of:

(1) Work requiring knowledge of an advance type in a field of science or learning customarily acquired by a prolonged course of specialized intellectual instruction and study, as distinguished from a general academic education and from an apprenticeship, and from training in the performance of routine mental, manual, or physical processes, or

Article 8-4   Continued

(2) Work that is original and creative in character in a recognized field of artistic endeavor (as opposed to work which can be produced by a person endowed with general manual or intellectual ability and training), and the result of which depends primarily on the invention, imagination, or talent of the employee, or

(3) Teaching, tutoring, instructing, or lecturing in the activity of imparting knowledge . . . , or

(4) Work that requires theoretical and practical application of highly-specialized knowledge in computer systems analysis, programming, and software engineering . . . ; and

(b) Whose work requires the consistent exercise of discretion and judgment in its performance; and

(c) Whose work is predominantly intellectual and varied in character (as opposed to routine mental, manual, mechanical, or physical work) and is of such character that the output produced or the result accomplished cannot be standardized in relation to a given period of time; and

(d) Who does not devote more than 20 percent of his hours worked in the workweek to activities which are not an essential part of and necessarily incident to the work described in paragraphs (a) through (c) of this section; and

(e) Who is compensated for services on a salary or fee basis at a rate of not less than $170 per week . . . exclusive of board, lodging, or other facilities: *Provided,* That this paragraph shall not apply in the case of an employee who is the holder of a valid license or certificate permitting the practice of law or medicine or any of their branches and who is actually engaged in the practice thereof, nor in the case of an employee who is the holder of the requisite academic degree for the general practice of medicine and is engaged in an internship or resident program pursuant to the practice of medicine or any of its branches, nor in the case of an employee employed and engaged as a teacher as provided in paragraph (a)(3) of this section: *Provided further,* That an employee who is compensated on a salary or fee basis at a rate of not less than $250 per week . . . exclusive of board, lodging, or other facilities, and whose primary duty consists of the performance either of work described in paragraph (a)(1), (3), or (4) of this section, which includes work requiring the consistent exercise of discretion and judgment, or of work requiring invention, imagination, or talent in a recognized field of artistic endeavor, shall be deemed to meet all of the requirements of this section . . .

29 C.F.R. § 541.3 (1995).

99. 29 C.F.R. § 541.301(b) (1995). *See also* Ernest N. Votaw, *The Professional Exemption in the Fair Labor Standards Act,* 5 VAL. U. L. REV. 511, 515 (1970) (discussing the education requirements of professional exemption). A letter ruling issued by the DOL's Wage and Hour Division determined that a bona fide professional employee should possess "at least a bachelor's degree." Priv. Ltr. Rul. (June 12, 1984) (no number assigned), *reprinted in* WAGE AND HOUR DIVISION, DEP'T OF LABOR, FAIR LABOR STANDARDS HANDBOOK app. III at 74–75 (1986) [hereinafter FLSA HANDBOOK]. The Administrator exempted physician's assistants from this requirement. *Id.*

100. *See* Votaw, *supra* note 99, at 515. Votaw disagrees with the use of education level to evaluate whether an employee is exempt. *Id.* at 516. He examines several areas that do not lend themselves to realistic classification under the Wage and Hour Division's criteria. Among these are journalism, computer science, electronics and engineering. *Id.* at 517–19. Votaw emphasizes the inequity of characterizing a job requiring two years of solid, hands-on experience as "non-professional," while characterizing a job with identical requirements, but necessitating a four-year degree, as "professional." *Id.* at 519.

101. 160 N.W.2d 691 (Minn. 1968).

102. *Id.* at 696.

103. *See supra* note 34.

104. 155 F.2d 832 (6th Cir. 1946), *vacated on other grounds sub nom. Morris v. McComb,* 332 U.S. 422 (1947).

105. *Id.* at 836.
106. *See supra* notes 6–8.
107. 29 U.S.C. § 216(b) (1988).
108. 29 U.S.C. § 216(e) (1988).
109. 834 F. Supp. 530 (D.N.H. 1993), *aff'd*, 44 F.3d 1060 (5th Cir. 1995).
110. *Id.* at 533.
111. *Id.* at 539–42.
112. For a description of the regulatory classification and requirements of executive, administrative, and professional exemption, see *supra* notes 41, 67 and 98.
113. This definition represents a compilation of definitions espoused by the National Federation of Paralegal Associations ("NFPA"), the ABA, and Black's Law Dictionary. The NFPA defines a paralegal/legal assistant as, "a person qualified through education, training or work experience to perform substantive legal work that requires knowledge of legal concepts and is customarily, but not exclusively, performed by a lawyer." *Workshops for Legal Assistants: 1995, NFPA Paralegal Responsibilities,* 525 A.L.I. 165 (1995) [hereinafter *Workshops for Legal Assistants*]. The ABA defines a legal assistant as:

    [A] person, qualified through education, training, or work experience, who is employed or retained by a lawyer, law office, governmental agency, or other entity in a capacity or function which involves the performance, under the ultimate direction and supervision of an attorney, specifically—delegated substantive legal work, which work, for the most part, requires a sufficient knowledge of legal concepts that, absent such assistant, the attorney would perform the task.

    Dominic Latorraca, *Regulation of Paralegals: An Upcoming Issue,* 22 Colo. Law 493 (Mar. 1993) (citing ABA Standing Committee on Legal Assistants, ABA Board of Governors (Feb. 1986) (unpublished policy paper)).

    In Black's Law Dictionary, a paralegal is defined as a "person with legal skills, but who is not an attorney, and who works under the supervision of a lawyer in performing various tasks relating to the practice of law or who is otherwise authorized by law to use those legal skills." Black's Law Dictionary 1111 (6th ed. 1990).
114. *See Paralegal Inst., Inc. v. American Bar Ass'n,* 475 F. Supp. 1123, 1126 (E.D.N.Y. 1979), *aff'd,* 622 F.2d 575 (2d Cir. 1980).
115. *Id.*
116. *Id.*
117. *See* Cassidy & Browning, *supra* note 12, at 32.
118. *See id.*
119. *See Paralegal Inst.,* 475 F. Supp. at 1127. As amended in 1990, the current ABA accreditation standards require that:

    An institution provide the necessary resources and administration to properly educate and train the legal assistants . . . .

    ABA Standing Comm. on Legal Assistants, Guidelines and Procedures for Obtaining ABA Approval of Legal Assistant Education Programs (1990) [hereinafter ABA Guidelines].
    This includes establishing a program designed to qualify graduates for work in all law-related occupations, as well as maintaining a curriculum consistent with an accrediting agency's requirements. *Id.* G-301, G-303(c). Institutions must be led by competent and qualified directors and instructors, and must provide students with adequate library facilities. *Id.* G-401, G-601.

Article 8-4   Continued

120. National Federation Of Paralegal Associations, Inc., Expanding the Paralegal Profession (June 1994).

121. Cassidy & Browning, *supra* note 12, at 32.

122. *Id.* The ABA Standing Committee on Legal Assistants estimates that there are over 172 paralegal schools or programs in the U.S. Teri L. Clarke, *How to Evaluate the Qualifications of Legal Assistants*, Ariz. Att'y, May 1994, at 28 (discussing paralegal training, certification and degree programs).

123. 491 U.S. 274 (1989).

124. *Id.* at 285. See also John S. Pierce & Beverly A. Brand, *Recent Developments in Attorney Fee Disputes*, 7 U.S. F. Mar. L.J. 205 (1994) (discussing paralegal fees and billing, and their relation to job assignments).

125. Tom Weidlich, *Surviving the Downturn: After Slump, Paralegal Work on Rebound; They Faced Less Dire Layoffs Than Associates and Billable Hours Are Up*, Nat'l L.J. Apr. 25, 1994, at 1.

126. *Id.*

127. *Id.*

128. *Id.*

129. For a proposal on uniform regulation of paralegal job descriptions, *see* Barbara L. Albert, Legal Assistant Program Proposal (PLI Litig. & Admin. Practice Course Handbook Series no. H4-5131, 1992).

130. See Carole A. Bruno, *Training Paralegals In-House*, Pa. Law., Mar. 1986, at 31 (suggesting training techniques for maximizing paralegal effectiveness and job satisfaction).

131. *Cf.* Jeffrey C. Freedman, *Overtime in the Law Office*, L.A. Law, July/Aug. 1988, at 24 (noting that state and federal law have similar exemptions but different requirements).

132. *See* ABA Guidelines, *supra* note 119, at 1–37.

133. *See* Bruno, *supra* note 130, at 31–36.

134. The Fifth Circuit enumerated paralegal duties of this latter nature in *Richardson v. Byrd*, 709 F.2d 1016, 1023 (5th Cir.), *cert. denied*, 464 U.S. 1009 (1983), *cited in* Cassidy & Browning, *supra* note 12, at 33. The Court acknowledged that the paralegals involved in the suit "assisted the lawyers at trial, organized and reviewed class members' claims, participated in telephone conferences with lawyers, witnesses, and class members, and performed complex statistical work." *Id.* at 1023. The Court included the value of the legal secretarys' [sic] work in the attorneys' fees award despite the fact that, without attorney supervision, this work may have constituted the unauthorized practice of law. *See infra* notes 138–52 and accompanying text.

135. *See* 29 U.S.C. § 213(a)(1) (1988); 29 C.F.R. §§ 541.1(d), 541.2(b), 541.301(2) (1995).

136. Consider Firm C which employs paralegals in *both* of these capacities.

137. Another relevant issue is paralegal ethics. Although paralegals may abide by the ABA Model Rules of Professional Conduct and the Model Code of Professional Responsibility, these regulations specifically govern the conduct of attorneys, not paralegals. *See generally* American Bar Ass'n, Model Rules of Professional Conduct (1983), *reprinted in* 1995 Selected Standards on Professional Responsibility 1–145 (Thomas O. Morgan & Ronald D. Rotunda eds., 1995) [hereinafter Selected Standards]; American Bar Ass'n, Model Code of Professional Responsibility (1981), *reprinted in* Selected Standards, *supra* at 146–538; *see also* Nat'l Fed'n of Paralegal Ass'ns, The Ethical Wall: It's [sic] Application to Paralegals (PLI Litig. & Admin. Practice Course Handbook Series No. H4-5192, 1993). [hereinafter Ethical Wall]. To remedy this problem, the NFPA adopted ethical standards for its members. Nat'l Fed'n of Paralegal Ass'ns, Model Code of Ethics and Professional Responsibility 9 (PLI Litig. & Admin. Practice Course Handbook Series No. H4-5174, 1993). For a discussion of the potential conflict of interest problems accompanying a paralegal's change in law firms, see Ethical Wall, *supra*, at 19; *see also Smart Indus. Corp. v. Superior Court*, 876 P.2d 1176, 1181 (Ariz. 1994) (finding ethical rules of imported disqualification applied to non-lawyers).

138. *See, e.g.,* Ala. Code §§ 34-3–1 (1991) (making it a misdemeanor to practice law without a license); Cal. Bus. & Prof. Code § 6002 (West 1990) (making it a misdemeanor to practice law without state bar membership); Ga. Code Ann. § 15-19-51 (1990) (making it unlawful to hold oneself out as an attorney); 705 ILCS 205/1 (Smith-Hurd 1995) (requiring a license to practice law); Me. Rev. Stat. Ann. tit. 4, § 807 (West 1989) (making it unlawful to practice law without admission to state bar); N.J. Stat. Ann. § 2C:21–22 (West 1995) (finding the UPL a "disorderly persons offense"); Tex. Gov't Code Ann. § 81.102 (West 1988) (requiring admission to state bar in order to practice law).

139. Ala. Code § 34-3-1 (1975). For example, Alabama's code states that:

If any person shall, without having become duly licensed to practice, or whose license to practice shall have expired either by disbarment, failure to pay his license fee within 30 days after the day it becomes due, or otherwise, practice or assume to act or hold himself out to the public as a person qualified to practice or carry on the calling of a lawyer, he shall be guilty of a misdemeanor and fined not to exceed $500.00, or be imprisoned for a period not to exceed six months, or both.

140. *Id.* Model Code of Professional Responsibility EC 3–5, 3–6 (1981), *reprinted in* 1995 Selected Standards, *supra* note 137, at 176.

141. *Id.* EC 3–5.

142. American Bar Ass'n, Model Guidelines for Utilization of Legal Assistant Services (1991), *reprinted in* Merle L. Isgett, *The Role of the Legal Assistant: What Constitutes the Unauthorized Practice of Law* at 18 (PLI Litig. & Admin. Practice Course Handbook Series No. H4-5118, 1991).

143. *Id.* Guideline 2 provides:

Provided the lawyer maintains responsibility for the work product, a lawyer may delegate to a legal assistant any task normally performed by the lawyer except those tasks proscribed to one not licensed as a lawyer by statute, court rule, administrative rule or regulation, controlling authority, the ABA Model Rules of Professional Conduct, or these Guidelines.

144. *Id. See generally* Isgett, *supra* note 142, at 7.

145. *See* Podgers, *supra* note 2, at 24. The author cites a Gallup poll, conducted for the A.B.A. Journal, in which 86% of the responding attorneys endorsed acting against paralegals engaging in the unauthorized practice of law. *Id,* at 24. According to Martin D. Omoto, the legislative director of the California Coalition for Legal Access, "Lawyers hate the fact that they've got to share their profession with someone who didn't go to law school." *Id.* at 28.

146. *See, e.g.,* Rose D. Ors, *Effective Paralegal Use Cuts Costs,* Nat'l L.J., Apr. 20, 1992, at 13, 31 (arguing paralegal use reduces client and firm costs, and promotes efficiency through organization and coordination of tasks); Barry Weisberg, *Cure for a System in Chaos,* Nat'l L.J., Oct. 19, 1992, at 13, 15 (proposing that an "extensive system of neighborhood paralegal advisers" would promote access to legal services for civil disputes).

147. *See* Podgers, *supra* note 2, at 26. Although UPL is recognized as a problem, one commentator pointed out that even bar leaders realize that rigid enforcement policies are unlikely to rectify this growing dilemma. *Id.*

148. *Id.* at 27. P. Terry Anderlini, former California State Bar President, questioned the ability of paralegals to adequately serve the public: "People don't show up with a nice, simple legal problem in a small neat box." *Id.* Anderlini expressed concern for paralegals' competency to "diagnose the problem in a complete sense." *Id.*

149. *Id.*

Article 8-4   Continued

150. *Id.* at 28. Frustration with attorneys is evidenced by the rise in citizen self-representation. *Id.* at 27 (citing an ABA report indicating that in Arizona, 15,939 divorces in 1990 involved at least one self-represented party).

151. *See* Cheryl Frank, *Paralegal Burnout: Challenging Work Wanted,* A.B.A. J., Dec. 1984, at 30 (discussing how paralegals desire challenging, responsible work).

152. For a discussion of the various definitions of paralegal, see *supra* note 113 and accompanying text.

153. No. 3:91-CV-2655-P, slip op. at 1 (N.D. Tex. March 10, 1994).

154. *Id.*

155. For a general overview of paralegals, exemption and overtime pay, *see* Patricia H. Hicks & Michelle R. Neal, *Wage & Hour Laws: A Potential Pitfall for Unsuspecting Law Firms,* NEV. LAW., Dec. 1993, at 30.

156. *See supra* notes 12–13 and accompanying text.

157. Marshall Interview, *supra* note 11.

158. *Id.*

159. Telephone interview with Lu Hangley, Managing Director, National Federation of Paralegal Associations, Missouri Office (Sept. 26, 1994).

160. *Id.*

161. Priv. Ltr. Rul. (Aug. 17, 1979) (no number assigned), *reprinted in* FLSA HANDBOOK, *supra* note 99, app. III at, 72.

162. *Id.*

163. *Id.*

164. Priv. Ltr. Rul. (Aug. 17, 1979) (no number assigned), *reprinted in* FLSA HANDBOOK, *supra* note 99, app. III, at 72–73.

165. *Id.*

166. Priv. Ltr. Rul. (June 12, 1984) (no number assigned), *reprinted in* FLSA HANDBOOK, *supra* note 99, at 74–75. For a brief endorsement of the DOL viewpoint, see Chris Quasebarth, *Paralegals Entitled to Overtime Rates,* W. VA. LAW Feb. 1992, at 21.

167. Telephone Interview with Jan L. Browning, Certified Legal Assistant, Page & Addison, P.C. (Oct. 28, 1994). In *Page & Addison,* Browning testified on behalf of the firm in arguing for exemption. She co-authored an article on the subject in response to the lawsuit. *See* Cassidy & Browning, *supra* note 12.

168. *Id.*

169. *Id.* One commentator espouses an analogous argument in a non-paralegal context. Marc Linder, *Labor Department is Subverting Wage Law,* NAT'L L.J., Jan. 17, 1994, at 15 (exploring the fairness of labeling over nine million employees "executives" and making them work overtime without pay).

170. For a discussion of UPL, see *supra* notes 138–52 and accompanying text.

171. Lawyers are more legitimately concerned with UPL among legal technicians who practice without attorney supervision. *See supra* note 2.

172. *See* Podgers, *supra* note 2, at 24.

173. *Id.* at 24, 25. *See also* Simmons, *supra* note 2, at 19 (describing Arizona's proposed rule regarding non-lawyer practitioners, and concluding that the rule is an appropriate response to the concerns of protecting public interests and increasing access to the judicial system); Meredith Ann Munro, *Deregulation of the Practice of Law: Panacea or Placebo?,* 42 HASTINGS L.J. 203–48 (1990) (discussing the California movement for deregulation of the legal profession). However, the majority of such movements have failed upon initiation within the states. *Id.* at 205. Only Washington has a statute allowing nonlawyer practice. *Id.* Connecticut, Montana, Nevada, New Mexico, Oregon, Texas and Utah recently rejected similar proposals. Podgers, *supra* note 2, at 25.

174. *See* Browning Interview, *supra* note 167.

175. For a discussion of these overtime pay methods, see *infra* notes 186–91 and accompanying text.

176. *See* Freedman, *supra* note 131, at 24 (noting that while paralegals often hold both college degrees and paralegal certification, these achievements are not required, and much of the work they perform does not require such advanced education).

177. For a discussion on possible ways to eliminate this disparity of duties dilemma, see *infra* notes 217–23.

178. *See* Browning Interview, *supra* note 167.

179. *Id.*

180. Frank, *supra* note 151, at 30.

181. *See* Browning Interview, *supra* note 167.

182. *Id.*

183. *Id.*

184. *See* Clyde Leland, *All in a Day's Work,* CA. LAW., Oct. 1985, at 19 (noting benefits of professional exemption for paralegals).

185. 29 U.S.C § 207(a)(1) (1988).

186. *See* Louis B. Livingston & Sharon Toncray-Parker, *Fair Labor Standards Act: Substance and Procedure, in* COMMITTEE ON CONTINUING PROFESSIONAL EDUC., AMERICAN LAW INST.—AM. BAR ASS'N, 2 RESOURCE MATERIALS: LABOR AND EMPLOYMENT LAW 1759, 1767–73 (6th ed. 1992) (explaining overtime pay calculations under various working conditions). Because paralegals work closely with attorneys, their hours likely correspond to the supervising attorney's caseload. Prior to a large trial, for example, paralegals may work longer hours preparing documents and exhibits. This renders overtime pay schedules more unpredictable and may lead to undercompensation.

187. *See* Browning Interview, *supra* note 167.

188. *See* Marc Linder, *Closing the Gap Between Reich and Poor: Which Side is the Department of Labor On?.* N.Y.U. REV. L. & SOC. CHANGE, at 1 (1993–94).

189. *See* Michael Faillace, FAIR LABOR STANDARDS ACT: RECENT CASE LAW DEVELOPMENT (PLI Litg. & Admin. Practice Course handbook Series no. H4-5219, 1995). For a complete discussion of overtime pay, see Roger J. Abrams & Dennis R. Nolan, *Time at a Premium: The Arbitration of Overtime and Premium Pay,* OHIO ST. L.J. at 837 (1984) (explaining overtime pay methods in relation to collective bargaining agreements).

190. *See* Brown Interview, *supra* note 167.

191. *See* Frank, *supra* note 151.

192. *Id.*

193. *Id.*

194. This argument is, of course, not unique to paralegals. It is self-evident that people generally seek happiness and gratification from their jobs and are more effective when they enjoy their work. Feelings of uselessness, worthlessness and boredom contribute to low output and high rates of resignation. *See* David I. Levine, REINVENTING THE WORKPLACE: HOW BUSINESSES AND EMPLOYEES CAN BOTH WIN, Washington, D.C., Brookings Inst. 1995; Frank J. Landy, PSYCHOLOGY OF WORK BEHAVIOR, Pacific Grove, Calif., Brooks/Cole Pub. Co. 1989, 4th ed.

195. *See* Browning Interview, *supra* note 167.

196. *See* Marshall Interview, *supra* note 11. Marshall believes that it is useful to compare duties performed by similar employees as a means of determining FLSA exemption.

197. Priv. Ltr. Rul. (May 13, 1974) (no number assigned), *cited in* Priv. Ltr. Rul. (June 12, 1984) (no number assigned), *reprinted in* FLSA HANDBOOK, *supra* note 99.

Article 8-4   Continued

198. *Id.*

199. *Id.*

200. *See Reich v. Page & Adison*, No. 3:91-CV-2655-P, slip op. at 1 (N.D. Tex. March 10, 1994). *See supra* notes 161–66 and accompanying text.

201. *Id.*

202. *Id.*

203. 29 C.F.R. §§ 541.1–541.3. See Linda S. Jevahirian, *More Firms Use Paralegal Managers,* NAT'L LAW J., Feb. 25, 1991, at 23.

204. *Javahirian, supra* note 203, at 23; *see also* Richard S. Granat & Dana K. Saewitz, *Paralegals Move up to Management,* NAT'L LAW J., Jan. 32, 1989, at 19. The benefits of using paralegal managers include providing enhanced career mobility to legal assistants and improving the overall quality of the paralegal staff. Jevaharian, *supra* note 203, at 23. Because paralegals are familiar with the responsibilities of the profession, they are most adept at managing and recruiting qualified paralegals for the particular firm. *Id.* In addition, promoting current paralegals to managerial positions assists the firm by giving authority to an individual already familiar with firm practices and personnel. Granat & Saewitz, *supra,* at 19. Furthermore, promoting from within eliminates the costs associated with seeking to fill the position and provides added work performance incentives to lower-level paralegals. *Id.*

205. For a description of the requirements for executive exemption under the FLSA, see *supra* notes 69–93 and accompanying text.

206. 29 C.F.R. § 541.2 (1995).

207. Cassidy & Browning, *supra* note 12, at 33 (citing Prentice-Hall GUIDE TO EMPLOYMENT LAW AND LABOR REGULATION, § 11.353.5).

208. 29 C.F.R. § 541.2 (1995).

209. See Browning Interview, *supra* note 167.

210. Cassidy & Browning, *supra* note 12, at 34.

211. *Id.*

212. *Id.*

213. *Oxman v. Hamilton & Samuels* (Cal. Labor Stds. Enforcement, Feb. 28, 1992), *cited in* Cassidy & Browning, *supra* note 12, at 34.

214. *Id.* The agency based its conclusion in part on the fact that the paralegals were all certified through an ABA-accredited program, compensated at a rate of $100 dollars per hour, and considered a "distinct group . . . with authority to delegate work . . . ." *Id.*

215. *Id.*

216. See Latorraca, *supra* note 113, at 493; *Workshops for Legal Assistants, supra* note 113, at 165.

217. See Latorraca, *supra* note 113.

218. Hope V. Samborn, *Legal Assistants: Has the Time Arrived for State-By-State Licensing?,* A.B.A. J., Dec. 1992, at 42.

219. *Id.*

220. For a discussion of the issues raised by the UPL, see *supra* notes 138–52 and accompanying text.

221. *See* Ors, *supra* note 146, at 31. The author describes a large firm that developed three tiers of paralegals: "entry-level paralegals," "senior paralegals" and third-level paralegals denoted "senior paralegal II" or "paralegal specialist." *Id.* A paralegal's duties and responsibilities increase proportionately with advancement to each level. *Id.*

222. By way of comparison, suppose the firm in question has a tiered system. *See supra* note 221. Do second-tier "senior paralegals" perform functions sufficient for exemption? Is exemption based on promotion alone? These questions suggest that creating tiers of paralegals only serves to further complicate an already complex issue.

223. *See* Priv. Ltr. Rul. (June 12, 1984) (no number assigned), *supra* note 197.

an active role in developing consistent, uniform standards for the profession in order to exempt all legal assistants. This conclusion brings the profession, once again, face-to-face with its professional identity issue.

The authors of Article 8-5 examine the exempt/nonexempt issue and urge the DOL to reexamine the issues. The authors conclude that whether a legal assistant is an exempt employee needs to be determined on a case-by-case basis.

Paralegal Overtime—Yes, No or Maybe?

Tax Bar Journal Jan '94

Richard T. Cassidy and Jan L. Browning, CLA

Paralegals—the growth industry of the 90's! Is this advertising hype for vocational schools or sound advice on law office management in today's legal market? If you use legal assistants in your practice, you probably realize the financial benefits you and your clients gain. Yet you may be unaware of the current controversy regarding whether legal assistants should be exempt or non-exempt from overtime pay under the Fair Labor Standards Act. This issue may affect your practice now and in the future.

Historical Perspective

Twenty-five years ago, the legal community was a respected profession. There was no formal advertising, no cutthroat competition for clients or associates and no legal assistants. Instead, the highly skilled legal secretary served as the boss's assistant. As technology made former methods of transacting business obsolete, traditional roles in the legal profession were challenged. Consumers did not bypass lawyers in their quest to assure value received for money spent. Fees were questioned and had to be explained, justified, and approved. Law firms found themselves competing in a business marketplace rather than relying on personal contacts and old school chums. Firms could no longer send out a statement with no explanation other than for "Professional Services Rendered."

The complexities of everyday business and personal dealings required more frequent advice, or even participation, of an attorney. Often, the result was that the legal services needed were beyond the financial reach of the average person. The resulting complaints forced the legal community to seek new solutions. Legal assistants became part of the solution.

In the past, experienced legal secretaries worked behind the scenes drafting documents, working with clients, and researching factual and legal issues. While young lawyers provided a similar service, the rapid acceleration in salaries paid to new associates altered their cost-effectiveness on some of these tasks. The market imperative to cut or contain costs was growing. Firms experimented with a variety of strategies to increase efficiency; the

---

Article 8-5 Paralegal Overtime—Yes, No, or Maybe

Richard T. Cassidy & Jan L. Browning, Paralegal Overtime—Yes, No or Maybe? Texas B.J., *Jan. 1994, at 32, 34. Courtesy of Richard T. Cassidy.*

result was that substantive work formerly done exclusively by attorneys was delegated to legal assistants and billed to clients at a substantially lower rate.

As the profession evolved, many legal assistants wore two hats, e.g., secretary and paralegal. Certain nonclerical functions were delegated to the secretary/legal assistant, but when production took priority, the legal assistant persona was pushed to the background so the secretarial persona could get the work out. Spurred by a desire for professional growth, legal assistants pushed for more opportunities to do substantive work and to educate attorneys and clients regarding the benefits to be derived from such delegation.

In 1975, the National Association of Legal Secretaries (NALS) recognized the trend toward the use of legal assistants and created the Legal Assistants Section of NALS. Less than a year later, the section was spun off into its own organization, the National Association of Legal Assistants (NALA). The National Federation of Paralegal Associations (NFPA) was also formed. The development of model standards and guidelines by NALA, NFPA, and the ABA, together with NALA's voluntary certification exam, helped ensure a high level of professionalism.

Legal ethics questions were raised and answered regarding what work could be delegated to legal assistants. As client acceptance of the legal assistant's role increased, so did the attorney's reliance on the legal assistant to promote client satisfaction while reducing overall legal expenses.

The courts recognized the value of paralegals by permitting inclusion of legal assistant time in the reimbursement of attorney's fees. MISSOURI V. JENKINS, 491 U.S. 274 (1989), held that a legal fee may include a charge for legal assistant services at market rates rather than actual cost, which further validated the legal assistants' role.

The question of legal assistant compensation became an issue. Were they to be paid as part of the general staff, with overtime payments as required, or as part of the professional staff, exempt from overtime requirements? Firms reached contradictory conclusions; and the issue divided attorneys and paralegals alike. In a survey by LEGAL ASSISTANT TODAY (May/June 1992), 58% of paralegals surveyed believed they should be paid overtime, while 63% responded their firms were not paying such overtime. As the editors noted, "This is a very complex issue which . . . may not be as black and white as our questions imply . . . Job duties and other factors can affect exempt/nonexempt status. Paralegal overtime and the laws surrounding it deserve a closer look . . . "

Fair Labor Standards Act

The Fair Labor Standards Act ("FLSA"), enacted in 1938 and enforced by the U.S. Department of Labor (the "DOL"), regulates minimum wage and overtime pay for hours worked in excess of forty hours per week in both private and public sectors. Applicable regulations (found in Title 29 of the Code of Federal Regulations, Part 541) provide for exemptions from the overtime provisions in three categories: executive, administrative, and professional.

Executive Exemption

An employee who is guaranteed a salary of at least $250.00 per week, whose primary duty is managing an enterprise or a recognized department or subdivision thereof, and who customarily and regularly directs the work of at least two other employees is exempt under the executive exemption with the proviso for high-salaried executives. This exemption might apply to a supervising legal assistant. It is generally a straightforward determination and leaves little room for argument. The administrative exemption, particularly as applied to legal assistants, has much more leeway for interpretation and argument.

Administrative Exemption

An employee who is guaranteed a salary of at least $250.00 per week, whose primary duty consists of performing office or nonmanual work directly related to the management policies or general business operations of the employer or the employee's clients, and who customarily and regularly exercises discretion and independent judgment is exempt under the administrative exemption with the proviso for high-salaried administrators.

Whereas the DOL agrees with the executive exemption if the circumstances fit the criteria, it has refused to recognize the administrative exemption for legal assistants. What part of this definition categorically excludes legal assistants?

The DOL's Position

From its first private letter ruling in 1977, the DOL has consistently maintained legal assistants are non-exempt, unless they are qualified under the executive exemption. The Department has repeated the same language in letter after letter:

> It is our further position that 'legal assistants' and 'paralegals' generally are not involved in the performance of duties requiring the exercise of discretion and independent judgment of the type required by section 541.3(b); they are, instead, involved in the use of skills rather than discretion and independent judgment. In our view, such employees generally are found to be highly trained and highly skilled specialists who, as such, would not qualify for the exemption as defined . . . in Regulations, Part 541. (Private letter rulings dated 11/9/77, 2/10/78, and 8/17/79 [Herbert J. Cohen]; 9/27/79 [C. Lamar Johnson]; 8/18/86 [Stephanie R. Giyear]; 4/23/84 and 6/12/84 [William M. Otter])

The DOL's position was established early in the development of the profession when standards, duties, training, and responsibilities were just beginning to evolve. Since then, it has become a definable, recognizable professional, supported by the ABA, NALA, NFPA, the State Bar of Texas Legal Assistants Division (created in 1981), and numerous local associations. Texas has led the nation in addressing issues relating to paralegals. Standards and guidelines for utilization of legal assistants have been developed. The ABA regularly reviews and oversees accredited programs of instruction. Legal assistants periodically attend and even serve as speakers at CLE seminars and enjoy associate membership in many state bar associations as well as the ABA. Duties and responsibilities have even been detailed by various court opinions. See, Gill Savings Assoc. v. International Supply Co., Inc., 759 S.W.2d 697 (Tex. App. Dallas, 1988, no writ); Richardson v. Byrd, 709 F.2d 1016 (5th cir.), cert. denied, 464 U.S. 1009, 104 S. Ct. 527, 78 L. Ed. 2d 710 (1983)

The DOL's position regarding the administrative exemption, unaltered from its inception, has ignored the evolution of the paralegal profession. With no political imperative to change, the Department remains adamant that the administrative exemption does not apply to legal assistants.

The Argument for the Administrative Exemption

(Directly Related to Management Policies or General Business Operations)

The first consideration is whether a legal assistant's "primary duties" consist of office work directly related to the management policies or general business operations of the law

Article 8-5 Continued

firm's clients. These duties must consume the majority of available time and must be more than simply clerical.

The activities contemplated under "directly related to management policies or general business operations" are administrative (as opposed to the production) activities. Illustration of this point is found in the Prentice-Hall's "Guide to Employment Law and Labor Regulation" ("P-H Guide"), Section 11,353.5:

> The test of 'directly related to management policies or general business operations' is also met by many persons employed as advisory specialists and consultants of various kinds . . . tax experts . . . and many others.
>
> Under Section 541.2 the 'managment policies or general business operations' may be those of the employer or the employer's customers. For example, **many bona fide administrative employees perform important functions as advisers and consultants but are employed by a concern engaged in furnishing such services for a fee**. . . . Such employees, if they meet the other requirements of Section 541.2, qualify for exemption regardless of whether the management policies or general business operations to which their work is directly related are those of their employer's clients or customers, or those of their employer. [Emphasis added.]

The requirement of "directly related to management policies of general business operations" also limits the acceptable work to activities which are of substantial importance to the management or operation of the business of the firm's clients. "Substantial importance" includes those employees responsible for carrying out the general business operations or management policies as well as those participating in the actual formulation of management policies or in the operation of the business as a whole. Thus, while legal assistants do not set management policies for a firm's clients, their work does carry out major and substantial assignments in the conduct of the client's operations.

P-H Guide, Section 11,353.5 is instructive on the question of "substantial importance:"

> . . . [I]t is clear that bookkeepers, secretaries, and clerks of various kinds hold the run-of-the-mine (sic) positions in any ordinary business and are not performing work directly related to management policies or general business operations. On the other hand, **a tax consultant employed** either by an individual company or **by a firm of consultants is ordinarily doing work of substantial importance to the management or operation of a business**.
>
> Some firms employ persons whom they describe as 'statisticians.' If all such a person does, in effect, is to tabulate data, [s]he is clearly not exempt. However, if such an employee **makes analyses of data and draws conclusions which are important to the determination of, or which, in fact, determine financial, merchandising, or other policy, clearly [s]he is doing work directly related to management policy or general business operations**. [Emphasis added.]

"CUSTOMARILY AND REGULARLY"

The employee must also "customarily and regularly" exercise discretion and independent judgment. Customarily and regularly does not mean "always," and it does not mean "occasional." P-H Guide addresses the meaning of this phrase in Section 11,353.7 as follows:

> The phrase 'customarily and regularly' signifies a frequency which must be greater than occasional but which, of course, may be less than constant. The requirement will be met by

the employee who normally and recurrently is called upon to exercise and does exercise discretion and independent judgment in the day-to-day performance of his duties.

"Discretion and Independent Judgment"

A legal assistant's position is not one which uses only certain skills in applying techniques, procedures or specific standards. Neither is it one in which there exists only limited discretionary leeway to perform the work within closely prescribed limits, or relies on rote memorization of standards to make decisions while calling such actions "discretion or independent judgment". P-H Guide, Section 11,353.7, provides a helpful example analogous to the type of performance required by a legal assistant:

> Every problem processed in a computer first must be carefully analyzed so that exact and logical steps for its solution can be worked out. When this preliminary work is done by a computer programmer he is exercising discretion and independent judgment. A computer programmer would also be using discretion and independent judgment when he determines exactly what information must be used to prepare the necessary documents and by ascertaining the exact form in which the information is to be presented.

In working on various real estate agreements, reviewing an opposing party's documents produced in discovery, or doing legal research, the paralegal's duties include a careful analysis of the problem, deciding what information is required for resolution, determining the form the resolution should take, or ascertaining the documentation required to prove a case. This is clearly the exercise of discretion and independent judgment.

> The regulations in Subpart A of this part also contemplate the kind of discretion and independent judgment exercised by an administrative assistant to an executive, **who without specific instructions or prescribed procedures, arranges interviews and meetings, and handles callers and meetings himself where the executive's personal attention is not required**. It includes the kind of discretion and independent judgment exercised by a customer's man in a brokerage house in deciding what recommendations to make to a customer for the purchase of securities. It may include the kind of discretion and judgment exercised by . . . persons who are given reasonable latitude in carrying on negotiations on behalf of their employers. [P-H Guide, Section 11,353.7. Emphasis added.]
>
> One phase of the work of an administrative assistant to a bona fide executive or administrative employee provides another illustration. **The work of determining whether to answer correspondence personally, call it to his superior's attention, or route it to someone else for reply requires the exercise of discretion and independent judgment and is exempt work of the kind described in Section 541.2**. Opening mail for the purpose of reading it to make the decisions indicated will be directly and closely related to the administrative work described. However, merely opening mail and placing it unread before his superior or some other person would be related only remotely, if at all, to any work requiring the exercise of discretion and independent judgment. [P-H Guide, Section 11,353.8. Emphasis added.]

"Final Decisions Not Necessary"

The DOL relies heavily on the requirement that a legal assistant's work must be reviewed by an attorney, arguing such review disproves discretion and independent judgment. This argument, however, is indicative of their fundamental misunderstanding concerning the work of legal assistants in particular and the legal profession in general.

Article 8-5 Continued

While a legal assistant's decisions are subject to review and may not be final, the same can be said of other exempt positions, including associates. Such review does not negate the exercise of discretion and independent judgment and the work of a legal assistant can simultaneously be directly related to the management policies or general business operations of the firm's clients and require the customary and regular exercise of discretion and independent judgment.

Discretion and independent judgment " . . . does not necessarily imply that the decisions made by the employee must have a finality that goes with unlimited authority and a complete absence of review . . . " [P-H Guide, Section 11,353.7]

Continuing, P-H Guide, Section 11,353.7 states:

> The decisions made as a result of the exercise of discretion and independent judgment may consist of recommendations for action rather than the actual taking of action. **The fact that an employee's decision may be subject to review and that upon occasion the decisions are revised or reversed after review does not mean that the employee is not exercising discretion and independent judgment within the meaning of the regulations in Subpart A of this part**. For example, the assistant to the president of a large corporation may regularly reply to correspondence addressed to the president. Typically, such an assistant will submit the more important replies to the president for review before they are sent out. Upon occasion, after review, the president may alter or discard the prepared reply and direct that another be sent instead. This action by the president would not, however, destroy the exempt character of the assistant's function, and does not mean that he does not exercise discretion and independent judgment in answering correspondence and in deciding which replies may be sent out without review by the president. [Emphasis added.]

Professional

The professional exemption contemplates work which requires a knowledge of an advanced type in a field of science or learning customarily acquired by a prolonged course of specialized intellectual instruction and study, as distinguished from a general academic education. While the Department has recognized law school as satisfying this requirement, it has not given similar recognition to paralegal programs. To date, this exemption has not been actively pursued for legal assistants.

The DOL did make an exception for a nurse/legal assistant in particular (See "To Be or Not to Be (Exempt)" by Diane Patrick, *Legal Assistant Today*, Sept/Oct 1992) and for physician's assistants generally. (See 6/12/84 private letter ruling.) In explaining its ruling, the Department said the exemption was justified because "the physician assistant is directly engaged in the practice of medicine, subject to the physician's approval, while performing duties requiring considerable analysis, interpretation and discretion." If this sounds to you a lot like the duties of a legal assistant, you might enjoy the DOL's attempt to make a distinction:

> The duties of the paralegal or legal assistant require the use of skills rather than discretion and independent judgment. The steps taken in legal research involve some judgment as to source material to be researched, steps to be taken, parties to be contacted, and the like, but such work does not involve the exercise of discretion and independent judgment at a level contemplated by the regulations.

In a new and interesting case, the California Division of Labor Standards Enforcement has radically departed from the DOL's position, deciding that an ABA-approved course of study for legal assistants does meet that criteria. In OXMAN V. HAMILTON & SAMUELS, decided February 28, 1992, Hamilton & Samuel's legal assistants were determined to be professionally exempt: they met the duties test and were cost-effective replacements for associates. The agency considered the fact that the firm required a certificate from an ABA-approved paralegal program. Moreover, the paralegals were a distinct group within the firm with authority to delegate work to the firm's secretaries and clerks. Another factor was that the firm's clients willingly paid the substantial hourly rates ($100.00/hour or more) for paralegals' independent judgment and discretion, but would no doubt have resisted such rates for clerical work.

The fact that a paralegal might choose to perform a clerical function in the course of the day to expedite the work, or do a necessary task after the departure of the clerical staff, did not alter the duties required for the job. Whether the job is exempt or non-exempt is based on the amount of discretion permitted and an entry level legal assistant would be allowed less discretionary authority than one with more advanced experience. The firm further argued that whether or not a paralegal is exempt is a rebuttable presumption, i.e., the paralegal should be classified under the professional exemption unless the duties show to the contrary.

The California decision stands in stark contrast to the usual position of the DOL, who clearly does not understand the nature and quality of work now being performed by legal assistants.

Time for Review

Continuing to categorically declare legal assistants non-exempt flies in the face of the FLSA's basic premise, i.e., the determination of whether or not one is exempt is a function of the duties performed, not the title of the position.

Obviously, not all legal assistants should be exempt. The determination should be based on duties and responsibilities and the degree of discretion and independent judgment exercised by the individual holding the paralegal position. It is well established that whether an employee is exempt under the Act is purely a question of fact to be determined on a case-by-case basis. ZACEK V. AUTOMATED SYSTEMS CORPORATION, 541 S.W.2d 516, 518 (Tex. Civ. App. 1976), citing WALLING V. GENERAL INDUSTRIES CO., 330 U.S. 545 (1947). This means a case by case determination. To attempt to rule categorically that most, if not all, legal assistants are non-exempt ignores the requirements of the FLSA as well as the substantive nature of a legal assistant's work.

The DOL should reexamine the issue with an eye toward creating clear guidelines by which firms can make a reasonable determination of the status of their paralegals. While the employer always carries the burden of proving the exemption (SEE, IDAHO SHEET METAL WORKS, INC. V. WIRTZ, 383 U.S. 190 (1966) and CRAIG V. FAR WEST ENGINEERING CO., 265 F.2d 251, 257 (9th Cir. 1959), the basis for a final determination should rest on something more current than recycled letter rulings from 1977. The decision should encompass the whole spectrum of current practice and utilization, the recognized status of the profession, the advanced education, continuing legal education, the substantive duties performed, and the degree to which a legal assistant exercises discretion and independent judgment in the performance of the job.

Article 8-5   Continued

CONCLUSION

The question of exemption for legal assistants under the FLSA remains controversial. Members of the profession have mixed feelings on the subject, the DOL has taken a very rigid stance in denying exempt status for legal assistants, and at least one jury has made a finding contrary to the DOL position. It is clear that not all legal assistants should be exempt and that a determination must be made on a case-by-case basis. The factors that will be considered in making that determination include the legal assistant's credentials, academic background, duties, and responsibilities, as well as the degree of discretion and independent judgment exercised in the performance of delegated duties.

DISCUSSION QUESTIONS

1. Consider the paralegal tasks that you have performed in your legal assistant position (or internship position as a legal assistant student). Under the *Reich v. Page & Addison* analysis discussed above, would you be considered an exempt employee under the FLSA?

2. Do you think it is logically consistent for a legal assistant to desire to be delegated paralegal tasks that require independent thinking, discretion, and judgment and to also take the position that the legal assistant should be paid overtime pay because the legal assistant is nonexempt under the FLSA?

3. Which position, exempt or nonexempt under the FLSA, is in the best interest of the legal assistant profession as a whole?

ENDNOTES

[1] 29 U.S.C. Sec. 201–219 (1988).

[2] Priv. Ltr. Rul. (May 13, 1974) (no number assigned), cited in Priv. Ltr. Rul. (June 12, 1984) (no number assigned), reprinted in WAGE AND HOUR DIVISION, U.S. DEPARTMENT OF LABOR, FAIR LABOR STANDARDS HANDBOOK, app. III at 74–75 (Private letter ruling is discussed and cited in footnotes 99 and 197–199 of Article 8-4 herein).

[3] Oxman v. Hamilton & Samuels (Cal. Labor Stds. Enforcement, Feb. 28, 1992).

[4] Reich v. Page & Addison, No. 3:91-CV-2655-P, slip op. (N.D. Tex. March 10, 1994).

[5] See generally, Gina Gladwell, *The Issues Affecting Paralegals Then & Now*, LEGAL ASSISTANT TODAY, Sept./Oct. 1997, at 65–68 (describing interview responses—excerpted portion Article 8-1 herein); Dorene Ridgway, *Exempt from Overtime Pay*, NATIONAL PARALEGAL REPORTER, Spring 1995, at 31 (citing surveys conducted—Article 8-2 herein); Xavier Rodriguez, *Paralegal Overtime— Yes, No, or Maybe?—an Update*, available at http://www.texasbar.com/newsinfo/about-statebar/committees/rodriguez.aps; Frances Beall Whiteside, *Exempt to Non-Exempt—a Blessing or a Curse?* NATIONAL PARALEGAL REPORTER, Winter 1994, at 28 (describing results of survey conducted in Summer 1994—Article 8-3 herein).

The Recovery of Legal Assistant Fees Issue

INTRODUCTION

Unlike the continuing issues of regulation and the exempt/non-exempt status of legal assistants, this question, "Is the time expended by a legal assistant recoverable as attorney fees and/or costs of a legal action?" was not an issue for the profession in the 1960s and 1970s. This issue came to the forefront in the 1980s and accelerated in the 1990s as the legal assistant profession evolved and as lawyers, judges, consumer groups, the general public, and legislators became more aware of the cost-saving benefits of proper utilization by lawyers of competent, qualified legal assistants. However, like many of the continuing issues facing the profession, this issue is intricately interwoven with the legal assistant identity and regulation issues. The development of the law on the recovery of legal assistant fees has enhanced the image and the status of the legal assistant profession. We predict that, as the profession continues to evolve and effectively deal with the identity and regulation issues, the issue of the recoverability of legal assistant fees will disappear.

ARE FEES CHARGED FOR LEGAL ASSISTANT WORK RECOVERABLE AS ATTORNEY FEES AND/OR COSTS?

At the federal level, legal assistant fees are recoverable in accordance with either specific statutory authority[1] or as authorized by federal case law interpreting federal statutes.[2] At the state level there is not uniformity on the issue. Since the state case law on the recoverability of legal assistant fees is not controlled by federal precedent, the states have not taken uniform positions on the issue. Some states allow recovery of legal assistant fees by specific statutory authority[3] or by case law interpreting state statutes.[4] However, some states do not allow the recovery of legal assistant fees either as attorney fees or as costs.[5] An analysis of the case law will be informative.

The seminal case on the issue of the recoverability of legal assistant fees is *Missouri v. Jenkins,* shown in Article 9-1.

The *Missouri v. Jenkins* case created federal precedent that interpreted the phrase "reasonable attorney fees," as utilized in a federal civil rights statute, to include a reasonable fee for the work product of a legal assistant, law clerk, and recent law graduate and thus allowed the legal assistant fee to be recovered under the statute. Additionally, the court held that the community's prevailing market rate for legal assistants would be the appropriate "reasonable" recoverable rate, not the actual cost of the legal assistant to the attorney. Other federal courts have followed this precedent in the interpretation of federal statutes.[6]

The federal precedent set by the United States Supreme Court in *Missouri v. Jenkins,* while persuasive authority at the state level, is not mandatory at the state level. Rather, absent a state statute which, by specific language, allows recovery of legal assistant fees as a component of attorney fees, the state court makes its determination of the issue on the recoverability of attorney fees based on the realities of cost-effective utilization of legal assistants and legislative intent. The state court cases in Articles 9-2 and 9-3 are provided as examples of the rationale utilized by state courts to establish precedent allowing legal assistant fees to be recovered as an element of attorney fees.

WHAT CRITERIA ARE USED BY THE COURT TO DETERMINE WHETHER LEGAL ASSISTANT FEES ARE RECOVERABLE?

Federal and state judicial opinions such as *Gill Savings Association*[7] and *Multi-Moto*[8] indicate specific criteria that are used in determining whether a specific legal assistant's fee was recoverable. Generally speaking, the courts in making this determination look at criteria in the following five areas:

- The legal assistant's credentials in terms of education and experience
- The specific type of tasks performed by the legal assistant
- The documentation of the legal assistant's separately billed time
- The reasonableness of the time
- The reasonableness of the fee

In *Absher Construction v. Kent School District,*[9] the court discussed the criteria that it felt were relevant in determining when an award for attorney fees may appropriately include legal assistant fees.

The cited cases note that the courts will review the educational credentials and the work experience of the legal assistant. The court will give significant weight to the legal assistant's education, experience, and credentials in determining whether the legal assistant is qualified to provide the service for which the recoverable fee is

Text continues on page 304

MISSOURI ET AL. *v.* JENKINS, BY HER FRIEND, AGYEI, ET AL.

CERTIORARI TO THE UNITED STATES COURT OF APPEALS FOR THE EIGHTH CIRCUIT

No. 88–64. Argued February 21, 1989—Decided June 19, 1989

In this major school desegregation litigation in Kansas City, Missouri, in which various desegregation remedies were granted against the State of Missouri and other defendants, the plaintiff class was represented by a Kansas City lawyer (Benson) and by the NAACP Legal Defense and Educational Fund, Inc. (LDF). Benson and the LDF requested attorney's fees under the Civil Rights Attorney's Fees Awards Act of 1976 (42 U. S. C. § 1988), which provides with respect to such litigation that the court, in its discretion, may allow the prevailing party, other than the United States, "a reasonable attorney's fee as part of the costs." In calculating the hourly rates for Benson's, his associates', and the LDF attorneys' fees, the District Court took account of delay in payment by using current market rates rather than those applicable at the time the services were rendered. Both Benson and the LDF employed numerous paralegals, law clerks, and recent law graduates, and the court awarded fees for their work based on market rates, again using current rather than historic rates in order to compensate for the delay in payment. The Court of Appeals affirmed.

Held:

1. The Eleventh Amendment does not prohibit enhancement of a fee award under § 1988 against a State to compensate for delay in payment. That Amendment has no application to an award of attorney's fees, ancillary to a grant of prospective relief, against a State, *Hutto v. Finney*, 437 U. S. 678, and it follows that the same is true for the calculation of the *amount* of the fee. An adjustment for delay in payment is an appropriate factor in determining what constitutes a reasonable attorney's fee under § 1988. Pp. 278–284.
2. The District Court correctly compensated the work of paralegals, law clerks, and recent law graduates at the market rates for their services, rather than at their cost to the attorneys. Clearly, "a reasonable attorney's fee" as used in § 1988 cannot have been meant to compensate only work performed personally by members of the bar. Rather, that term must refer to a reasonable fee for an attorney's work product, and thus must take into account the work not only of attorneys, but also the work of paralegals and the like. A reasonable attorney's fee under § 1988 is one calculated on the basis of rates and practices prevailing in the relevant market and one that grants the successful civil rights plaintiff a "fully compensatory fee," comparable to what "is traditional with attorneys compensated by a fee-paying client." In this case, where the practice in the relevant market is to bill the work of paralegals separately, the District Court's decision to award separate compensation for paralegals, law clerks, and

Article 9-1   Missouri et al. v. Jenkins, by her friend, Agyei, et al.

Missouri v. Jenkins, 491 U.S. 274, 105 L. Ed. 2d 229, 109 S. Ct. 2463 (1989).

recent law graduates at prevailing market rates was fully in accord with § 1988. Pp. 284–289.

838 F. 2d 260, affirmed.

BRENNAN, J., delivered the opinion of the Court, in which WHITE, BLACKMUN, STEVENS, and KENNEDY, JJ., joined, and in Parts I and III of which O'CONNOR and SCALIA, JJ., joined. O'CONNOR, J., filed an opinion concurring in part and dissenting in part, in which SCALIA, J., joined, and in which REHNQUIST, C. J., joined in part, *post*, p. 289. REHNQUIST, C. J., filed a dissenting opinion, *post*, p. 295. MARSHALL, J., took no part in the consideration or decision of the case.

Bruce Farmer, Assistant Attorney General of Missouri, argued the cause for petitioners. With him on the brief were *William L. Webster*, Attorney General, *Terry Allen*, Deputy Attorney General, and *Michael L. Boicourt* and *Bart A. Matanic*, Assistant Attorneys General.

Jay Topkis argued the cause for respondents. With him on the brief were *Julius LeVonne Chambers*, *Charles Stephen Ralston*, *Arthur A. Benson II*, *Russell E. Lovell II*, and *Theodore M. Shaw*.*

JUSTICE BRENNAN delivered the opinion of the Court.

This is the attorney's fee aftermath of major school desegregation litigation in Kansas City, Missouri. We granted certiorari, 488 U. S. 888 (1988), to resolve two questions relating to fees litigation under 90 Stat. 2641, as amended, 42 U. S. C. § 1988. First, does the Eleventh Amendment prohibit enhancement of a fee award against a State to compensate for delay in payment? Second, should the fee award compensate the work of paralegals and law clerks by applying the market rate for their work?

I

This litigation began in 1977 as a suit by the Kansas City Missouri School District (KCMSD), the school board, and the children of two school board members, against the State of Missouri and other defendants. The plaintiffs alleged that the State, surrounding school districts, and various federal agencies had caused and perpetuated a system of racial segregation in the schools of the Kansas City metropolitan area. They sought various desegregation remedies. KCMSD was subsequently realigned as a nominal defendant, and a class of present and future KCMSD students was certified as plaintiffs. After lengthy proceedings, including a trial that lasted 7 1/2 months during 1983 and 1984, the District Court found the State of Missouri and KCMSD liable, while dismissing the suburban school districts and the federal defendants. It ordered various intradistrict remedies, to be paid for by the State and KCMSD, including $260 million in capital improvements and a magnet-school plan costing over $200 million. See *Jenkins v. Missouri*, 807 F. 2d 657 (CA8 1986)(en banc), cert. denied, 484 U. S. 816 (1987); *Jenkins v. Missouri*, 855 F. 2d 1295 (CA8 1988), cert. granted, 490 U. S. 1034 (1989).

The plaintiff class has been represented, since 1979, by Kansas City lawyer Arthur Benson and, since 1982, by the NAACP Legal Defense and Educational Fund, Inc. (LDF). Benson and the LDF requested attorney's fees under the Civil Rights Attorney's Fees Awards Act of 1976, 42 U. S. C. § 1988.[1] Benson and his associates had devoted 10,875 attorney hours to the litigation, as well as 8,108 hours of paralegal and law clerk time. For the LDF the corresponding figures were 10,854 hours for attorneys and 15,517 hours for paralegals and law clerks. Their fee applications deleted from these totals 3,628 attorney hours and 7,046 paralegal hours allocable to unsuccessful claims against the suburban school districts. With additions for postjudgment monitoring and for preparation of the fee application, the District Court awarded Benson a total of approximately $1.7 million and the LDF $2.3 million. App. to Pet. for Cert. A22–A43.

In calculating the hourly rate for Benson's fees the court noted that the market rate in Kansas City for attorneys of Benson's qualifications was in the range of $125 to $175 per hour, and found that "Mr. Benson's rate would fall at the higher end of this range based upon his expertise in the area of civil rights." *Id.*, at A26. It calculated his fees on the basis of an even higher hourly rate of $200, however, because of three additional factors: the preclusion of other employment, the undesirability of the case, and the delay in payment for Benson's services. *Id.*, at A26–A27. The court also took account of the delay in payment in setting the rates for several of Benson's associates by using current market rates rather than those applicable at the time the services were rendered. *Id.*, at A28–A30. For the same reason, it calculated the fees for the LDF attorneys at current market rates. *Id.*, at A33.

Both Benson and the LDF employed numerous paralegals, law clerks (generally law students working part time), and recent law graduates in this litigation. The court awarded fees for their work based on Kansas City market rates for those categories. As in the case of the attorneys, it used current rather than historic market rates in order to compensate for the delay in payment. It therefore awarded fees based on hourly rates of $35 for law clerks, $40 for paralegals, and $50 for recent law graduates. *Id.*, at A29–A31, A34. The Court of Appeals affirmed in all respects. 838 F. 2d 260 (CA8 1988).

II

Our grant of certiorari extends to two issues raised by the State of Missouri. Missouri first contends that a State cannot, consistent with the principle of sovereign immunity this Court has found embodied in the Eleventh Amendment, be compelled to pay an attorney's fee enhanced to compensate for delay in payment. This question requires us to examine the intersection of two of our precedents, *Hutto v. Finney*, 437 U. S. 678 (1978), and *Library of Congress v. Shaw*, 478 U. S. 310 (1986).[2]

In *Hutto v. Finney*, the lower courts had awarded attorney's fees against the State of Arkansas, in part pursuant to § 1988, in connection with litigation over the conditions of confinement in that State's prisons. The State contended that any such award was subject to the Eleventh Amendment's constraints on actions for damages payable from a State's treasury. We relied, in rejecting that contention, on the distinction drawn in our earlier cases between "retroactive monetary relief" and "prospective injunctive relief." See *Edelman v. Jordan*, 415 U.S. 651 (1974); *Ex parte Young*, 209 U. S. 123 (1908). Attorney's fees, we held, belonged to the latter category, because they constituted reimbursement of "expenses incurred in litigation seeking only prospective relief," rather than "retroactive liability for prelitigation conduct." *Hutto*, 437 U. S., at 695; see also *id.*, at 690. We explained: "Unlike ordinary 'retroactive' relief such as damages or restitution, an award of costs does not compensate the plaintiff for the injury that first brought him into court. Instead, the award reimburses him for a portion of the expenses he incurred in seeking prospective relief." *Id.*, at 695, n. 24. Section 1988, we noted, fit easily into the long-standing practice of awarding "costs" against States, for the statute imposed the award of attorney's fees "as part of the costs." *Id.*, at 695–696, citing *Fairmont Creamery Co. v. Minnesota*, 275 U. S. 70 (1927).

After *Hutto*, therefore, it must be accepted as settled that an award of attorney's fees ancillary to prospective relief is not subject to the strictures of the Eleventh Amendment. And if the principle of making such an award is beyond the reach of the Eleventh Amendment, the same must also be true for the question of how a "reasonable attorney's fee" is to be calculated. See *Hutto, supra*, at 696–697.

Article 9-1   Continued

Missouri contends, however, that the principle enunciated in *Hutto* has been undermined by subsequent decisions of this Court that require Congress to "express its intention to abrogate the Eleventh Amendment in unmistakable language in the statute itself." *Atascadero State Hospital* v. *Scanlon*, 473 U. S. 234, 243 (1985); *Welsh* v. *Texas Dept. of Highways and Public Transportation*, 483 U. S. 468 (1987). See also *Dellmuth* v. *Muth, ante*, p. 223; *Pennsylvania* v. *Union Gas Co., ante*, p. 1. The flaw in this argument lies in its misreading of the holding of *Hutto*. It is true that in *Hutto* we noted that Congress could, in the exercise of its enforcement power under § 5 of the Fourteenth Amendment, set aside the States' immunity from retroactive damages, 437 U. S., at 693, citing *Fitzpatrick* v. *Bitzer*, 427 U. S. 445 (1976), and that Congress intended to do so in enacting § 1988, 437 U. S., at 693–694. But we also made clear that the application of § 1988 to the States did not depend on congressional abrogation of the States' immunity. We did so in rejecting precisely the "clear statement" argument that Missouri now suggests has undermined *Hutto*. Arkansas had argued that § 1988 did not plainly abrogate the States' immunity; citing *Employees* v. *Missouri Dept. of Public Health and Welfare*, 411 U. S. 279 (1973), and *Edelman* v. *Jordan, supra*, the State contended that "retroactive liability" could not be imposed on the States "in the absence of an extraordinarily explicit statutory mandate." *Hutto*, 437 U. S., at 695. We responded as follows: "[T]hese cases *[Employees* and *Edelman]* concern retroactive liability for prelitigation conduct rather than expenses incurred in litigation seeking only prospective relief. The Act imposes attorney's fees 'as part of the costs.' Costs have traditionally been awarded without regard for the States' Eleventh Amendment immunity." *Ibid.*

The holding of *Hutto*, therefore, was not just that Congress had spoken sufficiently clearly to overcome Eleventh Amendment immunity in enacting § 1988, but rather that the Eleventh Amendment did not apply to an award of attorney's fees ancillary to a grant of prospective relief. See *Maine* v. *Thiboutot*, 448 U. S. 1, 9, n. 7 (1980). That holding is unaffected by our subsequent jurisprudence concerning the degree of clarity with which Congress must speak in order to override Eleventh Amendment immunity, and we reaffirm it today.

Missouri's other line of argument is based on our decision in *Library of Congress* v. *Shaw*, *supra*. *Shaw* involved an application of the longstanding "no-interest rule," under which interest cannot be awarded against the United States unless it has expressly waived its sovereign immunity. We held that while Congress, in making the Federal Government a potential defendant under Title VII of the Civil Rights Act of 1964, had waived the United States' immunity from suit and from costs including reasonable attorney's fees, it had not waived the Federal Government's traditional immunity from any award of interest. We thus held impermissible a 30 percent increase in the "lodestar" fee to compensate for delay in payment. Because we refused to find in the language of Title VII a waiver of the United States' immunity from interest, Missouri argues, we should likewise conclude that § 1988 is not sufficiently explicit to constitute an abrogation of the States' immunity under the Eleventh Amendment in regard to any award of interest.

The answer to this contention is already clear from what we have said about *Hutto* v. *Finney*. Since, as we held in *Hutto*, the Eleventh Amendment does not bar an award of attorney's fees ancillary to a grant of prospective relief, our holding in *Shaw* has no application, even by analogy.[3] There is no need in this case to determine whether Congress has spoken sufficiently clearly to meet a "clear statement" requirement, and it is therefore irrelevant whether the Eleventh Amendment standard should be, as Missouri contends, as stringent as the one we applied for purposes of the no-interest rule in *Shaw*. Rather, the issue here—whether the "reasonable attorney's fee" provided for in § 1988 should be calculated in such a manner as to include an enhancement, where appropriate, for delay in payment—is a straightforward matter of statutory interpretation. For this question, it is of no relevance whether the party against which fees are awarded is a State. The question is what Congress intended—not whether it manifested "the clear affirmative intent . . . to waive the sovereign's immunity." *Shaw*, 478 U. S., at 321.[4]

This question is not a difficult one. We have previously explained, albeit in dicta, why an enhancement for delay in payment is, where appropriate, part of a "reasonable attorney's fee." In *Pennsylvania v. Delaware Valley Citizens' Council*, 483 U. S. 711 (1987), we rejected an argument that a prevailing party was entitled to a fee augmentation to compensate for the risk of nonpayment. But we took care to distinguish that risk from the factor of delay:

> "First is the matter of delay. When plaintiffs' entitlement to attorney's fees depends on success, their lawyers are not paid until a favorable decision finally eventuates, which may be years later. . . . Meanwhile, their expenses of doing business continue and must be met. In setting fees for prevailing counsel, the courts have regularly recognized the delay factor, either by basing the award on current rates or by adjusting the fee based on historical rates to reflect its present value. See, *e.g., Sierra Club v. EPA*, 248 U. S. App. D. C. 107, 120–121, 769 F. 2d 796, 809–810 (1985); *Louisville Black Police Officers Organization, Inc. v. Louisville*, 700 F. 2d 268, 276, 281 (CA6 1983). Although delay and the risk of nonpayment are often mentioned in the same breath, adjusting for the former is a distinct issue . . . . We do not suggest . . . that adjustments for delay are inconsistent with the typical fee-shifting statute." *Id.*, at 716.

The same conclusion is appropriate under § 1988.[5] Our cases have repeatedly stressed that attorney's fees awarded under this statute are to be based on market rates for the services rendered. See, *e. g., Blanchard v. Bergeron*, 489 U. S. 87 (1989); *Riverside v. Rivera*, 477 U. S. 561 (1986); *Blum v. Stenson*, 465 U. S. 886 (1984). Clearly, compensation received several years after the services were rendered—as it frequently is in complex civil rights litigation—is not equivalent to the same dollar amount received reasonably promptly as the legal services are performed, as would normally be the case with private billings.[6] We agree, therefore, that an appropriate adjustment for delay in payment—whether by the application of current rather than historic hourly rates or otherwise—is within the contemplation of the statute.

To summarize: We reaffirm our holding in *Hutto v. Finney* that the Eleventh Amendment has no application to an award of attorney's fees, ancillary to a grant of prospective relief, against a State. It follows that the same is true for the calculation of the *amount* of the fee. An adjustment for delay in payment is, we hold, an appropriate factor in the determination of what constitutes a reasonable attorney's fee under § 1988. An award against a State of a fee that includes such an enhancement for delay is not, therefore, barred by the Eleventh Amendment.

III

Missouri's second contention is that the District Court erred in compensating the work of law clerks and paralegals (hereinafter collectively "paralegals") at the market rates for their services, rather than at their cost to the attorney. While Missouri agrees that compensation for the cost of these personnel should be included in the fee award, it suggests that an hourly rate of $15—which it argued below corresponded to their salaries, benefits, and overhead—would be appropriate, rather than the market rates of $35 to $50. According to

Article 9-1   Continued

Missouri, § 1988 does not authorize billing paralegals' hours at market rates, and doing so produces a "windfall" for the attorney.[7]

We begin with the statutory language, which provides simply for "a reasonable attorney's fee as part of the costs." 42 U. S. C. § 1988. Clearly, a "reasonable attorney's fee" cannot have been meant to compensate only work performed personally by members of the bar. Rather, the term must refer to a reasonable fee for the work product of an attorney. Thus, the fee must take into account the work not only of attorneys, but also of secretaries, messengers, librarians, janitors, and others whose labor contributes to the work product for which an attorney bills her client; and it must also take account of other expenses and profit. The parties have suggested no reason why the work of paralegals should not be similarly compensated, nor can we think of any. We thus take as our starting point the self-evident proposition that the "reasonable attorney's fee" provided for by statute should compensate the work of paralegals, as well as that of attorneys. The more difficult question is how the work of paralegals is to be valued in calculating the overall attorney's fee.

The statute specifies a "reasonable" fee for the attorney's work product. In determining how other elements of the attorney's fee are to be calculated, we have consistently looked to the marketplace as our guide to what is "reasonable." In *Blum v. Stenson*, 465 U. S. 886 (1984), for example, we rejected an argument that attorney's fees for nonprofit legal service organizations should be based on cost. We said: "The statute and legislative history establish that 'reasonable fees' under § 1988 are to be calculated according to the prevailing market rates in the relevant community . . . . " *Id.*, at 895. See also, *e. g.*, *Delaware Valley*, 483 U. S., at 732 (O'CONNOR, J., concurring) (controlling question concerning contingency enhancements is "how the market in a community compensates for contingency"); *Rivera*, 477 U. S., at 591 (REHNQUIST, J., dissenting) (reasonableness of fee must be determined "in light of both the traditional billing practices in the profession, and the fundamental principle that the award of a 'reasonable' attorney's fee under § 1988 means a fee that would have been deemed reasonable if billed to affluent plaintiffs by their own attorneys"). A reasonable attorney's fee under § 1988 is one calculated on the basis of rates and practices prevailing in the relevant market, *i. e.*, "in line with those [rates] prevailing in the community for similar services by lawyers of reasonably comparable skill, experience, and reputation," *Blum, supra*, at 896, n. 11, and one that grants the successful civil rights plaintiff a "fully compensatory fee," *Hensley v. Eckerhart*, 461 U. S. 424, 435 (1983), comparable to what "is traditional with attorneys compensated by a fee-paying client." S. Rep. No. 94–1011, p. 6 (1976).

If an attorney's fee awarded under § 1988 is to yield the same level of compensation that would be available from the market, the "increasingly widespread custom of separately billing for the services of paralegals and law students who serve as clerks," *Ramos v. Lamm*, 713 F. 2d 546, 558 (CA10 1983), must be taken into account. All else being equal, the hourly fee charged by an attorney whose rates include paralegal work in her hourly fee, or who bills separately for the work of paralegals at cost, will be higher than the hourly fee charged by an attorney competing in the same market who bills separately for the work of paralegals at "market rates." In other words, the prevailing "market rate" for attorney time is not independent of the manner in which paralegal time is accounted for.[8] Thus, if the prevailing practice in a given community were to bill paralegal time separately at market rates, fees awarded the attorney at market rates for attorney time would not be fully compensatory if the court refused to compensate hours billed by paralegals or did so only at "cost." Similarly, the fee awarded would be too high if the court accepted separate billing for paralegal hours in a market where that was not the custom.

We reject the argument that compensation for paralegals at rates above "cost" would yield a "windfall" for the prevailing attorney. Neither petitioners nor anyone else, to our knowledge, has ever suggested that the hourly rate applied to the work of an associate attorney in a law firm creates a windfall for the firm's partners or is otherwise improper under § 1988, merely because it exceeds the cost of the attorney's services. If the fees are consistent with market rates and practices, the "windfall" argument has no more force with regard to paralegals than it does for associates. And it would hardly accord with Congress' intent to provide a "fully compensatory fee" if the prevailing plaintiff's attorney in a civil rights lawsuit were not permitted to bill separately for paralegals, while the defense attorney in the same litigation was able to take advantage of the prevailing practice and obtain market rates for such work. Yet that is precisely the result sought in this case by the State of Missouri, which appears to have paid its own outside counsel for the work of paralegals at the hourly rate of $35. Record 2696, 2699.[9]

Nothing in § 1988 requires that the work of paralegals invariably be billed separately. If it is the practice in the relevant market not to do so, or to bill the work of paralegals only at cost, that is all that § 1988 requires. Where, however, the prevailing practice is to bill paralegal work at market rates, treating civil rights lawyers' fee requests in the same way is not only permitted by § 1988, but also makes economic sense. By encouraging the use of lower cost paralegals rather than attorneys wherever possible, permitting market-rate billing of paralegal hours "encourages cost-effective delivery of legal services and, by reducing the spiraling cost of civil rights litigation, furthers the policies underlying civil rights statutes." *Cameo Convalescent Center, Inc. v. Senn*, 738 F. 2d 836, 846 (CA7 1984), cert. denied, 469 U. S. 1106 (1985).[10]

Such separate billing appears to be the practice in most communities today.[11] In the present case, Missouri concedes that "the local market typically bills separately for paralegal services," Tr. of Oral Arg. 14, and the District Court found that the requested hourly rates of $35 for law clerks, $40 for paralegals, and $50 for recent law graduates were the prevailing rates for such services in the Kansas City area. App. to Pet. for Cert. A29, A31, A34. Under these circumstances, the court's decision to award separate compensation at these rates was fully in accord with § 1988.

IV

The courts below correctly granted a fee enhancement to compensate for delay in payment and approved compensation of paralegals and law clerks at market rates. The judgment of the Court of Appeals is therefore

Affirmed.

JUSTICE MARSHALL took no part in the consideration or decision of this case.

JUSTICE O'CONNOR, with whom JUSTICE SCALIA joins, and with whom THE CHIEF JUSTICE joins in part, concurring in part and dissenting in part.

I agree with the Court that 42 U. S. C. § 1988 allows compensation for the work of paralegals and law clerks at market rates, and therefore join Parts I and III of its opinion. I do not join Part II, however, for in my view the Eleventh Amendment does not permit enhancement of attorney's fees assessed against a State as compensation for delay in payment.

The Eleventh Amendment does not, of course, provide a State with across-the-board immunity from all monetary relief. Relief that "serves directly to bring an end to a violation of federal law is not barred by the Eleventh Amendment even though accompanied by a substantial ancillary effect" on a State's treasury. *Papasan* v. *Allain*, 478 U.S. 265, 278 (1986). Thus, in *Milliken* v. *Bradley*, 433 U.S. 267, 289-290 (1977), the Court unanimously upheld a decision ordering a State to pay over $5 million to eliminate the effects of *de jure* segregation in certain school systems. On the other hand, "[r]elief that in essence serves to

Article 9-1 Continued

compensate a party injured in the past," such as relief "expressly denominated as damages," or "relief [that] is tantamount to an award of damages for a past violation of federal law, even though styled as something else," is prohibited by the Eleventh Amendment. *Papasan, supra*, at 278. The crucial question in this case is whether that portion of respondents' attorney's fees based on current hourly rates is properly characterized as retroactive monetary relief.

In *Library of Congress* v. *Shaw*, 478 U.S. 310 (1986), the Court addressed whether the attorney's fees provision of Title VII of the Civil Rights Act of 1964, 42 U. S. C. § 2000e-5(k), permits an award of attorney's fees against the United States to be enhanced in order to compensate for delay in payment. In relevant part, § 2000e-5(k) provides:

> "In any action or proceeding under this subchapter the court, in its discretion, may allow the prevailing party, other than the [Equal Employment Opportunity Commission (EEOC)] or the United States, a reasonable attorney's fees as part of the costs, and the [EEOC] and the United States shall be liable for costs the same as a private person."

The Court began its analysis in *Shaw* by holding that "interest is an element of damages separate from damages on the substantive claim." 478 U.S., at 314 (citing C. McCormick, Law of Damages § 50, p. 205 (1935)). Given the "no-interest" rule of federal sovereign immunity, under which the United States is not liable for interest absent an express statutory waiver to the contrary, the Court was unwilling to conclude that, by equating the United States' liability to that of private persons in § 2000e-5(k), Congress had waived the United States' immunity from interest. 478 U.S., at 314–319. The fact that § 2000e-5(k) used the word "reasonable" to modify "attorney's fees" did not alter this result, for the Court explained that it had "consistently . . . refused to impute an intent to waive immunity from interest into the ambiguous use of a particular word or phrase in a statute." *Id.*, at 320. The description of attorney's fees as costs in § 2000e-5(k) also did not mandate a contrary conclusion because "[p]rejudgment interest . . . is considered as damages, not a component of 'costs,'" and the "term 'costs' has *never* been understood to include any interest component." *Id.*, at 321 (emphasis added) (citing 10 C. Wright, A. Miller, & M. Kane, Federal Practice and Procedure §§ 2664, 2666, 2670 (2d ed. 1983); 2 A. Sedgwick & G. Van Nest, Sedgwick on Damages 157-158 (7th ed. 1880)). Finally, the Court rejected the argument that the enhancement was proper because the "no-interest" rule did not prohibit compensation for delay in payment: "Interest and a delay factor share an identical function. They are designed to compensate for the belated receipt of money." 478 U.S., at 322.

As the Court notes, *ante*, at 281, n. 3, the "no-interest" rule of federal sovereign immunity at issue in *Shaw* provided an "added gloss of strictness," 478 U.S., at 318, and may have explained the *result* reached by the Court in that case, *i. e.*, that § 2000e-5(k) did not waive the United States' immunity against awards of interest. But there is not so much as a hint anywhere in *Shaw* that the Court's discussions and definitions of interest and compensation for delay were dictated by, or limited to, the federal "no-interest" rule. As the quotations above illustrate, the Court's opinion in *Shaw* is filled with broad, unqualified language. The dissenters in *Shaw* did not disagree with the Court's sweeping characterization of interest and compensation for delay as damages. Rather, they argued only that § 2000e–5(k) had waived the immunity of the United States with respect to awards of interest. See *id.*, at 323–327 (BRENNAN, J., dissenting). I therefore emphatically disagree with the Court's statement that "*Shaw* . . . does not represent a general-purpose definition of compensation for delay that governs here." *Ante*, at 281, n. 3.

Two general propositions that are relevant here emerge from *Shaw*. First, interest is considered damages and not costs. Second, compensation for delay, which serves the same function as interest, is also the equivalent of damages. These two propositions make clear that enhancement for delay constitutes retroactive monetary relief barred by the Eleventh Amendment. Given my reading of *Shaw*, I do not think the Court's reliance on the cost rationale of § 1988 set forth in *Hutto v. Finney*, 437 U. S. 678 (1978), is persuasive. Because *Shaw* teaches that compensation for delay constitutes damages and cannot be considered costs, see 478 U. S., at 321–322, *Hutto* is not controlling. See *Hutto, supra,* at 697, n. 27 ("[W]e do not suggest that our analysis would be the same if Congress were to expand the concept of costs beyond the traditional category of litigation expenses"). Furthermore, *Hutto* does not mean that inclusion of attorney's fees as costs in a statute forecloses a challenge to the enhancement of fees as compensation for delay in payment. If it did, then *Shaw* would have been resolved differently, for § 2000e–5(k) lists attorney's fees as costs.

Even if I accepted the narrow interpretation of *Shaw* proffered by the Court, I would disagree with the result reached by the Court in Part II of its opinion. On its own terms, the Court's analysis fails. The Court suggests that the definitions of interest and compensation for delay set forth in *Shaw* would be triggered only by a rule of sovereign immunity barring awards of interest against the States: "Outside the context of the 'no-interest rule' of federal immunity, we see no reason why compensation for delay cannot be included within § 1988 attorney's fee awards." *Ante,* at 281, n. 3. But the Court does not inquire about whether such a rule exists. In fact, there is a federal rule barring awards of interest against States. See *Virginia v. West Virginia,* 238 U. S. 202, 234 (1915) ("Nor can it be deemed in derogation of the sovereignty of the State that she should be charged with interest *if* her agreement properly construed so provides") (emphasis added); *United States v. North Carolina,* 136 U. S. 211, 221 (1890) ("general principle" is that "an obligation of the State to pay interest, whether as interest or as damages, on any debt overdue, cannot arise *except* by the consent and contract of the State, manifested by statute, or in a form authorized by statute") (emphasis added). The Court has recently held that the rule of immunity set forth in *Virginia* and *North Carolina* is inapplicable in situations where the State does not retain any immunity, see *West Virginia v. United States,* 479 U. S. 305, 310–312 (1987) (State can be held liable for interest to the United States, against whom it has no sovereign immunity), but the rule has not otherwise been limited, and there is no reason why it should not be relevant in the Eleventh Amendment context presented in this case.

As *Virginia* and *North Carolina* indicate, a State can waive its immunity against awards of interest. See also *Clark v. Barnard,* 108 U. S. 436, 447 (1883). The Missouri courts have interpreted Mo. Rev. Stat. § 408.020 (1979 and Supp. 1989), providing for prejudgment interest on money that becomes due and payable, and § 408.040, providing for prejudgment interest on court judgments and orders, as making the State liable for interest. See *Denton Construction Co. v. Missouri State Highway Comm'n,* 454 S. W. 2d 44, 59–60 (Mo. 1970) (§ 408.020); *Steppelman v. State Highway Comm'n of Missouri,* 650 S. W. 2d 343, 345 (Mo. App. 1983)(§ 408.040). There can be no argument, however, that these Missouri statutes and cases allow interest to be awarded against the State here. A "State's waiver of sovereign immunity in its own courts is not a waiver of the Eleventh Amendment immunity in the federal courts." *Pennhurst State School and Hospital v. Halderman,* 465 U. S. 89, 99, n. 9 (1984).

The fact that a State has immunity from awards of interest is not the end of the matter. In a case such as this one involving school desegregation, interest or compensation for delay (in the guise of current hourly rates) can theoretically be awarded against a State despite the Eleventh Amendment's bar against retroactive monetary liability. The Court has held that Congress can set aside the States' Eleventh Amendment immunity in order

Article 9-1 Continued

to enforce the provisions of the Fourteenth Amendment. See *City of Rome v. United States*, 446 U. S. 156, 179 (1980); *Fitzpatrick v. Bitzer*, 427 U. S. 445, 456 (1976). Congress must, however, be unequivocal in expressing its intent to abrogate that immunity. See generally *Atascadero State Hospital v. Scanlon*, 473 U. S. 234, 243 (1985) ("Congress must express its intention to abrogate the Eleventh Amendment in unmistakable language in the statute itself").

In *Hutto* the Court was able to avoid deciding whether § 1988 met the "clear statement" rule only because attorney's fees (without any enhancement) are not considered retroactive in nature. See 437 U. S., at 695–697. The Court cannot do the same here, where the attorney's fees were enhanced to compensate for delay in payment. Cf. *Osterneck v. Ernst & Whinney*, 489 U. S. 169, 175 (1989) ("[U]nlike attorney's fees, which at common law were regarded as an element of costs, . . . prejudgment interest traditionally has been considered part of the compensation due [the] plaintiff").

In relevant part, § 1988 provides:

> "In any action or proceeding to enforce a provision of sections 1981, 1982, 1983, 1985, and 1986 of this title, title IX of Public Law 92–318, or title VI of the Civil Rights Act of 1964, the court, in its discretion, may allow the prevailing party, other than the United States, a reasonable attorney's fee as part of the costs."

In my view, § 1988 does not meet the "clear statement" rule set forth in *Atascadero*. It does not mention damages, interest, compensation for delay, or current hourly rates. As one federal court has correctly noted, "Congress has not yet made any statement suggesting that a § 1988 attorney's fee award should include prejudgment interest." *Rogers v. Okin*, 821 F. 2d 22, 27 (CA1 1987). A comparison of the statute at issue in *Shaw* also indicates that § 1988, as currently written, is insufficient to allow attorney's fees assessed against a State to be enhanced to compensate for delay in payment. The language of § 1988 is undoubtedly less expansive than that of § 2000e–5(k), for § 1988 does not equate the liability of States with that of private persons. Since § 2000e–5(k) does not allow enhancement of an award of attorney's fees to compensate for delay, it is logical to conclude that § 1988, a more narrowly worded statute, likewise does not allow interest (through the use of current hourly rates) to be tacked on to an award of attorney's fees against a State.

Compensation for delay in payment was *one* of the reasons the District Court used current hourly rates in calculating respondents' attorney's fees. See App. to Pet. for Cert. A26–A27; 838 F. 2d 260, 263, 265 (CA8 1988). I would reverse the award of attorney's fees to respondents and remand so that the fees can be calculated without taking compensation for delay into account.

CHIEF JUSTICE REHNQUIST, dissenting.

I agree with JUSTICE O'CONNOR that the Eleventh Amendment does not permit an award of attorney's fees against a State which includes compensation for delay in payment. Unlike JUSTICE O'CONNOR, however, I do not agree with the Court's approval of the award of law clerk and paralegal fees made here.

Title 42 U. S. C. § 1988 gives the district courts discretion to allow the prevailing party in an action under 42 U. S. C. § 1983 "a reasonable attorney's fee as part of the costs." The Court reads this language as authorizing recovery of "a 'reasonable' fee for the attorney's work product," *ante*, at 285, which, the Court concludes, may include separate compensation for the services of law clerks and paralegals. But the statute itself simply uses the very familiar term "a reasonable attorney's fee," which to those untutored in the Court's linguistic juggling means a fee charged for services rendered by an individual who has been licensed to practice law. Because law clerks and paralegals have not been licensed to practice law in Missouri, it is difficult to see how charges for their services may be separately billed as part of "attorney's fees." And since a prudent attorney customarily includes compensation for the cost of law clerk and paralegal services, like any other sort of office overhead—from secretarial staff, janitors, and librarians, to telephone service, stationery, and paper clips—in his own hourly billing rate, allowing the prevailing party to recover separate compensation for law clerk and paralegal services may result in "double recovery."

The Court finds justification for its ruling in the fact that the prevailing practice among attorneys in Kansas City is to bill clients separately for the services of law clerks and paralegals. But I do not think Congress intended the meaning of the statutory term "attorney's fee" to expand and contract with each and every vagary of local billing practice. Under the Court's logic, prevailing parties could recover at market rates for the cost of secretaries, private investigators, and other types of lay personnel who assist the attorney in preparing his case, so long as they could show that the prevailing practice in the local market was to bill separately for these services. Such a result would be a sufficiently drastic departure from the traditional concept of "attorney's fees" that I believe new statutory authorization should be required for it. That permitting separate billing of law clerk and paralegal hours at market rates might "'reduc[e] the spiraling cost of civil rights litigation'" by encouraging attorneys to delegate to these individuals tasks which they would otherwise perform themselves at higher cost, *ante*, at 288, and n. 10, may be a persuasive reason for Congress to enact such additional legislation. It is not, however, a persuasive reason for us to rewrite the legislation which Congress has in fact enacted. See *Badaracco v. Commissioner*, 464 U. S. 386, 398 (1984) ("Courts are not authorized to rewrite a statute because they might deem its effects susceptible of improvement").

I also disagree with the State's suggestion that law clerk and paralegal expenses incurred by a prevailing party, if not recoverable at market rates as "attorney's fees" under § 1988, are nonetheless recoverable at actual cost under that statute. The language of § 1988 expands the traditional definition of "costs" to include "a reasonable attorney's fee," but it cannot fairly be read to authorize the recovery of all other out-of-pocket expenses actually incurred by the prevailing party in the course of litigation. Absent specific statutory authorization for the recovery of such expenses, the prevailing party remains subject to the limitations on cost recovery imposed by Federal Rule of Civil Procedure 54(d) and 28 U. S. C. § 1920, which govern the taxation of costs in federal litigation where a cost-shifting statute is not applicable. Section 1920 gives the district court discretion to tax certain types of costs against the losing party in any federal litigation. The statute specifically enumerates six categories of expenses which may be taxed as costs: fees of the court clerk and marshal; fees of the court reporter; printing fees and witness fees; copying fees; certain docket fees; and fees of court-appointed experts and interpreters. We have held that this list is exclusive. *Crawford Fitting Co. v. J. T. Gibbons, Inc.*, 482 U. S. 437 (1987). Since none of these categories can possibly be construed to include the fees of law clerks and paralegals, I would also hold that reimbursement for these expenses may not be separately awarded at actual cost.

I would therefore reverse the award of reimbursement for law clerk and paralegal expenses.

*John A. DeVault III filed a brief for the National Association of Legal Assistants, Inc., as *amicus curiae* urging affirmance.

1. Section 1988 provides in relevant part: "In any action or proceeding to enforce a provision of sections 1981, 1982, 1983, 1985, and 1986 of this title, title IX of Public Law 92–318 [20 U. S. C. § 1681 *et seq.*], or title VI of the Civil Rights Act of 1964 [42 U. S. C. § 2000d *et seq.*], the court, in its discretion, may allow the prevailing party, other than the United States, a reasonable attorney's fee as part of the costs."

Article 9-1   Continued

2. The holding of the Court of Appeals on this point, 838 F. 2d, at 265–266, is in conflict with the resolution of the same question in *Rogers v. Okin*, 821 F. 2d 22, 26–28 (CA1 1987), cert. denied *sub nom. Commissioner, Massachusetts Dept. of Mental Health v. Rogers*, 484 U. S. 1010 (1988).

3. Our opinion in *Shaw* does, to be sure, contain some language that, if read in isolation, might suggest a different result in this case. Most significantly, we equated compensation for delay with prejudgment interest, and observed that "[p]rejudgment interest . . . is considered as damages, not a component of 'costs.' . . . Indeed, the term 'costs' has never been understood to include any interest component." *Library of Congress v. Shaw*, 478 U. S. 310, 321 (1986). These observations, however, cannot be divorced from the context of the special "no-interest rule" that was at issue in *Shaw*. That rule, which is applicable to the immunity of the United States and is therefore not at issue here, provides an "added gloss of strictness," *id.*, at 318, only where the United States' liability for interest is at issue. Our inclusion of compensation for delay within the definition of prejudgment interest in *Shaw* must be understood in light of this broad proscription of interest awards against the United States. *Shaw* thus does not represent a general-purpose definition of compensation for delay that governs here. Outside the context of the "no-interest rule" of federal immunity, we see no reason why compensation for delay cannot be included within § 1988 attorney's fee awards, which *Hutto* held to be "costs" not subject to Eleventh Amendment strictures.

    We cannot share JUSTICE O'CONNOR's view that the two cases she cites, *post*, at 293, demonstrate the existence of an equivalent rule relating to state immunity that embodies the same ultrastrict rule of construction for interest awards that has grown up around the federal no-interest rule. Cf. *Shaw, supra*, at 314–317 (discussing historical development of the federal no-interest rule).

4. In *Shaw*, which dealt with the sovereign immunity of the Federal Government, there was of course no prospective-retrospective distinction as there is when, as in *Hutto* and the present case, it is the Eleventh Amendment immunity of a State that is at issue.

5. *Delaware Valley* was decided under § 304(d) of the Clean Air Act, 42 U. S. C. § 7604(d). We looked for guidance, however, to § 1988 and our cases construing it. *Pennsylvania v. Delaware Valley Citizens' Council*, 483 U. S. 711, 713, n. 1 (1987).

6. This delay, coupled with the fact that, as we recognized in *Delaware Valley*, the attorney's *expenses* are not deferred pending completion of the litigation, can cause considerable hardship. The present case provides an illustration. During a period of nearly three years, the demands of this case precluded attorney Benson from accepting other employment. In order to pay his staff and meet other operating expenses, he was obliged to borrow $633,000. As of January 1987, he had paid over $113,000 in interest on this debt, and was continuing to borrow to meet interest payments. Record 2336–2339; Tr. 130–131. The LDF, for its part, incurred deficits of $700,000 in 1983 and over $1 million in 1984, largely because of this case. Tr. 46. If no compensation were provided for the delay in payment, the prospect of such hardship could well deter otherwise willing attorneys from accepting complex civil rights cases that might offer great benefit to society at large; this result would work to defeat Congress' purpose in enacting § 1988 of "encourag[ing] the enforcement of federal law through lawsuits filed by private persons." *Delaware Valley, supra*, at 737 (BLACKMUN, J., dissenting).

    We note also that we have recognized the availability of interim fee awards under § 1988 when a litigant becomes a prevailing party on one issue in the course of the litigation. *Texas State Teachers Assn. v. Garland Independent School Dist.*, 489 U. S. 782, 791–792 (1989). In economic terms, such an interim award does not differ from an enhancement for delay in payment.

7. The Courts of Appeals have taken a variety of positions on this issue. Most permit separate billing of paralegal time. See, *e. g., Save Our Cumberland Mountains, Inc. v. Hodel*, 263 U. S. App. D. C. 409, 420, n. 7, 826 F. 2d 43, 54, n. 7 (1987), vacated in part on other grounds, 273 U. S. App. D. C. 78, 857 F. 2d 1516 (1988) (en banc); *Jacobs v. Mancuso*, 825 F. 2d 559, 563, and n. 6

(CA1 1987) (collecting cases); *Spanish Action Committee of Chicago* v. *Chicago*, 811 F. 2d 1129, 1138 (CA7 1987); *Ramos* v. *Lamm*, 713 F. 2d 546, 558–559 (CA10 1983); *Richardson* v. *Byrd*, 709 F. 2d 1016, 1023 (CA5), cert. denied *sub nom. Dallas County Commissioners Court* v. *Richardson*, 464 U. S. 1009 (1983). See also *Riverside* v. *Rivera*, 477 U. S. 561, 566, n. 2 (1986) (noting lower court approval of hourly rate for law clerks). Some courts, on the other hand, have considered paralegal work "out-of-pocket expense," recoverable only at cost to the attorney. See, *e. g., Northcross* v. *Board of Education of Memphis City Schools*, 611 F. 2d 624, 639 (CA6 1979), cert. denied, 447 U. S. 911 (1980); *Thornberry* v. *Delta Air Lines, Inc.*, 676 F. 2d 1240, 1244 (CA9 1982), vacated, 461 U. S. 952 (1983). At least one Court of Appeals has refused to permit any recovery of paralegal expense apart from the attorney's hourly fee. *Abrams* v. *Baylor College of Medicine*, 805 F. 2d 528, 535 (CA5 1986).

8. The attorney who bills separately for paralegal time is merely distributing her costs and profit margin among the hourly fees of other members of her staff, rather than concentrating them in the fee she sets for her own time.

9. A variant of Missouri's "windfall" argument is the following: "If paralegal expense is reimbursed at a rate many times the actual cost, will attorneys next try to bill separately—and at a profit—for such items as secretarial time, paper clips, electricity, and other expenses?" Reply Brief for Petitioners 15–16. The answer to this question is, of course, that attorneys seeking fees under § 1988 would have no basis for requesting separate compensation of such expenses unless this were the prevailing practice in the local community. The safeguard against the billing at a profit of secretarial services and paper clips is the discipline of the market.

10. It has frequently been recognized in the lower courts that paralegals are capable of carrying out many tasks, under the supervision of an attorney, that might otherwise be performed by a lawyer and billed at a higher rate. Such work might include, for example, factual investigation, including locating and interviewing witnesses; assistance with depositions, interrogatories, and document production; compilation of statistical and financial data; checking legal citations; and drafting correspondence. Much such work lies in a gray area of tasks that might appropriately be performed either by an attorney or a paralegal. To the extent that fee applicants under § 1988 are not permitted to bill for the work of paralegals at market rates, it would not be surprising to see a greater amount of such work performed by attorneys themselves, thus increasing the overall cost of litigation.

    Of course, purely clerical or secretarial tasks should not be billed at a paralegal rate, regardless of who performs them. What the court in *Johnson* v. *Georgia Highway Express, Inc.*, 488 F. 2d 714, 717 (CA5 1974), said in regard to the work of attorneys is applicable by analogy to paralegals: "It is appropriate to distinguish between legal work, in the strict sense, and investigation, clerical work, compilation of facts and statistics and other work which can often be accomplished by non-lawyers but which a lawyer may do because he has no other help available. Such non-legal work may command a lesser rate. Its dollar value is not enhanced just because a lawyer does it."

11. *Amicus* National Association of Legal Assistants reports that 77 percent of 1,800 legal assistants responding to a survey of the association's membership stated that their law firms charged clients for paralegal work on an hourly billing basis. Brief for National Association of Legal Assistants as *Amicus Curiae* 11.

Article 9-1   Continued

**GILL SAVINGS
ASSOCIATION, Appellant,**

v.

**INTERNATIONAL SUPPLY
COMPANY, INC., Appellee.**

No. 05–87–01007–CV.

Court of Appeals of Texas,
Dallas.
Aug. 11, 1988.
Rehearing Denied Sept. 2, 1988.

Supplier brought action against project owner and contractor seeking establishment and foreclosure of mechanic's and materialman's lien. The 116th District Court, Dallas County, Hugh Snodgrass, J., granted judgment in favor of supplier. Project owner appealed. The Court of Appeals, Thomas, J., held that: (1) fact that supplier's attorney sought lien affidavit did not invalidate lien for removables; (2) fact that lien affidavit stated an amount in excess of what was owed did not render lien invalid; (3) compensation for legal assistant's work may be separately assessed and included in award of attorney fees if legal assistant performs work that has traditionally been done by any attorney; and (4) evidence was insufficient to support supplier's claim for compensation for legal assistants' work.

Affirmed in part and cause of action for attorney fees severed and remanded.

1. Mechanics' Liens ⚷ 154(3)

Mere fact that supplier's attorney signed mechanic's and materialman's lien affidavit without personal knowledge of matters stated in affidavit did not invalidate lien for removables; Property Code contains no affirmative personal knowledge requirement, supplier was corporation which had authorized attorney to make affidavit, and attorney had the means to, and could have become personally informed. V.T.C.A., Property Code §§ 53.054, 53.054(a).

2. Mechanics' Liens ⚷ 157(3)

Supplier's mechanic's and materialman's lien affidavit was in substantial compliance with Property Code when supplier filed lien for amount greater than actual amount reconciled by time of trial two years later; lender on project, which purchased property at foreclosure sale, was in no way a third-party stranger to dealings, discrepancy in amounts did not harm lender, and lender was in a better position than expected since lien was less than amount lender believed it to be at time it foreclosed on and bought project. V.T.C.A., Property Code § 53.054(a)(1).

3. Mechanics' Liens ⚷ 277(2)

Supplier claiming mechanic's and materialman's lien was not required to offer independent proof of having given project owner 36-day and 90-day notices of claims for materials

Article 9-2   Gill Savings Association, v. International Supply Company, Inc.

Gill Sav. Ass'n v. Int'l Supply Co., 759 S.W.2d 697 (Tex. App.—Dallas 1988).

furnished during one month where both supplier's original petition and first amended petition pled that all conditions precedent to project owner's liability and foreclosure of lien had been performed or had occurred and project owner did not specifically deny that supplier failed to give required notice. V.T.C.A., Property Code § 53.056(b); Vernon's Ann.Texas Rules Civ.Proc., Rule 54.

4. Mechanics' Liens ☞ 277(2)

Rule providing that in pleading performance or occurrence of conditions precedent, it shall be sufficient to aver generally that all conditions precedent have been performed or have occurred and when performances or occurrences have been so pled, party so pleading same shall be required to prove only such of them as are specifically denied by opposite party is applicable to notices required to be given in connection with mechanic's and materialmen's lien claims.

5. Mechanics' Liens ☞ 5

Mechanic's and materialmen's lien statutes are to be liberally construed for purpose of protecting laborers and materialmen.

6. Mechanics' Liens ☞ 277(2)

Proof of value of plumbing materials supplied as of date of trial to establish and foreclose mechanic's and materialman's lien was not an essential element of supplier's claim and did not render proof of amount of claim inadequate; value of removables as of date of trial was irrelevant because the only manner in which lien could be foreclosed was through judicial foreclosure sale. V.T.C.A., Property Code §§ 53.054(a)(1), 53.154.

7. Costs ☞ 194.18

Compensation for legal assistant's work may be separately assessed and included in award of attorney fees if legal assistant performs work that has traditionally been done by any attorney.

8. Costs ☞ 194.18

To recover compensation for legal assistant's work, party must present evidence establishing that legal assistant is qualified through education, training or work experience to perform substantive legal work, that substantive legal work was performed under direction and supervision of attorney, nature of legal work which was performed, hourly rate being charged for legal assistant, and number of hours expended by legal assistant.

9. Appeal and Error ☞ 931(1), 989

A "legally insufficient" point is a "no evidence" point presenting a question of law, and in deciding that question, Court of Appeals must consider only evidence and inferences tending to support finding and disregard all evidence and inferences to the contrary.

10. Appeal and Error ☞ 1175(1)

If a "no evidence" point is sustained and proper procedural steps have been taken, finding under attack may be disregarded entirely and judgment rendered for appellant unless interest of justice requires another trial.

11. Appeal and Error ☞ 989

In reviewing "factually insufficient evidence" points, Court of Appeals considers all the evidence, including any evidence contrary to the judgment.

Article 9-2 Continued

12. Mechanics' Liens ⌐⌐ 310(3)

Evidence was insufficient to support award of attorney fees in favor of supplier for services rendered by legal assistants in connection with action to establish and foreclose mechanic's and materialman's lien against property; testimony and exhibits did not provide any help in determining qualifications, if any, of legal assistants, whether tasks performed by legal assistants were of substantive legal nature or were performance of clerical duties, and hourly rate being charged for legal assistants.

13. Mechanics' Liens ⌐⌐ 310(3)

Failure of supplier to segregate attorney fees expended in its claim for establishment and foreclosure of mechanic's and materialman's lien against project owner and contractor was not error since claims arose out of same transaction and were so interrelated that their prosecution or defense entailed proof or denial of essentially the same facts.

14. Mechanics' Liens ⌐⌐ 310(3)

In view of fact that supplier's mechanic's and materialman's lien claim was valid and enforceable, project owner was not entitled to recover attorney fees or costs in defending foreclosure suit. V.T.C.A., Property Code § 53.156(b).

Paul T. Curl, San Antonio, for appellant.
Martin J. Lehman, David A. Miller, Dallas, for appellee.
Before WHITHAM, ROWE and THOMAS, JJ.
THOMAS, Justice.

Appellee, International Supply Company, Inc., instituted this action seeking the establishment and foreclosure of its statutory mechanic's and materialman's lien against property owned by appellant, Gill Savings Association. After the trial court granted judgment in favor of International, Gill brought this appeal complaining generally in four points of error that the trial court erred: 1) in ruling the mechanic's and materialman's lien to be valid; 2) in holding that International had proved the amount of its claim; 3) in awarding attorney's fees to International; and 4) in not awarding attorney's fees to Gill. For the reasons given below, we affirm the trial court's judgment except for the award of attorney's fees, which we reverse. We sever International's cause of action for attorney's fees and remand same to the trial court for determination of the reasonable amount of attorney's fees, if any, that International should recover from Gill.

FACTUAL BACKGROUND

Gentry Place, Ltd., a limited partnership, owned and constructed the Gentry Place Apartments. Gill held a first lien on the project as the construction lender. H & M, Ltd., the original contractor and a general partner of Gentry Place Ltd., entered into a contract with T.P. Mechanical, whereby T.P. Mechanical agreed to provide a complete plumbing system throughout the project which included the obligation to furnish and install all of the plumbing fixtures. T.P. Mechanical purchased the majority of the plumbing supplies, including such items as lavatories, water heaters, bar sinks and toilets, from International.

In order to perfect its lien to secure payment, International filed its mechanic's and materialmen's lien affidavit on June 21, 1985. Unable to collect the money which it was owed, International filed this suit on January 31, 1986, naming as defendants Gentry Place, Ltd., Martin K. Eby Construction, T.P. Mechanical, and Gill.[1] On or about October 7, 1986, Gill foreclosed its first lien on Gentry Place and purchased the apartments at the foreclosure sale.

VALIDITY OF THE LIEN

In the first point of error, Gill argues that the trial court erred in finding that International had a valid mechanic's and materialman's lien because the lien affidavit: (a) was signed by the attorney; (b) stated an amount far in excess of what was owed; and (c) included charges for items beyond the applicable notice and filing deadlines.

    A. *International's attorney signed the lien affidavit without having personal knowledge of the matters stated in the affidavit.*

        [1] In urging that the lien affidavit is void because it was signed by International's attorney, Gill argues that the holding in *Energy Fund of America, Inc. v. G.E.T. Service Co.*, 610 S.W.2d 833 (Tex.Civ.App.—Eastland 1980), *rev'd on other grounds sub nom. Ayco Development Corp. v. G.E.T. Service Co.*, 616 S.W.2d 184 (Tex.1981), is erroneous.[2] We disagree with Gill's arguments and hold that the mere fact that International's attorney signed the lien affidavit does not invalidate the lien for removables.

The Texas Property Code requires that the materialman's lien affidavit "must be signed by the person claiming the lien or by another person on the claimant's behalf . . . . " TEX.PROP.CODE ANN. § 53.054(a) (Vernon 1984). Section 53.054 sets out the contents required to be in a lien affidavit but does not specifically state whether such affidavit must be made on the personal knowledge of the one who signs it. Corporations, such as International, can act only through persons,[3] and it is undisputed that International designated its attorney, Martin Lehman, as being duly authorized to represent it for purposes of signing the lien affidavit.

In International's lien affidavit, the affiant Lehman states that he is "duly qualified and authorized to make [the] affidavit," and that he is acting as the "authorized representative" for International. The record demonstrates that Lehman's law firm had represented International for at least five years. John Vogt, the president of International, testified that Lehman prepared the lien affidavit at his [Vogt's] direction, that International authorized Lehman to sign the lien affidavit on its behalf, and that International had provided Lehman with various records prepared in the regular course of business prior to the time the affidavit was signed.

Because the property code contains no affirmative personal knowledge requirement, and because the record which reveals that Lehman had the means to, and could have become personally informed, as desired by Gill, we hold that the execution of the lien affidavit by International's attorney does not render it invalid. *See Energy Fund*, 610 S.W.2d 836–37; *Henry S. Miller Co.*, 573 S.W.2d at 555 (corporations can only act through persons); *Gex v. Texas Company*, 337 S.W.2d 820, 828 (Tex.Civ.App.—Amarillo 1960, writ ref'd n.r.e) (the affiant-attorney swore in the affidavit that he was duly authorized to make the affidavit, had read the motion, knew its contents, and knew that the facts therein were true and correct).

    B. *International's lien affidavit stated an amount far in excess of what it was owed.*

Section 53.054(a)(1) of the property code requires that the lien claimant file "a sworn statement of the claim, including the amount." Vogt testified that the $75,986.03 amount in International's lien affidavit, filed on June 21, 1985, failed to take into account a $15,678.00 credit received by International in early May, 1985, which credit was not applied to the account until sometime in August, 1985. An additional correction of approximately $3,000.00 was also made. Vogt admitted that the amount shown in the lien affidavit was incorrect; however, he testified at trial that the account had since been reconciled and that the sum due and owing amounted to $57,365.32 after all credits and corrections.

[2] Gill asserts that "[i]t is not unreasonable for the law to require that amount be correct, or at least much closer to correct than the amount stated in International's affidavit."

Article 9-2   Continued

Gill does not elaborate further on this complaint and neither party cited any authority beyond the statute itself. The statute, however, aids little in solving the issue of whether a lien affidavit that states more than the amount actually owed invalidates the lien. We hold that it does not.

Gill, as lender on the project, purchased and because the owner of Gentry Place through a foreclosure sale in October 1986, over one year after International filed its lien affidavit and over seven months after Gill made its appearance in this law suit. Further, Thomas Shockery, a vice-president of Gill, testified that when Gill bought Gentry Place, Gill knew International was claiming a lien. It is clear that Gill was in no way a third party stranger in its purchase of Gentry Place, and notwithstanding this fact, it is also clear that the discrepancy in amounts in no way harmed Gill, and Gill is actually in a better position than expected since the lien against Gentry Place is less than the amount that Gill believed it to be at the time it foreclosed on and bought the project.

We hold that under the facts of this case, International's lien affidavit was in substantial compliance with the property code statute when it filed its lien for an amount greater than the actual amount reconciled by the time of trial two years later. *See First National Bank in Graham v. Sledge*, 653 S.W.2d 283, 285 (Tex.1983) (a subcontractor's lien rights are totally dependent on compliance with the statutes authorizing the lien; however, substantial compliance is sufficient to perfect a lien); *see also and compare Mathews Construction Company, Inc. v. Jasper Housing Construction*, 528 S.W.2d 323, 329 (Tex.Civ.App.—Beaumont 1975, writ ref'd n.r.e) (holding that a "general statement" of the total price in lump sum is in substantial compliance with mechanic's and materialmen's lien statutes).

    C. *International's lien affidavit included charges for items supplied to Gentry Place beyond the applicable notice and filing deadlines.*

Gill's third argument is that the affidavit is invalid because International failed to timely perfect its lien claim as required by Section 53.056(b) of the Texas Property Code. Since the lien affidavit contained charges for materials delivered to Gentry Place in February 1985, Gill complains that the notices to the owner (dated June 20, 1985) and general contractor (dated May 13, 1985) were not timely. *See* TEX.PROP.CODE ANN. § 53.056(b) (Vernon 1984). Gill further contends that International did not timely file its lien affidavit. *See* TEX.PROP.CODE ANN. § 53.052(c) (Vernon 1984).

[3] International, on the other hand, claims that under Texas Rule of Civil Procedure 54, it was not required to offer any proof that it gave 36-day and 90-day notices of its claim for materials furnished during February 1985. Both International's Original Petition and First Amended Petition plead that "all conditions precedent to Defendants' liability and the foreclosure of International's lien have been performed or have occurred."

International contends that its pleadings are in accordance with Rule 54, which provides as follows:

> In pleading the performance or occurrence of conditions precedent, it shall be sufficient to aver generally that all conditions precedent have been performed or have occurred. When such performances or occurrences have been so plead, the party so pleading the same shall be required to prove only such of them as are *specifically* denied by the opposite party.

(Emphasis added.) The record shows that Gill did not specifically deny that International failed to give a 36-day notice to the original contractor or a 90-day notice to the owner for the materials delivered in February, 1985. Thus, we agree with International that it was not required to offer independent proof of having given the notices.

[4] Rule 54 is applicable to notices required to be given in connection with mechanic's and materialmen's lien claims. *Sunbelt Constr. Corp. v. S & D Mechanical Contractors, Inc.,*

668 S.W.2d 415, 417–18 (Tex.App.— Corpus Christi 1983, writ ref'd n.r.e); *Skinny's, Inc. v. Hicks Brothers Construction of Abilene, Inc.,* 602 S.W.2d 85, 90 (Tex.Civ.App.—Eastland 1980, no writ) (subcontractor required to prove only such conditions precedent as were specifically denied by owner, distinguishing and rejecting *Bunch Electric Co. v. Tex-Craft Builders, Inc.,* 480 S.W.2d 42, 46 (Tex.Civ.App.—Tyler 1972, no writ)); *Continental Contractors, Inc., v. Thorup,* 578 S.W.2d 864, 866–67 (Tex.Civ.App.—Houston [1st Dist.] 1979, no writ) (plaintiff not required to offer independent proof that he had given the required notice if plaintiff plead all relevant conditions precedent, also distinguishing and explaining *Bunch Electric* holding); *Yeager Electric & Plumbing Co. v. Ingleside Cove Lumber and Builders, Inc.,* 526 S.W.2d 738, 739–40 (Tex.Civ.App.— Corpus Christi 1975, no writ); *see also Investors, Inc. v. Hadley,* 738 S.W.2d 737, 741–42 (Tex.App.—Austin 1987, writ denied) (applying Rule 54 to the notice provisions of the Texas Deceptive Trade Practices Act, *citing Skinny's Inc., Continental Contractors, Inc.,* and *Yeager Electric & Plumbing Company, Inc.*).

Since Gill failed to specifically deny that International failed to give a 36-day notice to the original contractor and a 90-day notice to the owner for materials delivered in February 1985, International was not required, pursuant to Rule 54, to offer independent proof of having given the required notices. Gill has thereby waived its right to complain of any such failure on appeal. *Sunbelt Construction,* 668 S.W.2d at 418.

[5] The mechanic's and materialmen's lien statutes are to be liberally construed for the purpose of protecting laborers and materialmen. *Industrial Indemnity Co. v. Zack Burkett Co.,* 677 S.W.2d 493, 495 (Tex.1984). Moreover, the Texas Supreme Court has held that substantial compliance with statutes authorizing a subcontractor's lien is sufficient to perfect a lien. *First National Bank v. Sledge,* 653 S.W.2d at 285 (Tex.1983). Having found no merit in any of the three reasons offered by Gill to invalidate the lien, we hold that International's affidavit was in substantial compliance with the statutory requirements, and it therefore secured a valid lien. The first point of error is overruled.

PROOF OF AMOUNT OF CLAIM

[6] Gill's second point of error complains that the trial court erred in finding that International proved the amount of its claim. The essence of Gill's point of error is that International failed to establish the value of the plumbing materials it sought to remove *as of the date of trial.* We hold that proof of the value of the plumbing materials as of the date of trial is not an essential element of International's claim.

International is required to prove at trial *the amount* of its claim. *See* TEX.PROP.CODE ANN. § 53.054(a)(1) and discussion under point of error number one, *supra.* The record reveals through the testimony and exhibits that International made its proof, with the trial court finding that the principal unpaid balance owed to International as of the date of the trial was $57,365.32. The value of the removables as of the date of trial is irrelevant because the only manner in which the lien can be foreclosed is through a judicial foreclosure sale. TEX.PROP.CODE ANN. § 53.154 (Vernon 1984) ("A mechanic's lien may be foreclosed only on judgment of a court of competent jurisdiction foreclosing the lien and ordering the sale of the property subject to the lien."); *Exchange Savings v. Monocrete,* 629 S.W.2d 34, 38 (Tex.1982); *see Summerville v. King,* 98 Tex. 332, 339, 83 S.W. 680, 682 (Tex.1904).

Gill's reliance on this Court's case of *L & N Consultants, Inc. v. Sikes,* 648 S.W.2d 368 (Tex.App.—Dallas 1983, writ ref'd n.r.e.) is misplaced. In *Sikes,* this Court agreed with the contractor's contention that a mechanic's lien claimant is allowed to "recover the entire amount of his debt up to the total value of the removable improvements." *Sikes,* 648 S.W.2d at 370–71. That rule is correct (and was properly applied under the facts of that

Article 9-2   Continued

case), and it is not in conflict with the rule that the lien claimant's sole remedy is to have the removable items removed and sold through a judicial proceeding. *See* TEX.PROP.CODE ANN. § 53.154 (Vernon 1984). Accordingly, Gill's second point of error is overruled.

ATTORNEY'S FEES AWARDED TO INTERNATIONAL

[7, 8] Gill's third point of error is "the trial court erred in awarding attorney's fees to International." As a part of this assignment of error, Gill argues that (a) the award includes charges for legal assistant time, and (b) International failed to apportion its fees between its claims against T.P. Mechanical and Gill. For the reasons stated below, we overrule Gill's argument that, as a matter of law, a legal assistant's time is not includable as a part of an attorney's fees award. In this connection, we hold that compensation for a legal assistant's work may be separately assessed and included in the award of attorney's fees if a legal assistant performs work that has traditionally been done by any attorney. However, in order to recover such amounts, the evidence must establish: (1) that the legal assistant is qualified through education, training or work experience to perform substantive legal work; (2) that substantive legal work was performed under the direction and supervision of an attorney; (3) the nature of the legal work which was performed; (4) the hourly rate being charged for the legal assistant; and (5) the number of hours expended by the legal assistant. To the extent, however, that Gill argues that the evidence concerning the work performed by the legal assistants is legally insufficient to support the award, we sustain the point of error and reverse the trial court's judgment. Lastly, for the reasons stated below, we overrule the challenge concerning International's failure to apportion between Gill and T.P. Mechanical.

A.   *Legal Assistant's Time*

We have not been cited to any Texas state court decisions, nor have we found a decision which has dealt with the question of whether the value of legal work performed by legal assistants may be recovered as an element of attorney's fees.

The ever-increasing use of legal assistants by attorneys is recognized by the Texas legal community. In order to better define what legal assistants are and the general perimeters within which their services may be used, the Board of Directors of the State Bar of Texas has approved the General Guidelines for the Utilization of the Services of Legal Assistants by Attorneys. The Guidelines contain the following preliminary statement:

> Providing legal services to the public at an affordable price without reduction in the quality of services finds ample support in the purpose clause of the State Bar Act as well as in the Code of Professional Responsibility. It is a goal toward which the Bar is committed, both in principle and in practice. The utilization by attorneys of the services of legal assistants is recognized as one means by which the Bar may attain this goal. With direction and supervision by an attorney, legal assistants can perform a wide variety of tasks which may neither constitute the unauthorized practice of law nor require the traditional exercise of an attorney's training, experience, knowledge or professional judgment.

While the day-to-day duties of a legal assistant will vary from law firm to law firm, it is recognized that the legal assistant will perform work that has traditionally been done by an attorney, and the Guidelines so provide:

> A legal assistant is a person not admitted to the practice of law in Texas but ultimately subject to the definition of "the practice of law" as set forth in the law of the State of Texas, who has, through education, training and experience, demonstrated knowledge of the legal system, legal principles and procedures, and who

uses such knowledge in rendering paralegal assistance to an attorney in the representation of that attorney's clients. The attorney is responsible for the work of the legal assistant and the legal assistant remains, at all times, responsible to and under the supervision and direction of the attorney. The functions of a legal assistant are defined by the attorney responsible for the legal assistant's supervision and direction, and are limited only to the extent that they are limited by law.

We note further that General Guideline V states:

An attorney may charge and bill a client for a legal assistant's time, but the attorney may not share legal fees with a legal assistant under his or her supervision and direction.

In this action, International's right to recover attorney's fees arises from section 53.156(a) for the Texas Property Code, which provides:

If the lien provided under Section 53.021 is not paid before the 181st day the lien is fixed and secured under this Chapter, the claimant or owner of the lien is entitled to recover all reasonable costs of collection, including attorney's fees.

TEX.PROP.CODE ANN. § 53.156(a) (Vernon 1984). Thus, once International secured a lien under the Code, section 53.156 entitled it to recover the reasonable sums it had to expend in collecting upon the lien, including attorney's fees. Gill is correct in its assertion that the statute uses only the words "attorney's fees" and does not state "legal assistants' fees." For the reasons given below, though, we do not read the statute to preclude recovery for legal work properly performed by legal assistants.

In *Johnson v. Georgia Highway Express, Inc.*, 488 F.2d 714, 717–19 (5th Cir. 1974), the court established a twelve point test for determining what factors are necessary to ascertain reasonable attorney's fees, where such fees are allowed by federal law. These factors are: (1) the time and labor required; (2) the novelty and difficulty of the question; (3) the skill requisite to perform the legal service properly; (4) the preclusion of other employment by the attorney due to acceptance of the case; (5) the customary fee; (6) whether the fee is fixed or contingent; (7) time limitations imposed by the client or the circumstances; (8) the amount involved and the results obtained; (9) the experience, reputation and ability of the attorneys; (10) the "undesirability" of the case; (11) the nature and length of the professional relationship with the client; and (12) awards in similar cases. We note that this is consistent with the factors set out in Disciplinary Rule 2-106(B) of the Texas Code of Professional Responsibility.

Inasmuch as one of the elements is the time and labor required, we must look to the reasonableness of the labor and time expended in a case. Properly employed and supervised legal assistants can decrease litigation expense and improve an attorney's efficiency. As pointed out by one of our sister states, justice would not be served by requiring attorneys to perform tasks more properly performed by legal assistants solely to permit that time to be compensable in the event that a request for attorney's fees is ultimately submitted to the court. *See Continental Townhouses East v. Brockbank*, 733 P.2d 1120, 1126–27 (Ariz.App.1986). Indeed, the Guidelines suggest the inclusion of legal assistant services. Further, the purpose and objective of our legal system is to provide the most equitable, efficient adjudication of litigation at the least expense practicable. *See* TEX.R.CIV.P. 1. Likewise, as is suggested by the Guidelines, legal assistant charges are an appropriate component of attorney's fees since an attorney would have to have performed the services if a legal assistant had not been used.

Article 9-2   Continued

While the courts differ in their treatment of the time spent by non-lawyers in structuring fee awards, we note that our holding that work performed by legal assistants is compensable under statutes authorizing attorney's fees awards is supported by various federal court decisions. In *Jones v. Armstrong Cork Co.*, 630 F.2d 324 (5th Cir.1980), a civil rights action under 42 U.S.C.A. § 2000e–5(k), the district court's order denied the plaintiff's attorney's request for compensation for the work hours of Ethel Smith. In affirming the trial court's conclusion that it had not been established that Smith was a "paralegal," the court noted:

> Had Ms. Smith been a paralegal, then to the extent that she performed work that has traditionally been done by an attorney, Ms. Turner [plaintiff's attorney] would have been entitled to have compensation for that work separately assessed and included in her award.

630 F.2d at 325 (citations omitted). *See also Richardson v. Byrd*, 709 F.2d 1016, 1023 (5th Cir.), *cert. denied*, 464 U.S. 1009, 104 S.Ct. 527, 78 L.Ed.2d 710 (1983) (award of attorneys' fees to paralegals who performed work traditionally performed by attorneys was not error under 42 U.S.C.A. § 2000e); *Alter Financial Corp. v. Citizens & Southern International Bank*, 817 F.2d 349, 350 (5th Cir.1987) (award of attorney's fees properly included an assessment for work done by paralegals and a [sic] law clerk under 28 U.S.C.A. § 1927); *Jacobs v. Mancuso*, 825 F.2d 559 (1st Cir.1987) (in calculation of attorney's fee award under 42 U.S.C.A. § 1983, the use of paralegals should be encouraged by separate compensation and should not be considered part of the overhead included in counsel's fee); *Garmong v. Montgomery County*, 668 F.Supp. 1000, 1011 (S.D.Tex.1987) (award of attorney's fees allowed under 42 U.S.C.A. § 1988 to paraprofessional whose work replaced an attorney's efforts); *Zacharias v. Shell Oil Co.*, 627 F.Supp. 31, 34 (E.D.N.Y.1984) (defendant's inclusion of fees for paralegals in its request for reasonable fees under the Petroleum Marketing Practices Act 15 U.S.C.A. § 2805(d)(3) was proper); *Selzer v. Berkowitz*, 477 F.Supp. 686, 690–91 (E.D.N.Y.1979) (award of attorney's fees included charges for paralegals and such was reasonable in civil rights suit under 42 U.S.C.A. § 1988); *Entin v. Barg*, 412 F.Supp. 508, 519 (E.D.Pa.1976) (value of paralegal time computed on their normal hourly billing rate in case under the Securities Exchange Act of 1934 was allowable as a part of the attorney's fees).

The state courts have been divided on this issue. We note, however, that a growing number of our sister states have allowed recovery of "legal assistant" time in attorney's fee awards. *See Continental Townhouses East v. Brockbank*, 733 P.2d at 1127; *Aries v. Palmer Johnson, Inc.*, 735 P.2d 1373, 1384 (Ariz.App.1987) (value of legal work performed by legal assistants could be recovered as element of attorney fees under statute allowing award of attorney fees). *See also Williamette Prod. Credit v. Borg-Warner Acc.*, 706 P.2d 577, 580 (Or.App.1985) (in an action to foreclose livestock fee lien, charges for legal assistant time was properly considered in determining attorney fees); *In Re Marriage of Thornton*, 412 N.E.2d 1336, 1349 (Ill.App.1980) (services of a paralegal can be considered in determining a reasonable fee in a divorce action).

Having determined that a legal assistant's time is properly includable in an attorney's fee award under certain conditions, we turn to Gill's alternative argument that International did not put on the necessary proof to substantiate the award. Specifically, it is contended that there is no evidence regarding: 1) the specific tasks which were performed by the legal assistants; 2) the identity of all of the persons performing the various tasks; and 3) the charge for the legal assistant's work. Although not characterized as such, we will treat this as an assertion that the evidence is legally insufficient to support the award for legal assistant's services.

[9–11] A "legally insufficient" point is a "no evidence" point presenting a question of law. In deciding that question, we must consider only the evidence and the inferences tending to support the finding and disregard all evidence and inferences to the contrary. If a "no evidence" point is sustained and the proper procedural steps have been taken, the finding under attack may be disregarded entirely and judgment rendered for the appellant unless the interest of justice requires another trial. *Garza v. Alviar*, 395 S.W.2d 821, 823 (Tex.1965). In reviewing "factually insufficient evidence" points we consider all of the evidence, including any evidence contrary to the judgment. *Burnett v. Motyka*, 610 S.W.2d 735, 736 (Tex.1980). Applying these principles, we must determine if there is evidence of probative value to support the trial court's finding. It is fundamental that the finding must be upheld by this court if there is more than a scintilla of evidence in support thereof. *Stedman v. Georgetown Savings and Loan Association*, 595 S.W.2d 486, 288 (Tex.1979).

[12] Utilizing these principles, we examine the evidence presented by International in support of its request for attorney's fees. Copies of the monthly fee statements which were submitted to International by its counsel were admitted into evidence without objection. The following information is reflected on the statements: (1) the date the service was rendered; (2) a brief description of the work that was performed; (3) the time spent performing the particular task; (4) the initials of the person performing the work; and (5) the total amount due as a result of the services which were rendered. The testimony reflected that at least two of the sets of initials represent two of the attorneys who worked on the case and one of the sets of initials represents a "legal assistant." The testimony and exhibits however do not provide any help in determining: (1) the qualifications, if any, of the legal assistants; (2) whether the tasks performed by the legal assistants were of a substantive legal nature or were the performance of clerical duties; and (3) the hourly rate being charged for the legal assistant. Further, without the benefit of additional testimony identifying the different sets of initials, it is impossible to determine which class of professional is performing which task. Therefore, we hold that the evidence concerning the work performed by the legal assistants is legally insufficient to support the award. We sustain that portion of Gill's point of error complaining of the legal sufficiency of the evidence to support the attorney's fees award.

B. *Failure to Apportion Fees Between Claims*

[13] We find no error in International's failure to segregate the attorney's fees expended in its claim against T.P. Mechanical and its claim against Gill "since the claims arise out of the same transaction and are so interrelated that their prosecution or defense entails proof or denial of essentially the same facts." *See Flint & Associates v. Intercontinental Pipe & Steel, Inc.*, 739 S.W.2d 622 (Tex.App.—Dallas 1987, writ denied).

ATTORNEY'S FEES TO GILL

[14] In the final point of error, Gill complains that the trial court erred in not awarding it attorney's fees. Gill's right to recover attorney's fees arises from Section 53.156(b) which provides:

> If a claim for a lien provided under Section 53.021 *is not valid or enforceable* because of the failure to fix or secure the lien under this Chapter or for any other reason, the owner . . . is entitled to recover from the claimant all reasonable costs of defending against the lien claim, including attorney's fees.

TEX.PROP.CODE ANN. § 53.156(b) (Vernon 1984) (emphasis added). In view of the determination that International's lien claim is valid and enforceable, Gill is not entitled to

Article 9-2   Continued

recover its attorney's fees or costs in defending this suit, and the fourth point of error is overruled.

DISPOSITION

We affirm the trial court's judgment except as to the award of attorney's fees. We reverse the judgment insofar as it awards attorney's fees to International. Having prevailed on its "no evidence" point as to attorney's fees, Gill would ordinarily be entitled to the rendition of judgment in its favor. *National Life and Accident Ins. Co. v. Blagg*, 438 S.W.2d 905, 909 (Tex.1969); *Garza*, 395 S.W.2d at 823. However, the rules of appellate procedure authorize this court to remand for further proceedings "when it is necessary to remand . . . for further proceedings." TEX.R.APP.P. 81(c).

The precursor of rule 81 was rule 434 of the rules of civil procedure.[4] Under that rule, the supreme court has held that appellate courts have broad discretion to remand in the interest of justice. *Scott v. Liebman*, 404 S.W.2d 288, 294 (Tex.1966). As early as 1911, the supreme court laid down the rule to be followed in cases where a "no evidence" point has been sustained:

> [A]s long as there is a probability that a case has *for any reason* not been fully developed, this court will not render judgment on the insufficiency of the evidence. In other words, it must be apparent to the court that the case has been fully developed, and *that there is no probability* that any other evidence can be secured before it will render judgment.

Paris and G.N.R.R. v. Robinson, 104 Tex. 482, 492, 140 S.W. 434, 439 (1911) (emphasis added); *see also Morrow v. Shotwell*, 477 S.W.2d 538, 541–42 (Tex. 1972); *City of Lucas v. North Texas Municipal Water District*, 724 S.W.2d 811, 820 (Tex.App.—Dallas 1986, writ ref'd n.r.e.); *Zion Missionary Baptist Church v. Pearson*, 695 S.W.2d 609, 613 (Tex.App.—Dallas 1985 writ ref'd n.r.e.).

We can conceive of no case which better exemplifies the need to remand in the interest of justice than the case at bar. In this case of first impression, we have set out a rule for proving legal assistant's fees so that they are recoverable under a statute authorizing the award of attorney's fees. Because we have just enunciated this procedure, International had no reason to believe it was required to introduce the evidence we have now held necessary. Clearly, then, the case has not been fully developed as to attorney's fees.

Having found error in the judgment of the trial court on the issue of attorney's fees, we possess both the power and the obligation to remand because such recourse "will subserve better the ends of justice." *Zion Missionary Baptist Church*, 695 S.W.2d at 613, *quoting Massachusetts Mutual Life Ins. Co. v. Steves*, 472 S.W.2d 332, 333 (Tex.Civ.App.—Fort Worth 1971, no writ). Accordingly, we sever International's cause of action for attorney's fees and remand same to the trial court for a determination of the reasonable amount of attorney's fees, if any, that International should recover from Gill.

1. International also obtained judgments against Gentry Place, Ltd., Martin K. Eby Construction (the general contractor), and T.P. Mechanical. Those judgments have not been appealed.
2. *Energy Fund* involved several parties and Energy Fund itself did not take part in further appeal of the case to the Texas Supreme Court. *Ayco*, 616 S.W.2d 185. Thus, the Texas Supreme Court did not consider the Eastland Court's ruling on the propriety of an attorney signing a lien affidavit containing statements of which he has no personal knowledge.
3. *See Henry S. Miller Co. v. Treo Enterprises*, 573 S.W.2d 553, 555 (Tex.Civ.App.—Texarkana 1978), *aff'd*, 585 S.W.2d 674 (Tex.1979) (suit to recover balance due on promissory note representing a broker's commission on the sale of real estate).

4. Rule 434 required remand "when it is necessary that some matter of fact be ascertained or the damage to be assessed or the matter to be decreed is uncertain." Rule 81(c) of the rules of appellate procedure simply states that remand is allowed "when it is necessary to remand . . . for further proceedings." We consider the language of the two rules to be sufficiently similar that cases analyzing rule 434 also apply to our rule 81(c).

Article 9-2   Continued

MULTI-MOTO CORPORATION, d/b/a

Duncanville Suzuki, and Kenny Meazell, Appellants,

v.

ITT COMMERCIAL FINANCE CORPORATION, Appellee.

No. 05–89–00992–CV.

Court of Appeals of Texas,
Dallas.
Nov. 26, 1990.
Rehearing Denied Feb. 1, 1991.

Secured party brought action against motorcycle retailer after retailer had allegedly defaulted under wholesale financing agreement which granted secured party a purchase money security interest. Secured party obtained temporary restraining order and order for writ of sequestration. Constable executed writ and seized motorcycle. Thereafter secured party obtained second temporary restraining order and order of second writ of sequestration and recovered remaining motorcycles before the 298th District Court, Dallas County, William C. Black, J., and he appealed. The Court of Appeals, Kinkeade, J., held that: (1) retailer failed to establish necessity of notice; (2) retailer could not prevail on claim for wrongful sequestration; (3) trial court did not abuse its discretion in submitting secured party's waiver instruction rather than retailer's course of conduct instruction; and (4) evidence failed to identify reasonableness of constable's fee and included storage charge.

Modified, reformed, and affirmed.

1. Judgment ⌐⟶ 199(2)

Court may grant motion for judgment notwithstanding verdict when defect specifically identified in nonmovant's pleading makes it insufficient to support judgment; truth of

---

Article 9-3   Multi-Moto Corporation, d/b/a Duncanville Suzuki, and Kenny Meazell v. ITT Commercial Finance Corporation

Multi-Moto Corp. v. ITT Commercial Fin., 806 S.W.2d 560 (Tex. App.—Dallas 1990).

fact propositions, under substantive law, establishes right of movant; or evidence is insufficient to raise issue as to one or more fact propositions which nonmovant must establish for court to render judgment in its favor.

2. Appeal and Error ⌘ 934(1)

When trial court overrules motion for judgment notwithstanding verdict, Court of Appeals must consider evidence in light most favorable to jury finding, considering only evidence and inferences that support verdict and rejecting any contrary evidence and inferences.

3. Secured Transactions ⌘ 230

Ordinarily, when secured party disposes of collateral, it must give notice to debtors. V.T.C.A., Bus. & C. §§ 1.101 et seq., 9.504(c).

4. Secured Transactions ⌘ 230

Exception to rule that secured party must give notice to debtors when it disposes of collateral occurs when collateral transfer is under repurchase agreement or the like. V.T.C.A., Bus. & C. § 9.504(c, e).

5. Appeal and Error ⌘ 854(1)

Court of Appeals would affirm judgment of trial court that secured party was not required to give notice to debtor when it disposed of collateral—motorcycles—on any legal theory that was supported by the evidence, where debtor neglected to obtain ruling from trial court as to whether transfer constituted repurchase of motorcycles. V.T.C.A., Bus. & C. § 9.504(c, e).

6. Secured Transactions ⌘ 232

Finding that transfer of motorcycles seized by secured party pursuant to second writ of sequestration did not constitute private sale requiring secured party to give notice to debtor was supported by the evidence; evidence showed that motorcycle manufacturer could have felt itself obligated to accept transfer of motorcycles from secured party pursuant to original repurchase agreement. V.T.C.A., Bus. & C. § 9.504(e).

7. Trial ⌘ 139.1(14), 178

Court may grant directed verdict when evidence presented, viewed in light most favorable to nonmovant and after court indulges every reasonable inference in nonmovant's favor, raises no material fact issues.

8. Secured Transactions ⌘ 242

To succeed on counterclaim for wrongful sequestration, debtor was required to establish that secured party did not have reasonable grounds to believe that debtor might conceal, dispose of, ill-treat, waste, or destroy motorcycles as alleged in affidavit used to secure writ of sequestration and that debtor suffered damages as result of secured party's execution of writ.

9. Sequestration ⌘ 21

Wrongful sequestration results in conversion of property.

10. Trover and Conversion ⌘ 41

In action for wrongful conversion, measure of damages is sum of money necessary to compensate plaintiff for all of its actual losses or injuries sustained as natural and proximate result of defendant's wrong.

11. Pretrial Procedure ⌘ 313

When party fails to show good cause for its failure to designate witness in response to properly propounded interrogatory, court should exclude that witness' testimony.

12. Secured Transactions ⌖ 242

Debtor could not prevail on counterclaim for wrongful sequestration brought against secured party which obtained writs of sequestration for the collateral—motorcycles— debtor never paid for motorcycles, and secured party never obligated debtor to pay principal on motorcycle inventory until after inventory was sold.

13. Trial ⌖ 215, 252(1)

Proper instruction finds support in evidence or in inferences drawn from evidence and aids or assists jury in answering issue submitted. Vernon's Ann. Texas Rules Civ.Proc., Rule 277.

14. Trial ⌖ 215

Trial court does not abuse its discretion in refusing to give party's requested jury instruction absent showing of denial of party's rights that was reasonably calculated to cause and probably did cause rendition of improper verdict. Vernon's Ann. Texas Rules Civ.Proc., Rule 277.

15. Appeal and Error ⌖ 969

In determining whether trial court abused its discretion in refusing to give requested jury instruction, Court of Appeals may not substitute its judgment for that of trial court, and instead must decide only whether trial court's action was arbitrary or unreasonable. Vernon's Ann.Texas Rules Civ.Proc., Rule 277.

16. Secured Transactions ⌖ 242

Trial court did not abuse its discretion in submitting secured party's waiver instruction rather than debtor's course of conduct instruction in wrongful sequestration action, where evidence indicated that secured party changed payment procedures after bank dishonored one of debtor's checks, secured party alleged that it introduced new procedures in attempt to work out arrangement so that parties could continue to do business, and secured party stated that its decision to waive debtor's default and attempt to work out arrangement did not mean that it waived, or intended to waive, its right to take action on future defaults.

17. Appeal and Error ⌖ 989, 1003(6)

In examining insufficient evidence point, Court of Appeals must examine entire record as whole, including any evidence contrary to judgment and may set aside verdict only if it is so contrary to overwhelming weight of evidence as to be clearly wrong and unjust.

18. Secured Transactions ⌖ 242

In order to establish its right to recover compensatory damages, secured party was required to prove that it suffered some pecuniary loss as result of debtor's breach.

19. Secured Transactions ⌖ 227

Secured party has burden to prove reasonableness of expenses following breach of agreement by debtor, and evidence of amount paid is generally insufficient to establish such reasonableness.

20. Secured Transactions ⌖ 227

Debtor seeking to decrease damages for breach of agreement due to secured party's failure to mitigate was required to prove lack of diligence on part of secured party and amount by which secured party increased debtor's damages by its failure to mitigate.

Article 9-3   Continued

21. Contracts ⚯ 175(1), 187(1)

It is presumed that parties contract for themselves, and not for benefit of third party, unless contract states clear intention to contract for benefit to third party, and if any reasonable doubt exists as to intent to confer direct benefit, third-party beneficiary claim will fail.

22. Contracts ⚯ 187(1)

Debtor was not third-party beneficiary under secured party's repurchase agreements with manufacturer of motorcycles, but rather, debtor was at most incidental beneficiary; agreements in no way referenced debtor.

23. Secured Transactions ⚯ 240

Secured party had no mitigation obligation to debtor to seek reimbursement first from manufacturer of motorcycles, even though secured party had entered into repurchase agreements with manufacturer, but rather secured party merely had to show that debtor breached financing agreement and that deficiency remained after manufacturer repurchased goods; debtor was at most incidental beneficiary of agreements.

24. Secured Transactions ⚯ 227

Secured party was not entitled to recover constable's fee or storage charge from debtor, where secured party introduced no evidence of reasonableness of the expenses.

25. Costs ⚯ 194.18, 207

Party may separately assess and include in award of attorneys' fees compensation for legal assistant's work, if that assistant performs work traditionally done by attorney, and in order to recover such amounts, evidence must establish qualifications of legal assistant to perform substantive legal work, that legal assistant perform substantive legal work under direction and supervision of attorney, nature of legal work performed by assistant, assistant's hourly rate, and number of hours expended by assistant.

26. Costs ⚯ 194.32

Testimony introduced by secured party that it had incurred $65,000 in attorneys' fees up until first day of trial, that $65,000 was reasonable fee for services rendered, and that attorneys charged $110 an hour for work performed at trial was some evidence to support award of attorneys' fees.

27. Costs ⚯ 207

Evidence was sufficient to support attorneys' fee award to secured party, even though secured party's evidence as to attorneys' fees failed to specifically identify legal assistants or their qualifications; jury was not asked to take qualifications of legal assistants into consideration when setting reasonable fee.

Charles W. McGarry, Dallas, for appellants.
Robert M. O'Boyle, W. Alan Wright, Dallas, for appellee.
Before HOWELL, KINKEADE and BURNETT, JJ.

OPINION ON REHEARING

KINKEADE, Justice.
We withdraw this Court's opinion entered on August 20, 1990, and vacate the judgment entered on that same date. Both parties filed motions for rehearing. We grant ITT's

motion for rehearing in part and overrule it in part. We overrule Multi-Moto's motion for rehearing. The following is now the opinion of this Court.

Multi-Moto Corporation, d/b/a Duncanville Suzuki, and Kenny Meazell (collectively "Multi-Moto"), appeal the final judgment rendered by the trial court in favor of ITT Commercial Finance Corporation in this suit on a wholesale financing agreement and its guaranty. Multi-Moto argues that the trial court erred when it (1) refused to grant Multi-Moto's motion for judgment notwithstanding the verdict, (2) granted ITT a directed verdict on Multi-Moto's wrongful sequestration counterclaim, and (3) submitted an erroneous instruction on waiver to the jury. Multi-Moto further argues that there is insufficient evidence to support the jury's award of compensatory damages and either no evidence or insufficient evidence to support the jury's award of attorneys' fees. Because Multi-Moto failed to show the necessity of notice or present evidence of its damages incurred as a result of the alleged wrongful sequestration and ITT introduced sufficient evidence to support the jury's award of compensatory damages and attorneys' fees, we affirm the trial court's judgment.

FACTS AND PROCEDURAL HISTORY

Between 1984 and 1986, ITT, an inventory financing business, and Multi-Moto, a motorcycle retailer, entered into a wholesale financing agreement that enabled Multi-Moto to purchase directly from Suzuki an inventory of motorcycles for resale to the general public. Pursuant to this agreement, upon receipt of the motorcycles, Multi-Moto sent the invoices to ITT, which then paid Suzuki. Although the agreement provided that Multi-Moto owned the motorcycles, the agreement required that Multi-Moto grant ITT a purchase money security interest in all of its inventory. Additionally, Kenny Meazell, the president and sole shareholder of Multi-Moto, personally guaranteed the indebtedness.

The agreement provided for two separate accounts, special and regular. Under the special financing account, ITT provided a special eighteen month interest free financing arrangement that attracted Multi-Moto and allowed it to purchase and to retain the motorcycles interest free for a period of eighteen months. After the eighteen month period, payment for the motorcycles became due in full unless Multi-Moto transferred the motorcycles to a regular account. Under the regular account, Multi-Moto paid only the interest for an additional year before payment for an unsold motorcycle became due in full. The agreement also required Multi-Moto to report all sales to ITT and to pay ITT for each motorcycle when sold. A failure to report the sale or to pay for the motorcycle when sold constituted a default. Upon default, ITT had the option to accelerate the loan for the full amount due.

In February 1986 ITT conducted a routine floor inspection of Multi-Moto's facilities to check the presence and condition of its collateral. The inspection revealed that Multi-Moto had sold $35,000 of merchandise without informing or paying ITT. Although Multi-Moto's failure to notify ITT of the sales and failure to pay constituted a default, ITT did not call the loan due at that point, but instead allowed Multi-Moto to pay for the merchandise at that time and then continue operations. Initially, Multi-Moto issued a $35,000 check to ITT, which the bank returned for insufficient funds. Although unclear from the record, Multi-Moto apparently then deposited funds in its account, after which the bank honored the $35,000 check. At this time, ITT instituted a new payment procedure for Multi-Moto to follow in an attempt to avoid similar occurrences in the future.

On September 23, 1986, Multi-Moto wrote ITT a check for $3385 to pay for motorcycles it had sold. On October 14, 1986, after the bank returned that check because of insufficient

Article 9-3 Continued

funds, ITT conducted another floor inspection. This inspection revealed that Multi-Moto had not informed ITT of an additional $6547 worth of motorcycles it had sold. Upon further investigation, ITT determined that Multi-Moto also owed $2275.34 in insurance and interest payments to ITT and that $20,429.50 worth of Multi-Moto's merchandise had become payable in full.

On October 17, 1986, Multi-Moto sent ITT a cashier's check for $3385 to replace the previous insufficient funds check and a regular check for the $6547. The bank returned this latter check due to insufficient funds. On October 22, 1986, after the return of this last check and a complete review of Multi-Moto's file, ITT notified Multi-Moto that it intended to accelerate the loan and wanted to pick up the motorcycles. The terms of the agreement required Multi-Moto to voluntarily release the merchandise to ITT upon request. On October 28, 1986, ITT sued Multi-Moto under the agreement for $313,562.84, and on October 29, 1986, after Multi-Moto failed to voluntarily release the motorcycles, ITT obtained a temporary restraining order and an order for a writ of sequestration. The restraining order prohibited Multi-Moto from interfering with the execution of the writ and from selling, disposing of, or transferring the motorcycles.

On October 31, 1986, the constable executed the writ and seized 155 motorcycles. ITT transferred these motorcycles to Suzuki. Subsequently, ITT learned that the constable had failed to take possession of approximately thirty motorcycles, that Multi-Moto had transferred these motorcycles to a storage facility, and that Multi-Moto had apparently sold some of these motorcycles to a third party in violation of the restraining order. On December 19, 1986, ITT obtained a second temporary restraining order and an order for a second writ of sequestration. On December 24, 1986, the constable executed this second writ and recovered the remaining twenty-seven motorcycles relocated by Multi-Moto and placed them in storage. Several months later, ITT also transferred these motorcycles to Suzuki.

PROPER NOTICE OF SALE

In its first point of error, Multi-Moto contends that the trial court erred when it overruled Multi-Moto's motion for judgment notwithstanding the verdict. Multi-Moto argues that the transfer to Suzuki of the motorcycles seized pursuant to the second writ of sequestration constituted a private sale and that ITT failed to establish that it gave Multi-Moto proper notice of that alleged sale as required by the Texas Business and Commerce Code. *See* TEX. BUS. & COM.CODE ANN. § 9.504(c) (Vernon Supp.1991).

[1,2] A court may grant a motion for judgment notwithstanding the verdict when: (1) a defect specifically identified in the nonmovant's pleading makes it insufficient to support a judgment; (2) the truth of fact propositions, under the substantive law, establishes the right of the movant; or (3) the evidence is insufficient to raise an issue as to one or more fact propositions which the nonmovant must establish for the court to render judgment in its favor. *Rowland v. City of Corpus Christi*, 620 S.W.2d 930, 932–33 (Tex.Civ.App.—Corpus Christi 1981, writ ref'd n.r.e.). When the trial court overrules a motion for judgment notwithstanding the verdict, this Court must consider the evidence in a light most favorable to the jury finding, considering only the evidence and the inferences that support the verdict and rejecting any contrary evidence and inferences. *Fenwal, Inc. v. Mencio Security, Inc.*, 686 S.W.2d 660, 663 (Tex.App.—San Antonio 1985, writ ref'd n.r.e.).

[3,4] Ordinarily, when a secured party disposes of collateral, it must give notice to the debtors. An exception to this rule occurs when the collateral transfers under a repurchase agreement or the like. *Bexar County Nat'l Bank of San Antonio v. Hernandez*, 716 S.W.2d 938, 938–39 (Tex. 1986); *see* TEX. BUS. & COM.CODE ANN. § 9.504(c) & (e) (Vernon Supp.1991).

In consideration for ITT's grant of financing to Multi-Moto, Suzuki executed a repurchase agreement with ITT. Upon ITT's written request, this repurchase agreement obligated Suzuki to repurchase Multi-Moto's special inventory merchandise at 100 percent of the original invoice price. Subsequent to obtaining the first writ of sequestration, ITT sought an order to allow the pretrial disposition of the sequestered property. ITT asserted that the property consisted primarily of motorcycles that would greatly depreciate in value due to the passage of time pending a final disposition of the cause. The trial court granted the order allowing ITT to transfer the property under any repurchase agreements and to liquidate the remainder under applicable law. Pursuant to the repurchase agreement, ITT transferred all of the motorcycles seized under the first writ of sequestration to Suzuki. Multi-Moto does not challenge that Suzuki repurchased the motorcycles seized pursuant to the first writ of sequestration.

[5] After the execution of the second writ of sequestration, ITT stated that it entered into negotiations with Suzuki concerning the repurchase of the motorcycles seized thereunder. Multi-Moto had carried all of the motorcycles seized pursuant to this second writ in its regular account. Although the original repurchase agreement with Suzuki only obligated Suzuki to repurchase the special account inventory, Suzuki had the option to also repurchase the regular account inventory. Pursuant to the negotiations with ITT, Suzuki eventually repurchased the motorcycles seized as a result of the second writ of sequestration under the identical terms as it had repurchased the motorcycles seized as a result of the first writ of sequestration. Additionally, Multi-Moto stipulated at trial that whether the purchase of the second group of motorcycles constituted a repurchase by Suzuki was a question of law for the court to decide. Since Multi-Moto neglected to obtain a ruling from the trial court as to whether the transfer constituted a repurchase of the motorcycles, this Court "must affirm the judgment of the trial court on any legal theory that finds support in the evidence." *In the interest of W.E.R.*, 669 S.W.2d 716, 717 (Tex.1984).

[6] Reviewed in a light most favorable to the jury finding and considering only the evidence and the inferences that support the verdict, the evidence shows that Suzuki could have felt itself obligated to accept the transfer of these motorcycles from ITT pursuant to the original repurchase agreement. The Texas Business and Commerce Code specifically provides that a secured party's transfer of collateral pursuant to a repurchase agreement is not a sale or disposition subject to its provisions. *See* Tex. Bus. & Com.Code Ann. § 9.504(e) (Vernon Supp.1991). Because Multi-Moto failed to establish the necessity of notice, the trial court correctly overruled Multi-Moto's motion for judgment notwithstanding the verdict. We overrule Multi-Moto's first point of error.

WRONGFUL SEQUESTRATION

In its second point of error, Multi-Moto contends that the trial court erred when it granted ITT's directed verdict as to Multi-Moto's counterclaim for wrongful sequestration. Multi-Moto argues that ITT did not have reasonable grounds to believe the facts alleged in the affidavit used to secure its writ of sequestration. Multi-Moto further argues that it presented sufficient evidence of damages to support its counterclaim.

[7,8] A court may grant a directed verdict when the evidence presented, viewed in the light most favorable to the nonmovant and after the court indulges every reasonable inference in the nonmovant's favor, raises no material fact issues. *Anderson v. Moore*, 448 S.W.2d 105, 105–06 (Tex. 1969); *Guy v. Stubberfield*, 666 S.W.2d 176, 178 (Tex.App.—Dallas 1983, no writ). To succeed on its counterclaim for wrongful sequestration, Multi-Moto must establish that (1) ITT did not have reasonable grounds to believe that Multi-Moto might conceal, dispose of, ill-treat, waste, or destroy the motorcycles as alleged in the affidavit used to secure the writ of sequestration and (2) Multi-Moto suffered damages as a result of

Article 9-3   Continued

ITT's execution of the writ. *Edmondson v. Carroll*, 134 S.W.2d 378, 385 (Tex.Civ.App.—Fort Worth 1939, writ dism'd judgm't cor.).

[9,10] As part of the final judgment, the trial court granted ITT's motion for directed verdict on Multi-Moto's counterclaim for wrongful sequestration after making a determination that Multi-Moto presented no evidence of damages arising out of the alleged wrongful sequestration. A wrongful sequestration results in the conversion of property. *See Bloodgood v. B & L Sales Co.*, 436 S.W.2d 398, 399 (Tex.Civ.App.—Houston [14th Dist.] 1968, writ ref'd n.r.e.). In an action for wrongful conversion the measure of damages is the sum of money necessary to compensate the plaintiff for all of its actual losses or injuries sustained as a natural and proximate result of the defendant's wrong. TEX.CIV.PRAC. & REM.CODE ANN. § 62.045(a)(3) (Vernon Supp.1991); *see Groves v. Hanks*, 546 S.W.2d 638, 647 (Tex.Civ.App.—Corpus Christi 1976, writ ref'd n.r.e.).

[11] At trial, Multi-Moto attempted to call George Fettinger, a certified public accountant, to testify to the damages it allegedly suffered as a result of the wrongful sequestration. Prior to trial, ITT asked Multi-Moto in an interrogatory to designate any experts it intended to call to testify as to its alleged damages. Multi-Moto failed to do so. Therefore, ITT objected to Multi-Moto's attempted use of Fettinger or anyone else as a damages expert. Further, Multi-Moto failed to present any evidence of "good cause" why it had not designated a witness to testify as to its damages. When a party fails to show good cause for its failure to designate a witness in response to a properly propounded interrogatory, then the court should exclude that witness's testimony. *Gutierrez v. Dallas I.S.D.*, 729 S.W.2d 691, 693 (Tex.1987).

[12] Multi-Moto argues that it established the amount of its actual damages through Meazell's testimony and ITT's admissions at trial. *See Bloodgood*, 436 S.W.2d at 400; *Garlington v. Cotten*, 189 S.W. 294, 295 (Tex.Civ.App.—Texarkana 1916, no writ). Meazell testified as to his opinion of the retail and wholesale value of the sequestered motorcycles. Additionally, Multi-Moto contends that ITT's admission that the motorcycles sustained $388.97 worth of damages between the time ITT last inspected them and when Suzuki repurchased them was evidence of Multi-Moto's damages. Multi-Moto further contends that ITT's admission that the motorcycles depreciated in value while in storage was also evidence of its actual damages.

Multi-Moto misplaces it reliance on *Bloodgood* and *Garlington*. In both of those cases, the complaining party had already paid in full for the sequestered property. *Bloodgood*, 436 S.W.2d at 400; *Garlington*, 189 S.W. at 295. In the present case, Multi-Moto never paid for the motorcycles. ITT never obligated Multi-Moto to pay any principal on the inventory until after the inventory was sold. Further, Multi-Moto never established that the damages that the motorcycles sustained after their last floor inspection by Suzuki occurred as a result of the subsequent sequestration. Additionally, although ITT asserted that the motorcycles depreciated while in storage, no dollar figure was placed on this depreciation. Even viewing Meazell's testimony and ITT's admissions in the light most favorable to Multi-Moto, without additional expert testimony, the evidence was insufficient to establish that Multi-Moto incurred any actual damages. Because Multi-Moto failed to establish that it incurred any actual damages, the trial court correctly granted ITT's motion for directed verdict as to Multi-Moto's counterclaim for wrongful sequestration. We overrule Multi-Moto's second point of error.

ERRONEOUS JURY INSTRUCTION

In its third point of error, Multi-Moto contends that the trial court erred when it submitted an erroneous instruction on waiver to the jury. Multi-Moto argues that the trial court should have instructed the jury on waiver of strict compliance rather than waiver of the entire loan agreement.

Both the parties and the court chose to submit waiver as an instruction controlling the issue of default rather than as a separate special issue. The instruction submitted by the court to the jury read as follows:

> You are hereby instructed that Multi-Moto Corporation defaulted under its loan agreement with ITT unless ITT *waived* the loan agreement. You are also instructed that *waiver*, as that word is used in this written question means the intentional or voluntary relinquishment of a known right, or such conduct as warrants an inference of the relinquishment of such a right.

(Emphasis in original.) Multi-Moto objected to this instruction on the ground that it directs a verdict for ITT unless ITT waived the entire loan agreement. Multi-Moto further objected to this instruction on the ground that Multi-Moto only claimed a waiver of "strict compliance" implied from a course of conduct, and the existence of such a course of conduct entitled Multi-Moto to (1) advance notice that ITT would require strict compliance in the future, and (2) a reasonable opportunity to cure any default. Multi-Moto requested the court replace the above instruction with the following:

> A party, who accepts a course of performance or conduct of a contract that is not in strict compliance with the terms of a contract, waives the right to declare a default with respect thereto. In such a situation, the party who has not insisted upon strict compliance in the past, before he can declare a default for a subsequent failure to perform by the other party of the same nature, must give notice to the other party that strict compliance with the terms of the contract will be demanded in the future, and must furthermore give the other party a reasonable period of time to cure any then-existing breaches of the same nature.

[13–15] The Texas Rules of Civil Procedure require the trial court to "submit such explanatory instructions and definitions as shall be proper to enable the jury to render a verdict." TEX.R.CIV.P. 277. This rule gives the trial court considerable discretion in deciding which instructions are necessary and proper when submitting issues to the jury. *Security Sav. Ass'n v. Clifton*, 755 S.W.2d 925, 933 (Tex.App.—Dallas 1988, no writ). A proper instruction finds support in the evidence or in the inferences drawn from the evidence and aids or assists the jury in answering the issues submitted. *Miller v. Miller*, 700 S.W.2d 941, 952 (Tex.App.—Dallas 1985, writ ref'd n.r.e.). No abuse of discretion occurs absent the showing of a denial of a party's rights that was reasonably calculated to cause and probably did cause rendition of an improper verdict. *Security Sav.*, 755 S.W.2d at 933. In determining whether an abuse of discretion has occurred, this Court may not substitute its judgment for that of the trial court, and instead this Court must decide only whether the trial court's action was arbitrary or unreasonable. *Landry v. Traveler's Ins. Co.*, 458 S.W.2d 649, 651 (Tex.1970); *K-Mart Corp. v. Trotti*, 677 S.W.2d 632, 636 (Tex.App.—Houston [1st Dist.] 1984, writ ref'd n.r.e.).

[16] The evidence showed that after the bank dishonored Multi-Moto's check in February 1986, ITT introduced new payment procedures for Multi-Moto to follow. Multi-Moto alleged that these procedures, as well as ITT's acceptance of cashier's checks after the bank had dishonored Multi-Moto's checks for insufficient funds, constituted a new course of conduct. However, ITT stated that it introduced these procedures in an attempt to work out an arrangement so that the parties could continue to do business and that the agreement provided for this. ITT further stated that under the agreement Multi-Moto's action constituted a default. ITT stated the decision to waive this default and attempt a workout

Article 9-3 Continued

arrangement did not mean that it waived, or intended to waive, its right to take action on future defaults. Further, paragraph fifteen of the financing agreement provided that ITT's failure to take action when Multi-Moto defaulted did not prevent ITT from taking, or waive ITT's right to take, action as to any default or any later default. Although Multi-Moto alleged that ITT caused the last two defaults by not holding Multi-Moto's checks as promised, ITT stated that it never agreed to hold checks until Multi-Moto deposited funds into its account.

The evidence, and reasonable inferences drawn therefrom, show that ITT's change of payment procedures did not constitute a new course of conduct. ITT specifically included in the agreement the right to enter into a workout arrangement with Multi-Moto without relinquishing the right to declare a default in the future. Under Multi-Moto's theory of strict compliance, ITT would waive its right to strict compliance as to the payment procedure. Its theory would also waive the right to declare future defaults unless the parties significantly modified the agreement. The language of Multi-Moto's proposed instruction contained no clear definition of waiver. The proposed instruction failed to aid and assist the jury in understanding the legal concept of waiver and the effect of applicable law and presumptions. Additionally, Multi-Moto's instruction called undue attention to its affirmative defenses. *See Security Sav.*, 755 S.W.2d at 933; *Southern Pac. Transp. Co. v. Garrett*, 611 S.W.2d 670, 674 (Tex.Civ.App.—Corpus Christi 1980, no writ). Because Multi-Moto has failed to show that the trial court abused its discretion, the trial court did not err when it submitted ITT's waiver instruction rather than Multi-Moto's course of conduct instruction. We overrule Multi-Moto's third point of error.

SUFFICIENCY OF THE EVIDENCE

Compensatory Damages

In its fourth point of error, Multi-Moto contends that ITT's evidence as to compensatory damages was insufficient to support the jury's award because ITT failed to (1) establish that Multi-Moto proximately caused ITT's damages, (2) mitigate its own damages, or (3) show the reasonableness of the constable's fees and various costs of storage. First, Multi-Moto argues that the entire deficiency resulted from missing parts, and since the parts could have been lost after sequestration, ITT failed to prove Multi-Moto caused the deficiency when it did not inspect the motorcycles and record any damages at the time of sequestration. Second, Multi-Moto argues that ITT failed to mitigate its damages because under ITT's repurchase agreement with Suzuki, Suzuki agreed to pay 100 percent of the interest; insurance; returned check charges; dealer's net cost for each repossessed motorcycle, less any amount for damages; and any storage charges incurred thirty days after receiving the request for repurchase. Therefore, ITT should have first sought reimbursement for the constable's fee, including storage charge, and its attorneys' fees from Suzuki, and its failure to do so evidenced ITT's lack of diligence. With this last argument, Multi-Moto essentially asserts that it was a beneficiary of the repurchase agreement between ITT and Suzuki. *MJR Corp. v. B & B Vending Co.*, 760 S.W.2d 4, 10–12 (Tex.App.—Dallas 1988, writ denied).

[17,18] In examining an insufficient evidence point, the court must examine the entire record as a whole, including any evidence contrary to the judgment. *Plas-Tex, Inc. v. U.S. Steel Corp.*, 772 S.W.2d 442, 445 (Tex.1989). The court may set aside the verdict only if it is so contrary to the overwhelming weight of the evidence as to be clearly wrong and unjust. *Cain v. Bain*, 709 S.W.2d 175, 176 (Tex. 1986). In order to establish its right to recover compensatory damages ITT needed to prove that it suffered some pecuniary loss as a result of Multi-Moto's breach. *Braselton-Watson Builders, Inc. v. C.B. Burgess*, 567 S.W.2d 24, 28 (Tex.Civ.App.—Corpus Christi 1978, writ ref'd n.r.e.); *Stewart v. Basey*, 150 Tex. 666, 670, 245 S.W.2d 484, 486 (1952).

Rule 699 of the Texas Rules of Civil Procedure provides that only a sheriff or constable shall execute the writ of sequestration, take into his possession the property described in the application or affidavit, and keep the same subject to further orders of the court. TEX.R.CIV.P. 699. The rules that govern writs of sequestration are similar to those that govern writs of attachment. *Compare* TEX.R.CIV.P. 696–716 *with* TEX.R.CIV.P. 592–609; *Lawyers Civil Process, Inc. v. State ex rel. Vines*, 690 S.W.2d 939, 943 (Tex. App.—Dallas 1985, no writ). Neither party controls the manner in which the constable shall perform his obligation of looking after the property. Further, the constable acts as neither the agent nor the servant of either party. *Sorrells v. Irion*, 216 S.W.2d 1021, 1023 (Tex.Civ.App.—Amarillo 1948, writ dism'd). The statute that addresses compensation for constables fixes no fee for the care of the property by them, but it does provide for reasonable charges as allowed by the court. *See* TEX.CIV.PRAC. & REM.CODE ANN § 62.062(a) (Vernon 1986).

[19] The claimant has the burden to prove the reasonableness of expenses and evidence of the amount paid is generally insufficient to establish such reasonableness. *Cook Consultants, Inc. v. Larson*, 700 S.W.2d 231, 238 (Tex.App.—Dallas 1985, writ ref'd n.r.e.). At trial, ITT established that Multi-Moto defaulted under the agreement, and as a direct result of Multi-Moto's refusal to voluntarily release the motorcycles, ITT sought and obtained two writs of sequestration. Pursuant to the second writ, ITT had the constable seize the twenty-seven motorcycles and store them for approximately three months prior to delivery to Suzuki for repurchase. ITT introduced evidence that it expended $12,350.74, after reimbursement from Suzuki, for the constable's fee, which included charges for hauling the property to the warehouse, warehouse handling, three months' storage, and access to the storage. However, ITT introduced no evidence of the reasonableness of these expenses.

[20,21] ITT had a duty to minimize its loss. However, Multi-Moto had the burden to prove the extent to which ITT mitigated or could have mitigated its damages. *Town East Ford Sales, Inc. v. Gray*, 730 S.W.2d 796, 806 (Tex.App.—Dallas 1987, no writ). Therefore, Multi-Moto had to prove (1) lack of diligence on the part of ITT and (2) the amount by which ITT increased Multi-Moto's damages by its failure to mitigate. *Cocke v. White*, 697 S.W.2d 739, 744 (Tex.App.—Corpus Christi 1985, writ ref'd n.r.e.). The court presumes that parties contract for themselves, and not for the benefit of a third party, unless the contract states a clear intention to contract for a benefit to the third party. If any reasonable doubt exists as to an intent to confer a direct benefit, the third party beneficiary claim must fail. The courts will not create a third party beneficiary contract by implication. *MJR*, 760 S.W.2d at 10–12.

[22,23] Pursuant to the repurchase agreements with Suzuki, ITT requested that Suzuki repurchase the motorcycles and pay for a portion of the storage fees, which it did. The repurchase agreement between ITT and Suzuki did not confer a direct benefit on or reference Multi-Moto in any way. ITT introduced evidence which showed that, following Suzuki's repurchase under the agreement, Multi-Moto owed a total deficiency of $399.74, $390.97 for the special term inventory and $8.77 for the regular inventory. Since the repurchase agreements between ITT and Suzuki neither conferred a direct benefit on nor in any way referenced Multi-Moto, Multi-Moto misplaces its reliance on that agreement for its proposition that ITT failed to mitigate its damages. At most Multi-Moto was an incidental beneficiary of the repurchase agreement and as such had no right to enforce the agreement against either ITT or Suzuki. *See MJR*, 760 S.W.2d at 10. Therefore, ITT had no obligation to Multi-Moto to seek reimbursement from Suzuki first. ITT merely had to show that Multi-Moto breached the financing agreement and that a deficiency remained after

Article 9-3   Continued

Suzuki repurchased the goods. ITT did both. The burden then shifted to Multi-Moto to plead and to prove ITT's failure to mitigate. *See Town East Ford*, 730 S.W.2d at 806. Multi-Moto raised failure to mitigate for the first time on appeal. Further, Multi-Moto failed to show the amount, if any, by which ITT increased Multi-Moto's damages by the alleged failure.

[24] After examining the record as a whole, we find that ITT introduced sufficient evidence to show that Multi-Moto owed a deficiency of $399.74. Since ITT failed to establish the reasonableness of the constable's fee or storage charge, the evidence is insufficient to support these damages. We sustain Multi-Moto's fourth point of error only as to ITT's failure to establish the reasonableness of the unreimbursed $12,350.74 constable's fee and included storage charge.

Attorneys' Fees

[25] In its fifth point of error, Multi-Moto argues that ITT introduced no evidence to support the jury's award of attorneys' fees or that the evidence was insufficient because it failed to identify the attorney's legal assistants, their qualifications, the work they performed, or the customary and reasonable charge for legal assistants' work. A party may separately assess and include in the award of attorneys' fees compensation for a legal assistant's work, if that assistant performs work traditionally done by an attorney. In order to recover such amounts, the evidence must establish: (1) the qualifications of the legal assistant to perform substantive legal work; (2) that the legal assistant performed substantive legal work under the direction and supervision of an attorney; (3) the nature of the legal work performed; (4) the legal assistant's hourly rate; and (5) the number of hours expended by the legal assistant. *Gill Sav. Ass'n v. International Supply Co.*, 759 S.W.2d 697, 702 (Tex.App.—Dallas 1988, writ denied).

[26] On appeal, when the court reviews a no evidence challenge, it considers only the evidence and reasonable inferences drawn therefrom which, when viewed in their most favorable light, support the jury verdict. The court must disregard all evidence and inferences contrary to the fact finding. *Stafford v. Stafford*, 726 S.W.2d 14, 16 (Tex.1987). The instruction accompanying the jury question on attorneys' fees informed the jury that in setting a reasonable attorneys' fee they could consider the following factors: (1) the nature of the case, its difficulties, complexities, and importance; (2) the nature of the services required to be rendered by the attorneys; (3) the amount of money involved, the client's interest at stake, and the benefit derived by the client; and (4) the time reasonably spent by the attorneys, the responsibility imposed upon counsel, and the skill reasonably needed to perform the services. ITT introduced testimony that it had incurred $65,000 in attorneys' fees up until the first day of trial, that this was a reasonable fee for the services rendered, and that its attorneys charged $110 an hour for the work performed at trial. ITT also introduced detailed billing records, which delineated the work performed, the person performing the work by their initials and their hourly rate, the time spent performing the work, and a final total. Viewing this evidence in the light most favorable to the jury verdict, ITT produced some evidence to support the jury's award of attorneys' fees.

requested and to determine the reasonable market rate for the services. The stronger the legal assistant's educational background, work experience, and credentials, the more likely the legal assistant fee will be approved and will be held recoverable.

The courts have also focused on the specific types of tasks performed by the legal assistant to determine if it was appropriate to include the fee relating to the task as a recoverable fee. The trend is to allow recovery of legal assistant fees if the task performed by the legal assistant has traditionally been done by an attorney. The courts seem to use the "but-for test": but for the legal assistant, the task would have been performed by an attorney. If however, the tasks performed are deemed to be clerical in nature, the courts will generally not allow recovery of the portion of the fee related to the performance of clerical tasks.[10] *In fact, there are several cases where the courts have decreased an award of "attorney fees" where the duties performed by an attorney or a hearing officer were legal assistant in nature but the attorney or hearing officer had charged the full hourly rate of the attorney or hearing officer.* In other words, some courts have held that attorney time is not recoverable if it is spent in performing tasks that can and should be performed by a legal assistant.[11]

In a bankruptcy case, *In re Smuggler's Beach Properties, Inc.,* in which the amount of attorneys' fees was being contested, the court stated, "Performance of unnecessary work, inefficiency, and failure to delegate appropriate tasks to junior lawyers or paralegals also may warrant a reduction in fees."[12] Consider also the case of *In re S.T.N. Enterprises,* where the court so eloquently stated: "A Michelangelo charging Sistine Chapel rates should not be painting a farmer's barn."[13] The same court went on to warn that "[I]n the future . . . if the firm or law office has the personnel, this Court will reduce the rate of an attorney performing tasks appropriate to the paralegal or law clerk to the paraprofessionals' rate."[14]

The bankruptcy court in *In re Belknap, Inc.,* set out guidelines to be followed in future fee and expense applications filed in the federal bankruptcy court for the western district, which included the following:

2. Professionals and paraprofessionals should be utilized in such a way as to minimize the cost to the estate. Senior partners should not perform services which could be as competently performed by associates or paralegals; paralegals should not be used to perform tasks which are clerical in nature.

3. Out of state firms shall include proof of customary fees in their local legal community, including customary fees charged by paraprofessionals.[15]

Examples of the types of duties that courts have found appropriate to support a request for legal assistant fee recovery include the following: preparation of legal briefs;[16] conducting computerized legal research, conducting client interviews, analyzing discovery documents received, drafting discovery documents, preparing settlement documents, and participating in weekly meetings with attorney and client;[17] conducting fact investigation and legal research, summarizing depositions, checking citations, compiling statistical data, and compiling financial data;[18] drafting, reviewing, and revising pleadings, drafting motions and documents in opposition to motions;[19] and assisting attorney at trial.[20]

Another area of focus for the court in determining whether legal assistant fees are recoverable is the documentation of the legal assistant's separately billed time. Courts have held that it is proper to decline to make an award of legal assistant fees as a component of attorney fees if there is no documentation of the legal assistant's time. In the case of *Anderson v. Sec'y of Health and Human Serv.*, in refusing to award recovery of legal assistant fees, the court found that there was no separate documentation in the record for paralegal time other than an estimate made by the attorney of the amount of paralegal time that had been expended.[21]

Article 9-4 addresses the concept of documenting and "proving up" legal assistant time.

Legal assistants play a vital role in the delivery of legal services to the public. The profession continues to develop and the questions surrounding legal assistants' role in the legal system have become more complicated. This special section of the *Texas Bar Journal* discusses some of those issues and seeks to assist attorneys in their understanding of the legal assistant profession. In many jurisdictions serious consideration is being given to the relaxation of limitations on the unauthorized practice of law for legal assistants. So far, in Texas, attorneys remain responsible, under the Texas Disciplinary Rules of Professional Conduct, for their staff. This special section was coordinated by the State Bar Standing Committee on Legal Assistants, chaired by Xavier Rodriguez of San Antonio. Special thanks to the committee for its efforts in keeping legal assistants and lawyers up to date about issues surrounding the role of legal assistants in the delivery of legal services.

Legal Assistants

Special Section

Evidence Required to Prove the Validity Of Legal Assistant Fees as a Compensable Component of Attorney Fee Awards

By Vicki Kelly Brittain

The question used to be, whether a court or jury could properly include as a component of a reasonable attorney fees award, the hours incurred by a legal assistant for substantive paralegal work performed? During the last decade that question has been answered in the affirmative and consistent case law has been established in most jurisdictions nationwide. The current questions regarding the validity of inclusion of legal assistant fees in attorney fee awards, concerns the evidentiary showing that must be made to substantiate the award of legal assistant fees as a compensable component of attorney's fees.

Article 9-4   Evidence Required to Prove the Validity of Legal Assistant Fees as a Compensable Component of Attorney Fee Awards

Vicki Brittain, Evidence Required to Prove the Validity of Legal Assistant Fees as a Compensable Component of Attorney Fee Awards, Texas B.J. March 2000, at 260–264.

Review of Precedent

In 1978, the federal bankruptcy law was amended to specifically allow compensation for actual, necessary services rendered by a paraprofessional employed by an attorney.[1]

Subsequently, in 1989, the U.S. Supreme Court interpreted the phrase "attorney fees" as used in a federal statute as including the substantive legal work performed by legal assistants.[2] Since that date, federal courts have consistently found substantive legal work performed by legal assistants to be a proper, compensable element of attorney fee awards pursuant to federal statutes and private contracts that allow for the award of attorney fees.[3] At the state level, although not uniform,[4] the marked trend is to allow legal assistant fees incurred in the performance or substantive legal tasks as a component of attorney fee awards either pursuant to a state statute which specifies that a legislative reference to attorney fees includes paralegal fees[5] or pursuant to state case law which interprets the phrase "attorney fees," as used in a statute or in a private contract agreement, as including legal assistant fees.[6]

In 1988, the law in Texas on the issue of the recoverability of legal assistant fees was settled after the seminal case of *Gill Savings Association v. International Supply*.[7] In *Gill*, the court interpreted a statute which allowed the award of attorney fees. It held that legal assistant fees are a compensable component of attorney fees and are recoverable explaining that, "compensation for a legal assistant's work may be separately assessed and included in the award of attorney's fees if a legal assistant performs work traditionally done by an attorney."[8] Subsequently, the holding in *Gill* has been expanded to allow the recovery of legal assistant fees in a variety of statutory and contractual contexts in Texas.[9]

Evidence Required

In *Gill* the court held that, prior to the inclusion of legal assistant fees as a compensable component of attorney fees, the evidence must establish the following five factors: (1) that the legal assistant is qualified through education, training, or work experience to perform substantive legal work, (2) that substantive legal work was performed under the direction and supervision of an attorney, (3) the nature of the legal work which was performed, (4) the hourly rate being charged for the legal assistant, and (5) the number of hours expended by the legal assistant.[10] In the *Gill* case, the court held that the evidence presented was insufficient to support the inclusion of legal assistant fees and the case was remanded to the trial court for a determination of the attorney fee issue.[11]

Since the *Gill* decision, there have been more than 20 Texas cases that have either directly or indirectly involved issues relating to the recovery of legal assistant fees as a component of attorney fees.[12] An analysis of those cases indicates that several types of evidence have been used by attorneys in an attempt to make the necessary evidentiary showing. The categories of evidence that have been used include testimonial, documentary, and demonstrative. In the testimonial category the most common type of proof offered has been fact witness testimony by the supervising attorney, the legal assistant, and/or the client either on the witness stand or by affidavit.[13] However, in some cases, evidentiary foundation was laid to qualify the supervising attorney as an expert witness on the issue of attorney fees and expert testimony was offered into evidence to support the inclusion of legal assistant fees as a component of attorney fees.[14] In the documentary category, the following types of exhibits have been introduced into evidence to prove one or more of the five required factors: itemized billing statements, monthly fee statements, billing records, time records, and invoices.[15] Although no Texas case could be found, other jurisdictions have allowed legal assistant salary and market rate survey results;[16] and resumes and/or listing of legal assistant credentials[17] to be admitted into evidence to establish proof necessary to allow

Article 9-4 Continued

legal assistant fees to be recovered. In the demonstrative evidence category, attorneys offered exhibits including graphs, charts, and breakdowns as proof.[18] Attorneys have also, in an attempt to make the necessary evidentiary showing, asked the court to take judicial notice of other cases which approved specific market rates for legal assistants and/or approved the task as a substantive paralegal task.[19]

Further analysis of the Texas cases indicates that the evidentiary showing that the courts seem to prefer includes a combination of testimonial and documentary evidence.[20] In most of the cases where the court held that the evidence was sufficient to allow legal assistant fees to be included in the attorney fee award, there was testimonial evidence admitted to support some of the five factors and the evidence in record was not controverted.[21] Although there are some Texas cases which appear to have upheld the inclusion of legal assistant fees even when evidence was lacking as to one or more factors, in those cases the evidence that was presented was uncontroverted.[22] The factors that the courts have not been as focused on seem to be the qualifications of the legal assistant and the specific description of the substantive nature of the paralegal task involved. In most of the cases where the court disallowed the inclusion of the legal assistant fee, the evidence was held to be insufficient because it was vague or non-existent on the following three factors: the substantive work was done by the legal assistant under the supervision of the attorney, the hourly rate charged and its reasonableness in the market,[23] and the number of hours involved in the task performance.[24]

The law in Texas allowing the recovery of legal assistant fees as a component of attorney fees under certain circumstances and the requirement that there be sufficient evidence to support the award is consistent with the development found at both the state and federal levels. Courts in this decade have struggled with issues relating to the proper evidentiary showing. However, the field continues to evolve. The new question for the millennium will not be whether legal assistant fees are recoverable; rather, whether the court will reduce an attorney fee award because an attorney didn't delegate a paralegal task to a legal assistant and should have. Federal courts and the courts of other states have reduced attorney fee awards because the tasks performed by the attorney were paralegal in nature and should have been delegated to a legal assistant or done by the attorney at a reduced fee.[25] Although to date, no court in Texas has taken that position, it is a trend that needs to be acknowledged.

The recognition by the courts that legal assistants are income-producing members of the professional legal service delivery team, that they perform substantive legal tasks under the supervision of the attorney, and that their fees are properly included as a component in an award of attorney fees has done much to increase the status of the legal assistant profession. As the profession continues to define itself, as consumers of legal services become more aware of the economic benefits of a law firms utilization of competent, professional legal assistants, and as the legal community continues to expand its understanding of the credentials and competencies of qualified legal assistants, the legal assistant profession will attain its goal of being recognized as a [sic] integral part of the legal service delivery team.

1. 11 U.S.C. § 330 (a)(1999)
2. *Missouri v. Jenkins*, 491 U.S. 274, 105 L. Ed. 2d 229, 109 S. Ct. 2463 (1989).
3. *E.g., Mason v. Oklahoma Turnpike Auth.,* 1997 U.S. App. LEXIS 26399; 1997 WL 311880 (10th Cir. 1997); *In re Mullins,* 84 F.3d 459 (D.C. Cir. 1996); *Alter Fin. Corp. v. Citizens & S. Int'l Bank,* 817 F.2d 349 (5th Cir. 1987); *Jacobs v. Mancuso,* 825 F.2d 559 (1st Cir 1987); *Richardson v. Byrd,* 709 F.2d 1016 (5th Cir. 1983), *cert. denied,* 464 U.S. 1009, 104 S. Ct. 527, 78 L. Ed.2d 710 (1983); *Jones v. Armstrong Cork Co.,* 630 F.2d 324 (5th Cir.1980); *U.S. ex. rel. Garibaldi,* 46 F. Supp.2d 546 (E.D. La. 1999); *Corman v. Lifecare Acquisitions Corp.,* 1998 U.S. Dist. LEXIS 5423, 1998 WL 185517 (N.D. Tex.1998).

4. *E.g., Hines v. Hines,* 1997 WL 112346 (Idaho 1997) (Idaho Supreme Court interpreted an Idaho statute and held that fees for paralegal service rendered were not recoverable attorney fees or costs under F.R.C.P. 54(e)(3). The court reasoned that the rationale used by the U.S. Supreme Court in *Missouri v. Jenkins* was not applicable to Idaho.); *Joerger v. Gordon Food Service,* 224 Mich. App. 167, 568 N.W.2d 365 (Mich. Ct. App.1997) (The court acknowledged federal and sister state precedent which recognizes legal assistant fees as a separate element of attorney fees damages but found there was a lack of precedent in Michigan. The court urged the Michigan Legislature and the Supreme Court to address the issue.) *See also,* Annotation, *Attorneys Fees: Cost of Services Provided by Paralegals or the Like as Compensable Element of Award in State Court.* 73 A.L.R. 938.

5. 5 Ill. Comp.Stat.Ann. 70/1.35 (West 1999); Ind. Code § 1-1-4-6 (West 1999) (statutes clarify that a reference in an Act to attorney fee includes paralegal fees, recoverable at market rates).

6. *E.g., Aries v. Palmer Johnson, Inc.,* 153 Ariz. 250, 735 P.2d 1373 (Ariz. Ct. App. 1987); *Continental Townhouses East v. Brockbank,* 152 Ariz. 537, 733 P.2d 1120 (Ariz. Ct. App.1986); *Guinn v. Dotson,* 23 Cal. App. 4th 262, 28 Cal. Rptr.2d 409 (Cal. Ct. App., 1994); *Sundance v. Municipal Court,* 192 Cal. App. 3d 268, 237 Cal. Rptr. 269 (Cal. Ct. App. 1987); *In re First Interstate Bancorp Consolidated Shareholder Litigation,* 1999 Del. Ch. LEXIS 178 (Del. Ch. Aug. 26, 1999); *Sonet v. Plum Creek Timber Co.,* 1999 Del Ch. LEXIS 153 (Del. Ch. Aug.5, 1999); *Hampton Courts Tenants Ass'n v. District of Columbia Rental Housing Comm'n.,* 599 A.2d 1113 (D.C., 1991); *In Re Marriage of Thornton,* 89 Ill. App. 3d 1078, 412 N.E.2d 1336, 45 Ill. Dec. 612 (Ill. App. Ct.1980); *Attorney Grievance Comm'n of Maryland v. Wright,* 306 Md. 93, 507 A.2d 618 (Md. 1986); *Williamette Prod. Credit v. Borg-Warner Acc.,* 75 Or. App. 154, 706 P.2d 577 (Or. Ct. App.1985); *Multi-Moto Corporation v. ITT Commercial Fin.,* 806 S.W.2d 560 (Tex. App.—Dallas 1990); *Gill Savings Ass'n. v. International Supply,* 759 S.W.2d 697 (Tex. App.—Dallas 1988); *Holly Homes Inc. v. Urban Housing Group, Lts.,* 1997 Wash. App. LEXIS 5, 1997 WL 3199 (Wash. Ct. App. Jan. 3, 1997); *Absher Constr. Co. V. Kent Sch. District No. 415,* 79 Wash. App. 841, 917 P.2d 1086 (Wash. App. Div., 1995);. *See also,* Annotation, *Attorneys Fees: Cost of Services Provided by Paralegals or the Like as Compensable Element of Award in State Court.* 73 A.L.R. 938.

7. *Gill Savings Association v. International Supply,* 759 S.W.2d 697 (Tex. App.-Dallas 1988, writ denied).

8. *Id.* at 702.

9. *In the Interest of JLB,* 1999 Tex. App.LEXIS 4901 (Tex. App.—Houston [1st Dist.] July 1, 1999) (statute—T.F.C.); *Chevron Chemical Co. v. Southland Contracting, Inc.,* 1998 Tex. App. LEXIS 5902 (Tex. App.— Dallas Sept. 21, 1998, pet. denied) (statute—D.T.P.A.); *World Help v. Leisure Lifestyles, Inc.,* 977 S.W.2d 662 (Tex. App—Fort. Worth 1998 pet. denied) (loan contract); *In Re Cotton,* 972 S.W.2d 768 (Tex. App.—Corpus Christi 1998, pet. denied) (court sanction under T.R.A.P. 52.11); *Dickerson v. Debarbieris,* 964 S.W.2d 680 (Tex. App.—Houston [14th Dist.] 1998, no pet.) (contract); *Carlson's Hill Country Beverage, L.C. v. Westinghouse Road Joint Venture,* 957 S.W.2d 951(Tex. App.—Austin 1997, no pet.) (lease); *Clary Corp. v. Smith,* 949 S.W.2d 452 (Tex. App.—Fort. Worth, 1997, writ denied) (statute—D.T.P.A.); *Herring v. Bocquet,* 933 S.W.2d 611 (Tex. App.—San Antonio 1996), *rev'd,* 972 S.W.2d 19 (Tex. 1998) (statute—Declaratory Judgment Act); *Stamp-Ad, Inc. v. Barton Raben, Inc.,* 915 S.W.2d 932 (Tex. App.—Houston [1st Dist.], 1996, no pet.) (contract); *Contour Construction and Land Corp. v. Baxer County et al.,* 1996 Tex. App. LEXIS 3585 (Tex. App. San Antonio Aug. 14, 1996, no writ)(not designated for publication)) (construction contract); *Law Offices of Rodney K. Elkins v. Alexander,* 1996 Tex. App. LEXIS 1371 (Tex. App.— Dallas March 8, 1996) (not designated for publication) (contract); *Stewart Title Guaranty Co. v. Aiello,* 911 S.W.2d 463 (Tex. App.—El Paso 1995), *rev'd on other grounds,* 941 S.W.2d 68 (Tex. 1997) (statute—D.T.P.A.); *Richards v. Mena,* 907 S.W.2d 566 (Tex. App.—Corpus Christi 1995, writ dismissed by agr) (statute—Tex. Civil Practice and Remedies Code Sec. 38.004); *Great Global Assurance Co. v. Keltex Property,* 904 S.W.2d 771 (Tex. App.—Corpus Christi 1995, no writ)(statute—Tex. Turnover

Article 9-4 Continued

statute); *Arthur Anderson & Co. v. Perry Equipment Corp.*, 898 S.W.2d 914 (Tex. App.—Houston 1995), rev'd, 1987 Tex. LEXIS 6 (1997) (statute—D.T.P.A.); *Gilvarry v. Catalina*, 1994 Tex. App. LEXIS 1965 (Tex. App. Houston [1st Dist.] Aug. 4, 1994, writ denied) (not designated for publication) (contract); *Hanna v. Godwin*, 876 S.W.2d 454 (Tex. App.—El Paso 1994, no writ) (statute—workers' compensation); *Saxton v. Daggett*, 864 S.W.2d 729 (Tex. App.—Houston [1st Dist.] 1993, no writ) (statute—T.F.C.); *Moody v. EMC Services*, 828 S.W.2d 237 (Tex. App.—Houston [1st Dist.] 1992, writ denied) (construction contract); *Worley v. Butler*, 809 S.W.2d 242 (Tex. App.—Corpus Christi 1990, no writ); *Multi-Moto Corp. v. ITT Commercial Finance*, 806 S.W.2d 560 (Tex. App.—Dallas 1990, writ denied) (commercial financing contract); *Coke v. Coke*, 802 S.W.2d 270 (Tex. App.—Dallas 1990, writ denied) (statute—T.F.C.).

10. *Gill Savings Association v. International Supply*, 759 S.W.2d 697 (Tex. App.—Dallas 1988, writ denied).

11. *Id.*

12. *Supra* at footnote 9.

13. *Chevron Chemical Co.*, 1998 Tex. App. LEXIS 5902 (oral testimony of attorney); *World Help*, 977 S.W.2d 662 (oral testimony of attorney); *In Re Cotton*, 972 S.W.2d 769 (affidavit by attorney); *Dickerson*, 964 S.W.2d 680 (oral testimony of attorney); *Carlson's Hill Country Beverage, L.C.*, 957 S.W.2d 951(oral testimony of attorney); *Clary Corp.*, 949 S.W.2d 452 (oral testimony of attorney); *Herring*, 933 S.W.2d 611 (oral testimony of attorney); *Contour Construction and Land Corp.*, 1996 Tex. App. LEXIS 3585 (oral testimony of attorney and legal assistant); *Law Offices of Rodney K. Elkins*, 1996 Tex. App. LEXIS 1371 (oral testimony of attorney); *Stewart Title Guaranty Co.*, 911 S.W.2d 463 (oral testimony of attorneys); *Richards*, 907 S.W.2d 566 (oral testimony of attorneys); *Great Global Assurance Co.*, 904 S.W.2d 771 (oral testimony of attorney); *Gilvarry*, 1994 Tex. App. LEXIS 1965 (oral testimony of attorney); *Hanna*, 876 S.W.2d 454 (oral testimony of attorney); *Saxton*, 864 S.W.2d 729 (oral testimony of attorney); *Worley*, 809 S.W.2d 242 (oral testimony of attorney and client); *Multi-Moto Corp.*, 806 S.W.2d 560 (oral testimony of attorney); *Coke*, 802 S.W.2d 270 (oral testimony of attorney); *Gill Savings Association*, 759 S.W.2d 697 (oral testimony of attorney).

14. *In the Interest of JLB*, 1999 Tex. App. LEXIS 4901; *Stamp-Ad, Inc.*, 915 S.W.2d 932; *Arthur Anderson & Co.*, 898 S.W.2d 914.

15. *Chevron Chemical Co.*, 1998 Tex. App. LEXIS 5902 (invoices referenced but were not in evidence); *Dickerson*, 964 S.W.2d 680 (invoices); *Carlson's Hill Country Beverage, L.C.*, 957 S.W.2d 951 (fee billing statement); *Stamp-Ad, Inc.*, 915 S.W.2d 932 (time records); *Richards*, 907 S.W.2d 566 (time records); *Gilvarry*, 1994 Tex. App. LEXIS 1965 (billing statements); *Saxton*, 864 S.W.2d 729 (invoices); *Moody*, 828 S.W.2d 237 (invoices); *Multi-Moto Corp.*, 806 S.W.2d 560 (billing records); *Gill Savings Association*, 759 S.W.2d 697 (monthly fee statements).

16. *See e.g., Allen v. City of Chicago*, 1997 U.S. Dist. LEXIS 1299 (N.D. Ill.1997) (National Law Journal surveys).

17. *See e.g.,* Tirado v. Erosa, 1997 U.S. Dist. LEXIS 2753 (S.D.N.Y. March 6, 1997) (discussed lack of affidavit or resume specifying credentials).

18. *Dickerson*, 964 S.W.2d 680 (exhibit referenced as a breakdown of each income producers time, rate, total fee); *Coke*, 802 S.W.2d 270 (exhibit described as a summary of services rendered).

19. *In the Interest of JLB*, 1999 Tex. App. LEXIS 4901 (stipulations of parties as to qualifications, reasonableness of fees, and what substantive legal work required to represent clients); *Dickerson*, 964 S.W.2d 680 (court was asked to consider transcripts, pleadings, and motions on file); *Richards*, 907 S.W.2d 566 (argued that Tx. Civil Practice and Remedies Code Sec. 38.004 (Vernon's 1986) allows judicial notice of reasonableness of rates and hours and expert testimony is not required); *See also, Barvick v. Cisneros*, 1997 U.S. Dist. LEXIS 10904 (D. Kan. July 18, 1997) (Court cites prior cases as establishing reasonable market rate for legal assistant); *Lirette v. Delchamps*, 1997 U.S. Dist. LEXIS 8963 (E.D. La. June 25, 1997) (court referenced local cases finding various hourly rates to be reasonable); *Tirado*, 1997 U.S. Dist. LEXIS 2753 (referenced other cases).

20. *Clary Corp.*, 949 S.W.2d 452 (fee disallowed-evidence offered was only general attorney testimony); *Law Offices of Rodney K. Elkins*, 1996 Tex. App. LEXIS 1371 (fee disallowed-only evidence offered was attorney testimony); *Moody*, 828 S.W.2d 237 (fee disallowed-only evidence offered were invoices); *Gill Savings Association*, 759 S.W.2d 697 (evidence insufficient-only evidence offered was attorney testimony and monthly fee statements that were vague). *See supra* at footnote 21 for listing of fee allowed cases.

21. *In the Interest of JLB*, 1999 Tex. App. LEXIS 4901 (expert testimony and stipulations to qualifications); *World Help*, 977 S.W.2d 662 (fact witness testimony, uncontroverted); *In Re Cotton*, 972 S.W.2d 769 (uncontroverted affidavit of attorney); *Dickerson*, 964 S.W.2d 680 (fact witness testimony of attorney, invoices, transcripts, pleading documents, and breakdown chart of income producers); *Carlson's Hill Country Beverage, L.C.*, 957 S.W.2d 951 (fact witness testimony by attorney, fee billing statements, uncontroverted); *Herring*, 933 S.W.2d 611 (fact witness testimony of attorney); *Stamp-Ad, Inc.* 915 S.W.2d 932 (expert testimony and time records); *Contour Construction and Land Corp.*, 1996 Texas App. LEXIS 3585 (fact witness testimony of attorney and legal assistant); *Stewart Title Guaranty Co.*, 911 S.W.2d 463 (fact witness testimony of attorney, uncontroverted); *Richards*, 90 S.W.2d 566 (fact witness testimony from attorneys, judicial notice of many exhibits [not described], uncontroverted); *Great Global Assurance Co.*, 904 S.W.2d 771 (fact witness testimony of attorney, uncontroverted); *Arthur Anderson & Co.*, 898 S.W.2d 914 (expert witness testimony, uncontroverted); *Gilvarry*, 1994 Tex. App. LEXIS 1965 (fact witness testimony of attorney and billing statements); *Hanna*, 876 S.W.2d 454 (fact witness testimony of attorneys); *Saxton*, 864 S.W.2d 729 (fact witness testimony of attorney and invoice); *Worley*, 809 S.W.2d 242 (fact witness testimony by attorney and client, uncontroverted); *Coke*, 802 S.W.2d 270 (fact witness testimony and summary of services exhibit).

22. In the following cases the Texas court did not discuss any evidence that was presented relative to one or more of the five factors: *World Help*, 977 S.W.2d 662 (no discussion of evidence presented on qualifications but evidence presented was not controverted); *In Re Cotton*, 972 S.W.2d 769 (court described affidavit as including information on amount of time expended; court did not discuss evidence of qualification of legal assistant or the substantive nature of tasks performed); *Dickerson*, 964 S.W.2d 680 (Court did not discuss any evidence presented concerning qualifications); *Carlson's Hill Country Beverage, L.C.*, 957 S.W.2d 951 (Court did not discuss evidence of qualifications but evidence uncontroverted); *Herring*, 933 S.W.2d 611 (Court discussed the compensable nature of conferences held by attorneys and legal assistants. Court did not discuss evidence presented on any other factor); *Stamp-Ad, Inc.*, 915 S.W.2d 932 (Court did not discuss evidence of legal assistant qualifications); *Stewart Title Guaranty Co.*, 911 S.W.2d 463 (Court did not discuss evidence of qualification of legal assistant and court allowed fee award for legal assistant duties that were generally described in attorney fact witness testimony as "drafted pleadings and kept him organized); *Great Global Assurance Co.*, 904 S.W.2d 771 (Court cited testimony that seven legal assistants had worked on the case but did not discuss any of the five factors as applied to legal assistants); *Arthur Anderson & Co.*, 898 S.W.2d 914 (Court did not discuss legal assistant qualifications); *Gilvarry*, 1994 Tex. App. LEXIS 1965 (Court did not discuss legal assistant qualifications); *Hanna*, 876 S.W.2d 454 (only evidence discussed was number of hours by legal assistant); *Saxton*, 864 S.W.2d 729 (Court did not discuss qualifications of legal assistant); *Worley*, 809 S.W.2d 242 (no evidence of legal assistant qualifications discussed); *Coke*, 802 S.W.2d 270 (no evidence of legal assistant qualifications discussed but evidence uncontroverted). *But see, Chevron Chemical Co.*, 1998 Tex. App. LEXIS 5902 (court reviewed evidence presented regarding the legal assistant rate and the lack of identity of the legal assistant but found no evidence that jury had included the legal assistant time in the fee award and upheld award); *Clary Corp.*, 949 S.W.2d 452

Article 9-4   Continued

(fact witness testimony too general—no evidence of qualifications, total amount of fees, hourly billing rate, number of hours, no details of substantive nature of tasks performed); *Multi-Moto Corp.*, 806 S.W.2d 560 (fee allowed notwithstanding lack of evidence on each factor because there was a failure to object or to offer special instructions).

23. The Texas courts have approved the following legal assistant hourly rates as reasonable market rates: *In the Interest of JLB*, 1999 Tex. App. LEXIS 4901 ($90); *Chevron Chemical Co.*, 1998 Tex. App. LEXIS 5902 ($80 based on fact witness testimony however, court found that there was no evidence that jury included the legal assistant fee in the attorney fee award); *World Help*, 977 S.W.2d 662 ($55); *Carlson's Hill Country Beverage, L.C.*, 957 S.W.2d 951 ($60); *Stamp-Ad, Inc.*, 915 S.W.2d 932 ($35); *Contour Construction and Land Corp.*, 1996 Tex. App. LEXIS 3585 ($60); *Law Offices of Rodney K. Elkins*, 1996 Tex. App. LEXIS 1371 (testimony offered was $25–$45.00—court disallowed fee on other basis); *Worley*, 809 S.W.2d 242 ($25).

24. *Clary Corp.*, 949 S.W.2d 452 (fee disallowed-evidence offered was attorney testimony which was too general and vague); *Law Offices of Rodney K.Elkins*, 1996 Tex. App. LEXIS 1371 (fee disallowed-only evidence offered was attorney testimony in a general sense that legal assistant had worked on case and what rate would have been); *Moody*, 828 S.W.2d 237 (fee disallowed-only evidence offered were invoices which did not describe in detail the substantive nature of the work, the extent of the work, or the reasonableness of the tasks or the time); *Gills* [sic] *Savings Association*, 759 S.W.2d 697 (evidence insufficient—only evidence offered was attorney testimony and monthly fee statements that were vague, did not identify who performed the tasks, their qualifications, the substantive nature of the tasks, or the hourly rate for the legal assistant).

25. *E.g., Smith v. Roher*, 954 F. Supp. 359 (D.C. Cir. 1997); *Tirado*, 1997 U.S. Dist. Lexis 2753; *Miller v. Chater, Commissioner of Social Security*, 1997 U.S. Dist. Lexis 2837 (N.D.N.Y. Mar. 10, 1997); *Dimension Graphics, Inc. v. Paradise Magazine*, 1997 WL 298444 (D. Kan.) (May 27, 1997); *Holland v. Chrysler Corp.*, 1997 WL 256037 (E.D. Pa.) (May 9, 1997); *Barvick*, 1997 WL 417994; *Keller v. Illinois High Sch. Ass'n*, 1997 U.S. Dist. Lexis 7437 (1997); *Bourgal v. Atlas Transit Mix Corp.*, 196 WL 75290 (E.D.N.Y.) (Feb. 7, 1996); *In re Narragansett Clothing Co. Garb, Trustee, v. Marshall*, 210 B.R. 493 (1st Cir. BAP (R.I.) (1997); *In re Music Merchants, Inc. & Malpass*, 208 B.R. 944 (9TH Cir. BAP (Cal.) 1997); *In re Smuggler's Beach Properties, Inc.*, 149 B.R. 740, 745 (Bankr. D. Mass. 1993) (fee application should have been compiled by a paralegal not the attorney); *In re Kroh Bros. Development Co.*, 105 B.R. 515, 529 (Bankr. W.D. Mo., 1989) (administrative matters could and should have been performed by a legal assistant); *Foxley Cattle Co. v. Grain Dealers Mut. Ins. Co.*, 142 F.R.D. 677, 681 (S.D. Iowa 1992) (Motion to Dismiss/Compel Compliance could have been prepared by a legal assistant); *Attorney Grievance Comm'n. of Maryland v. Wright*, 507 A.2d 618, 622 (Md. 1986) (closing accounts, paying inheritance taxes should have been performed by paraprofessionals).

Vicki Kelly Brittain is an associate professor of political science at Southwest Texas State University in San Marcos. She earned a B.A. at Southwestern College and J.D. from Washburn University.

Consistent with its analysis of the reasonableness of the time spent per task by the attorney, the court, in making its determination of whether a fee for a specific task performed by a legal assistant should be recovered and at what rate, will also focus on the reasonableness of the time the legal assistant took to perform the task and the reasonableness of the legal assistant's fee for that task. To make this determination the court typically considers the customary time and fee rate as the market standard and rate in the community. In *Sundance v. Municipal Court*, the court stated that "awards of attorneys' fees for paralegal time have become commonplace, largely without protest . . . the amount of the award is to be made on the basis of the reasonable market value of the services rendered, and not on the salary paid."[22] This holding is consistent with the federal precedent established in *Missouri v. Jenkins* (see full text of opinion set out in Article 9-1).

CONCLUSION

As can be seen from this discussion, the legal assistant profession made substantial headway toward its goals of recognition and professional status during the 1980s and 1990s by obtaining favorable rulings relating to allowing recovery of legal assistant fees as an element of attorneys' fees and/or costs. This position is well established at the federal level. The trend is strong at the state level, although in some states where the issue has not yet been addressed it remains a gray area. The impact of this issue on the growth of the legal assistant profession is huge. It ties in with the fundamental legal assistant identity and regulation issues and, as such, is an issue that the profession must continue to address on the national, state, and local levels.

DISCUSSION QUESTIONS

1. Do you believe that courts should reduce attorney fee awards if the task performed by the attorney could have been delegated to a qualified, competent legal assistant?

2. In light of the documentation requirements to prove recoverablility of legal assistant fees, should a legal assistant maintain time records even though the legal assistant may not be working in a legal working environment that bills a client hourly for attorney and legal assistant time (such as a traditional plaintiff's law firm that is compensated by contingent fee rather than hourly fee, a corporate legal department, or an administrative agency)?

ENDNOTES

[1] In 1978, the federal bankruptcy law was rewritten to include a provision that the bankruptcy court could award reasonable compensation for actual, necessary services rendered by a paraprofessional employed by a trustee or attorney. 11 U.S.C. Sec. 330 (a).

[2] *Missouri v. Jenkins*, 491 U.S. 274, 105 L. Ed. 2d 229, 109 S. Ct. 2463 (1989).

[3] Illinois Rev. Stat. Ch. 5, para. 70/1.35 (1996); Indiana Code Sec. 1-1-4-6 (1993) (statutes clarify that a reference in an Act to attorney fee includes paralegal fees, recoverable at market rates).

[4] *E.g., Guinn v. Dotson*, 23 Cal. App. 4th 262 (1994); *Sundance v. Municipal Court*, 192 Cal. App. 3d 268, 237 Cal. Rptr. 26 (1987); *Hampton Courts Tenants Ass'n v. District of Columbia Rental Housing Comm'n*, 599 A.2d 1113 (D.C. 1991); *Attorney Grievance Comm'n of Maryland v. Wright*, 507 A.2d 618 (Md. 1986); *Multi-Moto Corp. v. ITT Commercial Finance*, 806 S.W.2d 560 (Tex. App.—Dallas 1990); *Gill Savings Ass'n v. International Supply*, 759 S.W.2d 697 (Tex. App.—Dallas 1988); *Absher Construction Co. v. Kent School District No. 415*, 79 Wn. App. 829 (Wash. App. Div. 1995); *Holly Homes Inc. v. Urban Housing Group*, Lts. 1997 WL 3199 (Wash. App. Div. 1995). *See also* 73 A.L.R. 938, annot., *Attorneys Fees: Cost of Services Provided by Paralegals or the Like as Compensable Element of Award in State Court.*

[5] *E.g., Hines v. Hines*, 1997 WL 112346 (1997) (Idaho Supreme Court interpreted an Idaho statute and held that fees for paralegal service rendered were not recoverable attorney fees or costs under I.R.C.P. 54 (e) (3). The court reasoned that the rationale used by the U.S. Supreme Court in *Missouri v. Jenkins* was not applicable to Idaho.); *Joerger v. Gordon Food Service*, 224 Mich. App. 167 (1997) (The court acknowledged federal and sister state precedent that recognizes legal assistant fees as a separate element of attorney fees damages but found there was a lack of precedent in Michigan. The court urged the Michigan legislature and the supreme court to address the issue.) *See also* 73 A.L.R. 938, annot., *Attorneys*

Fees: Cost of Services Provided by Paralegals or the Like as Compensable Element of Award in State Court.

[6] *E.g., Allen v. City of Chicago*, 197 U.S. Dist. Lexis 1299 (1997); *Lirette v. Delchamps, Inc.*, 1997 WL 358124 (E.D. La. 1997); *Smith v. Roher*, 1997 U.S. Dist. Lexis 1411 (1997); *Tirado v. Erosa*, 1997 U.S. Dist. Lexis 2753 (1997); *Miller v. Chater, Comm'r of Social Security*, 1997 U.S. Dist. Lexis 2837 (1997); *Dimension Graphics, Inc. v. Paradise Magazine*, 1997 WL 298444 (D. Kan. 1997); *Holland v. Chrysler Corp.*, 1997 WL 256037 (E.D. Pa. 1997); In re Narragansett Clothing Co. Garb, *Trustee v. Marshall*, 1997 WL348926 (1st Cir. BAP R.I. 1997); In re Music Merchants, Inc. & Malpass, 208 B.R. 944 (1997); *Barvick v. Cisneros*, 1997 WL 417994 (D. Kan. 1997); *Keller v. Illinois High Sch. Ass'n*, 1997 U.S. Dist. Lexis 7437 (1997); *Mason v. Oklahoma Turnpike Auth.*, 1997 WL 311880 (USCA 10th Cir. Okla. 1997); *People Who Care v. Rockford Bd. of Educ.*, Sch. Dist. No. 205, 90 F.3d 1307 (1996); *Berchin v. General Dynamics Corp.*, 1996 WL 465752 (S.D.N.Y. 1996); *Bourgal v. Atlas Transit Mix Corp.*, 196 WL 75290 (E.D.N.Y. 1996); *Berry v. New York Dep't of Corr. Servs.*, 947 F. Supp. 647 (N.Y. 1996); In re Continental Illinois Sec. Litig., 750 F. Supp. 868 (N.D. Ill. 1990).

[7] *Gill Sav. Ass'n v. Int'l Supply Co.*, 759 S.W.2d 697 (Tex. App.—Dallas 1988).

[8] *Multi-Moto Corp. v. ITT Commercial Fin.*, 806 S.W.2d 560 (Tex. App.—Dallas 1990).

[9] *Absher Constr. Co. v. Kent Sch. Dist. No. 415*, 79 Wn. App. 829 (Wash. App. 1995) and confirmed in *Absher Constr. Co. v. Kent Sch. Dist. No. 415*, 917 P.2d 1086 (Wash. App. 1996).

[10] *E.g., id.* See also, *Glen Cmty. Ass'n v. Kalaman*, 1996 WL 742394 (Wash App. Div. 1 1996); *Allen v. USDC for the N. Dist. of Illinois*, E. Div., (IL 1997); *Pierce Couch Hendrickson, Baysinger & Green v. Henry J. Freede*, 1997 Okla. Lexis 29 (OK 1997); *Dayco Products v. McLane*, 1997 WL 111326 (Fla. App. 1 Dist. 1997).

[11] *E.g., Smith v. Roher*, 1997 U.S. Dist. Lexis 1411 (1997); *Tirado v. Erosa*, 1997 U.S. Dist. Lexis 2753 (1997); *Miller v. Chater, Commissioner of*

Social Security, 1997 U.S. Dist. Lexis 2837 (1997); *Dimension Graphics, Inc. v. Paradise Magazine*, 1997 WL 298444 (D. Kan. 1997); *Holland v. Chrysler Corp.*, 1997 WL 256037 (E.D. Pa. 1997); In re *Narragansett Clothing Co. Garb, Trustee, v. Marshall*, 1997 WL348926 (1st Cir. BAP (R.I. 1997); In re Music Merchants, Inc. & Malpass, 208 B.R. 944 (1997); *Barvick v. Cisneros*, 1997 WL 417994 (D. Kn.) (1997); *Keller v. Illinois High School Ass'n.*, 1997 U.S. Dist. Lexis 7437 (1997); *Bourgal v. Atlas Transit Mix Corp.*, 196 WL 75290 (E.D.N.Y. 1996); In re Smuggler's Beach Properties, Inc., 149 B.R. 740, 745 (Bankr. D. Mass., 1993) (fee application should have been compiled by a paralegal, not the attorney); In re Kroh Bros. Development Co., 105 B.R. 515, 529 (Bankr. W.D. Mo. 1989) (administrative matters could and should have been performed by a legal assistant); *Foxley Cattle Co. v. Grain Dealers Mut. Ins. Co.*, 142 F.R.D. 677, 681 (S.D. Iowa 1992) (Motion to Dismiss/Compel Compliance could have been prepared by a legal assistant); *Attorney Grievance Comm'n of Maryland v. Wright*, 507 A.2d 618, 622 (Md. 1986) (closing accounts, paying inheritance taxes should have been performed by paraprofessionals).

12 In re Smuggler's Beach Properties, Inc., 149 B.R. 740, 743 (Bankr. D. Mass. 1993).

13 In re S.T.N. Enterprises, Inc., 70 B.R. 823, 842 (Bankr. D. Vt. 1987).

14 *Id.* at 842, fn16. *See also* In re Ginji Corp., 117 B.R. 983, 993–994, (Bankr. D. Nev.) (work which was done by an attorney which should have been done by a paralegal or nonprofessional should be billed at the lower rate); *Hampton Courts Tenants Ass'n v. District of Columbia Rental Housing Comm'n*, 599 A.2d 113, 1118 fn 14 (D.C. 1991) (quoting from 724 R.2d 211, 220–221, "Hours are not reasonably expended . . . if an attorney takes extra time due to inexperience, or if an attorney performs tasks that are normally performed by paralegals, clerical personnel or other nonattorneys.")

15 In re Belknap, Inc, 103 B.R. 842, 845 (Bankr. W.D. Ky., 1989)

16 *Absher Constr. Co. v. Kent Sch. Dist.*, *supra* note 9.

17 *Allen v. City of Chicago*, 1997 U.S. Dist. Lexis 1299 (1997).

18 *People Who Care v. Rockford Bd. of Educ.*, Sch. Dist. No. 205, 90 F.3d 1307 (1996).

19 *Berry v. New York Dep't of Corr. Servs.*, 947 F. Supp. 647 (N.Y. 1996).

20 *Lirette v. Delchamps, Inc.*, 1997 WL 358124 (E.D. La. 1997).

21 *Anderson v. Sec'y of Health and Human Serv.*, 80 F.3d 1500, 1507 (10th Cir. 1996).

22 *Sundance v. Mun. Ct.*, 192 Cal. App. 3d 268, 237 Cal. Rptr. 26 (1987).

The Non-Lawyer/
Non-Legal Assistant Issue

INTRODUCTION

Chapter 1 discusses the confusion created by the occupational titles "independent paralegal," "document preparer," "legal document assistant,"[1] and "legal technician." Generally, these titles refer to individuals who provide services directly to the general public and do not work under the supervision of a licensed attorney. Some courts have also referred to these individuals as "non-lawyer/non-legal assistants." These individuals are *not* legal assistants as defined by the various national organizations (such as the ABA, the NALA, the NFPA, the LAMA, and the AAfPE) because they practice independently of attorneys, they are not supervised by attorneys, and they provide services directly to the public. The movement to allow direct provision of services legal-in-nature to the public by non-lawyers has been referred to as the legal technician movement. It initially began at the behest of consumer advocacy groups such as Help Abolish Legal Tyranny (HALT) and was based on the premise that legal services were too expensive for members of the general public to afford and that made legal services inaccessible to poor and middle-class consumers. Provision of legal-type services directly to the general public by non-lawyers in specific areas of law was proposed as a solution to accessibility problem.

INDEPENDENT PARALEGALS

Article 10-1 addresses the rise of the independent paralegal movement, with its attendant concerns.

The Rise of Independents

Much of the movement toward paralegal regulation has been sparked by the activities of independent paralegals, those who, some allege, provide legal services directly to the public without attorney supervision. Independents typically fire back that they go out of their way to avoid the unauthorized practice of law (UPL) and limit their services to providing legal forms and information. They further argue that their existence opens up legal help to people who otherwise could not afford it. Whatever the merits of either argument, this much is clear: beloved by some and despised by others, both inside and outside the paralegal profession, independent paralegals have been the focus of unceasing attention over the past 15 years.

Virginia Simon is the owner of TLC Paralegal Service in Bakersfield, California. She began her paralegal career 16 years ago in the Kern County District Attorney's Office, working in the Family Support Division. Currently the vice president of the California Association of Independent Paralegals (CAIP), Simon received her paralegal certificate from the Paralegal Institute in Phoenix, Arizona, and has completed course work in advanced family law at Bakersfield Community College.

A decade ago, "there was an attorney who was trying to put us in jail every day," says Simon, "and a bankruptcy trustee sued me and two other paralegals for UPL (the unauthorized practice of law)." The case was dismissed and the paralegals were awarded $200 in attorneys fees. Since that time, Simon has made friends with the bankruptcy trustee and attorney, she says.

Rosemary Furman, owner of the Northside Secretarial Service, received national attention on "60 Minutes" and through a television docudrama for her battles against the Florida State Bar from 1977 to 1984. Charged repeatedly with the UPL, Furman was eventually sentenced to 120 days in jail for assisting in "do-it-yourself" divorce, adoption and other forms-preparation legal services. Twenty hours before she was to begin her sentence, on November 27, 1984, Florida's governor pardoned her, saying, "for millions of people, Rosemary Furman stands for the idea that you shouldn't have to pay a fortune for a simple legal matter."

While there are many other, equally critical issues facing the future of the paralegal profession, the ongoing press coverage afforded individuals providing "paralegal" services forces this particular issue into the limelight regularly. In 1992, the ABA formed the Commission on Non-Lawyer Practice to further study the issue and the impact of non-lawyers offering legal services directly to the public. Ten hearings and 12,000 pages of written statements later, the commission released its report in 1995. (For the report's recommendations and expected impact, see "A Quick Look At . . . " in the November/December 1995 issue of LEGAL ASSISTANT TODAY.)

Many traditional paralegals—meaning those who work under the supervision of an attorney—do not like the automatic affiliation bestowed on them by independent "paralegals." For one thing, many independent service providers have no legal training, background or experience, and simply bestow the title of "paralegal" upon themselves. For another, many paralegals, like Debbie Oaks of Dallas, Texas, say simply: "If you want to be a lawyer, go to law school."

Acknowledging that there are "a lot of people who are indigent that need help, and can't afford to hire an attorney," Patty L. Bondurant, CLA, a paralegal at Brooks, Pierce, McLendon, Humphrey & Leonard, L.L.P., in Greensboro, North Carolina, still fears that

---

Article 10-1   The Issues Affecting Paralegals Then and Now, p. 63–67

Gina Gladwell, The Issues Affecting Paralegals Then and Now, LEGAL ASSISTANT TODAY, Sept./Oct. 1997, at 63–65. Copyright 2002 James Publishing, Inc. Reprinted courtesy of LEGAL ASSISTANT TODAY magazine. For subscription information call (800) 394-2626, or visit www.legalassistanttoday.com.

there are "a lot of freelance paralegals holding themselves out as attorneys, and that's a bad reflection on the paralegal profession."

"The line is so narrow between answering a question on a form and giving legal advice—when the line's that thin, its too easy to step over it," agrees W. Susan Jones, a paralegal with the Benker Law Firm in Visalia, California. "We regularly have to go back and file motions to try and fix things that were either left out, ignored or handled incorrectly, either because the legal technician didn't know the law, or was unable to tell the client the law as it relates to their case."

California is one of a handful of states that regularly considers expanding the role of non-lawyers in providing legal services, legally, with proper monitoring, licensing and regulation. Simon, for one, believes that her services are invaluable to ensuring that access to justice is provided to the many people who need it. "There's a lot of people who absolutely can't afford even the small price we charge," she says. "(CAIP) set up a program with the Alliance Against Family Violence because of this, and each Kern County CAIP member provides two free restraining orders each month.

"We are not mini-lawyers and don't want to be," she adds. "I learned, especially through the advanced family law course, that there are matters more complex than I can handle, and I learned to spot them so that I can refer the customer to an attorney."

A good number of paralegals, managers, attorneys and educators believe it is only a matter of time before independent paralegal services are permitted for various, "simple" legal matters such as drafting wills or preparing bankruptcy or tax forms. Currently, 22 states allow some form of limited non-lawyer practice (see "News & Trends—National UPL Survey," LEGAL ASSISTANT TODAY, November/December 1996).

"The legal system is based on self help if you desire it. I think that's what the independent paralegals are providing—a better form of self help," says Thomas C. Holmes, a paralegal at Lane Powell Spears Lubersky, L.L.P. in Portland, Oregon. "They're providing you with forms, and knowledge of procedure, that will help you in the legal system. It's worth more to the public to have that available than to be forced to engage an attorney."

Paralegals, he adds, are "experts in procedure. What the current problem is in Oregon is that we have no regulation, so it's a grab bag—you have no idea what you're getting when you hire an independent paralegal."

Kim Kirkpatrick, CLA, a paralegal at Fingal Fahrney & Clark, L.L.P. in Newport Beach, California, says the same problem exists everywhere. "There's been a lot of publicity on this issue because the public has used these people and they've gotten angry because they didn't get the level of service they thought they were going to get," she says. "They thought they were going to get an attorney for a non-attorney price."

Stacey Hunt, CLA, a paralegal at Andre Morris & Buttery in San Luis Obispo, California, voices a popular sentiment about what the future may hold for independents: an entirely "independent" classification.

"I think there's a great need for them, but I think they are doing something different than what I view traditional paralegals doing," says Hunt. "I see them as a separate profession."

In the meantime, many more independent "paralegals" are likely to find themselves as defendants in a lawsuit or the bane of local attorneys—like Rosemary Furman before them—until sufficient regulations and standards regarding qualifications and services are in place.

For Simon, however, it will simply be business as usual. "I have worked very hard to earn (professional respect) in Kern County. We have made a practice of trying to meet with the county commissioners to let them know who we are and how we can make their jobs easier, and we have made the family law lawyers aware of CAIP and all the courses we take," she says. "I have become known, and attorneys refer cases to me. Likewise, we make sure we refer to attorneys."

Article 10-2 summarizes the results of a survey on independent paralegal services and the unauthorized practice of law concerns.

What You Had To Say:
Independent Paralegals

By Gina Farrell Gladwell

A majority say that paralegals can provide non-supervised legal services if clear regulations and standards are established.

Some people say that independent paralegal services will hurt the poor. Others believe they can provide much needed access to legal services for low-income families. The American Bar Association has not yet released the final opinion of their Commission on Nonlawyer Practice. But paralegals have made their opinions known—66 percent say paralegals should be permitted to provide defined legal services to the public without attorney supervision.

LEGAL ASSISTANT TODAY's November/December 1994 survey on independent paralegal services and the unauthorized practice of law (UPL) brought nearly 400 responses from paralegals, legal secretaries, students, teachers and attorneys across the country who spoke out on the benefits, drawbacks and important issues surrounding non-attorney legal services and their place in the legal arena.

In total, 68 percent of all respondents say that paralegals should be able to work without attorney supervision in some instances, though one in five say such services should be extremely limited. Another 30 percent say they do not support the idea of unsupervised provision of services, and 2 percent were undecided on the issue.

Respondents overwhelmingly agree that the legal system needs to provide more affordable and accessible services to consumers. "There are many mid- and low-income people who don't have access to legal representation because of the cost," says one litigation paralegal. "Independent paralegals would help fill that gap. There are many routine matters that paralegals could handle without direct attorney supervision."

Those who oppose the idea of independents also say that access is important. The issue, they argue, is making services affordable within the context of the current system. "A good working relationship between a paralegal and a supervising attorney will produce quality legal services at a reduced rate to the client without jeopardizing the client's rights or the profitability of the provider," says one bankruptcy/probate paralegal from Idaho.

Agrees another: "Paralegals working in law offices best serve the public. Paralegals do not have sufficient education to make independent judgment calls that could have an effect on someone's life or livelihood."

Are Paralegals "Independent" Now?

But many paralegals maintain that they are performing substantive legal services in their current positions anyway—even in traditional law-office support roles. "No matter how

---

Article 10-2   Independent Paralegals: What You Had To Say

Gina Gladwell, What You Had to Say: Independent Paralegals, LEGAL ASSISTANT TODAY, May/June 1995, at 62–67. Copyright 2002 James Publishing, Inc. Reprinted courtesy of LEGAL ASSISTANT TODAY magazine. For subscription information call (800) 394-2626, or visit www.legalassistanttoday.com.

one looks at it, the paralegal does the work of an attorney anyhow," says one civil litiga-tion paralegal. "The only drawback is that it is placing lawyers in a place they're not happy with!"

"I'm doing all of my boss's (attorney's) work, including writing motions and interview-ing clients; just using his name on everything," agrees another.

Over the past decade, legal assistant roles have expanded to the point where it is difficult to label the profession restrictively. In their *Discussion Draft for Comment: Nonlawyer Practice in the United States*, the ABA Commission on Nonlawyer Practice reports that witnesses to the Commission "testified that the trend within many firms now is to give paralegals signficant latitude in the work they do and that the level of supervision varies greatly."

"Many traditional paralegals testified that they already provide services directly to clients of law firms without any direct supervision by lawyers, including drafting simple wills, conducting title searches and real estate closings, and preparing bankruptcy petitions and tax forms," says the report.

An attorney respondent to *LAT*'s survey confirms such activities: "My paralegals cur-rently perform tasks of client interviewing and drafting simple wills and documents for uncontested divorces," he says. "I merely review notes and sign documents, (though) I do meet with clients to insure all bases have been covered and to explain the law to them."

In fact, say many, a paralegal's job is largely performing the substantive work for a case that will be turned over to an attorney for review and signatures only. If the attorney is an entry-level associate with little to no experience, then the major different in his or her qualifications is a juris doctorate degree.

"I've seen many paralegals with a better knowledge of the law in some areas than attor-neys with more years of practicing," says a 10-year litigation veteran. "Attorneys can say all they want that it is not about the money, but it is; otherwise the middle class would be receiving help."

Many lawyers emphatically deny that money is the issue. "There's a perception that lawyers are interested in turf protection, but the lawyers I talk with are not saying that," Armstrong, McCullen & Philpott attorney Owen McCullen told *LAT* last fall. "They're not concerned about the loss of business. They're concerned about peole who get themselves hurt and then come to a lawyer with a mess that can't be solved."

The ABA's Model Rules of Professional conduct, Rule 5.5, professes the same concern for consumers: "Limiting the practice of law to members of the bar protects the public against rendition of legal services by unqualified persons."

But the majority of survey respondents remain unconvinced. "The public gets incom-petent representation now, and pays a lot for what it gets," says a personal injury parale-gal with seven years' experience. "The benefits of making the legal system much more affordable greatly outweigh any drawbacks; and we all know that lawyers will scrutinize the independents very closely!"

Gauging Competency

Opinions on paralegal competency are divided. While nearly 70 percent of respondents say that paralegals are qualified to provide "scrivner" services for the public—essentially typ-ing and filling in forms with information provided by clients, or recording statements by clients—without attorney oversight, only 59 percent say that paralegals should provide expanded services. The main reasons: a lack of qualifications and absence of regulations and standards to ensure the public's protection.

"Paralegals are paralegals, not attorneys. If they want to independently practice law then they should go to law school," says a paralegal/adjunct professor of family law. "The paralegal profession is not designed for independent practice. We are not trained to know all the nuances and ramifications of the law. To open up this area screams for abuse of the public/consumer."

"There is currently no protection for the public for wrongdoings," agrees a nine-year paralegal. "At least with attorneys you can sue for malpractice."

Others say this doesn't have to be the case; consumer protection can be ensured through various other channels. "(A) self-serving concern for liability should minimize this problem," says one paralegal.

"I believe a competent legal assistant knows when she's in over her head and will refer those cases out," says another.

And respondents say with little exception that if paralegals are ever to offer services independently, stringent qualifications should be required. A combined 68 percent would mandate a minimum number of years' experience under a supervising attorney (28 percent say two years minimum, 40 percent say five years minimum); 62 percent would mandate state certification; and a whopping 74 percent say that a degree is necessary (26 percent advocate a two-year degree; 48 percent a four-year degree).

"By having high standards, it would eliminate these 'fly by night' people who call themselves paralegals," says a product liability/personal injury paralegal. "I have eight years' experience, a four-year degree, a one-year certificate, and am set to take the NALA (National Association of Legal Assistants) exam. All of this should be required to eliminate those not seriously qualified."

Agrees another: "With the proper training and oversight (combination of a four-year degree, state licensing and at least five years' paralegal experience under attorney supervision), qualified paralegals should be able to use their talents to the highest possible level."

A 'Two-Tier' Approach to Legal Services

The bottom-line issue seems to be whether legal services can be adequately provided at two levels. After all, paralegals are, simply put, not attorneys.

"This is a disservice to the public. A two-tier approach to the law means that if you have the money you can afford a lawyer; if not, then you can only afford a legal technician," says one litigation paralegal with 10 years' experience.

"Allowing paralegals to practice law undermines the attorney's profession. What then would be the purpose of going to law school?" asks another.

The medical community has had to ask itself the same question. Many individuals forgo much needed medical attention because the cost is too high, and physicians acknowledge this problem can lead to higher risks for patients and higher long-term costs for the American public.

One answer to this health care access problem has been an increased use of nurse practitioners and the creation of positions such as "nurse extenders"—or "cross-trained employees who perform many of the less-technical tasks once handled by RNs," (*Nursing94*, "The Changing Job Market: Views from the West," August 1994).

Law firms, too, have begun to categorize positions within the paralegal ranks. At Nelson Mullins Reilly and Scarbourough in Columbia, NC, for example, "project assistants" are used for Bates stamping and indexing tasks so that firm paralegals have time for more substantive duties.

But, can there be two levels of services—especially if one level is provided *without* attorney supervision?

"Yes," says one four-year paralegal from Wyoming. "If a system similar to the English system is implemented, paralegals (as solicitors), lawyers (as barristers), legal assistance

Article 10-2 Continued

and representation will become more accessible, while lawyers will be able to move a greater amount of cases through the courts without creating the current congestion."

Agrees another: "Many areas in the medical field are accomplished without a physician's supervision . . . and many specialties assist the physician in diagnosing and treating all types of patients."

To make this work in the legal arena will require a comprehensive system overhaul, however—not to mention an uphill battle by supporters against attorneys who will hear none of it. The New Jersey State Bar Association, for example, passed a resolution last July that condemned the ABA Commission on Nonlawyer Practice for "considering suggestions that certain fields of legal practice be opened to non-lawyers working without lawyer supervision." The resolution came after a review of the Commission's discussion draft, where the Commission took no formal stand but did state: "The Commission heard extensive testimony by witnesses that some non-lawyer practice meets legal needs that are not now being met by lawyers. In this connection, the Commission reviewed legal needs studies documenting the fact that low- and moderate-income persons have unmet legal needs."

Exactly, say supporters. "Most Legal Aid associations provide limited areas of help, such as only handling landlord/tenant disputes," says a paralegal from Oklahoma. "The Department of Human Services legal departments handle only collection of past due child support for clients receiving assistance and are greatly overworked and very understaffed. My county office has approximately 30,000 cases, with only two attorneys" and a handful of support staff.

"Paralegals who provide services directly to the public exist because there is a demand for them," agrees a litigation paralegal from Arizona. "State certification will help protect consumers of legal services."

But lawyers are not alone in their fear of legitimizing non-attorney legal services. NALA, representing over 15,000 members, "does not support the delivery of legal services to the public by paralegals without the supervision of a licensed attorney," (*LAT*, January/February 1995).

Thirty percent of survey respondents agree. "I have seen so many cases where independent 'paralegals' have prepared incorrect or invalid wills that once the person dies the beneficiaries are left out in the cold," says one nine-year estate planning paralegal.

Says another: "I have been working for an attorney for 12 years. I have seen basic documents being prepared by freelance paralegals that are totally incorrect. I don't think services should be rendered directly to the public without the supervision of an attorney. The drawbacks outweigh the benefits (cost savings)."

Setting Standards

Many respondents were quick to point out that the term "paralegal" should be used selectively, since "independent paralegal" reflects on the profession as a whole. "Please do not use the term 'paralegal'—use the term 'nonlawyer,'" a Certified Legal Assistant (CLA) asks.

Says another paralegal, who wants distance from independents: "It's to the public's detriment to use self-described 'independent paralegals' who don't have experience, education or any of the major qualifications it takes to be a professional paralegal."

A lack of definition for the paralegal profession as a whole—and for those who would hold themselves out to be independent paralegals—was a significant drawback cited by both supporters and detractors. "There must be qualified individuals holding themselves out as paralegals," says a 10-year civil litigation paralegal who supports some form of independent services. "(Right now) people can walk in off the street and hold themselves forth as paralegals."

An attorney opposed to independent paralegal services agrees: "Until paralegal training becomes more standardized, it is too risky—anyone calling themselves a paralegal could set up shop, whether or not they have any credentials," he says.

Three of five national associations interviewed by *LAT* in January/February 1995 have adopted no formal definition for paralegals. The two that have—NALA and the National Federation of Paralegal Associations (NFPA)—define paralegals as having education, training and experience in the legal field, and offer guidance on required numbers of educational semester hours. In addition, NALA offers the CLA voluntary nation certification exam, which has tested paralegal competency in various legal areas since 1976, and more recently, NFPA hired Professional Examination Service, an independent testing firm in Portland, OR, to develop the Paralegal Advance Competency Exam (PACE). As yet, however, there is no move by any organization to impose a set criteria and/or testing vehicle— i.e., certification or licensing—that would be *required* for one to be a paralegal, or an independent paralegal—something that more than 60 percent of respondents feel is necessary at least at the state level.

"I feel the state bar and state paralegal associations should work together to regulate independent legal services through testing, CLE, practical experience, etc.," says one practicing paralegal. Overall, more than one-third of respondents (36 percent) felt that regulation should come from state bar associations, another 23 percent from paralegal associations, and 15 percent from the two groups working together.

Avoiding UPL

Another worry for both those in support of and opposed to independent paralegal (non-attorney) services is that non-lawyer practitioners will overstep their bounds into the unauthorized practice of law.

"Since we cannot give legal advice, we are placed in sometimes awkward situations as to what we can and cannot say or do. Some people don't understand this," says one paralegal.

Agrees another: "There is too much danger of practicing law without a license, even in seemingly simple matters. It's too easy to think that you know more than you do."

Indeed, with the wide variations on what constitutes UPL from state to state and opinion to opinion, staying within legal boundaries today can be nearly impossible. In order for independent legal services to be successful, and successfully regulated, very clear guidelines would need to be established and enforced on what specific areas non-lawyers may provide services in, and what specific services they can provide. Inevitably, say some, this will need to include the ability to give limited legal advice.

"I don't think that paralegals can really advise clients of all they need to know without giving 'legal advice.' Legal services entail more than just the filling out of simple forms— even in wills, divorces and bankruptcies," says one corporate paralegal.

One way to make it work came from a former Social Security Disability Insurance (SSDI) examiner and current litigation paralegal, who sees attorneys and independent paralegals working together to improve access and cost-savings. "Wills, divorces and bankruptcies could be on referral from attorneys once it is established that a simple will, uncontested-no issue divorce or straight bankruptcy is in fact appropriate," he says.

And, says another, the scenario can work in reverse: "I see a paralegal more as working with the client, using forms, and then making a referral when and if necessary. A knowledgeable paralegal always knows when he or she is out of their depth legally and should immediately refer any case that warrants it to a specialized attorney."

Article 10-2 Continued

Without supervision? Yes, say many. "In less complex legal processes, generally the paralegal is very familiar with issues and court processes—sufficient to preclude attorney supervision."

But a number of respondents remain unconvinced that attorney oversight can dissappear entirely, even when they support the idea of independent services as a way to make legal aid affordable.

"Just as an obstetrical patient may choose to see a nurse practitioner under the supervision of an M.D., a paralegal must have a supervising attorney *available*," says one paralegal.

Agreed another: "Paralegals should always have a working relationship with an attorney for guidance and reference."

The Future

What the future holds remains, of course, to be seen. Large upheaval to the system is unlikely, but reforming legal-access problems is imminent. The ABA Commission on Nonlawyer Practice may set the stage for such reform in their final report (expected to be released this year). If it doesn't, then paralegals and others will undoubtedly take matters into their own hands.

"I see this as the beginning of major reform in the legal profession—that ultimately, one to two attorneys will oversee and supervise perhaps 10 to 12 (independent) paralegals," says one five-year veteran paralegal.

Says another: "As a paralegal, I intend to become self-employed one day. If paralegals can't work without supervision, then none of us can be self-employed without changing the profession.

"I think those of us who are competent and ambitious should be free to do what we do best, not restricted to having an attorney down the hall. If I had to run to my attorney with each task, I wouldn't consider myself a competent paralegal."

NON-LAWYER PRACTICE

In 1992, the ABA created a commission on non-lawyer practice in response to the perceived need to find a means to make the legal system more accessible to the general public. Subsequently, the ABA began conducting a series of public hearings throughout the United States, taking testimony concerning the pros and cons of non-lawyer practice. In June 1995, the ABA Commission on Nonlawyer Practice released its report with recommendations; excerpts from the report are shown in Article 10-3.

Prior to the ABA report, state legislatures and state bar organizations had begun to consider proposals concerning the regulation of nonlawyer practice.

Article 10-4 summarizes the proposals relating to regulation of non-lawyer practice that were made in the various states through 1999.

(Editor's Note: The complete report issued by the ABA Commission on Nonlawyer Practice is more than 250 pages long. Included in the complete report is an Executive Summary which highlights the Commission's findings and recommendations. Due to space limitations, the following excerpts were taken directly from the Executive Summary. In addition to the Commission's report, there were two minority reports issued. Both minority reports agreed with most of the Commission's recommendations, but disagreed with certain things. The first felt that the Report did not sufficiently emphasize that the protection of the public should be an essential factor in any proposal to increase the public's access to legal services. They disagreed that access to justice should be the paramount goal. The second minority report went even further. They felt that the ABA should take the lead in specifically defining the role of the lawyer and in distinguishing the differences between the lawyer, the paralegal, the legal assistant, the legal technician and the document preparer. They also felt that, given the overabundance of lawyers we have in this country, there are many ways to increase the public's access to justice and provide affordable lawyers, which the majority report ignored. At this time, the Bar has not reponded to the Commission's recommendations and it is uncertain if or when any action will be taken. For information on how to get a copy of the Commission's report and/or the Minority Reports (or just the Executive Summary), you may contact any of the TPJ editorial staff.

In 1992 the ABA established the Commission on Nonlawyer Practice, consisting of lawyers and nonlawyers with diverse backgrounds. The Commission was directed to "conduct research, hearings and deliberations to determine the implications of nonlawyer practice for society, the client and the legal profession."

A series of public hearings were held, beginning in December 1992 and continuing until August, 1994. The information received at the hearings was supplemented with extensive research. The Commission's report, first issued in April 1994 and revised in 1995, was titled "Nonlawyer Practice in the United States: Summary of the Factual Record Before the American Bar Association Commission on Nonlawyer Practice." Part One of the Report details the findings of the Commission. Part Two sets forth the Commission's analysis, conclusions and recommendations.

PART ONE: FINDINGS

Beginning in the 1930s, there were several decades in which the laws governing the unauthorized practice of law (UPL) were aggressively enforced. In the last 20 years, however, there has been a gradual decline in the enforcement of those laws. Today, individuals choose to act on their own behalf in many instances. The Commission found that an extensive array of federal and state administrative agencies allow nonlawyers to provide advice to self-represented persons and even to represent parties in agency proceedings. The Report categorizes these nonlawyers as "legal technicians."

Paralegals, as defined in the Report, are different from legal technicians by virtue of their working under the supervision of lawyers. They often perform complex substantive tasks or provide advice to clients with the supervision of a lawyer or for which a lawyer is accountable. An increasing number of paralegals have higher education, and two national paralegal organizations are urging broad adoption of voluntary certification systems for paralegals.

Article 10-3 ABA June 1995 report

Several states have recently examined nonlawyer activity. State legislatures have considered a wide variety of measures to regulate legal technicians. The thoughtfulness of the varied state task force reports bolsters the Commission's general belief that most of the issues discussed in those reports can best be addressed at the state level.

PART TWO: CONCLUSIONS AND RECOMMENDATIONS

The Commission reached three major conclusions when it analyzed the record:

- Increasing access to affordable assistance in law-related situations is an urgent goal of the legal profession and the states;
- Protecting the public from harm from persons providing assistance in law-related situations is also an urgent goal; and
- When adequate protection for the public is in place, nonlawyers have important roles to perform in providing affordable access to justice.

The most important conclusion of the Commission is that each state should conduct its own careful analytical examination, under the leadership of its supreme court, to determine whether and how to regulate the varied forms of nonlawyer activity that exist or are emerging in its jurisdiction.

The information that led the Commission to these conclusions also led it to formulate six major recommendations and to identify a variety of actions that practicing lawyers, bar associations, courts, law schools, and the federal and state governments might take. Part Two of the Commission's Report sets forth the bases for its conclusions, the recommendations they led to, and the actions that are needed to implement the recommendations.

A. Increasing the Public's Access to the Justice System and to Affordable Assistance with its Legal and Law-Related Needs is an Urgent Goal of the Legal Profession and the States.

B. Steps to Continue Improving Access to Justice.

A major opportunity for enhancing law practice and improving access to legal services involves more extensive utilization of paralegals. The Commission found that lawyers use the services of paralegals in innovative ways to save time and reduce costs to clients. Several lawyers recommended to the Commission that court rules be changed to permit paralegals to appear in court for their law firm employers on routine matters such as calendar calls or previously agreed to matters such as child support calculations and small estate probate hearings.

C. The Protection of the Public from Harm Arising from Incompetent and Unethical Conduct by Persons Providing Legal or Law-Related Services is an Urgent Goal of Both the Legal Profession and the States. When Adequate Protections for the Public are in Place, Nonlawyers have Important Roles to Perform in Providing the Public with Access to Justice.

The record before the Commission makes it clear that the expansion of access to justice through the services of document preparers, legal technicians, or other nonlawyer service providers carries with it both the risk of incompetent or even fraudulent services and the promise of excellent and high quality services. The states will have to take both risk and promise into account in their assessments.

D. As to Nonlawyers Whose Services are not Already Authorized Under Current States or Other Law, the Commission Recommends that States Should Assess Whether and How to Regulate Their Activities. The Commission recommends a specific analytical approach for use by the states in determining what level of regulation, if any, is appropriate. The approach will help in assessing whether a particular activity should be unregulated, regulated, or prohibited.

CONCLUSION

The Commission's Report amply demonstrates that nonlawyers provide services that in many instances impact upon or relate to the practice law . . . The factual findings of the Commission demonstrate that nonlawyers, both as paralegals accountable to lawyers and in other roles permitted by law, have become an important part of the delivery of legal services. This has contributed to improvements in public access to affordable legal services. The work of the Commission has also uncovered imperfections among lawyers in providing professional services that give rise to increasing dissatisfaction with our profession by the public. The delivery of law-related services and their cost is a concern that will be debated by the public, not just by the legal profession. This Report should be viewed by the bar as an opportunity to take those steps that will protect the public and at the same time provide increased access. If this Report is to have any value, it will be in the thoughtful consideration of it by the bar, the judiciary and the public. In the first instance, the bar must continue to take the lead to assure that legal services are rendered in a manner that will enhance public respect for the institutions of justice.

Recommendations

1. The American Bar Association, state, local and specialty bar associations, the practicing bar, courts, law schools, and the federal and state governments should continue to develop and finance new and improved ways to provide access to justice to help the public meet its legal and law-related needs.
2. The range of activities of traditional paralegals should be expanded, with lawyers remaining accountable for their activities.
3. States should consider allowing nonlawyer representation of individuals in state administrative agency proceedings. Nonlawyer representatives should be subject to the agencies' standards of practice and discipline.
4. The American Bar Association should examine its ethics rules, policies and standards to ensure that they promote the delivery of affordable competent services and access to justice.
5. The activities of nonlawyers who provide assistance, advice and representation authorized by statute, court rule or agency regulation should be continued, subject to review by the entity under whose authority the services are performed.
6. With regard to activities of all other nonlawyers, states should adopt an analytical approach in assessing whether and how to regulate varied forms of nonlawyer activity that exist or are emerging in their respective jurisdictions. Criteria for this analysis should include the risk of harm these activities present. The highest courts should take the lead in examining specific nonlawyer activities within their jurisdictions with the active support and participation of the Bar and the public.

Article 10-3   Continued

News Around the Country

Paralegal Regulation

By Pamela Young

The paralegal profession has championed a significant status in our states' and national legal community. As this profession becomes increasingly more adept in providing skillful and necessary assistance to attorneys it desires definition, educational standards, expanded responsibilities and recognition.

At the threshold of the millennium the regulation of this profession is a "hot topic." It is inevitable that every state will adopt some form of regulation involving this profession within the next five to ten years. This is a positive course which will channel future growth and development of the paralegal career.

Regulation of the paralegal profession is a growing topic of discussion in many state legislative bodies and within many paralegal asociation and related organizations. The most familiar terms of regulation include (1) voluntary certification; (2) voluntary registration; and (3) licensure. Other regulatory terms or discussion directives include restriction of the term/use of "legal assistant/paralegal," accreditation, exit assessment, court rules and/or legislative definition.

The majority of the states, through their respective legislative bodies and/or supportive state bar associations, have already adopted a definition of the term "paralegal or legal assistant." Many have already adopted guidelines for utilization. Some states, and paralegal organizations, have incorporated a voluntary certification program where paralegal candidates who meet certain criteria, must pass an exam prior to receiving a special paralegal designation. There is also discussion and activity in some states centering around paralegal licensure.

In the last 15 to 18 months, there has been regulation activity in the following states:

California	Senate Bill 1418 concerning registration of legal document Assistants was signed by the Governor of California in September, 1998. The law became effective January 1, 2000. A legal document assistant is a person who provides or assists in providing any self help services to a member of the public who is representing himself or herself in a legal matter. The legal document assistant can be compensated for these services.
New Jersey	In 1998, the New Jersey Supreme Court Committee on Paralegal Education and Regulation issued a report which sets forth several recommendations concerning attorneys' use of paralegals. The report appears to identify individuals who meet a set of educational requirements and who also pass a written exam on the subject of ethics and to qualify them to work as paralegals under the supervision of licensed attorneys. The Court rejected its own specially appointed Commission's recommendation for mandatory licensing of Legal Assistants. The Court

Article 10-4   News Around the Country: Paralegal Regulation

Pamela Young, News Around the Country: Paralegal Regulation (1999) (unpublished manuscript). Courtesy of Pamela Young.

claimed—whether employed by a law firm or working as independent contractors—work is best done through direct supervision by the attorneys for whom they are working. The Court did encourage the development of a "credentialing" system which would provide a means of recognizing qualified paralegals. The Justices asked the New Jersey State Bar Association to work with paralegal organizations to come up with specific guidelines both for paraprofessionals and for their supervisors.

(In 1994, the Minnesota Legislature considered the same matter as New Jersey, where a special Committee was appointed to study the feasibility of the delivery of legal services by those who would be called specialized legal assistants. The Committee was requested to consider a licensure procedure. A committee report was issued and concluded that *licensing legal assistants does not fit into the analytical framework created by the Minnesota statute because the practice of law is already a regulated profession.*)

Nevada
Nevada Governor Kenny Guinn signed a bill into law on May 28, 1999 increasing the penalty for anyone found guilty of illegally practicing law. The new law will also restrict services offered by paralegals and legal assistants who do not operate under the supervision of an attorney. The new measure becomes effective October 1, 1999.

Florida
On April 9, 1999, Florida's State Bar Board of Governors changed Bar Rule 4.5-3 to now state that persons using either of or similar titles (paralegal or legal assistant) who provide services to the public must work for or under the direction or supervision of a lawyer or an authorized business entity. This rule now goes to the Supreme Court for approval.

The rule change also modifies and expands the responsibilities of legal assistants who are working under the supervision of attorneys. A legal assistant may now perform the duties delegated to them by the supervising attorney without the presence or active involvement of the attorney. However, the attorney will continue to be ultimately held responsible and accountable for the paralegal work product.

Utah
Utah State Bar is studying licensing. Utah, like Texas, has a Legal Assistants Division. To join the Division, an individual must meet certain education or experience requirements. The requirements include completing a paralegal program sanctioned by the ABA; passing an exam given by National Association Of Legal Assistants ("NALA") or another recognized industry group; working at least 5 years as a paralegal under the supervision of a licensed attorney; or holding a bachelor's degree with 2 years' experience as a paralegal. According to Kim Morris of The Department of Commerce the State Of Utah does not plan to license paralegals.

In 1999, Utah Legislature passed a bill creating a Legislative Committee to approve occupations for licensing. At this time no occupations have gone before the Committee.

Maine
Maine Governor signed on June 2, 1999 into law a bill which was enacted by the Maine Legislature that clearly defines the role of para-

Article 10-4 Continued

	legals and legal assistants.

legals and legal assistants.

Legislative Document #724 restricts the use of titles "paralegal" and "legal assistant" to a *person qualified by education training or work experience who is employed by an attorney...or other entity and who performs specifically delegated substantive legal work for which an attorney is responsible.*

Missouri   An ad hoc committee on educational standards for the Missouri State Bar Committee on Paralegals met for the first time in April, 1999 to renew its discussions again and work on developing educational guidelines that will be presented to the Bar for approval. The Paralegal Committee has debated the issue of licensure for more than a decade.

Outside of the United States, there are other provinces involved in the regulation of the paralegal profession:

Ontario, Canada   In 1990 a provincial task force report called for the regulation of paralegals. In a recent 1999 Court of Appeals ruling however relating to a criminal case where a defendant, convicted in 1998 of failing to remain at the scene of an accident after a collision with an off-duty police officer's car, was represented by a paralegal in the criminal case. When the case reached the Ontario Court of Appeals, the Canadian Bar and Ontario's Criminal Lawyers Association intervened asking the Court to declare paralegals cannot represent people charged with crimes. In its decision, the Court ruled parliament had the authority to give nonlawyers the right to act as paid agents for accused people in criminal trials, but imposed a requirement that trial judges can bar paralegals from trials by virtue of their authority to control their courtrooms and

Japan   In 1999, Japan is considering paralegal certification.

National associations, bar associations, legislatures, and supreme courts have addressed the definition of legal assistants and paralegals. In the last decade, there are similarities in the identification and duties and all are consistent with the supervision or direction of an attorney. The ABA amended its definition in 1997:

"A legal assistant or paralegal is a person qualified by education, training or work experience who is employed or retained by a lawyer, law office, corporation, governmental agency or other entity who performs specifically delegated substantive legal work for which a lawyer is responsible."

States introducing similar definitions through legislative bodies are:

Florida, Indiana, Montana, Oklahoma, California, Illinois, Pennsylvania, and Maine

State Supreme Courts addressing the definition and some via bar associations adoption but regulated by Supreme Courts are:

Kentucky, Rhode Island, New Mexico, New Hampshire, South Dakota, Indiana, North Dakota, Virginia.

Bar Associations who have defined legal assistants as qualified and educated individuals working under the supervision of attorneys are the following states:

Alaska, Arizona, California (Santa Barbara Bar), Colorado Connecticut, Florida, Illinois, Iowa, Kansas, Kentucky, Massachusetts, Michigan, Minnesota, Missouri, New Mexico, New Hampshire, North Carolina, North Dakota, Ohio, Oregon, Rhode Island, South Carolina, South Dakota, Tennessee, Texas, Virginia, and Wisconsin

States where there are Supreme Court cases or rules relating to legal assistant/paralegal definitions:

Illinois, Indiana, Iowa, Kentucky, Missouri, New Hampshire, New Mexico, North Dakota, Rhode Island, South Dakota and Virginia.

On October 8, 1999, the National Federation of Paralegal Associations ("NFPA") met in Atlanta to discuss and possibly vote on whether to increase their effort to establish state by state regulatory guidelines for paralegals.

Each year representatives of five national law related professional associations discuss and share information about the paralegal profession. This joint effort of these five national associations is called the Conclave. Attendees at this Conclave are representatives from the American Bar Association ("ABA"), the American Bar Association's Standing Committee on Legal Assistants, the American Association for Paralegal Education ("AAfPE"), the Legal Assistant Managers Association ("LAMA"), the National Association of Legal Assistants ("NALA") and the National Federation of Paralegal Associations ("NFPA"). A unified definition of the term "paralegal" is among the projects this Conclave is addressing. It is hoped that a unified definition may lead to the adoption of a unified model code of ethics for the paralegal profession.

Pamela Young holds the position of Legal Administrator for JCPenney Co., Inc. Corporate Headquarters, Plano, Texas; Ms. Young has held membership on the State Bar of Texas Standing Committee on Legal Assistants since 1988 and has chaired the Subcommittee monitoring Paralegal Regulation and Career Development since 1990; Ms. Young has also held membership since 1989, on the Unauthorized Practice of Law Committee, as appointed by the Texas Supreme Court.

Article 10-4 Continued

Although many regulations, legislative proposals, and proposals by state bar associations have been considered, to date no state has passed legislation allowing non-lawyers to provide "legal services" directly to the public. However the state of California has taken a step in that direction by passing legislation, which was effective January 1, 2000, that allows individuals who meet certain eligibility standards and who register under the statute as "legal document assistants" to provide "self-help" services directly to the general public for a fee.[2] Any type of legislation to recognize and regulate non-lawyers and allow independent paralegals and/or legal technicians to provide services directly to the public, would need to address the current definitional and administrative issues. A literature review confirms that commentators continue to address the advantages and disadvantages of non-lawyer delivery of legal services. For example, in Article 10-5, the author makes a case for the regulation of non-lawyers.

Rethinking Barriers to Legal Practice

81 JUDICATURE 100–103 (1997)

Instead of Being Prohibited From Providing Legal Services, Nonlawyers Should be Regulated and Controlled, Just Like Lawyers

Herbert M. Kritzer

Introduction

Throughout the 20th century, the legal profession has worked hard to create an expansive definition of what constitutes the practice of law and to exclude all nonlawyers from activities falling within that definition. Critics maintain that the only real reason for restrictions on who can provide legal services is the protection of lawyers from competition. One witness at a public hearing of the American Bar Association Commission on Nonlawyer Practice referred to the profession as a "greedy lawyer cartel" that sells justice to the highest bidder.[1] Others have made similar, though less strident, observations. For example, law professor Richard Abel develops a strong case that historically the profession sought to limit both the "production of producers" of legal services (i.e., limiting entry into the profession) and the "production [of legal services] by producers" (i.e., limiting who provides services and the nature of what is provided).[2]

While the profession has largely lost control of the production of producers, lawyers continue to try to limit the opportunities for nonlawyers to provide legal services. The profession continues to fall back on the standard rhetoric about "protecting the public" from incompetent providers, even in the absence of systematic evidence that the quality of routine services delivered by nonlawyers is substantially below that delivered by lawyers. While lawyers can provide anecdotal evidence of errors by nonlawyers, professional disciplinary bodies can provide similar evidence of errors by lawyers. There is no evidence that the presence of a disciplinary body actually reduces the number of errors of legal service providers.

A recent detailed study of legal advocacy in four settings in which lawyers and nonlawyers regularly appear examined the likelihood of success of various types of advocates, observed advocates at work in a variety of types of hearings, and interviewed advocates, adjudicators, and clients.[3] This systematic research makes it clear that nonlawyers can be effective advocates and, in some situations, better advocates than licensed attorneys. The assertions by members of the legal profession that the public is protected when only licensed attorneys provide legal services is not supported by what happens when specialized nonlawyers are permitted to represent clients.

Herbert M. Kritzer, a professor of political science and law, is chair of the Department of Political Science at the University of Wisconsin.

Article 10-5   Rethinking Barriers to Legal Practice

Toward nonlawyer practice

Does this mean that anyone should be permitted to offer legal services? Some countries allow anyone to do exactly this, subject to very specific exclusions. In England, for example, one of the biggest providers of legal advice is the Citizens' Advice Bureau. The CABs are locally funded dispensers of a wide range of advice, much of which would, at least in the United States, be labeled legal advice. In fact, while the managers of CABs are usually salaried employees, trained volunteers handle most of the actual client contacts, with professionals (including volunteer solicitors) often available for backup or more specialized advice. The issue of unauthorized practice of law is not relevant, because anyone in England may dispense legal advice or assist with a claim pursued outside the courts.

Research shows that formal legal training is only one path to the skills and knowledge necessary for competent legal assistance and representation. The image of legal services still revolves around the general practitioner who is there to help individuals with the full range of legal needs. If, however, one thinks of legal practice in terms of specialized areas rather than as general practice, it is clear that a person can acquire specialized representational competency, both in terms of the legal substance and the legal process/procedures, through a variety of avenues. Furthermore, traditional legal training in the United States equips a person with only some parts of this competency, and that training primarily serves to prepare the practitioner to acquire specialized competency.

Specialized experience and training other than law school can probably be as effective in preparing a person to provide representation in a narrow, specific area. For many contexts, such as unemployment compensation, social security disability, tax appeals, and labor grievance arbitration, the key to effective representation is the combination of three types of expertise: knowledge about the substance of the area, an understanding of the procedures used, and familiarity with the other regular players in the process. The latter can come only with experience, but the first two (substantive and procedural expertise) could be imparted through one-year, specialized training programs for paralegals, legal technicians, and licensed advocates. The expertise necessary to handle specialized proceedings or tasks can also be acquired experientially, either through an apprentice-like process or by parallel experience.

Error and redress

Defenders of restrictions raise two questions about the idea of opening up specialized legal services to nonlawyers: Would the nonlawyers be more prone to error than are lawyers? In what ways should the nonlawyers be regulated, particularly with regard to recourse for dissatisfied clients?

In discussing nonlawyer practice, lawyers tell of such experiences as a client who had first gone to a nonlawyer who made errors the lawyer now had to clean up. The assumption is that a lawyer would not have made such mistakes. Interestingly, we know almost nothing about the frequency of "legal error," a term that parallels the idea of "medical error."

How frequent is error in the provision of legal services? The answer is simply unknown. One might speculate that in comparing three groups—nonlawyer specialists, lawyer specialists, and lawyer generalists—the latter would be the most likely to make an error. If this speculation is correct, then the logic of excluding nonlawyers (assuming their error rate is higher than that for lawyer specialists) would also dictate allowing only lawyer specialists to handle matters within their area of specialization.

Article 10-5   Continued

How might nonlawyer practitioners be regulated to provide redress for dissatisfied consumers? Can the regulation of lawyers provide a model for regulating nonlawyers? There are three separate mechanisms currently used to regulate lawyers.[4]

- Institutional controls, in which institutional forums within which the lawyers work take some responsibility for uncovering and sanctioning lawyer misconduct (in the federal courts this is exemplified by Rule 11 sanctions for filing frivolous cases, unsupported claims, and motions);
- Liability controls, in which disgruntled clients can seek compensation by bringing a claim for professional malpractice; and
- Disciplinary controls, in which independent agencies (often a part of the state bar) investigate and prosecute violations of rules of professional conduct (with the final disciplinary authority typically resting with the state supreme court).

All three of these are currently or potentially applicable to nonlawyer advocates.

Institutional controls

Many agencies already have the power to regulate both lawyers and nonlawyers who appear before them. For example, many federal administrative agencies, including the Social Security Administration, have broad latitude to regulate advocates (both in permitting nonlawyers to appear and in disciplining advocates who appear before them). State agencies often have similar powers. At least one state agency in Wisconsin, which handles appeals concerning unemployment compensation, has disciplinary powers in this sense. Another example of a state agency with extensive licensing and disciplinary powers is the New York State Workers' Compensation Board, which has procedures for examining, licensing, and disciplining nonlawyers who appear in its proceedings.

The experience of agencies with disciplinary power is interesting. The Wisconsin Unemployment Compensation Bureau's administrative rules were put into place years ago because of problems with one nonlawyer advocate, but no one at the bureau could recall the rules actually being invoked to discipline an advocate. The Social Security Administration initiates "only a few dozen cases each year,"[5] and there is no indication that there are more problems with nonlawyers than with lawyers. As of the mid-1980s nonlawyers constituted 16.5 percent of those registered to practice before the Trademark and Patent Office, and about one-sixth of the disciplinary matters initiated during that period pertained to nonlawyer practitioners.[6]

The New York State Workers' Compensation Board, whose procedures require nonlawyers to pass an examination covering workers' compensation law and procedures before being allowed to appear as representatives, initiates disciplinary proceedings against few nonlawyers. One official noted that there are probably more complaints about nonspecialist lawyers than about nonlawyers who have passed the board's examination. Thus, where there is experience with institutional regulation, there is no evidence that it is used disproportionately to discipline nonlawyers.

Liability controls

In principle, liability controls ought to be available in any venue for any type of representative, on simple consumer-protection grounds. In the same way that one would have recourse against a plumber who made a faulty repair that led to substantial expense, one could seek damages against an advocate who failed to provide competent services. The dilemma is that of standards against which to measure performance, but this is also a problem in legal malpractice because of the difficulty in separating performance of the advo-

Recommendations of the ABA Commission on Nonlawyer Practice

- The range of activities of traditional paralegals should be expanded, with lawyers remaining accountable for their activities.
- States should consider allowing nonlawyer representation of individuals in state administrative agency proceedings. Nonlawyers should be subject to the agencies' standards of practice and discipline.
- The activities of nonlawyers who provide assistance, advice, and representation authorized by statute, court rule, or agency regulation should be continued, subject to review by the entity under whose authority the services are performed.
- With regard to the activities of all other nonlawyers, states should adopt an analytical approach in assessing whether and how to regulate varied forms of nonlawyer activity that exist or are emerging in their respective jurisdictions. Criteria for this analysis should include the risk of harm these activities present, whether consumers can evaluate providers' qualifications, and whether the net effect of regulating the activities will be a benefit to the public. State supreme courts should take the lead in examining specific nonlawyer activities within their jurisdictions with the active support and participation of the bar and public.
- The American Bar Association, state, local, and specialty bar associations, the practicing bar, courts, law schools, and the federal and state governments should continue to develop and finance new and improved ways to provide access to justice to help the public meet its legal and law-related needs.
- The American Bar Association should examine its ethical rules, policies and standards to ensure that they promote the delivery of affordable competent services and access to justice.

cate from the outcome of the matter. Obvious things, such as missing filing deadlines and the like, can be applied just as easily to nonlawyer advocates as to lawyer advocates.

The major reason that liability controls are not frequently used with regard to nonlawyers (except, perhaps, for accountants) is the question of available sources of compensation for damages. Lawyers (and many other professionals) typically carry professional liability insurance. In fact, many states require at least some types of service providers to carry insurance or to be bonded, although only one state—Oregon—requires that lawyers carry liability insurance.

Licensing often provides a mechanism for enforcing an insurance requirement. (In fact, this may well be the most important aspect of some licensing systems.) Devising some type of licensing system for nonlawyer advocates who offer their services to the public could be justified on the grounds of providing an insurance mechanism (but this would probably also require imposing an insurance requirement on attorneys). With an insurance mechanism in place covering the work of nonlawyer advocates, there is no reason that the liability system would work any less well for nonlawyers than it currently does for lawyers.

Article 10-5   Continued

Disciplinary controls

The last mechanism, disciplinary controls, goes hand-in-hand with licensing. Here, however, the licensing authority assumes responsibility for discipline, while the liability system relies entirely upon the dissatisfied client. The central component of this system is some mechanism for identifying possible problems, investigating and prosecuting problems, and imposing disciplinary sanctions upon proof that the problems are real. As with the liability mechanism, disciplinary controls rely on the existence of some type of standards. For most professions and occupations subject to licensing and regulation, executive agencies of the various states handle the licensing and disciplinary process. In most states, the state supreme court oversees the licensing of legal professionals because they are deemed to be "officers of the court."

There are a variety of ways to organize the licensing and disciplining of nonlawyer advocates, either through some central agency or through venue-specific offices. One might complain that such mechanisms would be costly for the public, but there is no reason that the license fees could not be set at a level that covers the cost of administration. Nonlawyer advocates might object to bearing this cost on the ground that it would make their costs of practice so high that they could not compete with lawyers. If this is true, it in effect means that their current costs fail to reflect the "real costs" of their practice, because it does not take into account the need to protect clients from unethical behavior or to compensate clients for practitioner errors.

The politics of change

The need to regulate and control nonlawyer advocates is real; it is also feasible. The same types of mechanisms and protections for clients available with regard to legal professionals would work (and in some settings already exist) for nonlawyer advocates. The failure of these mechanisms to be further developed reflects the relatively small stakes involved in large numbers of cases, the absence of apparent and recurring problems with nonlawyer advocates, and continuing unwillingness of the legal profession to accept and deal with the reality of nonlawyer practice. The latter of these may be the most important: the continued focus on the idea that the work of nonlawyer advocates represents the unauthorized practice of law results in the pursuit of traditional responses (i.e., seeking to suppress such work), rather than systematically investigating the nature of problems created by such activities and designing mechanisms to regulate the providers and protect their clients.

Beginning in the late 1980s, various groups within the legal profession have considered nonlawyer practice. In California, bar committees studied the problems and potential of nonlawyer provision of legal services. Those committees generally concluded it is time to recognize both that such practice exists and that it should, and probably will, expand.

The response to these reports from the bar associations that spawned them have generally been hostile. In California, when the Commission on Legal Technicians developed proposals that would permit limited practice by nonlawyers and provide for the regulation of those practitioners, segments of the bar succeeded in blocking the proposals both before the bar and in the legislature.

In 1994 the American Bar Association Commission on Nonlawyer Practice published a document summarizing its findings that nonlawyer practice was already widespread and that there was no support for the traditional contention that such practice resulted in widespread abuse.[7] In response, and in anticipation of a formal report and recommendation, ABA members hostile to the direction the commission was moving mobilized in opposition. The National Caucus of State Bar Associations adopted a resolution against any plan that would permit legal technicians to offer their services to the public.[8]

The commission's final recommendations recognize the current reality, but refrain from strongly advocating major extensions of that reality, with one exception. The commission apparently was impressed that nonlawyer practice permitted under the federal Administrative Procedures Act had shown that nonlawyers could effectively practice in administrative agencies. This seems to have led to their recommendation that state administrative agencies be similarly opened to nonlawyer practice. Beyond this, the commission stated that nonlawyers could be effective, but recommended no action other than that the states take an "analytical approach" in considering whether to extend rights of nonlawyer practice and how to regulate that practice. Despite calls that the ABA act upon and adopt the commission's recommendations,[9] no action has been taken, and none appears contemplated. The commission's recommendations are quickly being forgotten.

The research on which this essay is based produced findings that are consistent with those reported by the commission. Both the research and the commission's findings make it clear that it is time to abandon the existing rules regarding "unauthorized practice of law." It is time instead to consider the nature of legal services in an age of specialized tasks and specialized training. All providers of legal services should be subject to appropriate regulation and discipline. Within the proper framework, the public can be well served by nonlawyer providers. Consumers of legal services, from whatever source, must have suitable recourse should the services fall below some established standard. In this regard, nonlawyer providers are no different from members of the legal profession.

Footnotes

1. Quoted in NONLAWYER PRACTICE IN THE UNITED STATES: SUMMARY OF THE FACTUAL RECORD BEFORE THE AMERICAN BAR ASSOCIATION COMMISSION ON NONLAWYER PRACTICE, discussion draft for comment (Chicago: American Bar Association, April 1994), A.TX-2.
2. See Abel, AMERICAN LAWYERS (New York: Oxford University Press, 1989).
3. The details appear in Kritzer, LEGAL ADVOCACY: LAWYERS AND NONLAWYERS AT WORK (University of Michigan Press, forthcoming, 1998).
4. Wilkins, Who Should Regulate Lawyers?, 105 HARV. L. REV. 801-887 (1992).
5. See Wolf, Nonlawyer Practice Before the Social Security Administration, 37 ADMIN. L. REV. 415 (1985).
6. Quigg, Nonlawyer Practice Before the Patent and Trademark Office, 37 ADMIN. L. REV. 410 (1985).
7. See supra n. 1, at A.CA-8f.
8. See France, Bar Chiefs Protect the Guild, *National Law Journal*, August 7, 1995, at 28.
9. See Rhode, Meet Needs with Nonlawyers: It Is Time to Accept Lay Practitioners—and Regulate Them, *ABA Journal*, January 1996, at 82.

Article 10-5   Continued

CONCLUSION

The delivery of legal services directly to the public by non-lawyers will continue to be an important issue and will continue to have an enormous impact on the legal assistant profession. The legal assistant profession must distinguish itself as separate and apart from this alternative method of obtaining equal access to justice.

DISCUSSION QUESTIONS

1. Do you think a non-lawyer/non-legal assistant should be allowed to deliver legal services directly to the general public for compensation? If so, what type of legal services should they be allowed to provide? Should they be regulated and how?

2. Reflect on your educational background and work experience. What legal services do you would feel comfortable in delivering to the general public without supervision by an attorney?

3. What remedies, if any, should the public have if damaged by the misinformation, misadvice, and/or malpractice of a non-lawyer/non-legal assistant?

4. What would be the appropriate standard of care for a non-lawyer/non-legal assistant provider of legal services?

ENDNOTES

[1] California Business and Professions Code, Section 6400(c) (contains statutory definition of Legal Document Assistant).

[2] *Id. See infra.* Chapter 1 at n. 15–17.

Legal Working Environments and Survival Skills

One of the most exciting aspects of the legal assistant profession is the variety of legal working environments that utilize the skills of professional, competent legal assistants. This fact allows each legal assistant the opportunity to find employment in a legal working environment that best suits his or her individual desires, skills, and goals. In addition, within each category of legal working environments there are a variety of legal assistant utilization structures and a diversity of types of paralegal tasks that are delegated to legal assistants. A legal assistant can find employment in positions that would be considered traditional for legal assistants and can also find many opportunities to utilize his or her skills in environments and organizations that would be considered non-traditional legal assistant settings. The chapters in this section examine the types of legal working environments for legal assistants and the skills that a legal assistant needs in order to survive and succeed in those environments.

Legal Working Environments

INTRODUCTION

There are a variety of legal working environments available in the legal service delivery system in the United States. The various types fall into the following four categories:

- Private law firm
- Corporate and/or business organization legal department
- Administrative agency
- Legal aid clinic or public interest law service

Legal assistants are employed in all categories of legal working environments. The tasks delegated to and performed by legal assistants in the various legal working environments will depend on the type of legal services provided within that environment, the organizational structure and policies that exist within the environment, the credentials of the legal assistant, and the personnel involved in the delegation decisions. This analysis of the four categories of legal working environments provides comparison and contrast in the six following areas:

- Size of working environment
- Legal assistant's role within environment
- Hierarchy within environment
- Typical legal assistant utilization within environment
- Salary/compensation systems within environment
- Expectations employers have for legal assistant employees

LEGAL ASSISTANT OPPORTUNITIES IN PRIVATE LAW FIRMS

Like lawyers, most legal assistants will choose to work in a private law firm. According to statistics released in 1996 by the U.S. Department of Labor, the number of practicing legal assistants in the United States was expected to increase from 90,000 in 1990 to 167,000 in 2005.[1] This study predicted that private law firms would continue to be the largest employers of legal assistants.[2] There are an infinite variety of private law firm environments; in fact, no two private law firms are alike. Since a private law firm is a private business, the owners of the business have discretion to organize the working environment to meet their business needs. Therefore, the following analysis of private law firm working environments is at best a stereotypical presentation and will not be precisely correct for every private law firm. However, this analysis should prove helpful for the legal assistant wanting to explore the contrasts between the various types of legal working environments.

What is the Size of the Typical Legal Assistant Staff in a Private Law Firm?

Private law firms range in size from the small, solo-practice law firm with one lawyer, to the medium-size law firm in which a group of lawyers practice, to the large-size law firm in which a large group of lawyers practice, to the enormous, factory-type law firm. The size of the legal assistant staff within a private firm will generally bear some relationship to the number of lawyers working within the firm. The average ratio of attorneys to legal assistants is about two to one.

What Is the Legal Assistant's Role within the Private Law Firm?

The role of the legal assistant within the private firm depends on many factors. The most significant factor is the view of legal assistants that is held by the owners of the law firm. To illustrate, consider the variety of employees of a typical private law firm and classify them according to the following four categories:

- Income-producer or overhead-expense employee
- Professional-side or business-side employee
- Exempt or non-exempt employee
- Owner employee or non-owner employee

As with any business, a law firm ensures its existence by making a profit on the services that it sells to its clients. A private law firm offers clients legal services in the form of advice, representation, and document production. Some employees of a private firm have jobs that are of critical importance to the delivery of legal services but are clerical and/or administrative in nature and, as such, they are not "legal services," which are separately billed to a client. Rather, they are support services that are considered necessary overhead expenses. An "overhead-expense employee" is not expected to bring in money to the law firm. Other employees in a private firm are the actual producers and deliverers of legal services and so are considered to be income-producers as opposed to overhead-expense employees. An employee who is considered an "income-producer" is expected to bring money into the firm through billable-hour production. In a typical law firm, the income-producers would include the attorneys, legal assistants who perform non-clerical tasks that are legal-in-nature (but do not require a law degree) under the supervision of an attorney, and law clerks. Typical overhead-expense employees would include the clerical support staff, bookkeeping staff, office runners, librarian, computer-service staff, and law office management staff. Not all law firms classify their legal assistants as income-producers, but law firms that are utilizing competent, professional legal assistants would realize more financial rewards if their qualified legal assistants were utilized as and were expected to be income-producers.

The management of the law firm typically views the employees as falling on either the "professional" side or the "business" side. Professional-side employees usually include all income-producers. The hiring, firing, and supervision of professional-side employees are usually done by the attorney-owners of the law firm. In contrast, a business-side employee is usually an employee who provides support services; the hiring, firing, and supervision of a business-side employee is often delegated to a business-side office manager. A law firm that understands the economic justification for legal assistants and correctly utilizes their legal assistant employees expects those employees to be income-producers, accords them the status of other income-producers, and classifies them as professional-side employees.

Under the Fair Labor Standards Act (FLSA), all employees are classified as either "exempt" or "non-exempt" employees. An exempt employee is exempt from the minimum wage and hour provisions of the Act and is not paid overtime, whereas a non-exempt employee must be paid minimum wage and, in addition, overtime compensation if he or she works more than 40 hours a week. Consistent with this Act, all employees of a private law firm will be classified in one of these two categories. Typically, the attorneys, department heads, law office managers, and supervisors are considered to be exempt employees and the non-supervisory support staff are considered to be non-exempt. Whether a legal assistant is an exempt or non-exempt employee is a legal determination that needs to be made on a case-by-case basis. (Chapter 8 of this book contains a discussion concerning whether a legal assistant is an exempt or non-exempt employee.) The bottom line of the discussion is that the more academic and experiential credentials the legal assistant holds and the more tasks the legal assistant performs that require independent judgment and discretion, the more likely it is that the legal assistant will be considered an exempt employee under the Act. The classification as an exempt employee would put the legal assistant in the same classification as the other professional-side income-producers.

Employees of the law firm are also classified based on whether they have an ownership interest in the private law firm. Some employees of the law firm are also owners of the law firm. The private law firm is often organized as a partnership, corporation, corporation, professional corporation, and/or limited liability company. The owners of the actual business entity are one or more of the attorneys in active practice in the law firm or of-counsel to the law firm. Not all of the attorneys are business owners. Some of the attorneys, referred to as "associates," are not owners of the law firm; rather, they are non-owner employees. A legal assistant would be classified as a non-owner employee.

Having made and explained these four employee classifications within the context of a private law firm, consider the role of the legal assistant.

If the owners of the law firm believe that the legal assistant is an income-producer for the law firm, then the law firm will maintain rigorous hiring standards that demand strong academic qualifications, professional work experience, and excellence in work product. A legal assistant who works in this type of legal working environment can expect to be delegated tasks that require independent judgment and discretion and that would, absent the legal assistant, be performed by an attorney income-producer within the firm. A legal assistant who is considered an income-producer within the firm has ideally the same status as any of the income-producers within the law firm, including the law clerks, associate attorneys, and partner and/or shareholder attorneys. A legal assistant with these strong credentials and consistent delegation of billable-hour work would generally be considered an exempt employee under the FLSA. A private law firm that has income-producing expectations for their legal assistants would typically classify them as professional-side employees in terms of status, compensation, and benefits. Accordingly, their role in the law firm would be the role of a professional income-producer for the law firm.

On the other hand, if the owners of the law firm believe that the legal assistant is an overhead-expense employee and the services rendered by the legal assistant are more clerical in nature, then the legal assistant's time should not be separately billed and the role of the legal assistant would be better described an administrative assistant/secretary. The status of a legal assistant working under this belief system would be the same as that of other overhead-expense employees, and would probably be considered as non-exempt under the FLSA. A private law firm that does not have income-producing expectations for their legal assistants and delegates only clerical tasks to them would typically classify them as business-side employees in terms of status, compensation, and benefits. Accordingly, their role in the law firm would be that of business-side, overhead-expense employees.

Then there are those private law firms that "want to have their cake and eat it too." These private law firms hire qualified, competent, professional legal assistants and expect them to be income-producers and exempt employees under the FLSA, but treat them as business-side employees for the purpose of status, compensation, and benefits. That's not fair.

Some legal assistants work for private law firms who also "want to have their cake and eat it too." These legal assistants are qualified, competent, professional legal assistants who want the status, compensation, and benefits of a professional-side income-producing employee, but don't want the "burden" of having to produce a certain amount of billable hours each month and they want to be paid overtime. That's not fair either.

How the law firm classifies the legal assistant employee in the four areas discussed here needs to be discussed during the interviewing and compensation negotiation process before the legal assistant accepts the position. This discussion ensures that both the owners of the law firm and the legal assistant understand the status and role of the legal assistant within the firm.

What Is the Hierarchy within a Private Law Firm?

Most private law firms have a typical hierarchy. Although it is rarely discussed, it is understood among the employees that it exists. Unless the legal assistant has worked in a private law firm environment in another role, he or she would only acquire this information by learning about it in an academic environment, by doing an internship in a private law firm environment, or by learning about it on the job. The typical hierarchy in a law firm is diagrammed in Figure 11-1.

To understand the typical hierarchy in a law firm, it is critical to know who the business owners are and that they all have a major interest in the productivity of all employees, because the business owners will receive their portion of the net profits of the business only if the gross profits exceed the expenses of the law firm. The law firm's expenses include all wages paid to all employees, the office rent, the library, computer, equipment, supplies, and other overhead expenses. For this reason, the business owners structure the hierarchy of the business such that they have control

SENIOR PARTNERS/
MAJORITY SHAREHOLDERS

BUSINESS OWNERS

JUNIOR PARTNERS/
MINORITY SHAREHOLDERS

LAW OFFICE MANAGER

ASSOCIATES

LEGAL ASSISTANTS/
LAW CLERKS

EMPLOYEES

CLERICAL STAFF

OTHER SUPPORT STAFF

Figure 11-1 Law firm hierarchy.

over both the professional side and the business side of the law firm. Owner control of both sides ensures that the firm maintains a strong client-base by delivering quality legal services in a cost-effective manner, while tightly controlling overhead expenses.

If a legal assistant understands these basic business facts, then the need for the hierarchy makes sense. It will also make more sense to the legal assistant that an attorney who "they don't work for" has the audacity to question his/her billable hour production or use of time. It may be that the attorney raising the question does not directly supervise that legal assistant's work, so in that sense he/she doesn't work for that attorney. However, if that attorney is a business-owner, then in reality he/she does work for that attorney, as does everyone else in the law firm.

How Are Legal Assistants Utilized in a Private Law Firm?

The previous discussion shows why this question will be difficult to answer. The fact of the matter is that utilization of legal assistants within law firms will vary from one law firm to another. It will vary based on the beliefs of the owners concerning the role of the legal assistant; it will also depend on the academic credentials, experience, and the skills of the legal assistant. Another factor bearing on utilization is the area of law being practiced and the needs of the client. Rather than discuss the infinite variety of legal assistant job descriptions that might be revealed in a survey of law firms, it might be more productive to focus on the prominent utilization systems in law firms with legal assistant employees. The following three different utilization systems are typical in private law firms:

- Team system
- Pool system
- Tier system

If a law firm uses the team system, it organizes the law office staff into legal service delivery teams composed of attorneys, legal assistants, and clerical support staff. Some law firms assign staff to a particular team that always works together on the same legal matters. Under this structure, a legal assistant would be a member of only one team. Other law firms using the team method custom-design a legal service delivery team to meet the particular needs of each specific legal matter; thus, the legal assistant may be a member of several different teams. Under either team system, the legal assistant would begin work on the legal matter from the first day and would be able to perform tasks associated with that legal matter until the matter was finally resolved. Many legal assistants believe that the team system allows them to utilize a wider range of legal assistant skills, to establish stronger rapport with the client, and to provide more consistent, cost-effective delivery of legal services.

An alternate utilization method is the pool system. Under the pool system, legal assistants are grouped together (sometimes even physically grouped together in terms of where their offices are maintained) and, as paralegal tasks are needed by an attorney, the attorney identifies the needed task and requests the assistance of a legal assistant. The pool supervisor will, after receipt of a request, determine which legal assistant is available to perform the task. The legal assistant will then be delegated the task and supervised by the attorney making the request. When the task has been completed, the legal assistant is once again available to the pool. Under the pool system, the legal assistant works with many attorneys within the firm and will often be delegated a wide variety of tasks. Many legal assistants enjoy these advantages. Disadvantages cited to the pool system include that a legal assistant does not get to see a particular legal matter from beginning to the end and coming in and out of a particular matter so often it is difficult to establish a rapport with the client and with the supervising attorney.

Another system utilized by some private law firms is referred to as a tier system. Under a tier system, legal assistants are classified on a particular "tier" level based on their academic credentials, experience, and skill levels. The higher tier levels will be populated by the most qualified legal assistants and the tasks delegated to the highest-tier legal assistant will be those paralegal tasks that require the most independent judgment and discretion. The highest-tier-level legal assistants most likely will be classified as exempt employees under the FLSA, will be considered professional-side employees and income-producers, and will be given the status, compensation, and benefits to match those classifications. On the other hand, the lower tier levels will be populated by the legal assistants who have fewer qualifications and credentials. These legal assistants might be considered as business-side, non-exempt, overhead-expense employees, and so would be paid an hourly wage and would be entitled to overtime compensation. A law firm could use a combination of a tier system and a pool system or a tier system and a team system.

What Is the Salary/Compensation System Used within a Private Law Firm?

The salary/compensation system used with legal assistant employees within a private law firm will also vary from law firm to law firm. As you might expect, if the owners of the law firm classify the legal assistants as income-producers, if they use rigorous hiring standards to assure that their legal assistant employees have strong academic and experiential credentials and skills, and if they correctly delegate billable-hour tasks to the legal assistant, the salary/compensation system used for professional legal assistants should be the same system used for the attorneys within the law firm. That is not to say that the amount of compensation is the same, because the billable-hour rates for attorneys and legal assistants are not the same; rather, what is the same is the system itself. The bottom line in that system is that a legal assistant's compensation is in direct relationship to their productivity: The more billable hours a legal assistant produces, the more money they should be paid. This system is used to compensate associate attorneys in the law firm, and it is also used by the owners of the law firm to justify maintaining their percentage of ownership.

However, if the owners of the law firm classify the legal assistant as an overhead-expense employee and merely delegate non-billable-hour, clerical-in-nature tasks, the typical salary compensation is an hourly wage plus overtime.

What Billable-Hour Expectations Do Private Law Firms Have for Their Legal Assistant Employees?

Most law firms now hire legal assistants who are considered professional-side employees and income-producers. This is the trend especially in view of the economic justification for legal assistants and the availability of high-quality educational programs that offer intense academic and practical education, as well as college and advanced graduate degrees for legal assistants. The private law firm expects legal assistant income-producers to bring in more money through their billable hours than the law firm pays them in salary, thus allowing the law firm to realize a net profit from their effort. The expectation is referred to as the "Rule of Three": A law firm expects a legal assistant to bring in, through billable hours, three times their gross salary. The logic is that the *first* time the legal assistant brings in his or her salary through billable hours, the law firm is losing money on that income-producer because it has only recouped the salary and not the amount of money that the law firm has had to expend to provide overhead support to the legal assistant through his or her share of the office rent, library expense, clerical support expense, equipment cost, and supply expenses. The logic continues that the *second* time the legal assistant brings in his or her salary through billable hours, the law firm has broken even because it has then recouped the salary and the legal assistant's share of the overhead expenses. Therefore, the *third* time the legal assistant brings in his or her salary, the legal assistant has finally produced net profit for the owners of the business.

This is the same system used to compensate associate attorneys within a law firm, but the multiplier is usually different. For an associate attorney, a law firm is more likely to use the Rule of Five. As an alternative to utilizing the Rule of Three or the Rule of Five, some private law firms establish billable-hour expectations for each income-producer in the law firm, including the lawyers and the legal assistants. The number of billable hours expected is computed to allow the law firm to realize a net profit per income-producer.

By understanding the economics of the salary/compensation system, legal assistants will realize how important time management, timekeeping, and billable-hour production is to them and to the owners of the business. Legal assistants should keep strong documentation of billable- and non-billable-hour tasks performed in order to develop documentary evidence not only to justify the award by the court of legal assistant fees, but also to justify a salary increase based on billable-hour production or, if necessary, to identify problems with billable-hour production, such as failure of the attorney to delegate billable-hour tasks.

LEGAL ASSISTANT OPPORTUNITIES IN CORPORATE LEGAL DEPARTMENTS

Many legal assistants are now interested in working in corporate legal working environments. The 1996 update of the 1994 U.S. Department of Labor study predicted that business organizations such as corporate legal departments, insurance companies, banks, title insurance companies, and real estate businesses would provide increasing job opportunities for legal assistants.[3] A corporation or other business entity in need of legal advice and assistance has the option to hire a private outside counsel, a private outside general counsel, or a legal service team of employees to provide legal services in-house. Many corporations and business entities have determined that hiring an in-house legal service delivery team is more cost-effective for the business.[4] As corporations have begun to hire in-house counsel and the in-house attorneys have become overwhelmed by legal work, many of the in-house general counsel are beginning to hire legal assistants to help them because it is more cost-effective than hiring another attorney. This trend helps prove the point that, wherever there is an overworked attorney, there is a need for a qualified, competent, professional legal assistant.

As with any business, corporations and business organizations come in a variety of sizes and organizational structures. Therefore, the following analysis of corporate legal department working environments is a stereotypical presentation and will not be precisely correct for every corporate legal department. However, this analysis should prove helpful for the legal assistant wanting to explore the contrasts between the various types of legal working environments.

What Is the Size of the Typical Legal Assistant Staff in a Corporate Legal Department?

The size of the typical legal assistant staff in a corporate legal department varies from corporation to corporation. The size of the legal assistant staff is related to the number of attorneys on staff in the legal department.

What Is the Legal Assistant's Role within the Corporate Legal Department?

The legal assistant in a corporate legal department provides direct assistance to the attorneys on staff. Often a corporate legal department is composed of various divisions, including the following: corporate records, litigation, real estate, acquisition, compliance, taxation, licensing, copyright/patent, and securities. Each division is generally headed by an assistant general counsel who works under the general counsel for the whole legal department. The legal assistant generally works within a specific division of the legal department.

The issue of whether a legal assistant is considered to be a professional-side income-producer or a business-side, overhead-expense employee does not exist in a corporate working environment. All employees of the legal department are considered to be a necessary corporate overhead expense and part of the support staff for the corporation as a whole. However, the issue of whether a legal assistant employee is classified as an exempt or non-exempt employee under the FLSA remains an issue in a corporate legal department. As discussed previously in relation to private law firms, whether a legal assistant is an exempt or non-exempt employee is a legal determination that needs to be made on a case-by-case basis. As with legal assistants in private law firms, the bottom line is that the more academic and experiential credentials the legal assistant holds and the more tasks the legal assistant performs that require independent judgment and discretion, the more likely it is that the legal assistant will be considered an exempt employee under the FLSA. Chapter 8 of this book discusses whether a legal assistant is an exempt or non-exempt employee. Many of the cases cited involved legal assistants who were working in a corporate legal department when the determination was made and the resolution of the issue was made based on the type of tasks performed by the legal assistant.

The role of each member of the legal service delivery team in a corporate legal department often depends on the philosophy of the board of directors and the officers of the corporation concerning the role of the corporate legal department as a whole. The typical philosophies found in corporations are as follows:

- The corporate legal department should function as legal advisors.
- The corporate legal department should function as corporate policemen.
- The corporate legal department should be directly involved in business management decisions.

In a corporation holding the philosophy that the legal department functions as corporate legal advisors, the legal service delivery team resolves legal issues and concerns that are brought to them. The legal staff working in the department do not become involved in management or business decisions. Rather, they advise corporate management on the legal ramifications of a particular course of action, and the management of the corporation considers the advice and decides how to proceed. The legal service delivery team under this philosophy is expected to solve legal problems after they arise and are brought to their attention.

By contrast, in a corporation with the philosophy that the corporate legal department functions as corporate policemen, management expects the legal service delivery team to be proactive and knowledgeable about all aspects, components, and operations of the corporation. All members of the legal service delivery team work to ensure that the corporation operates within appropriate legal parameters and to evaluate legal implications before corporate management acts. The legal service delivery team, under this philosophy, is expected to practice preventative law to help the corporation avoid legal entanglements and concerns, as well as resolve legal problems as they arise.

Some corporations operate under the philosophy that the corporate legal department is to be directly involved in corporate management and corporate decision-making. In these corporations, the legal staff is expected not only to provide legal advice but also to assist the management of the corporation in making business decisions. In this type of corporation, members of the legal service delivery team are typically promoted to management positions outside the corporate legal department. The legal service delivery team under this philosophy has a very broad role. It is expected to help the corporation avoid legal problems, resolve legal issues as they arise, and help make the business management decisions of the corporation. Unique ethical concerns arise when the legal staff members step out of the role of legal advisors and into the role of management, including a concern regarding the attorney-client privilege and possible conflict-of-interest problems.

What Is the Hierarchy within a Corporate Legal Department?

Two organizational schemes are generally utilized by corporations with internal legal departments, as follows:

- Centralized corporate legal departments
- Decentralized corporate legal departments

Many corporations have centralized corporate legal departments. The centralized corporate legal department is usually located in the corporate headquarters or home office, providing legal services to all operating divisions and units of the corporation notwithstanding the physical location of the operating units. The general counsel for the corporation supervises the legal service delivery team.

Decentralized legal departments are often created by corporations with many outlying operating units. A decentralized legal department may have regional counsel who provides legal services to the operating units within a particular geographic region or alternatively the corporation could assign a legal service delivery team (attorneys and legal assistants) to a particular division or operating unit. In a decentralized legal department the subdivisions operate relatively independently, although they might still be accountable to the corporate general counsel.

The actual hierarchy or organization within the corporate legal department varies from one corporation to another. Generally, the organizational structure within the corporate legal department mirrors the organizational structure within the other departments and divisions of the corporation.

A legal assistant working in a corporate legal department is supervised by one or more of the corporate attorneys in the legal department. The diagram in Figure 11-2 depicts the common chain of command for a legal assistant working in a corporate legal department.

As in large private law firms, large corporate legal departments now tend to hire professional law office managers to handle the day-to-day business-side management of the corporate legal department. The corporate law department manager performs functions such as hiring, firing, and supervision of clerical and administrative staff members within the department; administrative recordkeeping and reporting; budget and financial matters; and supply, equipment, and location needs. The corporate law department manager is expected to free up the staff attorneys to allow them to use their expertise and devote their energies to the legal issues and concerns of the corporation.

If a corporate legal department is managed by a corporate law department manager, it could change the "chain of command" or "reporting line" for the legal assistant, but it is important for the legal assistant's paralegal work to still be supervised by one or more staff attorneys. Although it is possible, depending on the type of tasks

CORPORATE GENERAL COUNSEL			
ASSISTANT GENERAL COUNSEL			
PATENT & TRADEMARK COUNSEL	CORPORATE RECORDS COUNSEL	LITIGATION COUNSEL	REAL ESTATE COUNSEL
ATTORNEY	ATTORNEY	ATTORNEY	ATTORNEY
LEGAL ASSISTANT	LEGAL ASSISTANT	LEGAL ASSISTANT	LEGAL ASSISTANT

Figure 11-2 Corporate legal department hierarchy.

delegated to the legal assistant, to be supervised by both the staff attorneys and the non-lawyer, law department manager, it is never ideal to answer to two bosses. In the case of a legal assistant, it could raise ethical issues. As in any legal working environment, in order to function effectively and efficiently, the legal assistant must understand the hierarchy and chain of command.

How Are Legal Assistants Utilized in a Corporate Legal Department?

Utilization of legal assistants within corporate legal departments varies from one corporation to another. The scope of the actual paralegal tasks that can be delegated to the legal assistant remains very broad in a corporate legal department. The utilization decision includes the academic credentials, work experience, and skills of the legal assistant, as well as the needs of the corporate legal department and/or subdivisions.

The legal assistant utilization systems in corporate law departments include the three discussed previously for private law firms: the team system, the pool system, and the tier system. What is perhaps unique to corporate legal departments, compared to solo, small, and medium-size private firms, is that the corporate legal department is often subdivided into specialized divisions and each division may use a different utilization system within the division. A legal assistant is usually assigned to a particular division, specializing in particular areas of law and the legal assistant gains expertise within that division. As the legal assistant gains expertise, it becomes increasingly unlikely that he or she would be "loaned" to another division. Some legal assistants believe that this would be a disadvantage because their experience would be narrow. However, the sure cure for that would be to request a corporate transfer to another division within the corporate legal department.

What Is the Salary/Compensation System Used within a Corporate Legal Department?

A corporation generally uses the same salary/compensation system with all its employees, typically referred to as a "lockstep" system. In a lockstep salary system, each job title has a defined salary range. Unlike a private law firm salary/compensation system, the legal assistant's salary is not dependent on productivity in terms of billable hours. However, a more productive legal assistant in terms of work product is a more valued employee and will generally be paid at the high end of the salary range for the position.

In most corporate legal departments the professional, competent legal assistant is paid a salary as opposed to an hourly wage. If the legal assistant is performing paralegal tasks that qualify him or her as an exempt employee under FLSA, then the legal assistant will not be paid overtime. Rather, the exempt employee typically receives the same types of benefits that other exempt employees receive, such as access to the pension plan, the stock option plan, and bonus programs.

What Billable-Hour Expectations Do Corporations Have for their Legal Assistant Employees?

Corporations expect legal assistants in the corporate legal department to focus on the quality of the work product. Unlike a private law firm, the legal department has only one client (the corporation), so there are not expectations about billable hours. However, the amount of time that a legal assistant takes to perform a paralegal task is still scrutinized as part of the overall assessment of the quality of his or her work.

LEGAL ASSISTANT OPPORTUNITIES IN ADMINISTRATIVE AGENCIES

Many legal assistants are employed by governmental administrative agencies at the federal, state, and local levels. The U.S. Department of Labor study predicted that federal, state, and local government agencies and courts would continue to hire legal assistants in increasing numbers.[5] This is wonderful news for legal assistants and for the taxpayers.

Governmental employers have realized that legal assistants are important members of the legal service delivery team and that, when the legal staff has more work than it can handle, hiring a legal assistant is a less expensive alternative.

What Is the Size of the Typical Legal Assistant Staff in an Administrative Agency?

The size of the legal assistant staff in an administrative agency depends on the size of the agency itself, the number of divisions within the agency that utilizes the legal service delivery team, and the number of attorney staff members. Some governmental agencies are quite small and some are exceptionally large.

What Is the Legal Assistant's Role in an Administrative Agency?

To understand the role of the legal assistant in an administrative agency, it is necessary to understand how an administrative agency functions and the various roles that the staff attorneys play in an administrative agency. Typically an administrative agency is delegated authority in the following three areas:

- Rule-making: creating rules and regulations to implement legislation
- Enforcement: enforcing the agency rules and regulations
- Hearings: interpreting rules and regulations as applied in particular fact patterns

If a large administrative agency has authority in all three of these areas, it typically will hire separate legal staff to assist in each distinct area. In a small agency, the legal staff may have responsibility for all three areas. The role of the legal service delivery team varies depending on which of these three areas of responsibility are within the purview of the legal service delivery team.

If the legal service delivery team is working in the area of rule-making, the staff attorneys and legal assistants work with the non-legal rule-making staff members to ensure that the rules are properly drafted and are implemented in accord with the applicable administrative procedure act requirements.

If the legal service delivery team is working in the area of enforcement, the staff attorneys and legal assistants work with the non-legal staff members to ensure that the inspections, licensing, recordkeeping, audits, and reviews of the individuals and entities subject to the agency regulations are performed and executed in accord with the applicable administrative procedure act and other constitutional, statutory, and common law requirements.

If the legal service delivery team is working in the area of hearings, the staff attorneys and legal assistants work in conjunction with the non-legal staff members to schedule and hold hearings and make decisions that resolve disputes arising between the agency and the individual and/or the entity that is subject to the agency regulation. The hearing and decision process is governed by the applicable administrative procedure act and other constitutional, statutory, and common law requirements. The staff attorneys' and legal assistants' roles are to ensure compliance with these laws by the agency.

What Is the Hierarchy within an Administrative Agency?

The organizational structure within a governmental administrative agency depends on the scope of duties delegated to the agency and the size of the agency. Like corporate legal departments, agencies can utilize either a centralized or decentralized organizational structure. In a centralized organizational structure, the legal service delivery team staff is grouped into the same department or division within the main headquarters of the administrative agency. When legal issues and concerns arise in any of the other departments or divisions, the legal matter is referred to the agency legal department or division. Alternatively, some administrative agencies have a decentralized organizational structure, in which legal service delivery staff members are assigned to particular departments and/or divisions that have a consistent need for legal services.

The legal assistant performs paralegal tasks under the supervision of an attorney under either the centralized or decentralized organizational scheme. The legal assistant may also be supervised in a more general sense by the non-lawyer management staff in the agency. This raises the concern that a legal assistant may have two bosses, which could create a difficult working environment and could raise ethical concerns. The bottom line is that the paralegal tasks performed by the legal assistant must be supervised by an attorney. In many agencies, legal staff members may also be working in areas that involve non-legal matters and often are promoted from the legal department and/or division into agency management positions.

How Are Legal Assistants Utilized in an Administrative Agency?

Legal assistants employed by administrative agencies are usually delegated a broad range of paralegal tasks directly relating to the responsibilities of the entire legal staff within the agency. For example, if the legal staff assists in the rule-making functions of the agency, then the legal assistant will be delegated the following types of tasks: legal research; rule drafting; drafting, filing, and publishing notice of rule-making; reviewing and drafting responses to public comment; making rule revisions; providing information to governmental officials in the executive and legislative branches of government; and monitoring legislation. If the legal staff assists in the enforcement functions of the agency, then the legal assistant will be expected to perform the following types of tasks: conducting legal research; fact investigation; records review and analysis; participating in investigation and audit procedures; reviewing license and/or rate-making applications; and drafting agency documents. If the legal staff assists in the hearings function of the agency, the legal assistant will often be delegated the following types of tasks: drafting, review, and analysis of notice of hearing; preparation for the hearing either as an advocate for the agency or as an assistant to the agency hearing officer; analysis of data; gathering and indexing of exhibits; summarizing depositions; legal research; drafting decisions; and participating in the evidentiary hearing.

What Is the Salary/Compensation System Used by an Administrative Agency?

A governmental entity receives its funding during a set funding cycle based on the proposed budget that the agency submitted. In the proposed budget, agency management has determined the number and type of personnel that will be needed during the next fiscal cycle and has established a pay range for each position. After the budget has been accepted, it is difficult for the governmental entity to increase its budget or change the number of positions allocated to any specific subdivision until the next budget cycle. Most governmental agencies have a classified employee system where each job title/category has a set job description and established pay range. A legal assistant who accepts employment for an agency will be hired into a specific job classification and the salary paid to the legal assistant can be negotiated within the pay range established for that position based on the credentials and experience of the legal assistant.

What Billable-Hour Expectations Do Administrative Agencies Have for their Legal Assistant Employees?

Legal assistants employed by governmental agencies are not expected to bring in any billable hours. The legal staff of an agency has only one client, the agency. The legal assistant works for a salary and is evaluated based on the quality of his or her work product and the use of time-management skills.

LEGAL ASSISTANT OPPORTUNITIES IN PUBLIC INTEREST LAW ENTITIES

One of the conclusions reached in the U.S. Department of Labor study was that there would be expanded job opportunities for legal assistants in the public sector. The study reported, "Community legal service programs, which provide assistance to the poor, aged, minorities, and middle-income families, operate on limited budgets. They will seek to employ additional legal assistants in order to minimize expenses and serve the most people."[6] Legal assistants have historically been employed by entities created to provide legal services to individuals who cannot afford legal representation. These entities go by different names, but they share the same public interest purpose. The entity may be called a legal clinic, a public interest law firm, a legal services corporation, a legal aid society, or a pro bono legal service firm.

At one point, Congress recognized a need to make legal services accessible to those who could not afford private legal services, so it provided funding for the Legal Service Corporation, a nonprofit corporation set up to provide legal services to poor people. During the Reagan administration, however, funding was drastically reduced, causing a major cutback in legal services being provided to the poor. Since that time, public interest law entities have had to seek funding from other sources. Many public interest law entities currently receive their funding from state and local levels of government. Other public interest law entities receive funding from private foundations, church organizations, or state bar associations, or they simply operate by volunteer assistance in the form of pro bono work by attorneys and legal assistants.

Public interest law entities are still needed, but funding remains a crisis for most of these entities. Those entities that continue to operate do so on a shoestring. As a result of this economic reality, it behooves the entity to maximize its use of legal assistants in its efforts to provide legal services to the greatest number of people.

What Is the Size of the Typical Legal Assistant Staff in a Public Interest Law Entity?

Currently, most public interest law entities are small to medium-size organizations. The case load is high and the number of staff attorneys is low. The ratio of legal assistants to attorneys is much higher in a public interest law entity than in any other legal working environment.

What Is the Legal Assistant's Role within a Public Interest Law Entity?

The legal assistant in a public interest law entity plays an integral role in the delivery of legal services to the poor. The legal assistant who performs paralegal tasks involving independent judgment and discretion must work under the supervision of an attorney. As a result of the economics of the situation, it is typical for the attorney staff member to supervise the work of several legal assistants and to delegate a very wide range of tasks to the legal assistant staff members.

What Is the Hierarchy within a Public Interest Law Entity?

Unlike the other legal working environments that have been discussed, a public interest law entity has a minimal structure. There is a hierarchy in any organization; however, the funding for a public interest law entity is generally so limited that, although a larger entity might have a non-lawyer manager, most of the small and medium-size entities generally have just the legal service delivery team members and a small clerical support staff.

How Are Legal Assistants Utilized in a Public Interest Law Entity?

This is the exciting part of public interest law work for legal assistants. The legal assistant is probably utilized best in this environment because the demand for services is so high, there is so much legal work that needs to be done, and there are so few staff lawyers to do it. As a result, the staff lawyers delegate well. A legal assistant in this legal working environment usually has an opportunity to use all of his or her paralegal skills and enjoys a wide variety of cases and clients. A legal assistant in this environment generally has more client contact than would be realized in the other legal working environments.

What Is the Salary/Compensation System Used by a Public Interest Law Entity?

This is the not-so-exciting part of public interest law work for legal assistants. Legal assistants working in a public interest law entity are paid a salary but it will typically be a salary below market rate. The staff attorneys working for a public law entity will also be working for a below-market salary. In fact, funding is at such a crisis level in some public law entities that they exist only because of pro bono contributions of time from attorneys and legal assistants. There are tremendous rewards for attorneys and legal assistants who work for public interest law entities, but those rewards are not generally monetary.

What Billable-Hour Expectations Does a Public Interest Law Entity Have for Its Legal Assistant Employees?

There are no billable-hour expectations in a public interest law entity for either the attorneys or the legal assistants. The focus on productivity is not measured by the amount of money brought in but by whether the legal service delivery team is able to meet the demand for services and by the cost-effective delivery of quality legal services.

CONCLUSION

The legal assistant profession offers opportunities for legal assistants in a variety of legal working environments, enough to match anyone's individual needs and personal workplace expectations. A legal assistant should explore the various legal working environments and determine which environments will not only match his/her interests and expectations, but will also allow full utilization of his/her skills, academic background, and experience.

DISCUSSION QUESTIONS

1. What type of legal working environment would provide you with the most job satisfaction?
2. What type of legal assistant utilization system (team, pool, or tier) would you like the best and why?

ENDNOTES

[1] Robert Sperber, *58% Paralegal Job Increase by Year 2005*, LEGAL ASSISTANT TODAY, May/June 1997, at 24 (citing statistics compiled by the Bureau of Labor Statistics, U.S. Department of Labor). See the U.S. DOL Bureau of Labor Standards Web site at http://www.bls.gov, which contains updated occupational outlook information, projections, and employment and wage estimates for paralegals and legal assistants (SOC Code number 23-2011).

[2] *Id.*

[3] *Id.*

[4] *See* M. ALTMAN & R. WEIL, HOW TO MANAGE YOUR LAW OFFICE (Matthew Bender 1986) (Chapter 3 contains a full discussion of the organization of corporate legal and patent departments).

[5] *Supra* n. 1, at 25.

[6] *Id.*

Legal Assistant Survival Skills

INTRODUCTION

Legal working environments are business environments. Legal assistants, in order to be successful in their working environment, must have survival skills that will ensure their ability to meet the business needs and goals of the organization. The survival skills that are necessary in legal working environments include a solid understanding of the economic justification for legal assistants within the environment, knowledge of timekeeping and skills involved in documenting billable hours, time-management skills, delegation skills, and interpersonal dynamics skills.

UNDERSTANDING THE ECONOMIC UTILIZATION OF LEGAL ASSISTANTS WITHIN LEGAL WORKING ENVIRONMENTS

The economic justification for the utilization of qualified, competent, professional legal assistants is based on two premises, as follows:

- Legal assistants are income-producers.
- Legal assistants save attorney time.

The implication of these premises is that if a law firm correctly utilizes legal assistants by delegating billable-hour, paralegal tasks to them and if the legal assistants are qualified and competent, everyone involved in the legal service delivery system wins, including the attorneys, the legal assistants, and the clients.

The attorneys benefit from the economic utilization of legal assistants in two ways. First, the overburdened attorney can delegate tasks that, but for the legal assistant, he/she would have to perform. The attorney can focus more time and effort on tasks that require a law degree and involve direct client representation and advising. The time that the attorney spends in this manner can then be billed out to the client at the full attorney hourly rate. Second, the attorney will make money on the legal assistant because the time the legal assistant devotes to performing paralegal tasks for a client will be billed out to the client at the legal assistant hourly rate, which is lower than the attorney's hourly rate but higher than the actual cost of the legal assistant to the attorney or law firm. In this way, both the attorney and the legal assistant are able to fully utilize their billable-hour potential and maximize profit to the law firm.

Legal assistants benefit from economic utilization in two ways. First, legal assistants reap the rewards of being delegated paralegal tasks that are not clerical in nature and allow them to use their intelligence, education, and experience. Legal assistants who perform tasks that require independent judgment and discretion, and which are recognized as billable-hour tasks, feel more satisfied with their jobs and professional career choices. Second, the income-producing legal assistants, as they become more and more profitable to the law firm, will be able to negotiate higher salaries based on their productivity. The law firm will want to reward their productivity to motivate them to continue to perform at optimal levels. The law firm will realize that if they fail to reward productivity, then the productive legal assistant will seek employment in a different law firm that wants to increase its profitability by adding them to its staff.

The client is the ultimate beneficiary of the economic utilization of legal assistants because he or she receives the same high quality of legal services at a reduced rate. The client will be charged the higher attorney hourly rate only for the provision of legal services that required a law degree. The client will be charged the lower legal assistant hourly rate for all paralegal tasks that were performed by the legal assistant but were supervised by the attorney. Thus, the client realizes a cost-containment benefit without any risk of reduced quality of legal services.

Two contingencies must be met in order for this economic utilization for legal assistants to work, as follows:

- The legal assistant must be competent and must have the credentials and skills to perform paralegal tasks that require independent judgment and discretion.
- The attorney must consistently delegate non-clerical, paralegal tasks to the legal assistant rather than perform the tasks himself.

If both of these contingencies are met, the law firm will be in a position to maximize its utilization of all income-producing employees. It will also maximize the client's ability to convince the court to award legal assistant fees as a meaningful component of attorney fees if the court requires the opposing party to pay costs and attorney fees.

In fact, the economic justification for maximum utilization of legal assistants is so strong, that if a law office does not correctly utilize legal assistants, it will not only lose profit potential but it will not be able to compete for clients in the legal marketplace.

DISCUSSION QUESTIONS

1. Consider the contrasting expectations in a legal working environment relative to the income-producing members of the legal service delivery team and the non-income-producing members.

2. How would you explain the economic justification of utilization of legal assistants to a client?

3. How would you explain the economic justification of utilization of legal assistants to a potential employer?

4. Who benefits from the utilization of qualified, competent legal assistants as members of a legal service delivery team?

UNDERSTANDING BILLABLE HOURS AND TIMEKEEPING

Every legal assistant in every legal working environment should maintain time records that document the date, client, client matter, task performed, and time to perform the task. This should occur whether the legal assistant is expected to be a billable-hour income-producer or not. The four reasons legal assistants should document their time are as follows:

- To have documentary evidence that can be used to prove the legal assistant's time in a situation where the court is asked to award attorney fees (which can include legal assistant fees if proper documentation is maintained)

- To have documentary evidence that can be used by the legal assistant to prove the type and quantity of billable versus non-billable tasks that were delegated

- To have documentary evidence to assist the office in the event of a fee dispute with the client

- To have documentary evidence to use to bill the client for services performed

Many courts, when asked to assess costs and attorney fees against the opposing side, will include legal assistant fees as a component of costs and/or attorney fees.[1] However, in order for a court to allow legal assistant fees to be recovered, legal assistant fees must be separately billed and documented. The documentation required includes the date, the name of the legal assistant, a description of the paralegal tasks performed, and the time taken to perform the task. For this reason alone, a legal assistant should maintain detailed time records even if working in an environment that does not routinely bill clients by the hour for legal services rendered.

Often legal assistants need to justify their productivity or explain their lack of productivity. If a legal assistant has not maintained time records, then he or she has only his/her memory to rely on, along with the very weak argument that he/she either "billed out a lot of time consistently" or that "the reason he/she was unable to meet the billable hour expectations is because he/she was being delegated clerical, non-billable hour tasks." Making either of these arguments to a employer without evidence to support the argument makes the legal assistant sound like he or she is exaggerating or whining or both. A much more credible presentation will be made if legal assistants are able to support their position on delegation with documentary evidence. Legal assistants should never forget that attorneys prefer documentary evidence.

On rare occasions, after a client receives a bill, a dispute arises concerning the fee. In that situation all of the income-producers who have provided legal services to the client must be able to prove the date it was done, the type of legal services provided, and the amount of time it took. This documentary evidence will be relied upon by the law firm to resolve the fee dispute. In addition to fee dispute situations, the time records also document all of the efforts of the legal service delivery team in a grievance or malpractice action.

The most common use of manually maintained or computer-generated time records is to provide documentary evidence of the time that has been expended by all of the income-producers on the legal services delivery team on the client's behalf. Based on these time records, the law firm generates a client bill or statement for legal services rendered. Other administrative reports are also generated based on these time records. For example, the owners of a law firm typically have monthly meetings when they review financial matters. Usually one of the reports that the owners review shows the billable-hour production of each income-producer. If the billable-hour production for a legal assistant income-producer is less than expected, generally the supervising attorney is charged with the task of working with that legal assistant to increase the billable-hour production. As with the attorney income-producers, a legal assistant wants to be in a position to answer for their billable-hour production should it come into question. A review of the time records usually indicates whether the billable-hour problem was caused by the legal assistant's inefficiency and time-management problems or if it was created by the attorney's failure to properly delegate non-clerical, billable-hour, paralegal tasks to the legal assistant.

The bottom line is that no matter what type of legal working environment legal assistants choose to work in, they need to document their time using a convenient timekeeping system. Timekeeping is a legal assistant survival skill. As such, accurate timekeeping must be a normal part of the legal assistant's daily routine.

DISCUSSION QUESTIONS

1. Why would a legal assistant who works in a legal environment that does not bill a client hourly for legal services need to keep time records?

2. List the various ways in which time records can be used by a legal assistant.

3. How could time records help a legal assistant negotiate future compensation?

UNDERSTANDING TIME-MANAGEMENT PRINCIPLES _____

Time is the basic commodity of the legal working environment. If those environments and the individuals who work in those environments have learned to manage the use of time carefully, they will achieve better client service and higher financial rewards. All employees in legal working environments must have an understanding of the value of time, the cost of wasting time, and techniques available to improve time management.

What Is the Value of Time in a Legal Working Environment?

In a time-management book written by Alan Lakein, the author emphasizes the value of time by philosophically stating: "Time is life. It is irreversible and irreplaceable. To waste time is to waste your life, but to master your time is to master your life and make the most of it."[2] In another popular time-management book published by the American Management Association, the author, Alec MacKenzie, states the following about time:

> Most of us sense something else about time: It is a resource. Moreover, it is a unique resource. It cannot be accumulated like money or stockpiled like raw materials. We are forced to spend it, whether we chose to or not, at a fixed rate of 60 seconds every minute. It cannot be turned on and off like a machine or replaced like a man. It is irretrievable . . . . We can, however, determine the way we spend it. Like other resources, time is either managed effectively or it is mismanaged.[3]

We all have the same amount of time in a day and each day we all have many demands on our time. Often those demands on our time exceed the amount of tasks that can realistically be performed within 24 hours. We have all said at one time or another, "I can't do that because I don't have time." Although at the moment we made that statement we thought it was true, the reality is that it is never true. We have time. We all have the same amount of time. Time itself is not the problem. The problem is that we must consciously choose how to use our time. This process requires us to prioritize the items that are on our list to do and to choose which items can be accomplished within the 24 hours that we have to spend that day. Often the demands on our time are excessive and we have to take responsibility for deciding which demands we will be able to respond to immediately and which demands we will not be able to respond to until a later date. This conscious process of deciding how to use our time is the process of time management.

It is incumbent on all employees in all working environments to become efficient in the use of their time. It is particularly important for employees who work in a service-providing business, where the commodity being sold is time, to be efficient time managers, for two reasons. First, in order for the legal working environment to remain financially stable, the time expended by the legal service delivery team must be recouped in terms of client-paid billable hours. Second, in order to ensure competitive ability in the legal marketplace, the legal working environment must deliver legal services in a timely, cost-effective manner.

Waste of Time by a Legal Assistant: What Is the Cost to the Legal Working Environment?

Waste of time or inefficient use of time by a legal assistant or attorney member of the legal service delivery team has an enormous cost to the business. To understand the full cost of the waste of time to the legal working environment, the following factors need to be considered:

- The cost in terms of loss of wage dollars paid to the non-productive employee
- The cost in terms of the loss of income caused by the loss of billable-hour time by the non-productive employee
- The cost in terms of client loss resulting from delay of provision of legal services caused by the non-productive employee

All employees in the legal working environment are paid wages. Looking at a worst-case scenario, if an employee comes to the job and does not perform his/her delegated work, then the employer received no benefit from the wages paid. The employer lost all of the wage dollars paid and gained nothing in return. In a more usual situation, the employee comes to work and wastes some amount of time. In that situation, the employer still loses wage dollars relative to the time that was wasted by the employee. To get an idea of how much that waste of time may cost a business in terms of loss of wage dollars paid to the employee, let's look at the following scenario:

Calculation of Loss of Wage Dollars

You have been asked to calculate the amount of wasted wage dollars per year to your law firm if each employee in the firm wasted only one hour per day. There are 20 employees including 10 attorneys, 5 legal assistants, and 5 support staff. The estimated average hourly wage would be $20.00 per hour. You follow these steps to arrive at the lost wage dollar amount:

Step 1: Determine the number of approximate working days per year for one employee.

Average working days, less weekends	=	260
minus paid holidays		–10
minus average vacation		–14
minus authorized sick leave		–7
Approximate working days for each employee	=	229

Step 2: Determine the total number of employees. = 20

Step 3: Compute the wasted time hours for one employee by multiplying the average number of working days times one wasted hour per day.

Wasted hours by one employee in one year	=	229 hours

Step 4: Determine the hours wasted by all employees during the year by multiplying the number of employees times the hours wasted per employee.

Total time wasted by all employees in one year	=	4,580 hours

Step 5: Determine the dollar value of wages paid for wasted time by computing the estimated average hourly wage and multiply the total wasted time by all employees times the average hourly wage.

Total wasted wage dollars per year	=	$91,600.00

Under the preceding scenario, the law firm would have lost $91,600.00 of wages paid to employees who wasted only one hour per day. This is the cost the law firm incurs anytime any employee wastes time. As the time waste increases, so do the costs to the law firm.

The cost of the waste of time by an income-producing employee, the attorney and/or the legal assistant, is even greater. Not only does the legal working environment experience the loss of "wage dollars" described in the preceding paragraph, the legal working environment also experiences a loss of income because of the fees that it could have billed out to clients if the time had been correctly utilized and not wasted. Let's continue to look at the preceding scenario and determine the "loss of income" cost associated with each of the income-producers in the law firm wasting one hour each day.[4]

Calculation of Loss of Income

You have now been asked to calculate the amount of loss of income per year to your law firm if each income-producer, the attorneys and legal assistants, wastes only one hour per year. Remember there are 20 employees: 10 attorneys, 5 legal assistants, and 5 overhead-expense support staff. Assume that the average attorney billable-hour rate is $200.00 per hour and the average legal assistant billable-hour rate is $75.00 per hour. Follow these steps to arrive at the loss-of-income figure:

Step 1: Determine the number of approximate working days per year for one employee.

Average working days, less weekends	=	260
minus paid holidays		–10
minus average vacation		–14
minus authorized sick leave		–7
		———

Approximate working days for each income-producing employee	=	229
Step 2: Determine the total number of income-producing employees.	=	10 attorneys 5 legal assistants

Step 3: Compute the wasted non-billed hours for one employee by multiplying the average number of working days times one wasted non-billed hour per day.

Wasted non-billed hours by one income-producing employee in one year	=	229 non-billed hours

Step 4: Determine the hours wasted and not billed by all income-producing employees during the year by multiplying the number of attorney employees times the hours wasted per employee and then multiply the number of legal assistant employees times the hours wasted per legal assistant employee.

Total time wasted by all attorney income-producing employees in one year	=	2,290 hours
Total time wasted by all legal assistant income-producing employees in one year	=	1,145 hours

Step 5: Determine the dollar value of loss of income to the firm caused by wasted time of the attorney income-producers by multiplying the total wasted time by all attorneys, times the average attorney billable hour rate of $200.00.   = $458,000.00

Step 6: Determine the dollar value of loss of income to the firm caused by wasted time of the legal assistant income-producers by multiplying the total wasted time by all legal assistants times the average legal assistant billable hour rate of $75.00.   = $85,875.00

Total loss of income due to waste of time by all income-producers in one year	=	$543,875.00

Under this scenario, if all employees waste one hour per day per year, the law firm will experience an annual loss of wage dollars paid of $91,600.00. In addition, the law firm will experience a loss of income caused by waste of time by all income-producers of $543,875.00. The total monetary cost to the law firm that results from each employee wasting 1 hour per day each day of the year is $635,475.00.

Another cost to the law firm or other legal environment that is caused by the waste of time by employees is often a loss of client base. The waste of time causes a delay in the provision of legal services and that delay will cause frustration for the client; in today's competitive legal marketplace, it may cause the firm to lose that client to another legal service provider that can meet the client expectation in terms of timeliness of legal services.

What Are the Most Common Time-Wasters?

The most common time-wasters in working environments include the following:

1. Telephone interruptions
2. Visitors dropping in without appointments
3. Meetings, both scheduled and unscheduled
4. Crisis situation for which no plans were possible
5. Lack of objectives, priorities, and deadlines
6. Cluttered desk and personal disorganization
7. Involvement in routine and detail that should be delegated to others
8. Attempting too much at once and underestimating the time it takes to do it
9. Failure to set up clear lines of responsibility and authority
10. Inadequate, inaccurate, or delayed information from others
11. Indecision and procrastination
12. Lack of or unclear communication and instruction
13. Inability to say "No"
14. Lack of standards and progress reports that enable a manager to keep track of developments
15. Fatigue[5]

All of these possible time-wasters exist inside and outside the legal working environment. If a legal assistant experiences problems with efficient use of time, a good strategy would to review this list and attempt to identify the time-wasters.

What Strategy Can Legal Assistants Use to Better Manage their Time?

Since, by definition, a legal assistant works under the supervision of an attorney, a legal assistant who experiences time-management problems must first do an analysis to determine what the time-wasters are and who is causing them. Many of the identified time-wasters may be "internal" problems that the legal assistant has personal responsibility for and will need to take action to correct. Other identified time-wasters may be "external" problems belonging to someone else in the legal working environment. An external time-waster is more difficult to resolve because it requires the legal assistant to confront someone else in the environment and persuade them to solve their time-waster problem so that it does not continue to adversely impact the legal assistant. After the time-wasters have been identified, the legal assistant can take steps to correct the problems. A legal assistant should employ the following four-step strategy to identify and resolve the time-waster problems in the working environment.

Step 1: Identify the time-wasters in the environment.

Step 2: Classify each identified time-waster as either an internal or an external time-management problem.

Step 3: Utilize time-management techniques to resolve internal time-management problems.

Step 4: Address external time-management problems.

Step 1 requires the legal assistant to identify the time-wasters in the legal working environment before trying to resolve them. If this step is skipped, often the legal assistant resolves only the symptoms of the problems and not the core time-wasters themselves. This step requires the legal assistant to do fact research, using the following tools: (1) A self-assessment (a good place to start is the list of the 15 most common time-wasters); and (2) a review of time records, to help uncover problems and to identify how the legal assistant uses time each day.

Once the time-wasters have been identified, the legal assistant is ready for Step 2, classifying each identified time-waster as internal or external. An *internal time-waster* is personal to the legal assistant, a problem that causes difficulty in time management. None of us likes to discover and admit to our own personal problems, but in this situation it is a joy to discover that the time-waster is internal because the legal assistant will have total control over its resolution. By contrast, an *external time-waster* is someone else's time-waster that adversely impacts the legal assistant's use of time. For example, the legal assistant may identify and classify as an external time-waster the personal disorganization of a clerical support staff member. As a result of the support staff's disorganization, case files get lost and both the support staff and the legal assistant have to spend time each week trying to find lost files. This causes the legal assistant to waste billable-hour time on the non-billable-hour task of finding a lost file. Another example of an external time-waster would be the procrastination of the supervising attorney. As a result of the supervising attorney's procrastination, the legal assistant is always working in crisis mode because the supervising attorney delegates a task at the very last minute rather than when he/she first becomes aware of the deadline.

After a time-waster has been identified and classified, the legal assistant moves to Steps 3 and 4. The technique and approach used to resolve a time-waster depends on whether it is internal or external. Let's first discuss the technique and approach for resolving an internal time-waster. Since the time-waster is the legal assistant's own personal problem, he/she has total control over its resolution. Research and self-help work well for most legal assistants. Time-management techniques and coping skills to deal with internal time-wasters can be found in many books and articles.[6] For each time-waster, several proposed solutions can be found in the wealth of literature. This area of self-improvement will make the legal assistant a more efficient and effective person both inside and outside the legal working environment. Examples of suggested time-management techniques include making "to do" lists; using calendar and diary systems; establishing an orderly organization for case files; and establishing internal deadlines that are well in advance of externally imposed deadlines for the completion of a particular project.

A different strategy and approach is in order to resolve an external time-waster because the actual problem is someone else's and the legal assistant's task is to decide how and when to best approach the other person and get them to change their pattern of behavior. This is particularly difficult if the other person is up the chain of command, like a supervising attorney. The legal assistant will need to use a five-step strategy to resolve an external time-waster, as follows:

- Document the external time-waster and the actual time wasted.
- Research solutions to the time-waster.
- Schedule an appointment to discuss the time-management issue with the other person.
- Gently confront the other person with the problem and the proposed solution.
- Work together to implement the agreed-upon solution.

Before you confront another person about a problem that you perceive that they have, it is best to make sure that you can *document and prove that the problem exists.* Often we think in absolute terms and perceive problems that may or may not really exist. For example, a legal assistant may think that the secretary "always" loses case files and that causes the legal assistant to waste time helping the secretary find the case files. Having identified that as an external time-waster, before the legal assistant confronts the secretary it would be a good idea to go back over the time records for the last two months to determine if that perceived time-waster really exists before confronting the secretary. It could be that as the legal assistant reviews the past two months of time records, it becomes apparent that the legal assistant did not, in fact, lose billable-hour time because of that, so the problem is not really a problem. Or it may become apparent that the legal assistant needs to do a better job of documenting non-billable time because the time records do not document the perceived problem. Or it may become apparent that in the last two months the legal assistant has used a total of two non-billable hours helping the secretary find lost case files. If the time-waster cannot be "proven" or documented, it would be better to wait until the problem can be documented before confronting the other person. If, on the other hand, the problem is documented, then the legal assistant has "evidence" to prove the time-waster problem exists and to explain its adverse impact on the legal assistant's billable-hour production.

After documenting the time-waster, the next step is to do *research possible solutions to the time-waster.* This may simply involve critical and creative thinking or it may involve research on various time-management techniques that have been suggested.

A legal assistant should discover solutions to the problem before confronting another person. If a legal assistant confronts another person with documentation of an existing problem and also proposes a solution to the problem, he/she will be viewed in a more positive light by all individuals involved. If the legal assistant only presents the problem without a solution, he/she may be perceived as a griper or complainer. No one wants to work with a griper or complainer.

After the legal assistant has identified and documented the external time-waster and has arrived at a workable solution to propose, the next step is to *schedule an appointment* to discuss the situation with the other person. It is always better to approach the other person when the legal assistant is feeling calm and the other person is not in the middle of another task, is feeling calm, and is ready to have a scheduled discussion. On the date and at the time of the scheduled appointment the legal assistant needs to present the situation to the other person in such a way that the other person will not react defensively but will be open to change and resolution. Often the direct approach is the best approach, although the legal assistant will need to be gentle and use tact while explaining the identified time-waster and how it adversely impacts the legal assistant. When *gently confronting the other person* and proposing and discussing a solution, it is always best for the legal assistant to be ready to assist in the implementation. If tension begins to develop during the discussion, it could be reduced by discussing common goals that both parties need to cooperate to attain, such as timely delivery of high-quality legal services to clients in a cost-effective manner. After agreeing to a solution, the final step is to *assist in implementing the agreed-upon solution.*

To use the example of an external time-waster discussed previously involving a perceived problem of a procrastinating supervising attorney: As a result of the supervising attorney's procrastination, the legal assistant is always working in crisis mode because the supervising attorney delegates a task at the very last minute rather than when he/she first becomes aware of the deadline. If the legal assistant used the suggested five-step approach to resolving this external time-waster, he/she would first go to the time records to see if the time-waster could be documented. This type of time-waster could also be documented with the calendars of the secretary, the legal assistant, and the supervising attorney. The legal assistant needs to find concrete examples of the procrastination of the supervising attorney and the actual time-management problem that was created for the other members of the legal service delivery team. If the past records do not document the problem the legal assistant may need to reassess whether the problem actually exists; if it does, then the legal assistant needs to work in the future to document the time-waster each time it occurs so that later he/she will have sufficient documentation to resolve the problem.

If the legal assistant can document several concrete examples of the supervising attorney's procrastination and its adverse affects, then he/she should move to the next step by researching possible solutions. The research may reveal a possible solution by changing the calendaring of deadlines. For example, when an external deadline is established by the court or other source, the supervising attorney notifies the secretary of the deadline and the secretary then puts the deadline on the calendar for the legal assistant and for the supervising attorney. In addition, the secretary would create tickler slips that would notify both the legal assistant and the attorney at regular intervals before the deadline.

After arriving at a suitable solution to propose, the legal assistant should schedule an appointment with the supervising attorney to discuss "a new system idea that would increase the efficiency of the legal service delivery team." It is always better to state the subject matter of the meeting in the most positive terms. The next step is to gently confront the supervising attorney with the identified time-waster, the adverse affect it has on the legal service delivery team, and the proposed solution. This approach, if done with tact and timing, should provide the legal assistant with the best opportunity to create a positive change in the legal working environment. If done correctly, the supervising attorney will appreciate the efforts of the legal assistant to improve the working relationship and the environment.

DISCUSSION QUESTIONS

1. What are your personal, internal time-management problems?

2. If you are working, consider whether external time-management problems exist in your legal working environment. If so, what strategy can you put in place to document the problem and resolve it?

UNDERSTANDING HOW TO DELEGATE TASKS

A legal assistant who functions in a paralegal capacity as an income-producer, performing tasks that require independent judgment and discretion, will generally have authority to delegate clerical tasks to support staff members. In some situations, a legal assistant may have the authority to delegate paralegal tasks to other legal assistants, investigators, and/or law clerks. There is an art to delegation that the legal assistant must understand in order to be an efficient, responsible delegator.

What Are the Ground Rules in Delegation?

To effectively delegate, the delegator must have a clear understanding of the task to be delegated, he/she must effectively communicate the task to the delegate, the delegate must agree to perform the task, and the delegate must agree to give the delegator a status report at regular intervals. The person doing the delegation must delegate both the responsibility for performing the task and the authority to perform the task requested; however, he/she cannot delegate accountability for the performance of the task. Ultimately, "the buck stops" with the delegator, so it is incumbent on the delegator to periodically check with the delegate to make sure the task is being performed correctly and in a timely manner.

Why Should a Legal Assistant Delegate Tasks?

The legal assistant, if it is possible and within his or her authority, should delegate all clerical tasks to non-income-producing support staff because it is non-billable time. If a legal assistant performs the clerical task instead of income-producing paralegal tasks, it will have an adverse impact on his or her billable-hour production. If the clerical support staff is overloaded with clerical work, it is a better business decision for the management in the legal working environment to hire temporary clerical assistance than to misuse an income-producer. The loss of income occasioned by the loss of the billable-hour productivity of an income-producer will very quickly economically justify the hiring of an hourly wage temporary clerical assistant during peak times.

In some legal working environments and on various levels of the legal assistant career path within the organization, a legal assistant may have authority to delegate paralegal tasks to other legal assistants, investigators, and/or law clerks. If a legal assistant has this authority, delegation should occur. Many benefits will be reaped by effective delegation, including the following:

- *More will be accomplished*   When there is no delegation, legal assistants are limited by what they can accomplish alone. When legal assistants delegate, they are limited only by what they can control.
- *Better ideas*   Delegation allows all members of the legal service delivery team to have input and to contribute new ideas. The old adage is true: Two heads are better than one!
- *Better team effort*   When the legal assistants delegate to other members of the legal service delivery team, it shows trust and confidence in the other members of the team and they respond to this vote of confidence by higher-level team performance.
- *Stimulates delegates*   Delegation stimulates those receiving the delegation. It makes them think and increases their involvement and commitment to the project and to the legal service delivery team.
- *Organizes work to be done*   When legal assistants delegate, they must communicate clearly and in precise terms the task to be performed. As a part of this delegation process, the legal assistant clarifies the job in his/her own mind and often is able to reorganize it more effectively prior to the delegation.

Why Don't Legal Assistants Delegate Tasks?

Some legal assistants find it difficult to delegate tasks to others. If the legal assistant has authority to delegate tasks, then he or she will be expected to delegate tasks so that the benefits of delegation can actually occur. A legal assistant might hesitate to delegate for many reasons, including the following:

- *Uncertainty about how, what, or when to delegate*   A legal assistant may never have had the opportunity to learn to delegate tasks. It is a learning process and much of the learning will be by trial and error. The legal assistant needs to jump in and start learning by doing.

- *Fear that mistakes will be made*   Since the legal assistant remains accountable for the work product, he or she may be reluctant to delegate because of worry that the task will be done wrong. However, the more work is delegated to other staff members, the more experience they will get, and the fewer mistakes they will make.

- *Fear of delegating oneself out of a job*   It is very common for the legal assistant to feel a need to be essential. The legal assistant may fear that if others on the legal service delivery team develop the same level of skills and competence, that will make the legal assistant less essential. This fear is unfounded and runs contrary to the team approach to the delivery of legal services. It should be the goal of all team members to increase the competency of one another so the team can function at an optimal level.

- *Fear of losing prestige or privileges*   It is true that a status is connected with being selected to attend particular meetings or perform particular tasks and a legal assistant may enjoy that special status and be reluctant to let go of any of those particular tasks. However, if the legal assistant has the authority to delegate those particular tasks and refuses to do so, the other members of the legal service delivery team will feel that the legal assistant does not have confidence in them and may distrust the legal assistant's motives.

- *Feeling that he or she can do the job faster*   This is a very common reason for failure to delegate. The legal assistant may feel that it would take more time to delegate the task than to just do it him/herself. This is a dangerous precedent to establish because, if followed, the legal assistant never stops to take the time to train another staff member to perform the task. Once others on the team learn to perform the task, then it will not be faster for the legal assistant to do it; what the legal assistant can accomplish will be limited only by what he or she can control.

- *Fear of losing an enjoyable part of the job*   Often a legal assistant does not want to give up a particular task that is enjoyable. If this fear inhibits delegation, the legal assistant will limit his/her experiences by not opening up to learn new tasks and face new challenges that will raise his/her level of competence and skills.

- *Feeling that team members already have too much to do*   There is a old adage that work expands to fill the time available. Even if team members already fill their time, adding additional tasks by delegation will encourage the team member to reorganize their time to accomplish the new tasks. The team member might also find the new delegation to be stimulating, rewarding, and confidence-building.

- *Feeling that the team members do not want more responsibility*   This feeling may be more of a reflection of the legal assistant's failure to delegate. The fact of the matter is that most team members enjoy new responsibility and it is invigorating.

- *Fear of supervising attorney*   A legal assistant may be afraid to delegate a particular task because of worry that the supervising attorney might ask for a report and he or she will not be able to respond. This fear is unfounded if the legal assistant follows up the delegation with control and keeps apprised of the status of the delegated project. Most supervising attorneys are more interested in the job being done than in who does it. Also, if the legal assistant is expected to delegate to other legal service delivery team members, and does so with control, the supervising attorney will generally be pleased with the delegation.

What Common Mistakes Do Legal Assistants Make while Delegating Tasks?

Delegation is a learned skill. The more a person practices, the better he or she gets. Several mistakes are commonly made during the process of delegation, including the following:

- *Delegating without retaining control*   Since a legal assistant is always accountable for a particular task even if the performance of the task has been delegated to another, the legal assistant must delegate tasks with control. That generally means that as a part of the delegation, the legal assistant and the delegate agree on reporting deadlines and status reports at regular intervals. These types of controls build in checkpoints where the legal assistant can assess the quality and progress of the work.

- *Delegating with too much control*   Sometimes a legal assistant is so nervous about the delegation that he or she literally stands over the shoulder of the delegate to make sure the task is done correctly. This problem usually makes the person receiving the delegation feel distrusted and does not save the legal assistant any time. A legal assistant must delegate with control but the level of control needs to be well-balanced in order to achieve the benefits of delegation.

- *Falling prey to reverse delegation*   Reverse delegation occurs when the delegate comes back to the legal assistant who originally delegated the task and asks for clarification, and in the process of providing clarification, the legal assistant finds him/herself actually doing the task originally delegated. If this occurs, the benefits of delegation go out the window.

- *Failure to communicate important information*   When delegating a task the legal assistant must be careful to fully communicate all relevant information. Remember that communication is a two-way street. A good delegation technique is to communicate the task and then ask the person who received the delegation to give you feedback about what they heard to make sure that good communication actually occurred.

- *Failure to clarify the extent of authority being delegated*   An important part of delegation is to be certain that the delegate understands the full extent of delegated authority so that his/her actions will stay within the expected parameters of the delegation. If this is left unclear, the person receiving the delegation may either over-step his/her authority or fail to take necessary action.

- *Overreacting to errors*   We are all human and we all err. If a legal assistant over-reacts to an error made by the delegate, it may cause future problems for the legal service delivery team. Certainly the error needs to be addressed and corrected, but the legal assistant needs to do so in a tactful, constructive manner.

- *Discourage new ideas and innovations*   The legal assistant needs to be open to new ideas and techniques offered by the delegate. By doing so, the work product of the entire legal service delivery team continues to improve and positive team-building occurs.

How Can a Legal Assistant Improve Delegation Skills?

We can all improve our delegation skills, even the most experienced at delegation. The team-building benefits of effective delegation are so positive in a legal working environment that legal assistants need to constantly work at improving their delegation skills. The following are ideas to improve delegation skills:

- *Stand behind what you say*   If you tell the delegate that he/she has full authority to do a particular thing or decide on a particular reporting format, then stand behind that. If instead you redo it, then you begin to lose credibility with the other person. If the person is not experienced enough to have the authority, do not give him/her full authority until he/she is ready for it.

- *Be a clear communicator*   When a legal assistant delegates a task, the delegate must understand the goals and objectives as well as the specific steps that you expect him/her to follow to accomplish the task. Ask the delegate to give you oral feedback about his/her understanding of the task to make sure that effective communication occurred.

- *Ask for ideas*   When delegating a task, ask the delegate for input about whether he/she can handle the task. Also ask for additional ideas about how the task can be accomplished.

- *Delegate the tasks that you know best*   It is easier to control and supervise the delegation if the task that was delegated is one that you have experience in doing. It will also allow the legal assistant delegating the tasks to have time to take on new challenges and continue to improve his/her skills.

- *Delegate consistently*   The more the legal assistant delegates, the easier it will become. Consistently delegating also will assist in the team-building process with the other members of the legal service delivery team.

- *Keep your door open*   The individuals receiving the delegation will feel more supported if they are free to return to you and ask you for assistance and clarification. Just be careful of reverse delegation.

- *Help others learn from mistakes*   A constructive approach to use when a delegate makes an error is to talk about what the team learned from the error rather than getting angry and engaging in non-constructive discussion.

- *Allow the task to be done in a new way*   A legal assistant who remains open to new ideas and new ways of doing a task will obtain all the benefits of delegation. Although some tasks must be performed in a particular manner, other tasks do not have to be. Everyone has their own way of working. Unless a particular procedure is required, allow the person performing the task to use his or her judgment and discretion. He or she may have a procedure that is more efficient than old one.

- *Follow up the delegation with an evaluation*   After the delegated task has been completed, give the person who performed the task feedback. If the performance was less than expected, have a constructive discussion with the person about how the performance could have been improved so that he/she learns and will do better next time. If the performance met or exceeded expectations, reward the performance with praise.

DISCUSSION QUESTIONS

1. After reviewing the list of reasons given for why a legal assistant does not delegate tasks, if you are a practicing legal assistant, consider your own delegation pattern and determine how you could become a better delegator. How could your supervising attorney become a better delegator?

2. Identify two situations in the legal working environment in which you work, where better delegation (by you or by someone else) would have enhanced the working relationship, the quality of work product, and/or the timely delivery of the work product to the client.

3. What types of tasks can a legal assistant delegate to clerical support staff members?

UNDERSTANDING INTERPERSONAL DYNAMICS IN A LEGAL WORKING ENVIRONMENT

Because there are people in every working environment, there is a need for the people to be able to work together and to relate together in such a way that the objectives of the work environment are met. As a part of the process of working together and relating to one another, various interpersonal dynamics naturally develop and form an essential part of the environment. There are positive and negative aspects to the concept of interpersonal dynamics. The positive aspect is that the dynamics ideally help the work group to function as a cohesive whole and accomplish the common objectives of the group. In a legal working environment the common objective would be the timely delivery of high-quality legal services in a cost-effective manner. The negative aspect of the dynamics is what is commonly referred to as "office politics." Office politics is a reality in almost every working environment, often unconsciously generated by the group process. Office politics is generally invisible and is felt before it can be identified, but it is rarely discussed and can be quite dangerous to an employee who fails to recognize it and act in a "politically expected" manner. A successful legal assistant attempts to identify and understand both the positive and negative interpersonal dynamics that exist in the legal working environment and acts to avoid any conflicts that could be created as a result of office politics.

What Are the Potential Problem Areas between Staff within a Legal Working Environment?

The usual reason for interpersonal relationship problems is the friction created when two or more people attempt to cooperate to achieve a particular result. That friction could be created by the stress or deadline pressure involved in the situation; by personality conflicts between the individuals involved; by personal feelings such as jealousy, anger, distrust, misperception, fear, or bad moods; or by adverse conditions in the work environment such as overcrowding, lack of adequate supplies and equipment, insufficient staffing, or inadequate climate control. There are many reasons why people in the workplace have difficulty getting along with one another. When this friction exists for whatever reason, it robs the workplace of constructive positive energy and creates negativity. All employees in the legal working environment need to remain alert for this type of friction and when discovered, they should ideally attempt to dispel it. If that is not possible, they should at least not add fuel to the fire.

The following is an analysis of the potential friction or problem areas that could exist for a legal assistant in a legal working environment. Don't let this discussion become a self-fulfilling prophecy, because in many legal working environments none of the potential problems will ever be encountered.

The Attorney and the Legal Assistant.   Occasionally an interpersonal dynamics problem arises between one or more of the attorneys and a legal assistant. Since the legal assistant works under the supervision of the attorneys this can be a significant problem for the legal assistant. Such a problem also interferes with the ability of the entire legal service delivery team to meet their ultimate goal of timely delivery of high-quality legal services to clients in a cost-effective manner. The legal assistant may perceive that the attorney is acting cold, not communicating, not delegating, and strident. When this sort of friction is identified by the legal assistant, the natural response is often to take it personally and to feel that the behavior is due to the fact that the attorney does not like the legal assistant. Often that is not the case. Before jumping to that conclusion, it would be better for the legal assistant to consider other possible reasons for the attorney's behavior, including any or all of the following:

- The attorney might merely be responding to the pressure of time demands. Remember that the attorney's salary and promotion is dependent on his or her productivity. Many attorneys feel an enormous billable-hour pressure. The billable-hour expectation on the attorneys is even greater than the billable-hour expectation of legal assistants. In responding to this pressure, the attorney stays focused on the task at hand and this strong focus may be perceived by others in the environment as being cold, non-communicative, and strident, which is not the perception intended by the attorney.

- The attorney remains fully accountable and liable for the acts of the legal assistant. As a result of that accountability the attorney may hesitate to fully delegate paralegal tasks until he or she is completely confident that the legal assistant is ready for the delegation.

- The attorney may not have learned how to delegate. As was pointed out earlier in this chapter, delegation is learned and it must be practiced. An attorney does not learn delegation in law school; delegation usually is learned on the job. An inexperienced attorney is just learning how to practice law and also how to delegate, and a legal assistant working for that attorney needs to understand that the attorney is going through a major learning curve. However, delegation problems are not limited to inexperienced attorneys. Often attorneys who are very busy say they don't have time to sit down and figure out what to delegate and that it is faster and easier for them to do it themselves. While this type of thinking is counterproductive and creates a vicious non-delegation cycle, the attorney in the midst of the cycle often feels he/she can't stop it. That makes the attorney work faster, talk less, worry more, become more strident, delegate less, communicate less, and seem cold and uncaring, when really he/she is just trying to keep his/her head above water. It would be easy for a legal assistant working with this attorney to take this personally unless he/she could view the situation objectively. If the legal assistant was able to correctly identify the cause, it may be that he/she could take action to stop the non-delegation cycle by becoming more self-motivated and initiating self-delegation of tasks that would relieve pressure on the attorney.

- The attorney may have organizational problems. When an attorney is disorganized a lot of time is spent trying to figure out the status of various projects, where the files are, and what needs to be done. This type of attorney often works under deadline pressure created by the disorganization, feeling frustrated and overworked. A legal assistant may perceive his or her behavior as cold, uncaring, and lacking in trust in the legal assistant. In reality, the attorney may simply be responding to his or her own internal organizational problem. If the legal assistant could correctly identify the cause of the attorney's behavior, the legal assistant may be able to set up systems that would assist the attorney to be better organized.

- It will take some time for a mutual trust relationship to fully develop between the attorney and the legal assistant. Until that trust relationship matures, the attorney is unlikely to fully delegate all possible tasks to the legal assistant. If a legal assistant perceives that the attorney is hesitant to delegate tasks, the legal assistant should not assume that the attorney doesn't like him or her or that the attorney dislikes the quality of his or her work. The legal assistant just needs to give the relationship time to mature and, during that time, build the attorney's confidence with efficient production of a quality work product.

- It could be that the attorney does not understand what a competent, qualified legal assistant is capable of doing. If the attorney does not understand the range of skills and educational background that the legal assistant has, the attorney may not understand what tasks the legal assistant is capable of performing. If a legal assistant identifies that as the problem causing the friction or the lack of delegation, the legal assistant can cure that problem by educating the attorney about his or her areas of competence and skill. Sometimes this educational process will require the legal assistant to be self-motivated enough to initiate the delegation of tasks to show the attorney his or her skill level.

- Another possible explanation for the attorney's behavior may be that the attorney has a problem communicating either because he or she is so busy or because at the time the task is being delegated, the attorney has not clarified the task in his or her own mind so the delegation is incomplete, fuzzy, or lacks sufficient information. If this is the root problem, then the legal assistant should not take it personally. The legal assistant, having identified this as the problem, may need to take more initiative to learn the additional information required by going directly to the case file or the prior case files, and getting information from the clerical support staff.

The Clerical Support Staff Member and the Legal Assistant. The interpersonal relationship that exists between a legal assistant and the clerical support members of the legal service delivery team is critical. Sometimes a problem exists between a clerical support staff member and the legal assistant. Curiously, sometimes the problem exists on the first day before the clerical staff member and the legal assistant even get to know each other or really have a chance to work together. It is normal for a legal assistant who perceives friction in a relationship with a clerical support staff member to take it personally and think that the clerical staff member does not like him or her. That, however, should be the last assumption made. It is more typical for one of the following reasons to underlie the friction:

- The legal assistant may have a condescending attitude toward the clerical support staff. This type of "I am better and more important than you" attitude will definitely adversely affect the working relationship between the clerical support staff members and the legal assistant. If that is identified as the problem, the solution is that the legal assistant needs to change that attitude or that perception. The reality of the situation is that all members of the legal service delivery team are critically important to the common goals of the team. No one member is better than another member; each member has a different role and a different job to do.

- Another possible reason for the friction could be that the clerical support staff member had a bad experience in the past working with a legal assistant and is incorrectly assuming that he or she will always have difficulty working with all legal assistants. If this is the cause of the friction, the legal assistant needs to work hard to reassure the clerical staff member that he or she hopes and expects them to be able to work together as equal team members in the legal service delivery team.

- It is also possible that the clerical support staff member may be worried that he or she will be replaced or that some of the tasks that the attorney previously delegated to the clerical support staff member would be delegated to the legal assistant instead. If this is the cause of the interpersonal problem, then both the attorney and the legal assistant need to provide reassurance to the clerical support staff member of his or her value and integral role in the legal service delivery team, which assures him or her of job security and stability.

- Another possibility is that the clerical support staff member has jealous feelings toward the legal assistant. The jealousy may relate to the type of work that is delegated to the legal assistant or to the time the supervising attorney spends with the legal assistant. If this is the cause of the friction, then the best the legal assistant can do is to be pleasant, supportive, and reassuring. Responding in that fashion makes it possible for the clerical support staff member to let go of jealous feelings and be a productive member of the team.

The Legal Assistant Relationship with other Legal Assistants. It is possible that some friction could exist between the various legal assistant employees within the legal working environment. This is particularly true in environments that provide career tracks for legal assistants, have "exempt" and "non-exempt" tiers of legal assistant employees, have employees share clerical staff resources, or have open "billable-hour" competition between income-producers. As with all other interpersonal relationships, the cause of the friction could be any number of factors. Potential problems in the interpersonal interaction between legal assistants include the following:

- Unequal workload distribution between legal assistants can cause friction. Often this problem is caused by the unique utilization patterns of the separate attorneys supervising each legal assistant. If this is the case, the legal assistants themselves will not be able to resolve this friction by themselves. If this is the cause of the friction, then the legal assistants should attempt to discuss the matter among themselves and propose a solution to the supervising attorneys that would allow the legal assistant with the lesser workload to provide assistance to the other legal assistant during peak times.

- In environments that require legal assistants to share clerical staff resources, a common source of friction is caused by the issue of which legal assistant's work should be considered a priority for the clerical staff member. If this is the cause of the friction, the legal assistants should be able to discuss the matter and design a prioritizing system that they can agree upon. The clerical support staff member who is caught in the middle of this friction will no doubt welcome the solution.

- Another possible cause of friction is jealous feelings caused by one legal assistant receiving delegation that is perceived to be better than that which another legal assistant receives. This different utilization and delegation may be correctly based on the difference in credentials, academic background, and experiential background of the legal assistants involved. If that is the case, then the delegation would be proper and the jealous feelings are unfounded. However, just because they are unfounded does not mean they will go away. The legal assistant who identifies this as a cause of a co-worker's negative feelings should continue to be positive, friendly, reassuring, and supportive and hope the other legal assistant will be able to deal effectively with his or her own feelings. If the different utilization is not credential-based, but a result of the ability or lack of ability of the supervising attorney to properly delegate, the legal assistant who seeks to improve the delegation should direct constructive energy toward educating the attorney and assisting him or her in improving the delegation.

The Legal Assistant and the Law Clerk. On some occasions there are interpersonal problems between legal assistants and law clerks. To understand the possible causes for the friction, it is first important to understand the difference between the education and skill levels of the law clerk and the legal assistant. A law clerk is typically a student with a four-year college degree who is attending law school. The law clerk has an in-depth theoretical background in the various areas of law but generally has not developed many practical skills through the law school experience. A law clerk is generally delegated legal research tasks. By contrast, today's legal assistant, as a general rule, has a four-year college degree, but instead of attending law school attended a specialized educational program that provided a general knowledge of legal theory and lots of practical skills. Interpersonal problems between a legal assistant and a law clerk might have any number of causes, including the following:

- The law clerk may have a condescending attitude toward the legal assistant. This attitude will create friction between the law clerk and the legal assistant. If a legal assistant perceives friction and believes this is the cause, the best course of action for the legal assistant may be to "rise above it," view it as the law clerk's problem, and go about his or her business of creating a quality work product. As the law clerk continues to work with a professional legal assistant and views the quality of his or her work, the law clerk might begin to revise his or her opinion of the status and value of the legal assistant to the legal service delivery team.

- The law clerk may not understand the education, credentials, and competencies of the legal assistant. This is not generally a topic that is taught in law school. Most practical information about the legal working environment the law clerk will learn on the job. If this is identified as the problem, the legal assistant can begin to educate the law clerk concerning the legal assistant profession; the role the legal assistant plays on the legal service delivery team; the qualifications, education, and skills of the legal assistant; and the paralegal tasks appropriately delegated to legal assistants.

- Another possible cause of friction between the law clerk and the legal assistant is a worry, on the part of the law clerk, that legal assistants are taking "their jobs." Their concern is that if the attorneys in the environment have more legal work than they can handle, it is a better business decision to hire a legal assistant than to hire an attorney. This is often true. However, there are and there will remain job opportunities for high-quality attorneys.

What Can a Legal Assistant Do to Avoid Interpersonal Problems in a Legal Working Environment?

A legal assistant can be proactive in such a way as to avoid many potential interpersonal problems or, alternatively, can act quickly to resolve the problem when it arises. There are nine steps that a legal assistant can take to have a positive affect on his or her working environment, as follows:

- *Adopt a team approach.*   A legal assistant who sees him/herself as an integral part of the legal service delivery team and projects a team attitude will enhance the positive aspects of interpersonal dynamics within the firm.

- *Direct energy and interpersonal relationships toward the common goals.*   Rather than get bogged down and directly involved in the negative energy that is often generated by office politics, legal assistants should direct their energies in a constructive positive direction. When being engaged by another and encouraged to speak negatively about another team member or take sides in an interpersonal dispute, the team member should direct the conversation back to the common group goals that all team members share: to deliver high-quality legal services to clients in a timely, cost-effective manner.

- *Maintain a good attitude.*   A legal assistant should maintain an attitude at the work place that is professional, objective, non-condescending, non-judgmental, and positive. This type of attitude helps maintain a balance in the working environment and tends to offset the negative energy created by office politics.

- *Develop strong communication skills.*   A legal assistant with strong oral and written communication skills is often able to use those skills to positively influence a conversation or situation that is being driven by negative office politics.

- *Be self-motivated.*   A legal assistant who is self-motivated will always have plenty of paralegal work to do because the legal assistant acts in such a manner that he or she will find work to do even if it is not delegated. Members of the team appreciate a team member who can look around, see what needs to be done, and do it.

- *Always produce a quality work product.* If a legal assistant consistently produces a quality work product, it will be difficult for "office politics" to ever detract from the work product. A quality work product is the legal assistant's best protection.

- *Respect the chain of command.* A legal assistant can avoid interpersonal problems by always following the correct chain of command to address or resolve any issue that arises in the legal working environment. In most situations this means that the legal assistant will take an issue directly to his or her supervising attorney. In some organizational structures, the person in the direct supervision line may be the law office manager instead of the supervising attorney.

- *Respect the time of others.* Since time is the commodity of legal working environments, it is critical that the legal assistant respect the time of other income-producers on the legal service delivery team. Often this means going to the case file to gather information rather than expecting the supervising attorney to spend his or her time explaining the facts of a particular case. It may also mean that a lot of communication among the income-producers will be in written format that is concise, complete, and in a format that is easy to skim-read.

- *Use planning skills to avoid interpersonal problems.* Many interpersonal problems can be avoided by using good planning skills. Planning skills involve determining the proper "timing" of acts. A destructive confrontation might be avoided by determining the proper timing for the conversation and scheduling an appointment for the discussion at a time when all of the people involved will have had time to reflect rather than deciding to speak in the heat of the moment.

CONCLUSION

Throughout our lives we have all learned many valuable lessons about successfully dealing with and working in cooperation with other people. We need to marshal all of the skills we have learned to enjoy the positive aspects of interpersonal dynamics in the legal working environment and avoid the negative aspects involved in office politics.

DISCUSSION QUESTIONS

1. Compare and contrast the interpersonal dynamics problems that have arisen in the various legal and nonlegal working environments in which you have worked.

2. Consider your personal characteristics and determine which of them assist you in dealing with interpersonal dynamics problems in working environments.

3. Consider your personal characteristics and determine which have caused or could cause interpersonal dynamics problems in a working environment.

ENDNOTES

[1] *Infra* at Chapter 9 (discussion of the "Fee Recovery Issue").

[2] ALAN LAKEIN, HOW TO GET CONTROL OF YOUR TIME AND YOUR LIFE (Peter Wydent 1973).

[3] R. ALEC MACKENZIE, THE TIME TRAP (American Management Association 1972).

[4] The formula analysis reflected in the following scenario was originally proposed by M. Altman and R.Weil in a presentation at the American Association for Paralegal Educators Annual Meeting held in San Francisco, California, in October 1980.

[5] *See generally,* R. ALEC MACKENZIE, THE TIME TRAP (American Management Association, 1972); R. Alec MacKenzie, *How to Make the Most of Your Time,* U.S. NEWS AND WORLD REPORT, December 3, 1973.

[6] *See, e.g.,* EDWIN C. BLISS, GETTING THINGS DONE: THE ABCS OF TIME MANAGEMENT (Charles Scribner's Sons 1976); J.H. Jackson & R.L. Hayen, *Rationing the Scarcest Resource: A Manager's Time,* PERSONAL JOURNAL, October 1974, at 752–756; ALAN LAKEIN, HOW TO GET CONTROL OVER YOUR TIME AND YOUR LIFE (Peter Wydent 1973); R. ALEC MACKENZIE, THE TIME TRAP (American Management Association 1972); R. Alec MacKenzie, *Time Management: From Principle to Practice,* TRAINING AND DEVELOPMENT JOURNAL, July 1978, at 34–35; R. ALEC MACKENZIE, MANAGEMENT TIME AT THE TOP (The President's Association 1970); DONALD P. MACKINTOSH, MANAGEMENT BY EXCEPTION: A HANDBOOK OF FORMS (Prentice-Hall 1978); DALE D. MCCONKEY, NO-NONSENSE DELEGATION (American Management Association 1974); W. Oncken, Jr. & D.L. Wass, *Management Time: Who's Got the Monkey,* HARVARD BUSINESS REVIEW, November 1974, at 75–80; Norman V. Peale, *You Can Stop Being a Procrastinator,* READER'S DIGEST, January 1972; H.C. Rotenbury, *Time Management and the Organization,* MANAGEMENT WORLD, July 1978, at 25–26; ROSS A. WEBBER, TIME AND MANAGEMENT (Van Nostrand Reinhold 1972).

Legal Assistant Career Opportunities

C areer opportunities for legal assistants abound. The trick is to find a career opportunity that will provide a legal assistant with personal and professional satisfaction. In order to secure such a career opportunity, a legal assistant must first engage in a self-assessment process that will allow him/her to identify his or her personal and professional wants, needs, skills, goals, and dreams. After taking that step, a legal assistant must follow a systematic approach that will allow him/her to determine all career opportunities available within the parameters of the self-assessment, then begin the process of narrowing down those opportunities to the ones that he/she wants to pursue, and finally follow the steps necessary to secure the desired position. The chapters in this section set out a process that can lead to a satisfying career opportunity.

Exploring Career Opportunities

INTRODUCTION

The focus of this chapter is the exploration of career opportunities for competent, professional legal assistants. The word "exploration" is meant to convey an active, participatory process in which the legal assistant is directly involved in self-analysis, assessment, planning, research, contemplation, preparation, interviewing, negotiating, weighing, and deciding. The exploration process is ongoing for a legal assistant. Ideally it leads a new legal assistant to enter the profession and an experienced legal assistant to seek new opportunities and outlets for his or her creative energies and well-honed skills.

FIND A LEGAL ASSISTANT CAREER OPPORTUNITY . . . NOT JUST A JOB

The exploration process requires a participant who wants more than just a "job." A job is defined as "a piece of work undertaken or employment."[1] It is true that, unless money is no object, legal assistants all want to find a job so that they are employed and are generating money to provide financial security for them and their families. But is a job enough? Will a legal assistant be satisfied after securing a job that will allow them to move closer to their goal of financial security? What about a legal assistant's other personal and professional goals not directly linked to money?

This exploration process, if undertaken as suggested, will help the participant discover more than just a job. It will help him or her to discover career opportunities. A career is defined as "an occupation forming the object of one's life."[2] The broader search for a career is designed to enable the participant to identify all of the personal and professional goals in his or her life and to explore the variety of opportunities in the marketplace that will enable a satisfying level of occupational involvement in the legal system, while maintaining a holistic balance in both personal and professional lives. In view of the number of years most legal assistants will be occupationally involved, it only makes sense to search for the most satisfying career opportunities, rather than settle for the less onerous task of just finding the perfect job.

The career exploration process suggested in this section requires that the participant follow nine steps, as follows:[3]

- Self-assessment and identification of goals, skills, and priorities
- Research regarding career opportunities within the perimeters of identified goals, skills, and priorities
- Planning a systematic approach to maximize exploration of career opportunities discovered by research
- Preparing an effective resume and cover letter
- Following up after delivery of resumes
- Interviewing
- Following up after the interviews
- Negotiating compensation
- Making the employment decision

ASSESS PERSONAL AND PROFESSIONAL GOALS, SKILLS, AND PRIORITIES

Many legal assistants have entered the profession by searching for a job, landing a job, and then finding out that the job they landed left them feeling dissatisfied or burned out after a short time. What looked like a "perfect job" was not. Often the reason the job was dissatisfying had little to do with the compensation, which was a known factor at the time the job was accepted. The dissatisfaction had more to do with esoteric factors involving the personal and professional goals of the legal assistant that were not being met in the legal working environment, perhaps goals that had not been identified and assessed prior to the initial search, in which the legal assistant just wanted to find a job. Running head-first into the job market may help a participant get a job faster, but it will generally not help a legal assistant find a satisfying career opportunity that will provide holistic occupational satisfaction for the long term.

Assessing personal and professional goals, skills, and priorities *at the very beginning of the career exploration process* enables the legal assistant to come face-to-face with him/herself. From this honest, introspective process will emerge the skeleton of the evolving spirit: the legal assistant's wants, needs, aspirations, requirements, dreams, fears, skills, and ultimately goals. During the introspection process, it is common to identify areas of conflict . . . those areas where we want it all. As those areas of conflict are identified, the legal assistant must face the reality that he or she might not be able to have it all, and in those situations might be forced to make choices and establish priorities. The good news is that these choices and priorities are never set in stone, and as our lives evolve, we may find ourselves beginning another career exploration process, repeating this self-assessment to face ourselves once again, re-identify our goals and conflicts, make new choices, and set new priorities.

The introspection process should include a realistic analysis of your personal goals, hopes, wishes, dreams, and fears and should take into account all facets of yourself, including your physical, mental, emotional, and spiritual well-being. It should identify what is important to you personally in your life right now and what you believe will be important to you in 5 years, in 10 years, and in 20 years. During this process, conflicts may be detected, and they will need to be resolved, at least for the moment. For example, you might identify as an important personal goal that you want to begin a family, have a child, and spend a maximum amount of time with the child; you might identify as another personal goal that you want to spend time alone with your spouse to develop a more solid marriage relationship while you both work, using your professional credentials to gather assets in order to be more financially secure before you have a family. These goals will generally be in conflict with one another . . . and you can't have it all during the same period of time. The legal assistant in this situation, as a part of the introspective process, will need to resolve the conflict by prioritizing goals before searching for a career opportunity to match them. If the conflict is not resolved prior to the search, the legal assistant will not be in touch with what career opportunity would really be satisfying, both personally and professionally, and that unresolved conflict will cause problems not only in the interviewing process but after an employment decision is made.

The introspection process requires not only the assessment of personal goals but also the realistic assessment of professional goals and the identification of skills. It should identify what is important to you professionally in your life right now and what you believe will be important to you in five years, in ten years, and in twenty years. Part of this identification process involves an honest assessment of your good points, bad points, strong skills, weak skills, areas of law that you enjoy, and areas of the law that you do not enjoy. It should involve consideration of your financial goals, the type of working environments that you enjoy, the hours you are willing to work, the geographic area where you want to live, and the type of work you want to do. During this process, conflicts may be detected, and they will need to be resolved, at least for the moment. For example, you might identify as an important professional goal that you want to work in a small private law firm that specializes in patent and copyright legal work in a small, rural community in the western part of Texas. There are inherent conflicts in this goal. It is unlikely that such a career opportunity exists, because in the geographic area identified, there is not much, if any, demand for patent and copyright legal services. Choices will have to be made and priorities established to make this a more realistic professional goal. It may be possible to maintain this goal by switching geographic priorities to a small community outside of Houston, Texas.

After coming to terms with personal and professional goals, often conflicts can be seen between the two. Conflicting goals must also be identified and resolved before continuing the career exploration process. For example, you might identify as important personal goals that you want to begin a family, have a child, and spend a maximum amount of time with the child; you might also identify as an important professional goal that you want to be a litigation legal assistant in a large firm working directly with the trial team in major litigation matters. It is unlikely that you will be able to achieve both of these goals during the same time period. Choices will need to be made and priorities established to resolve the conflict, at least for the occupational time period being assessed.

To assist in the self-assessment process, write down specific goals in timeframe increments in the following areas: Personal, Professional, Family, Recreation/Leisure, Professional, Geographic, Environment, and Areas of Law. See Figure 13-1.

In addition to the written goal-and-target-date assessment tool in Figure 13-1, a self-assessment questionnaire may prove helpful to more specifically identify goals and conflicts between personal and professional goals. A self-assessment questionnaire is provided in Figure 13-2.

WRITTEN GOALS ASSESSMENT				
GOALS	NOW	5 YEARS	10 YEARS	20 YEARS
PERSONAL:				
FINANCIAL:				
FAMILY:				
RECREATION/LEISURE:				
PROFESSIONAL:				
GEOGRAPHIC:				
ENVIRONMENT:				
AREAS OF LAW:				

Figure 13-1 Written goals assessment.

SELF-ASSESSMENT QUESTIONNAIRE

1. On a scale of 1 to 10 with 1 being the best, I rate my skill level in the following areas as:

legal research	___	oral communication	___
legal drafting	___	written communication	___
fact investigation	___	interpersonal people skills	___
direct client contact	___	attention to detail	___
drafting documents	___	drafting contracts	___
interviewing	___	organization	___
analysis of data	___	persuasive communication	___
discovery planning	___	informative communication	___

2. Other skills that I possess include: (describe in detail)

computer: _____

language: _____

engineering: _____

alternate dispute resolution: _____

counseling: _____

artistic: _____

other: _____

_____

_____

_____

_____

3. On a scale of 1 to 10 with 1 being the best, I rate my interest level in the following areas as:

legal research	___	real estate law	___
legal drafting	___	corporate law	___
litigation	___	wills and estate law	___
criminal law	___	administrative law	___
social legislation	___	contract law	___
tort law	___	employment law	___
health law	___	family law	___
copyright/patent	___	intellectual property	___

Figure 13-1 Written goals assessment.

4. I consider the following to be my strong points or the things I am good at and enjoy:

5. I consider the following to be my weak points or the things I am not good at and do not enjoy:

6. I "need" to make a salary of _____ to meet my financial obligations.

7. I "want" to make a salary of _____.

8. On a scale of 1 to 10 with 1 being the best, I rate my interest level in the following legal working environments as:

small private law firm	___	corporate legal department	___
medium private law firm	___	state administrative agency	___
large private law firm	___	federal administrative agency	___
public interest law clinic	___	bank	___
insurance company	___	real estate corporation	___
state court	___	federal court	___
county/district attorney	___	U.S. attorney	___

other: _____

_____

9. I am willing to accept a job and live in the following geographic locations:

10. I am not willing to accept a job and live in the following geographic locations:

11. I want to have ____ hours per week for personal recreation and leisure.

Figure 13-2 Continued

12. Three years from now I will be ____ years old and at that time I will want to be and to have the following options.

13. Five years from now I will be _____ years old and at that time I will want to be and to have the following options::

14. Ten years from now I will be ____ years old and at that time I will want to be and to have the following options:

15. Twenty years from now I will be ____ years old and at that time I will want to be and to have the following options:

16. I see the following competing interests with my goals and skills. I know I will need to make choices and prioritize to resolve these conflicts for the present (knowing that I can revisit these decisions later as my life continues to change and evolve):

     _____   v   _____
     _____   v   _____
     _____   v   _____
     _____   v   _____
     _____   v   _____
     _____   v   _____

17. My current priorities, among the competing interests listed above are:

18. Based on this self-assessment, I would like to explore the following types of career opportunities in the following geographic areas: (list the preferred legal working environments and the preferred geographic areas)

DISCUSSION QUESTIONS

1. Fill out Figure 13-1.
2. Fill out Figure 13-2.
3. Based on your self-analysis, list the discoveries that you have made concerning the types of legal working environments, geographical areas, and skill utilization that you prefer in your career as a legal assistant.

RESEARCH CAREER OPPORTUNITIES WITHIN THE ENVIRONMENTAL AND GEOGRAPHIC PARAMETERS DICTATED BY THE SELF-ASSESSMENT

After completing the self-assessment, the legal assistant will have weighed personal and professional strengths, weaknesses, interests, desires, and goals and decided priorities among conflicting interests and goals. The result of that analysis is an informed decision by the legal assistant concerning what types of legal working environments in which geographic areas the legal assistant will want to explore during the next step in the career exploration process. This step requires the legal assistant to engage in research to determine all possible occupational opportunities and options that exist within the legal working environments and geographical areas the legal assistant has decided to explore.

Do not skip this research step. Yes, it will take time. However, if research is not done, the legal assistant will not discover the full range of occupational opportunities available. Failure to discover employment options due to lack of research is a fatal step, for the obvious reason that if you do not explore and discover the option, you cannot apply for and secure the employment opportunity! Remember that very few occupational opportunities fall out of the sky directly into the lap of the seeker.

Researching employment opportunities in specific geographic areas for legal assistants in selected legal working environments generally involves using non-legal reference materials, books, directories, and sources. These types of reference materials can usually be found in public libraries, as well as law libraries. Some of this material might be available through the Internet and other computer databases. The following information in this chapter summarizes the suggested research resources available for discovering potential employers in the various types of legal working environments.

What Research Sources Can Be Used to Discover Potential Private Law Firm Employers?

The best research source for discovering information about potential private law firm employers is the *Martindale-Hubbell Law Directory,* which is published annually and consists of several large volumes. It is the most complete, readily accessible source of information about law firms in the United States and the individual attorneys in each law firm, and it also contains legal assistant information. Most major law firms in

```
┌─────────────────────────────────────────────────────────────────────┐
│                    POTENTIAL EMPLOYER LOG                             │
│                                                                       │
│  Name,         Contact      Resume (&      Interview (&      Other    │
│  Address, Zip, Person (&    Follow Up)     Follow Up)                 │
│  Phone and     Why)                                                   │
│  Facsimile                                                            │
│  Numbers &                                                            │
│  Areas of Law                                                         │
│  Practice                                                             │
│                                                                       │
└─────────────────────────────────────────────────────────────────────┘
```

Figure 13-3 Potential employer log.

each state in the United States are included in the directory, paying a fee to be listed. The volumes are organized by state and within each state volume, each law firm is listed alphabetically by city. The entry for each firm includes the name, address, telephone and fax numbers, branch offices, areas of practice, representative clients, and biographical information for each individual attorney in the law firm. Biographical information includes birth date, dates of bar admissions, educational information, honors, bar memberships, and publications.

The information contained in the law firm listing can help the legal assistant determine whether the attorneys in the law firm practice in the areas of law that are of most interest. To effectively utilize the information presented in the law firm listing, once the legal assistant has found the correct state volume and the correct city or cities to be explored, he or she should read about each law firm listed, noting the size of the law firm and the areas of practice in order to determine whether it fits the parameters established for the search. If it does, then the legal assistant should write down the relevant information so that it will be ready for the next step, the planning stage. The legal assistant should write the information down in a *Potential Employer Log*, as shown in Figure 13-3. This information can be manually written in the Potential Employer Log or in a computerized database that the legal assistant has ready access to during the career opportunities exploration process.

The relevant information to note includes the name, address, zip code, and telephone and fax numbers for the law firm. It is also important to determine which attorney the legal assistant believes would be the best contact person within the law firm to send the cover letter and resume to. Usually it is best to send the resume and cover letter to a junior partner in the law firm. A junior partner is an owner of the law firm and is usually more involved in the management of the law firm's business than are the senior partners. You can look at birthdate information and the bar admission date to figure out the age and experience of each of the partners in the law firm. Do not send a resume to an associate of the law firm, because an associate is an employee and usually does not have authority to hire other employees. Once you have determined who the junior partners are, look at their biographical sketches and determine what, if anything, you may have in common with them. Did you graduate from the same undergraduate college? Were you in the same social fraternity? Do you have the same home town? If you have anything in common with any of the partner attorneys, note the name of the partner and what you have in common on the Potential Employer Log (Figure 13-3). If you do not find anything in common with any of the junior partners, then simply choose the partner you would prefer to send the cover letter and resume to and write that name down in the log.

Other national, state, and local attorney directories may be used as reference sources, but they are generally not as complete as the *Martindale-Hubbell Law Directory*, so the same commitment of time may yield less information. Examples of other directories include: *American Bar Reference Handbook, Attorney's Directory of Services and Information, Best Lawyers in America, Best's Directory of Recommended Insurance Attorneys, Lawyer's Register by Specialty and Field of Law,* and *Who's Who in American Law.*

The local telephone book should not be used as a source in and of itself because the information it contains is limited to the names, address, and telephone number. However, depending on the publication date of the telephone book, it may be a good source for updating and validating the telephone number of the law firm. Also, not all small firms pay to be listed in the various law directories and might only be listed in the local telephone book.

What Research Sources Can Be Used to Discover Potential Corporate Employers?

Several sources can be used to research potential corporate employers in specific geographic areas. Among the research sources available is the *Martindale-Hubbell Law Directory* discussed previously, which also lists corporate legal departments alphabetically by corporate name. Under the corporate listing, it specifies the geographic location(s) of its main legal department and other regional corporate legal departments. In addition to this source, several corporate reference directories are available in most public libraries, as follows:

- *Standard & Poor's Register of Corporations, Directors and Executives*   This annually published directory alphabetically lists approximately 55,000 corporations located in the United States and contains information about business and management personnel. To identify legal staff, look for the individuals designated as General Counsel.

- *Moody's Industrial Manual* and the *Moody's Bank and Financial Manual*   These manuals contain an alphabetical listing of corporations in the United States and provide information concerning the corporation, including the general counsel.

- *Dun & Bradstreet Million Dollar Directory*   This annual national directory contains information regarding businesses and management personnel. The information provided about the management personnel is not as complete as either *Standard & Poor's Register* or *Moody's Industrial Manual.*

- *Dun's Reference Book of Corporate Management*   This national directory has a great deal of information about management personnel. It lists corporations alphabetically.

- *Directory of Corporate Counsel,* published by *Dun's Marketing Service Books.*

- *Walker's Manual of Western Corporations*   This manual lists all corporations in the western United States in alphabetical order by regions.

- *Ward's Business Directory of U.S. Public and Private Companies*   This directory is helpful because it lists corporations both alphabetically and geographically. It also includes the names of the corporate officers.

While using these sources, when the legal assistant locates a potential employer that has a corporate legal department in the geographic location desired, the relevant information concerning the potential corporate employer, including the name of the corporate attorney to send the resume and cover letter to, should be entered in the Potential Employer Log (see Figure 13-3). Many corporations also have personnel departments and may have employment applications to fill out. The legal assistant should send a resume and cover letter to both the corporate attorney and to the director of human resources.

What Research Sources Can Be Used to Discover Potential Governmental Employers?

Several sources are available for discovering career opportunities with government employers. Determining which sources are appropriate depends upon the categories of governmental employers being explored. The categories of governmental employers include federal, state, and local government entities.

Legal Assistant Opportunities in the Federal Government: To obtain information about career opportunities and specific job openings available with the federal government, the legal assistant should contact the Federal Job Information Center (FJIC) which has several Offices of Personnel Management (OPM) nationwide. The telephone numbers for these centers can be found in most telephone books listed under "U.S. Government." Other reference sources that can be used to explore legal assistant opportunities in the federal government include the following:

- *Electronic Federal Job Opportunity List Service*   This continuously updated, on-line data base lists all federal governmental employment openings and applicable deadlines.

- *The Paralegal's Guide to U.S. Government Jobs: How to Land a Job in 70 Law-Related Fields*   This booklet describes the hiring standards and procedures used by the federal government. It can be ordered from Federal Reports, 1010 Vermont Avenue NW, Suite 408, Washington, D.C. 20005, (202) 313-3311.

- *Law and Lobbying in the Nation's Capitol*   This weekly newspaper provides information concerning career opportunities in the federal government and has a nationwide circulation.

Legal assistant positions with federal agencies vary in both job titles and in the nature of the paralegal duties delegated. The following federal government job titles require legal assistant education and training:

- Paralegal Specialist
- Legal Technician
- Litigation Support Technician

The Paralegal Specialist job title is used for positions that involve the delegation of paralegal tasks but do not require professional legal competence. The work requires discretion and independent judgment in the application of specialized knowledge of particular laws, regulations, precedents, or agency practices based thereon. The type of delegated tasks include legal research, selecting, assembling, summarizing, and compiling substantive legal information, case preparation, analyzing facts, and drafting responses to legal questions. The GS levels are 5/7/9, which means that the pay ranges for these positions are from approximately $17,000 to $25,700 per year.

The Legal Technician/Legal Clerk job title includes all classes of positions, the duties of which are to perform or supervise legal, clerical, or technical work. The work requires a specialized knowledge of legal documents and processes and the ability to apply established instructions, rules, and regulations, precedents, and procedures pertaining to legal activities. The GS levels are 5/6/7, which means the pay for these positions ranges from approximately $17,000 to $21,023 per year.

The Litigation Support Technician also requires legal assistant education and training and the paralegal duties delegated focus on providing litigation support for the litigation divisions within the governmental unit.

Testing is usually required for governmental positions. The tests are generally conducted by the Office of Personnel Management (OPM) and the applicant must fill out an application prior to the test, form OPM-5000B for an entry-level legal assistant position. Once the examination is passed, the applicant's name will be placed on a list that can be accessed by federal governmental agencies as vacancies arise.

Some federal government positions require not only testing but security clearance. The security clearance process will take additional time and will be done by federal security employees.

If the legal assistant applies for a specific opening with a federal agency, the agency usually requires the applicant to fill out an SF-171, a Personal Qualifications Statement. This form is considered to be the federal government's job application form. The applicant may also be asked to submit an OPM Form 1170-17, which requires a listing of college classes taken; often a college transcript can be submitted in lieu of OPM Form 1170-17. In addition to these forms, the applicant will be asked to submit a resume. When filling out these forms and communicating with the federal agency, be sure to make very specific reference to the job title, job number, position, grade level, and job announcement for which you are applying. Another must is to carefully observe the closing date or deadline for applications for the job. If an application is received after the deadline, it cannot be considered.

Remember that the federal government is a huge organization and is very structured. There are forms and more forms, tests, and security clearances. Obtaining a job with the federal government takes patience, attention to detail, following procedures, filling out forms, and lots of waiting. Perseverance is the key!

Legal Assistant Opportunities in State and Local Governments   Most state and local governments have a specific procedure for hiring employees in any particular position. The procedure usually involves publication of the job opening for a certain time period, accepting employment applications and resumes from the date the job is posted until the closing date, reviewing the log of applicants for the position, narrowing down the applicants based on the applications and resumes, conducting interviews, and making the hiring decision. The best sources of information concerning job openings are the official job posting sites used by the state or local government. The state administrative code lists each state administrative agency as well as the rules and regulations of each agency. Local governments usually have directories listing each entity within the local government. Telephone books can be used to obtain the telephone numbers for these state and local entities. By calling the personnel department, the legal assistant could easily determine the official job posting sites used by the state or local entity. Many state and local entities also provide on-line access to job information. Other reference sources for state and local government information include the *Attorney's Directory of Service and Information* and the *Municipal/County Executive Directory Annual* (published by Carroll Publishing Company, 1058 Thomas Jefferson St., NW, Washington, D.C. 20077), which contains listings of both elected and appointed officials at all levels of government.

What Research Sources Can Be Used to Discover Potential Public Interest Law Employers?

Public interest law clinics hire legal assistants and often broadly delegate tasks to their legal assistant employees. They are usually organized as private law firms and concentrate on handling legal problems of middle-class individuals.

Legal Services Corporation is a federally funded corporation that provides legal assistance to low-income individuals. There are many offices located within each state. The best source of information concerning the location of these entities is the *Attorney's Directory of Services and Information*. Usually bilingual (Spanish) ability is preferred or required, particularly in the Southwest. Knowledge of other languages such as Korean or Chinese may be valuable in other areas of the United States.

Many of the legal clinics and legal services corporations will continue to experience funding cuts, which will require them to reduce their services. This concern might, however, increase the need for legal assistants within these organizations.

What Other Sources Can Be Used to Discover Existing Job Opportunities in a Specific Geographic Area?

Several reference sources can be consulted for information about legal assistant occupational opportunities in specific geographic areas, as follows:

- Job banks are listings of legal assistant positions that are collected by private sources. For example, both national paralegal organizations have job banks that can be accessed by their membership. Many legal assistant educational facilities also have a job bank that is accessible to their current and former students. Local legal assistant organizations also have job banks containing information about legal assistant openings within the local area. Many state bar associations, especially those with legal assistant divisions, have job banks containing statewide job listings.

- Newspapers are also sources of information concerning local job openings. It is a mistake, however, to consult only this source because many employers do not publicize professional job openings in the newspaper.

- Newsletters published by legal-based entities that have a circulation with the legal community may contain information about specific job openings.

- Networking is an excellent source of information concerning legal assistant openings. Many, many legal assistant positions, particularly in private law firms, are publicized by word-of-mouth. For this reason, among others, it is an excellent idea to join national and local legal assistant organizations where you can meet and interact with other legal assistants.

CONCLUSION

Exploring career opportunities requires a lot of work because it is a participatory process. An effective search that will yield the maximum number of personally and professionally satisfying career opportunities for a legal assistant begins with an intense self-assessment process and includes broad research designed to identify all available legal working environments within the parameters of the self-assessment.

DISCUSSION QUESTIONS

1. What strategy would be the best for you to use to research employment opportunities in the legal working environments and geographic locations you would like to explore?

2. Examine the Potential Employer Log in Figure 13-3 and consider how you might use it to better organize your search for legal assistant career opportunities.

ENDNOTES

[1] Webster Encyclopedic Dictionary of the English Language (Consolidated Book Publishers 1979), at 464.

[2] Id., at 123.

[3] The systematic approach to exploring and securing career opportunities reflected in Chapters 13 and 14 of this book are based upon concepts and information that was originally obtained from Therese A. Cannon at a workshop presentation made at the American Association for Paralegal Educators Annual Meeting held in San Francisco, California, in October 1980.

Securing Legal Assistant Career Opportunities

INTRODUCTION

After completing the self-assessment and research steps discussed in Chapter 13, a legal assistant continues the search process by taking systematic steps to secure a satisfying career opportunity in one of the available legal working environments previously identified. The steps discussed in this chapter include planning the time and manner in which to approach potential employers, developing an effective resume and cover letter, using the resume and cover letter to full advantage, following up the resume and cover letter with personal contact, preparing for the interview, interviewing for the position, graciously following up after the interview, and negotiating acceptable compensation prior to acceptance of the position.

PLAN A BROAD SEARCH TO DISCOVER SATISFYING CAREER OPPORTUNITIES

After finishing the self-assessment and research steps outlined in Chapter 13, the legal assistant will have a list of potential employers and the relevant information on each recorded on the Potential Employer Log (Figure 13-3). The next step is to plan a broad search to discover all career opportunities in the chosen legal working environments in the selected geographic areas. This search requires the legal assistant to establish and follow a specific strategy to systematically explore each potential occupational opportunity. The suggested strategy is to plan the timeframe for the search and the uniform steps that will be followed in making contact with each potential employer.

For example, the plan could be that the legal assistant will send out all resumes and cover letters to potential employers by June 1, then will make follow-up telephone calls to each potential employer on June 5, and will track each contact on the Potential Employer Log (Figure 13-3). The plan will need to become more generalized as some of the follow-up contacts result in interviews and some do not, however, each contact's status can still be noted on the log. By using planning skills, the legal assistant can establish a systematic strategy in order to effectively utilize his or her time and to ensure that none of the potential employer searches fall through the cracks. Conduct a broad search to develop all potential occupational opportunities rather than putting all of your eggs in one basket.

DISCUSSION QUESTIONS

1. Examine the strategy that you created in response to the discussion questions on Chapter 13. In light of this discussion about strategy, what would you change and why?

2. Reflect on your previous employment searches. What strategies did you employ to determine where to send your resumes?

PREPARE AN EFFECTIVE RESUME FOR LEGAL WORKING ENVIRONMENTS

Once a plan is in place for conducting the search, the next step is the development of an effective resume. Drafting a resume that is effective in a legal working environment requires the legal assistant to consider the unique characteristics of that environment and the perceptions and needs of the legal audience recipients of the resume. The following discussion will first focus on the purpose of the resume, the major parts of a resume, and the contents to include in each part in order to tailor the resume to the legal environment and audience. It continues with a practical focus on improving the appearance and effectiveness of the resume and concludes with information about the appropriate use of the resume and cover letter.

What Is the Purpose of a Resume?

The purpose of a resume is to introduce the applicant to the potential employer. It is a tool used by the applicant to make the first impression that will, hopefully, open the door to a subsequent job interview. It must present the applicant in a positive, favorable manner. Unlike lengthy job applications, the resume is not expected to account for everything that the applicant has done since 1965. Rather, the resume should pinpoint key facts about the applicant's education, past employment, and special skills. The effective resume for a legal working environment must be drafted so that it will be easily understood by a legal audience who, in view of the enormous ongoing reading burden experienced by the average attorney and the unusually large number of resumes that are generally received, will probably "skim-read" the resume.

What Are the Major Parts of a Resume?

A well-drafted, skim-able resume includes the following five major parts:

- Personal information
- Educational background
- Work experience
- Honors and awards, professional associations, or career distinctions
- Other skills

Before discussing each of the major parts, note what information the well-drafted, skim-able resume should *not* include. It should not include the following:

- *The title "Resume"*   It will be obvious to the potential employer that the document is a resume without wasting the space required to write the title on the top of it. Space will be a premium because the well-drafted, skim-able resume should be only one page long.

- *A "Hobbies and Interests" section*   This information will be viewed as not relevant and, depending on the hobbies and interests listed, may actually distract the reader from the applicant's relevant credentials. On occasion, an applicant may have a hobby or interest that would relate to the type of legal work the employer does; for example, if an applicant is a private pilot and is applying for a legal assistant position with a law firm that handles aviation law matters. If this is the case, the applicant should consider putting that information in the "Other Skills" section of the resume and also mentioning it in the cover letter that accompanies the resume.

- *Non-job-related personal information*   Information concerning the applicant's physical description, a photograph of the applicant, age, marital status, spouse's occupation, health, religion, sexual preference, birth control preference, children, or any other non-job-related personal information is inappropriate for a potential employer to use as a basis for hiring.

- *A "Career Objectives" section*   Since this resume is being used to open up professional career opportunities in the legal field, it is not necessary to state this objective in the resume. Usually such statements simply waste space because they are too general in nature and do not add or pinpoint specific information for the reader. If the applicant wants to make a specific statement about career objectives in a particular legal working environment, that statement should be included in the cover letter that accompanies the resume.

- *The phrase "References Available On Request"*   This is a known fact and need not be stated in the resume. It will simply waste space and does not pinpoint specific relevant information.

- *A list of specific individuals as references*   There will be a time in the process for using a list of specific individuals as references and making the list available to the potential employer. However, it is not at the "resume and cover letter" stage. Rather, the reference list will be used after the interview and should be taken to the job interview in case it is requested at that time. Most employers will not check references until they have interviewed the applicants and have narrowed the search to the finalists.

What Should Be Included in the Major Parts of the Well-Drafted, Skim-able Resume?

The following is a discussion of the contents of each of the five parts of an effective resume. Each of the following parts includes substantive suggestions about appropriate elements to include and exclude in view of the unique characteristics of the legal environment and legal audience readers. In addition, practical suggestions help the legal assistant design a resume that reflects his/her unique self.

Personal Information.   The first major part of a well-drafted, skim-able resume will consist of personal information about the applicant. This information should be clearly set out and formatted in such a way that it is easily identified by the skim-reader. The applicant should list his or her name, address, zip code, telephone number(s) with area codes, and e-mail address either in the upper left-hand corner of the page or centered in the middle of the page, using capital letters and/or boldface type for the name. The legal assistant applicant should carefully consider which address to use and which telephone numbers to list, based on the timeframe for the search. If the applicant is a student at the time the resume is prepared but has graduated and moved by the time the resume is received, the person who receives the resume will not be able to call or otherwise contact the applicant if he or she used a student address and telephone number. Updatintg the address and telephone number in a cover letter would not help because the potential employer might not keep both documents stapled together and even if they did, they might not always read both documents. The resume will be the most used document and should always contain the best, most updated personal information.

The telephone numbers listed on the resume must always be answered either by a person or by voice mail (an answering machine or a message service). Usually the potential employer receives a large number of resumes to skim-read as a part of the narrowing process, then they call the surviving applicants to schedule interviews. If the potential employer calls and no one answers, they will probably not try again. They will simply interview the applicants who answered the call and forget about the applicant who did not bother to provide a valid telephone contact number; for this reason, the applicant should list not only the home telephone number but also a message number. An answering/message service is best but not always financially feasible, so an answering machine or voice mail could be used. In addition, the applicant could list as a message number the telephone number of a relative or friend who is at that number "all the time" and will agree to take messages.

Most legal working environments are technologically advanced and most potential employers are accustomed to using electronic mail to communicate, so the applicant should list a current e-mail address. However, if the e-mail address is listed, then the applicant must regularly check his or her e-mail and reply to any e-mail messages received.

Educational Background.   Lawyers and managers in legal working environments are increasingly interested in hiring legal assistants with strong academic backgrounds. This is particularly true for the employer hiring a professional legal assistant who will be expected to be an exempt employee and income-producer. The trend in the profession is to require, as a minimum educational credential, a four-year college degree, but more legal assistants are now entering the profession with advanced, graduate-level coursework, such as a Masters in Legal Studies. In view of this trend and the increased focus on academic credentials, the legal assistant applicant should pay special attention to the "educational background" portion of the resume. The educational background portions should be drafted in such a way as to pinpoint all aspects of the applicant's education, including not only college-level coursework, but also proprietary legal assistant training, continuing legal education training, and seminars. Do not list pre-collegiate education. If the applicant's academic background includes graduate-level degrees and coursework in legal studies or paralegal training, that should be emphasized by separating the educational portion into the following components: graduate education, undergraduate education, and continuing legal education.

As a practical matter, the applicant should list the educational background within each category in reverse chronological order, stating the name of the academic institution (university, college, or school), the degree earned, the major and minor, and the date of graduation or completion of the degree. The applicant should only include the grade point average earned if it is very high (over 3.0). In addition, the applicant may choose to list specific courses that are particularly applicable to a legal assistant position or which taught them skills that are directly applicable to the legal working environment. Use the full name of the academic institution without abbreviations, because they may not be understood by the reader. Listing specific paralegal skills acquired in paralegal training is usually not useful and should not be done unless the applicant lacks significant work experience.

Work Experience.   A potential employer will focus particularly on this area of the resume, because most legal working environment employers prefer not only a strong academic background, but also an impressive experiential background. The legal assistant applicant should work hard to develop the "work experience" section of the resume so that it clearly highlights both paralegal skills (legal research, drafting, fact investigation, etc.) and functional skills that are a normal part of a legal assistant's job (organization, analysis, detail-oriented tasks, logic, written communication, oral communication, public relations, dispute resolution, supervision, administrative reporting and recordkeeping, accounting, computer skills, etc.). Remember, even if the applicant is just entering the legal assistant profession and does not have work experience as a legal assistant, he or she generally has worked in other jobs (in paid or volunteer capacities) that have developed and used transferable skills. These skills should be included in the functional description of the applicant's work experience.

As a practical matter, when drafting the work experience portion of the resume, the legal assistant should follow these two principles: (1) List work experience in *reverse chronological order* with the most recent work experience first and (2) use a *functional description* to pinpoint specific skills that were utilized in that work experience that would also be used by the legal assistant in the legal working environment.

When listing work experience in reverse chronological order, provide the following information for each job listed:

- Dates of employment
- Name of company
- Location of company (city and state only)
- Job title
- Functional description of job duties and responsibilities

Internships and volunteer experience can also be included in the work experience portion of the resume.

One of the most critical components of the work experience section is a powerful, skim-able, functional description of job duties and responsibilities. It is easier to set forth a functional description of work experience in a paralegal job because the legal-oriented reader will be familiar with paralegal tasks. However, as this section is being drafted the legal assistant needs to understand that the person reading the resume will usually have a legal orientation or background and may not understand all of the functional skills utilized by a person working in non-legal jobs such as retail sales, manufacturing, teaching, library science, nursing, waitress work, March of Dimes neighborhood coordination, business management, banking, insurance, real estate, and even various clerical support jobs. The legal assistant must carefully pinpoint the specific skills that were developed and utilized in the non-legal work experience in order to allow the legal-oriented reader to clearly see the transferability of the actual work experience to a legal assistant position.

For example, suppose Jill Smith worked as a clerical assistant to a loan counselor at Acme Mortgage Company from 1995–1997. Among her duties were using Dictaphone equipment to type letters for her employer, answering telephones to take messages for her employer, responding to routine inquiries from customers, keeping an appointment calendar, maintaining records on the status of accounts and foreclosures, preparing periodic reports based on records she maintained, relieving the switchboard operator, and filing and preparing a variety of forms. Jill's work experience could be functionally described as follows:

1995–1997   Acme Mortgage Loan Company. Los Angeles, California.
                 Assistant to Loan Counselor.

Job responsibilities included: Preparing initial foreclosure and loan documents, maintaining records regarding status of accounts, preparing monthly and semi-annual reports, handling inquiries from borrowers and lenders, and performing general office work.

In summary, a functional job description should indicate the skills developed and utilized in the applicant's work experience, as those skills relate to what is expected of a legal assistant in a legal working environment. If possible, describe work experience within the context of writing, organizing, researching (fact and law), analyzing, and relating to people (client contact). Describe skills that reflect the use of independent judgment, discretion, responsibility for other workers, accountability for results (financial, inventory, nightly lock-up), preparing demonstrative presentations of analysis (graph, charts, spreadsheets, visual aids, overheads, educational handouts, and other types of exhibits), and administrative responsibilities.

When describing the work experience, the functional skills listed should be described in an active voice for a more powerful impact on the reader. It is also important to use a consistent format and parallel construction as the various different jobs are described. Consistency and parallel construction will help the skim-reader more quickly assimilate the information and understand the depth of the combined job experience. It will also impress the legal-oriented reader who values good writing, organization, and drafting techniques.

Honors and Awards, Professional Associations, or Career Distinctions.   The exact title that the legal assistant uses for this section of the resume depends on what he or she has accomplished that can be included. The title of the section should be a fair summary of the content of the section. Often this kind of information is impressive to potential employers if it is substantive in the context of the legal working environment. However, listing honors, awards, achievements, associations, or distinctions that are of an insignificant nature appears pretentious. For example, it is certainly an honor to have been named and crowned as "Miss Peach 1999" in the Georgia Peach Beauty Competition; however, such an award is so unrelated to the skills needed in a legal working environment that it would be insignificant in the legal assistant employment context.

As a general rule, if the honor, award, association, or distinction is based on academic performance, functional skill assessment, merit, excellence in job performance, knowledge, peer recognition, and academic class standing, it would be a good idea to include it in this section. If a legal assistant has taken and passed legal assistant certification examinations given by the national legal assistant associations, is a member of a national legal assistant association, is board-certified as a legal assistant by a state bar association, or is a member of a division and/or section of a state bar association, that should be noted. If the legal assistant has held office in any organization that would be viewed as a substantive organization in an employment context, the legal assistant could note that information under this section.

If a legal assistant does not have any substantive information to include in this section, then this entire section should be omitted, rather than put the title and write the word "none" under it.

Other Skills.   The "other skills" portion of the resume can be used by the legal assistant to inform the potential employer of specialized non-legal skills that are relevant and would be considered helpful in a legal working environment. The following types of skills would fall in this category:

- *Military experience* could be listed in this category. If listed the applicant should include the branch of service, dates, rank at the time of discharge (if significant), and a functional description of areas of responsibility (with emphasis on transferable skills)

- *Foreign language* oral and written communication skills should be listed in this category. These skills are becoming increasingly important in all work environments in view of the global economy and the need to be able to communicate with all individuals within and outside of the United States. Remember that "sign language" is considered a special language skill also.

- *Photography or other artistic and/or computer graphics* skills are particularly helpful to a litigation law firm that creates demonstrative evidence.

- *Computer-related skills,* including experience with word processing, spreadsheets, automated litigation support software, the Internet, designing and creating Web pages, and various computer software is definitely a plus in any legal working environment. Most legal assistants and lawyers have computer terminals in their offices for their own word processing and electronic communication, working on- and off-line.

If the legal assistant has skills to include in this portion, the descriptions should be clear and specific. If the legal assistant does not have skills to list in this area of the resume, it should be omitted.

How Should a Well-Drafted, Skim-able Resume Look?

Remember that a resume is a reflection of the applicant. Think of the resume as a "picture" of the applicant: If the resume is well organized, concise, consistent in format, detail-oriented, grammatically correct, relevant to the legal working environment, and aesthetically appealing, it will impress the legal reader and will be more likely to open the door to a job interview. The reader will, upon review of this type of resume, assume that the legal assistant has, in addition to the education, experience, and skills listed, all of the other qualities reflected in the appearance of the resume: intelligence, organization, detail orientation, excellent written communication skills, independent judgment, and an understanding of the needs of a legal working environment. On the other hand, if the resume is not organized well, is verbose, contains matter that is not substantial in nature, is inconsistent in format, contains spelling and/or grammatical errors, and is not aesthetically appealing, the legal reader will assume that the legal assistant applicant is not qualified for the position because the applicant lacks intelligence, organization, detail orientation, written communication skills, independent judgment, and an understanding of the realities of a legal working environment, notwithstanding the education, experience, and skills listed in the resume.

How Long Should the Resume Be?

In every legal working environment there is too much information and there are too many documents to read! Given this reality, the legal assistant preparing a resume will understand the value of achieving the perfect balance between completeness and conciseness in every legal drafting process . . . including the drafting of a resume. *A resume should not be more than one page in length!* Even if the legal assistant has worlds of education, experience, honors, and skills, the resume must reflect the quality and quantity of the legal assistant's credentials in a one-page, clear, well-organized, concise, skim-able format.

A legal assistant with the maximum amount of academic and experiential credentials will have the wonderful task of condensing all of these credentials into a one-page format. This task will require careful use spacing, tabs, indenting, and choice of fonts, in addition to condensing information into very concise packages that remain clear and complete. It is a wonderful task compared to the more difficult task facing a legal assistant with the minimum amount of academic and experiential credentials. The less-credentialed legal assistant must expand the relevant, substantive information to fill at least one full page, requiring the careful use of spacing, tabs, indenting, and choice of fonts in addition to the creative functional expansion of the descriptions of academic and experiential credentials.

The purpose of the resume is to open the door to a job interview by making the legal reader so interested in the applicant that he or she wants to talk to the applicant to learn more details . . . the resume merely needs to pique the reader's interest in the applicant, not answer all questions the reader may have about the applicant. The resume must make the applicant "stand out from the crowd" in a positive manner. The ability of a resume to portray the applicant as someone who stands out, above the individuals portrayed in other resumes, enables the applicant to survive the resume-screening process and make it to the job-interview stage. A well-drafted, concise, one-page resume is more likely to help the legal assistant achieve the goal of persuading the reader to call the applicant and schedule an interview to learn more about his or her credentials, qualifications, and personality.

What Organization and Format Should Be Used for the Resume?

No single organization and/or format is suggested for all legal assistants. This decision requires the independent judgment of the legal assistant based on the quality and quantity of information to be included in the resume. A typical outline reflects the preferred order of the five main portions of the resume itself, first setting out relevant personal information, then educational background, then work experience, then honors and awards, and finally other skills. However, within this framework, the legal assistant must use discretion to organize the relevant information to be included and to determine the specific format. In making organizational and formatting decisions, the following factors should be considered:

- Margins
- Fonts
- Parallel construction within each of the major parts of the resume
- Consistent format among major parts of the resume

It is customary to have one-inch margins on each side of a document (including top and bottom). However, if space is a premium because of the quantity of information that the legal assistant is attempting to include in the resume, using smaller side margins may be an option. It is advisable to use a consistent margin for all sides of the document because the information will look more centered on the page and be more aesthetically appealing. On the other hand, if the legal assistant has more space on one page than needed for the quantity of information to be included, the margins could be enlarged to give the appearance that the full page is being utilized. The key idea is to have the final product centered in an aesthetically appealing manner on the page.

Font options include typeface, size, style, and appearance. These options enable the legal assistant to emphasize and pinpoint specific information by varying the font used in order to draw the skim-reader's eye to the information. Font decisions need to be carefully made; if the applicant uses font changes indiscriminately or too often, it will reflect poorly on the applicant because the effect will be to make the resume look too confusing and/or too busy. However, consistent use of font options will enhance to appearance of a resume; font options can be an organizational tool to help the reader skim organizationally similar information. For example, if the legal assistant uses a bold font style for the title of each of the five major portions of the resume, it will help the reader quickly see the overall organizational structure of the resume.

The *font face* needs to be one that is easily skim-read; some font faces are easier to read than others. A typical font face used in legal document drafting is Times New Roman. The *font size* typically used in legal documents is 12-point or 10-point. If the font size gets too small it will be difficult to skim-read, especially by a reader who wears glasses or needs to wear glasses and doesn't. *Font style and appearance* options can be used by the legal assistant to draw attention to specific categories of information that the legal assistant wants to pinpoint for the reader. The options typically used include boldface, underlining, double underlining, and italics. These options can be quite effective if used with consistency and discretion, but overuse of font style and appearance option can distract the reader. The key is to use font style and appearance consciously and purposefully to emphasize information, to draw the reader's attention to information, and/or to organize information.

The resume will be more aesthetically appealing if the legal assistant uses the legal drafting principle of parallel construction within each of the major parts of the resume. The parallel construction principle requires the drafter to list and provide similar information in the same order using the same word or phrases, if appropriate, within each part of the resume. Parallel construction principles can also be used in formatting by using the same spacing, indenting, and font choices. For example, in the work experience portion of the resume, the introduction of each separate job should provide the same category of information in the same order using the same phraseology, when appropriate, and using parallel construction in formatting. The following two work experience descriptions illustrate the principle of parallel construction:

WORK EXPERIENCE:

1998–1999   Brown and True, P.C. San Antonio, Texas.
                 Legal Assistant.

Job responsibilities included: Conducting legal research, analyzing documents and records, creating demonstrative exhibits, drafting pleading and discovery documents, preparing witnesses to testify, summarizing depositions, developing trial notebooks, providing second-chair assistance at trial, and performing general paralegal tasks.

1995–1997   Acme Mortgage Loan Company. Los Angeles, California.
                 Assistant to Loan Counselor.

Job responsibilities included: Preparing initial foreclosure and loan documents, maintaining records regarding status of accounts, preparing monthly and semi-annual reports, handling inquiries from borrowers and lenders, and performing general office work.

Consistent format among major parts of the resume is also desirable. Consistency in format will improve the aesthetic appeal of the resume, enabling the reader to skim-read to identify and assimilate relevant information in each part more quickly. The consistency principle can be applied in a variety of ways to achieve this result: An example would be to use the same font appearance for all headings, sub-headings, and similar categories of information, as well as using the same spacing, indenting, and ordering of information. The following example of the educational background and work experience portions of a resume will illustrate this concept.

EDUCATION:

Graduate Education: Southwest Texas State University, San Marcos, Texas.
                         Master of Arts in Legal Studies received May, 1999.

Undergraduate Education: University of Texas, Austin, Texas.
                         Bachelor of Arts, Political Science received May, 1995.

WORK EXPERIENCE:

1998–1999   Brown and True, P.C. San Antonio, Texas.
                 Legal Assistant.

Job responsibilities included: Conducting legal research, analyzing documents and records, creating demonstrative exhibits, drafting pleading and discovery documents, preparing witnesses to testify, summarizing depositions, developing trial notebooks, providing second-chair assistance at trial, and performing general paralegal tasks.

1995–1997   Acme Mortgage Loan Company. Los Angeles, California.
                 Assistant to Loan Counselor.

Job responsibilities included: Preparing initial foreclosure and loan documents, maintaining records regarding status of accounts, preparing monthly and semi-annual reports, handling inquiries from borrowers and lenders, and performing general office work.

What Proofreading Process Is Appropriate to Ensure Quality in the Resume?

The legal assistant should use the same proofreading process in resume drafting that is used in any type of legal drafting: Proofread, then proofread again, then have another person proofread, then have a final proofreading by the drafter. At each stage of the proofreading process, the proofreader should do both a *horizontal proofing* and a *vertical proofing*. Horizontal proofing requires the proofreader to read the content of the resume line-by-line, checking for clarity, readability, accuracy of information, and typographical and grammatical errors. Vertical proofing requires the proofreader to once again look at the document from the top down, checking for consistency in format, parallel construction, uniformity in presentation, and other aesthetic considerations.

Even if the resume is typed or printed by another person, the legal assistant remains responsible and accountable for the content and appearance of the resume. The legal assistant will be judged by the final product; therefore, the legal assistant needs to be the first and the final proofreader of the resume.

What Type and Color of Paper Should Be Used for the Resume?

The *type* of paper used for a professional resume should be of high quality. Often a resume is routed from one office to another and is touched by many different individuals in the legal working environment. To ensure that the resume continues to look good as it moves from office to office, the legal assistant should use a higher quality of paper, at least 25 percent rag, which resists crumpling. Avoid using photocopy paper.

The best *color* choice for a legal working environment is white paper and black print. This combination is a traditional choice for legal working environments; it would be suitable and expected. Some legal assistants like their resumes to stand out from the others in the stack, opting to use colored paper. If the legal assistant makes this choice, the colored paper selected should be lightly colored and a soft shade. Remember that most legal working environments are conservative environments, so if one chooses to take the path least traveled, it should be a very conservative path: ivory paper with black print or butter-colored paper with brown print.

How Should a Resume Be Produced and Reproduced?

The three typical methods used to produce and reproduce a resume include the following: (1) typing or word-processing and photocopying, (2) typing or word-processing and instant printing, and (3) typesetting and printing. There are advantages and disadvantages to each and each involves different costs.

The least expensive method is typing or word-processing and photocopying the resume. The typing can be done on a typewriter but is best done by using a word-processing program on the computer. If a typewriter must be used, an office typewriter such as an IBM Selectric or Executive should be used, or use a professional typing service. Excellent computer software word-processing programs are available that allow a choice of fonts, which will improve the aesthetic appeal of the resume. Once the resume has been typed or word-processed, the original can be photocopied. Remember not to use typical-grade photocopy paper; use paper that is at least 25 percent rag for the copies. However, even with better quality paper, the photocopy process lends itself to spots and blurs.

Another option is to type or word-process the resume and instant-copy the resume. In this case, the legal assistant first types or word-processes the resume and proofreads it to be sure it is in "camera-ready" form. Then the finished resume is taken to a printing service, which will instant-copy the resume using the quality of paper chosen by the legal assistant. The instant-printing process is better than the photocopy process, which is more likely to have spotting and blurring problems. However, the quality of instant copies will be no better than the quality of the original. If this process is used, the legal assistant should have enough resumes made for the scope of the job search as identified during the planning stage. Between 100 and 200 instant copies should be made, because it is more effective than later returning and having additional copies made.

The most expensive option is having the resume typeset and printed. However, the quality of the finished product is usually superior. If this method is used, the original used by the printer does not need to be in camera-ready form because the type will be set by the printer to specially run the resume, resulting in a cleaner copy. It is a good method to use if the legal assistant has to condense a large amount of information onto one page, because the printer can assist in selecting different sizes of small type. On the other hand, if the legal assistant has to expand the information so it will fill up one page, the printer can assist by selecting different sizes of large and small type. The printing process also offers the options of boldface and larger type for emphasis. If this process is used, the legal assistant must effectively communicate with the printer concerning what the finished product should look like. The cost of the first several copies of a typeset, printed resume will be expensive, but the cost of additional copies will not be as much if they are ordered at the same time as the original run.

Should a Cover Letter Accompany a Resume when Mailed to a Potential Employer?

After the resume is completed, the legal assistant should develop cover letters to send to potential employers along with the resume. To determine what cover letters will be required, the legal assistant should look back at the plans that were established during the planning stage and at the Potential Employer Log (Figure 13-3). Form cover letters should be developed for the different categories of legal working environments being explored. The form cover letters should then be personalized for each separate potential employer by inserting the correct name and address and inserting in the body of the letter the reason why the applicant desires employment in that specific environment.

The appropriate, personalized cover letter and finished resume should then be mailed to each potential employer on the log and the legal assistant should note the mailing date on the log. About a week after mailing the cover letter and resume, the legal assistant should follow up by calling the potential employer to make sure they received the cover letter and communicating once again his or her desire to meet personally with them to discuss employment opportunities. Don't wait for the potential employer to call you! Many legal assistants make a mistake by simply mailing out the cover letter and the resume and not following up. If the legal assistant understands how busy a legal working environment is, he or she will understand why it is necessary for an applicant to be assertive and make the additional effort to open the door to the job interview. All follow-up contacts should be noted on the Potential Employer Log, along with the names of the individuals spoken with during the follow-up.

DISCUSSION QUESTIONS

1. Is your resume skim-able? If not, what could you do to make it easier to read rapidly?

2. Does the work experience portion of the resume contain a clear, complete functional description of each of your jobs, including all tasks that you performed in your previous jobs that required the same type of skills that you will need to perform a legal assistant task?

3. Develop cover letters that can be used to explore career opportunities with each of the potential employers that you discovered during the research step.

INTERVIEW FOR EMPLOYMENT IN LEGAL WORKING ENVIRONMENTS

One of the most exciting events during the search for the best career opportunity is receiving telephone calls and/or e-mails seeking to schedule job interviews. The discussion that follows provides practical information to help the legal assistant prepare in advance of the job interview, be successful during the job interview, follow up after the job interview, and negotiate appropriate compensation.

What Should a Legal Assistant Do to Prepare for a Job Interview?

After mailing out cover letters and resumes and while making follow-up contacts, the legal assistant should make final preparations for the job interview. Three tasks need to be completed in order to fully prepare for a job interview in a legal working environment, as follows:

- Prepare a portfolio to take to the job interview.
- Research specifics on the potential employer.
- Develop responses to expected questions and questions to ask.

Completing the three-step preparation process will prepare the legal assistant for the interview and improve his or her ability to make a good impression. During the interview the legal assistant will attempt to provide the potential employer with as much positive information as possible about his or her qualifications and skills. Sometimes the individual conducting the job interview is an experienced interviewer who knows how to ask open, yet probing, questions that allow the interviewee a chance to talk about and sell him/herself. Other times, the individual conducting the job interview does not have good interviewing skills and he/she does most of the talking, which does not allow the legal assistant a good chance to sell him/herself. The three-step preparation process prepares the legal assistant to excel in either interviewing situation.

The first step is the preparation of a portfolio for the job interview. Many employers do not understand the educational background, credentialing system (or lack thereof), scope of appropriate paralegal tasks, and competencies of legal assistants. The portfolio is a physical tool that the legal assistant should prepare, carry into the job interview, and use during the job interview to educate the potential employer as necessary concerning the legal assistant's educational background, experiential background, skills, and competencies. Think of the portfolio as an evidence file, an organizational tool to enable you to get to any necessary exhibit within three seconds. A well-organized, complete portfolio enables the legal assistant to quickly access information and examples to not only sell him/herself to a potential employer but also point to the documentary evidence to prove it.

By definition, a portfolio is "a hinged cover or flexible case for carrying loose papers."[1] The portfolio container for a legal working environment is an expandable red-roper folder containing several separate manila file folders with identifying tabs. This is the type of portfolio container used in all legal working environments to organize case files. Since it is traditionally used, a legal assistant using the same portfolio container system will look like he or she fits right into the environment! Separate manila file folders should be tabbed, filled with appropriate content, and inserted into the expandable red-roper folder. The legal assistant should create the following separate manila folders:

Resumes	Although the potential employer had a cover letter and resume at one time, it may have been shared with others or misplaced. Always bring extra resumes to leave with the potential employer.
Transcripts	Have the original and several extra copies of all collegiate transcripts, including undergraduate and graduate transcripts, inserted into this file folder. A copy may need to be left for the potential employer to review. Never leave your originals; leave a copy.
Certificates	If the legal assistant has received any special certificates issued by educational institutions, state bar associations, legal assistant divisions or associations, copies of the certificates should be inserted into this file folder to show as documentation of that fact.
Academic Institution Information	This file folder should contain information concerning the academic institution and degree program that provided the educational background for the legal assistant. If the entire undergraduate or graduate catalog is too bulky to insert, then photocopy the relevant pages including the description of each course taken to earn the degree. Make sure there are extra copies of this information in the folder because a copy might need to be left for review by the potential employer.
Reference List	The legal assistant should create a list of references, individuals who have agreed to serve as personal, professional, and/or character references for them during the job search. The list should include the name, address, and telephone number of each reference, and the position that the reference holds. Never use an individual as a reference unless you ask permission and know that he or she will give you a positive, favorable, unqualified recommendation. Keep several copies of the reference list in this folder, since you will want to leave a copy for the potential employer. If desired, a legal assistant could also keep reference letters in this portfolio. Never give the employer the original reference let-

ter; make sure to have a photocopy of it to leave with the potential employer.

Paralegal Course Work A separate manila file folder should be prepared for each separate substantive paralegal course taken. Into each separate course folder, the legal assistant should insert the following: (1) the course syllabus, (2) complete course assignments, (3) course hand-outs, and (4) examples of the legal assistant's writing and drafting skills related to that course work.

Writing Samples Many potential employers ask to see writing samples. A separate file folder should be set up with exemplary writing samples placed in the folder. It is a good idea to have several copies of the writing samples because the legal assistant may want to leave a copy for the potential employer to review.

Form Notebooks Develop a separate manila folder for each form notebook included. Be sure to take the form notebooks that would be most relevant to the potential employer.

Billable-Hour Statistics An experienced legal assistant who has been functioning as a income-producer should include billable-hour reports or statistics for a reasonable time period preceding the job interview. These may be needed to evidence the billable-hour production ability of the legal assistant. A caveat here is that the billable-hour report or statistic must be in a format that will protect the confidentiality and privacy of both the client and the members of the prior (or current) legal working environment.

Client List An experienced legal assistant or clerical support staff member who has been working in other legal working environments must be careful to avoid any conflict-of-interest problem or staff-side-switching problems. At some point in the hiring process, the applicant may need to disclose a list of clients served by his or her supervising attorney(s). This list should not be disclosed until necessary and should not be copied and left with the potential employer.

After the portfolio is completed, the next step is to research the potential employer. This step will refresh the legal assistant's recollection concerning the legal working environment in which the interview will take place, the reasons why the environment was chosen, and why the cover letter and resume was sent to the specific attorney. If the legal assistant made good notes during the research stage, this task will be as simple as going back and reviewing those notes. If the legal assistant's notes are incomplete, this task will require the legal assistant to go back and use the original resource reference book or directory to once again acquaint him/herself with the facts. It is amazing how many job applicants go into a job interview having failed to do research to acquaint themselves with the areas of law practiced, the size of the law firm or legal department, and the specifics concerning the attorneys working in the environment. When an uninformed legal assistant goes into a job interview without bothering to prepare him/herself for the specifics of the legal working environment, he or she has made a fatal error. He or she has overlooked an opportunity to prove to the potential employer that he or she is detail-oriented, intelligent, astute, on-the-ball, and motivated to work in that particular environment.

After the portfolio and research steps are complete, the last preparation task is to consider appropriate responses to expected questions and to develop appropriate questions that the legal assistant can ask. During the job interview, the legal assistant will have only seconds to respond to questions that are asked. Some of the questions posed can be difficult to answer unless they have been thought about beforehand. To prepare for the interview the legal assistant should consider what responses they would give to expected questions. The following is a list of common questions that are typically asked:

- How did you find out about this job?
- Why did you decide to apply for this job?
- Why did you decide to become a paralegal?
- Are you a paralegal or a legal assistant?
- Where would you like to be in five years?
- What are your professional plans?
- Do you plan to go to law school?
- Can you type?
- What are your personal plans?
- Tell me about yourself.
- What is your philosophy of life?
- What are your strong points?
- What are your weak points?
- What have you learned about (litigation, personal injury, preparing corporate minutes, real estate, administrative law, etc.)?
- How do you work under pressure?
- How do you work in a structured (unstructured) environment?
- What did you like least about your former boss?

- Will you work overtime?
- How would you describe your work ethic?
- Can you travel?
- What did you like best (least) about your past jobs?
- How much do you expect to be paid?
- What is the least salary you would consider?
- How do you work with large numbers of people?
- Do you consider yourself a team player and why?
- Are you a self-starter?
- Do you have good organizational skills? Give examples.
- Do you write well? Give examples.
- Will commuting be difficult for you?
- How much money do you expect to make five years from now?
- Why do you think you want to work for us?
- Now that I've told you all these things about the job and firm, are you still interested and why?
- What can you do for us?
- What are your hobbies?
- When can you begin?
- What do paralegals do?
- What type of training do you have?
- You've never worked as a paralegal; how do you know you can do the job?

Not only should the legal assistant develop appropriate responses to the common questions listed, the legal assistant should also *develop intelligent questions to ask the potential employer*. Often during the interview the potential employer will ask the legal assistant if he or she has any questions. It would give a more positive, interested, alert, and intelligent impression for the legal assistant to say "yes" than to say "no." For that reason, the legal assistant should think of two or three questions to ask and formulate them before the interview. These questions should not relate to salary, vacation time, or time off—those questions would leave a bad taste in the mouth of a potential employer. Appropriate questions should relate to substantive matters such as the status of the legal assistant as an income-producer in the law firm, whether the law firm considers the legal assistant as an exempt employee under the Fair Labor Standards Act, and what legal assistant utilization approach is used by the firm (pool system, tier system, or team system). If these types of questions are asked, it may begin a discussion that would prove educational for the attorney interviewer and would give the legal assistant a chance to impress the interviewer with his or her knowledge of the subject.

What Should a Legal Assistant Know about Participating in a Job Interview?

Most legal assistant job applicants have had prior jobs and this will not be a first job interview. However, it may be a first job interview in a legal working environment. Often the job interview in a legal working environment will be conducted by an attorney. Occasionally the interview will be conducted by a legal assistant or by a nonlawyer law office manager. All interviewers expect a legal assistant to be efficient, organized, honest, self-confident, intelligent, healthy, clean, neat, professional, positive, logical, clear-headed, stable, rational, skilled, detail-oriented, able to communicate, and motivated. In short, *perfect*!

During the job interview, the legal assistant's appearance, dress, responses, lack of responses, and body language will give the potential employer information about him or her. From that information, the potential employer will decide whether the applicant can do the job, whether the applicant is the type of person who will fit in with the existing staff, and whether the clients will feel comfortable with the applicant. These are critical decisions made by the interviewer. The legal assistant will want to participate in the interview in such as way as to portray characteristics that will cause the interviewer to decide favorably on behalf of him or her.

Appearance.   Many law firms, corporations, businesses, and governmental agencies have unwritten but apparent standards of dress. Traditionally, the dress code in most legal working environments is conservative and businesslike. Occasionally, some law firms have a more relaxed dress code but that is not the general rule. For the job interview, conventional and understated business attire is recommended for all job interviews in any legal working environment. For men, this means a business suit and tie or at least a sport jacket and tie. For women, business suits with skirts, not pants, are recommended.

Attitude.   The words and phrases that potential employers use to describe the type of employee they prefer include intelligence, enthusiasm, confidence, positive attitude, and willingness to learn. No one wants to add a negative, complaining, whining individual to the staff. It is imperative that during the job interview the legal assistant in all circumstances maintain a positive, can-do, glad-to-be-alive attitude. Often the search for the perfect career opportunity is very hard, time-consuming, tedious, frustrating work. It is natural to have moments of self-doubt and anxiety during the job search. However, set those feelings aside and mentally prepare yourself and your frame of mind to be successful in the job interview by portraying a positive, self-confident attitude during the job interview.

What to Take into the Interview.   The legal assistant should bring the portfolio prepared for the job interview that contains all relevant and necessary material. The portfolio should be attractive and well organized to make a good impression, as discussed earlier in this chapter. A man should not carry anything else, leaving one hand free to shake hands. A woman could take a purse, if necessary; however, the female applicant needs to have a hand free to shake hands with the potential employer, so she should choose a purse that can be carried on the shoulder.

Number of Interviews.   Often a job applicant might have several interviews, sometimes in the same day. Usually several individuals are involved in the hiring decision in a legal working environment, so the legal assistant applicant needs to be prepared for more than one interview. It has become common at many firms for a legal assistant or non-lawyer law office manager to conduct the initial screening interviews, then later to refer several applicants to an attorney for a second round of interviews before offering a job to any of the applicants.

Interview Format and Topics.   Unfortunately for the legal assistant attempting to prepare for the job interview, there is not a general or uniform format used for the job interview. Often the interviewer will describe the law firm, the type of law firm practice (or legal department/division practice), and what tasks are usually assigned to legal assistants. Other topics that should be covered during an interview are the identity of the legal assistant supervisor, how assignments will be given, benefits, bonuses, continuing education programs, office space, secretarial assistance, and frequency and time of salary reviews. Salary and benefits information may not be discussed in the initial interview, but generally are discussed in the final interview.

Meeting other Staff Members.   Many interviewers have the legal assistant applicant talk with other staff members as a part of the interview. This is a wonderful opportunity to explore the realities of the legal working environment, but be careful. Remember what you say and do can and will be held against you! Maintain a positive, can-do attitude in all interactions with all staff members in the legal working environment. They are all interviewing you.

Participating in the Job Interview.   During some interviews, the interviewer does not provide the information the applicant wants to know about the legal working environment or does not allow applicant an adequate opportunity to give the interviewer relevant information about the applicant's qualifications, experience, and skills. If either of these situations arise, the applicant should very tactfully and carefully bring up the topic or provide additional information. It is important for the applicant to participate in the interview but the applicant should not control the interview. The applicant must appear to be interested and motivated without seeming demanding, negative, or overbearing.

What Should a Legal Assistant Do after the Job Interview?   Immediately after the job interview, the legal assistant should write down relevant impressions of the legal working environment on the Potential Employer Log (Figure 13-3) including the names of all staff members he or she spoke to during the interview process. Then the legal assistant should write thank-you notes to all individuals who participated in the interview process. The thank-you note should not only thank the person for their time but should also contain information about what impressed the applicant about the job and environment. It should not be verbose, but could also include a brief discussion of the applicant's credentials and experience that would make him or her a good fit in the environment. Many applicants make the mistake of failing to follow up the job interview with a thank-you note. Don't make that mistake. The thank-you note may make the difference between you and another applicant.

DISCUSSION QUESTIONS

1. Based on your prior interviewing experience and the information in this section, what can you do to prepare for a future job interview as a legal assistant?

2. Based on your prior interviewing experience, what problems did you experience and how can you overcome them in the next interview?

3. Identify the questions or inquiries that may cause you the most trouble in a job interview. How will you deal with those questions or inquiries?

NEGOTIATING FOR COMPENSATION IN LEGAL WORKING ENVIRONMENTS

During the final job interview the interviewer usually will discuss compensation. Some legal working environments have established salary policies and the salary is not negotiable. However, in most legal working environments starting salaries are negotiable. The legal assistant must be ready to negotiate for compensation that includes both base salary and benefits.

The salary negotiation portion of the final interview serves several functions, including the following: (1) giving the employer information about the applicant's expectations regarding salary, benefits, promotion possibilities; (2) giving the applicant information about the employer's salary policies and ability and willingness to meet the applicant's expectations; and (3) establishing a mutually agreed-upon policy regarding the applicant's starting salary, benefits, first salary review, and expected performance measures.

The legal assistant must prepare for the salary negotiation session in advance. It usually occurs in a final or later interview, but occasionally it occurs at the first interview. To prepare for the salary negotiation session the legal assistant must establish the salary range that is acceptable to him or her, by first determining the lowest acceptable salary and then determining the highest salary that he or she could reasonably expect to get in the legal working environment in question. To establish these low and high numbers, the legal assistant should consider his or her own needs, which may be as simple as returning to the Self-Assessment Questionnaire (Figure 13-2) if the legal assistant has followed the systematic approach to the job search suggested in this section. If not, the legal assistant needs to come to terms with these questions at this point in the job search. In addition to determining his or her own needs and wants, the legal assistant should determine the competitive salaries that are being paid to legal assistants with the same or similar credentials in the geographic marketplace. This information can be obtained by looking at the ongoing salary surveys that are performed in most metropolitan areas by local and national legal assistant associations. The legal assistant should also consider the value of any special skills and expertise that he or she will bring to the work environment and what other elements, beyond monthly salary, are important components to the total compensation packet. After this analysis, the legal assistant should be clear about his or her own personal salary range and the factors relevant to the negotiation process.

During the salary negotiation process, the potential employer's goal will be to hire the most qualified person for the least salary. The goal of the applicant is to obtain the desired job at the highest salary possible. With these competing goals, one of the early problems of salary negotiation is to get one of the parties to actually commit to a salary figure from which to begin the negotiation. If the applicant is the first to commit to a salary figure, it should be the highest realistic salary figure, because the negotiation from that first figure will be downward. In other words, the applicant will never be offered more money than the first salary figure that he or she committed to, which is why the applicant must know his or her range prior to the salary negotiation session. The most successful negotiator will be the applicant who can think logically and can set forth reasons and factors to support his or her stated salary figure. Remember that most salary negotiation is done with lawyers, and they are best persuaded by logic and evidence.

CONCLUSION

The process of securing a legal assistant career opportunity that will be personally and professionally satisfying requires motivation, hard work, and dedication. A legal assistant who follows the systematic procedure discussed in this section, taking each thoughtful step one at a time, will enhance both his/her professional and personal lives for years to come.

DISCUSSION QUESTIONS

1. In the past, what difficulties, if any, did you experience in negotiation of a compensation package?
2. What negotiation skills can you now employ to overcome any hurdles that may exist in the area of compensation negotiation?

ENDNOTE

[1]WEBSTER ENCYCLOPEDIC DICTIONARY OF THE ENGLISH LANGUAGE (Consolidated Book Publishers 1979), at 646.

Index